Chinese Myths & Folk Tales

Chinese Myths
& Folk Tales
Barnes & Noble
NEW YORK

This 2020 edition printed for Barnes & Noble Booksellers, Inc. by Sterling Publishing Co., Inc.

ISBN 978-1-4351-6985-2

Barnes & Noble Booksellers, Inc.
122 Fifth Avenue
New York, NY 10011

Manufactured in China

6 8 10 9 7 5

sterlingpublishing.com

Cover illustration by Freki Wodenswolf Jungnickel
Endpaper art adapted from Owen Jones's *Examples of Chinese Ornament*

Contents

Note on the Text x

Strange Stories from a Chinese Studio

Examination for the Post of Guardian Angel 3
The Talking Pupils 4
The Painted Wall 6
Planting a Pear-Tree 8
The Taoist Priest of Lao-shan 9
The Buddhist Priest of Ch'ang-ch'ing 12
The Marriage of the Fox's Daughter 13
Miss Chiao-no 16
Magical Arts 23
Joining the Immortals 25
The Fighting Quails 31
The Painted Skin 37
The Trader's Son 40
Judge Lu 44
Miss Ying-ning, or the Laughing Girl 50
The Magic Sword 58
The *Shui-mang* Plant 64
Little Chu 68
Miss Quarta Hu 72
Mr. Chu, the Considerate Husband 75
The Magnanimous Girl 76
The Boon-Companion 78
Miss Lien-hsiang 79
Miss A-pao; or, Perseverance Rewarded 87
Jen Hsiu 92
The Lost Brother 94
The Three Genii 99
The Singing Frogs 101
The Performing Mice 101
The Tiger of Chao-ch'êng 101
A Dwarf 103
Hsiang-ju's Misfortunes 103
Chang's Transformation 109
A Taoist Priest 113
The Fight with the Foxes 115
The King 117
Engaged to a Nun 120
The Young Lady of the Tung-t'ing Lake 124
The Man Who Was Changed into a Crow 127
The Flower Nymphs 131
Ta-nan in Search of His Father 137
The Wonderful Stone 141
The Quarrelsome Brothers 144
The Young Gentleman Who Couldn't Spell 150
The Tiger Guest 152
The Sisters 155
Foreign Priests 158
The Self-Punished Murderer 158
The Master Thief 159
A Flood 160
Death by Laughing 160

CONTENTS

Playing at Hanging 161
The Rat Wife 161
The Man Who Was Thrown Down a Well 166
The Virtuous Daughter-in-Law 170
Dr. Tsêng's Dream 176
The Country of the Cannibals 180
Foot-ball on the Tung-t'ing Lake 185
The Thunder God 187
The Gambler's Talisman 190
The Husband Punished 191
The Marriage Lottery 194
The Lo-ch'a Country and the Sea-market 196
The Fighting Cricket 203
Taking Revenge 207
The Tipsy Turtle 208
The Magic Path 212
The Faithless Widow 213
The Princess of the Tung-t'ing Lake 214
The Princess Lily 220
The Donkey's Revenge 224
The Wolf Dream 229
The Unjust Sentence 231
A Rip Van Winkle 233
The Three States of Existence 235
In the Infernal Regions 237
Singular Case of Ophthalmia 241
Chou K'o-ch'ang and His Ghost 242
The Spirits of the Po-yang Lake 244
The Stream of Cash 244
The Injustice of Heaven 244
The Sea-Serpent 245
The Magic Mirror 245
Courage Tested 246
The Disembodied Friend 247
The Cloth Merchant 251
A Strange Companion 252
Spiritualistic Séances 252
The Mysterious Head 253
The Spirit of the Hills 254
Ingratitude Punished 254
Smelling Essays 255
His Father's Ghost 256
The Boat-Girl Bride 259
The Two Brides 263
A Supernatural Wife 267
Bribery and Corruption 268
A Chinese Jonah 270
Chang Pu-liang 271
The Dutch Carpet 271
Carrying a Corpse 272
A Taoist Devotee 272
Justice for Rebels 272
Killing a Serpent 273
The Resuscitated Corpse 274
The Fisherman and His Friend 276
The Priest's Warning 279
Metempsychosis 280
The Forty Strings of Cash 281
Saving Life 282
The Salt Smuggler 283
Collecting Subscriptions 284
Taoist Miracles 286
Arrival of Buddhist Priests 288
The Stolen Eyes 289
The Invisible Priest 289
The Censor in Purgatory 290
Mr. Willow and the Locusts 292
Mr. Tung, or Virtue Rewarded 292
The Dead Priest 293
The Flying Cow 294
The "Mirror-and-Listen" Trick 294
The Cattle Plague 295
The Marriage of the Virgin Goddess 296
The Wine Insect 297

CONTENTS

The Faithful Dog 298
An Earthquake 298
Making Animals 299
Cruelty Avenged 300
The Wei-ch'i Devil 300
The Fortune-Hunter Punished 301
Life Prolonged 302
The Clay Image 303
Dishonesty Punished 304
The Mad Priest 305
Feasting the Ruler of Purgatory 306
The Picture Horse 307
The Butterfly's Revenge 308
The Doctor 308
Snow in Summer 309
Planchette 310
Friendship with Foxes 311
The Great Rat 312
Wolves 313
Singular Verdict 313
The Grateful Dog 314
The Great Test 315
The Alchemist 316
Raising the Dead 318
Fêng-Shui 319
The Lingering Death 320
Dreaming Honors 321
The She-Wolf and the Herd-Boys 322
Adulteration Punished 323
A Chinese Solomon 324
The Roc 326
The Faithful Gander 327
The Elephants and the Lion 327
The Hidden Treasure 328
The Boatmen of Lao-lung 329
The Pious Surgeon 330
Another Solomon 332
The Incorrupt Official 333

Chinese Folk Tales

The Infamous Chow Sin and the Beautiful T'a Ki 337
The Love Adventures of the Fox Fairy, Prince Hu 343
Yu Kong the Athlete 352
Li, the Man with the Iron Staff 356
Wong Sing; or, How the Fortunes of a Royal Family Were Restored by a Fairy 362
The Stirring Adventures of the Scholar Wang 370
The Mysterious Peach 377
The Strange Adventures of the Scholar Siu 384
The Romantic Story of the Phoenix Fairy 390
Mr. Tang, the Filial Son 398
Soat-Lip and the Youthful Fairy 407
The King of the Nine Mountains 414
The Fairy Scholar 423
Phoenix, the Beautiful Fox Fairy 431
The Scholar Hai, and the Fairy Songster, Lady Kwey 437
Mr. Wang and the Taoist Abbot 445
The King of the Snakes 453
How an Expectant Prime Minister Was Cured of His Ambition by the Ingenious Device of a Fairy 461

Chinese Fairy Tales

Nursery Fairy Tales

Women's Words Part Flesh and Blood 477
The Three Rhymsters 478
How Greed for a Trifling Thing Led a Man to Lose a Great One 480
Who Was the Sinner? 482

CONTENTS

The Magic Cask 482
The Favorite of Fortune and the Child of Ill Luck 483
The Bird with Nine Heads 484
The Cave of the Beasts 486
The Panther 488
The Great Flood 490
The Fox and the Tiger 492
The Tiger's Decoy 493
The Fox and the Raven 493
Why Dog and Cat Are Enemies 494

Legends of the Gods

How the Five Ancients Became Men 495
The Herd Boy and the Weaving Maiden 496
Yang Oerlang 499
Notscha 500
The Lady of the Moon 505
The Morning and the Evening Star 506
The Girl with the Horse's Head; or, The Silkworm Goddess 507
The Queen of Heaven 508
The Fire-God 509
The Three Ruling Gods 510
A Legend of Confucius 511
The God of War 512

Tales of Saints and Magicians

The Halos of the Saints 514
Laotsze 515
The Ancient Man 516
The Eight Immortals (I) 516
The Eight Immortals (II) 520
The Two Scholars 521
The Miserly Farmer 523
Sky O'Dawn 525
King Mu of Dschou 527
The King of Huai Nan 530
Old Dschang 532
The Kindly Magician 535

Nature and Animal Tales

The Flower-Elves 540
The Spirit of the Wu-Lian Mountain 543
The King of the Ants 543
The Little Hunting Dog 545
The Dragon After His Winter Sleep 546
The Spirits of the Yellow River 547
The Dragon-Princess 551
Help in Need 554
The Disowned Princess 559
Fox-Fire 565

Ghost Stories

The Talking Silver Foxes 567
The Constable 569
The Dangerous Reward 572
Retribution 574
The Ghost Who Was Foiled 576
The Punishment of Greed 579
The Night on the Battlefield 580
The Kingdom of the Ogres 581
The Maiden Who Was Stolen Away 586
The Flying Ogre 587
Black Arts 588

Historic Legends

The Sorcerer of the White Lotus Lodge 593
The Three Evils 594
How Three Heroes Came by Their Deaths Because of Two Peaches 596
How the River-God's Wedding Was Broken Off 598
Dschang Liang 600

Old Dragonbeard 601
How Molo Stole the Lovely Rose-Red 606
The Golden Canister 609
Yang Gui Fe 612
The Monk of the Yangtze-kiang 614

Literary Fairy Tales
The Heartless Husband 619
Giauna the Beautiful 625
The Frog Princess 631
Rose of Evening 636
The Ape Sun Wu Kung 641

CHINESE FABLES
How the Moon Became Beautiful 667
The Animals' Peace Party 668
The Widow and Her Son 670
The Evergreen Tree and the Wilderness Marigold 672
The Snail and the Bees 673
The Proud Chicken 676
The Lemon Tree and the Pumelo 678
Woo Sing and the Mirror 679
Two Mothers and a Child 680
A Boy Who Would Not Tell a Lie 683
A Great Repentance and a Great Forgiveness 685
The Man Who Loved Money Better than Life 687
The Hen and the Chinese Mountain Turtle 687
The Boy of Perfect Disposition 690
What the Yen Tzi Taught the Hunter 691
A Lesson from Confucius 692
The Wind, the Clouds, and the Snow 694
The Fish and the Flowers 698
The Hen, the Cat, and the Birds 699
The Boy Who Wanted the Impossible 701
The Boy Who Became Hsao-Tsze 703
The Hunter, the Snipe, and the Bivalve 707
The Mule and the Lion 709
The Fa-Nien-Ts'ing and the Mön-Tien-Sing 711
The Body that Deserted the Stomach 714
The Proud Fox and the Crab 715
A Little Chinese Rose 716
The Eagle and the Rice Birds 717
The Children and the Dog 720
The Two Mountains 722
A Chinese Prodigal Son 725
The Lion and the Mosquitoes 728
The Thief and the Elephant 730
The General, the Bird, and the Ant 732
The Three Girls Who Went to a Boys' School 734
The Rattan Vine and the Rose Tree 736
The Melon and the Professor 738

SOME CHINESE GHOSTS
The Soul of the Great Bell 741
The Story of Ming-Y 744
The Legend of Tchi-Niu 755
The Return of Yen-Tchin-King 760
The Tradition of the Tea-Plant 765
The Tale of the Porcelain-God 772

Note on the Text

The stories published in this volume have been adapted from the following sources:

Davis, Mary Hayes and Chow-Leung. *Chinese Fables and Folk Stories.* New York: American Book Company, 1908.

Giles, Herbert A. *Strange Stories from a Chinese Studio*, Volumes I and II. London: Thos. De la Rue & Co., 1880.

Hearn, Lafcadio. *Some Chinese Ghosts*. Boston: Little, Brown, and Company, 1906.

Macgowan, John. *Chinese Folk-Lore*. Shanghai: North-China Daily News & Herald Ltd., 1910.

Wilhelm, Dr. R. (ed.) *The Chinese Fairy Book*. New York: Frederick A. Stokes Company, 1921.

Strange Stories from a Chinese Studio

Examination for the Post of Guardian Angel

My eldest sister's husband's grandfather, named Sung Tao, was a graduate. One day, while lying down from indisposition, an official messenger arrived, bringing the usual notification in his hand and leading a horse with a white forehead, to summon him to the examination for his master's degree. Mr. Sung here remarked that the Grand Examiner had not yet come, and asked why there should be this hurry. The messenger did not reply to this, but pressed so earnestly that at length Mr. Sung roused himself, and getting upon the horse rode with him. The way seemed strange, and by-and-by they reached a city which resembled the capital of a prince. They then entered the Prefect's *yamên*, the apartments of which were beautifully decorated; and there they found some ten officials sitting at the upper end, all strangers to Mr. Sung, with the exception of one whom he recognized to be the God of War.

In the verandah were two tables and two stools, and at the end of one of the former a candidate was already seated, so Mr. Sung sat down alongside of him. On the table were writing materials for each, and suddenly down flew a piece of paper with a theme on it, consisting of the following eight words:—"One man, two men; by intention, without intention." When Mr. Sung had finished his essay, he took it into the hall. It contained the following passage:— "Those who are virtuous by intention, though virtuous, shall not be rewarded. Those who are wicked without intention, though wicked, shall receive no punishment." The presiding deities praised this sentiment very much, and calling Mr. Sung to come forward, said to him, "A Guardian Angel is wanted in Honan. Go you and take up the appointment."

Mr. Sung no sooner heard this than he bowed his head and wept, saying, "Unworthy though I am of the honor you have conferred upon me, I should not venture to decline it but that my aged mother has reached her seventh decade, and there is no one now to take care of her. I pray you let me wait until she has fulfilled her destiny, when I will hold myself at your disposal." Thereupon one of the deities, who seemed to be the chief, gave instructions to search out his mother's term of life, and a long-bearded attendant forthwith brought in the Book of Fate. On turning it over, he declared that she still had nine years to live; and then a consultation was held among the deities, in the middle of which the God of War said, "Very well. Let Mr. graduate Chang take the post, and be relieved in nine years' time." Then, turning to Mr. Sung, he continued, "You ought to proceed without delay to your post; but as a reward for your filial piety, you are granted a furlough of nine years. At the expiration of that time you will receive another summons."

He next addressed a few kind words to Mr. Chang; and the two candidates, having made their *kotow*, went away together. Grasping Mr. Sung's hand, his companion, who gave "Chang Ch'i of Ch'ang-shan" as his name and address, accompanied him beyond the city walls and gave him a stanza of poetry at parting. I cannot recollect it all, but in it occurred this couplet:—

With wine and flowers we chase the hours,
In one eternal spring:
No moon, no light, to cheer the night—
Thyself that ray must bring.

Mr. Sung here left him and rode on, and before very long reached his own home; here he awaked as if from a dream, and found that he had been dead three days, when his mother, hearing a groan in the coffin, ran to it and helped him out. It was some time before he could speak, and then he at once inquired about Ch'ang-shan, where, as it turned out, a graduate named Chang had died that very day.

Nine years afterward, Mr. Sung's mother, in accordance with fate, passed from this life; and when the funeral obsequies were over, her son, having first purified himself, entered into his chamber and died also. Now his wife's family lived within the city, near the western gate; and all of a sudden they beheld Mr. Sung, accompanied by numerous chariots and horses with carved trappings and red-tasseled bits, enter into the hall, make an obeisance, and depart. They were very much disconcerted at this, not knowing that he had become a spirit, and rushed out into the village to make inquiries, when they heard he was already dead. Mr. Sung had an account of his adventure written by himself; but unfortunately after the insurrection it was not to be found. This is only an outline of the story.

The Talking Pupils

At Ch'ang-ngan there lived a scholar, named Fang Tung, who though by no means destitute of ability was a very unprincipled rake, and in the habit of following and speaking to any woman he might chance to meet. The day before the spring festival of Clear Weather, he was strolling about outside the city when he saw a small carriage with red curtains and an embroidered awning, followed by a crowd of waiting-maids on horseback, one of whom was exceedingly pretty, and riding on a small palfrey. Going closer to get a better view, Mr. Fang noticed that the carriage curtain was partly open, and inside he beheld a beautifully dressed girl of about sixteen, lovely beyond anything he had ever seen. Dazzled by the sight, he could not take his eyes off her; and, now before, now behind, he followed the carriage for many a mile. By-and-by he heard the young lady call out to her maid, and, when the latter came alongside, say to her, "Let down the screen for me. Who is this rude fellow that keeps on staring so?" The maid accordingly let down the screen, and looking angrily at Mr. Fang, said to him, "This is the bride of the Seventh Prince in the City of Immortals going home to see her parents, and no village girl that you should stare at her thus." Then taking a handful of dust, she threw it at him and blinded him. He rubbed his eyes and looked round, but the carriage and horses were gone.

This frightened him, and he went off home, feeling very uncomfortable about the eyes. He sent for a doctor to examine his eyes, and on the pupils was found a small film, which had increased by next morning, the eyes watering incessantly all the time. The film went on growing, and in a few days was as thick as a cash. On the right pupil there came a kind of spiral, and as no medicine was of any avail, the sufferer gave himself up to grief and wished for death. He then bethought himself of repenting of his misdeeds, and hearing that the *Kuang-ming* sutra could relieve misery, he got a copy and hired a man to teach it to him. At first it was very tedious work, but by degrees he became more composed, and spent every evening in a posture of devotion, telling his beads.

At the end of a year he had arrived at a state of perfect calm, when one day he heard a small voice, about as loud as a fly's, calling out from his left eye:—"It's horridly dark in here." To this he heard a reply from the right eye, saying, "Let us go out for a stroll, and cheer ourselves up a bit." Then he felt a wriggling in his nose which made it itch, just as if something was going out of each of the nostrils; and after a while he felt it again as if going the other way. Afterward he heard a voice from one eye say, "I hadn't seen the garden for a long time: the epidendrums are all withered and dead." Now Mr. Fang was very fond of these epidendrums, of which he had planted a great number, and had been accustomed to water them himself; but since the loss of his sight he had never even alluded to them. Hearing, however, these words, he at once asked his wife why she had let the epidendrums die. She inquired how he knew they were dead, and when he told her she went out to see, and found them actually withered away. They were both very much astonished at this, and his wife proceeded to conceal herself in the room.

She then observed two tiny people, no bigger than a bean, come down from her husband's nose and run out of the door, where she lost sight of them. In a little while they came back and flew up to his face, like bees or beetles seeking their nests. This went on for some days, until Mr. Fang heard from the left eye, "This roundabout road is not at all convenient. It would be as well for us to make a door." To this the right eye answered, "My wall is too thick; it wouldn't be at all an easy job." "I'll try and open mine," said the left eye, "and then it will do for both of us." Whereupon Mr. Fang felt a pain in his left eye as if something was being split, and in a moment he found he could see the tables and chairs in the room. He was delighted at this and told his wife, who examined his eye and discovered an opening in the film, through which she could see the black pupil shining out beneath, the eyeball itself looking like a cracked pepper-corn. By next morning the film had disappeared, and when his eye was closely examined it was observed to contain two pupils. The spiral on the right eye remained as before; and then they knew that the two pupils had taken up their abode in one eye. Further, although Mr. Fang was still blind of one eye, the sight of the other was better than that of the two together. From this time he was more careful of his behavior, and acquired in his part of the country the reputation of a virtuous man.

The Painted Wall

A Kiang-si gentleman, named Mêng Lung-t'an, was lodging at the capital with a Mr. Chu, M.A., when one day chance led them to a certain monastery, within which they found no spacious halls or meditation chambers, but only an old priest in *deshabille*. On observing the visitors, he arranged his dress and went forward to me et them, leading them round and showing whatever there was to be seen.

In the chapel they saw an image of Chih Kung, and the walls on either side were beautifully painted with life-like representations of men and things. On the east side were pictured a number of fairies, among whom was a young girl whose maiden tresses were not yet confined by the matron's knot. She was picking flowers and gently smiling, while her cherry lips seemed about to move, and the moisture of her eyes to overflow. Mr. Chu gazed at her for a long time without taking his eyes off, until at last he became unconscious of anything but the thoughts that were engrossing him. Then, suddenly, he felt himself floating in the air, as if riding on a cloud, and found himself passing through the wall, where halls and pavilions stretched away one after another, unlike the abodes of mortals. Here an old priest was preaching the Law of Buddha, surrounded by a large crowd of listeners. Mr. Chu mingled with the throng, and after a few moments perceived a gentle tug at his sleeve. Turning round, he saw the young girl above-mentioned, who walked laughing away. Mr. Chu at once followed her, and passing a winding balustrade arrived at a small apartment beyond which he dared not venture further. But the young lady, looking back, waved the flowers she had in her hand as though beckoning him to come on. He accordingly entered and found nobody else within. Then they fell on their knees and worshipped heaven and earth together, and rose up as man and wife, after which the bride went away, bidding Mr. Chu keep quiet until she came back. This went on for a couple of days, when the young lady's companions began to smell a rat and discovered Mr. Chu's hiding-place. Thereupon they all laughed and said, "My dear, you are now a married woman, and should leave off that maidenly *coiffure*." So they gave her the proper hair-pins and head ornaments, and bade her go bind her hair, at which she blushed very much but said nothing. Then one of them cried out, "My sisters, let us be off. Two's company, more 's none." At this they all giggled again and went away.

Mr. Chu found his wife very much improved by the alteration in the style of her hair. The high top-knot and the coronet of pendants were very becoming to her. But suddenly they heard a sound like the tramping of heavy-soled boots, accompanied by the clanking of chains and the noise of angry discussion. The bride jumped up in a fright, and she and Mr. Chu peeped out. They saw a man clad in golden armor, with a face as black as jet, carrying in his hand chains and whips, and surrounded by all the girls. He asked, "Are you all here?"

"All," they replied.

"If," said he, "any mortal is here concealed amongst you, denounce him at once, and lay not up sorrow for yourselves."

Here they all answered as before that there was no one.

The man then made a movement as if he would search the place, upon which the bride was dreadfully alarmed, and her face turned the color of ashes. In her terror she said to Mr. Chu, "Hide yourself under the bed," and opening a small lattice in the wall, disappeared herself.

Mr. Chu in his concealment hardly dared to draw his breath; and in a little while he heard the boots tramp into the room and out again, the sound of the voices getting gradually fainter and fainter in the distance. This reassured him, but he still heard the voices of people going backward and forward outside; and having been a long time in a cramped position, his ears began to sing as if there was a locust in them, and his eyes to burn like fire. It was almost unbearable; however, he remained quietly awaiting the return of the young lady without giving a thought to the why and wherefore of his present position.

Meanwhile, Mêng Lung-t'an had noticed the sudden disappearance of his friend, and thinking something was wrong, asked the priest where he was.

"He has gone to hear the preaching of the Law," replied the priest.

"Where?" said Mr. Mêng.

"Oh, not very far," was the answer.

Then with his finger the old priest tapped the wall and called out, "Friend Chu! what makes you stay away so long?"

At this, the likeness of Mr. Chu was figured upon the wall, with his ear inclined in the attitude of one listening.

The priest added, "Your friend here has been waiting for you some time"; and immediately Mr. Chu descended from the wall, standing transfixed like a block of wood, with starting eyeballs and trembling legs.

Mr. Mêng was much terrified, and asked him quietly what was the matter. Now the matter was that while concealed under the bed he had heard a noise resembling thunder and had rushed out to see what it was.

Here they all noticed that the young lady on the wall with the maiden's tresses had changed the style of her *coiffure* to that of a married woman. Mr. Chu was greatly astonished at this and asked the old priest the reason.

He replied, "Visions have their origin in those who see them: what explanation can I give?"

This answer was very unsatisfactory to Mr. Chu; neither did his friend, who was rather frightened, know what to make of it all; so they descended the temple steps and went away.

Planting a Pear-Tree

A COUNTRYMAN WAS ONE DAY SELLING HIS PEARS IN THE MARKET. THEY WERE UNUSUALLY sweet and fine flavored, and the price he asked was high. A Taoist priest in rags and tatters stopped at the barrow and begged one of them. The countryman told him to go away, but as he did not do so he began to curse and swear at him.

The priest said, "You have several hundred pears on your barrow; I ask for a single one, the loss of which, Sir, you would not feel. Why then get angry?"

The lookers-on told the countryman to give him an inferior one and let him go, but this he obstinately refused to do. Thereupon the beadle of the place, finding the commotion too great, purchased a pear and handed it to the priest. The latter received it with a bow and turning to the crowd said, "We who have left our homes and given up all that is dear to us are at a loss to understand selfish niggardly conduct in others. Now I have some exquisite pears which I shall do myself the honor to put before you."

Here somebody asked, "Since you have pears yourself, why don't you eat those?"

"Because," replied the priest, "I wanted one of these pips to grow them from." So saying, he munched up the pear; and when he had finished took a pip in his hand, unstrapped a pick from his back, and proceeded to make a hole in the ground, several inches deep, wherein he deposited the pip, filling in the earth as before. He then asked the bystanders for a little hot water to water it with, and one among them who loved a joke fetched him some boiling water from a neighboring shop. The priest poured this over the place where he had made the hole, and every eye was fixed upon him when sprouts were seen shooting up, and gradually growing larger and larger. By-and-by, there was a tree with branches sparsely covered with leaves; then flowers, and last of all fine, large, sweet-smelling pears hanging in great profusion. These the priest picked and handed round to the assembled crowd until all were gone, when he took his pick and hacked away for a long time at the tree, finally cutting it down. This he shouldered, leaves and all, and sauntered quietly away.

Now, from the very beginning, our friend the countryman had been among the crowd, straining his neck to see what was going on, and forgetting all about his business. At the departure of the priest he turned round and discovered that every one of his pears was gone. He then knew that those the old fellow had been giving away so freely were really his own pears. Looking more closely at the barrow he also found that one of the handles was missing, evidently having been newly cut off. Boiling with rage, he set out in pursuit of the priest, and just as he turned the corner he saw the lost barrow-handle lying under the wall, being in fact the very pear-tree that the priest had cut down. But there were no traces of the priest—much to the amusement of the crowd in the market-place.

The Taoist Priest of Lao-shan

There lived in our village a Mr. Wang, the seventh son in an old family. This gentleman had a *penchant* for the Taoist religion; and hearing that at Lao-shan there were plenty of Immortals, shouldered his knapsack and went off for a tour thither. Ascending a peak of the mountain he reached a secluded monastery where he found a priest sitting on a rush mat, with long hair flowing over his neck, and a pleasant expression on his face. Making a low bow, Wang addressed him thus:—

"Mysterious indeed is the doctrine: I pray you, Sir, instruct me therein."

"Delicately-nurtured and wanting in energy as you are," replied the priest, "I fear you could not support the fatigue."

"Try me," said Wang. So when the disciples, who were very many in number, collected together at dusk, Wang joined them in making obeisance to the priest, and remained with them in the monastery.

Very early next morning the priest summoned Wang, and giving him a hatchet sent him out with the others to cut firewood. Wang respectfully obeyed, continuing to work for over a month until his hands and feet were so swollen and blistered that he secretly meditated returning home.

One evening when he came back he found two strangers sitting drinking with his master. It being already dark, and no lamp or candles having been brought in, the old priest took some scissors and cut out a circular piece of paper like a mirror, which he proceeded to stick against the wall. Immediately it became a dazzling moon, by the light of which you could have seen a hair or a beard of corn.

The disciples all came crowding round to wait upon them, but one of the strangers said, "On a festive occasion like this we ought all to enjoy ourselves together." Accordingly he took a kettle of wine from the table and presented it to the disciples, bidding them drink each his fill; whereupon our friend Wang began to wonder how seven or eight of them could all be served out of a single kettle.

The disciples, too, rushed about in search of cups, each struggling to get the first drink for fear the wine should be exhausted. Nevertheless, all the candidates failed to empty the kettle, at which they were very much astonished, when suddenly one of the strangers said, "You have given us a fine bright moon; but it's dull work drinking by ourselves. Why not call Ch'ang-ngo to join us?" He then seized a chop-stick and threw it into the moon, whereupon a lovely girl stepped forth from its beams. At first she was only a foot high, but on reaching the ground lengthened to the ordinary size of women. She had a slender waist and a beautiful neck, and went most gracefully through the Red Garment figure. When this was finished she sang the following words:—

"Ye fairies! ye fairies! I'm coming back soon,
Too lonely and cold is my home in the moon."

Her voice was clear and well sustained, ringing like the notes of a flageolet, and when she had concluded her song she pirouetted round and jumped up on the table, where, with every eye fixed in astonishment upon her, she once more became a chop-stick.

The three friends laughed loudly, and one of them said, "We are very jolly to-night, but I have hardly room for any more wine. Will you drink a parting glass with me in the palace of the moon?" They then took up the table and walked into the moon where they could be seen drinking so plainly, that their eyebrows and beards appeared like reflections in a looking-glass.

By-and-by the moon became obscured; and when the disciples brought a lighted candle they found the priest sitting in the dark alone. The viands, however, were still upon the table and the mirror-like piece of paper on the wall. "Have you all had enough to drink?" asked the priest; to which they answered that they had.

"In that case," said he, "you had better get to bed, so as not to be behindhand with your wood-cutting in the morning."

So they all went off, and among them Wang, who was delighted at what he had seen, and thought no more of returning home. But after a time he could not stand it any longer; and as the priest taught him no magical arts he determined not to wait, but went to him and said, "Sir, I traveled many long miles for the benefit of your instruction. If you will not teach me the secret of Immortality, let me at any rate learn some trifling trick, and thus soothe my cravings for a knowledge of your art. I have now been here two or three months, doing nothing but chop firewood, out in the morning and back at night, work to which I was never accustomed in my own home."

"Did I not tell you," replied the priest, "that you would never support the fatigue? To-morrow I will start you on your way home."

"Sir," said Wang, "I have worked for you a long time. Teach me some small art, that my coming here may not have been wholly in vain."

"What art?" asked the priest.

"Well," answered Wang, "I have noticed that whenever you walk about anywhere, walls and so on are no obstacle to you. Teach me this, and I'll be satisfied."

The priest laughingly assented, and taught Wang a formula which he bade him recite. When he had done so he told him to walk through the wall; but Wang, seeing the wall in front of him, didn't like to walk at it. As, however, the priest bade him try, he walked quietly up to it and was there stopped.

The priest here called out, "Don't go so slowly. Put your head down and rush at it." So Wang stepped back a few paces and went at it full speed; and the wall yielding to him as he passed, in a moment he found himself outside. Delighted at this, he went in to thank the priest, who told him to be careful in the use of his power, or otherwise there would be no response, handing him at the same time some money for his expenses on the way.

When Wang got home, he went about bragging of his Taoist friends and his contempt for walls in general; but as his wife disbelieved his story, he set about going through the performance as before. Stepping back from the wall, he rushed at it full speed with his head down; but coming in contact with the hard bricks, finished up in a heap on the floor. His wife picked him up and found he had a bump on his forehead as big as a large egg, at which she roared with laughter; but Wang was overwhelmed with rage and shame, and cursed the old priest for his base ingratitude

The Buddhist Priest of Ch'ang-ch'ing

At Ch'ang-ch'ing there lived a Buddhist priest of exceptional virtue and purity of conduct, who, though over eighty years of age, was still hale and hearty. One day he fell down and could not move; and when the other priests rushed to help him up, they found he was already gone. The old priest was himself unconscious of death, and his soul flew away to the borders of the province of Honan.

Now it chanced that the scion of an old family residing in Honan, had gone out that very day with some ten or a dozen followers to hunt the hare with falcons; but his horse having run away with him he fell off and was killed. Just at that moment the soul of the priest came by and entered into the body, which thereupon gradually recovered consciousness.

The servants crowded round to ask him how he felt, when opening his eyes wide, he cried out, "How did I get here?" They assisted him to rise, and led him into the house, where all his ladies came to see him and inquire how he did. In great amazement he said, "I am a Buddhist priest. How came I hither?" His servants thought he was wandering, and tried to recall him by pulling his ears. As for himself, he could make nothing of it, and closing his eyes refrained from saying anything further. For food, he would only eat rice, refusing all wine and meat; and avoided the society of his wives.

After some days he felt inclined for a stroll, at which all his family were delighted; but no sooner had he got outside and stopped for a little rest than he was besieged by servants begging him to take their accounts as usual. However, he pleaded illness and want of strength, and no more was said. He then took occasion to ask if they knew the district of Ch'ang-ch'ing, and on being answered in the affirmative expressed his intention of going thither for a trip, as he felt dull and had nothing particular to do, bidding them at the same time look after his affairs at home. They tried to dissuade him from this on the ground of his having but recently risen from a sick bed; but he paid no heed to their remonstrances, and on the very next day set out.

Arriving in the Ch'ang-ch'ing district, he found everything unchanged; and without being put to the necessity of asking the road, made his way straight to the monastery. His former disciples received him with every token of respect as an honored visitor; and in reply to his question as to where the old priest was, they informed him that their worthy teacher had been dead for some time. On asking to be shown his grave, they led him to a spot where there was a solitary mound some three feet high, over which the grass was not yet green. Not one of them knew his motives for visiting this place; and by-and-by he ordered his horse, saying to the disciples, "Your master was a virtuous priest. Carefully preserve whatever relics of him you may have, and keep them from injury."

They all promised to do this, and he then set off on his way home. When he arrived there, he fell into a listless state and took no interest in his family affairs. So much so, that after a few months he ran away and went straight to his former home at the monastery, telling the disciples that he was their old master. This they refused to believe, and laughed among themselves at his pretensions; but he told them the whole story, and recalled many incidents of his previous life among them, until at last they were convinced. He then occupied his old bed and went through the same daily routine as before, paying no attention to the repeated entreaties of his family, who came with carriages and horses to beg him to return.

About a year subsequently, his wife sent one of the servants with splendid presents of gold and silk, all of which he refused with the exception of a single linen robe. And whenever any of his old friends passed this monastery, they always went to pay him their respects, finding him quiet, dignified, and pure. He was then barely thirty, though he had been a priest for more than eighty years.

The Marriage of the Fox's Daughter

A president of the Board of Civil Office, named Yin, and a native of Li-ch'êng, when a young man, was very badly off, but was endowed with considerable physical courage. Now in his part of the country there was a large establishment, covering several acres, with an unbroken succession of pavilions and verandahs, and belonging to one of the old county families; but because ghosts and apparitions were frequently seen there, the place had for a long time remained untenanted, and was overgrown with grass and weeds, no one venturing to enter in even in broad daylight.

One evening when Yin was carousing with some fellow-students, one of them jokingly said, "If anybody will pass a night in the haunted house, the rest of us will stand him a dinner."

Mr. Yin jumped up at this, and cried out, "What is there difficult in that?"

So, taking with him a sleeping-mat, he proceeded thither, escorted by all his companions as far as the door, where they laughed and said, "We will wait here a little while. In case you see anything, shout out to us at once."

"If there are any goblins or foxes," replied Yin, "I'll catch them for you."

He then went in, and found the paths obliterated by long grass, which had sprung up, mingled with weeds of various kinds. It was just the time of the new moon, and by its feeble light he was able to make out the door of the house. Feeling his way, he walked on until he reached the back pavilion, and then went up on to the Moon Terrace, which was such a pleasant spot that he determined to stop there. Gazing westward, he sat for a long time looking at the moon—a single thread of light embracing in its horns the peak of a hill—without hearing anything at all unusual; so, laughing to himself at the nonsense people talked, he spread his mat upon the floor, put a stone under his head for a pillow, and lay down to sleep.

He had watched the stars until they were just disappearing, and was on the point of dropping off, when suddenly he heard footsteps down below coming up the stairs. Pretending to be asleep, he saw a servant enter, carrying in his hand a lotus-shaped lantern, who, on observing Mr. Yin, rushed back in a fright, and said to someone behind, "There is a stranger here!"

The person spoken to asked who it was, but the servant did not know; and then up came an old gentleman, who, after examining Mr. Yin closely, said, "It's the future President: he's as drunk as can be. We needn't mind him; besides, he's a good fellow, and won't give us any trouble." So they walked in and opened all the doors; and by-and-by there were a great many other people moving about, and quantities of lamps were lighted, till the place was as light as day.

About this time Mr. Yin slightly changed his position, and sneezed; upon which the old man, perceiving that he was awake, came forward and fell down on his knees, saying, "Sir, I have a daughter who is to be married this very night. It was not anticipated that Your Honor would be here. I pray, therefore, that we may be excused." Mr. Yin got up and raised the old man, regretting that, in his ignorance of the festive occasion, he had brought with him no present.

"Ah, Sir," replied the old man, "your very presence here will ward off all noxious influences; and that is quite enough for us."

He then begged Mr. Yin to assist in doing the honors, and thus double the obligation already conferred. Mr. Yin readily assented, and went inside to look at the gorgeous arrangements they had made. He was here met by a lady, apparently about forty years of age, whom the old gentleman introduced as his wife; and he had hardly made his bow when he heard the sound of flageolets, and someone came hurrying in, saying, "He has come!" The old gentleman flew out to meet this personage, and Mr. Yin also stood up, awaiting his arrival.

In no long time, a bevy of people with gauze lanterns ushered in the bridegroom himself, who seemed to be about seventeen or eighteen years old, and of a most refined and prepossessing appearance. The old gentleman bade him pay his respects first to their worthy guest; and upon his looking toward Mr. Yin, that gentleman came forward to welcome him on behalf of the host. Then followed ceremonies between the old man and his son-in-law; and when these were over, they all sat down to supper. Hosts of waiting-maids brought in profuse quantities of wine and meats, with bowls and cups of jade or gold, till the table glittered again. And when the wine had gone round several times, the old gentleman told one of the maids to summon the bride. This she did, but some time passed and no bride came. So the old man rose and drew aside the curtain, pressing the young lady to come forth; whereupon a number of women escorted out the bride, whose ornaments went *tinkle tinkle* as she walked along, sweet perfumes being all the time diffused around. Her father told her to make the proper salutation, after which she went and sat by her mother.

Mr. Yin took a glance at her, and saw that she wore on her head beautiful ornaments made of kingfisher's feathers, her beauty quite surpassing anything he had ever seen. All this time they had been drinking their wine out of golden goblets big enough to hold several pints, when it flashed across him that one of these goblets would be a capital thing to carry back to his companions in evidence of what he had seen. So he secreted it in his sleeve, and, pretending to be tipsy, leaned forward with his head upon the table as if going off to sleep.

"The gentleman is drunk," said the guests; and by-and-by Mr. Yin heard the bridegroom take his leave, and there was a general trooping downstairs to the tune of a wedding march.

When they were all gone the old gentleman collected the goblets, one of which was missing, though they hunted high and low to find it. Someone mentioned the sleeping guest; but the old gentleman stopped him at once for fear Mr. Yin should hear, and before long silence reigned throughout.

Mr. Yin then arose. It was dark, and he had no light; but he could detect the lingering smell of the food, and the place was filled with the fumes of wine. Faint streaks of light now appearing in the east, he began quietly to make a move, having first satisfied himself that the goblet was still in his sleeve. Arriving at the door, he found his friends already there; for they had been afraid he might come out after they left, and go in again early in the morning. When he produced the goblet they were all lost in astonishment; and on hearing his story, they were fain to believe it, well knowing that a poor student like Yin was not likely to have such a valuable piece of plate in his possession.

Later on Mr. Yin took his doctor's degree, and was appointed magistrate over the district of Fei-ch'iu, where there was an old-established family of the name of Chu. The head of the family asked him to a banquet in honor of his arrival, and ordered the servants to bring in the large goblets. After some delay a slave-girl came and whispered something to her master which seemed to make him very angry. Then the goblets were brought in, and Mr. Yin was invited to drink. He now found that these goblets were of precisely the same shape and pattern as the one he had at home, and at once begged his host to tell him where he had had these made.

"Well," said Mr. Chu, "there should be eight of them. An ancestor of mine had them made, when he was a minister at the capital, by an experienced artificer. They have been handed down in our family from generation to generation, and have now been carefully laid by for some time; but I thought we would have them out to-day as a compliment to your Honor. However, there are only seven to be found. None of the servants can have touched them, for the old seals of ten years ago are still upon the box, unbroken. I don't know what to make of it."

Mr. Yin laughed, and said, "It must have flown away! Still, it is a pity to lose an heir-loom of that kind; and as I have a very similar one at home, I shall take upon myself to send it to you."

When the banquet was over, Mr. Yin went home, and taking out his own goblet, sent it off to Mr. Chu. The latter was somewhat surprised to find that it was identical with his own, and hurried away to thank the magistrate for his gift, asking him at the same time how it had come into his possession. Mr. Yin told him the whole story, which proves conclusively that although a fox may obtain possession of a thing, even at a distance of many hundred miles, he will not venture to keep it altogether.

Miss Chiao-no

K'UNG HSÜEH-LI WAS A DESCENDANT OF CONFUCIUS. HE WAS A MAN OF CONSIDERABLE ability, and an excellent poet. A fellow-student, to whom he was much attached, became magistrate at T'ien-t'ai, and sent for K'ung to join him. Unfortunately, just before K'ung arrived his friend died, and he found himself without the means of returning home; so he took up his abode in a Buddhist monastery, where he was employed in transcribing for the priests.

Several hundred paces to the west of this monastery there was a house belonging to a Mr. Shan, a gentleman who had known better days, but who had spent all his money in a heavy law-suit; and then, as his family was a small one, had gone away to live in the country and left his house vacant. One day there was a heavy fall of snow which kept visitors away from the monastery; and K'ung, finding it dull, went out. As he was passing by the door of the house above-mentioned, a young man of very elegant appearance came forth, who, the moment he saw K'ung, ran up to him and, with a bow, entered into conversation, asking him to be pleased to walk in.

K'ung was much taken with the young man, and followed him inside. The rooms were not particularly large, but adorned throughout with embroidered curtains, and from the walls hung scrolls and drawings by celebrated masters. On the table lay a book, the title of which was, *Jottings from Paradise*; and turning over its leaves, K'ung found therein many strange things. He did not ask the young man his name, presuming that as he lived in the Shan family mansion, he was necessarily the owner of the place. The young man, however, inquired what he was doing in that part of the country, and expressed great sympathy with his misfortunes, recommending him to set about taking pupils.

"Alas!" said K'ung, "who will play the Mæcenas to a distressed wayfarer like myself?"

"If," replied the young man, "you would condescend so far, I for my part would gladly seek instruction at your hands."

K'ung was much gratified at this, but said he dared not arrogate to himself the position of teacher, and begged merely to be considered as the young man's friend. He then asked him why the house had been shut up for so long; to which the young man replied, "This is the Shan family mansion. It has been closed all this time because of the owner's removal into the country. My surname is Huang-fu, and my home is in Shen-si; but as our house has been burnt down in a great fire, we have put up here for a while." Thus Mr. K'ung found out that his name was not Shan.

That evening they spent in laughing and talking together, and K'ung remained there for the night. In the morning a lad came in to light the fire; and the young man, rising first, went into the private part of the house.

Mr. K'ung was sitting up with the bed-clothes still huddled round him, when the lad looked in and said, "Master's coming!" So he jumped up with a start, and in came an old man with a silvery beard, who began to thank him, saying, "I am very much obliged to you for your condescension in becoming my son's tutor. At present he writes a villainous hand; and I can only hope you will not allow the ties of friendship to interfere with discipline."

Thereupon, he presented Mr. K'ung with an embroidered suit of clothes, a sable hat, and a set of shoes and stockings; and when the latter had washed and dressed himself he called for wine and food. K'ung could not make out what the valances of the chairs and tables were made of: they were so very bright-colored and dazzling. By-and-by, when the wine had circulated several times, the old gentleman picked up his walking-stick and took his leave.

After breakfast, the young man handed in his theme, which turned out to be written in an archaic style, and not at all after the modern fashion of essay-writing. K'ung asked him why he had done this, to which the young man replied that he did not contemplate competing at the public examinations. In the evening they had another drinking-bout, but it was agreed that there should be no more of it after that night.

The young man then called the boy and told him to see if his father was asleep or not; adding, that if he was, he might quietly summon Miss Perfume. The boy went off, first taking a guitar out of a very pretty case; and in a few minutes in came a very nice-looking young girl. The young man bade her play the *Death of Shun*; and seizing an ivory plectrum she swept the chords, pouring forth a vocal melody of exquisite sweetness and pathos. He then gave her a goblet of wine to drink, and it was midnight before they parted.

Next morning they got up early and settled down to work. The young man proved an apt scholar; he could remember what he had once read, and at the end of two or three months had made astonishing progress. Then they agreed that every five days they would indulge in a symposium, and that Miss Perfume should always be of the party.

One night when the wine had gone into K'ung's head, he seemed to be lost in a reverie; whereupon his young friend, who knew what was the matter with him, said, "This girl was brought up by my father. I know you find it lonely, and I have long been looking out for a nice wife for you."

"Let her only resemble Miss Perfume," said K'ung, "and she will do."

"Your experience," said the young man, laughing, "is but limited, and, consequently, anything is a surprise to you. If Miss Perfume is your beau ideal, why it will not be difficult to satisfy you."

Some six months had passed away, when one day Mr. K'ung took it into his head that he would like to go out for a stroll in the country. The entrance, however, was carefully closed; and on asking the reason, the young man told him that his father wished to receive no guests for fear of causing interruption to his studies. So K'ung thought no more about it; and by-and-by, when the heat of summer came on, they moved their study to a pavilion in the garden.

At this time Mr. K'ung had a swelling on the chest about as big as a peach, which, in a single night, increased to the size of a bowl. There he lay groaning with the pain, while his pupil waited upon him day and night. He slept badly and took hardly any food; and in a few days the place got so much worse that he could neither eat nor drink.

The old gentleman also came in, and he and his son lamented over him together. Then the young man said, "I was thinking last night that my sister, Chiao-no, would be able to cure Mr. K'ung, and accordingly I sent over to my grandmother's asking her to come. She ought to be here by now."

At that moment a servant entered and announced Miss Chiao-no, who had come with her cousin, having been at her aunt's house. Her father and brother ran out to meet her, and then brought her in to see Mr. K'ung. She was between thirteen and fourteen years old, and had beautiful eyes with a very intelligent expression in them, and a most graceful figure besides. No sooner had Mr. K'ung beheld this lovely creature than he quite forgot to groan, and began to brighten up.

Meanwhile the young man was saying, "This respected friend of mine is the same to me as a brother. Try, sister, to cure him."

Miss Chiao-no immediately dismissed her blushes, and rolling up her long sleeves approached the bed to feel his pulse. As she was grasping his wrist, K'ung became conscious of a perfume more delicate than that of the epidendrum; and then she laughed, saying, "This illness was to be expected; for the heart is touched. Though it is severe, a cure can be effected; but, as there is already a swelling, not without using the knife."

Then she drew from her arm a gold bracelet which she pressed down upon the suffering spot, until by degrees the swelling rose within the bracelet and overtopped it by an inch and more, the outlying parts that were inflamed also passing under, and thus very considerably reducing the extent of the tumor. With one hand she opened her robe and took out a knife with an edge as keen as paper, and pressing the bracelet down all the time with the other, proceeded to cut lightly round near the root of the swelling. The dark blood gushed forth, and stained the bed and the mat; but Mr. K'ung was delighted to be near such a beauty,—not only felt no pain, but would willingly have continued the operation that she might sit by him a little longer. In a few moments the whole thing was removed, and the place looked like the knot on a tree where a branch has been cut away.

Here Miss Chiao-no called for water to wash the wound, and from between her lips she took a red pill as big as a bullet, which she laid upon the flesh, and, after drawing the skin together, passed round and round the place. The first turn felt like the searing of a hot iron; the second like a gentle itching; and at the third he experienced a sensation of lightness and coolness which penetrated into his very bones and marrow. The young lady then returned the pill to her mouth, and said, "He is cured," hurrying away as fast as she could.

Mr. K'ung jumped up to thank her, and found that his complaint had quite disappeared. Her beauty, however, had made such an impression on him that his troubles were hardly at an end. From this moment he gave up his books, and took no interest in anything.

This state of things was soon noticed by the young man, who said to him, "My brother, I have found a fine match for you."

"Who is it to be?" asked K'ung.

"Oh, one of the family," replied his friend.

Thereupon Mr. K'ung remained some time lost in thought, and at length said, "Please don't!" Then turning his face to the wall, he repeated these lines:—

"Speak not of lakes and streams to him who once has seen the sea;
The clouds that circle Wu's peak are the only clouds for me."

The young man guessed to whom he was alluding, and replied, "My father has a very high opinion of your talents, and would gladly receive you into the family, but that he has only one daughter, and she is much too young. My cousin, Ah-sung, however, is seventeen years old, and not at all a bad-looking girl. If you doubt my word, you can wait in the verandah until she takes her daily walk in the garden, and thus judge for yourself." This Mr. K'ung acceded to, and accordingly saw Miss Chiao-no come out with a lovely girl—her black eyebrows beautifully arched, and her tiny feet encased in phoenix-shaped shoes—as like one another as they well could be. He was of course delighted, and begged the young man to arrange all preliminaries; and the very next day his friend came to tell him that the affair was finally settled. A portion of the house was given up to the bride and bridegroom, and the marriage was celebrated with plenty of music and hosts of guests, more like a fairy wedding than anything else.

Mr. K'ung was very happy, and began to think that the position of Paradise had been wrongly laid down, until one day the young man came to him and said, "For the trouble you have been at in teaching me, I shall ever remain your debtor. At the present moment, the Shan family law-suit has been brought to a termination, and they wish to resume possession of their house immediately. We therefore propose returning to Shen-si, and as it is unlikely that you and I will ever meet again, I feel very sorrowful at the prospect of parting."

Mr. K'ung replied that he would go too, but the young man advised him to return to his old home. This, he observed, was no easy matter; upon which the young man said, "Don't let that trouble you: I will see you safe there."

By-and-by his father came in with Mr. K'ung's wife, and presented Mr. K'ung with one hundred ounces of gold; and then the young man gave the husband and wife each one of his hands to grasp, bidding them shut their eyes. The next instant they were floating away in the air, with the wind whizzing in their ears. In a little while he said, "You have arrived," and opening his eyes, K'ung beheld his former home. Then he knew that the young man was not a human being.

Joyfully he knocked at the old door, and his mother was astonished to see him arrive with such a nice wife. They were all rejoicing together, when he turned round and found that his friend had disappeared. His wife attended on her mother-in-law with great devotion, and acquired a reputation both for virtue and beauty, which was spread round far and near. Some time passed away, and then Mr. K'ung took his doctor's degree, and was appointed Governor of the Gaol in Yen-ngan. He proceeded to his post with his wife only, the journey being too long for his mother, and by-and-by a son was born. Then he got into trouble by being too honest an official, and threw up his appointment; but had not the wherewithal to get home again.

One day when out hunting he met a handsome young man riding on a nice horse, and seeing that he was staring very hard looked closely at him. It was young Huang-fu. So they drew bridle, and fell to laughing and crying by turns,—the young man then inviting K'ung to go along with him. They rode on together until they had reached a village thickly shaded with trees, so that the sun and sky were invisible overhead, and entered into a most elaborately-decorated mansion, such as might belong to an old-established family. K'ung asked after Miss Chiao-no, and heard that she was married; also that his own mother-in-law was dead, at which tidings he was greatly moved.

Next day he went back and returned again with his wife. Chiao-no also joined them, and taking up K'ung's child played with it, saying, "Your mother played us truant."

Mr. K'ung did not forget to thank her for her former kindness to him, to which she replied, "You're a great man now. Though the wound has healed, haven't you forgotten the pain yet?" Her husband, too, came to pay his respects, returning with her on the following morning.

One day the young Huang-fu seemed troubled in spirit, and said to Mr. K'ung, "A great calamity is impending. Can you help us?" Mr. K'ung did not know what he was alluding to, but readily promised his assistance. The young man then ran out and summoned the whole family to worship in the ancestral hall, at which Mr. K'ung was alarmed, and asked what it all meant.

"You know," answered the young man, "I am not a man but a fox. To-day we shall be attacked by thunder; and if only you will aid us in our trouble, we may still hope to escape. If you are unwilling, take your child and go, that you may not be involved with us."

Mr. K'ung protested he would live or die with them, and so the young man placed him with a sword at the door, bidding him remain quiet there in spite of all the thunder. He did as he was told, and soon saw black clouds obscuring the light until it was all as dark as pitch. Looking round, he could see that the house had disappeared, and that its place was occupied by a huge mound and a bottomless pit. In the midst of his terror, a fearful peal was heard which shook the very hills, accompanied by a violent wind and driving rain. Old trees were torn up, and Mr. K'ung became both dazed and deaf. Yet he stood firm until he saw in a dense black column of smoke a horrid thing with a sharp beak and long claws, with which it snatched some one from the hole, and was disappearing up with the smoke. In an instant K'ung knew by her clothes and shoes that the victim was no other than Chiao-no, and instantly jumping up he struck the devil violently with his sword, and cut it down. Immediately the mountains were riven, and a sharp peal of thunder laid K'ung dead upon the ground. Then the clouds cleared away, and Chiao-no gradually came round, to find K'ung dead at her feet. She burst out crying at the sight, and declared that she would not live since K'ung had died for her. K'ung's wife also came out, and they bore the body inside.

Chiao-no then made Ah-sung hold her husband's head, while her brother prized open his teeth with a hair-pin, and she herself arranged his jaw. She next put a red pill into his mouth, and bending down breathed into him. The pill went along with the current of air, and presently there was a gurgle in his throat, and he came round. Seeing all the family about him, he was disturbed as if waking from a dream. However they were all united together, and fear gave place to joy; but Mr. K'ung objected to live in that out-of-the-way place, and proposed that they should return with him to his native village. To this they were only too pleased to assent—all except Chiao-no; and when Mr. K'ung invited her husband, Mr. Wu, as well, she said she feared her father and mother-in-law would not like to lose the children. They had tried all day to persuade her, but without success, when suddenly in rushed one of the Wu family's servants, dripping with perspiration and quite out of breath. They asked what was the matter, and the servant replied that the Wu family had been visited by a calamity on the very same day, and had every one perished. Chiao-no cried very bitterly at this, and could not be comforted; but now there was nothing to prevent them from all returning together.

Mr. K'ung went into the city for a few days on business, and then they set to work packing-up night and day. On arriving at their destination, separate apartments were allotted to young Mr. Huang-fu, and these he kept carefully shut up, only opening the door to Mr. K'ung and his wife. Mr. K'ung amused himself with the young man and his sister Chiao-no, filling up the time with chess, wine, conversation, and good cheer, as if they had been one family. His little boy, Huan, grew up to be a handsome young man, with a fox-like *penchant* for roaming about; and it was generally known that he was actually the son of a fox.

Magical Arts

A CERTAIN MR. YÜ WAS A SPIRITED YOUNG FELLOW, FOND OF BOXING AND TRIALS OF strength. He was able to take two kettles and swing them round about with the speed of the wind. Now, during the reign of Ch'ung Chêng, when up for the final examination at the capital, his servant became seriously ill. Much troubled at this, he applied to a necromancer in the market-place who was skillful at determining the various leases of life allotted to men.

Before he had uttered a word, the necromancer asked him, saying, "Is it not about your servant, Sir, that you would consult me?"

Mr. Yü was startled at this, and replied that it was.

"The sick man," continued the necromancer, "will come to no harm; you, Sir, are the one in danger."

Mr. Yü then begged him to cast his nativity, which he proceeded to do, finally saying to Mr. Yü, "You have but three days to live!"

Dreadfully frightened, he remained some time in a state of stupefaction, when the necromancer quietly observed that he possessed the power of averting this calamity by magic, and would exert it for the sum of ten ounces of silver. But Mr. Yü reflected that Life and Death are already fixed, and he didn't see how magic could save him. So he refused, and was just going away, whereupon the necromancer said, "You grudge this trifling outlay. I hope you will not repent it."

Mr. Yü's friends also urged him to pay the money, advising him rather to empty his purse than not secure the necromancer's compassion. Mr. Yü, however, would not hear of it and the three days slipped quickly away. Then he sat down calmly in his inn to see what was going to happen. Nothing did happen all day, and at night he shut his door and trimmed the lamp; then, with a sword at his side, he awaited the approach of death.

By-and-by, the clepsydra showed that two hours had already gone without bringing him any nearer to dissolution; and he was thinking about lying down, when he heard a scratching at the window, and then saw a tiny little man creep through, carrying a spear on his shoulder, who, on reaching the ground, shot up to the ordinary height. Mr. Yü seized his sword and at once struck at it; but only succeeded in cutting the air. His visitor instantly shrunk down small again, and made an attempt to escape through the crevice of the window; but Yü redoubled his blows and at last brought him to the ground.

Lighting the lamp, he found only a paper man, cut right through the middle. This made him afraid to sleep, and he sat up watching, until in a little time he saw a horrid hobgoblin creep through the same place. No sooner did it touch the ground than he assailed it lustily with his sword, at length cutting it in half. Seeing, however, that both halves kept on wriggling about, and fearing that it might get up again, he went on hacking at it. Every blow told, giving forth a hard sound, and when he came to examine his work, he found a clay image all knocked to pieces. Upon this he moved his seat near to the window, and kept his eye fixed upon the crack.

After some time, he heard a noise like a bull bellowing outside the window, and something pushed against the window-frame with such force as to make the whole house tremble and seem about to fall. Mr. Yü, fearing he should be buried under the ruins, thought he could not do better than fight outside; so he accordingly burst open the door with a crash and rushed out. There he found a huge devil, as tall as the house, and he saw by the dim light of the moon that its face was as black as coal. Its eyes shot forth yellow fire: it had nothing either upon its shoulders or feet; but held a bow in its hand and had some arrows at its waist.

Mr. Yü was terrified; and the devil discharged an arrow at him which he struck to the ground with his sword. On Mr. Yü preparing to strike, the devil let off another arrow which the former avoided by jumping aside, the arrow quivering in the wall beyond with a smart crack. The devil here got very angry, and drawing his sword flourished it like a whirlwind, aiming a tremendous blow at Mr. Yü. Mr. Yü ducked, and the whole force of the blow fell upon the stone wall of the house, cutting it right in two. Mr. Yü then ran out from between the devil's legs, and began hacking at its back—whack!—whack! The devil now became furious, and roared like thunder, turning round to get another blow at his assailant.

But Mr. Yü again ran between his legs, the devil's sword merely cutting off a piece of his coat. Once more he hacked away—whack!—whack!—and at length the devil came tumbling down flat. Mr. Yü cut at him right and left, each blow resounding like the watchman's wooden gong; and then, bringing a light, he found it was a wooden image about as tall as a man. The bow and arrows were still there, the latter attached to its waist. Its carved and painted features were most hideous to behold; and wherever Mr. Yü had struck it with his sword, there was blood. Mr. Yü sat with the light in his hand till morning, when he awaked to the fact that all these devils had been sent by the necromancer in order to kill him, and so evidence his own magical power.

The next day, after having told the story far and wide, he went with some others to the place where the necromancer had his stall; but the latter, seeing them coming, vanished in the twinkling of an eye. Some one observed that the blood of a dog would reveal a person who had made himself invisible, and Mr. Yü immediately procured some and went back with it. The necromancer disappeared as before, but on the spot where he had been standing they quickly threw down the dog's blood. Thereupon they saw his head and face all smeared over with the blood, his eyes glaring like a devil's; and at once seizing him, they handed him over to the authorities, by whom he was put to death.

Joining the Immortals

A Mr. Chou, of Wên-têng, had in his youth been fellow-student with a Mr. Ch'êng, and a firm friendship was the result. The latter was poor, and depended very much upon Chou, who was the elder of the two. He called Chou's wife his "sister," and had the run of the house just as if he was one of the family. Now this wife happening to die in child-bed, Chou married another named Wang; but as she was quite a young girl, Ch'êng did not seek to be introduced.

One day her younger brother came to visit her, and was being entertained in the "inner" apartments when Ch'êng chanced to call. The servant announced his arrival, and Chou bade him ask Mr. Ch'êng in. But Ch'êng would not enter, and took his leave. Thereupon Chou caused the entertainment to be moved into the public part of the house, and, sending after Ch'êng, succeeded in bringing him back.

They had hardly sat down before some one came in to say that a former servant of the establishment had been severely beaten at the magistrate's *yamên*; the facts of the case being that a cow-boy of the Huang family connected with the Board of Rites had driven his cattle across the Chou family's land, and that words had arisen between the two servants in consequence; upon which the Huang family's servant had complained to his master, who had seized the other and had sent him in to the magistrate's, where he had been bambooed.

When Mr. Chou found out what the matter was, he was exceedingly angry, and said, "How dares this pig-boy fellow behave thus? Why, only a generation ago his master was my father's servant! He emerges a little from his obscurity, and immediately thinks himself I don't know what!"

Swelling with rage, he rose to go in quest of Huang, but Ch'êng held him back, saying, "The age is corrupt: there is no distinction between right and wrong. Besides, the officials of the day are half of them thieves, and you will only get yourself into hot water." Chou, however, would not listen to him; and it was only when tears were added to remonstrances that he consented to let the matter drop. But his anger did not cease, and he lay tossing and turning all night.

In the morning he said to his family, "I can stand the insults of Mr. Huang; but the magistrate is an officer of the Government, and not the servant of influential people. If there is a case of any kind, he should hear both plaintiff and defendant, and not act like a dog, biting anybody he is set upon. I will bring an action against the cow-boy, and see what the magistrate will do to him." As his family rather egged him on, he accordingly proceeded to the magistrate's and entered a formal plaint; but that functionary tore up his petition, and would have nothing to do with it. This roused Chou's anger, and he told the magistrate plainly what he thought of him, in return for which contempt of court he was at once seized and bound.

During the forenoon Mr. Ch'êng called at his house, where he learnt that Chou had gone into the city to prosecute the cow-boy, and immediately hurried after him with a view to stop proceedings. But his friend was already in the gaol, and all he could do was to stamp his foot in anger.

Now it happened that three pirates had just been caught; and the magistrate and Huang, putting their heads together, bribed these fellows to say that Chou was one of their gang, whereupon the higher authorities were petitioned to deprive him of his status as a graduate, and the magistrate then had him most unmercifully bambooed. Mr. Ch'êng gained admittance to the gaol, and, after a painful interview, proposed that a petition should be presented direct to the Throne.

"Alas!" cried Chou, "here am I bound and guarded, like a bird in a cage. I have indeed a young brother, but it is as much as he can do to provide me with food."

Then Ch'êng stepped forward, saying, "I will perform this service. Of what use are friends who will not assist in the hour of trouble?" So away he went, and

Chou's son provided him with money to defray his expenses. After a long journey he arrived at the capital, where he found himself quite at a loss as to how he should get the petition presented. However, hearing that the Emperor was about to set out on a hunting tour, he concealed himself in the market-place, and when His Majesty passed by, prostrated himself on the ground with loud cries and gesticulations. The Emperor received his petition, and sent it to the Board of Punishments, desiring to be furnished with a report on the case. It was then more than ten months since the beginning of the affair, and Chou, who had been made to confess to this false charge, was already under sentence of death; so that the officers of the Board were very much alarmed when they received the Imperial instructions, and set to work to re-hear the case in person.

Huang was also much alarmed, and devised a plan for killing Mr. Chou by bribing the gaolers to stop his food and drink; so that when his brother brought provisions he was rudely thrust back and prevented from taking them in. Mr. Ch'êng complained of this to the Viceroy of the province, who investigated the matter himself, and found that Chou was in the last stage of starvation, for which the gaolers were bambooed to death. Terrified out of his wits, Huang, by dint of bribing heavily, succeeded in absconding and escaping a just punishment for his crimes. The magistrate, however, was banished for perversion of the law, and Chou was permitted to return home, his affection for Ch'êng being now very much increased. But ever after the prosecution and his friend's captivity, Mr. Ch'êng took a dismal view of human affairs, and one day invited Chou to retire with him from the world. The latter, who was deeply attached to his young wife, threw cold water on the proposition, and Mr. Ch'êng pursued the subject no farther, though his own mind was fully made up.

Not seeing him for some days afterward, Mr. Chou sent to inquire about him at his house; but there they all thought he was at Chou's, neither family, in fact, having seen anything of him. This looked suspicious, and Chou, aware of his peculiarity, sent off people to look for him, bidding them search all the temples and monasteries in the neighborhood. He also from time to time supplied Ch'êng's son with money and other necessaries.

Eight or nine years had passed away when suddenly Ch'êng re-appeared, clad in a yellow cap and stole, and wearing the expression of a Taoist priest. Chou was delighted, and seized his arm, saying, "Where have you been?—letting me search for you all over the place."

"The solitary cloud and the wild crane," replied Ch'êng, laughing, "have no fixed place of abode. Since we last met my equanimity has happily been restored."

Chou then ordered wine, and they chatted together on what had taken place in the interval. He also tried to persuade Ch'êng to detach himself from the Taoist persuasion, but the latter only smiled and answered nothing.

"It is absurd!" argued Chou. "Why cast aside your wife and child as you would an old pair of shoes?"

"Not so," answered Ch'êng; "a man may wish to cast aside his son, but how can he do so?" Chou asked where he lived, to which he replied, "In the Great Pure Mansion on Mount Lao."

They then retired to sleep on the same bed; and by-and-by Chou dreamt that Ch'êng was lying on his chest so that he could not breathe. In a fright he asked him what he was doing, but got no answer; and then he waked up with a start. Calling to Ch'êng and receiving no reply, he sat up and stretched out his hand to touch him. The latter, however, had vanished, he knew not whither. When he got calm, he found he was lying at Ch'êng's end of the bed, which rather startled him. "I was not tipsy last night," reflected he; "how could I have got over here?"

He next called his servants, and when they came and struck a light, lo! he was Ch'êng. Now Chou had had a beard, so he put up his hand to feel for it, but found only a few straggling hairs. He then seized a mirror to look at himself, and cried out in alarm: "If this is Mr. Ch'êng, where on earth am I?"

By this time he was wide awake, and knew that Ch'êng had employed magic to induce him to retire from the world. He was on the point of entering the ladies' apartments; but his brother, not recognizing who he was, stopped him, and would not let him go in; and as he himself was unable to prove his own identity, he ordered his horse that he might go in search of Ch'êng.

After some days' journey he arrived at Mount Lao; and, as his horse went along at a good rate, the servant could not keep up with him. By-and-by he rested awhile under a tree, and saw a great number of Taoist priests going backward and forward, and among them was one who stared fixedly at him. So he inquired of him where he should find Ch'êng; whereat the priest laughed and said, "I know the name. He is probably in the Great Pure Mansion." When he had given this answer he went on his way, Chou following him with his eyes about a stone's throw, until he saw him speak with some one else, and, after saying a few words, proceed onwards as before.

The person whom he had spoken with came on to where Chou was, and turned out to be a fellow-townsman of his. He was much surprised at meeting Chou, and said, "I haven't seen you for some years. They told me you had gone to Mount Lao to be a Taoist priest. How is it you are still amusing yourself among mortals?"

Chou told him who he really was; upon which the other replied, "Why, I thought the gentleman I just met was you! He has only just left me, and can't have got very far."

"Is it possible," cried Chou, "that I didn't know my own face?"

Just then the servant came up, and away they went full speed, but could not discover the object of their search. All around them was a vast desert, and they were at a loss whether to go on or to return. But Chou reflected that he had no longer any home to receive him, and determined to carry out his design to the bitter end; but as the road was dangerous for riding, he gave his horse to the servant, and bade him go back.

On he went cautiously by himself, until he spied a boy sitting by the wayside alone. He hurried up to him and asked the boy to direct him where he could find Mr. Ch'êng. "I am one of his disciples," replied the lad; and, shouldering Chou's bundle, started off to show the way.

They journeyed on together, taking their food by the light of the stars, and sleeping in the open air, until, after many miles of road, they arrived in three days at their destination. But this Great Pure locality was not like that generally spoken of in the world. Though as late as the middle of the tenth moon, there was a great profusion of flowers along the road, quite unlike the beginning of winter. The lad went in and announced the arrival of a stranger, whereupon Mr. Ch'êng came out, and Chou recognised his own features. Ch'êng grasped his hand and led him inside, where he prepared wine and food, and they began to converse together.

Chou noticed many birds of strange plumage, so tame that they were not afraid of him; and these from time to time would alight on the table and sing with voices like Pan-pipes. He was very much astonished at all this, but a love of mundane pleasures had eaten into his soul, and he had no intention of stopping. On the ground were two rush-mats, upon which Ch'êng invited his friend to sit down with him. Then about midnight a serene calm stole over him; and while he was dozing off for a moment, he seemed to change places with Ch'êng. Suspecting what had happened, he put his hand up to his chin, and found it covered with a beard as before.

At dawn he was anxious to return home, but Ch'êng pressed him to stay; and when three days had gone by Ch'êng said to him, "I pray you take a little rest now: to-morrow I will set you on your way." Chou had barely closed his eyelids before he heard Ch'êng call out, "Everything is ready for starting!" So he got up and followed him along a road other than that by which he had come, and in a very short time he saw his home in the distance.

In spite of Chou's entreaties, Ch'êng would not accompany him so far, but made Chou go, waiting himself by the roadside. So the latter went alone, and when he reached his house, knocked at the door. Receiving no answer, he determined to get over the wall, when he found that his body was as light as a leaf, and with one spring he was over. In the same manner he passed several inner walls, until he reached the ladies' apartments, where he saw by the still burning lamp that the inmates had not yet retired for the night. Hearing people talking within, he licked a hole in the paper window and peeped through, and saw his wife sitting drinking with a most disreputable-looking fellow. Bursting with rage, his first impulse was to surprise them in the act; but seeing there were two against one, he stole away and let himself out by the entrance-gate, hurrying off to Ch'êng, to whom he related what he had seen, and finally begged his assistance. Ch'êng willingly went along with him; and when they reached the room, Chou seized a big stone and hammered loudly at the door. All was then confusion inside, so Chou hammered again, upon which the door was barricaded more strongly than before. Here Ch'êng came forward with his sword, and burst the door open with a crash. Chou rushed in, and the man inside rushed out; but Ch'êng was there, and with his sword cut his arm right off. Chou rudely seized his wife, and asked what it all meant; to which she replied that the man was a friend who sometimes came to take a cup of wine with them. Thereupon Chou borrowed Ch'êng's sword and cut off her head, hanging up the trunk on a tree in the court-yard. He then went back with Ch'êng.

By-and-by he awaked and found himself on the bed, at which he was somewhat disturbed, and said, "I have had a strangely-confused dream, which has given me a fright."

"My brother," replied Ch'êng, smiling, "you look upon dreams as realities: you mistake realities for dreams." Chou asked what he meant by these words; and then Ch'êng showed him his sword besmeared with blood. Chou was terrified, and sought to destroy himself; but all at once it occurred to him that Ch'êng might be deceiving him again. Ch'êng divined his suspicions, and made haste at once to see him home.

In a little while they arrived at the village-gate, and then Ch'êng said, "Was it not here that, sword in hand, I awaited you that night? I cannot look upon the unclean spot. I pray you go on, and let me stay here. If you do not return by the afternoon, I will depart alone." Chou then approached his house, which he found all shut up as if no one was living there; so he went into his brother's.

The latter, when he beheld Chou, began to weep bitterly, saying, "After your departure, thieves broke into the house and killed my sister-in-law, hanging her body upon a tree. Alas! alas! The murderers have not yet been caught." Chou then told him the whole story of his dream, and begged him to stop further proceedings; at all of which his brother was perfectly lost in astonishment.

Chou then asked after his son, and his brother told the nurse to bring him in; whereupon the former said, "Upon this infant are centered the hopes of our race. Tend him well; for I am going to bid adieu to the world."

He then took his leave, his brother following him all the time with tears in his eyes to induce him to remain. But he heeded him not; and when they reached the village-gate his brother saw him go away with Ch'êng. From afar he looked back and said, "Forbear, and be happy!"

His brother would have replied; but here Ch'êng whisked his sleeve, and they disappeared. The brother remained there for some time, and then went back overwhelmed with grief. He was an unpractical man, and before many years were over all the property was gone and the family reduced to poverty. Chou's son, who was growing up, was thus unable to secure the services of a tutor, and had no one but his uncle to teach him.

One morning, on going into the school-room, the uncle found a letter lying on his desk addressed to himself in his brother's handwriting. There was, however, nothing in it but a finger-nail about four inches in length. Surprised at this, he laid the nail down on the ink-slab while he went out to ask whence the letter had come. This no one knew; but when he went back he found that the ink-stone had been changed into a piece of shining yellow gold. More than ever astonished, he tried the nail on copper and iron things, all of which were likewise turned to gold. He thus became very rich, sharing his wealth with Chou's son; and it was bruited about that the two families possessed the secret of transmutation.

The Fighting Quails

WANG CH'ENG BELONGED TO AN OLD FAMILY IN P'ING-YÜAN, BUT WAS SUCH AN IDLE fellow that his property gradually disappeared, until at length all he had left was an old tumble-down house. His wife and he slept under a coarse hempen coverlet, and the former was far from sparing of her reproaches.

At the time of which we are speaking the weather was unbearably hot; and Wang went to pass the night with many other of his fellow-villagers in a pavilion which stood among some dilapidated buildings belonging to a family named Chou. With the first streaks of dawn his comrades departed; but Wang slept well on till about nine o'clock, when he got up and proceeded leisurely home. All at once he saw in the grass a gold hair-pin; and taking it up to look at it, found engraved thereon in small characters—"The property of the Imperial family." Now Wang's own grandfather had married into the Imperial family, and consequently he had formerly possessed many similar articles; but while he was thinking it over up came an old woman in search of the hair-pin, which Wang, who though poor was honest, at once produced and handed to her. The old woman was delighted, and thanked Wang very much for his goodness, observing that the pin was not worth much in itself, but was a relic of her departed husband. Wang asked what her husband had been; to which she replied, "His name was Wang Chien-chih, and he was connected by marriage with the Imperial family."

"My own grandfather!" cried Wang, in great surprise; "how could you have known him?"

"You, then," said the old woman, "are his grandson. I am a fox, and many years ago I was married to your grandfather; but when he died I retired from the world. Passing by here I lost my hair-pin, which destiny conveyed into your hands."

Wang had heard of his grandfather's fox-wife, and believing therefore the old woman's story, invited her to return with him, which she did. Wang called his wife out to receive her; but when she came in rags and tatters, with unkempt hair and dirty face, the old woman sighed, and said, "Alas! Alas! has Wang Chien-chih's grandson come to this?" Then looking at the broken, smokeless stove, she added, "How, under these circumstances, have you managed even to support life?"

Here Wang's wife told the tale of their poverty, with much sobbing and tears; whereupon the old woman gave her the hair-pin, bidding her go pawn it, and with the proceeds buy some food, saying that in three days she would visit them again. Wang pressed her to stay, but she said, "You can't even keep your wife alive; what would it benefit you to have me also dependent on you?" So she went away, and then Wang told his wife who she was, at which his wife felt very much alarmed; but Wang was so loud in her praises, that finally his wife consented to treat her with all proper respect.

In three days she returned as agreed, and, producing some money, sent out for a hundred-weight of rice and a hundred-weight of corn. She passed the night with them, sleeping with Mrs. Wang, who was at first rather frightened, but who soon laid aside her suspicions when she found that the old lady meant so well toward them. Next day, the latter addressed Wang, saying, "My grandson, you must not be so lazy. You should try to make a little money in some way or other."

Wang replied that he had no capital; upon which the old lady said, "When your grandfather was alive, he allowed me to take what money I liked; but not being a mortal, I had no use for it, and consequently did not draw largely upon him. I have, however, saved from my pin-money the sum of forty ounces of silver, which has long been lying idle for want of an investment. Take it, and buy summer cloth, which you may carry to the capital and re-sell at a profit."

So Wang bought some fifty pieces of summer cloth; and the old lady made him get ready, calculating that in six or seven days he would reach the capital. She also warned him, saying,

"Be neither lazy nor slow—
For if a day too long you wait,
Repentance comes a day too late."

Wang promised all obedience, and packed up his goods and went off. On the road he was overtaken by a rain-storm which soaked him through to the skin; and as he was not accustomed to be out in bad weather, it was altogether too much for him. He accordingly sought shelter in an inn, but the rain went on steadily till night, running over the eaves of the house like so many ropes.

Next morning the roads were in a horrible state; and Wang, watching the passers-by slipping about in the slush, unable to see any path, dared not face it all, and remained until noon, when it began to dry up a little. Just then, however, the clouds closed over again, and down came the rain in torrents, causing him to stay another night before he could go on. When he was nearing the capital, he heard to his great joy that summer cloth was at a premium; and on arrival proceeded at once to take up his quarters at an inn. There the landlord said it was a pity he had come so late, as communications with the south having been only recently opened, the supply of summer cloth had been small; and there being a great demand for it among the wealthy families of the metropolis, its price had gone up to three times the usual figure. "But," he added, "two days ago several large consignments arrived, and the price went down again, so that the late comers have lost their market."

Poor Wang was thus left in the lurch, and as every day more summer cloth came in, the value of it fell in a corresponding ratio. Wang would not part with his at a loss, and held on for some ten days, when his expenses for board and lodging were added to his present distress. The landlord urged him to sell even at a loss, and turn his attention to something else, which he ultimately did, losing over ten ounces of silver on his venture. Next day he rose in the morning to depart, but on looking in his purse found all his money gone. He rushed away to tell the landlord, who, however, could do nothing for him. Some one then advised him to take out a summons and make the landlord reimburse him; but he only sighed, and said, "It is my destiny, and no fault of the landlord's." Thereupon the landlord was very grateful to him, and gave him five ounces of silver to enable him to go home.

He did not care, however, to face his grandmother empty-handed, and remained in a very undecided state, until suddenly he saw a quail-catcher winning heaps of money by fighting his birds, and selling them at over 100 *cash* a-piece. He then determined to lay out his five ounces of silver in quails, and pay back the landlord out of the profits. The latter approved very highly of this plan, and not only agreed to lend him a room but also to charge him little or nothing for his board. So Wang went off rejoicing, and bought two large baskets of quails, with which he returned to the city, to the great satisfaction of the landlord who advised him to lose no time in disposing of them.

All that night it poured in torrents, and the next morning the streets were like rivers, the rain still continuing to fall. Wang waited for it to clear up, but several days passed and still there were no signs of fine weather. He then went to look at his quails, some of which he found dead and others dying. He was much alarmed at this, but was quite at a loss what to do; and by the next day a lot more had died, so that only a few were left, which he fed all together in one basket. The day after this he went again to look at them, and lo! there remained but a single quail. With tears in his eyes he told the landlord what had happened, and he, too, was much affected.

Wang then reflected that he had no money left to carry him home, and that he could not do better than cease to live. But the landlord spoke to him and soothed him, and they went together to look at the quail. "This is a fine bird," said the landlord, "and it strikes me that it has simply killed the others. Now, as you have got nothing to do, just set to work and train it; and if it is good for anything, why you'll be able to make a living out of it."

Wang did as he was told; and when the bird was trained, the landlord bade him take it into the street and gamble for something to eat. This, too, he did, and his quail won every main; whereupon the landlord gave him some money to bet with the young fellows of the neighborhood. Everything turned out favorably, and by the end of six months he had saved twenty ounces of silver, so that he became quite easy in his mind and looked upon the quail as a dispensation of his destiny.

Now one of the princes was passionately fond of quail-fighting, and always at the Feast of Lanterns anybody who owned quails might go and fight them in the palace against the prince's birds. The landlord therefore said to Wang, "Here is a chance of enriching yourself by a single stroke; only I can't say what your luck will do for you." He then explained to him what it was, and away they went together, the landlord saying, "If you lose, burst out into lamentations; but if you are lucky enough to win, and the prince wishes, as he will, to buy your bird, don't consent. If he presses you very much watch for a nod from me before you agree."

This settled, they proceeded to the palace where they found crowds of quail-fighters already on the ground; and then the prince came forth, heralds proclaiming to the multitude that any who wished to fight their birds might come up. Some man at once stepped forward, and the prince gave orders for the quails to be released; but at the first strike the stranger's quail was knocked out of time. The prince smiled, and by-and-by won several more mains, until at last the landlord said, "Now's our time," and went up together with Wang.

The Prince looked at their bird and said, "It has a fierce-looking eye and strong feathers. We must be careful what we are doing." So he commanded his servants to bring out Iron Beak to oppose Wang's bird; but, after a couple of strikes, the Prince's quail was signally defeated. He sent for a better bird, but that shared the same fate; and then he cried out, "Bring the Jade Bird from the palace!" In a little time it arrived, with pure white feathers like an egret, and an unusually martial appearance.

Wang was much alarmed, and falling on his knees prayed to be excused this main, saying, "Your highness's bird is too good. I fear lest mine should be wounded, and my livelihood be taken from me."

But the Prince laughed and said, "Go on. If your quail is killed I will make it up to you handsomely."

Wang then released his bird and the Prince's quail rushed at it at once; but when the Jade Bird was close by, Wang's quail awaited its coming head down and full of rage. The former made a violent peck at its adversary, and then sprung up to swoop down on it. Thus they went on up and down, backward and forward, until at length they got hold of each other, and the Prince's bird was beginning to show signs of exhaustion. This enraged it all the more, and it fought more violently than ever; but soon a perfect snowstorm of feathers began to fall, and, with drooping wings, the Jade Bird made its escape.

The spectators were much moved by the result; and the Prince himself, taking up Wang's bird, examined it closely from beak to claws, finally asking if it was for sale. "My sole dependence," replied Wang, "is upon this bird. I would rather not part with it."

"But," said the Prince, "if I give you as much as the capital, say of an ordinary tradesman, will not that tempt you?"

Wang thought some time, and then answered, "I would rather not sell my bird; but as your highness has taken a fancy to it I will only ask enough to find me in food and clothes."

"How much do you want?" inquired the Prince; to which Wang replied that he would take a thousand ounces of silver.

"You fool!" cried the Prince; "do you think your bird is such a jewel as all that?"

"If your highness," said Wang, "does not think the bird a jewel, I value it more than that stone which was priced at fifteen cities."

"How so?" asked the Prince.

"Why," said Wang, "I take my bird every day into the market-place. It there wins for me several ounces of silver, which I exchange for rice; and my family, over ten in number, has nothing to fear from either cold or hunger. What jewel could do that?"

"You shall not lose anything," replied the Prince; "I will give you two hundred ounces."

But Wang would not consent, and then the prince added another hundred; whereupon Wang looked at the landlord, who, however, made no sign. Wang then offered to take nine hundred; but the prince ridiculed the idea of paying such a price for a quail, and Wang was preparing to take his leave with the bird, when the Prince called him back, saying, "Here! here! I will give you six hundred. Take it or leave it as you please."

Wang here looked at the landlord, and the landlord remained motionless as before. However, Wang was satisfied himself with this offer, and being afraid of missing his chance, said to his friend, "If I get this price for it I shall be quite content. If we go on haggling and finally come to no terms, that will be a very poor end to it all." So he took the Prince's offer, and the latter, overjoyed, caused the money to be handed to him.

Wang then returned with his earnings; but the landlord said to him, "What did I say to you? You were in too much of a hurry to sell. Another minute, and you would have got eight hundred." When Wang got back he threw the money on the table and told the landlord to take what he liked; but the latter would not, and it was only after some pressing that he would accept payment for Wang's board.

Wang then packed up and went home, where he told his story and produced his silver to the great delight of all of them. The old lady counseled the purchase of a quantity of land, the building of a house, and the purchase of implements; and in a very short time they became a wealthy family. The old lady always got up early in the morning and made Wang attend to the farm, his wife to her spinning; and rated them soundly at any signs of laziness. The husband and wife henceforth lived in peace, and no longer abused each other, until at the expiration of three years the old lady declared her intention of bidding them adieu. They both tried to stop her, and with the aid of tears succeeded in persuading her; but the next day she had disappeared.

The Painted Skin

At T'ai-yüan there lived a man named Wang. One morning he was out walking when he met a young lady carrying a bundle and hurrying along by herself. As she moved along with some difficulty, Wang quickened his pace and caught her up, and found she was a pretty girl of about sixteen. Much smitten he inquired whither she was going so early, and no one with her.

"A traveler like you," replied the girl, "cannot alleviate my distress; why trouble yourself to ask?"

"What distress is it?" said Wang; "I'm sure I'll do anything I can for you."

"My parents," answered she, "loved money, and they sold me as concubine into a rich family, where the wife was very jealous, and beat and abused me morning and night. It was more than I could stand, so I have run away."

Wang asked her where she was going; to which she replied that a runaway had no fixed place of abode.

"My house," said Wang, "is at no great distance; what do you say to coming there?" She joyfully acquiesced; and Wang, taking up her bundle, led the way to his house. Finding no one there, she asked Wang where his family were; to which he replied that that was only the library.

"And a very nice place, too," said she; "but if you are kind enough to wish to save my life, you mustn't let it be known that I am here." Wang promised he would not divulge her secret, and so she remained there for some days without anyone knowing anything about it.

He then told his wife, and she, fearing the girl might belong to some influential family, advised him to send her away. This, however, he would not consent to do; when one day, going into the town, he met a Taoist priest, who looked at him in astonishment, and asked him what he had met.

"I have met nothing," replied Wang.

"Why," said the priest, "you are bewitched; what do you mean by not having met anything?" But Wang insisted that it was so, and the priest walked away, saying, "The fool! Some people don't seem to know when death is at hand."

This startled Wang, who at first thought of the girl; but then he reflected that a pretty young thing as she was couldn't well be a witch, and began to suspect that the priest merely wanted to do a stroke of business. When he returned, the library door was shut, and he couldn't get in, which made him suspect that something was wrong; and so he climbed over the wall, where he found the door of the inner room shut too. Softly creeping up, he looked through the window and saw a hideous devil, with a green face and jagged teeth like a saw, spreading a human skin upon the bed and painting it with a paint-brush. The devil then threw aside the brush, and giving the skin a shake out, just as you would a coat, threw it over its shoulders, when, lo! it was the girl.

Terrified at this, Wang hurried away with his head down in search of the priest who had gone he knew not whither; subsequently finding him in the fields, where he threw himself on his knees and begged the priest to save him.

"As to driving her away," said the priest, "the creature must be in great distress to be seeking a substitute for herself; besides, I could hardly endure to injure a living thing." However, he gave Wang a fly-brush, and bade him hang it at the door of the bedroom, agreeing to meet again at the Ch'ing-ti temple.

Wang went home, but did not dare enter the library; so he hung up the brush at the bedroom door, and before long heard a sound of footsteps outside. Not daring to move, he made his wife peep out; and she saw the girl standing looking at the brush, afraid to pass it. She then ground her teeth and went away; but in a little while came back, and began cursing, saying, "You priest, you won't frighten me. Do you think I am going to give up what is already in my grasp?" Thereupon, she tore the brush to pieces, and bursting open the door, walked straight up to the bed, where she ripped open Wang and tore out his heart, with which she went away.

Wang's wife screamed out, and the servant came in with a light; but Wang was already dead and presented a most miserable spectacle. His wife, who was in an agony of fright, hardly dared cry for fear of making a noise; and next day she sent Wang's brother to see the priest. The latter got into a great rage, and cried out, "Was it for this that I had compassion on you, devil that you are?" proceeding at once with Wang's brother to the house, from which the girl had disappeared without anyone knowing whither she had gone. But the priest, raising his head, looked all round, and said, "Luckily she's not far off." He then asked who lived in the apartments on the south side, to which Wang's brother replied that he did; whereupon the priest declared that there she would be found.

Wang's brother was horribly frightened and said he did not think so; and then the priest asked him if any stranger had been to the house. To this he answered that he had been out to the Ch'ing-ti temple and couldn't possibly say; but he went off to inquire, and in a little while came back and reported that an old woman had sought service with them as a maid-of-all-work, and had been engaged by his wife. "That is she," said the priest, as Wang's brother added she was still there; and they all set out to go to the house together. Then the priest took his wooden sword, and standing in the middle of the court-yard, shouted out, "Base-born fiend, give me back my fly-brush!"

Meanwhile the new maid-of-all-work was in a great state of alarm, and tried to get away by the door; but the priest struck her and down she fell flat, the human skin dropped off, and she became a hideous devil. There she lay grunting like a pig, until the priest grasped his wooden sword and struck off her head. She then became a dense column of smoke curling up from the ground, when the priest took an uncorked gourd and threw it right into the midst of the smoke. A sucking noise was heard, and the whole column was drawn into the gourd; after which the priest corked it up closely and put it in his pouch. The skin, too, which was complete even to the eyebrows, eyes, hands, and feet, he also rolled up as if it had been a scroll, and was on the point of leaving with it, when Wang's wife stopped him, and with tears entreated him to bring her husband to life.

The priest said he was unable to do that; but Wang's wife flung herself at his feet, and with loud lamentations implored his assistance. For some time he remained immersed in thought, and then replied, "My power is not equal to what you ask. I myself cannot raise the dead; but I will direct you to some one who can, and if you apply to him properly you will succeed."

Wang's wife asked the priest who it was; to which he replied, "There is a maniac in the town who passes his time groveling in the dirt. Go, prostrate yourself before him, and beg him to help you. If he insults you, show no sign of anger." Wang's brother knew the man to whom he alluded, and accordingly bade the priest adieu, and proceeded thither with his sister-in-law.

They found the destitute creature raving away by the road side, so filthy that it was all they could do to go near him. Wang's wife approached him on her knees; at which the maniac leered at her, and cried out, "Do you love me, my beauty?" Wang's wife told him what she had come for, but he only laughed and said, "You can get plenty of other husbands. Why raise the dead one to life?" But Wang's wife entreated him to help her; whereupon he observed, "It's very strange: people apply to me to raise their dead as if I was king of the infernal regions." He then gave Wang's wife a thrashing with his staff, which she bore without a murmur, and before a gradually increasing crowd of spectators. After this he produced a loathsome pill which he told her she must swallow, but here she broke down and was quite unable to do so. However, she did manage it at last, and then the maniac crying out, "How you do love me!" got up and went away without taking any more notice of her. They followed him into a temple with loud supplications, but he had disappeared, and every effort to find him was unsuccessful. Overcome with rage and shame, Wang's wife went home, where she mourned bitterly over her dead husband, grievously repenting the steps she had taken, and wishing only to die. She then bethought herself of preparing the corpse, near which none of the servants would venture; and set to work to close up the frightful wound of which he died.

While thus employed, interrupted from time to time by her sobs, she felt a rising lump in her throat, which by-and-by came out with a pop and fell straight into the dead man's wound. Looking closely at it, she saw it was a human heart; and then it began as it were to throb, emitting a warm vapor like smoke. Much excited, she at once closed the flesh over it, and held the sides of the wound together with all her might. Very soon, however, she got tired, and finding the vapor escaping from the crevices, she tore up a piece of silk and bound it round, at the same time bringing back circulation by rubbing the body and covering it up with clothes. In the night, she removed the coverings, and found that breath was coming from the nose; and by next morning her husband was alive again, though disturbed in mind as if awaking from a dream and feeling a pain in his heart. Where he had been wounded, there was a cicatrix about as big as a cash, which soon after disappeared.

The Trader's Son

In the province of Hunan there dwelt a man who was engaged in trading abroad; and his wife, who lived alone, dreamt one night that some one was in her room. Waking up, she looked about, and discovered a small creature which on examination she knew to be a fox; but in a moment the thing had disappeared, although the door had not been opened.

The next evening she asked the cook-maid to come and keep her company; as also her own son, a boy of ten, who was accustomed to sleep elsewhere. Toward the middle of the night, when the cook and the boy were fast asleep, back came the fox; and the cook was waked up by hearing her mistress muttering something as if she had nightmare. The former then called out, and the fox ran away; but from that moment the trader's wife was not quite herself. When night came she dared not blow out the candle, and bade her son be sure and not sleep too soundly. Later on, her son and the old woman having taken a nap as they leaned against the wall, suddenly waked up and found her gone. They waited some time, but she did not return, and the cook was too frightened to go and look after her; so her son took a light, and at length found her fast asleep in another room. She didn't seem aware that anything particular had happened, but she became queerer and queerer every day, and wouldn't have either her son or the cook to keep her company any more. Her son, however, made a point of running at once into his mother's room if he heard any unusual sounds; and though his mother always abused him for his pains, he paid no attention to what she said. At the same time, the more people urged him on to keep a sharp look-out, the more eccentric were his mother's ways.

One day she played at being a mason, and piled up stones upon the window-sill, in spite of all that was said to her; and if anyone took away a stone, she threw herself on the ground, and cried like a child, so that nobody dared go near her. In a few days she had got both windows blocked up and the light excluded; and then she set to filling up the chinks with mud. She worked hard all day without minding the trouble, and when it was finished she smoothed it off with the kitchen chopper. Everyone who saw her was disgusted with such antics, and would take no notice of her. At night her son darkened his lamp, and, with a knife concealed on his person, sat waiting for his mother to mutter. As soon as she began he uncovered his light, and, blocking up the doorway, shouted out at the top of his voice. Nothing, however, happened, and he moved from the door a little way, when suddenly out rushed something like a fox, which was disappearing through the door, when he made a quick movement and cut off about two inches of its tail, from which the warm blood was still dripping as he brought the light to bear upon it. His mother hereupon cursed and reviled him, but he pretended not to hear her, regretting only as he went to bed that he hadn't hit the brute fair. But he consoled himself by thinking that although he hadn't killed it outright, he had done enough to prevent it coming again.

On the morrow he followed the tracks of blood over the wall and into the garden of a family named Ho; and that night, to his great joy, the fox did not reappear. His mother was meanwhile prostrate, with hardly any life in her, and in the midst of it all his father came home. The boy told him what had happened, at which he was much alarmed, and sent for a doctor to attend his wife; but she only threw the medicine away, and cursed and swore horribly. So they secretly mixed the medicine with her tea and soup, and in a few days she began to get better, to the inexpressible delight of both her husband and son.

One night, however, her husband woke up and found her gone; and after searching for her with the aid of his son, they discovered her sleeping in another room. From that time she became more eccentric than ever, and was always being found in strange places, cursing those who tried to remove her. Her husband was at his wits' end. It was no use keeping the door locked, for it opened of itself at her approach; and he had called in any number of magicians to exorcise the fox, but without obtaining the slightest result.

One evening her son concealed himself in the Ho family garden, and lay down in the long grass with a view to detecting the fox's retreat. As the moon rose he heard the sound of voices, and, pushing aside the grass, saw two people drinking, with a long-bearded servant pouring out their wine, dressed in an old dark-brown coat. They were whispering together, and he could not make out what they said; but by-and-by he heard one of them remark, "Get some white wine for to-morrow," and then they went away, leaving the long-bearded servant alone. The latter then threw off his coat, and lay down to sleep on the stones; whereupon the trader's son eyed him carefully, and saw that he was like a man in every respect except that he had a tail. The boy would then have gone home; but he was afraid the fox might hear him, and accordingly remained where he was till near dawn, when he saw the other two come back, one at a time, and then they all disappeared among the bushes.

On reaching home his father asked him where he had been, and he replied that he had stopped the night with the Ho family. He then accompanied his father to the town, where he saw hanging up at a hat-shop a fox's tail, and finally, after much coaxing, succeeded in making his father buy it for him. While the latter was engaged in a shop, his son, who was playing about beside him, availed himself of a moment when his father was not looking and stole some money from him, and went off and bought a quantity of white wine, which he left in charge of the wine-merchant.

Now an uncle of his, who was a sportsman by trade, lived in the city, and thither he next betook himself. His uncle was out, but his aunt was there, and inquired after the health of his mother. "She has been better the last few days," replied he; "but she is now very much upset by a rat having gnawed a dress of hers, and has sent me to ask for some poison." His aunt opened the cupboard and gave him about the tenth of an ounce in a piece of paper, which he thought was very little; so, when his aunt had gone to get him something to eat, he took the opportunity of being alone, opened the packet, and abstracted a large handful. Hiding this in his coat, he ran to tell his aunt that she needn't prepare anything for him, as his father was waiting in the market, and he couldn't stop to eat it. He then went off; and having quietly dropped the poison into the wine he had bought, went sauntering about the town.

At nightfall he returned home, and told his father that he had been at his uncle's. This he continued to do for some time, until one day he saw amongst the crowd his long-bearded friend. Marking him closely, he followed him, and at length entered into conversation, asking him where he lived.

"I live at Pei-ts'un," said he; "where do you live?"

"I," replied the trader's son, falsely, "live in a hole on the hill-side." The long-bearded man was considerably startled at his answer, but much more so when he added, "We've lived there for generations: haven't *you*?"

The other then asked his name, to which the boy replied, "My name is Hu. I saw you with two gentlemen in the Ho family garden, and haven't forgotten you." Questioning him more fully, the long-bearded man was still in a half-and-half state of belief and doubt, when the trader's son opened his coat a little bit, and showed him the end of the tail he had bought, saying, "The like of us can mix with ordinary people, but unfortunately we can never get rid of this."

The long-bearded man then asked him what he was doing there, to which he answered that his father had sent him to buy wine; whereupon the former remarked that that was exactly what he had come for, and the boy then inquired if he had bought it yet or not. "We are poor," replied the stranger, "and as a rule I prefer to steal it."

"A difficult and dangerous job," observed the boy. "I have my master's instructions to get some," said the other, "and what am I to do?"

The boy then asked him who his masters were, to which he replied that they were the two brothers the boy had seen that night. "One of them has bewitched a lady named Wang; and the other, the wife of a trader who lives near. The son of the last-mentioned lady is a violent fellow, and cut off my master's tail, so that he was laid up for ten days. But he is putting her under spells again now."

He was then going away, saying he should never get his wine; but the boy said to him, "It's much easier to buy than steal. I have some at the wine-shop there which I will give to you. My purse isn't empty, and I can buy some more." The long-bearded man hardly knew how to thank him; but the boy said, "We're all one family. Don't mention such a trifle. When I have time I'll come and take a drink with you."

So they went off together to the wine-shop, where the boy gave him the wine and they then separated. That night his mother slept quietly and had no fits, and the boy knew that something must have happened. He then told his father, and they went to see if there were any results; when lo! they found both foxes stretched out dead in the arbour. One of the foxes was lying on the grass, and out of its mouth blood was still trickling. The wine-bottle was there; and on shaking it they heard that some was left. Then his father asked him why he had kept it all so secret; to which the boy replied that foxes were very sagacious, and would have been sure to scent the plot. Thereupon his father was mightily pleased, and said he was a perfect Ulysses for cunning.

They then carried the foxes home, and saw on the tail of one of them the scar of a knife-wound. From that time they were left in peace; but the trader's wife became very thin, and though her reason returned, she shortly afterward died of consumption. The other lady, Mrs. Wang, began to get better as soon as the foxes had been killed; and as to the boy, he was taught riding and archery by his proud parent, and subsequently rose to high rank in the army.

Judge Lu

At Ling-yang there lived a man named Chu Erh-tan, whose literary designation was Hsiao-ming. He was a fine manly fellow, but an egregious dunce, though he tried hard to learn. One day he was taking wine with a number of fellow-students, when one of them said to him, by way of a joke, "People credit you with plenty of pluck. Now, if you will go in the middle of the night to the Chamber of Horrors, and bring back the Infernal Judge from the left-hand porch, we'll all stand you a dinner." For at Ling-yang there was a representation of the Ten Courts of Purgatory, with the Gods and devils carved in wood, and almost life-like in appearance; and in the eastern vestibule there was a full-length image of the Judge with a green face, and a red beard, and a hideous expression in his features. Sometimes sounds of examination under the whip were heard to issue during the night from both porches, and persons who went in found their hair standing on end from fear; so the other young men thought it would be a capital test for Mr. Chu. Thereupon Chu smiled, and rising from his seat went straight off to the temple; and before many minutes had elapsed they heard him shouting outside, "His Excellency has arrived!" At this they all got up, and in came Chu with the image on his back, which he proceeded to deposit on the table, and then poured out a triple libation in its honor.

His comrades who were watching what he did, felt ill at ease, and did not like to resume their seats; so they begged him to carry the Judge back again. But he first poured some wine upon the ground, invoking the image as follows:—

"I am only a fool-hardy, illiterate fellow: I pray Your Excellency excuse me. My house is close by, and whenever Your Excellency feels so disposed I shall be glad to take a cup of wine with you in a friendly way."

He then carried the Judge back, and the next day his friends gave him the promised dinner, from which he went home half-tipsy in the evening. But not feeling that he had had enough, he brightened up his lamp, and helped himself to another cup of wine, when suddenly the bamboo curtain was drawn aside, and in walked the Judge.

Mr. Chu got up and said, "Oh, dear! Your Excellency has come to cut off my head for my rudeness the other night."

The Judge parted his thick beard, and smiling, replied, "Nothing of the kind. You kindly invited me last night to visit you; and as I have leisure this evening, here I am."

Chu was delighted at this, and made his guest sit down, while he himself wiped the cups and lighted a fire. "It's warm weather," said the Judge; "let's drink the wine cold." Chu obeyed, and putting the bottle on the table, went out to tell his servants to get some supper. His wife was much alarmed when she heard who was there, and begged him not to go back; but he only waited until the things were ready, and then returned with them.

They drank out of each other's cups, and by-and-by Chu asked the name of his guest. "My name is Lu," replied the Judge; "I have no other names." They then conversed on literary subjects, one capping the other's quotation as echo responds to sound.

The Judge then asked Chu if he understood composition; to which he answered that he could just tell good from bad; whereupon the former repeated a little infernal poetry which was not very different from that of mortals. He was a deep drinker, and took off ten goblets at a draught; but Chu who had been at it all day, soon got dead drunk and fell fast asleep with his head on the table. When he waked up the candle had burned out and day was beginning to break, his guest having already departed; and from this time the Judge was in the habit of dropping in pretty often, until a close friendship sprang up between them. Sometimes the latter would pass the night at the house, and Chu would show him his essays, all of which the Judge scored and underlined as being good for nothing.

One night Chu got tipsy and went to bed first, leaving the Judge drinking by himself. In his drunken sleep he seemed to feel a pain in his stomach, and waking up he saw that the Judge, who was standing by the side of the bed, had opened him, and was carefully arranging his inside.

"What harm have I done you?" cried Chu, "that you should thus seek to destroy me?"

"Don't be afraid," replied the Judge, laughing, "I am only providing you with a more intelligent heart." He then quietly put back Chu's viscera, and closed up the opening, securing it with a bandage tied tightly round his waist. There was no blood on the bed, and all Chu felt was a slight numbness in his inside. Here he observed the Judge place a piece of flesh upon the table, and asked him what it was. "Your heart," said the latter, "which wasn't at all good at composition, the proper orifice being stuffed up. I have now provided you with a better one, which I procured from Hades, and I am keeping yours to put in its place." He then opened the door and took his leave.

In the morning Chu undid the bandage, and looked at his waist, the wound on which had quite healed up, leaving only a red seam. From that moment he became an apt scholar, and found his memory much improved; so much so, that a few days afterward he showed an essay to the Judge for which he was very much commended. "However," said the latter, "your success will be limited to the master's degree. You won't get beyond that."

"When shall I take it?" asked Chu.

"This year," replied the Judge.

And so it turned out. Chu passed first on the list for the bachelor's degree, and then among the first five for the master's degree. His old comrades, who had been accustomed to make a laughing-stock of him, were now astonished to find him a full blown M.A., and when they learned how it had come about, they begged Chu to speak to the Judge on their behalf. The Judge promised to assist them, and they made all ready to receive him; but when in the evening he did come, they were so frightened at his red beard and flashing eyes that their teeth chattered in their heads, and one by one they stole away. Chu then took the Judge home with him to have a cup together, and when the wine had mounted well into his head, he said, "I am deeply grateful to Your Excellency's former kindness in arranging my inside; but there is still another favor I venture to ask which possibly may be granted." The Judge asked him what it was; and Chu replied, "If you can change a person's inside, you surely could also change his face. Now my wife is not at all a bad figure, but she is very ugly. I pray Your Excellency try the knife upon her." The Judge laughed, and said he would do so, only it would be necessary to give him a little time.

Some days subsequently, the Judge knocked at Chu's door toward the middle of the night; whereupon the latter jumped up and invited him in. Lighting a candle, it was evident that the Judge had something under his coat, and in answer to Chu's inquiries, he said, "It's what you asked me for. I have had great trouble in procuring it." He then produced the head of a nice-looking young girl, and presented it to Chu, who found the blood on the neck was still warm. "We must make haste," said the Judge, "and take care not to wake the fowls or dogs."

Chu was afraid his wife's door might be bolted; but the Judge laid his hand on it and it opened at once. Chu then led him to the bed where his wife was lying asleep on her side; and the Judge, giving Chu the head to hold, drew from his boot a steel blade shaped like the handle of a spoon. He laid this across the lady's neck, which he cut through as if it had been a melon, and the head fell over the back of the pillow. Seizing the head he had brought with him, he now fitted it on carefully and accurately, and pressing it down to make it stick, bolstered the lady up with pillows placed on either side. When all was finished, he bade Chu put his wife's old head away, and then took his leave.

Soon after Mrs. Chu waked up, and perceived a curious sensation about her neck, and a scaly feeling about the jaws. Putting her hand to her face, she found flakes of dry blood; and much frightened called a maid-servant to bring water to wash it off. The maid-servant was also greatly alarmed at the appearance of her face, and proceeded to wash off the blood, which colored a whole basin of water; but when she saw her mistress's new face she was almost frightened to death. Mrs. Chu took a mirror to look at herself, and was staring at herself in utter astonishment, when her husband came in and explained what had taken place. On examining her more closely, Chu saw that she had a well-featured pleasant face, of a medium order of beauty; and when he came to look at her neck, he found a red seam all round, with the parts above and below of a different colored flesh.

Now the daughter of an official named Wu was a very nice-looking girl who, though nineteen years of age, had not yet been married, two gentlemen who were engaged to her having died before the day. At the Feast of Lanterns, this young lady happened to visit the Chamber of Horrors, whence she was followed home by a burglar, who that night broke into the house and killed her. Hearing a noise, her mother told the servant to go and see what was the matter; and the murder being thus discovered, every member of the family got up. They placed the body in the hall, with the head alongside, and gave themselves up to weeping and wailing the livelong night.

Next morning, when they removed the coverings, the corpse was there but the head had disappeared. The waiting-maids were accordingly flogged for neglect of duty, and consequent loss of the head, and Mr. Wu brought the matter to the notice of the Prefect. This officer took very energetic measures, but for three days no clue could be obtained; and then the story of the changed head in the Chu family gradually reached Mr. Wu's ears. Suspecting something, he sent an old woman to make inquiries; and she at once recognised her late young mistress's features, and went back and reported to her master. Thereupon Mr. Wu, unable to make out why the body should have been left, imagined that Chu had slain his daughter by magical arts, and at once proceeded to the house to find out the truth of the matter; but Chu told him that his wife's head had been changed in her sleep, and that he knew nothing about it, adding that it was unjust to accuse him of the murder. Mr. Wu refused to believe this, and took proceedings against him; but as all the servants told the same story, the Prefect was unable to convict him.

Chu returned home and took counsel with the Judge, who told him there would be no difficulty, it being merely necessary to make the murdered girl herself speak. That night Mr. Wu dreamt that his daughter came and said to him, "I was killed by Yang Ta-nien, of Su-ch'i. Mr. Chu had nothing to do with it; but desiring a better-looking face for his wife, Judge Lu gave him mine, and thus my body is dead while my head still lives. Bear Chu no malice." When he awaked, he told his wife, who had dreamt the same dream; and thereupon he communicated these facts to the officials. Subsequently, a man of that name was captured, who confessed under the bamboo that he had committed the crime; so Mr. Wu went off to Chu's house, and asked to be allowed to see his wife, regarding Chu from that time as his son-in-law. Mrs. Chu's old head was fitted on to the young lady's body, and the two parts were buried together.

Subsequent to these events Mr. Chu tried three times for his doctor's degree, but each time without success, and at last he gave up the idea of entering into official life. Then when thirty years had passed away, Judge Lu appeared to him one night, and said, "My friend, you cannot live for ever. Your hour will come in five days' time." Chu asked the Judge if he could not save him; to which he replied, "The decrees of Heaven cannot be altered to suit the purposes of mortals. Besides, to an intelligent man life and death are much the same. Why necessarily regard life as a boon and death as a misfortune?" Chu could make no reply to this, and forthwith proceeded to order his coffin and shroud; and then, dressing himself in his grave-clothes, yielded up the ghost.

Next day, as his wife was weeping over his bier, in he walked at the front door, to her very great alarm. "I am now a disembodied spirit," said Chu to her, "though not different from what I was in life; and I have been thinking much of the widow and orphan I left behind." His wife, hearing this, wept till the tears ran down her face, Chu all the time doing his best to comfort her.

"I have heard tell," said she, "of dead bodies returning to life; and since your vital spark is not extinct, why does it not resume the flesh?"

"The ordinances of Heaven," replied her husband, "may not be disobeyed." His wife here asked him what he was doing in the infernal regions; and he said that Judge Lu had got him an appointment as Registrar, with a certain rank attached, and that he was not at all uncomfortable.

Mrs. Chu was proceeding to inquire further, when he interrupted her, saying, "The Judge has come with me; get some wine ready and something to eat." He then hurried out, and his wife did as he had told her, hearing them laughing and drinking in the guest chamber just like old times come back again. About midnight she peeped in, and found that they had both disappeared; but they came back once in every two or three days, often spending the night, and managing the family affairs as usual.

Chu's son was named Wei, and was about five years old; and whenever his father came he would take the little boy upon his knee. When he was about eight years of age, Chu began to teach him to read; and the boy was so clever that by the time he was nine he could actually compose. At fifteen he took his bachelor's degree, without knowing all this time that he had no father. From that date Chu's visits became less frequent, occurring not more than once or so in a month; until one night he told his wife that they were never to meet again. In reply to her inquiry as to whither he was going, he said he had been appointed to a far-off post, where press of business and distance would combine to prevent him from visiting them any more. The mother and son clung to him, sobbing bitterly; but he said, "Do not act thus. The boy is now a man, and can look after your affairs. The dearest friends must part some day." Then, turning to his son, he added, "Be an honorable man, and take care of the property. Ten years hence we shall meet again." With this he bade them farewell, and went away.

Later on, when Wei was twenty-two years of age, he took his doctor's degree, and was appointed to conduct the sacrifices at the Imperial tombs. On his way thither he fell in with a retinue of an official, proceeding along with all the proper insignia, and, looking carefully at the individual sitting in the carriage, he was astonished to find that it was his own father. Alighting from his horse, he prostrated himself with tears at the side of the road; whereupon his father stopped and said, "You are well spoken of. I now take leave of this world."

Wei remained on the ground, not daring to rise; and his father, urging on his carriage, hurried away without saying any more. But when he had gone a short distance, he looked back, and unloosing a sword from his waist, sent it as a present to his son, shouting out to him, "Wear this and you will succeed." Wei tried to follow him; but, in an instant, carriage, retinue, and horses, had vanished with the speed of wind. For a long time his son gave himself up to grief, and then seizing the sword began to examine it closely.

It was of exquisite workmanship, and on the blade was engraved this legend:—*"Be bold, but cautious; round in disposition, square in action."* Wei subsequently rose to high honors, and had five sons named Ch'ên, Ch'ien, Wu, Hun, and Shên. One night he dreamt that his father told him to give the sword to Hun, which he accordingly did; and Hun rose to be a Viceroy of great administrative ability.

Miss Ying-ning, or the Laughing Girl

At Lo-tien, in the province of Shantung, there lived a youth named Wang Tzŭ-fu, who had been left an orphan when quite young. He was a clever boy, and took his bachelor's degree at the age of fourteen, being quite his mother's pet, and not allowed by her to stray far away from home. One young lady to whom he had been betrothed having unhappily died, he was still in search of a wife when, on the occasion of the Feast of Lanterns, his cousin Wu asked him to come along for a stroll. But they had hardly got beyond the village before one of his uncle's servants caught them up and told Wu he was wanted. The latter accordingly went back; but Wang, seeing plenty of nice girls about and being in high spirits himself, proceeded on alone.

Among others, he noticed a young lady with her maid. She had just picked a sprig of plum-blossom, and was the prettiest girl he had ever heard of—a perfect bunch of smiles. He stared and stared at her quite regardless of appearances; and when she had passed by, she said to her maid, "That young fellow has a wicked look in his eyes." As she was walking away, laughing and talking, the flower dropped out of her hand; and Wang, picking it up, stood there disconsolate as if he had lost his wits. He then went home in a very melancholy mood; and, putting the flower under his pillow, lay down to sleep. He would neither talk nor eat; and his mother became very anxious about him, and called in the aid of the priests. By degrees, he fell off in flesh and got very thin; and the doctor felt his pulse and gave him medicines to bring out the disease. Occasionally, he seemed bewildered in his mind, but in spite of all his mother's inquiries would give no clue as to the cause of his malady.

One day when his cousin Wu came to the house, Wang's mother told him to try and find out what was the matter; and the former, approaching the bed, gradually and quietly led up to the point in question. Wang, who had wept bitterly at the sight of his cousin, now repeated to him the whole story, begging him to lend some assistance in the matter.

"How foolish you are, cousin," cried Wu; "there will be no difficulty at all, I'll make inquiries for you. The girl herself can't belong to a very aristocratic family to be walking alone in the country. If she's not already engaged, I have no doubt we can arrange the affair; and even if she is unwilling, an extra outlay will easily bring her round. You make haste and get well: I'll see to it all." Wang's features relaxed when he heard these words; and Wu left him to tell his mother how the case stood, immediately setting on foot inquiries as to the whereabouts of the girl. All his efforts, however, proved fruitless, to the great disappointment of Wang's mother; for since his cousin's visit Wang's color and appetite had returned.

In a few days Wu called again, and in answer to Wang's questions falsely told him that the affair was settled. "Who do you think the young lady is?" said he. "Why, a cousin of ours, who is only waiting to be betrothed; and though you two are a little near, I daresay the circumstances of the case will be allowed to overrule this objection."

Wang was overjoyed, and asked where she lived; so Wu had to tell another lie, and say, "On the south-west hills, about ten miles from here." Wang begged him again and again to do his best for him, and Wu undertook to get the betrothal satisfactorily arranged. He then took leave of his cousin, who from this moment was rapidly restored to health. Wang drew the flower from underneath his pillow, and found that, though dried up, the leaves had not fallen away. He often sat playing with this flower and thinking of the young lady; but by-and-by, as Wu did not reappear, he wrote a letter and asked him to come. Wu pleaded other engagements, being unwilling to go; at which Wang got in a rage and quite lost his good spirits; so that his mother, fearing a relapse, proposed to him a speedy betrothal in another quarter. Wang shook his head at this, and sat day after day waiting for Wu, until his patience was thoroughly exhausted. He then reflected that ten miles was no great distance, and that there was no particular reason for asking anybody's aid; so, concealing the flower in his sleeve, he went off in a huff by himself without letting it be known. Having no opportunity of asking the way, he made straight for the hills; and after about ten miles walking found himself right in the midst of them, enjoying their exquisite verdure, but meeting no one, and with nothing better than mountain paths to guide him.

Away down in the valley below, almost buried under a densely luxuriant growth of trees and flowers, he espied a small hamlet, and began to descend the hill and make his way thither. He found very few houses, and all built of rushes, but otherwise pleasant enough to look at. Before the door of one, which stood at the northern end of the village, were a number of graceful willow trees, and inside the wall plenty of peach and apricot trees, with tufts of bamboo between them, and birds chirping on the branches. As it was a private house he did not venture to go in, but sat down to rest himself on a huge smooth stone opposite the front door.

By-and-by he heard a girl's voice from within calling out Hsiao-jung; and, noticing that it was a sweet-toned voice, set himself to listen, when a young lady passed with a bunch of apricot-flowers in her hand, and occupied in putting hair-pins into her downcast head. As soon as she raised her face she saw Wang, and stopped putting in hair-pins; then, smothering a laugh, picked a few flowers and ran in. Wang perceived to his intense delight that she was none other than his heroine of the Feast of Lanterns; but recollecting that he had no right to follow her in, was on the point of calling after her as his cousin. There was no one, however, in the street, and he was afraid lest he might have made a mistake; neither was there anybody at the door of whom he could make inquiries. So he remained there in a very restless state till the sun was well down in the west, and his hopes were almost at an end, forgetting all about food and drink.

He then saw the young lady peep through the door, apparently very much astonished to find him still there; and in a few minutes out came an old woman leaning on a stick, who said to him, "Whence do you come, Sir? I hear you have been here ever since morning. What is it you want? Aren't you hungry?" Wang got up, and making a bow, replied that he was in search of some relatives of his; but the old woman was deaf and didn't catch what he said, so he had to shout it out again at the top of his voice. She asked him what their names were, but he was unable to tell her; at which she laughed and said, "It is a funny thing to look for people when you don't know their names. I am afraid you are an unpractical gentleman. You had better come in and have something to eat; we'll give you a bed and you can go back to-morrow and find out the names of the people you are in quest of."

Now Wang was just beginning to get hungry, and, besides, this would bring him nearer to the young lady; so he readily accepted and followed the old woman in. They walked along a paved path banked on both sides with hibiscus, the leaves of which were scattered about on the ground; and passing through another door, entered a court-yard full of trained creepers and other flowers. The old woman showed Wang into a small room with beautifully white walls and a branch of a crab-apple tree coming through the window, the furniture being also nice and clean. They had hardly sat down when it was clear that some one was taking a peep through the window; whereupon the old woman cried out, "Hsiao-jung! make haste and get dinner," and a maid from outside immediately answered, "Yes, ma'am."

Meanwhile, Wang had been explaining who he was; and then the old lady said, "Was your maternal grandfather named Wu?"

"He was," replied Wang.

"Well, I never!" cried the old woman, "he was my uncle, and your mother and I are cousins. But in consequence of our poverty, and having no sons, we have kept quite to ourselves, and you have grown to be a man without my knowing you."

"I came here," said Wang, "about my cousin, but in the hurry I forgot your name."

"My name is Ch'in," replied the old lady; "I have no son: only a girl, the child of a concubine, who, after my husband's death, married again and left her daughter with me. She's a clever girl, but has had very little education; full of fun and ignorant of the sorrows of life. I'll send for her by-and-by to make your acquaintance."

The maid then brought in the dinner—a large dish full of choice morsels of fowl—and the old woman pressed him to eat. When they had finished, and the things were taken away, the old woman said, "Call Miss Ning," and the maid went off to do so. After some time there was a giggling at the door, and the old woman cried out, "Ying-ning! your cousin is here." There was then a great tittering as the maid pushed her in, stopping her mouth all the time to try and keep from laughing. "Don't you know better than to behave like that?" asked the old woman, "and before a stranger, too." So Ying-ning controlled her feelings, and Wang made her a bow, the old woman saying, "Mr. Wang is your cousin: you have never seen him before. Isn't that funny?" Wang asked how old his cousin was, but the old woman didn't hear him, and he had to say it again, which sent Ying-ning off into another fit of laughter.

"I told you," observed the old woman, "she hadn't much education; now you see it. She is sixteen years old, and as foolish as a baby."

"One year younger than I am," remarked Wang. "Oh, you're seventeen are you? Then you were born in the year ——, under the sign of the horse." Wang nodded assent, and then the old woman asked who his wife was, to which Wang replied that he had none. "What! a clever, handsome young fellow of seventeen not yet engaged? Ying-ning is not engaged either: you two would make a nice pair if it wasn't for the relationship."

Wang said nothing, but looked hard at his cousin; and just then the maid whispered to her, "It is the fellow with the wicked eyes! He's at his old game." Ying-ning laughed, and proposed to the maid that they should go and see if the peaches were in blossom or not; and off they went together, the former with her sleeve stuffed into her mouth until she got outside, where she burst into a hearty fit of laughing.

The old woman gave orders for a bed to be got ready for Wang, saying to him, "It's not often we meet: you must spend a few days with us now you are here, and then we'll send you home. If you are at all dull, there's a garden behind where you can amuse yourself, and books for you to read."

So next day Wang strolled into the garden, which was of moderate size, with a well-kept lawn and plenty of trees and flowers. There was also an arbor consisting of three posts with a thatched roof, quite shut in on all sides by the luxurious vegetation. Pushing his way among the flowers, Wang heard a noise from one of the trees, and looking up saw Ying-ning, who at once burst out laughing and nearly fell down. "Don't! don't!" cried Wang, "you'll fall!" Then Ying-ning came down, giggling all the time, until, when she was near the ground, she missed her hold, and tumbled down with a run. This stopped her merriment, and Wang picked her up, gently squeezing her hand as he did so. Ying-ning began laughing again, and was obliged to lean against a tree for support, it being some time before she was able to stop. Wang waited till she had finished, and then drew the flower out of his sleeve and handed it to her. "It's dead," said she; "why do you keep it?"

"You dropped it, cousin, at the Feast of Lanterns," replied Wang, "and so I kept it." She then asked him what was his object in keeping it, to which he answered, "To show my love, and that I have not forgotten you. Since that day when we met, I have been very ill from thinking so much of you, and am quite changed from what I was. But now that it is my unexpected good fortune to meet you, I pray you have pity on me."

"You needn't make such a fuss about a trifle," replied she, "and with your own relatives, too. I'll give orders to supply you with a whole basketful of flowers when you go away." Wang told her she did not understand, and when she asked what it was she didn't understand, he said, "I didn't care for the flower itself; it was the person who picked the flower."

"Of course," answered she, "everybody cares for their relations; you needn't have told me that."

"I wasn't talking about ordinary relations," said Wang, "but about husbands and wives."

"What's the difference?" asked Ying-ning.

"Why," replied Wang, "husband and wife are always together."

"Just what I shouldn't like," cried she, "to be always with anybody."

At this juncture up came the maid, and Wang slipped quietly away. By-and-by they all met again in the house, and the old woman asked Ying-ning where they had been; whereupon she said they had been talking in the garden. "Dinner has been ready a long time. I can't think what you have had to say all this while," grumbled the old woman.

"My cousin," answered Ying-ning, "has been talking to me about husbands and wives." Wang was much disconcerted, and made a sign to her to be quiet, so she smiled and said no more; and the old woman luckily did not catch her words, and asked her to repeat them. Wang immediately put her off with something else, and whispered to Ying-ning that she had done very wrong. The latter did not see that; and when Wang told her that what he had said was private, answered him that she had no secrets from her old mother. "Besides," added she, "what harm can there be in talking on such a common topic as husbands and wives?"

Wang was angry with her for being so dull, but there was no help for it; and by the time dinner was over he found some of his mother's servants had come in search of him, bringing a couple of donkeys with them. It appeared that his mother, alarmed at his non-appearance, had made strict search for him in the village; and when unable to discover any traces of him, had gone off to the Wu family to consult. There her nephew, who recollected what he had previously said to young Wang, advised that a search should be instituted in the direction of the hills; and accordingly the servants had been to all the villages on the way until they had at length recognized him as he was coming out of the door. Wang went in and told the old woman, begging that he might be allowed to take Ying-ning with him. "I have had the idea in my head for several days," replied the old woman, overjoyed; "but I am a feeble old thing myself, and couldn't travel so far. If, however, you will take charge of my girl and introduce her to her aunt, I shall be very pleased." So she called Ying-ning, who came up laughing as usual; whereupon the old woman rebuked her, saying, "What makes you always laugh so? You would be a very good girl but for that silly habit. Now, here's your cousin, who wants to take you away with him. Make haste and pack up." The servants who had come for Wang were then provided with refreshment, and the old woman bade them both farewell, telling Ying-ning that her aunt was quite well enough off to maintain her, and that she had better not come back. She also advised her not to neglect her studies, and to be very attentive to her elders, adding that she might ask her aunt to provide her with a good husband.

Wang and Ying-ning then took their leave; and when they reached the brow of the hill, they looked back and could just discern the old woman leaning against the door and gazing toward the north. On arriving at Wang's home, his mother, seeing a nice-looking young girl with him, asked in astonishment who she might be; and Wang at once told her the whole story. "But that was all an invention of your cousin Wu's," cried his mother; "I haven't got a sister, and consequently I can't have such a niece."

Ying-ning here observed, "I am not the daughter of the old woman; my father was named Ch'in and died when I was a little baby, so that I can't remember anything."

"I *had* a sister," said Wang's mother, "who actually did marry a Mr. Ch'in, but she died many years ago, and can't be still living, of course." However, on inquiring as to facial appearance and characteristic marks, Wang's mother was obliged to acknowledge the identity, wondering at the same time how her sister could be alive when she had died many years before.

Just then in came Wu, and Ying-ning retired within; and when he heard the story, remained some time lost in astonishment, and then said, "Is this young lady's name Ying-ning?" Wang replied that it was, and asked Wu how he came to know it. "Mr. Ch'in," answered he, "after his wife's death was bewitched by a fox, and subsequently died. The fox had a daughter named Ying-ning, as was well known to all the family; and when Mr. Ch'in died, as the fox still frequented the place, the Taoist Pope was called in to exorcise it. The fox then went away, taking Ying-ning with it, and now here she is."

While they were thus discussing, peals of laughter were heard coming from within, and Mrs. Wang took occasion to remark what a foolish girl she was. Wu begged to be introduced, and Mrs. Wang went in to fetch her, finding her in an uncontrollable fit of laughter, which she subdued only with great difficulty, and by turning her face to the wall. By-and-by she went out; but, after making a bow, ran back and burst out laughing again to the great discomfiture of all the ladies. Wang then said he would go and find out for them all about Ying-ning and her queer story, so as to be able to arrange the marriage; but when he reached the spot indicated, village and houses had all vanished, and nothing was to be seen except hill-flowers scattered about here and there. Wu recollected that Mrs. Ch'in had been buried at no great distance from that spot; he found, however, that the grave had disappeared, and he was no longer able to determine its position.

Not knowing what to make of it all, he returned home, and then Mrs. Wang told him she thought the girl must be a disembodied spirit. Ying-ning showed no signs of alarm at this remark; neither did she cry at all when Mrs. Wang began to condole with her on no longer having a home. She only laughed in her usual silly way, and fairly puzzled them all. Sharing Miss Wang's room, she now began to take her part in the duties of a daughter of the family; and as for needlework, they had rarely seen anything like hers for fineness. But she could not get over that trick of laughing, which, by the way, never interfered with her good looks, and consequently rather amused people than otherwise, among others a young married lady who lived next door.

Wang's mother fixed an auspicious day for the wedding, but still feeling suspicious about Ying-ning, was always secretly watching her. Finding, however, that she had a proper shadow, and that there was nothing extraordinary in her behavior, she had her dressed up when the day came, in all the finery of a bride; and would have made her perform the usual ceremonies, only Ying-ning laughed so much she was unable to kneel down. They were accordingly obliged to excuse her, but Wang began to fear that such a foolish girl would never be able to keep the family counsel. Luckily, she was very reticent and did not indulge in gossip; and moreover, when Mrs. Wang was in trouble or out of temper, Ying-ning could always bring her round with a laugh. The maid-servants, too, if they expected a whipping for anything, would always ask her to be present when they appeared before their mistress, and thus they often escaped punishment.

Ying-ning had a perfect passion for flowers. She got all she could out of her relations, and even secretly pawned her jewels to buy rare specimens; and by the end of a few months the whole place was one mass of flowers. Behind the house there was one especial tree which belonged to the neighbors on that side; but Ying-ning was always climbing up and picking the flowers, for which Mrs. Wang rebuked her severely, though without any result. One day the owner saw her, and gazed at her some time in rapt astonishment; however, she didn't move, deigning only to laugh. The gentleman was much smitten with her; and when she smilingly descended the wall on her own side, pointing all the time with her finger to a spot hard by, he thought she was making an assignation. So he presented himself at nightfall at the same place, and sure enough Ying-ning was there. Seizing her hand, to tell his passion, he found that he was grasping only a log of wood which stood against the wall; and the next thing he knew was that a scorpion had stung him violently on the finger. There was an end of his romance, except that he died of the wound during the night, and his family at once commenced an action against Wang for having a witch-wife.

The magistrate happened to be a great admirer of Wang's talent, and knew him to be an accomplished scholar; he therefore refused to grant the summons, and ordered the prosecutor to be bambooed for false accusation. Wang interposed and got him off this punishment, and returned home himself. His mother then scolded Ying-ning well, saying, "I knew your too playful disposition would some day bring sorrow upon you. But for our intelligent magistrate we should have been in a nice mess. Any ordinary hawk-like official would have had you publicly interrogated in court; and then how could your husband ever have held up his head again?" Ying-ning looked grave and did not laugh this time; and Mrs. Wang continued, "There's no harm in laughing as long as it is seasonable laughter"; but from that moment Ying-ning laughed no more, no matter what people did to make her, though at the same time her expression was by no means gloomy.

One evening she went in tears to her husband, who wanted to know what was the matter. "I couldn't tell you before," said she, sobbing; "we had known each other such a short time. But now that you and your mother have been so kind to me, I will keep nothing from you, but tell you all. I am the daughter of a fox. When my mother went away she put me in the charge of the disembodied spirit of an old woman, with whom I remained for a period of over ten years. I have no brothers: only you to whom I can look. And now my foster-mother is lying on the hill-side with no one to bury her and appease her discontented shade. If not too much, I would ask you to do this, that her spirit may be at rest, and know that it was not neglected by her whom she brought up."

Wang consented, but said he feared they would not be able to find her grave; on which Ying-ning said there was no danger of that, and accordingly they set forth together. When they arrived, Ying-ning pointed out the tomb in a lonely spot amidst a thicket of brambles, and there they found the old woman's bones. Ying-ning wept bitterly, and then they proceeded to carry her remains home with them, subsequently interring them in the Ch'in family vault. That night Wang dreamt that the old woman came to thank him, and when he waked he told Ying-ning, who said that she had seen her also, and had been warned by her not to frighten Mr. Wang. Her husband asked why she had not detained the old lady; but Ying-ning replied, "She is a disembodied spirit, and would be ill at ease for any time surrounded by so much life." Wang then enquired after Hsiao-jung, and his wife said, "She was a fox too, and a very clever one. My foster-mother kept her to wait on me, and she was always getting fruit and cakes for me, so that I have a friendship for her and shall never forget her. My foster-mother told me yesterday she was married."

After this, whenever the great fast-day came round, husband and wife went off without fail to worship at the Ch'in family tomb; and by the time a year had passed she gave birth to a son, who wasn't a bit afraid of strangers, but laughed at everybody, and in fact took very much after his mother.

The Magic Sword

NING LAI-CH'ÊN WAS A CHEKIANG MAN, AND A GOOD-NATURED, HONORABLE FELLOW, fond of telling people that he had only loved once. Happening to go to Chinhua, he took shelter in a temple to the north of the city; very nice as far as ornamentation went, but overgrown with grass taller than a man's head, and evidently not much frequented. On either side were the priest's apartments, the doors of which were ajar, with the exception of a small room on the south side, where the lock had a new appearance.

In the east corner he espied a group of bamboos, growing over a large pool of water-lilies in flower; and, being much pleased with the quiet of the place, determined to remain; more especially as, the Grand Examiner being in the town, all lodgings had gone up in price. So he roamed about waiting till the priests should return; and in the evening, a gentleman came and opened the door on the south side. Ning quickly made up to him, and with a bow informed him of his design.

"There is no one here whose permission you need ask," replied the stranger; "I am only lodging here, and if you don't object to the loneliness, I shall be very pleased to have the benefit of your society."

Ning was delighted, and made himself a straw bed, and put up a board for a table, as if he intended to remain some time; and that night, by the beams of the clear bright moon, they sat together in the verandah and talked. The stranger's name was Yen Ch'ih-hsia, and Ning thought he was a student up for the provincial examination, only his dialect was not that of a Chekiang man. On being asked, he said he came from Shensi; and there was an air of straightforwardness about all his remarks.

By-and-by, when their conversation was exhausted, they bade each other good night and went to bed; but Ning, being in a strange place, was quite unable to sleep; and soon he heard sounds of voices from the room on the north side. Getting up, he peeped through a window, and saw, in a small court-yard the other side of a low wall, a woman of about forty with an old maid-servant in a long faded gown, humped-backed and feeble-looking. They were chatting by the light of the moon; and the mistress said, "Why doesn't Hsiao-ch'ien come?"

"She ought to be here by now," replied the other.

"She isn't offended with you; is she?" asked the lady.

"Not that I know of," answered the old servant; "but she seems to want to give trouble."

"Such people don't deserve to be treated well," said the other; and she had hardly uttered these words when up came a young girl of seventeen or eighteen, and very nice looking. The old servant laughed, and said, "Don't talk of people behind their backs. We were just mentioning you as you came without our hearing you; but fortunately we were saying nothing bad about you. And, as far as that goes," added she, "if I were a young fellow why I should certainly fall in love with you."

"If *you* don't praise me," replied the girl, "I'm sure I don't know who will"; and then the lady and the girl said something together, and Mr. Ning, thinking they were the family next door, turned round to sleep without paying further attention to them. In a little while no sound was to be heard; but, as he was dropping off to sleep, he perceived that somebody was in the room. Jumping up in great haste, he found it was the young lady he had just seen; and detecting at once that she was going to attempt to bewitch him, sternly bade her begone. She then produced a lump of gold which he threw away, and told her to go after it or he would call his friend. So she had no alternative but to go, muttering something about his heart being like iron or stone.

Next day, a young candidate for the examination came and lodged in the east room with his servant. He, however, was killed that very night, and his servant the night after; the corpses of both showing a small hole in the sole of the foot as if bored by an awl, and from which a little blood came. No one knew who had committed these murders, and when Mr. Yen came home, Ning asked him what he thought about it. Yen replied that it was the work of devils, but Ning was a brave fellow, and that didn't frighten him much. In the middle of the night Hsiao-ch'ien appeared to him again, and said, "I have seen many men, but none with a steel cold heart like yours. You are an upright man, and I will not attempt to deceive you. I, Hsiao-ch'ien, whose family name is Nieh, died when only eighteen, and was buried alongside of this temple. A devil then took possession of me, and employed me to bewitch people by my beauty, contrary to my inclination. There is now nothing left in this temple to slay, and I fear that imps will be employed to kill you."

Ning was very frightened at this, and asked her what he should do. "Sleep in the same room with Mr. Yen," replied she.

"What!" asked he, "cannot the spirits trouble Yen?"

"He is a strange man," she answered, "and they don't like going near him."

Ning then inquired how the spirits worked.

"I bewitch people," said Hsiao-ch'ien, "and then they bore a hole in the foot which renders the victim senseless, and proceed to draw off the blood, which the devils drink. Another method is to tempt people by false gold, the bones of some horrid demon; and if they receive it, their hearts and livers will be torn out. Either method is used according to circumstances." Ning thanked her, and asked when he ought to be prepared; to which she replied, "To-morrow night."

At parting she wept, and said, "I am about to sink into the great sea, with no friendly shore at hand. But your sense of duty is boundless, and you can save me. If you will collect my bones and bury them in some quiet spot, I shall not again be subject to these misfortunes." Ning said he would do so, and asked where she lay buried. "At the foot of the aspen-tree on which there is a bird's nest," replied she; and passing out of the door, disappeared.

The next day Ning was afraid that Yen might be going away somewhere, and went over early to invite him across. Wine and food were produced toward noon; and Ning, who took care not to lose sight of Yen, then asked him to remain there for the night. Yen declined, on the ground that he liked being by himself; but Ning wouldn't hear any excuses, and carried all Yen's things to his own room, so that he had no alternative but to consent. However, he warned Ning, saying, "I know you are a gentleman and a man of honor. If you see anything you don't quite understand, I pray you not to be too inquisitive; don't pry into my boxes, or it may be the worse for both of us."

Ning promised to attend to what he said, and by-and-by they both lay down to sleep; and Yen, having placed his boxes on the window-sill, was soon snoring loudly. Ning himself could not sleep; and after some time he saw a figure moving stealthily outside, at length approaching the window to peep through. It's eyes flashed like lightning, and Ning in a terrible fright was just upon the point of calling Yen, when something flew out of one of the boxes like a strip of white silk, and dashing against the window-sill returned at once to the box, disappearing very much like lightning. Yen heard the noise and got up, Ning all the time pretending to be asleep in order to watch what happened. The former then opened the box, and took out something which he smelt and examined by the light of the moon. It was dazzlingly white like crystal, and about two inches in length by the width of an onion leaf in breadth. He then wrapped it up carefully and put it back in the broken box, saying, "A bold-faced devil that, to come so near my box"; upon which he went back to bed; but Ning, who was lost in astonishment, arose and asked him what it all meant, telling at the same time what he himself had seen. "As you and I are good friends," replied Yen, "I won't make any secret of it. The fact is I am a Taoist priest. But for the window-sill the devil would have been killed; as it is, he is badly wounded." Ning asked him what it was he had there wrapped up, and he told him it was his sword, on which he had smelt the presence of the devil. At Ning's request he produced the weapon, a bright little miniature of a sword; and from that time Ning held his friend in higher esteem than ever.

Next day he found traces of blood outside the window which led round to the north of the temple; and there among a number of graves he discovered the aspen-tree with the bird's nest at its summit. He then fulfilled his promise and prepared to go home, Yen giving him a farewell banquet, and presenting him with an old leather case which he said contained a sword, and would keep at a distance from him all devils and bogies. Ning then wished to learn a little of Yen's art; but the latter replied that although he might accomplish this easily enough, being as he was an upright man, yet he was well off in life, and not in a condition where it would be of any advantage to him. Ning then pretending he had to go and bury his sister, collected Hsiao-ch'ien's bones, and, having wrapped them up in grave-clothes, hired a boat, and set off on his way home. On his arrival, as his library looked towards the open country, he made a grave hard by and buried the bones there, sacrificing, and invoking Hsiao-ch'ien as follows:—"In pity for your lonely ghost, I have placed your remains near my humble cottage, where we shall be near each other, and no devil will dare annoy you. I pray you reject not my sacrifice, poor though it be."

After this, he was proceeding home when he suddenly heard himself addressed from behind, the voice asking him not to hurry; and turning round he beheld Hsiao-ch'ien, who thanked him, saying, "Were I to die ten times for you I could not discharge my debt. Let me go home with you and wait upon your father and mother; you will not repent it." Looking closely at her, he observed that she had a beautiful complexion, and feet as small as bamboo shoots, being altogether much prettier now that he came to see her by daylight. So they went together to his home, and bidding her wait awhile, Ning ran in to tell his mother, to the very great surprise of the old lady.

Now Ning's wife had been ill for a long time, and his mother advised him not to say a word about it to her for fear of frightening her; in the middle of which in rushed Hsiao-ch'ien, and threw herself on the ground before them. "This is the young lady," said Ning; whereupon his mother in some alarm turned her attention to Hsiao-ch'ien, who cried out, "A lonely orphan, without brother or sister, the object of your son's kindness and compassion, begs to be allowed to give her poor services as some return for favors shown."

Ning's mother, seeing that she was a nice pleasant-looking girl, began to lose fear of her, and replied, "Madam, the preference you show for my son is highly pleasing to an old body like myself; but this is the only hope of our family, and I hardly dare agree to his taking a devil-wife." "I have but one motive in what I ask," answered Hsiao-ch'ien, "and if you have no faith in disembodied people, then let me regard him as my brother, and live under your protection, serving you like a daughter."

Ning's mother could not resist her straightforward manner, and Hsiao-ch'ien asked to be allowed to see Ning's wife, but this was denied on the plea that the lady was ill. Hsiao-ch'ien then went into the kitchen and got ready the dinner, running about the place as if she had lived there all her life. Ning's mother was, however, much afraid of her, and would not let her sleep in the house; so Hsiao-ch'ien went to the library, and was just entering when suddenly she fell back a few steps, and began walking hurriedly backward and forward in front of the door. Ning seeing this, called out and asked her what it meant; to which she replied, "The presence of that sword frightens me, and that is why I could not accompany you on your way home." Ning at once understood her, and hung up the sword-case in another place; whereupon she entered, lighted a candle, and sat down. For some time she did not speak: at length asking Ning if he studied at night or not—"For," said she, "when I was little I used to repeat the Lêng-yen *sutra*;

but now I have forgotten more than half, and, therefore, I should like to borrow a copy, and when you are at leisure in the evening you might hear me." Ning said he would, and they sat silently there for some time, after which Hsiao-ch'ien went away and took up her quarters elsewhere.

Morning and night she waited on Ning's mother, bringing water for her to wash in, occupying herself with household matters, and endeavouring to please her in every way. In the evening before she went to bed, she would always go in and repeat a little of the *sutra*, and leave as soon as she thought Ning was getting sleepy. Now the illness of Ning's wife had given his mother a great deal of extra trouble—more, in fact, than she was equal to; but ever since Hsiao-ch'ien's arrival all this was changed, and Ning's mother felt kindly disposed to the girl in consequence, gradually growing to regard her almost as her own child, and forgetting quite that she was a spirit. Accordingly, she didn't make her leave the house at night; and Hsiao-ch'ien, who being a devil had not tasted meat or drink since her arrival, now began at the end of six months to take a little thin gruel. Mother and son alike became very fond of her, and henceforth never mentioned what she really was; neither were strangers able to detect the fact.

By-and-by, Ning's wife died, and his mother secretly wished him to espouse Hsiao-ch'ien, though she rather dreaded any unfortunate consequences that might arise. This Hsiao-ch'ien perceived, and seizing an opportunity said to Ning's mother, "I have been with you now more than a year, and you ought to know something of my disposition. Because I was unwilling to injure travelers I followed your son hither. There was no other motive; and, as your son has shown himself one of the best of men, I would now remain with him for three years in order that he may obtain for me some mark of Imperial approbation which will do me honor in the realms below." Ning's mother knew that she meant no evil, but hesitated to put the family hopes of a posterity into jeopardy. Hsiao-ch'ien, however, reassured her by saying that Ning would have three sons, and that the line would not be interrupted by his marrying her.

On the strength of this the marriage was arranged to the great joy of Ning, a feast prepared, and friends and relatives invited; and when in response to a call the bride herself came forth in her gay wedding-dress, the beholders took her rather for a fairy than for a devil. After this, numbers of congratulatory presents were given by the various female members of the family, who vied with one another in making her acquaintance; and these Hsiao-ch'ien returned by gifts of paintings of flowers, done by herself, in which she was very skillful, the receivers being extremely proud of such marks of her friendship.

One day she was leaning at the window in a despondent mood, when suddenly she asked where the sword-case was. "Oh," replied Ning, "as you seemed afraid of it, I moved it elsewhere."

"I have now been so long under the influence of surrounding life," said Hsiao-ch'ien, "that I shan't be afraid of it any more. Let us hang it on the bed."

"Why so?" asked Ning.

"For the last three days," explained she, "I have been much agitated in mind; and I fear that the devil at the temple, angry at my escape, may come suddenly and carry me off."

So Ning brought the sword-case, and Hsiao-ch'ien, after examining it closely, remarked, "This is where the magician puts people. I wonder how many were slain before it got old and worn out as it is now. Even now when I look at it my flesh creeps."

The case was then hung up, and next day removed to over the door. At night they sat up and watched, Hsiao-ch'ien warning Ning not to go to sleep; and suddenly something fell down flop like a bird. Hsiao-ch'ien in a fright got behind the curtain; but Ning looked at the thing, and found it was an imp of darkness, with glaring eyes and a bloody mouth, coming straight to the door. Stealthily creeping up it made a grab at the sword-case, and seemed about to tear it in pieces, when bang!—the sword-case became as big as a wardrobe, and from it a devil protruded part of his body and dragged the imp in. Nothing more was heard, and the sword-case resumed its original size. Ning was greatly alarmed, but Hsiao-ch'ien came out rejoicing, and said, "There's an end of my troubles." In the sword-case they found only a few quarts of clear water; nothing else.

After these events Ning took his doctor's degree and Hsiao-ch'ien bore him a son. He then took a concubine, and had one more son by each, all of whom became in time distinguished men.

The *Shui-mang* Plant

The *shui-mang* is a poisonous herb. It is a creeper, like the bean, and has a similar red flower. Those who eat of it die, and become *shui-mang* devils, tradition asserting that such devils are unable to be born again unless they can find some one else who has also eaten of this poison to take their place. These *shui-mang* devils abound in the province of Hunan, where, by the way, the phrase "same-year man" is applied to those born in the same year, who exchange visits and call each other brother, their children addressing the father's "brother" as uncle. This has now become a regular custom there.

A young man named Chu was on his way to visit a same-year friend of his, when he was overtaken by a violent thirst. Suddenly he came upon an old woman sitting by the roadside under a shed and distributing tea gratis, and immediately walked up to her to get a drink. She invited him into the shed, and presented him with a bowl of tea in a very cordial spirit; but the smell of it did not seem like the smell of ordinary tea, and he would not drink it, rising up to go away. The old woman stopped him, and called out, "San-niang! bring some good tea." Immediately a young girl came from behind the shed, carrying in her hands a pot of tea. She was about fourteen or fifteen years old, and of very fascinating appearance, with glittering rings and bracelets on her fingers and arms. As Chu received the cup from her his reason fled; and drinking down the tea she gave him, the flavor of which was unlike any other kind, he proceeded to ask for more. Then, watching for a moment when the old woman's back was turned, he seized her wrist and drew a ring from her finger. The girl blushed and smiled; and Chu, more and more inflamed, asked her where she lived. "Come again this evening," replied she, "and you'll find me here."

Chu begged for a handful of her tea, which he stowed away with the ring, and took his leave. Arriving at his destination, he felt a pain in his heart, which he at once attributed to the tea, telling his friend what had occurred. "Alas! you are undone," cried the other; "they were *shui-mang* devils. My father died in the same way, and we were unable to save him. There is no help for you."

Chu was terribly frightened, and produced the handful of tea, which his friend at once pronounced to be leaves of the *shui-mang* plant. He then showed him the ring, and told him what the girl had said; whereupon his friend, after some reflection, said, "She must be San-niang, of the K'ou family."

"How could you know her name?" asked Chu, hearing his friend use the same words as the old woman. "Oh," replied he, "there was a nice-looking girl of that name who died some years ago from eating of the same herb. She is doubtless the girl you saw."

Here some one observed that if the person so entrapped by a devil only knew its name, and could procure an old pair of its shoes, he might save himself by boiling them in water and drinking the liquor as medicine. Chu's friend thereupon rushed off at once to the K'ou family, and implored them to give him an old pair of their daughter's shoes; but they, not wishing to prevent their daughter from finding a substitute in Chu, flatly refused his request. So he went back in anger and told Chu, who ground his teeth with rage, saying, "If I die, she shall not obtain her transmigration thereby." His friend then sent him home; and just as he reached the door he fell down dead.

Chu's mother wept bitterly over his corpse, which was in due course interred; and he left behind one little boy barely a year old. His wife did not remain a widow, but in six months married again and went away, putting Chu's son under the care of his grandmother, who was quite unequal to any toil, and did nothing but weep morning and night. One day she was carrying her grandson about in her arms, crying bitterly all the time, when suddenly in walked Chu. His mother, much alarmed, brushed away her tears, and asked him what it meant.

"Mother," replied he, "down in the realms below I heard you weeping. I am therefore come to tend you. Although a departed spirit, I have a wife, who has likewise come to share your toil. Therefore do not grieve."

His mother inquired who his wife was, to which he replied, "When the K'ou family sat still and left me to my fate I was greatly incensed against them; and after death I sought for San-niang, not knowing where she was. I have recently seen my old same-year friend, and he told me where she was. She had come to life again in the person of the baby-daughter of a high official named Jen; but I went thither and dragged her spirit back. She is now my wife, and we get on extremely well together."

A very pretty and well-dressed young lady here entered, and made obeisance to Chu's mother, Chu saying, "This is San-niang, of the K'ou family"; and although not a living being, Mrs. Chu at once took a great fancy to her. Chu sent her off to help in the work of the house, and, in spite of not being accustomed to this sort of thing, she was so obedient to her mother-in-law as to excite the compassion of all. The two then took up their quarters in Chu's old apartments, and there they continued to remain.

Meanwhile San-niang asked Chu's mother to let the K'ou family know; and this she did, notwithstanding some objections raised by her son. Mr. and Mrs. K'ou were much astonished at the news, and, ordering their carriage, proceeded at once to Chu's house. There they found their daughter, and parents and child fell into each other's arms. San-niang entreated them to dry their tears; but her mother, noticing the poverty of Chu's household, was unable to restrain her feelings. "We are already spirits," cried San-niang; "what matters poverty to us? Besides, I am very well treated here, and am altogether as happy as I can be." They then asked her who the old woman was; to which she replied, "Her name was Ni. She was mortified at being too ugly to entrap people herself, and got me to assist her. She has now been born again at a soy-shop in the city." Then, looking at her husband, she added, "Come, since you are the son-in-law, pay the proper respect to my father and mother, or what shall I think of you?"

Chu made his obeisance, and San-niang went into the kitchen to get food ready for them, at which her mother became very melancholy, and went away home, whence she sent a couple of maid-servants, a hundred ounces of silver, and rolls of cloth and silk, besides making occasional presents of food and wine, so that Chu's mother lived in comparative comfort. San-niang also went from time to time to see her parents, but would never stay very long, pleading that she was wanted at home, and such excuses; and if the old people attempted to keep her, she simply went off by herself. Her father built a nice house for Chu with all kinds of luxuries in it; but Chu never once entered his father-in-law's door.

Subsequently a man of the village who had eaten *shui-mang*, and had died in consequence, came back to life, to the great astonishment of everybody. However, Chu explained it, saying, "I brought him back to life. He was the victim of a man named Li Chiu; but I drove off Li's spirit when it came to make the other take his place." Chu's mother then asked her son why he did not get a substitute for himself; to which he replied, "I do not like to do this. I am anxious to put an end to, rather than take advantage of, such a system. Besides, I am very happy waiting on you, and have no wish to be born again." From that time all persons who had poisoned themselves with *shui-mang* were in the habit of feasting Chu and obtaining his assistance in their trouble. But in ten years' time his mother died, and he and his wife gave themselves up to sorrow, and would see no one, bidding their little boy put on mourning, beat his breast, and perform the proper ceremonies.

Two years after Chu had buried his mother, his son married the granddaughter of a high official named Jen. This gentleman had had a daughter by a concubine, who had died when only a few months old; and now, hearing the strange story of Chu's wife, came to call on her and arrange the marriage. He then gave his granddaughter to Chu's son, and a free intercourse was maintained between the two families. However, one day Chu said to his son, "Because I have been of service to my generation, God has appointed me Keeper of the Dragons; and I am now about to proceed to my post." Thereupon four horses appeared in the court-yard, drawing a carriage with yellow hangings, the flanks of the horses being covered with scale-like trappings. Husband and wife came forth in full dress, and took their seats, and, while son and daughter-in-law were wee ping their adieus, disappeared from view. That very day the K'ou family saw their daughter arrive, and, bidding them farewell, she told them the same story. The old people would have kept her, but she said, "My husband is already on his way," and, leaving the house, parted from them for ever. Chu's son was named Ngo, and his literary name was Li-ch'ên. He begged San-niang's bones from the K'ou family, and buried them by the side of his father's.

Little Chu

A man named Li Hua dwelt at Ch'ang-chou. He was very well off, and about fifty years of age, but he had no sons; only one daughter, named Hsiao-hui, a pretty child on whom her parents doted. When she was fourteen she had a severe illness and died, leaving their home desolate and depriving them of their chief pleasure in life. Mr. Li then bought a concubine, and she by-and-by bore him a son, who was perfectly idolized, and called Chu, or the Pearl. This boy grew up to be a fine manly fellow, though so extremely stupid that when five or six years old he didn't know pulse from corn, and could hardly talk plainly. His father, however, loved him dearly, and did not observe his faults.

Now it chanced that a one-eyed priest came to collect alms in the town, and he seemed to know so much about everybody's private affairs that the people all looked upon him as superhuman. He himself declared he had control over life, death, happiness, and misfortune; and consequently no one dared refuse him whatever sum he chose to ask of them. From Li he demanded one hundred ounces of silver, but was offered only ten, which he refused to receive. This sum was increased to thirty ounces, whereupon the priest looked sternly at Li and said, "I must have one hundred; not a fraction less." Li now got angry, and went away without giving him any, the priest, too, rising up in a rage and shouting after him, "I hope you won't repent."

Shortly after these events little Chu fell sick, and crawled about the bed scratching the mat, his face being of an ashen paleness. This frightened his father, who hurried off with eighty ounces of silver, and begged the priest to accept them. "A large sum like this is no trifling matter to earn," said the priest, smiling; "but what can a poor recluse like myself do for you?" So Li went home, to find that little Chu was already dead; and this worked him into such a state that he immediately laid a complaint before the magistrate. The priest was accordingly summoned and interrogated; but the magistrate wouldn't accept his defense, and ordered him to be bambooed. The blows sounded as if falling on leather, upon which the magistrate commanded his lictors to search him; and from about his person they drew forth two wooden men, a small coffin, and five small flags. The magistrate here flew into a passion, and made certain mystic signs with his fingers, which when the priest saw he was frightened, and began to excuse himself; but the magistrate would not listen to him, and had him bambooed to death. Li thanked him for his kindness, and, taking his leave, proceeded home.

In the evening, after dusk, he was sitting alone with his wife, when suddenly in popped a little boy, who said, "Pa! why did you hurry on so fast? I couldn't catch you up." Looking at him more closely, they saw that he was about seven or eight years old, and Mr. Li, in some alarm, was on the point of questioning him, when he disappeared, re-appearing again like smoke, and, curling round and round, got upon the bed. Li pushed him off, and he fell down without making any sound, crying out, "Pa! why do you do this?" and in a moment he was on the bed again. Li was frightened, and ran away with his wife, the boy calling after them, "Pa! Ma! boo-oo-oo."

They went into the next room, bolting the door after them; but there was the little boy at their heels again. Li asked him what he wanted, to which he replied, "I belong to Su-chou; my name is Chan; at six years of age I was left an orphan; my brother and his wife couldn't bear me, so they sent me to live at my maternal grandfather's. One day, when playing outside, a wicked priest killed me by his black art underneath a mulberry-tree, and made of me an evil spirit, dooming me to everlasting devildom without hope of transmigration. Happily you exposed him; and I would now remain with you as your son."

"The paths of men and devils," replied Li, "lie in different directions. How can we remain together?"

"Give me only a tiny room," cried the boy, "a bed, a mattress, and a cup of cold gruel every day. I ask for nothing more."

So Li agreed, to the great delight of the boy, who slept by himself in another part of the house, coming in the morning and walking in and out like any ordinary person. Hearing Li's concubine crying bitterly, he asked how long little Chu had been dead, and she told him seven days. "It's cold weather now," said he, "and the body can't have decomposed. Have the grave opened, and let me see it; if not too far gone, I can bring him to life again." Li was only too pleased, and went off with the boy; and when they opened the grave they found the body in perfect preservation; but while Li was controlling his emotions, lo! the boy had vanished from his sight. Wondering very much at this, he took little Chu's body home, and had hardly laid it on the bed when he noticed the eyes move. Little Chu then called for some broth, which put him into a perspiration, and then he got up. They were all overjoyed to see him come to life again; and, what is more, he was much brighter and cleverer than before. At night, however, he lay perfectly stiff and rigid, without showing any signs of life; and, as he didn't move when they turned him over and over, they were much frightened, and thought he had died again. But toward daybreak he awaked as if from a dream, and in reply to their questions said that when he was with the wicked priest there was another boy named Ko-tzŭ; and that the day before, when he had been unable to catch up his father, it was because he had stayed behind to bid adieu to Ko-tzŭ; that Ko-tzŭ was now the son of an official in Purgatory named Chiang, and very comfortably settled; and that he had invited him (Chan) to go and play with him that evening, and had sent him back on a white-nosed horse. His mother then asked him if he had seen little Chu in Purgatory; to which he replied, "Little Chu has already been born again. He and our father here had not really the destiny of father and son. Little Chu was merely a man named Yen Tzŭ-fang, from Chin-ling, who had come to reclaim an old debt."

Now Mr. Li had formerly traded to Chin-ling, and actually owed money for goods to a Mr. Yen; but he had died, and no one else knew anything about it, so that he was now greatly alarmed when he heard this story. His mother next asked (the quasi) little Chu if he had seen his sister, Hsiao-hui; and he said he had not, promising to go again and inquire about her. A few days afterward he told his mother that Hsiao-hui was very happy in Purgatory, being married to a son of one of the Judges; and that she had any quantity of jewels, and crowds of attendants when she went abroad.

"Why doesn't she come home to see her parents?" asked his mother.

"Well," replied the boy, "dead people, you know, haven't got any flesh or bones; however, if you can only remind them of something that happened in their past lives, their feelings are at once touched. So yesterday I managed, through Mr. Chiang, to get an interview with Hsiao-hui; and we sat together on a coral couch, and I spoke to her of her father and mother at home, all of which she listened to as if she was asleep. I then remarked, 'Sister, when you were alive you were very fond of embroidering double-stemmed flowers; and once you cut your finger with the scissors, and the blood ran over the silk, but you brought it into the picture as a crimson cloud. Your mother has that picture still, hanging at the head of her bed, a perpetual souvenir of you. Sister, have you forgotten this?' Then she burst into tears, and promised to ask her husband to let her come and visit you."

His mother asked when she would arrive; but he said he could not tell. However, one day he ran in and cried out, "Mother, Hsiao-hui has come, with a splendid equipage and a train of servants; we had better get plenty of wine ready." In a few moments he came in again, saying, "Here is my sister," at the same time asking her to take a seat and rest. He then wept; but none of those present saw anything at all.

By-and-by he went out and burned a quantity of paper money and made offerings of wine outside the door, returning shortly and saying he had sent away her attendants for a while. Hsiao-hui then asked if the green coverlet, a small portion of which had been burnt by a candle, was still in existence. "It is," replied her mother, and, going to a box, she at once produced the coverlet. "Hsiao-hui would like a bed made up for her in her old room," said her (quasi) brother; "she wants to rest awhile, and will talk with you again in the morning."

Now their next-door neighbor, named Chao, had a daughter who was formerly a great friend of Hsiao-hui's, and that night she dreamt that Hsiao-hui appeared with a turban on her head and a red mantle over her shoulders, and that they talked and laughed together precisely as in days gone by. "I am now a spirit," said Hsiao-hui, "and my father and mother can no more see me than if I was far separated from them. Dear sister, I would borrow your body, from which to speak to them. You need fear nothing."

On the morrow when Miss Chao met her mother, she fell on the ground before her and remained some time in a state of unconsciousness, at length saying, "Madam, it is many years since we met; your hair has become very white."

"The girl's mad," said her mother, in alarm; and, thinking something had gone wrong, proceeded to follow her out of the door. Miss Chao went straight to Li's house, and there with tears embraced Mrs. Li, who did not know what to make of it all.

"Yesterday," said Miss Chao, "when I came back, I was unhappily unable to speak with you. Unfilial wretch that I was, to die before you, and leave you to mourn my loss. How can I redeem such behavior?"

Her mother thereupon began to understand the scene, and, weeping, said to her, "I have heard that you hold an honorable position, and this is a great comfort to me; but, living as you do in the palace of a Judge, how is it you are able to get away?"

"My husband," replied she, "is very kind; and his parents treat me with all possible consideration. I experience no harsh treatment at their hands." Here Miss Chao rested her cheek upon her hand, exactly as Hsiao-hui had been wont to do when she was alive; and at that moment in came her brother to say that her attendants were ready to return. "I must go," said she, rising up and weeping bitterly all the time; after which she fell down, and remained some time unconscious as before.

Shortly after these events Mr. Li became dangerously ill, and no medicines were of any avail, so that his son feared they would not be able to save his life. Two devils sat at the head of his bed, one holding an iron staff, the other a nettle-hemp rope four or five feet in length. Day and night his son implored them to go, but they would not move; and Mrs. Li in sorrow began to prepare the funeral clothes. Toward evening her son entered and cried out, "Strangers and women, leave the room! My sister's husband is coming to see his father-in-law." He then clapped his hands, and burst out laughing.

"What is the matter?" asked his mother.

"I am laughing," answered he, "because when the two devils heard my sister's husband was coming, they both ran under the bed, like terrapins, drawing in their heads." By-and-by, looking at nothing, he began to talk about the weather, and ask his sister's husband how he did, and then he clapped his hands, and said, "I begged the two devils to go, but they would not; it's all right now." After this he went out to the door and returned, saying, "My sister's husband has gone. He took away the two devils tied to his horse. My father ought to get better now. Besides, Hsiao-hui's husband said he would speak to the Judge, and obtain a hundred years' lease of life both for you and my father." The whole family rejoiced exceedingly at this, and, when night came, Mr. Li was better, and in a few days quite well again. A tutor was engaged for (the quasi) little Chu, who showed himself an apt pupil, and at eighteen years of age took his bachelor's degree. He could also see things of the other world; and when anyone in the village was ill, he pointed out where the devils were, and burned them out with fire, so that everybody got well. However, before long he himself became very ill, and his flesh turned green and purple; whereupon he said, "The devils afflict me thus because I let out their secrets. Henceforth I shall never divulge them again."

Miss Quarta Hu

MR. SHANG WAS A NATIVE OF T'AI-SHAN, AND LIVED QUIETLY WITH HIS BOOKS ALONE. One autumn night when the Silver River was unusually distinct and the moon shining brightly in the sky, he was walking up and down under the shade, with his thoughts wandering somewhat at random, when lo! a young girl leaped over the wall, and, smiling, asked him, "What are you thinking about, Sir, all so deeply?" Shang looked at her, and seeing that she had a pretty face, asked her to walk in. She then told him her name was Hu, and that she was called Tertia; but when he wanted to know where she lived, she laughed and would not say. So he did not inquire any further; and by degrees they struck up a friendship, and Miss Tertia used to come and chat with him every evening.

He was so smitten that he could hardly take his eyes off her, and at last she said to him, "What *are* you looking at?"

"At you," cried he, "my lovely rose, my beautiful peach. I could gaze at you all night long."

"If you think so much of poor me," answered she, "I don't know where your wits would be if you saw my sister Quarta."

Mr. Shang said he was sorry he didn't know her, and begged that he might be introduced; so next night Miss Tertia brought her sister, who turned out to be a young damsel of about fifteen, with a face delicately powdered and resembling the lily, or like an apricot-flower seen through mist; and altogether as pretty a girl as he had ever seen. Mr. Shang was charmed with her, and inviting them in, began to laugh and talk with the elder, while Miss Quarta sat playing with her girdle, and keeping her eyes on the ground.

By-and-by Miss Tertia got up and said she was going, whereupon her sister rose to take leave also; but Mr. Shang asked her not to be in a hurry, and requested the elder to assist in persuading her. "You needn't hurry," said she to Miss Quarta; and accordingly the latter remained chatting with Mr. Shang without reserve, and finally told him she was a fox. However, Mr. Shang was so occupied with her beauty, that he didn't pay any heed to that; but she added, "And my sister is very dangerous; she has already killed three people. Any one bewitched by her has no chance of escape. Happily, you have bestowed your affections on me, and I shall not allow you to be destroyed. You must break off your acquaintance with her at once."

Mr. Shang was very frightened, and implored her to help him; to which she replied, "Although a fox, I am skilled in the arts of the Immortals; I will write out a charm for you which you must paste on the door, and thus you will keep her away." So she wrote down the charm, and in the morning when her sister came and saw it, she fell back, crying out, "Ungrateful minx! you've thrown me up for him, have you? You two being destined for each other, what have I done that you should treat me thus?"

She then went away; and a few days afterward Miss Quarta said she too would have to be absent for a day, so Shang went out for a walk by himself, and suddenly beheld a very nice-looking young lady emerge from the shade of an old oak that was growing on the hill-side. "Why so dreadfully pensive?" said she to him; "those Hu girls can never bring you a single cent." She then presented Shang with some money, and bade him go on ahead and buy some good wine, adding, "I'll bring something to eat with me, and we'll have a jolly time of it." Shang took the money and went home, doing as the young lady had told him; and by-and-by in she herself came, and threw on the table a roast chicken and a shoulder of salt pork, which she at once proceeded to cut up. They now set to work to enjoy themselves, and had hardly finished when they heard some one coming in, and the next minute in walked Miss Tertia and her sister. The strange young lady didn't know where to hide, and managed to lose her shoes; but the other two began to revile her, saying, "Out upon you, base fox; what are you doing here?" They then chased her away after some trouble, and Shang began to excuse himself to them, until at last they all became friends again as before.

One day, however, a Shensi man arrived, riding on a donkey, and coming to the door said, "I have long been in search of these evil spirits: now I have got them." Shang's father thought the man's remark rather strange, and asked him whence he had come. "Across much land and sea," replied he; "for eight or nine months out of every year I am absent from my native place. These devils killed my brother with their poison, alas! alas! and I have sworn to exterminate them; but I have traveled many miles without being able to find them. They are now in your house, and if you do not cut them off, you will die even as my brother."

Now Shang and the young ladies had kept their acquaintanceship very dark; but his father and mother had guessed that something was up, and, much alarmed, bade the Shensi man walk in and perform his exorcisms. The latter then produced two bottles which he placed upon the ground, and proceeded to mutter a number of charms and cabalistic formulas; whereupon four wreaths of smoke passed two by two into each bottle. "I have the whole family," cried he, in an ecstasy of delight; as he proceeded to tie down the mouths of the bottles with pig's bladder, sealing them with the utmost care. Shang's father was likewise very pleased, and kept his guest to dinner; but the young man himself was sadly dejected, and approaching the bottles unperceived, bent his ear to listen. "Ungrateful man," said Miss Quarta from within, "to sit there and make no effort to save me." This was more than Shang could stand, and he immediately broke the seal, but found that he couldn't untie the knot. "Not so," cried Miss Quarta; "merely lay down the flag that now stands on the altar, and with a pin prick the bladder, and I can get out." Shang did as she bade him, and in a moment a thin streak of white smoke issued forth from the hole and disappeared in the clouds. When the Shensi man came out, and saw the flag lying on the ground, he started violently, and cried out, "Escaped! This must be your doing, young Sir." He then shook the bottle and listened, finally exclaiming, "Luckily only one has got away. She was fated not to die, and may therefore be pardoned." Thereupon he took the bottles and went his way.

Some years afterward Shang was one day superintending his reapers cutting the corn, when he descried Miss Quarta at a distance, sitting under a tree. He approached, and she took his hand, saying, "Ten years have rolled away since last we met. Since then I have gained the prize of immortality; but I thought that perhaps you had not quite forgotten me, and so I came to see you once more." Shang wished her to return home with him; to which she replied, "I am no longer what I was that I should mingle in the affairs of mortals. We shall meet again." And as she said this, she disappeared; but twenty years later, when Shang was one day alone, Miss Quarta walked in. Shang was overjoyed, and began to address her; but she answered him, saying, "My name is already enrolled in the Register of the Immortals, and I have no right to return to earth. However, out of gratitude to you I determined to announce to you the date of your dissolution that you might put your affairs in order. Fear nothing; I will see you safely through to the happy land." She then departed, and on the day named Shang actually died. A relative of a friend of mine, Mr. Li Wên-yü, frequently met the above-mentioned Mr. Shang.

Mr. Chu, the Considerate Husband

At the village of Chu in Chi-yang, there was a man named Chu, who died at the age of fifty and odd years. His family at once proceeded to put on their mourning robes, when suddenly they heard the dead man cry out. Rushing up to the coffin, they found that he had come to life again; and began, full of joy, to ask him all about it. But the old gentleman replied only to his wife, saying, "When I died I did not expect to come back. However, by the time I had got a few miles on my way, I thought of the poor old body I was leaving behind me, dependent for everything on others, and with no more enjoyment of life. So I made up my mind to return, and take you away with me."

The bystanders thought this was only the disconnected talk of a man who had just regained consciousness, and attached no importance to it; but the old man repeated it, and then his wife said, "It's all very well, but you have only just come to life; how can you go and die again directly?"

"It is extremely simple," replied her husband; "you go and pack up everything ready."

The old lady laughed and did nothing; upon which Mr. Chu urged her again to prepare, and then left the house. In a short time he returned, and his wife pretended that she had done what he wanted. "Then you had better dress," said he; but Mrs. Chu did not move until he pressed her again and again, after which she did not like to cross him, and by-and-by came out all fully equipped. The other ladies of the family were laughing on the sly, when Mr. Chu laid his head upon the pillow, and told his wife to do likewise. "It's too ridiculous," she was beginning to say, when Mr. Chu banged the bed with his hand, and cried out, "What is there to laugh at in dying?" upon which the various members of the family, seeing the old gentleman was in a rage, begged her to gratify his whim.

Mrs. Chu then lay down alongside of her husband, to the infinite amusement of the spectators; but it was soon noticed that the old lady had ceased to smile, and by-and-by her two eyes closed. For a long time not a sound was heard, as if she was fast asleep; and when some of those present approached to touch her, they found she was as cold as ice, and no longer breathing; then, turning to her husband, they perceived that he also had passed away.

This story was fully related by a younger sister-in-law of Mr. Chu's, who, in the twenty-first year of the reign K'ang Hsi, was employed in the house of a high official named Pi.

The Magnanimous Girl

At Chin-ling there lived a young man named Ku, who had considerable ability but was very poor; and having an old mother, he was very loath to leave home. So he employed himself in writing or painting for people, and gave his mother the proceeds, going on thus till he was twenty-five years of age without taking a wife. Opposite to their house was another building, which had long been untenanted; and one day an old woman and a young girl came to occupy it, but there being no gentleman with them young Ku did not make any inquiries as to who they were or whence they hailed.

Shortly afterward it chanced that just as Ku was entering the house he observed a young lady come out of his mother's door. She was about eighteen or nineteen, very clever and refined looking, and altogether such a girl as one rarely sets eyes on; and when she noticed Mr. Ku, she did not run away, but seemed quite self-possessed. "It was the young lady over the way; she came to borrow my scissors and measure," said his mother, "and she told me that there was only her mother and herself. They don't seem to belong to the lower classes. I asked her why she didn't get married, to which she replied that her mother was old. I must go and call on her to-morrow, and find out how the land lies. If she doesn't expect too much, you could take care of her mother for her."

So next day Ku's mother went, and found that the girl's mother was deaf, and that they were evidently poor, apparently not having a day's food in the house. Ku's mother asked what their employment was, and the old lady said they trusted for food to her daughter's ten fingers. She then threw out some hints about uniting the two families, to which the old lady seemed to agree; but, on consultation with her daughter, the latter would not consent. Mrs. Ku returned home and told her son, saying, "Perhaps she thinks we are too poor. She doesn't speak or laugh, is very nice-looking, and as pure as snow; truly no ordinary girl."

There ended that; until one day, as Ku was sitting in his study, up came a very agreeable young fellow, who said he was from a neighboring village, and engaged Ku to draw a picture for him. The two youths soon struck up a firm friendship and met constantly, when it happened that the stranger chanced to see the young lady of over the way. "Who is that?" said he, following her with his eyes. Ku told him, and then he said, "She is certainly pretty, but rather stern in her appearance."

By-and-by Ku went in, and his mother told him the girl had come to beg a little rice, as they had had nothing to eat all day. "She's a good daughter," said his mother, "and I'm very sorry for her. We must try and help them a little." Ku thereupon shouldered a peck of rice, and, knocking at their door, presented it with his mother's compliments. The young lady received the rice but said nothing; and then she got into the habit of coming over and helping Ku's mother with her work and household affairs, almost as if she had been her daughter-in-law, for which Ku was very grateful to her, and whenever he had anything nice he always sent some of it in to her mother, though the young lady herself never once took the trouble to thank him.

So things went on until Ku's mother got an abscess on her leg, and lay writhing in agony day and night. Then the young lady devoted herself to the invalid, waiting on her and giving her medicine with such care and attention that at last the sick woman cried out, "Oh, that I could secure such a daughter-in-law as you, to see this old body into its grave!" The young lady soothed her, and replied, "Your son is a hundred times more filial than I, a poor widow's only daughter." "But even a filial son makes a bad nurse," answered the patient; "besides, I am now drawing toward the evening of my life, when my body will be exposed to the mists and the dews, and I am vexed in spirit about our ancestral worship and the continuance of our line."

As she was speaking Ku walked in; and his mother, weeping, said, "I am deeply indebted to this young lady; do not forget to repay her goodness." Ku made a low bow, but the young lady said, "Sir, when you were kind to my mother, I did not thank you; why, then, thank me?" Ku thereupon became more than ever attached to her; but could never get her to depart in the slightest degree from her cold demeanor toward himself. One day, however, he managed to squeeze her hand, upon which she told him never to do so again; and then for some time he neither saw nor heard anything of her. She had conceived a violent dislike to the young stranger above-mentioned; and one evening when he was sitting talking with Ku, the young lady reappeared. After a while she got angry at something he said, and drew from her robe a glittering knife about a foot long. The young man, seeing her do this, ran out in a fright and she after him, only to find that he had vanished. She then threw her dagger up into the air, and whish! a streak of light like a rainbow, and something came tumbling down with a flop. Ku got a light, and ran to see what it was; and lo! there lay a white fox, head in one place and body in another. "There is your *friend*," cried the girl; "I knew he would cause me to destroy him sooner or later." Ku dragged it into the house, and said, "Let us wait till to-morrow to talk it over; we shall then be more calm."

Next day the young lady arrived, and Ku inquired about her knowledge of the black art; but she told Ku not to trouble himself about such affairs, and to keep it secret or it might be prejudicial to his happiness. Ku then entreated her to consent to their union, to which she replied that she had already been as it were a daughter-in-law to his mother, and there was no need to push the thing further. "Is it because I am poor?" asked Ku. "Well, I am not rich," answered she, "but the fact is I had rather not." She then took her leave, and the next evening when Ku went across to their house to try once more to persuade her, the young lady had disappeared, and was never seen again.

The Boon-Companion

Once upon a time there was a young man named Ch'ê, who was not particularly well off, but at the same time very fond of his wine; so much so, that without his three stoups of liquor every night, he was quite unable to sleep, and bottles were seldom absent from the head of his bed. One night he had waked up and was turning over and over, when he fancied some one was in the bed with him; but then, thinking it was only the clothes which had slipped off, he put out his hand to feel, and, lo! he touched something silky like a cat, only larger. Striking a light, he found it was a fox, lying in a drunken sleep like a dog; and then looking at his wine bottle he saw that it had been emptied. "A boon-companion," said he, laughing, as he avoided startling the animal, and covering it up, lay down to sleep with his arm across it, and the candle alight so as to see what transformation it might undergo.

About midnight, the fox stretched itself, and Ch'ê cried, "Well, to be sure, you've had a nice sleep!" He then drew off the clothes, and beheld an elegant young man in a scholar's dress; but the young man jumped up, and making a low obeisance, returned his host many thanks for not cutting off his head. "Oh," replied Ch'ê, "I am not averse to liquor myself; in fact they say I'm too much given to it. You shall play Pythias to my Damon; and if you have no objection, we'll be a pair of bottle-and-glass chums." So they lay down and went to sleep again, Ch'ê urging the young man to visit him often, and saying that they must have faith in each other. The fox agreed to this, but when Ch'ê awoke in the morning his bedfellow had already disappeared. So he prepared a goblet of first-rate wine in expectation of his friend's arrival, and at nightfall sure enough he came. They then sat together drinking, and the fox cracked so many jokes that Ch'ê said he regretted he had not known him before.

"And truly I don't know how to repay your kindness," replied the former, "in preparing all this nice wine for me."

"Oh," said Ch'ê, "what's a pint or so of wine?—nothing worth speaking of."

"Well," rejoined the fox, "you are only a poor scholar, and money isn't so easily to be got. I must try if I can't secure a little wine capital for you."

Next evening when he arrived, he said to Ch'ê, "Two miles down toward the southeast you will find some silver lying by the wayside. Go early in the morning and get it."

So on the morrow Ch'ê set off and actually obtained two lumps of silver with which he bought some choice morsels to help them out with their wine that evening. The fox now told him that there was a vault in his back-yard which he ought to open; and when he did so, he found therein more than a hundred strings of cash. "Now then," cried Ch'ê, delighted, "I shall have no more anxiety about funds for buying wine with all this in my purse."

"Ah," replied the fox, "the water in a puddle is not inexhaustible. I must do something further for you."

Some days afterward the fox said to Ch'ê, "Buckwheat is very cheap in the market just now. Something is to be done in this line." Accordingly, Ch'ê bought over forty tons, and thereby incurred general ridicule; but by-and-by there was a bad drought and all kinds of grain and beans were spoiled. Only buckwheat would grow, and Ch'ê sold off his stock at a profit of one thousand per cent. His wealth thus began to increase; he bought two hundred acres of rich land, and always planted his crops, corn, millet, or what not, upon the advice of the fox secretly given him beforehand. The fox looked on Ch'ê's wife as a sister, and on Ch'ê's children as his own; but when, subsequently, Ch'ê died, it never came to the house again.

Miss Lien-hsiang

There was a young man named Sang Tzŭ-ming, a native of I-chou, who had been left an orphan when quite young. He lived near the Saffron market, and kept himself very much to himself, only going out twice a day for his meals to a neighbor's close by, and sitting quietly at home all the rest of his time. One day the said neighbor called, and asked him in joke if he wasn't afraid of devil-foxes, so much alone as he was. "Oh," replied Sang, laughing, "what has the superior man to fear from devil-foxes. If they come as men, I have here a sharp sword for them; and if as women, why, I shall open the door and ask them to walk in." The neighbor went away, and having arranged with a friend of his, they got a young lady of their acquaintance to climb over Sang's wall with the help of a ladder, and knock at the door. Sang peeped through, and called out, "Who's there?" to which the girl answered, "A devil!" and frightened Sang so dreadfully that his teeth chattered in his head. The girl then ran away, and next morning when his neighbor came to see him, Sang told him what had happened, and said he meant to go back to his native place. The neighbor then clapped his hands, and said to Sang, "Why didn't you ask her in?" Whereupon Sang perceived that he had been tricked, and went on quietly again as before.

Some six months afterward, a young lady knocked at his door; and Sang, thinking his friends were at their old tricks, opened it at once, and asked her to walk in. She did so; and he beheld to his astonishment a perfect Helen for beauty. Asking her whence she came, she replied that her name was Lien-hsiang, and that she lived not very far off, adding that she had long been anxious to make his acquaintance.

After that she used to drop in every now and again for a chat; but one evening when Sang was sitting alone expecting her, another young lady suddenly walked in. Thinking it was Lien-hsiang, Sang got up to meet her, but found that the new-comer was somebody else. She was about fifteen or sixteen years of age, wore very full sleeves, and dressed her hair after the fashion of unmarried girls, being otherwise very stylish-looking and refined, and apparently hesitating whether to go on or go back. Sang, in a great state of alarm, took her for a fox; but the young lady said, "My name is Li, and I am of a respectable family. Hearing of your virtue and talent, I hope to be accorded the honor of your acquaintance." Sang laughed, and took her by the hand, which he found was as cold as ice; and when he asked the reason, she told him that she had always been delicate, and that it was very chilly outside. She then remarked that she intended to visit him pretty frequently, and hoped it would not inconvenience him; so he explained that no one came to see him except another young lady, and that not very often. "When she comes, I'll go," replied the young lady, "and only drop in when she's not here." She then gave him an embroidered slipper, saying that she had worn it, and that whenever he shook it she would know that he wanted to see her, cautioning him at the same time never to shake it before strangers. Taking it in his hand he beheld a very tiny little shoe almost as fine pointed as an awl, with which he was much pleased; and next evening, when nobody was present, he produced the shoe and shook it, whereupon the young lady immediately walked in. Henceforth, whenever he brought it out, the young lady responded to his wishes and appeared before him. This seemed so strange that at last he asked her to give him some explanation; but she only laughed, and said it was mere coincidence.

One evening after this Lien-hsiang came, and said in alarm to Sang, "Whatever has made you look so melancholy?" Sang replied that he did not know, and by-and-by she took her leave, saying, they would not meet again for some ten days.

During this period Miss Li visited Sang every day, and on one occasion asked him where his other friend was. Sang told her; and then she laughed and said, "What is your opinion of me as compared with Lien-hsiang?"

"You are both of you perfection," replied he, "but you are a little *colder* of the two."

Miss Li didn't much like this, and cried out, "*Both of us perfection* is what you say to *me*. Then she must be a downright Cynthia, and I am no match for her." Somewhat out of temper, she reckoned that Lien-hsiang's ten days had expired, and said she would have a peep at her, making Sang promise to keep it all secret.

The next evening Lien-hsiang came, and while they were talking she suddenly exclaimed, "Oh, dear! how much worse you seem to have become in the last ten days. You must have encountered something bad." Sang asked her why so; to which she answered, "First of all your appearance; and then your pulse is very thready. You've got the devil-disease."

The following evening when Miss Li came, Sang asked her what she thought of Lien-hsiang. "Oh," said she, "there's no question about her beauty; but she's a fox. When she went away I followed her to her hole on the hill side." Sang, however, attributed this remark to jealousy, and took no notice of it; but the next evening when Lien-hsiang came, he observed, "I don't believe it myself, but some one has told me you are a fox." Lien-hsiang asked who had said so, to which Sang replied that he was only joking; and then she begged him to explain what difference there was between a fox and an ordinary person.

"Well," answered Sang, "foxes frighten people to death, and, therefore, they are very much dreaded."

"Don't you believe that!" cried Lien-hsiang; "and now tell me who has been saying this of me."

Sang declared at first that it was only a joke of his, but by-and-by yielded to her instances, and let out the whole story. "Of course I saw how changed you were," said Lien-hsiang; "she is surely not a human being to be able to cause such a rapid alteration in you. Say nothing, to-morrow I'll watch her as she watched me."

The following evening Miss Li came in; and they had hardly interchanged half-a-dozen sentences when a cough was heard outside the window, and Miss Li ran away. Lien-hsiang then entered and said to Sang, "You are lost! She is a devil, and if you do not at once forbid her coming here, you will soon be on the road to the other world."

"All jealousy," thought Sang, saying nothing, as Lien-hsiang continued, "I know that you don't like to be rude to her; but I, for my part, cannot see you sacrificed, and to-morrow I will bring you some medicine to expel the poison from your system. Happily, the disease has not yet taken firm hold of you, and in ten days you will be well again."

The next evening she produced a knife and chopped up some medicine for Sang, which made him feel much better; but, although he was very grateful to her, he still persisted in disbelieving that he had the devil-disease. After some days he recovered and Lien-hsiang left him, warning him to have no more to do with Miss Li. Sang pretended that he would follow her advice, and closed the door and trimmed his lamp. He then took out the slipper, and on shaking it Miss Li appeared, somewhat cross at having been kept away for several days. "She merely attended on me these few nights while I was ill," said Sang; "don't be angry." At this Miss Li brightened up a little; but by-and-by Sang told her that people said she was a devil. "It's that nasty fox," cried Miss Li, after a pause, "putting these things into your head. If you don't break with her, I won't come here again." She then began to sob and cry, and Sang had some trouble in pacifying her.

Next evening Lien-hsiang came and found out that Miss Li had been there again; whereupon she was very angry with Sang, and told him he would certainly die. "Why need you be so jealous?" said Sang, laughing; at which she only got more enraged, and replied, "When you were nearly dying the other day and I saved you, if I had not been jealous, where would you have been now?" Sang pretended he was only joking, and said that Miss Li had told him his recent illness was entirely owing to the machinations of a fox; to which she replied, "It's true enough what you say, only you don't see *whose* machinations. However, if any thing happens to you, I should never clear myself even had I a hundred mouths; we will, therefore, part. A hundred days hence I shall see you on your bed." Sang could not persuade her to stay, and away she went; and from that time Miss Li became a regular visitor.

Two months passed away, and Sang began to experience a feeling of great lassitude, which he tried at first to shake off, but by-and-by he became very thin, and could only take thick gruel. He then thought about going back to his native place; however, he could not bear to leave Miss Li, and in a few more days he was so weak that he was unable to get up. His friend next door, seeing how ill he was, daily sent in his boy with food and drink; and now Sang began for the first time to suspect Miss Li. So he said to her, "I am sorry I didn't listen to Lien-hsiang before I got as bad as this." He then closed his eyes and kept them shut for some time; and when he opened them again Miss Li had disappeared. Their acquaintanceship was thus at an end, and Sang lay all emaciated as he was upon his bed in his solitary room longing for the return of Lien-hsiang.

One day, while he was still thinking about her, some one drew aside the screen and walked in. It was Lien-hsiang; and approaching the bed she said with a smile, "Was I then talking such nonsense?" Sang struggled a long time to speak; and, at length, confessing he had been wrong, implored her to save him. "When the disease has reached such a pitch as this," replied Lien-hsiang, "there is very little to be done. I merely came to bid you farewell, and to clear up your doubts about my jealousy." In great tribulation, Sang asked her to take something she would find under his pillow and destroy it; and she accordingly drew forth the slipper, which she proceeded to examine by the light of the lamp, turning it over and over.

All at once Miss Li walked in, but when she saw Lien-hsiang she turned back as though she would run away, which Lien-hsiang instantly prevented by placing herself in the doorway. Sang then began to reproach her, and Miss Li could make no reply; whereupon Lien-hsiang said, "At last we meet. Formerly you attributed this gentleman's illness to me; what have you to say now?" Miss Li bent her head in acknowledgment of her guilt, and Lien-hsiang continued, "How is it that a nice girl like you can thus turn love into hate?"

Here Miss Li threw herself on the ground in a flood of tears and begged for mercy; and Lien-hsiang, raising her up, inquired of her as to her past life. "I am a daughter of a petty official named Li, and I died young, leaving the web of my destiny incomplete, like the silkworm that perishes in the spring. To be the partner of this gentleman was my ardent wish; but I had never any intention of causing his death."

"I have heard," remarked Lien-hsiang, "that the advantage devils obtain by killing people is that their victims are ever with them after death. Is this so?"

"It is not," replied Miss Li; "the companionship of two devils gives no pleasure to either. Were it otherwise, I should not have wanted for friends in the realms below. But tell me, how do foxes manage not to kill people?"

"You allude to such foxes as suck the breath out of people?" replied Lien-hsiang; "I am not of that class. Some foxes are harmless; no devils are, because of the dominance of the *yin* in their compositions."

Sang now knew that these two girls were really a fox and a devil; however, from being long accustomed to their society, he was not in the least alarmed. His breathing had dwindled to a mere thread, and at length he uttered a cry of pain.

Lien-hsiang looked round and said, "How shall we cure him?" upon which Miss Li blushed deeply and drew back; and then Lien-hsiang added, "If he does get well, I'm afraid you will be dreadfully jealous."

Miss Li drew herself up, and replied, "Could a physician be found to wipe away the wrong I have done to this gentleman, I would bury my head in the ground. How should I look the world in the face?"

Lien-hsiang here opened a bag and drew forth some drugs, saying, "I have been looking forward to this day. When I left this gentleman I proceeded to gather my samples, as it would take three months for the medicine to be got ready; but then, should the poison have brought anyone even to death's door, this medicine is able to call him back. The only condition is that it be administered by the very hand which wrought the ill." Miss Li did as she was told and put the pills Lien-hsiang gave her one after another into Sang's mouth. They burned his inside like fire; but soon vitality began to return, and Lien-hsiang cried out, "He is cured!"

Just at this moment Miss Li heard the cock crow and vanished, Lien-hsiang remaining behind in attendance on the invalid, who was unable to feed himself. She bolted the outside door and pretended that Sang had returned to his native place, so as to prevent visitors from calling. Day and night she took care of him, and every evening Miss Li came in to render assistance, regarding Lien-hsiang as an elder sister, and being treated by her with great consideration and kindness. Three months afterward Sang was as strong and well as ever he had been, and then for several evenings Miss Li ceased to visit them, only staying a few moments when she did come, and seeming very uneasy in her mind.

One evening Sang ran after her and carried her back in his arms, finding her no heavier than so much straw; and then, being obliged to stay, she curled herself up and lay down, to all appearance in a state of unconsciousness, and by-and-by she was gone. For many days they heard nothing of her, and Sang was so anxious that she should come back that he often took out her slipper and shook it. "I don't wonder at your missing her," said Lien-hsiang, "I do myself very much indeed."

"Formerly," observed Sang, "when I shook the slipper she invariably came. I thought it very strange, but I never suspected her of being a devil. And now, alas! all I can do is to sit and think about her with this slipper in my hand." He then burst into a flood of tears.

Now a young lady named Yen-êrh, belonging to the wealthy Chang family, and about fifteen years of age, had died suddenly, without any apparent cause, and had come to life again in the night, when she got up and wished to go out. They barred the door and would not hear of her doing so; upon which she said, "I am the spirit daughter of a petty magistrate. A Mr. Sang has been very kind to me, and I have left my slipper at his house. I am really a spirit; what is the use of keeping me in?" There being some reason for what she said, they asked her why she had come there; but she only looked up and down without being able to give any explanation. Some one here observed, that Mr. Sang had already gone home, but the young lady utterly refused to believe them. The family was much disturbed at all this; and when Sang's neighbor heard the story, he jumped over the wall, and peeping through beheld Sang sitting there chatting with a pretty-looking girl. As he went in, there was some commotion, during which Sang's visitor had disappeared, and when his neighbor asked the meaning of it all, Sang replied, laughing, "Why, I told you if any ladies came I should ask them in." His friend then repeated what Miss Yen-êrh had said; and Sang, unbolting his door, was about to go and have a peep at her, but unfortunately had no means of so doing.

Meanwhile Mrs. Chang, hearing that he had not gone away, was more lost in astonishment than ever, and sent an old woman-servant to get back the slipper. Sang immediately gave it to her, and Miss Yen-êrh was delighted to recover it, though when she came to try it on it was too small for her by a good inch. In considerable alarm, she seized a mirror to look at herself; and suddenly became aware that she had come to life again in some one else's body. She therefore told all to her mother, and finally succeeded in convincing her, crying all the time because she was so changed for the worse as regarded personal appearance from what she had been before. And whenever she happened to see Lien-hsiang, she was very much disconcerted, declaring that she had been much better off as a devil than now as a human being. She would sit and weep over the slipper, no one being able to comfort her; and finally, covering herself up with bed-clothes, she lay all stark and stiff, positively refusing to take any nourishment. Her body swelled up, and for seven days she refused all food, but did not die; and then the swelling began to subside, and an intense hunger to come upon her which made her once more think about eating. Then she was troubled with a severe irritation, and her skin peeled entirely away; and when she got up in the morning, she found that the shoes had fallen off. On trying to put them on again, she discovered that they did not fit her any longer; and then she went back to her former pair which were now exactly of the right size and shape. In an ecstasy of joy, she grasped her mirror, and saw that her features had also changed back to what they had formerly been; so she washed and dressed herself and went in to visit her mother. Every one who met her was much astonished; and when Lien-hsiang heard the strange story, she tried to persuade Mr. Sang to make her an offer of marriage. But the young lady was rich and Sang was poor, and he did not see his way clearly. However, on Mrs. Chang's birthday, when she completed her cycle of sixty-one years, Sang went along with the others to wish her many happy returns of the day; and when the old lady knew who was coming, she bade Yen-êrh take a peep at him from behind the curtain. Sang arrived last of all; and immediately out rushed Miss Yen-êrh and seized his sleeve, and said she would go back with him. Her mother scolded her well for this, and she ran in abashed; but Sang, who had looked at her closely, began to weep, and threw himself at the feet of Mrs. Chang who raised him up without saying anything unkind. Sang then took his leave, and got his uncle to act as medium between them; the result being that an auspicious day was fixed upon for the wedding.

At the appointed time Sang proceeded to the house to fetch her; and when he returned he found that, instead of his former poor-looking furniture, beautiful carpets were laid down from the very door, and thousands of colored lanterns were hung about in elegant designs. Lien-hsiang assisted the bride to enter, and took off her veil, finding her the same bright girl as ever. She also joined them while drinking the wedding cup, and inquired of her friend as to her recent transmigration; and Yen-êrh related as follows:—"Overwhelmed with grief, I began to shrink from myself as some unclean thing; and, after separating from you that day, I would not return any more to my grave. So I wandered about at random, and whenever I saw a living being, I envied its happy state. By day I remained among trees and shrubs, but at night I used to roam about anywhere. And once I came to the house of the Chang family, where, seeing a young girl lying upon the bed, I took possession of her mortal coil, unknowing that she would be restored to life again."

When Lien-hsiang heard this she was for some time lost in thought; and a month or two afterward became very ill. She refused all medical aid and gradually got worse and worse, to the great grief of Mr. Sang and his wife, who stood weeping at her bed-side. Suddenly she opened her eyes, and said, "You wish to live; I am willing to die. If fate so ordains it, we shall meet again ten years hence." As she uttered these words, her spirit passed away, and all that remained was the dead body of a fox. Sang, however, insisted on burying it with all the proper ceremonies.

Now his wife had no children; but one day a servant came in and said, "There is an old woman outside who has got a little girl for sale." Sang's wife gave orders that she should be shown in; and no sooner had she set eyes on the girl than she cried out, "Why, she's the image of Lien-hsiang!" Sang then looked at her, and found to his astonishment that she was really very like his old friend. The old woman said she was fourteen years old; and when asked what her price was, declared that her only wish was to get the girl comfortably settled, and enough to keep herself alive, and ensure not being thrown out into the kennel at death. So Sang gave a good price for her; and his wife, taking the girl's hand, led her into a room by themselves. Then, chucking her under the chin, she asked her, smiling, "Do you know me?" The girl said she did not; after which she told Mrs. Sang that her name was Wei, and that her father, who had been a pickle-merchant at Hsü-ch'êng, had died three years before. Mrs. Sang then calculated that Lien-hsiang had been dead just ten years; and, looking at the girl, who resembled her so exactly in every trait, at length patted her on the head, saying, "Ah, my sister, you promised to visit us again in ten years, and you have not played us false." The girl here seemed to wake up as if from a dream, and, uttering an exclamation of surprise, fixed a steady gaze upon Sang's wife. Sang himself laughed, and said, "Just like the return of an old familiar swallow." "Now I understand," cried the girl, in tears; "I recollect my mother saying that when I was born I was able to speak; and that, thinking it an inauspicious manifestation, they gave me dog's blood to drink, so that I should forget all about my previous state of existence. Is it all a dream, or are you not the Miss Li who was so ashamed of being a devil?" Thus they chatted of their existence in a former life, with alternate tears and smiles; but when it came to the day for worshipping at the tombs, Yen-êrh explained that she and her husband were in the habit of annually visiting and mourning over her grave. The girl replied that she would accompany them; and when they got there they found the whole place in disorder, and the coffin wood all warped. "Lien-hsiang and I," said Yen-êrh to her husband, "have been attached to each other in two states of existence. Let us not be separated, but bury my bones here with hers." Sang consented, and opening Miss Li's tomb, took out the bones and buried them with those of Lien-hsiang, while friends and relatives, who had heard the strange story, gathered round the grave in gala dress to the number of many hundreds.

I learned the above when traveling through I-chou, where I was detained at an inn by rain, and read a biography of Mr. Sang written by a comrade of his named Wang Tzŭ-chang. It was lent me by a Mr. Liu Tzŭ-ching, a relative of Sang's, and was quite a long account. This is merely an outline of it.

Miss A-pao; or, Perseverance Rewarded

In the province of Kuang-si there lived a scholar of some reputation, named Sun Tzŭ-ch'u. He was born with six fingers, and such a simple fellow was he that he readily believed any nonsense he was told. Very shy with the fair sex, the sight of a woman was enough to send him flying in the opposite direction; and once when he was inveigled into a room where there were some young ladies, he blushed down to his neck and the perspiration dripped off him like falling pearls. His companions laughed heartily at his discomfiture, and told fine stories of what a noodle he looked, so that he got the nickname of Silly Sun.

In the town where our hero resided, there was a rich trader whose wealth equaled that of any prince or nobleman, and whose connections were all highly aristocratic. He had a daughter, A-pao, of great beauty, for whom he was seeking a husband; and the young men of position in the neighborhood were vying with each other to obtain her hand, but none of them met with the father's approval.

Now Silly Sun had recently lost his wife; and some one in joke persuaded him to try his luck and send in an application. Sun, who had no idea of his own shortcomings, proceeded at once to follow this advice; but the father, though he knew him to be an accomplished scholar, rejected his suit on the ground of poverty. As the go-between was leaving the house, she chanced to meet A-pao, and related to her the object of her visit. "Tell him," cried A-pao, laughing, "that if he'll cut off his extra finger, I'll marry him." The old woman reported this to Sun, who replied, "That is not very difficult"; and, seizing a chopper, cut the finger clean off. The wound was extremely painful and he lost so much blood that he nearly died, it being many days before he was about again. He then sought out the go-between, and bade her inform Miss A-pao, which she did; and A-pao was taken rather aback, but she told the old woman to go once more and bid him cut off the "silly" from his reputation. Sun got much excited when he heard this, and denied that he was silly; however, as he was unable to prove it to the young lady herself, he began to think that probably her beauty was over-stated, and that she was giving herself great airs. So he ceased to trouble himself about her until the following spring festival, when it was customary for both men and women to be seen abroad, and the young rips of the place would stroll about in groups and pass their remarks on all and sundry.

Sun's friends urged him to join them in their expedition, and one of them asked him with a smile if he did not wish to look out for a suitable mate. Sun knew they were chaffing him, but he thought he should like to see the girl that had made such a fool of him, and was only too pleased to accompany them. They soon perceived a young lady resting herself under a tree, with a throng of young fellows crowding round her, and they immediately determined that she must be A-pao, as in fact they found she was. Possessed of peerless beauty, the ring of her admirers gradually increased, till at last she rose up to go. The excitement among the young men was intense; they criticized her face and discussed her feet, Sun only remaining silent; and when they had passed on to something else, there they saw Sun rooted like an imbecile to the same spot. As he made no answer when spoken to, they dragged him along with them, saying, "Has your spirit run away after A-pao?" He made no reply to this either; but they thought nothing of that, knowing his usual strangeness of manner, so by dint of pushing and pulling they managed to get him home. There he threw himself on the bed and did not get up again for the rest of the day, lying in a state of unconsciousness just as if he were drunk. He did not wake when called; and his people, thinking that his spirit had fled, went about in the fields calling out to it to return. However, he showed no signs of improvement; and when they shook him, and asked him what was the matter, he only answered in a sleepy kind of voice, "I am at A-pao's house"; but to further questions he would not make any reply, and left his family in a state of keen suspense.

Now when Silly Sun had seen the young lady get up to go, he could not bear to part with her, and found himself first following and then walking along by her side without anyone saying anything to him. Thus he went back with her to her home, and there he remained for three days, longing to run home and get something to eat, but unfortunately not knowing the way. By that time Sun had hardly a breath left in him; and his friends, fearing that he was going to die, sent to beg of the rich trader that he would allow a search to be made for Sun's spirit in his house. The trader laughed and said, "He wasn't in the habit of coming here, so he could hardly have left his spirit behind him"; but he yielded to the entreaties of Sun's family, and permitted the search to be made. Thereupon a magician proceeded to the house, taking with him an old suit of Sun's clothes and some grass matting; and when Miss A-pao heard the reason for which he had come, she simplified matters very much by leading the magician straight to her own room. The magician summoned the spirit in due form, and went back toward Sun's house. By the time he had reached the door, Sun groaned and recovered consciousness; and he was then able to describe all the articles of toilette and furniture in A-pao's room without making a single mistake. A-pao was amazed when the story was repeated to her, and could not help feeling kindly toward him on account of the depth of his passion. Sun himself, when he got well enough to leave his bed, would often sit in a state of abstraction as if he had lost his wits; and he was for ever scheming to try and have another glimpse at A-pao.

One day he heard that she intended to worship at the Shui-yüeh temple on the 8th of the fourth moon, that day being the Wash-Buddha festival; and he set off early in the morning to wait for her at the roadside. He was nearly blind with straining his eyes, and the sun was already past noontide before the young lady arrived; but when she saw from her carriage a gentleman standing there, she drew aside the screen and had a good stare at him. Sun followed her in a great state of excitement, upon which she bade one of her maids to go and ask his name. Sun told her who he was, his perturbation all the time increasing; and when the carriage drove on he returned home. Again he became very ill, and lay on his bed unconscious, without taking any food, occasionally calling on A-pao by name, at the same time abusing his spirit for not having been able to follow her as before. Just at this juncture a parrot that had been long with the family died; and a child, playing with the body, laid it upon the bed. Sun then reflected that if he was only a parrot one flap of his wings would bring him into the presence of A-pao; and while occupied with these thoughts, lo! the dead body moved and the parrot flew away. It flew straight to A-pao's room, at which she was delighted; and catching it, tied a string to its leg, and fed it upon hemp-seed.

"Dear sister," cried the bird, "do not tie me by the leg: I am Sun Tzŭ-ch'u." In great alarm A-pao untied the string, but the parrot did not fly away.

"Alas!" said she, "your love has engraved itself upon my heart; but now you are no longer a man, how shall we ever be united together?"

"To be near your dear self," replied the parrot, "is all I care about." The parrot then refused to take food from anyone else, and kept close to Miss A-pao wherever she went, day and night alike.

At the expiration of three days, A-pao, who had grown very fond of her parrot, secretly sent some one to ask how Mr. Sun was; but he had already been dead three days, though the part over his heart had not grown cold. "Oh! come to life again as a man," cried the young lady, "and I swear to be yours for ever."

"You are surely not in earnest," said the parrot, "are you?" Miss A-pao declared she was, and the parrot, cocking its head aside, remained some time as if absorbed in thought.

By-and-by A-pao took off her shoes to bind her feet a little tighter; and the parrot, making a rapid grab at one, flew off with it in its beak. She called loudly after it to come back, but in a moment it was out of sight; so she next sent a servant to inquire if there was any news of Mr. Sun, and then learned that he had come round again, the parrot having flown in with an embroidered shoe and dropped down dead on the ground. Also, that directly he regained consciousness he asked for the shoe, of which his people knew nothing; at which moment her servant had arrived, and demanded to know from him where it was. "It was given to me by Miss A-pao as a pledge of faith," replied Sun; "I beg you will tell her I have not forgotten her promise." A-pao was greatly astonished at this, and instructed her maid to divulge the whole affair to her mother, who, when she had made some inquiries, observed that Sun was well known as a clever fellow, but was desperately poor, and "to get such a son-in-law after all our trouble would give our aristocratic friends the laugh against us." However, A-pao pleaded that with the shoe there as a proof against her, she would not marry anybody else; and, ultimately, her father and mother gave their consent. This was immediately announced to Mr. Sun, whose illness rapidly disappeared in consequence. A-pao's father would have had Sun come and live with them; but the young lady objected, on the score that a son-in-law should not remain long at a time with the family of his wife, and that as he was poor he would lower himself still more by doing so. "I have accepted him," added she, "and I shall gladly reside in his humble cottage, and share his poor fare without complaint."

The marriage was then celebrated, and bride and bridegroom met as if for the first time in their lives. The dowry A-pao brought with her somewhat raised their pecuniary position, and gave them a certain amount of comfort; but Sun himself stuck only to his books, and knew nothing about managing affairs in general. Luckily his wife was clever in that respect, and did not bother him with such things; so much so that by the end of three years they were comparatively well off, when Sun suddenly fell ill and died. Mrs. Sun was inconsolable, and refused either to sleep or take nourishment, being deaf to all entreaties on the subject; and before long, taking advantage of the night, she hanged herself. Her maid, hearing a noise, ran in and cut her down just in time: but she still steadily refused all food. Three days passed away, and the friends and relatives of Sun came to attend his funeral, when suddenly they heard a sigh proceeding forth from the coffin. The coffin was then opened and they found that Sun had come to life again. He told them that he had been before the Great Judge, who, as a reward for his upright and honorable life, had conferred upon him an official appointment. "At this moment," said Sun, "it was reported that my wife was close at hand, but the Judge, referring to the register, observed that her time had not yet come. They told him she had taken no food for three days; and then the Judge, looking at me, said that as a recompense for her wifely virtues she should be permitted to return to life. Thereupon he gave orders to his attendants to put to the horses and see us safely back."

From that hour Sun gradually improved, and the next year went up for his master's degree. All his old companions chaffed him exceedingly before the examination, and gave him seven themes on out-of-the-way subjects, telling him privately that they had been surreptitiously obtained from the examiners. Sun believed them as usual, and worked at them day and night until he was perfect, his comrades all the time enjoying a good laugh against him. However, when the day came it was found that the examiners, fearing lest the themes they had chosen in an ordinary way should have been dishonestly made public, took a set of fresh ones quite out of the common run—in fact, on the very subjects Sun's companions had given to him. Consequently, he came out at the head of the list; and the next year, after taking his doctor's degree, he was entered among the Han-lin Academicians. The Emperor, too, happening to hear of his curious adventures, sent for him and made him repeat his story; subsequently, summoning A-pao and making her some very costly presents.

Jen Hsiu

Jen Chien-chih was a native of Yü-t'ai, and a dealer in rugs and furs. One day he set off for Shensi, taking with him every penny he could scrape together; and on the road he met a man who told him that his name was Shên Chu-t'ing, and his native place Su-ch'ien. These two soon became firm friends, and entered into a masonic bond with each other, journeying on together by the same stages until they reached their destination.

By-and-by Mr. Jen fell sick, and his companion had to nurse him, which he did with the utmost attention, but for ten days he gradually got worse and worse, and at length said to Shên, "My family is very poor. Eight mouths depend upon my exertions for food; and now, alas! I am about to die, far from my own home. You and I are brothers. At this distance there is no one else to whom I can look. Now in my purse you will find two hundred ounces of silver. Take half, and when you have defrayed my funeral expenses, use the balance for your return journey; and give the other half to my family, that they may be able to send for my coffin. If, however, you will take my mortal remains with you home to my native place, these expenses need not be incurred." He then, with the aid of a pillow, wrote a letter, which he handed to Shên, and that evening he died. Thereupon Shên purchased a cheap coffin for some five or six ounces of silver; and, as the landlord kept urging him to take away the body, he said he would go out and seek for a temple where it might be temporarily deposited. But he ran away and never went back to the inn; and it was more than a year before Jen's family knew what had taken place. His son was just about seventeen years of age, and had recently been reading with a tutor; but now his books were laid aside, and he proposed to go in search of his father's body. His mother said he was too young; and it was only when he declared he would rather not live than stay at home, that with the aid of the pawn-shop enough money was raised to start him on his way. An old servant accompanied him, and it was six months before they returned and performed the last ceremonies over Jen's remains. The family was thus reduced to absolute destitution; but happily young Hsiu was a clever fellow, and when the days of mourning were over, took his bachelor's degree. On the other hand, he was somewhat wild and very fond of gambling; and although his mother strictly prohibited such diversions, all her prohibitions were in vain.

By-and-by the Grand Examiner arrived, and Hsiu came out in the fourth class. His mother was extremely angry, and refused to take food, which brought young Hsiu to his senses, and he promised her faithfully he would never gamble again. From that day he shut himself up, and the following year took a first class degree, coming out among the "senior" graduates. His mother now advised him to take pupils, but his reputation as a disorderly fellow stuck to him, and no one would entrust their sons to his care.

Just then an uncle of his, named Chang, was about to start with merchandise for the capital, and recommended that Hsiu should go along with him, promising himself to pay all expenses, an offer which Hsiu was only too pleased to accept. When they reached Lin-ch'ing, they anchored outside the Custom House, where they found a great number of salt-junks, in fact a perfect forest of masts; and what with the noise of the water and the people it was quite impossible to sleep. Besides, as the row was beginning to subside, the clear rattle of dice from a neighboring boat fell upon Hsiu's ear, and before long he was itching to be back again at his old games. Listening to hear if all around him were sound asleep, he drew forth a string of cash that he had brought with him, and thought he would just go across and try his luck. So he got up quietly with his money, and was on the point of going, when he suddenly recollected his mother's injunctions, and at once tying his purse-strings laid himself down to sleep. He was far too excited, however, to close his eyes; and after a while got up again and re-opened his purse. This he did three times, until at last it was too much for him, and off he went with his money. Crossing over into the boat whence the sounds proceeded, he beheld two persons engaged in gambling for high stakes; so throwing his money on the table, he begged to be allowed to join. The others readily consented, and they began to play, Hsiu winning so rapidly that soon one of the strangers had no money left, and was obliged to get the proprietor of the boat to change a large piece of silver for him, proceeding to lay down as much as several ounces of silver for a single stake.

As the play was in full swing another man walked in, who after watching for some time at length got the proprietor to change another lump of silver for him of one hundred ounces in weight, and also asked to be allowed to join. Now Hsiu's uncle, waking up in the middle of the night, and finding his nephew gone, and hearing the sound of dice-throwing hard by, knew at once where he was, and immediately followed him to the boat with a view of bringing him back. Finding, however, that Hsiu was a heavy winner, he said nothing to him, only carrying off a portion of his winnings to their own boat and making the others of his party get up and help him to fetch the rest, even then leaving behind a large sum for Hsiu to go on with.

By-and-by the three strangers had lost all their ready money, and there wasn't a farthing left in the boat: upon which one of them proposed to play for lumps of silver, but Hsiu said he never went so high as that. This made them a little quarrelsome, Hsiu's uncle all the time trying to get him away; and the proprietor of the boat, who had only his own commission in view, managed to borrow some hundred strings of cash from another boat, and started them all again. Hsiu soon took this out of them; and, as day was beginning to dawn and the Custom House was about to open, he went off with his winnings back to his own boat.

The proprietor of the gambling-boat now found that the lumps of silver which he had changed for his customers were nothing more than so much tinsel, and rushing off in a great state of alarm to Hsiu's boat, told him what had happened and asked him to make it good; but when he discovered he was speaking to the son of his former traveling companion, Jen Chien-chih, he hung his head and slunk away covered with shame. For the proprietor of that boat was no other than Shên Chu-t'ing, of whom Hsiu had heard when he was in Shensi; now, however, that with supernatural aid the wrongs of his father had been avenged, he determined to pursue the man no further. So going into partnership with his uncle, they proceeded north together; and by the end of the year their capital had increased five-fold. Hsiu then purchased the status of chien-shêng, and by further careful investment of his money ultimately became the richest man in that part of the country.

The Lost Brother

In Honan there lived a man named Chang, who originally belonged to Shantung. His wife had been seized and carried off by the soldiery during the period when Ching Nan's troops were overrunning the latter province; and as he was frequently in Honan on business, he finally settled there and married a Honan wife, by whom he had a son named Na. By-and-by this wife died, and he took another, who bore him a son named Ch'êng. The last-mentioned lady was from the Niu family, and a very malicious woman. So jealous was she of Na, that she treated him like a slave or a beast of the field, giving him only the coarsest food, and making him cut a large bundle of wood every day, in default of which she would beat and abuse him in a most shameful manner. On the other hand she secretly reserved all the tit-bits for Ch'êng, and also sent him to school. As Ch'êng grew up, and began to understand the meaning of filial piety and fraternal love, he could not bear to see this treatment of his elder brother, and spoke privately to his mother about it; but she would pay no heed to what he said.

One day, when Na was on the hills performing his task, a violent storm came on, and he took shelter under a cliff. However, by the time it was over the sun had set, and he began to feel very hungry. So, shouldering his bundle, he wended his way home, where his step-mother, displeased with the small quantity of wood he had brought, refused to give him anything to eat. Quite overcome with hunger, Na went in and lay down; and when Ch'êng came back from school, and saw the state he was in, he asked him if he was ill. Na replied that he was only hungry, and then told his brother the whole story; whereupon Ch'êng colored up and went away, returning shortly with some cakes, which he offered to Na.

"Where did you get them?" asked the latter.

"Oh," replied Ch'êng, "I stole some flour and got a neighbor's wife to make them for me. Eat away, and don't talk." Na ate them up; but begged his brother not to do this again, as he might get himself into trouble. "I shan't die," added he, "if I only get one meal a-day."

"You are not strong," rejoined Ch'êng, "and shouldn't cut so much wood as you do."

Next day, after breakfast, Ch'êng slipped away to the hills, and arrived at the place where Na was occupied with his usual task, to the great astonishment of the latter, who inquired what he was going to do.

"To help you cut wood," replied Ch'êng.

"And who sent you?" asked his brother.

"No one," said he; "I came of my own accord."

"Ah," cried Na, "you can't do this work; and even if you can you must not. Run along home again."

Ch'êng, however, remained, aiding his brother with his hands and feet alone, but declaring that on the morrow he would bring an axe. Na tried to stop him, and found that he had already hurt his finger and worn his shoes into holes; so he began to cry, and said, "If you don't go home directly, I'll kill myself with my axe." Ch'êng then went away, his brother seeing him half-way home, and going back to finish his work by himself. He also called in the evening at Ch'êng's school, and told the master his brother was a delicate boy, and should not be allowed to go on the hills, where, he said, there were fierce tigers and wolves. The master replied that he didn't know where Ch'êng had been all the morning, but that he had caned him for playing truant. Na further pointed out to Ch'êng that by not doing as he had told him, he had let himself in for a beating. Ch'êng laughed, and said he hadn't been beaten; and the very next day off he went again, and this time with a hatchet.

"I told you not to come," cried Na, much alarmed; "why have you done so?"

Ch'êng made no reply, but set to work chopping wood with such energy that the perspiration poured down his face; and when he had cut about a bundle he went away without saying a word. The master caned him again, and then Ch'êng told him how the matter stood, at which the former became full of admiration for his pupil's kind behavior, and no longer prevented him from going. His brother, however, frequently urged him not to come, though without the slightest success; and one day, when they went with a number of others to cut wood, a tiger rushed down from the hills upon them. The wood-cutters hid themselves, in the greatest consternation; and the tiger, seizing Ch'êng, ran off with him in his mouth. Ch'êng's weight caused the tiger to move slowly; and Na, rushing after them, hacked away at the tiger's flanks with his axe. The pain only made the tiger hurry off, and in a few minutes they were out of sight. Overwhelmed with grief, Na went back to his comrades, who tried to soothe him; but he said, "My brother was no ordinary brother, and, besides, he died for me; why, then, should I live?" Here, seizing his hatchet, he made a great chop at his own neck, upon which his companions prevented him from doing himself any more mischief. The wound, however, was over an inch deep, and blood was flowing so copiously that Na became faint, and seemed at the point of death. They then tore up their clothes, and, after having bandaged his neck, proceeded to carry him home.

His step-mother cried bitterly, and cursed him, saying, "You have killed my son, and now you go and cut your neck in this make-believe kind of way."

"Don't be angry, mother," replied Na; "I will not live now that my brother is dead."

He then threw himself on the bed; but the pain of his wound was so great he could not sleep, and day and night he sat leaning against the wall in tears. His father, fearing that he too would die, went every now and then and gave him a little nourishment; but his wife cursed him so for doing it, that at length Na refused all food, and in three days he died.

Now in the village where these events took place there was a magician who was employed in certain devil-work among mortals, and Na's ghost, happening to fall in with him, related the story of its previous sorrows, winding up by asking where his brother's ghost was. The magician said he didn't know, but turned round with Na and showed him the way to a city where they saw an official servant coming out of the city gates. The magician stopped him, and inquired if he could tell them anything about

Ch'êng; whereupon the man drew out a list from a pouch at his side, and, after carefully examining it, replied that among the male and female criminals within there was no one of the name of Chang. The magician here suggested that the name might be on another list; but the man replied that he was in charge of that road, and surely ought to know. Na, however, was not satisfied, and persuaded the magician to enter the city, where they met many new and old devils walking about, among whom were some Na had formerly known in life. So he asked them if they could direct him to his brother but none of them knew where he was; and suddenly there was a great commotion, the devils on all sides crying out, "P'u-sa has come!" Then, looking up, Na beheld a most beautiful man descending from above, encircled by rays of glory, which shot forth above and below, lighting up all around him.

"You are in luck's way, Sir," said the magician to Na; "only once in many thousand years does P'u-sa descend into hell and banish all suffering. He has come to-day."

He then made Na kneel, and all the devils began with clasped hands to sing songs of praise to P'u-sa for his compassion in releasing them from their misery, shaking the very earth with the sound. P'u-sa himself, seizing a willow-branch, sprinkled them all with holy water; and when this was done the clouds and glory melted away, and he vanished from their sight. Na, who had felt the holy water fall upon his neck, now became conscious that the axe-wound was no longer painful; and the magician then proceeded to lead him back, not quitting him until within sight of the village gate.

In fact, Na had been in a trance for two days, and when he recovered he told them all that he had seen, asserting positively that Ch'êng was not dead. His mother, however, looked upon the story as a make-up, and never ceased reviling him; and, as he had no means of proving his innocence, and his neck was now quite healed, he got up from the bed and said to his father, "I am going away to seek for my brother throughout the universe; if I do not find him, never expect to see me again, but I pray you regard me as dead." His father drew him aside and wept bitterly. However, he would not interfere with his son's design, and Na accordingly set off. Whenever he came to a large town or populous place he used to ask for news of Ch'êng; and by-and-by, when his money was all spent, he begged his way on foot.

A year had passed away before he reached Nanking, and his clothes were all in tatters as ragged as a quail's tail, when suddenly he met some ten or a dozen horsemen, and drew away to the roadside. Among them was a gentleman of about forty, who appeared to be a mandarin, with numerous lusty attendants and fiery steeds accompanying him before and behind. One young man on a small palfrey, whom Na took to be the mandarin's son, and at whom, of course, he did not venture to stare, eyed him closely for some time, and at length stopped his steed, and, jumping off, cried out, “Are you not my brother?” Na then raised his head, and found that Ch‘êng stood before him. Grasping each other’s hands, the brothers burst into tears, and at length Ch‘êng said, “My brother, how is it you have strayed so far as this?” Na told him the circumstances, at which he was much affected; and Ch‘êng’s companions, jumping off their horses to see what was the matter, went off and informed the mandarin. The latter ordered one of them to give up his horse to Na, and thus they rode together back to the mandarin’s house. Ch‘êng then told his brother how the tiger had carried him away, and how he had been thrown down in the road, where he had passed a whole night; also how the mandarin, Mr. Chang, on his return from the capital, had seen him there, and, observing that he was no common-looking youth, had set to work and brought him round again. Also how he had said to Mr. Chang that his home was a great way off, and how Mr. Chang had taken him to his own home, and finally cured him of his wounds; when, having no son of his own, he had adopted him. And now, happening to be out with his father, he had caught sight of his brother.

As he was speaking Mr. Chang walked in, and Na thanked him very heartily for all his kindness; Ch‘êng, meanwhile, going into the inner apartments to get some clothes for his brother. Wine and food was placed on the table; and while they were chatting together the mandarin asked Na about the number of their family in Honan.

“There is only my father,” replied Na, “and he is a Shantung man who came to live in Honan.”

“Why, I am a Shantung man too,” rejoined Mr. Chang; “what is the name of your father’s native place?”

“I have heard that it was in the Tung-ch‘ang district,” replied Na.

“Then we are from the same place,” cried the mandarin.

“Why did your father go away to Honan?”

“His first wife,” said Na, “was carried off by soldiers, and my father lost everything he possessed; so, being in the habit of trading to Honan, he determined to settle down there for good.”

The mandarin then asked what his father’s other name was, and when he heard, he sat some time staring at Na, and at length hurried away within. In a few moments out came an old lady, and when they had all bowed to her, she asked Na if he was Chang Ping-chih’s grandson. On his replying in the affirmative, the old lady wept, and, turning to Mr. Chang, said, “These two are your younger brothers.” And then she explained to Na and Ch‘êng as follows:—“Three years after my marriage with your father, I was carried off to the north and made a slave in a mandarin’s family. Six months afterward your elder brother here was born, and in another six months the mandarin died. Your elder brother being his heir, he received this appointment, which he is now resigning. I have often thought of my native place, and have not unfrequently sent people to inquire about my husband, giving them the full particulars as to name and clan; but I could never hear anything of him. How should I know that he had gone to Honan?"

Then, addressing Mr. Chang, she continued, "That was rather a mistake of yours, adopting your own brother."

"He never told me anything about Shantung," replied Mr. Chang; "I suppose he was too young to remember the story; and I only looked at the difference between our ages." For he, the elder of the brothers, was forty-one; Ch'êng, the younger, being only sixteen; and Na, twenty years of age. Mr. Chang was very glad to get two young brothers; and when he heard the tale of their separation, proposed that they should all go back to their father. Mrs. Chang was afraid her husband would not care to receive her back again; but her eldest son said, "We will cast our lot together; all or none. How can there be a country where fathers are not valued?" They then sold their house and packed up, and were soon on the way to Honan.

When they arrived, Ch'êng went in first to tell his father, whose third wife had died since Na left, and who now was a desolate old widower, left alone with only his own shadow. He was overjoyed to see Ch'êng again, and, looking fondly at his son, burst into a flood of tears. Ch'êng told him his mother and brothers were outside, and the old man was then perfectly transfixed with astonishment, unable either to laugh or to cry. Mr. Chang next appeared, followed by his mother; and the two old people wept in each other's arms, the late solitary widower hardly knowing what to make of the crowd of men and women-servants that suddenly filled his house. Here Ch'êng, not seeing his own mother, asked where she was; and when he heard she was dead, he fainted away, and did not come round for a good half-hour. Mr. Chang found the money for building a fine house, and engaged a tutor for his two brothers. Horses pranced in the stables, and servants chattered in the hall—it was quite a large establishment.

The Three Genii

THERE WAS A CERTAIN SCHOLAR WHO, PASSING THROUGH SU-CH'IEN ON HIS WAY TO Nanking, where he was going to try for his master's degree, happened to fall in with three other gentlemen, all graduates like himself, and was so charmed with their unusual refinement that he purchased a quantity of wine, and begged them to join him in drinking it. While thus pleasantly employed, his three friends told him their names.

One was Chieh Ch'in-hêng; the second, Ch'ang Fêng-lin; and the other, Ma Hsi-ch'ih. They drank away and enjoyed themselves very much, until evening had crept upon them unperceived, when Chieh said, "Here we, who ought to have been playing the host, have been feasting at a stranger's expense. This is not right. But, come, my house is close by; I will provide you with a bed." Ch'ang and Ma got up, and, taking our hero by the arm, bade his servant come along with them.

When they reached a hill to the north of the village, there before them was a house and grounds, with a stream of clear water in front of the door, all the apartments within being beautifully clean and nice. Chieh then gave orders to light the lamps and see after his visitor's servant; whereupon Ma observed, "Of old it was customary to set intellectual refreshments before one's friends; let us not miss the opportunity of this lovely evening, but decide on four themes, one for each of us; and then, when we have finished our essays, we can set to work on the wine." To this the others readily agreed; and each wrote down a theme and threw it on the table. These were next divided among them as they sat, and before the second watch was over the essays were all completed and handed round for general inspection; and our scholar was so struck with the elegance and vigor of those by his three friends, that he ran off a copy of them and put it in his pocket. The host then produced some excellent wine, which was drunk by them in such bumpers that soon they were all tolerably tipsy. The other two now took their leave; but Chieh led the scholar into another room, where, so overcome was he with wine, that he went to bed in his boots and clothes.

The sun was high in the heavens when our hero awaked, and, looking round, he saw no house or grounds, only a dell on the hill-side, in which he and his servant had been sleeping. In great alarm he called out to the servant, who also got up, and then they found a hole with a rill of water trickling down before it. Much astonished at all this, he felt in his pocket, and there, sure enough, was the paper on which he had copied the three essays of his friends. On descending the hill and making inquiries, he found that he had been to the Grotto of the Three Genii—namely, Crab, Snake, and Frog, three very wonderful beings, who often came out for a stroll, and were occasionally visible to mortal eyes. Subsequently, when our hero entered the examination hall, lo! the three themes set were those of the Three Genii, and he came out at the top of the list.

The Singing Frogs

Wang Tzŭ-sun told me that when he was at the capital he saw a man in the street who gave the following performance:—He had a wooden box, divided by partitions into twelve holes, in each of which was a frog; and whenever he tapped any one of these frogs on the head with a tiny wand, the frog so touched would immediately begin to sing. Some one gave him a piece of silver, and then he tapped the frogs all round, just as if he was striking a gong; whereupon they all sang together, with their *Do, Ré, Mi, Fa*, in perfect time and harmony.

The Performing Mice

Mr. Wang also told me that there was a man at Ch'ang-an who made his living by exhibiting performing mice. He had a pouch on his back in which he kept some ten of these little animals; and whenever he got among a number of people he would fix a little frame on his back, exactly resembling a stage. Then beating a drum he would sing some old theatrical melody, at the first sounds of which the mice would issue forth from the pouch, and then, with masks on their faces, and arrayed in various costumes, they would climb up his back on to the stage, where standing on their hind-legs they would go through a performance portraying the various emotions of joy and anger, exactly like human actors of either sex.

The Tiger of Chao-ch'êng

At Chao-ch'êng there lived an old woman more than seventy years of age, who had an only son. One day he went up to the hills and was eaten by a tiger, at which his mother was so overwhelmed with grief that she hardly wished to live. With tears and lamentations she ran and told her story to the magistrate of the place, who laughed and asked her how she thought the law could be brought to bear on a tiger. But the old woman would not be comforted, and at length the magistrate lost his temper and bade her begone. Of this, however, she took no notice; and then the magistrate, in compassion for her great age and unwilling to resort to extremities, promised her that he would have the tiger arrested. Even then she would not go until the warrant had been ac tually issued; so the magistrate, at a loss what to do, asked his attendants which of them would undertake the job. Upon this one of them, Li Nêng, who happened to be gloriously drunk, stepped forward and said that he would; whereupon the warrant was immediately issued and the old woman went away. When our friend, Li Nêng, got sober, he was sorry for what he had done; but reflecting that the whole thing was a mere trick of his master's to get rid of the old woman's importunities, did not trouble himself much about it, handing in the warrant as if the arrest had been made. "Not so," cried the magistrate, "you said you could do this, and now I shall not let you off." Li Nêng was at his wits' end, and begged that he might be allowed to impress the hunters of the district. This was conceded; so collecting together these men, he proceeded to spend day and night among the hills in the hope of catching a tiger, and thus making a show of having fulfilled his duty.

A month passed away, during which he received several hundred blows with the bamboo, and at length, in despair, he betook himself to the Ch'êng-huang temple in the eastern suburb, where, falling on his knees, he prayed and wept by turns. By-and-by a tiger walked in, and Li Nêng, in a great fright, thought he was going to be eaten alive. But the tiger took no notice of anything, remaining seated in the doorway. Li Nêng then addressed the animal as follows:—"O tiger, if thou didst slay that old woman's son, suffer me to bind thee with this cord"; and, drawing a rope from his pocket, threw it over the animal's neck. The tiger drooped its ears, and allowing itself to be bound, followed Li Nêng to the magistrate's office. The latter then asked it, saying, "Did you eat the old woman's son?" to which the tiger replied by nodding its head; whereupon the magistrate rejoined, "That murderers should suffer death has ever been the law. Besides, this old woman had but one son, and by killing him you took from her the sole support of her declining years. But if now you will be as a son to her, your crime shall be pardoned." The tiger again nodded assent, and accordingly the magistrate gave orders that he should be released, at which the old woman was highly incensed, thinking that the tiger ought to have paid with its life for the destruction of her son.

Next morning, however, when she opened the door of her cottage, there lay a dead deer before it; and the old woman, by selling the flesh and skin, was able to purchase food. From that day this became a common event, and sometimes the tiger would even bring her money and valuables, so that she became quite rich, and was much better cared for than she had been even by her own son. Consequently, she became very well-disposed to the tiger, which often came and slept in the verandah, remaining for a whole day at a time, and giving no cause of fear either to man or beast. In a few years the old woman died, upon which the tiger walked in and roared its lamentations in the hall. However, with all the money she had saved, she was able to have a splendid funeral; and while her relatives were standing round the grave, out rushed a tiger, and sent them all running away in fear. But the tiger merely went up to the mound, and, after roaring like a thunder-peal, disappeared again. Then the people of that place built a shrine in honor of the Faithful Tiger, and it remains there to this day.

A Dwarf

In the reign of K'ang Hsi, there was a magician who carried about with him a wooden box, in which he had a dwarf not much more than a foot in height. When people gave him money he would open the box and bid the little creature come out. The dwarf would then sing a song and go in again. Arriving one day at Yeh, the magistrate there seized the box, and taking it into his *yamên* asked the dwarf whence he came. At first he dared not reply, but on being pressed told the magistrate everything. He said he belonged to a respectable family, and that once when returning home from school he was stupified by the magician, who gave him some drug which made his limbs shrink, and then took him about to exhibit to people. The magistrate was very angry and had the magician beheaded, himself taking charge of the dwarf. He was subsequently very anxious to get him cured, but unable to obtain the proper prescription.

Hsiang-ju's Misfortunes

At Kuang-p'ing there lived an old man named Fêng, who had an only son called Hsiang-ju. Both of them were graduates; and the father was very particular and strict, though the family had long been poor. Mrs. Fêng and Hsiang-ju's wife had died one shortly after the other, so that the father and son were obliged to do their household work for themselves.

One night Hsiang-ju was sitting out in the moonlight, when suddenly a young lady from next door got on the wall to have a look at him. He saw she was very pretty, and as he approached her she began to laugh. He then beckoned to her with his hand; but she did not move either to come or to go away. At length, however, she accepted the invitation, and descended the ladder that he had placed for her. In reply to Hsiang-ju's inquiries, the young lady said her name was Hung-yü, and that she lived next door; so Hsiang-ju, who was much taken with her beauty, begged her to come over frequently and have a chat. To this she readily assented, and continued to do so for several months, until one evening old Mr. Fêng, hearing sounds of talking and laughing in his son's room, got up and looked in. Seeing Miss Hung-yü, he was exceedingly angry, and called his son out, saying, "You good-for-nothing fellow! poor as we are, why aren't you at your books, instead of wasting your time like this? A pretty thing for the neighbors to hear of!—and even if they don't hear of it, somebody else will, and shorten your life accordingly."

Hsiang-ju fell on his knees, and with tears implored forgiveness; whereupon his father turned to the young lady, and said, "A girl who behaves like this disgraces others as well as herself; and if people find this out, we shan't be the only ones to suffer."

The old man then went back to bed in a rage, and Miss Hung-yü, weeping bitterly, said to Hsiang-ju, "Your father's reproaches have overwhelmed me with shame. Our friendship is now at an end."

"I could say nothing," replied he, "as long as my father was here; but if you have any consideration for me, I pray you think nothing of his remarks."

Miss Hung-yü protested, however, that they could meet no more, and then Hsiang-ju also burst into tears. "Do not weep," cried she, "our friendship was an impossible one, and time must sooner or later have put an end to these visits. Meanwhile, I hear there is a very good match to be made in the neighborhood." Hsiang-ju replied that he was poor; but Miss Hung-yü told him to meet her again the following evening, when she would endeavor to do something for him.

At the appointed time she arrived, and, producing forty ounces of silver, presented them to Hsiang-ju; telling him that at a village some distance off there was a Miss Wei, eighteen years of age, who was not yet married because of the exorbitant demands of her parents, but that a little extra outlay would secure for him the young lady's hand. Miss Hung-yü then bade him farewell, and Hsiang-ju went off to inform his father, expressing a desire to go and make inquiries, but saying nothing about the forty ounces. His father, thinking that they were not sufficiently well off, urged him not to go; however, by dint of argument, he finally persuaded the old man that, at any rate, there was no harm in trying. So he borrowed horses and attendants, and set off to the house of Mr. Wei, who was a man of considerable property; and when he got there he asked Mr. Wei to come outside and accord him a few minutes' conversation. Now the latter knew that Hsiang-ju belonged to a very good family; and when he saw all the retinue that Hsiang-ju had brought with him, he inwardly consented to the match, though he was afraid that perhaps his would-be son-in-law might not be as liberal as he would like. Hsiang-ju soon perceived what Mr. Wei's feelings were, and emptied his purse on the table, at which Mr. Wei was delighted, and begged a neighbor to allow the marriage contract to be drawn up in his house.

Hsiang-ju then went in to pay his respects to Mrs. Wei, whom he found in a small, miserable room, with Miss Wei hiding behind her. Still he was pleased to see that, in spite of her homely toilette, the young lady herself was very nice-looking; and, while he was being entertained in the neighbor's house, the old lady said, "It will not be necessary for you, Sir, to come and fetch our daughter. As soon as we have made up a small trousseau for her, we will send her along to you." Hsiang-ju then agreed with them upon a day for the wedding, and went home and informed his father, pretending that the Wei family only asked for respectability, and did not care about money. His father was overjoyed to hear this; and when the day came, the young lady herself arrived. She proved to be a thrifty housekeeper and an obedient wife, so that she and her husband got along capitally together.

In two years she had a son, who was called Fu-êrh. And once, on the occasion of the great spring festival, she was on her way to the family tombs, with her boy in her arms, when she chanced to meet a man named Sung, who was one of the gentry of the neighborhood. This Mr. Sung had been a Censor, but had purchased his retirement, and was now leading a private life, characterized by many overbearing and violent acts. He was returning from his visit to the graves of his ancestors when he saw Hsiang-ju's wife, and, attracted by her beauty, found out who she was; and imagining that, as her husband was a poor scholar, he might easily be induced for a consideration to part with the lady, sent one of his servants to find out how the land lay. When Hsiang-ju heard what was wanted, he was very angry; but, reflecting on the power of his adversary, controlled his passion, and passed the thing off with a laugh. His father, however, to whom he repeated what had occurred, got into a violent rage, and, rushing out, flung his arms about, and called Mr. Sung every name he could lay his tongue to. Mr. Sung's emissary slunk off and went home; and then a number of men were sent by the enraged Sung, and these burst into the house and gave old Fêng and his son a most tremendous beating.

In the middle of the hubbub Hsiang-ju's wife ran in, and, throwing her child down on the bed, tore her hair and shrieked for help. Sung's attendants immediately surrounded her and carried her off, while there lay her husband and his father, wounded on the ground and the baby squalling on the bed. The neighbors, pitying their wretched condition, helped them up on to the couches, and by the next day Hsiang-ju could walk with a stick; however, his father's anger was not to be appeased, and, after spitting a quantity of blood, he died. Hsiang-ju wept bitterly at this, and, taking his child in his arms, used every means to bring the offenders to justice, but without the slightest success. He then heard that his wife had put an end to her own existence, and with this his cup of misery was full. Unable to get his wrongs redressed, he often meditated assassinating Sung in the open street, but was deterred from attempting this by the number of his retainers and the fear of leaving his son with no one to protect him.

Day and night he mourned over his lot, and his eyelids were never closed in sleep, when suddenly in walked a personage of striking appearance to condole with him on his losses. The stranger's face was covered with a huge curly beard; and Hsiang-ju, not knowing who he was, begged him to take a seat, and was about to ask whence he came, when all at once he began, "Sir! have you forgotten your father's death, your wife's disgrace?" Thereupon Hsiang-ju, suspecting him to be a spy from the Sung family, made some evasive reply, which so irritated the stranger that he roared out, "I thought you were a man; but now I know that you are a worthless, contemptible wretch." Hsiang-ju fell on his knees and implored the stranger to forgive him, saying, "I was afraid it was a trick of Sung's: I will speak frankly to you. For days I have lain, as it were, upon thorns, my mouth filled with gall, restrained only by pity for this little one and fear of breaking our ancestral line. Generous friend, will you take care of my child if I fall?" "That," replied the stranger, "is the business of women; I cannot undertake it. But what you wish others to do for you, do yourself; and that which you would do yourself, I will do for you." When Hsiang-ju heard these words he knocked his head upon the ground; but the stranger took no more notice of him, and walked out. Following him to the door, Hsiang-ju asked his name, to which he replied, "If I cannot help you I shall not wish to have your reproaches; if I do help you, I shall not wish to have your gratitude." The stranger then disappeared, and Hsiang-ju, having a presentiment that some misfortune was about to happen, fled away with his child.

When night came, and the members of the Sung family were wrapped in sleep, some one found his way into their house and slew the ex-Censor and his two sons, besides a maid-servant and one of the ladies. Information was at once given to the authorities; and as the Sung family had no doubt that the murderer was Hsiang-ju, the magistrate, who was greatly alarmed, sent out lictors to arrest him. Hsiang-ju, however, was nowhere to be found, a fact which tended to confirm the suspicions of the Sung family; and they, too, despatched a number of servants to aid the mandarin in effecting his capture.

Toward evening the lictors and others reached a hill, and, hearing a child cry, made for the sound, and thus secured the object of their search, whom they bound and led away. As the child went on crying louder than ever, they took it from him and threw it down by the wayside, thereby nearly causing Hsiang-ju to die of grief and rage. On being brought before the magistrate he was asked why he had killed these people; to which he replied that he was falsely accused, "For," said he, "they died in the night, whereas I had gone away in the daytime. Besides," added he, "how, with a crying baby in my arms, could I scale walls and kill people?"

"If you didn't kill people," cried the magistrate, "why did you run away?"

Hsiang-ju had no answer to make to this, and he was accordingly ordered to prison; whereupon he wept and said, "I can die without regret; but what has my child done that he, too, should be punished?"

"You," replied the magistrate, "have slain the children of others; how can you complain if your child meets the same fate?" Hsiang-ju was then stripped of his degree and subjected to all kinds of indignities, but they were unable to wring a confession from his lips; and that very night, as the magistrate lay down, he heard a sharp noise of something striking the bed, and, jumping up in a fright, found, by the light of a candle, a small, keen blade sticking in the wood at the head of his couch so tightly that it could not be drawn out. Terribly alarmed at this, the magistrate walked round the room with a spear over his shoulder, but without finding anything; and then, reflecting that nothing more was to be feared from Sung, who was dead, as well as his two sons, he laid Hsiang-ju's case before the higher authorities, and obtained for him an acquittal.

Hsiang-ju was released and went home. His cupboard, however, was empty, and there was nothing except his own shadow within the four walls of his house. Happily, his neighbors took pity on him and supplied him with food; and whenever he thought upon the vengeance that had been wreaked, his countenance assumed an expression of joy; but as often as his misfortunes and the extinction of his family came into his mind, his tears would begin to flow. And when he remembered the poverty of his life and the end of his ancestral line, he would seek out some solitary spot, and there burst into an ungovernable fit of grief.

Thus things went on for about six months, when the search after the murderer began to be relaxed; and then Hsiang-ju petitioned for the recovery of his wife's bones, which he took home with him and buried. His sorrows made him wish to die, and he lay tossing about on the bed without any object in life, when suddenly he heard somebody knock at the door. Keeping quiet to listen, he distinguished the sound of a voice outside talking with a child; and, getting up to look, he perceived a young lady, who said to him, "Your great wrongs are all redressed, and now, luckily, you have nothing to ail you." The voice seemed familiar to him, but he could not at the moment recall where he had heard it; so he lighted a candle, and Miss Hung-yü stood before him. She was leading a small, happy-looking child by the hand; and after she and Hsiang-ju had expressed their mutual satisfaction at meeting once more, Miss Hung-yü pushed the boy forward, saying, "Have you forgotten your father?" The boy clung to her dress, and looked shyly at Hsiang-ju, who, on examining him closely, found that he was Fu-êrh.

"Where did he come from?" asked his father, in astonishment, not unmingled with tears.

"I will tell you all," replied Miss Hung-yü. "I was only deceiving you when I said I belonged to a neighboring family. I am really a fox, and, happening to go out one evening, I heard a child crying in a ditch. I took him home and brought him up; and, now that your troubles are over, I return him to you, that father and son may be together."

Hsiang-ju wiped away his tears and thanked her heartily; but Fu-êrh kept close to Miss Hung-yü, whom he had come to regard as a mother, and did not seem to recognize his father again. Before day-break Miss Hung-yü said she must go away; but Hsiang-ju fell upon his knees and entreated her to stop, until at last she said she was only joking, adding that, in a new establishment like theirs, it would be a case of early to rise and late to bed. She then set to work cutting fuel and sweeping it up, toiling hard as if she had been a man, which made Hsiang-ju regret that he was too poor to have all this done for her. However, she bade him mind his books, and not trouble himself about the state of their affairs, as they were not likely to die of hunger. She also produced some money, and bought implements for spinning, besides renting a few acres of land and hiring laborers to till them. Day by day she would shoulder her hoe and work in the fields, or employ herself in mending the roof, so that her fame as a good wife spread abroad, and the neighbors were more than ever pleased to help them. In half-a-year's time their home was like that of a well-to-do family, with plenty of servants about; but one day Hsiang-ju said to Miss Hung-yü, "With all that you have accomplished on my behalf, there is still one thing left undone." On her asking him what it was, he continued: "The examination for master's degree is at hand, and I have not yet recovered the bachelor's degree of which I was stripped."

"Ah," replied she, "some time back I had your name replaced upon the list; had I waited for you to tell me, it would have been too late."

Hsiang-ju marveled very much at this, and accordingly took his master's degree. He was then thirty-six years of age, the master of broad lands and fine houses; and Miss Hung-yü, who looked delicate enough to be blown away by the wind, and yet worked harder than an ordinary laborer's wife, keeping her hands smooth and nice in spite of winter weather, gave herself out to be thirty-eight, though no one took her to be much more than twenty.

Chang's Transformation

Chang Yü-tan, of Chao-yuan, was a wild fellow, who pursued his studies at the Hsiao temple. Now it chanced that the magistrate of the district, Mr. Tsêng of San-han, had a daughter who was very fond of hunting, and that one day young Chang met her in the fields, and was much struck with her great beauty. She was dressed in an embroidered sable jacket, and rode about on a small palfrey, for all the world like a girl in a picture. Chang went home with the young lady still in his thoughts, his heart being deeply touched; but he soon after heard, to his infinite sorrow and dismay, that Miss Tsêng had died suddenly. Their own home being at a distance, her father deposited the coffin in a temple; the very temple, in fact, where her lover was residing. Accordingly Chang paid to her remains the same respect he would have offered to a god; he burned incense every morning, and poured out libations at every meal, always accompanied by the following invocation:—"I had hardly seen you when your spirit became ever present to me in my dreams. But you passed suddenly away; and now, near as we are together, we are as far apart as if separated by hills and rivers. Alas! alas! In life you were under the control of your parents; now, however, there is nothing to restrain you, and with your supernatural power, I should be hearing the rustle of your robe as you approach to ease the sorrow of my heart." Day and night he prayed thus, and when some six months had passed away, and he was one night trimming his lamp to read, he raised his head and saw a young lady standing, all smiles, before him. Rising up, he inquired who she was; to which his visitor replied, "Grateful to you for your love of me, I was unable to resist the temptation of coming to thank you myself." Chang then offered her a seat, and they sat together chatting for some time.

From this date the young lady used to come in every evening, and on one occasion said to Chang, "I was formerly very fond of riding and archery, shooting the musk and slaying the deer; it is a great sorrow to me to be deprived of these pleasures by death. If you have any friendly feelings toward me, I pray you recite for me the Diamond *sutra* five thousand and forty-eight times, and I will never forget your kindness." Chang did as he was asked, getting up every night and telling his beads before the coffin, until the occasion of a certain festival, when he wished to go home to his parents, and take the young lady with him. Miss Tsêng said she was afraid her feet were too tender to walk far; but Chang offered to carry her, to which she laughingly assented. It was just like carrying a child, she was so light; and by degrees Chang got so accustomed to taking her about with him, that when he went up for his examination she went in too. The only thing was she could not travel except at night. Later on, Chang would have gone up for his master's degree, but the young lady told him it was of no use to try, for it was not destined that he should pass; and accordingly he desisted from his intention. Four or five years afterward, Miss Tsêng's father resigned his appointment, and so poor was he that he could not afford to pay for the removal of his daughter's coffin, but wanted to bury it economically where it was. Unfortunately, he had no ground of his own, and then Chang came forward and said that a friend of his had a piece of waste land near the temple, and that he might bury it there. Mr. Tsêng was very glad to accept, and Chang kindly assisted him with the funeral,—for what reason the former was quite unable to guess.

One night after this, as Miss Tsêng was sitting by Chang's side, her father having already returned home, she burst into a flood of tears, and said, "For five years we have been good friends; we must now part. I can never repay your goodness to me." Chang was alarmed, and asked her what she meant; to which she replied, "Your sympathy has told for me in the realms below. The sum of my *sutras* is complete, and to-day I am to be born again in the family of a high official, Mr. Lu, of Ho-pei. If you do not forget the present time, meet me there in fifteen years from now, on the 16th of the 8th moon."

"Alas!" cried Chang, "I am already over thirty, and in fifteen years more I shall be drawing near the wood. What good will our meeting do?"

"I can be your servant," replied Miss Tsêng, "and so make some return to you. But come, escort me a few miles on my way; the road is beset with brambles, and I shall have some trouble with my dress."

So Chang carried her as before, until they reached a high road, where they found a number of carriages and horses, the latter with one or two riders on the backs of each, and three or four, or even more persons, in every carriage. But there was one richly-decorated carriage, with embroidered curtains and red awnings, in which sat only one old woman, who, when she saw Miss Tsêng, called out, "Ah, there you are."

"Here I am," replied Miss Tsêng; and then she turned to Chang and said, "We must part here; do not forget what I told you." Chang promised he would remember; and then the old woman helped her up into the carriage, round went the wheels, off went the attendants, and they were gone. Sorrowfully Chang wended his way home, and there wrote upon the wall the date mentioned by Miss Tsêng; after which, bethinking himself of the efficacy of prayer, he took to reciting *sutras* more energetically than ever.

By-and-by he dreamed that an angel appeared to him, and said, "The bent of your mind is excellent indeed, but you must visit the Southern Sea." Asking how far off the Southern Sea was, the angel informed him it was close by; and then waking up, and understanding what was required of him, he fixed his sole thoughts on Buddha, and lived a purer life than before. In three years' time his two sons, Ming and Chêng, came out very high on the list at the examination for the second degree, in spite of which worldly successes Chang continued to lead his usual holy life.

Then one night he dreamed that another angel led him among beautiful halls and palaces, where he saw a personage sitting down who resembled Buddha himself. This personage said to him, "My son, your virtue is a matter of great joy; unhappily your term of life is short, and I have, therefore, made an appeal to God on your behalf." Chang prostrated himself, and knocked his head upon the ground; upon which he was commanded to rise, and was served with tea, fragrant as the epidendrum. A boy was next instructed to take him to bathe in a pool, the water of which was so exquisitely clear that he could count the fishes swimming about therein. He found it warm as he walked in, and scented like the leaves of the lotus-flower; and gradually the water got deeper and deeper, until he went down altogether and passed through with his head under water. He then waked up in a fright; but from this moment he became more robust and his sight improved. As he stroked his beard the white hairs all came out, and by-and-by the black ones too; the wrinkles on his face were smoothed away, and in a few months he had the beardless face of a boy of fifteen or sixteen. He also grew very fond of playing about like other boys, and would sometimes tumble head over heels, and be picked up by his sons.

Soon afterward his wife died of old age, and his sons begged him to marry again into some good family; but he said he should be obliged to go to Ho-pei first; and then, calculating his dates, found that the appointed time had arrived. So he ordered his horses and servants, and set off for Ho-pei, where he discovered that there actually was a high official named Lu. Now Mr. Lu had a daughter, who when born was able to talk, and became very clever and beautiful as she grew up. She was the idol of her parents, and had been asked in marriage by many suitors, but would not accept any of them; and when her father and mother inquired her motives for refusal, she told them the story of her engagement in her former life. "Silly child," said they, reckoning up the time, and laughing at her; "that Mr. Chang would now be about fifty years of age, a changed and feeble old man. Even if he is still alive, his hair will be white and his teeth gone." But their daughter would not listen to them; and, finding her so obstinate in her determination, they instructed the doorkeeper to admit no strangers until the appointed time should have passed, that thus her expectations might be brought to naught.

Before long, Chang arrived, but the doorkeeper would not let him in, and he went back to his inn in great distress, not knowing what to do. He then took to walking about the fields, and secretly making inquiries concerning the family. Meanwhile Miss Tsêng thought that he had broken his engagement, and refused all food, giving herself up to tears alone. Her mother argued that he was probably dead, or in any case that the breach of engagement was no fault of her daughter's; to none of which, however, would Miss Tsêng listen, lying where she was the livelong day. Mr. Lu now became anxious about her, and determined to see what manner of man this Chang might be; so, on the plea of taking a walk, he went out to meet him in the fields, and to his astonishment found quite a young man. They sat down together on some leaves, and after chatting awhile Mr. Lu was so charmed with his young friend's bearing that he invited him to his house.

No sooner had they arrived, than Mr. Lu begged Chang to excuse him a moment, and ran in first to tell his daughter, who exerted herself to get up and take a peep at the stranger. Finding, however, that he was not the Chang she had formerly known, she burst into tears and crept back to bed, upbraiding her parents for trying to deceive her thus. Her father declared he was no other than Chang, but his daughter replied only with tears; and then he went back very much upset to his guest, whom he treated with great want of courtesy. Chang asked him if he was not the Mr. Lu, of such and such a position, to which he replied in a vacant kind of way that he was, looking the other way all the time and paying no attention to Chang. The latter did not approve of this behavior, and accordingly took his leave; and in a few days Miss Tsêng had cried herself to death. Chang then dreamed that she appeared to him, and said, "Was it you after all that I saw? You were so changed in age and appearance that when I looked upon your face I did not know you. I have already died from grief; but if you make haste to the little street shrine and summon my spirit back, I may still recover. Be not late!" Chang then waked, and immediately made inquiries at Mr. Lu's house, when he found that the young lady had been dead two days. Telling her father his dream, they went forth to summon the spirit back; and on opening the shroud, and throwing themselves with lamentations over the corpse, a noise was heard in the young lady's throat, and her cherry lips parted. They moved her on to a bed, and soon she began to moan, to the great joy of Mr. Lu, who took Chang out of the room and, over a bumper of wine, asked some questions about his family. He was glad to find that Chang was a suitable match for his daughter, and an auspicious day was fixed for the wedding.

In a fortnight the event came off, the bride being escorted to Chang's house by her father, who remained with them six months before going home again. They were a youthful pair, and people who didn't know the story mistook Chang's son and daughter-in-law for his father and mother. A year later Mr. Lu died; and his son, a mere child, having been badly wounded by some scoundrels, and the family property being almost gone, Chang made him come and live with them, and be one of their own family.

A Taoist Priest

ONCE UPON A TIME THERE WAS A MR. HAN, WHO BELONGED TO A WEALTHY FAMILY, AND was fond of entertaining people. A man named Hsü, of the same town, frequently joined him over the bottle; and on one occasion when they were together a Taoist priest came to the door with his alms-bowl in his hand. The servants threw him some money and food, but the priest would not accept them, neither would he go away; and at length they would take no more notice of him. Mr. Han heard the noise of the priest knocking his bowl going on for a long time, and asked his servants what was the matter; and they had hardly told him when the priest himself walked in. Mr. Han begged him to be seated; whereupon the priest bowed to both gentlemen and took his seat. On making the usual inquiries, they found that he lived at an old tumble-down temple to the east of the town, and Mr. Han expressed regret at not having heard sooner of his arrival, so that he might have shown him the proper hospitality of a resident. The priest said that he had only recently arrived, and had no friends in the place; but hearing that Mr. Han was a jovial fellow, he had been very anxious to take a glass with him. Mr. Han then ordered wine, and the priest soon distinguished himself as a hard drinker; Mr. Hsü treating him all the time with a certain amount of disrespect in consequence of his shabby appearance, while Mr. Han made allowances for him as being a traveler. When he had drunk over twenty large cups of wine, the priest took his leave, returning subsequently whenever any jollification was going on, no matter whether it was eating or drinking.

Even Han began now to tire a little of him; and on one occasion Hsü said to him in raillery, "Good priest, you seem to like being a guest; why don't you play the host sometimes for a change?"

"Ah," replied the priest, "I am much the same as yourself—a mouth carried between a couple of shoulders." This put Hsü to shame, and he had no answer to make; so the priest continued, "But although that is so, I have been revolving the question with myself for some time, and when we do meet I shall do my best to repay your kindness with a cup of my own poor wine."

When they had finished drinking, the priest said he hoped he should have the pleasure of their company the following day at noon; and at the appointed time the two friends went together, not expecting, however, to find anything ready for them. But the priest was waiting for them in the street; and passing through a handsome court-yard, they beheld long suites of elegant apartments stretching away before them. In great astonishment, they remarked to the priest that they had not visited this temple for some time, and asked when it had been thus repaired; to which he replied that the work had been only lately completed. They then went inside, and there was a magnificently-decorated apartment, such as would not be found even in the houses of the wealthy. This made them begin to feel more respect for their host; and no sooner had they sat down than wine and food were served by a number of boys, all about sixteen years of age, and dressed in embroidered coats, with red shoes. The wine and the eatables were delicious, and very nicely served; and when the dinner was taken away, a course of rare fruits was put on the table, the names of all of which it would be impossible to mention. They were arranged in dishes of crystal and jade, the brilliancy of which lighted up the surrounding furniture; and the goblets in which the wine was poured were of glass, and more than a foot in circumference.

The priest here cried out, "Call the Shih sisters," whereupon one of the boys went out, and in a few moments two elegant young ladies walked in. The first was tall and slim like a willow wand; the other was short and very young, both being exceedingly pretty girls. Being told to sing while the company were drinking, the younger beat time and sang a song, while the elder accompanied her on the flageolet. They acquitted themselves admirably; and, when the song was over, the priest holding his goblet bottom upward in the air, challenged his guests to follow his example, bidding his servants pour out more wine all round. He then turned to the girls, and remarked that they had not danced for a long time, asking if they were still able to do so; upon which a carpet was spread by one of the boys, and the two young ladies proceeded to dance, their long robes waving about and perfuming the air around. The dance concluded, they leaned against a painted screen, while the two guests gradually became more and more confused, and were at last irrecoverably drunk.

The priest took no notice of them; but when he had finished drinking, he got up and said, "Pray, go on with your wine; I am going to rest awhile, and will return by-and-by." He then went away, and lay down on a splendid couch at the other end of the room; at which Hsü was very angry, and shouted out, "Priest, you are a rude fellow," at the same time making toward him with a view of rousing him up. The priest then ran out, and Han and Hsü lay down to sleep, one at each end of the room, on elaborately-carved couches covered with beautiful mattresses. When they woke up, they found themselves lying in the road, Mr. Hsü with his head in a dirty drain. Hard by were a couple of rush huts; but everything else was gone.

The Fight with the Foxes

In the province of Chih-li, there was a wealthy family in want of a tutor. One day a graduate presented himself at the door, and was asked by the master of the house to walk in; and he conversed so pleasantly that in a short time it was clear to both sides that they were mutually pleased with each other. The tutor said his name was Hu; and when the usual present had been made to him, he was forthwith provided with apartments, and entered very energetically upon his duties, proving himself a scholar of no mean order. He was, however, very fond of roaming, and generally came back in the middle of the night, not troubling himself to knock if the door was locked but suddenly appearing on the inside. It was therefore suspected that he was a fox, though as his intentions seemed to be harmless, he was treated extremely well, and not with any want of courtesy as if he had been something uncanny. By-and-by he discovered that his master had a daughter, and being desirous of securing the match was always dropping hints to that effect, which his master, on the other hand, invariably pretended not to understand.

One day he went off for a holiday, and on the next day a stranger called; who, tying a black mule at the door, accepted the invitation of the master to take a seat within. He was about fifty years of age, very neat and clean in his dress, and gentlemanly in his manners. When they were seated, the stranger began by saying that he was come with proposals of marriage on behalf of Mr. Hu; to which his host, after some consideration, replied that he and Mr. Hu got along excellently well as friends, and there was no object in bringing about a closer connection.

"Besides," added he, "my daughter is already betrothed, and I beg you, therefore, to ask Mr. Hu to excuse me."

The stranger said he was quite sure the young lady was not engaged, and inquired what might be the objection to the match: but it was all of no avail, until at length he remarked, "Mr. Hu is of a good family; I see no reason why you should have such an aversion to him."

"Well, then," replied the other, "I will tell you what it is. We don't like his *species*."

The stranger here got very angry, and his host also lost his temper, so that they came to high words, and were already on the way to blows, when the latter bade his servants give the stranger a beating and turn him out. The stranger then retired, leaving his mule behind him; and when they drew near to look at it they found a huge creature with black hair, drooping ears, and a long tail. They tried to lead it away, but it would not move; and on giving it a shove with the hand from behind, it toppled over and was discovered to be only of straw.

In consequence of the angry words that had been said, the master of the house felt sure that there would be an attempt at revenge, and accordingly made all preparations; and sure enough the next day a whole host of fox-soldiers arrived, some on horseback, some on foot, some with spears, and others with cross-bows, men and horses trampling along with an indescribable din. The family were afraid to leave the house, and the foxes shouted out to set the place on fire, at which the inmates were dreadfully alarmed; but just then one of the bravest of them rushed forth with a number of the servants to engage the foxes. Stones and arrows flew about in all directions, and many on both sides were wounded; at length, however, the foxes drew off leaving their swords on the field. These glittered like frost or snow, but when picked up turned out to be only millet-stalks. "Is this all their cunning?" cried their adversary, laughing, at the same time making still more careful preparations in case the foxes should come again.

Next day they were deliberating together, when suddenly a giant descended upon them from the sky. He was over ten feet in height by several feet in breadth, and brandished a sword as broad as half a door; but they attacked him so vigorously with arrows and stones that he was soon stretched dead upon the ground, when they saw that he was made of grass. Our friends now began to make light of their fox-foes, and as they saw nothing more of them for three days their precautions were somewhat relaxed. The foxes, however, soon reappeared, armed with bows and arrows, and succeeded in shooting the master of the house in the back, disappearing when he summoned his servants and proceeded to attack them. Then, drawing the arrow from his back, he found it was a long thorn; and thus the foxes went on for a month or so, coming and going, and making it necessary to take precautions, though not really inflicting any serious injury. This annoyed the master of the family very much, until one day Mr. Hu himself appeared with a troop of soldiers at his back, and he immediately went out to meet him. Mr. Hu withdrew among his men, but the master called to him to come forth, and then asked him what he had done that soldiers should be thus brought against his family. The foxes were now on the point of discharging their arrows; Mr. Hu, however, stopped them; whereupon he and his old master shook hands, and the latter invited him to walk into his old room. Wine being served, his host observed, "You, Mr. Hu, are a man of intelligence, and I trust you will make allowances for me. Friends as we were, I should naturally have been glad to form a connection with you; your carriages, however, horses, houses, etc., are not those of ordinary mortals; and even had my daughter consented, you must know the thing would have been impossible, she being still a great deal too young." Mr. Hu was somewhat disconcerted at this, but his host continued, "It's of no consequence; we can still be friends as before, and if you do not despise us earthly creatures, there is my son whom you have taught; he is fifteen years old, and I should be proud to see him connected with you if such an arrangement should be feasible."

Mr. Hu was delighted, and said, "I have a daughter one year younger than your son; she is neither ugly nor stupid. How would she do?" His host got up and made a low bow, which Mr. Hu forthwith returned, and they then became the best of friends, forgetting all about the former unpleasantness. Wine was given to Mr. Hu's attendants, and every one was made happy. The host now inquired where Mr. Hu lived, that the ceremony of pouring out a libation to the geese might be performed; but Mr. Hu said this would not be necessary, and remained drinking till night, when he went away again.

From this time there was no more trouble; and a year passed without any news of Mr. Hu, so that it seemed as if he wished to get out of his bargain. The family, however, went on waiting, and in six months more Mr. Hu reappeared, when, after a few general remarks, he declared that his daughter was ready, and requested that an auspicious day might be fixed for her to come to her husband's home. This being arranged, the young lady arrived with a retinue of sedan-chairs, and horses, and a beautiful trousseau that nearly filled a room. She was unusually respectful to her father and mother in-law, and the former was much pleased with the match. Her father and a younger brother of his had escorted her to the house, and conversing away in a most refined style they sat drinking till daybreak before they went away. The bride herself had the gift of foreknowing whether the harvest would be good or bad, and her advice was always taken in such matters. Mr. Hu and his brother, and also their mother, often came to visit her in her new home, and were then very frequently seen by people.

The King

A CERTAIN GOVERNOR OF HU-NAN DESPATCHED A MAGISTRATE TO THE CAPITAL IN CHARGE of treasure to the amount of six hundred thousand ounces of silver. On the road the magistrate encountered a violent storm of rain, which so delayed him that night came on before he was able to reach the next station. He therefore took refuge in an old temple; but, when morning came, he was horrified to find that the treasure had disappeared. Unable to fix the guilt on any one, he returned forthwith to the Governor and told him the whole story. The latter, however, refused to believe what the magistrate said, and would have had him severely punished, but that each and all of his attendants stoutly corroborated his statements; and accordingly he bade him return and endeavor to find the missing silver.

When the magistrate got back to the temple, he met an extraordinary-looking blind man, who informed him that he could read people's thoughts, and further went on to say that the magistrate had come there on a matter of money. The latter replied that it was so, and recounted the misfortune that had overtaken him; whereupon the blind man called for sedan-chairs, and told the magistrate to follow and see for himself, which he accordingly did, accompanied by all his retinue. If the blind man said east, they went east; or if north, north; journeying along for five days until far among the hills, where they beheld a large city with a great number of inhabitants. They entered the gates and proceeded on for a short distance, when suddenly the blind man cried, "Stop!" and, alighting from his chair, pointed to a lofty door facing the west, at which he told the magistrate to knock and make what inquiries were necessary. He then bowed and took his leave, and the magistrate obeyed his instructions, whereupon a man came out in reply to his summons. He was dressed in the fashion of the Han dynasty, and did not say what his name was; but as soon as the magistrate informed him wherefore he had come, he replied that if the latter would wait a few days he himself would assist him in the matter. The man then conducted the magistrate within, and giving him a room to himself, provided him regularly with food and drink.

One day he chanced to stroll away to the back of the building, and there found a beautiful garden with dense avenues of pine-trees and smooth lawns of fine grass. After wandering about for some time among the arbours and ornamental buildings, the magistrate came to a lofty kiosque, and mounted the steps, when he saw hanging on the wall before him a number of human skins, each with its eyes, nose, ears, mouth, and heart. Horrified at this, he beat a hasty retreat to his quarters, convinced that he was about to leave his own skin in this out-of-the-way place, and giving himself up for lost. He reflected, however, that he should probably gain nothing by trying to escape, and made up his mind to wait; and on the following day the same man came to fetch him, saying he could now have an audience. The magistrate replied that he was ready; and his conductor then mounted a fiery steed, leaving the other to follow on foot.

By-and-by they reached a door like that leading into a Viceroy's *yamên*, where stood on either side crowds of official servants, preserving the utmost silence and decorum. The man here dismounted and led the magistrate inside; and after passing through another door they came into the presence of a king, who wore a cap decorated with pearls, and an embroidered sash, and sat facing the south. The magistrate rushed forward and prostrated himself on the ground; upon which the king asked him if he was the Hu-nan official who had been charged with the conveyance of treasure. On his answering in the affirmative, the king said, "The money is all here; it's a mere trifle, but I have no objection to receive it as a present from the Governor." The magistrate here burst into tears, and declared that his term of grace had already expired: that he would be punished if he went back thus, especially as he would have no evidence to adduce in substantiation of his story. "That is easy enough," replied the king, and put into his hands a thick letter, which he bade him give to the Governor, assuring him that this would prevent him from getting into any trouble. He also provided him with an escort; and the magistrate, who dared not argue the point further, sorrowfully accepted the letter and took his departure.

The road he traveled along was not that by which he had come; and when the hills ended, his escort left him and went back. In a few days more he reached Ch'ang-sha, and respectfully informed the Governor of what had taken place; but the Governor thought he was telling more lies, and in a great rage bade the attendants bind him hand and foot. The magistrate then drew the letter forth from his coat; and when the Governor broke the seal and saw its contents, his face turned deadly pale. He gave orders for the magistrate to be unbound, remarking that the loss of the treasure was of no importance, and that the magistrate was free to go. Instructions were next issued that the amount was to be made up in some way or other and forwarded to the capital; and meanwhile the Governor fell sick and died.

Now this Governor had had a wife of whom he was dotingly fond; and one morning when they waked up, lo! all her hair was gone. The whole establishment was in dismay, no one knowing what to make of such an occurrence. But the letter abovementioned contained that hair, accompanied by the following words:—"Ever since you first entered into public life your career has been one of peculation and avarice. The six hundred thousand ounces of silver are safely stored in my treasury. Make good this sum from your own accumulated extortions. The officer you charged with the treasure is innocent; he must not be wrongly punished. On a former occasion I took your wife's hair as a gentle warning. If now you disobey my injunctions, it will not be long before I have your head. Herewith I return the hair as an evidence of what I say." When the Governor was dead, his family divulged the contents of the letter; and some of his subordinates sent men to search for the city, but they only found range upon range of inaccessible mountains, with nothing like a road or path.

Engaged to a Nun

AT I-LING, IN HUPEI, THERE LIVED A YOUNG MAN NAMED CHÊN YÜ, THE SON OF A graduate. He was a good scholar and a handsome fellow, and had made a reputation for himself even before he arrived at manhood. When quite a boy, a physiognomist had predicted that he would marry a Taoist nun; but his parents regarded it only as a joke, and made several attempts to get him a different kind of wife. Their efforts, however, had not hitherto proved successful, the difficulty being to find a suitable match.

Now his maternal grandmother lived at Huang-kang; and on one occasion, when young Chên was paying her a visit, he heard some one say that of the four Yüns at Huang-chou the youngest had no peer. This remark referred to some very nice-looking nuns who lived in a temple a few miles from his grandmother's house; and accordingly Chên secretly set off to see them, and, knocking at the door, was very cordially received by the four ladies, who were persons of considerable refinement. The youngest was a girl of incomparable beauty, and Chên could not keep his eyes off her, until at last she put her hand up to her face and looked the other way. Her companions now going out of the room to get tea for their visitor, Chên availed himself of the opportunity to ask the young lady's name; to which she replied that she was called Yün-ch'i, and that her surname was Ch'ên. "How extraordinary!" cried Chên; "and mine is P'an." This made her blush very much, and she bent her head down and made no answer; by-and-by rising up and going away.

The tea then came in, accompanied by some nice fruit, and the nuns began telling him their names. One was Pai Yün-shên, and thirty odd years of age; another was Shêng Yün-mien, just twenty; and the third was Liang Yün-tung, twenty-four or five years old, but the junior in point of religious standing. Yün-ch'i did not re-appear, and at length Chên grew anxious to see her again, and asked where she was. Miss Pai told him her sister was afraid of strangers, and Chên then got up and took his leave in spite of their efforts to detain him. "If you want to see Yün-ch'i you had better come again to-morrow," said Miss Pai; and Chên, who went home thinking of nothing but Yün-ch'i, did return to the temple on the following day.

All the nuns were there except Yün-ch'i, but he hardly liked to begin by inquiring after her; and then they pressed him to stay and take dinner with them, accepting no excuses, Miss Pai herself setting food and chop-sticks before him, and urging him to eat. When he asked where Yün-ch'i was, they said she would come directly; but evening gradually drew on and Chên rose to go home. Thereupon they all entreated him to stay, promising that if he did so they would make Yün-ch'i come in. Chên then agreed to remain; the lamps were lighted, and wine was freely served round, until at last he said he was so tipsy he couldn't take any more. "Three bumpers more," cried Miss Pai, "and then we will send for Yün-ch'i." So Chên drank off his three cups, whereupon Miss Liang said he must also drink three with her, which he did, turning his wine-cup down on the table and declaring that he would have no more. "The gentleman won't condescend to drink with us," said Miss Pai to Miss Liang, "so you had better call in Yün-ch'i, and tell the fair Eloïsa that her Abelard is awaiting her."

In a few moments Miss Liang came back and told Chên that Yün-ch'i would not appear; upon which he went off in a huff, without saying a word to either of them, and for several days did not go near the place again. He could not, however, forget Yün-ch'i, and was always hanging about on the watch, until one afternoon he observed Miss Pai go out, at which he was delighted, for he wasn't much afraid of Miss Liang, and at once ran up to the temple and knocked at the door. Yün-mien answered his knock, and from her he discovered that Miss Liang had also gone out on business. He then asked for Yün-ch'i, and Yün-mien led him into another court-yard, where she called out, "Yün-ch'i! here's a visitor." At this the door of the room was immediately slammed, and Yün-mien laughed and told Chên she had locked herself in.

Chên was on the point of saying something, when Yün-mien moved away, and a voice was heard from the other side of the window, "They all declare I'm setting my cap at you, Sir; and if you come here again, I cannot answer for my safety. I do not wish to remain a nun, and if I could only meet with a gentleman like you, Mr. P'an, I would be a handmaid to him all the days of my life." Chên offered his hand and heart to the young lady on the spot; but she reminded him that her education for the priesthood had not been accomplished without expense, "and if you truly love me," added she, "bring twenty ounces of silver wherewith to purchase my freedom. I will wait for you three years with the utmost fidelity." Chên assented to this, and was about to tell her who he really was, when Yün-mien returned and they all went out together, Chên now bidding them farewell and going back to his grandmother's.

After this he always had Yün-ch'i in his thoughts, and wanted very much to get another interview with her and be near her once again, but at this juncture he heard that his father was dangerously ill, and promptly set off on his way home, traveling day and night. His father died, and his mother who then ruled the household was such a severe person that he dared not tell her what was nearest to his heart. Meanwhile he scraped together all the money he could; and refused all proposals of marriage on the score of being in mourning for his father. His mother, however, insisted on his taking a wife; and he then told her that when he was with his grandmother at Huang-kang, an arrangement had been made that he was to marry a Miss Ch'ên, to which he himself was quite ready to accede; and that now, although his father's death had stopped all communications on the subject, he could hardly do better than pay a visit to his grandmother and see how matters stood, promising that if the affair was not actually settled he would obey his mother's commands. His mother consented to this, and off he started with the money he had saved; but when he reached Huang-kang and went off to the temple, he found the place desolate and no longer what it had been. Entering in, he saw only one old priestess employed in cooking her food; and on making inquiries of her, she told him that the Abbess had died in the previous year, and that the four nuns had gone away in different directions. According to her, Yün-ch'i was living in the northern quarter of the city, and thither he proceeded forthwith; but after asking for her at all the temples in the neighborhood, he could get no news of her, and returned sorrowfully home, pretending to his mother that his uncle had said Mr. Ch'ên had gone away, and that as soon as he came back they would send a servant to let him know.

Some months after these events, Chên's mother went on a visit to her own home, and mentioned this story in conversation with her old mother, who, to her astonishment, knew nothing at all about it, but suggested that Chên and his uncle must have concocted the thing together. Luckily, however, for Chên his uncle was away at that time, and they had no means of getting at the real truth. Meanwhile, Chên's mother went away to the Lily Hill to fulfill a vow she had made, and remained all night at an inn at the foot of the hill. That evening the landlord knocked at her door and ushered in a young priestess to share the room. The girl said her name was Yün-ch'i; and when she heard that Chên's mother lived at I-ling, she went and sat by her side, and poured out to her a long tale of tribulation, finishing up by saying that she had a cousin named P'an, at I-ling, and begging Chên's mother to send some one to tell him where she would be found. "Every day I suffer," added she, "and each day seems like a year. Tell him to come quickly, or I may be gone." Chên's mother inquired what his other name might be, but she said she did not know; to which the old lady replied that it was of no consequence, as, being a graduate, it would be easy to find him out.

Early in the morning Chên's mother bade the girl farewell, the latter again begging her not to forget; and when she reached home she told Chên what had occurred. Chên threw himself on his knees, and told his mother that he was the P'an to whom the young lady alluded; and after hearing how the engagement had come about, his mother was exceedingly angry, and said, "Undutiful boy! how will you face your relations with a nun for a wife?" Chên hung his head and made no reply; but shortly afterward when he went up for his examination, he presented himself at the address given by Yün-ch'i—only, however, to find that the young lady had gone away a fortnight before. He then returned home and fell into a bad state of health, when his grandmother died and his mother set off to assist at her funeral. On her way back she missed the right road and reached the house of some people named Ching, who turned out to be cousins of hers. They invited her in, and there she saw a young girl of about eighteen sitting in the parlor, and as great a beauty as she had ever set eyes on.

Now, as she was always thinking of making a good match for her son, and curing him of his settled melancholy, she asked who the young lady might be; and they told her that her name was Wang,—that she was a connection of their own, and that her father and mother being dead, she was staying temporarily with them. Chên's mother inquired the name of Miss Wang's betrothed, but they said she was not engaged; and then taking her hand, she entered into conversation, and was very much charmed with her. Passing the night there, Chên's mother took her cousin into her confidence, and the latter agreed that it would be a capital match; "but," added she, "this young lady is somewhat ambitious, or she would hardly have remained single so long. We must think about it." Meanwhile, Chên's mother and Miss Wang got on so extremely well together that they were already on the terms of mother and daughter; and Miss Wang was invited to accompany her home. This invitation she readily accepted, and next day they went back; Chên's mother, who wished to see her son free from his present trouble, bidding one of the servants tell him that she had brought home a nice wife for him; Chên did not believe this; but on peeping through the window beheld a young lady much prettier even than Yün-ch'i herself. He now began to reflect that the three years agreed upon had already expired; that Yün-ch'i had gone no one knew whither, and had probably by this time found another husband; so he had no difficulty in entertaining the thought of marrying this young lady, and soon regained his health.

His mother then caused the young people to meet, and be introduced to one another; saying to Miss Wang, when her son had left the room, "Did you guess why I invited you to come home with me?"

"I did," replied the young lady, "but I don't think you guessed what was *my* object in coming. Some years ago I was betrothed to a Mr. P'an, of I-ling. I have heard nothing of him for a long time. If he has found another wife I will be your daughter-in-law; if not, I will ever regard you as my own mother, and endeavor to repay you for your kindness to me."

"As there is an actual engagement," replied Chên's mother, "I will say no more; but when I was at the Lily Hill there was a Taoist nun inquiring after this Mr. P'an, and now you again, though, as a matter of fact, there is no Mr. P'an in I-ling at all."

"What!" cried Miss Wang, "are you that lady I met? I am the person who inquired for Mr. P'an."

"If that is so," replied Chên's mother with a smile, "then your Mr. P'an is not far off."

"Where is he?" said she; and then Chên's mother bade a maid-servant lead her out to her son and ask him.

"Is your name Yün-ch'i?" said Chên, in great astonishment; and when the young lady asked him how he knew it, he told her the whole story of his pretending to be a Mr. P'an. But when Yün-ch'i found out to whom she was talking, she was abashed, and went back and told his mother, who inquired how she came to have two names.

"My real name is Wang," replied the young lady; "but the old Abbess, being very fond of me, made me take her own name." Chên's mother was overjoyed at all this, and an auspicious day was immediately fixed for the celebration of their marriage.

The Young Lady of the Tung-t'ing Lake

THE SPIRITS OF THE TUNG-T'ING LAKE ARE VERY MUCH IN THE HABIT OF BORROWING boats. Sometimes the cable of an empty junk will cast itself off, and away goes the vessel over the waves to the sound of music in the air above. The boatmen crouch down in one corner and hide their faces, not daring to look up until the trip is over and they are once more at their old anchorage.

Now a certain Mr. Lin, returning home after having failed at the examination for master's degree, was lying down very tipsy on the deck of his boat, when suddenly strains of music and singing began to be heard. The boatmen shook Mr. Lin, but failing to rouse him, ran down and hid themselves in the hold below. Then some one came and lifted him up, letting him drop again on to the deck, where he was allowed to remain in the same drunken sleep as before.

By-and-by the noise of the various instruments became almost deafening, and Lin, partially waking up, smelt a delicious odour of perfumes filling the air around him. Opening his eyes, he saw that the boat was crowded with a number of beautiful girls; and knowing that something strange was going on, he pretended to be fast asleep. There was then a call for Chih-ch'eng, upon which a young waiting-maid came forward and stood quite close to Mr. Lin's head. Her stockings were the color of the kingfisher's wing, and her feet encased in tiny purple shoes, no bigger than one's finger. Much smitten with this young lady, he took hold of her stocking with his teeth, causing her, the next time she moved, to fall forward flat on her face. Some one, evidently in authority, asked what was the matter; and when he heard the explanation, was very angry, and gave orders to take off Mr. Lin's head.

Soldiers now came and bound Lin, and on getting up he beheld a man sitting with his face to the south, and dressed in the garments of a king. "Sire," cried Lin, as he was being led away, "the king of the Tung-t'ing lake was a mortal named Lin; your servant's name is Lin also. His Majesty was a disappointed candidate; your servant is one too. His Majesty met the Dragon Lady, and was made immortal; your servant has played a trick upon this girl, and he is to die. Why this inequality of fortunes?"

When the king heard this, he bade them bring him back, and asked him, saying, "Are you, then, a disappointed candidate?" Lin said he was; whereupon the king handed him writing materials, and ordered him to compose an ode upon a lady's head-dress.

Some time passed before Lin, who was a scholar of some repute in his own neighborhood, had done more than sit thinking about what he should write; and at length the king upbraided him, saying, "Come, come, a man of your reputation should not take so long."

"Sire," replied Lin, laying down his pen, "it took ten years to complete the Songs of the Three Kingdoms; whereby it may be known that the value of compositions depends more upon the labor given to them than the speed with which they are written."

The king laughed and waited patiently from early morning till noon, when a copy of the verses was put into his hand, with which he declared himself very pleased. He now commanded that Lin should be served with wine; and shortly after there followed a collation of all kinds of curious dishes, in the middle of which an officer came in and reported that the register of people to be drowned had been made up.

"How many in all?" asked the king.

"Two hundred and twenty-eight," was the reply; and then the king inquired who had been deputed to carry it out; whereupon he was informed that the generals Mao and Nan had been appointed to do the work. Lin here rose to take leave, and the king presented him with ten ounces of pure gold and a crystal square, telling him that it would preserve him from any danger he might encounter on the lake. At this moment the king's retinue and horses ranged themselves in proper order upon the surface of the lake; and His Majesty, stepping from the boat into his sedan-chair, disappeared from view.

When everything had been quiet for a long time, the boatmen emerged from the hold, and proceeded to shape their course northward. The wind, however, was against them, and they were unable to make any headway; when all of a sudden an iron cat appeared floating on the top of the water. "General Mao has come," cried the boatmen, in great alarm; and they and all the passengers on board fell down on their faces. Immediately afterward a great wooden beam stood up from the lake, nodding itself backward and forward, which the boatmen, more frightened than ever, said was General Nan. Before long a tremendous sea was raging, the sun was darkened in the heavens, and every vessel in sight was capsized. But Mr. Lin sat in the middle of the boat, with the crystal square in his hand, and the mighty waves broke around without doing them any harm. Thus were they saved, and Lin returned home; and whenever he told his wonderful story he would assert that, although unable to speak positively as to the facial beauty of the young lady he had seen, he dared say that she had the most exquisite pair of feet in the world.

Subsequently, having occasion to visit the city of Wu-ch'ang, he heard of an old woman who wished to sell her daughter, but was unwilling to accept money, giving out that any one who had the fellow of a certain crystal square in her possession should be at liberty to take the girl. Lin thought this very strange; and taking his square with him sought out the old woman, who was delighted to see him, and told her daughter to come in. The young lady was about fifteen years of age, and possessed of surpassing beauty; and after saying a few words of greeting, she turned round and went within again. Lin's reason had almost fled at the sight of this peerless girl, and he straightway informed the old woman that he had such an article as she required, but could not say whether it would match hers or not. So they compared their squares together, and there was not a fraction of difference between them, either in length or breadth. The old woman was overjoyed, and inquiring where Lin lived, bade him go home and get a bridal chair, leaving his square behind him as a pledge of his good faith. This he refused to do; but the old woman laughed, and said, "You are too cautious, Sir; do you think I should run away for a square?" Lin was thus constrained to leave it behind him, and hurrying away for a chair, made the best of his way back. When, however, he got there, the old woman was gone. In great alarm he inquired of the people who lived near as to her whereabouts; no one, however, knew; and it being already late he returned disconsolately to his boat.

On the way, he met a chair coming toward him, and immediately the screen was drawn aside, and a voice cried out, "Mr. Lin! why so late?" Looking closely, he saw that it was the old woman, who, after asking him if he hadn't suspected her of playing him false, told him that just after he left she had had the offer of a chair; and knowing that he, being only a stranger in the place, would have some trouble in obtaining one, she had sent her daughter on to his boat. Lin then begged she would return with him, to which she would not consent; and accordingly, not fully trusting what she said, he hurried on himself as fast as he could, and, jumping into the boat, found the young lady already there. She rose to meet him with a smile, and then he was astonished to see that her stockings were the color of a kingfisher's wing, her shoes purple, and her appearance generally like that of the girl he had met on the Tung-t'ing lake. While he was still confused, the young lady remarked, "You stare, Sir, as if you had never seen me before!" but just then Lin noticed the tear in her stocking made by his own teeth, and cried out in amazement, "What! are you Chih-ch'eng?"

The young lady laughed at this; whereupon Lin rose, and, making her a profound bow, said, "If you are that divine creature, I pray you tell me at once, and set my anxiety at rest."

"Sir," replied she, "I will tell you all. That personage you met on the boat was actually the king of the Tung-t'ing lake. He was so pleased with your talent that he wished to bestow me upon you; but, because I was a great favorite with Her Majesty the Queen, he went back to consult with her. I have now come at the Queen's own command." Lin was highly pleased; and washing his hands, burnt incense, with his face toward the lake, as if it were the Imperial Court, and then they went home together.

Subsequently, when Lin had occasion to go to Wu-ch'ang, his wife asked to be allowed to avail herself of the opportunity to visit her parents; and when they reached the lake, she drew a hair-pin from her hair, and threw it into the water. Immediately a boat rose from the lake, and Lin's wife, stepping into it, vanished from sight like a bird on the wing. Lin remained waiting for her on the prow of his vessel, at the spot where she had disappeared; and by-and-by, he beheld a house-boat approach, from the window of which there flew a beautiful bird which was no other than Chih-ch'eng. Then some one handed out from the same window gold and silk, and precious things in great abundance, all presents to them from the Queen. After this, Chih-ch'eng went home regularly twice every year, and Lin soon became a very rich man, the things he had being such as no one had ever before seen or heard of.

The Man Who Was Changed into a Crow

MR. YÜ JUNG WAS A HU-NAN MAN. THE PERSON WHO TOLD ME HIS STORY DID NOT recollect from what department or district he came. His family was very poor; and once, when returning home after failure at the examination, he ran quite out of funds. Being ashamed to beg, and feeling uncomfortably hungry, he turned to rest awhile in the Wu Wang temple, where he poured out all his sorrows at the feet of the God. His prayers over, he was about to lie down in the outer porch, when suddenly a man took him and led him into the presence of Wu Wang; and then, falling on his knees, said, "Your Majesty, there is a vacancy among the black-robes; the appointment might be bestowed on this man." The King assented, and Yü received a suit of black clothes; and when he had put these on he was changed into a crow, and flew away.

Outside he saw a number of fellow-crows collected together, and immediately joined them, settling with them on the masts of the boats, and imitating them in catching and eating the meat or cakes which the passengers and boatmen on board threw up to them in the air. In a little while he was no longer hungry, and, soaring aloft, alighted on the top of a tree quite satisfied with his change of condition. Two or three days passed, and the King, now pitying his solitary state, provided him with a very elegant mate, whose name was Chu-ch'ing, and who took every opportunity of warning him when he exposed himself too much in search of food. However, he did not pay much attention to this, and one day a soldier shot him in the breast with a cross-bow; but luckily Chu-ch'ing got away with him in her beak, and he was not captured. This enraged the other crows very much, and with their wings they flapped the water into such big waves that all the boats were upset. Chu-ch'ing now procured food and fed her husband; but his wound was a severe one, and by the end of the day he was dead—at which moment he waked, as it were, from a dream, and found himself lying in the temple. The people of the place had found Mr. Yü to all appearance dead; and not knowing how he had come by his death, and finding that his body was not quite cold, had set some one to watch him. They now learned what had happened to him, and making up a purse between them, sent him away home.

Three years afterward he was passing by the same spot, and went in to worship at the temple; also preparing a quantity of food, and inviting the crows to come down and eat it. He then prayed, saying, "If Chu-ch'ing is among you, let her remain." When the crows had eaten the food they all flew away; and by-and-by Yü returned, having succeeded in obtaining his master's degree. Again he visited Wu Wang's temple, and sacrificed a calf as a feast for the crows; and again he prayed as on the previous occasion.

That night he slept on the lake, and, just as the candles were lighted and he had sat down, suddenly there was a noise as of birds settling, and lo! some twenty beautiful young ladies stood before him. "Have you been quite well since we parted?" asked one of them; to which Yü replied that he should like to know whom he had the honor of addressing.

"Don't you remember Chu-ch'ing?" said the young lady; and then Yü was overjoyed, and inquired how she had come.

"I am now," replied Chu-ch'ing, "a spirit of the Han river, and seldom go back to my old home; but in consequence of what you did on two occasions, I have come to see you once more."

They then sat talking together like husband and wife reunited after long absence, and Yü proposed that she should return with him on his way south. Chu-ch'ing, however, said she must go west again, and upon this point they could not come to any agreement. Next morning, when Yü waked up, he found himself in a lofty room with two large candles burning brightly, and no longer in his own boat. In utter amazement he arose and asked where he was. "At Han-yang," replied Chu-ch'ing; "my home is your home; why need you go south?"

By-and-by, when it got lighter, in came a number of serving-women with wine, which they placed on a low table on the top of a broad couch; and then husband and wife sat down to drink together.

"Where are all my servants?" asked Yü; and when he heard they were still on the boat, he said he was afraid the boat people would not be able to wait.

"Never mind," replied Chu-ch'ing; "I have plenty of money, and I'll help you to make it up to them." Yü therefore remained with her, feasting and enjoying himself, and forgetting all about going home. As for the boatmen, when they waked up and found themselves at Han-yang, they were greatly astonished; and, seeing that the servants could find no trace of their missing master, they wished to go about their own business.

They were unable, however, to undo the cable, and so they all remained there together for more than a couple of months, by the end of which time Mr. Yü became anxious to return home, and said to Chu-ch'ing, "If I stay here, my family connections will be completely severed. Besides, as we are husband and wife, it is only right that you should pay a visit to my home."

"That," replied Chu-ch'ing, "I cannot do; and even were I able to go, you have a wife there already, and where would you put me? It is better for me to stop where I am, and thus you will have a second family."

Yü said she would be so far off that he could not always be dropping in; whereupon Chu-ch'ing produced a black suit, and replied, "Here are your old clothes. Whenever you want to see me, put these on and come, and on your arrival I will take them off for you."

She then prepared a parting feast for her husband, at which he got very tipsy; and when he waked up he was on board his boat again, and at his old anchorage on the lake. The boatmen and his servants were all there, and they looked at one another in mutual amazement; and when they asked Yü where he had been, he hardly knew what to say. By the side of his pillow he discovered a bundle in which were some new clothes Chu-ch'ing had given him, shoes, stockings, etc.; and folded up with them was the suit of black. In addition to these he found an embroidered belt for tying round the waist, which was stuffed full of gold. He now started on his way south, and, when he reached the end of his journey, dismissed the boatmen with a handsome present.

After being at home for some months, his thoughts reverted to Han-yang; and, taking out the black clothes, he put them on, when wings immediately grew from his ribs, and with a flap he was gone. In about four hours he arrived at Han-yang, and, wheeling round and round in the air, espied below him a solitary islet, on which stood a house, and there he proceeded to alight. A maid-servant had already seen him coming, and cried out, "Here's master!" and in a few moments out came Chu-ch'ing, and bade the attendants take off Mr. Yü's feathers. They were not long in setting him free, and then, hand in hand, he and Chu-ch'ing went into the house together.

"You have come at a happy moment," said his wife, as they sat down to tell each other all the news; and in three days' time she gave birth to a boy, whom they called Han-ch'an, which means "born on the Han river." Three days after the event all the river-nymphs came to congratulate them, and brought many handsome presents. They were a charming band, not one being over thirty years of age; and, going into the bedroom and approaching the bed, each one pressed her thumb on the baby's nose, saying, "Long life to thee, little one!" Yü asked who they all were, and Chu-ch'ing told him they belonged to the same family of spirits as herself; "And the two last of all," said she, "dressed in white like the lily, are the nymphs who gave away their girdles at Hankow."

A few months passed away, and then Chu-ch'ing sent her husband back in a boat to his old home. No sails or oars were used, but the boat sped along of itself; and at the end of the river journey there were men waiting with horses to convey him to his own door. After this he went backward and forward very frequently; and in time Han-ch'an grew up to be a fine boy, the apple of his father's eye. Unhappily his first wife had no children, and she was extremely anxious to see Han-ch'an; so Yü communicated this to Chu-ch'ing, who at once packed up a box and sent him back with his father, on the understanding that he was to return in three months. However, the other wife became quite as fond of him as if he had been her own child, and ten months passed without her being able to bear the thought of parting with him.

But one day Han-ch'an was taken violently ill, and died; upon which Yü's wife was overwhelmed with grief, and wished to die too. Yü then set off for Han-yang, to carry the tidings to Chu-ch'ing; and when he arrived, lo! there was Han-ch'an, with his shoes and socks off, lying on the bed. He was greatly rejoiced at this, and asked Chu-ch'ing what it all meant. "Why," replied she, "the term agreed upon by us had long expired, and, as I wanted my boy, I sent for him." Yü then told her how much his other wife loved Han-ch'an, but Chu-ch'ing said she must wait until there was another child, and then she should have him. Later on Chu-ch'ing had twins, a boy and a girl, the former named Han-shêng and the latter Yü-p'ei; whereupon Han-ch'an went back again with his father, who, finding it inconvenient to be traveling backward and forward three or four times in a year, removed with his family to the city of Han-yang. At twelve years of age Han-ch'an took his bachelor's degree; and his mother, thinking there was no girl among mortals good enough for her son, sent for him to come home, that she herself might find a wife for him, which she did in the person of a Miss Chih-niang, who was the daughter of a spirit like herself. Yü's first wife then died, and the three children all went to mourn her loss, Han-ch'an remaining in Hu-nan after the funeral, but the other two returning with their father, and not leaving their mother again.

The Flower Nymphs

At the lower temple on Mount Lao the camellias are twenty feet in height, and many spans in circumference. The peonies are more than ten feet high; and when the flowers are in bloom the effect is that of gorgeous tapestry.

There was a Mr. Huang, of Chiao-chow, who built himself a house at that spot, for the purposes of study; and one day he saw from his window a young lady dressed in white wandering about among the flowers. Reflecting that she could not possibly belong to the monastery, he went out to meet her, but she had already disappeared. After this he frequently observed her, and once hid himself in a thick-foliaged bush, waiting for her to come. By-and-by she appeared, bringing with her another young lady dressed in red, who, as he noticed from his distant point of observation, was an exceedingly good-looking girl. When they approached nearer, the young lady in the red dress ran back, saying, "There is a man here!" whereupon Mr. Huang jumped out upon them, and away they went in a scare, with their skirts and long sleeves fluttering in the breeze, and perfuming the air around. Huang pursued them as far as a low wall, where they suddenly vanished from his gaze. In great distress at thus losing the fair creatures, he took a pencil and wrote upon a tree the following lines:—

"The pangs of love my heart enthrall
As I stand opposite this wall.
I dread some hateful tyrant's power,
With none to save you in that hour."

Returning home he was absorbed in his own thoughts, when all at once the young lady walked in, and he rose up joyfully to meet her. "I thought you were a brigand," said his visitor, smiling; "you nearly frightened me to death. I did not know you were a great scholar whose acquaintance I now hope to have the honor of making."

Mr. Huang asked the young lady her name, etc., to which she replied, "My name is Hsiang-yü, and I belong to P'ing-k'ang-hsiang; but a magician has condemned me to remain on this hill much against my own inclination."

"Tell me his name," cried Huang, "and I'll soon set you free."

"There is no need for that," answered the young lady; "I suffer no injury from him, and the place is not an inconvenient one for making the acquaintance of such worthy gentlemen as yourself."

Huang then inquired who was the young lady in red, and she told him that her name was Chiang-hsüeh, and that they were half-sisters; "and now," added she, "I will sing you a song; but please don't laugh at me." She then began as follows:—

"In pleasant company the hours fly fast,
And through the window daybreak peeps at last.
Ah, would that, like the swallow and his mate,
To live together were our happy fate."

Huang here grasped her hand and said, "Beauty without and intellect within—enough to make a man love you and forget all about death, regarding one day's absence like the separation of a thousand years. I pray you come again whenever an opportunity may present itself."

From this time the young lady would frequently walk in to have a chat, but would never bring her sister with her in spite of all Mr. Huang's entreaties. Huang thought they weren't friends, but Hsiang said her sister did not care for society in the same way that she herself did, promising at the same time to try and persuade her to come at some future day.

One evening Hsiang-yü arrived in a melancholy frame of mind, and told Huang that he was wanting more when he couldn't even keep what he had got; "for to-morrow," said she, "we part." Huang asked what she meant; and then wiping away her tears with her sleeve, Hsiang-yü declared it was destiny, and that she couldn't well tell him. "Your former prophecy," continued she, "has come too true; and now it may well be said of me—

"'Fallen into the tyrant's power,
With none to save me in that hour.'"

Huang again tried to question her, but she would tell him nothing; and by-and-by she rose and took her leave. This seemed very strange; however, next day a visitor came, who, after wandering round the garden, was much taken with a white peony, which he dug up and carried away with him. Huang now awaked to the fact that Hsiang-yü was a flower nymph, and became very disconsolate in consequence of what had happened; but when he subsequently heard that the peony only lived a few days after being taken away, he wept bitterly, and composed an elegy in fifty stanzas, besides going daily to the hole from which it had been taken, and watering the ground with his tears.

One day, as he was returning thence, he espied the young lady of the red clothes also wiping away her tears alongside the hole, and immediately walked back gently toward her. She did not run away, and Huang, grasping her sleeve, joined with her in her lamentations. When these were concluded he invited her to his house, and then she burst out with a sigh, saying, "Alas! that the sister of my early years should be thus suddenly taken from me. Hearing you, Sir, mourn as you did, I have also been moved to tears. Those you shed have sunk down deep to the realms below, and may perhaps succeed in restoring her to us; but the sympathies of the dead are destroyed for ever, and how then can she laugh and talk with us again?"

"My luck is bad," said Huang, "that I should injure those I love, neither can I have the good fortune to draw toward me another such a beauty. But tell me, when I often sent messages by Hsiang-yü to you, why did you not come?"

"I knew," replied she, "what nine young fellows out of ten are; but I did not know what you were." She then took leave, Huang telling her how dull he felt without Hsiang-yü, and begging her to come again.

For some days she did not appear; and Huang remained in a state of great melancholy, tossing and turning on his bed and wetting the pillow with his tears, until one night he got up, put on his clothes, and trimmed the lamp; and having called for pen and ink, he composed the following lines:—

"On my cottage roof the evening raindrops beat;
I draw the blind and near the window take my seat.
To my longing gaze no loved one appears;
Drip, drip, drip, drip: fast flow my tears."

This he read aloud; and when he had finished, a voice outside said, "You want some one to cap your verses there!" Listening attentively, he knew it was Chiang-hsüeh; and opening the door he let her in. She looked at his stanza, and added impromptu—

"She is no longer in the room;
A single lamp relieves the gloom;
One solitary man is there;
He and his shadow make a pair."

As Huang read these words his tears fell fast; and then, turning to Chiang-hsüeh, he upbraided her for not having been to see him. "I can't come so often as Hsiang-yü did," replied she, "but only now and then when you are very dull."

After this she used to drop in occasionally, and Huang said Hsiang-yü was his beloved wife, and she his dear friend, always trying to find out every time she came which flower in the garden she was, that he might bring her home with him, and save her from the fate of Hsiang-yü. "The old earth should not be disturbed," said she, "and it would not do any good to tell you. If you couldn't keep your wife always with you, how will you be sure of keeping a friend?" Huang, however, paid no heed to this, and seizing her arm, led her out into the garden, where he stopped at every peony and asked if this was the one; to which Chiang-hsüeh made no reply, but only put her hand to her mouth and laughed.

At New Year's time Huang went home, and a couple of months afterwards he dreamt that Chiang-hsüeh came to tell him she was in great trouble, begging him to hurry off as soon as possible to her rescue. When he woke up, he thought his dream a very strange one; and ordering his servant and horses to be ready, started at once for the hills. There he found that the priests were about to build a new room; and finding a camellia in the way, the contractor had given orders that it should be cut down. Huang now understood his dream, and immediately took steps to prevent the destruction of the flower.

That night Chiang-hsüeh came to thank him, and Huang laughed and said, "It serves you right for not telling me which you were. Now I know you, and if you don't come and see me, I'll get a firebrand and make it hot for you."

"That's just why I didn't tell you before," replied she.

"The presence of my dear friend," said Huang, after a pause, "makes me think more of my lost wife. It is long since I have mourned for her. Shall we go and bemoan her loss together?" So they went off and shed many a tear on the spot where formerly Hsiang-yü had stood, until at last Chiang-hsüeh wiped her eyes and said it was time to go.

A few evenings later Huang was sitting alone when suddenly Chiang-hsüeh entered, her face radiant with smiles. "Good news!" cried she, "the Flower-God, moved by your tears, has granted Hsiang-yü a return to life."

Huang was overjoyed, and asked when she would come; to which Chiang-hsüeh replied, that she could not say for certain, but that it would not be long. "I came here on your account," said Huang; "don't let me be duller than you can help."

"All right," answered she, and then went away, not returning for the next two evenings. Huang then went into the garden and threw his arms around her plant, entreating her to come and see him, though without eliciting any response. He accordingly went back, and began twisting up a torch, when all at once in she came, and snatching the torch out of his hand, threw it away, saying, "You're a bad fellow, and I don't like you, and I shan't have any more to do with you." However, Huang soon succeeded in pacifying her, and by-and-by in walked Hsiang-yü herself. Huang now wept tears of joy as he seized her hand, and drawing Chiang-hsüeh toward them, the three friends mingled their tears together.

They then sat down and talked over the miseries of separation, Huang meanwhile noticing that Hsiang-yü seemed to be unsubstantial, and that when he grasped her hand his fingers seemed to close only on themselves, and not as in the days gone by. This Hsiang-yü explained, saying, "When I was a flower-nymph I had a body; but now I am only the disembodied spirit of that flower. Do not regard me as a reality, but rather as an apparition seen in a dream."

"You have come at the nick of time," cried Chiang-hsüeh; "your husband there was just getting troublesome."

Hsiang-yü now instructed Huang to take a little powdered white-berry, and mixing it with some sulfur, to pour out a libation to her, adding, "This day next year I will return your kindness." The young ladies then went away, and next day Huang observed the shoots of a young peony growing up where Hsiang-yü had once stood. So he made the libation as she had told him, and had the plant very carefully tended, even building a fence all round to protect it. Hsiang-yü came to thank him for this, and he proposed that the plant should be removed to his own home; but to this she would not agree, "for," said she, "I am not very strong, and could not stand being transplanted. Besides, all things have their appointed place; and as I was not originally intended for your home, it might shorten my life to be sent there. We can love each other very well here."

Huang then asked why Chiang-hsüeh did not come; to which Hsiang-yü replied that they must make her, and proceeded with him into the garden, where, after picking a blade of grass, she measured upward from the roots of Chiang-hsüeh's plant to a distance of four feet six inches, at which point she stopped, and Huang began to scratch a mark on the place with his nails.

At that moment Chiang-hsüeh came from behind the plant, and in mock anger cried out, "You hussy you! what do you aid that wretch for?"

"Don't be angry, my dear," said Hsiang-yü; "help me to amuse him for a year only, and then you shan't be bothered any more."

So they went on, Huang watching the plant thrive, until by the spring it was over two feet in height. He then went home, giving the priests a handsome present, and bidding them take great care of it. Next year, in the fourth moon, he returned and found upon the plant a bud just ready to break; and as he was walking round, the stem shook violently as if it would snap, and suddenly the bud opened into a flower as large as a plate, disclosing a beautiful maiden within, sitting upon one of the pistils, and only a few inches in height. In the twinkling of an eye she had jumped out, and lo! it was Hsiang-yü. "Through the wind and the rain I have waited for you," cried she; "why have you come so late?" They then went into the house, where they found Chiang-hsüeh already arrived, and sat down to enjoy themselves as they had done in former times. Shortly afterward Huang's wife died, and he took up his abode at Mount Lao for good and all. The peonies were at that time as large round as one's arm; and whenever Huang went to look at them, he always said, "Some day my spirit will be there by your side"; to which the two girls used to reply with a laugh, and say, "Mind you don't forget." Ten years after these events, Huang became dangerously ill, and his son, who had come to see him, was very much distressed about him. "I am about to be born," cried his father; "I am not going to die. Why do you weep?" He also told the priests that if later on they should see a red shoot, with five leaves, thrusting itself forth alongside of the peony, that would be himself. This was all he said, and his son proceeded to convey him home, where he died immediately on arrival.

Next year a shoot did come up exactly as he had mentioned; and the priests, struck by the coincidence, watered it and supplied it with earth. In three years it was a tall plant, and a good span in circumference, but without flowers. When the old priest died, the others took no care of it; and as it did not flower they cut it down. The white peony then faded and died; and before long the camellia was dead too.

Ta-nan in Search of His Father

HSI CH'ÊNG-LIEH WAS A CH'ÊNG-TU MAN. HE HAD A WIFE AND A CONCUBINE, THE LATTER named Ho Chao-jung. His wife dying, he took a second by name Shên, who bullied the concubine dreadfully, and by her constant wrangling made his life perfectly unbearable, so that one day in a fit of anger he ran away and left them. Shortly afterward Ho gave birth to a son, and called him Ta-nan; but as Hsi did not return, the wife Shên turned them out of the house, making them a daily allowance of food. By degrees Ta-nan became a big boy; and his mother, not daring to ask for an increase of victuals, was obliged to earn a little money by spinning. Meanwhile, Ta-nan, seeing all his companions go to school and learn to read, told his mother he should like to go too; and accordingly, as he was still very young, she sent him for a few days' probation. He turned out to be so clever that he soon beat the other boys; at which the master of the school was much pleased, and offered to teach him for nothing. His mother, therefore, sent him regularly, making what trifling presents she could to the master; and by the end of two or three years he had a first-rate knowledge of the Sacred Books.

One day he came home and asked his mother, saying, "All the fellows at our school get money from their fathers to buy cakes. Why don't I?"

"Wait till you are grown up," replied his mother, "and I will explain it to you."

"Why, mother," cried he, "I'm only seven or eight years old. What a time it will be before I'm grown up."

"Whenever you pass the temple of the God of War on your way to school," said his mother, "you should go in and pray awhile; that would make you grow faster."

Ta-nan believed she was serious; and every day, going and coming, he went in and worshipped at that temple. When his mother found this out, she asked him how soon he was praying to be grown up; to which he replied that he only prayed that by the following year he might be as big as if he were fifteen or sixteen years old. His mother laughed; but Ta-nan went on, increasing in wisdom and stature alike, until by the time he was ten, he looked quite thirteen or fourteen, and his master was no longer able to correct his essays. Then he said to his mother, "You promised me that when I grew up you would tell me where my father is. Tell me now."

"By-and-by, by-and-by," replied his mother; so he waited another year, and then pressed her so eagerly to tell him that she could no longer refuse, and related to him the whole story. He heard her recital with tears and lamentations, and expressed a wish to go in search of his father; but his mother objected that he was too young, and also that no one knew where his father was. Ta-nan said nothing; however, in the middle of the day he did not come home as usual, and his mother at once sent off to the school, where she found he had not shown himself since breakfast. In great alarm, and thinking that he had been playing truant, she paid some people to go and hunt for him everywhere, but was unable to obtain the slightest clue to his whereabouts.

As to Ta-nan himself, when he left the house he followed the road without knowing whither he was going, until at length he met a man who was on his way to K'uei-chou, and said his name was Ch'ien. Ta-nan begged of him something to eat, and went along with him; Mr. Ch'ien even procuring an animal for him to ride because he walked too slowly. The expenses of the journey were all defrayed by Ch'ien; and when they arrived at K'uei-chou they dined together, Ch'ien secretly putting some drug in Ta-nan's food which soon reduced him to a state of unconsciousness. Ch'ien then carried him off to a temple, and, pretending that Ta-nan was his son, offered him to the priests on the plea that he had no money to continue his journey. The priests, seeing what a nice-looking boy he was, were only too ready to buy him; and when Ch'ien had got his money he went away. They then gave Ta-nan a draught which brought him round; but as soon as the abbot heard of the affair and saw Ta-nan himself, he would not allow them to keep him, sending him away with a purse of money in his pocket.

Ta-nan next met a gentleman named Chiang, from Lu-chou, who was returning home after having failed at the examination; and this Mr. Chiang was so pleased with the story of his filial piety that he took him to his own home at Lu-chou. There he remained for a month and more, asking everybody he saw for news of his father, until one day he was told that there was a man named Hsi among the Fokien traders. So he bade good-by to Mr. Chiang, and set off for Fokien, his patron providing him with clothes and shoes, and the people of the place making up a subscription for him.

On the road he met two traders in cotton cloth who were going to Fu-ch'ing, and he joined their party; but they had not traveled many stages before these men found out that he had money, and taking him to a lonely spot, bound him hand and foot and made off with all he had. Before long a Mr. Ch'ên, of Yung-fu, happened to pass by, and at once unbound him, and giving him a seat in one of his own vehicles, carried him off home. This Mr. Ch'ên was a wealthy man, and in his house Ta-nan had opportunities of meeting with traders from all quarters. He therefore begged them to aid him by making inquiries about his father, himself remaining as a fellow student with Mr. Ch'ên's sons, and roaming the country no more, neither hearing any news of his former and now distant home.

Meanwhile, his mother, Ho, had lived alone for three or four years, until the wife, Shên, wishing to reduce the expenses, tried to persuade her to find another husband. As Ho was now supporting herself, she steadfastly refused to do this; and then Shên sold her to a Chung-ch'ing trader, who took her away with him. However, she so frightened this man by hacking herself about with a knife, that when the wounds were healed he was only too happy to get rid of her to a trader from Yen-t'ing, who in his turn, after Ho had nearly disemboweled herself, readily listened to her repeated cries that she wished to become a nun. However, he persuaded her to hire herself out as housekeeper to a friend of his, as a means of reimbursing himself for his outlay in purchasing her; but no sooner had she set eyes on the gentleman in question than she found it was her own husband. For Hsi had given up the career of a scholar, and gone into business; and as he had no wife, he was consequently in want of a housekeeper.

They were very glad to see each other again; and on relating their several adventures, Hsi knew for the first time that he had a son who had gone forth in search of his father. Hsi then asked all the traders and commercial travelers to keep a look out for Ta-nan, at the same time raising Ho from the status of concubine to that of wife. In consequence, however, of the many hardships Ho had gone through, her health was anything but good, and she was unable to do the work of the house; so she advised her husband to buy a concubine. This he was most unwilling to do, remembering too well the former squabbling he had to endure; but ultimately he yielded, asked a friend to buy for him an oldish woman—at any rate more than thirty years of age. A few months afterward his friend arrived, bringing with him a person of about that age; and on looking closely at her, Hsi saw that she was no other than his own wife Shên!

Now this lady had lived by herself for a year and more when her brother Pao advised her to marry again, which she accordingly agreed to do. She was prevented, however, by the younger branches of the family from selling the landed property; but she disposed of everything else, and the proceeds passed into her brother's hands. About that time a Pao-ning trader, hearing that she had plenty of money, bribed her brother to marry her to himself; and afterward, finding that she was a disagreeable woman, took possession of everything she had, and advertised her for sale. No one caring to buy a woman of her age, and her master being on the eve of starting for K'uei-chou, took her with him, finally getting rid of her to Hsi, who was in the same line of business as himself. When she stood before her former husband, she was overwhelmed with shame and fear, and had not a word to say; but Hsi gathered an outline of what had happened from the trader, and then said to her, "Your second marriage with this Pao-ning gentleman was doubtless contracted after you had given up all hope of seeing me again. It doesn't matter in the least, as now I am not in search of a wife but only of a concubine. So you had better begin by paying your respects to your mistress here, my wife Ho Chao-jung."

Shên was ashamed to do this: but Hsi reminded her of the time when she had been in the wife's place, and in spite of all Ho's intercession insisted that she should do so, stimulating her to obedience by the smart application of a stick. Shên was therefore compelled to yield, but at the same time she never tried to gain Ho's favor, and kept away from her as much as possible. Ho, on the other hand, treated her with great consideration, and never took her to task on the performance of her duties; whilst Hsi himself, whenever he had a dinner-party, made her wait at table, though Ho often entreated him to hire a maid.

Now the magistrate at Yen-t'ing was named Ch'ên Tsung-ssŭ, and once when Hsi had some trifling difficulty with one of the neighbors he was further accused to this official of having forced his wife to assume the position of concubine. The magistrate, however, refused to take up the case, to the great satisfaction of Hsi and his wife, who lauded him to the skies as a virtuous mandarin. A few nights after, at rather a late hour, the servant knocked at the door, and called out, "The magistrate has come!" Hsi jumped up in a hurry, and began looking for his clothes and shoes; but the magistrate was already in the bedroom without either of them understanding what it all meant: when suddenly Ho, examining him closely, cried out, "It is my son!" She then burst into tears, and the magistrate, throwing himself on the ground, wept with his mother. It seemed he had taken the name of the gentleman with whom he had lived, and had since entered upon an official career. That on his way to the capital he had made a *détour* and visited his old home, where he heard to his infinite sorrow that both his mothers had married again; and that his relatives, finding him already a man of position, had restored to him the family property, of which he had left some one in charge in the hope that his father might return. That then he had been appointed to Yen-t'ing, but had wished to throw up the post and travel in search of his father, from which design he had been dissuaded by Mr. Ch'ên. Also that he had met a fortune-teller from whom he had obtained the following response to his inquiries:—"The lesser is the greater; the younger is the elder. Seeking the cock, you find the hen; seeking one, you get two. Your official life will be successful." Ch'ên then took up his appointment, but not finding his father he confined himself entirely to a vegetable diet, and gave up the use of wine. The above-mentioned case had subsequently come under his notice, and seeing the name Hsi, he quietly sent his private servant to find out, and thus discovered that this Hsi was his father.

At night-fall he set off himself, and when he saw his mother he knew that the fortune-teller had told him true. Bidding them all say nothing to anybody about what had occurred, he provided money for the journey, and sent them back home. On arriving there, they found the place newly painted, and with their increased retinue of servants and horses, they were quite a wealthy family. As to Shên when she found what a great man Ta-nan had become, she put still more restraint upon herself; but her brother Pao brought an action for the purpose of reinstating her as wife. The presiding official happened to be a man of probity, and delivered the following judgment:—"Greedy of gain you urged your sister to re-marry. After she had driven Hsi away, she took two fresh husbands. How have you the face to talk about reinstating her as wife?" He thereupon ordered Pao to be severely bambooed, and from this time there was no longer any doubt about Shên's *status*. She was the lesser and Ho the greater; and yet in the matter of clothes and food Ho showed herself by no means grasping. Shên was at first afraid that Ho would pay her out, and was consequently more than ever repentant; and Hsi himself, letting by-gones be by-gones, gave orders that Shên should be called *madam* by all alike, though of course she was excluded from any titles that might be gained for them by Ta-nan.

The Wonderful Stone

In the prefecture of Shun-t'ien there lived a man named Hsing Yün-fei, who was an amateur mineralogist and would pay any price for a good specimen. One day as he was fishing in the river, something caught his net, and diving down he brought up a stone about a foot in diameter, beautifully carved on all sides to resemble clustering hills and peaks. He was quite as pleased with this as if he had found some precious stone; and having had an elegant sandal-wood stand made for it, he set his prize upon the table. Whenever it was about to rain, clouds, which from a distance looked like new cotton wool, would come forth from each of the holes or grottoes on the stone, and appear to close them up.

By-and-by an influential personage called at the house and begged to see the stone, immediately seizing it and handing it over to a lusty servant, at the same time whipping his horse and riding away. Hsing was in despair; but all he could do was to mourn the loss of his stone, and indulge his anger against the thief. Meanwhile, the servant, who had carried off the stone on his back, stopped to rest at a bridge; when all of a sudden his hand slipped and the stone fell into the water. His master was extremely put out at this, and gave him a sound beating; subsequently hiring several divers, who tried every means in their power to recover the stone, but were quite unable to find it. He then went away, having first published a notice of reward, and by these means many were tempted to seek for the stone.

Soon after, Hsing himself came to the spot, and as he mournfully approached the bank, lo! the water became clear, and he could see the stone lying at the bottom. Taking off his clothes he quickly jumped in and brought it out, together with the sandal-wood stand which was still with it. He carried it off home, but being no longer desirous of showing it to people, he had an inner room cleaned and put it in there.

Some time afterward an old man knocked at the door and asked to be allowed to see the stone; whereupon Hsing replied that he had lost it a long time ago. "Isn't that it in the inner room?" said the old man, smiling. "Oh, walk in and see for yourself if you don't believe me," answered Hsing; and the old man did walk in, and there was the stone on the table. This took Hsing very much aback; and the old man then laid his hand upon the stone and said, "This is an old family relic of mine: I lost it many months since. How does it come to be here? I pray you now restore it to me." Hsing didn't know what to say, but declared he was the owner of the stone; upon which the old man remarked, "If it is really yours, what evidence can you bring to prove it?" Hsing made no reply; and the old man continued, "To show you that I know this stone, I may mention that it has altogether ninety-two grottoes, and that in the largest of these are five words:—

" 'A stone from Heaven above.' "

Hsing looked and found that there were actually some small characters, no larger than grains of rice, which by straining his eyes a little he managed to read; also, that the number of grottoes was as the old man had said. However, he would not give him the stone; and the old man laughed, and asked, "Pray, what right have you to keep other people's things?"

He then bowed and went away, Hsing escorting him as far as the door; but when he returned to the room, the stone had disappeared. In a great fright, he ran after the old man, who had walked slowly and was not far off, and seizing his sleeve entreated him to give back the stone. "Do you think," said the latter, "that I could conceal a stone a foot in diameter in my sleeve?" But Hsing knew that he must be superhuman, and led him back to the house, where he threw himself on his knees and begged that he might have the stone.

"Is it yours or mine?" asked the old man.

"Of course it is yours," replied Hsing, "though I hope you will consent to deny yourself the pleasure of keeping it."

"In that case," said the old man, "it is back again"; and going into the inner room, they found the stone in its old place.

"The jewels of this world," observed Hsing's visitor, "should be given to those who know how to take care of them. This stone can choose its own master, and I am very pleased that it should remain with you; at the same time I must inform you that it was in too great a hurry to come into the world of mortals, and has not yet been freed from all contingent calamities. I had better take it away with me, and three years hence you shall have it again. If, however, you insist on keeping it, then your span of life will be shortened by three years, that your terms of existence may harmonize together. Are you willing?" Hsing said he was; whereupon the old man with his fingers closed up three of the stone's grottoes, which yielded to his touch like mud. When this was done, he turned to Hsing and told him that the grottoes on that stone represented the years of his life; and then he took his leave, firmly refusing to remain any longer, and not disclosing his name.

More than a year after this, Hsing had occasion to go away on business, and in the night a thief broke in and carried off the stone, taking nothing else at all. When Hsing came home, he was dreadfully grieved, as if his whole object in life was gone; and made all possible inquiries and efforts to get it back, but without the slightest result. Some time passed away, when one day going into a temple Hsing noticed a man selling stones, and amongst the rest he saw his old friend. Of course he immediately wanted to regain possession of it; but as the stone-seller would not consent, he shouldered the stone and went off to the nearest mandarin. The stone-seller was then asked what proof he could give that the stone was his; and he replied that the number of grottoes was eighty-nine. Hsing inquired if that was all he had to say, and when the other acknowledged that it was, he himself told the magistrate what were the characters inscribed within, also calling attention to the finger marks at the closed-up grottoes. He therefore gained his case, and the mandarin would have bambooed the stone-seller, had he not declared that he bought it in the market for twenty ounces of silver,—whereupon he was dismissed.

A high official next offered Hsing one hundred ounces of silver for it; but he refused to sell it even for ten thousand, which so enraged the would-be purchaser that he worked up a case against Hsing, and got him put in prison. Hsing was thereby compelled to pawn a great deal of his property; and then the official sent some one to try if the affair could not be managed through his son, to which Hsing, on hearing of the attempt, steadily refused to consent, saying that he and the stone could not be parted even in death. His wife, however, and his son, laid their heads together, and sent the stone to the high official, and Hsing only heard of it when he arrived home from the prison. He cursed his wife and beat his son, and frequently tried to make away with himself, though luckily his servants always managed to prevent him from succeeding. At night he dreamt that a noble-looking personage appeared to him, and said, "My name is Shih Ch'ing-hsü—(Stone from Heaven). Do not grieve. I purposely quitted you for a year and more; but next year on the 20th of the eighth moon, at dawn, come to the Hai-tai Gate and buy me back for two strings of cash." Hsing was overjoyed at this dream, and carefully took down the day mentioned. Meanwhile the stone was at the official's private house; but as the cloud manifestations ceased, the stone was less and less prized; and the following year when the official was disgraced for maladministration and subsequently died, Hsing met some of his servants at the Hai-tai Gate going off to sell the stone, and purchased it back from them for two strings of cash.

Hsing lived till he was eighty-nine; and then having prepared the necessaries for his interment, bade his son bury the stone with him, which was accordingly done. Six months later robbers broke into the vault and made off with the stone, and his son tried in vain to secure their capture; however, a few days afterward, he was traveling with his servants, when suddenly two men rushed forth dripping with perspiration, and looking up into the air, acknowledged their crime, saying, "Mr. Hsing, please don't torment us thus! We took the stone, and sold it for only four ounces of silver." Hsing's son and his servants then seized these men, and took them before the magistrate, where they at once acknowledged their guilt. Asking what had become of the stone, they said they had sold it to a member of the magistrate's family; and when it was produced, that official took such a fancy to it that he gave it to one of his servants and bade him place it in the treasury. Thereupon the stone slipped out of the servant's hand and broke into a hundred pieces, to the great astonishment of all present. The magistrate now had the thieves bambooed and sent them away; but Hsing's son picked up the broken pieces of the stone, and buried them in his father's grave.

The Quarrelsome Brothers

At K'un-yang there lived a wealthy man named Tsêng. When he died, and before he was put in the coffin, tears were seen to gush forth from both eyes of the corpse, to the infinite amazement of his six sons. His second son, T'i, otherwise called Yu-yü, who had gained for himself the reputation of being a scholar, said it was a bad omen, and warned his brothers to be careful and not give cause for sorrow to the dead,—at which the others only laughed at him as an idiot.

Tsêng's first wife and eldest son having been carried off by the rebels when the latter was only seven or eight years old, he married a second wife, by whom he had three sons, Hsiao, Chung, and Hsin; besides three other sons by a concubine—namely, the above-mentioned T'i, or Yu-yü, Jen, and Yi. Now the three by the second wife banded themselves together against the three by the concubine, saying that the latter were a base-born lot; and whenever a guest was present and either of them happened to be in the room, Hsiao and his two brothers would not take the slightest notice of them. This enraged Jen and Yi very much, and they went to consult with Yu-yü as to how they should avenge themselves for such slights. Yu-yü, however, tried every means in his power to pacify them, and would not take part in any plot; and, as they were much younger than he, they took his advice, and did nothing.

Hsiao had a daughter, who died shortly after her marriage to a Mr. Chou; and her father begged Yu-yü and his other brothers to go with him and give his late daughter's mother-in-law a sound beating. Yu-yü would not hear of it for a moment; so Hsiao in a rage got his brothers Chung and Hsin, with a lot of rowdies from the neighborhood, and went off and did it themselves, scattering the goods and chattels of the family about, and smashing everything they could lay their hands on. An action was immediately brought by the Chou family, and Hsiao and his two brothers were thrown into prison by the angry mandarin, who purposed sending the case before a higher tribunal. Yu-yü, however, whose high character was well known to that official, interceded for them, and himself went to the Chou family and tendered the most humble apologies for what had occurred. The Chou family, out of respect for Yu-yü, suffered the case to drop, and Hsiao regained his liberty, though he did not evince the slightest gratitude for his brother's exertions.

Shortly after, Yu-yü's mother died; but Hsiao and the other two refused to put on mourning for her, going on with their usual feasting and drinking as if nothing had happened. Jen and Yi were furious at this; but Yu-yü only observed, "What they do is their own indecorous behavior; it does not injure us." Then, again, when the funeral was about to take place, Hsiao, Chung, and Hsin stood before the door of the vault, and would not allow the others to bury their mother there. So Yu-yü buried her alongside the principal grave. Before long Hsiao's wife died, and Yu-yü told Jen and Yi to accompany him to the house and condole with the widower; to which they both objected, saying, "He would not wear mourning for our mother; shall we do so for his wife?"

Ultimately Yu-yü had to go alone; and while he was pouring forth his lamentations beside the bier, he heard Jen and Yi playing drums and trumpets outside the door.

Hsiao flew into a tremendous passion, and went after them with his own two brothers to give them a good thrashing. Yu-yü, too, seized a big stick and accompanied them to the house where Jen and Yi were; whereupon Jen made his escape; but as Yi was clambering over the wall, Yu-yü hit him from behind and knocked him down. Hsiao and the others then set upon him with their fists and sticks, and would never have stopped but that Yu-yü interposed his body between them and made them desist. Hsiao was very angry at this, and began to abuse Yu-yü, who said, "The punishment was for want of decorum, for which death would be too severe. I can neither connive at their bad behavior, nor at your cruelty. If your anger is not appeased, strike me." Hsiao now turned his fury against Yu-yü, and being well seconded by his two brothers, they beat Yu-yü until the neighbors separated them and put an end to the row. Yu-yü at once proceeded to Hsiao's house to apologize for what had occurred; but Hsiao drove him away, and would not let him take part in the funeral ceremonies.

Meanwhile, as Yi's wounds were very severe, and he could neither eat nor drink, his brother Jen went on his behalf to the magistrate, stating in the petition that the accused had not worn mourning for their father's concubine. The magistrate issued a warrant; and, besides causing the arrest of Hsiao, Chung, and Hsin, he ordered Yu-yü to prosecute them as well. Yu-yü, however, was so much cut about the head and face that he could not appear in court, but he wrote out a petition, in which he begged that the case might be quashed; and this the magistrate consented to do.

Yi soon got better, the feeling of hatred and resentment increasing in the family day by day; while Jen and Yi, who were younger than the others, complained to Yu-yü of their recent punishment, saying, "The relationship of elder and younger brothers exists for others, why not for us?"

"Ah," replied Yu-yü, "that is what I might well say; not you."

Yu-yü then tried to persuade them to forget the past; but, not succeeding in his attempt, he shut up his house, and went off with his wife to live somewhere else, about twenty miles away. Now, although when Yu-yü was among them he did not help the two younger ones, yet his presence acted as some restraint upon Hsiao and the other two; but now that he was gone their conduct was beyond all bounds. They sought out Jen and Yi in their own houses, and not only reviled them, but abused the memory of their dead mother, against which Jen and Yi could only retaliate by keeping the door shut against them. However, they determined to do them some injury, and carried knives about with them wherever they went for that purpose.

One day the eldest brother, Ch'êng, who had been carried off by the rebels, returned with his wife; and, after three days' deliberation, Hsiao and the other two determined that, as he had been so long separated from the family, he had no further claims upon them for house-room, etc. Jen and Yi were secretly delighted at this result, and at once inviting Ch'êng to stay with them, sent news of his arrival to Yu-yü, who came back directly, and agreed with the others to hand over a share of the property to their elder brother. Hsiao and his clique were much enraged at this purchase of Ch'êng's good will, and, hurrying to their brothers' houses, assailed them with every possible kind of abuse. Ch'êng, who had long been accustomed to scenes of violence among the rebels, now got into a great passion, and cried out, "When I came home none of you would give me a place to live in. Only these younger ones recognized the ties of blood, and you would punish them for so doing. Do you think to drive me away?" Thereupon he threw a stone at Hsiao and knocked him down; and Jen and Yi rushed out with clubs and gave the three of them a severe thrashing.

Ch'êng did not wait for them to lay a plaint, but set off to the magistrate on the spot, and preferred a charge against his three brothers. The magistrate, as before, sent for Yu-yü to ask his opinion, and Yu-yü had no alternative but to go, entering the *yamên* with downcast head, his tears flowing in silence all the while. The magistrate inquired of him how the matter stood; to which he replied only by begging His Honor to hear the case; which the magistrate accordingly did, deciding that the whole of the property was to be divided equally among the seven brothers. Thenceforth Jen and Yi became more and more attached to Ch'êng; and one day, in conversation, they happened to tell him the story of their mother's funeral. Ch'êng was exceedingly angry, and declared that such behavior was that of brute beasts, proposing at the same time that the vault should be opened and that she should be re-buried in the proper place.

Jen and Yi went off and told this to Yu-yü, who immediately came and begged Ch'êng to desist from his scheme; to which, however, he paid no attention, and fixed a day for her interment in the family vault. He then built a hut near by, and, with a knife lopping the branches off the trees, informed the brothers that any of them who did not appear at the funeral in the usual mourning would be treated by him in a manner similar to the trees. So they were all obliged to go, and the obsequies were conducted in a fitting manner. The brothers were now at peace together, Ch'êng keeping them in first-rate order, and always treating Hsiao, Chung, and Hsin with much more severity than the others. To Yu-yü he showed a marked deference, and, whenever he was in a rage, would always be appeased by a word from him. Hsiao, too, was always going to Yu-yü to complain of the treatment he received at Ch'êng's hands when he did anything that Ch'êng disapproved of; and then, if Yu-yü quietly reproved him, he would be dissatisfied, so that at last Yu-yü could stand it no longer, and again went away and took a house at a considerable distance, where he remained almost entirely cut off from the others.

By the time two years had passed away Ch'êng had completely succeeded in establishing harmony amongst them, and quarrels were of rare occurrence. Hsiao was then forty-six years old, and had five sons; Chi-yeh and Chi-tê, the first and third, by his wife; Chi-kung and Chi-chi, the second and fourth, by a concubine; and Chi-tsu, by a slave. They were all grown up, and exactly imitated their father's former behavior, banding themselves together one against the other, and so on, without their father being able to make them behave better. Chi-tsu had no brothers of his own, and, being the youngest, the others bullied him dreadfully; until at length, being on a visit to his wife's family, who lived not far from Yu-yü's house, he went slightly out of his way to call and see his uncle. There he found his three cousins living peaceably together and pursuing their studies, and was so pleased that he remained with them some time, and said not a word as to returning home. His uncle urged him to go back, but he entreated to be allowed to stay; and then his uncle told him it was not that he grudged his daily food: it was because his father and mother did not know where he was.

Chi-tsu accordingly went home, and a few months afterward, when he and his wife were on the point of starting to congratulate his wife's mother on the anniversary of her birthday, he explained to his father that he should not come home again. When his father asked him why not, he partly divulged his reasons for going; whereupon his father said he was afraid his uncle would bear malice for what happened in the past, and that he would not be able to remain there long. "Father," replied Chi-tsu, "uncle Yu-yü is a good and virtuous man." He set out with his wife, and when they arrived Yu-yü gave them separate quarters, and made Chi-tsu rank as one of his own sons, making him join the eldest, Chi-san, in his studies. Chi-tsu was a clever fellow, and now enrolled himself as a resident of the place where his uncle lived.

Meanwhile, his brothers went on quarreling among themselves as usual; and one day Chi-kung, enraged at an insult offered to his mother, killed Chi-yeh. He was immediately thrown into prison, where he was severely bambooed, and in a few days he died. Chi-yeh's wife, whose maiden name was Fêng, now spent the days of mourning in cursing her husband's murderer; and when Chi-kung's wife heard this, she flew into a towering passion, and said to her, "If your husband is dead, mine isn't alive." She then drew a knife and killed her, completing the tragedy by herself committing suicide in a well.

Mr. Fêng, the father of the murdered woman, was very much distressed at his daughter's untimely end; and, taking with him several members of the family with arms concealed under their clothes, they proceeded to Hsiao's house, and there gave his wife a most terrific beating. It was now Ch'êng's turn to be angry. "The members of my family are dying like sheep," cried he; "what do you mean by this, Mr. Fêng?" He then rushed out upon them with a roar, accompanied by all his own brothers and their sons; and the Fêng family was utterly routed. Seizing old Fêng himself, Ch'êng cut off both his ears; and when his son tried to rescue him, Chi-chi ran up and broke both his legs with an iron crowbar. Every one of the Fêng family was badly wounded, and thus dispersed, leaving old Fêng's son lying in the middle of the road. The others not knowing what to do with him, Ch'êng took him under his arm, and, having thrown him down in the Fêng village, returned home, giving orders to Chi-chi to go immediately to the authorities and enter their plaint the first.

The Fêng family had, however, anticipated them, and all the Tsêngs were accordingly thrown into prison, except Chung, who managed to escape. He ran away to the place where Yu-yü lived, and was pacing backward and forward before the door, afraid lest his brother should not have forgiven past offenses, when suddenly Yu-yü, with his son and nephew, arrived, on their return from the examination. "What do you want, my brother?" asked Yu-yü; whereupon Chung prostrated himself at the roadside, and then Yu-yü, seizing his hand, led him within to make further inquiries. "Alas! alas!" cried Yu-yü, when he had heard the story, "I knew that some dreadful calamity would be the result of all this wicked behavior. But why have you come hither? I have been absent so long that I am no more acquainted with the local authorities; and if I now went to ask a favor of them, I should probably only be insulted for my pains. However, if none of the Fêng family die of their wounds, and if we three may chance to be successful in our examination, something may perhaps be done to mitigate this calamity." Yu-yü then kept Chung to dinner, and at night he shared their room, which kind treatment made him at once grateful and repentant. By the end of ten days he was so struck with the behavior of the father, sons, uncle, nephew, and cousins, one toward the other, that he burst into tears, and said, "Now I know how badly I behaved in days gone by." His uncle was overjoyed at his repentance, and sympathized with his feelings, when suddenly it was announced that Yu-yü and his son had both passed the examination for master's degree, and that Chi-tsu was *proximé accessit*. This delighted them all very much. They did not, however, attend the Fu-t'ai's congratulatory feast, but went off first to worship at the tombs of their ancestors.

Now, at the time of the Ming dynasty a man who had taken his master's degree was a very considerable personage, and the Fêngs accordingly began to draw in their horns. Yu-yü, too, met them half-way. He got a friend to convey to them presents of food and money to help them in recovering from their injuries, and thus the prosecution was withdrawn. Then all his brothers implored him with tears in their eyes to return home, and, after burning incense with them, and making them enter into a bond with him that by-gones should be by-gones, he acceded to their request. Chi-tsu, however, would not leave his uncle; and Hsiao himself said to Yu-yü, "I don't deserve such a son as that. Keep him, and teach him as you have done hitherto, and let him be as one of your own children; but if at some future time he succeeds in his examination, then I will beg you to return him to me." Yu-yü consented to this; and three years afterward Chi-tsu did take his master's degree, upon which he sent him back to his own family.

Both husband and wife were very loath to leave their uncle's house, and they had hardly been at home three days before one of their children, only three years old, ran away and went back, returning to his great-uncle's as often as he was recaptured. This induced Hsiao to remove to the next house to Yu-yü's, and, by opening a door between the two, they made one establishment of the whole. Ch'êng was now getting old, and the family affairs devolved entirely upon Yu-yü, who managed things so well that their reputation for filial piety and fraternal love was soon spread far and wide.

The Young Gentleman Who Couldn't Spell

At Chia-p'ing there lived a certain young gentleman of considerable talent and very prepossessing appearance. When seventeen years of age he went up for his bachelor's degree; and as he was passing the door of a house, he saw within a pretty-looking girl, who not only riveted his gaze, but also smiled and nodded her head at him. Quite pleased at this, he approached the young lady and began to talk, she, meanwhile, inquiring of him where he lived, and if alone or otherwise. He assured her he was quite by himself; and then she said, "Well, I will come and see you, but you mustn't let any one know." The young gentleman agreed, and when he got home he sent all the servants to another part of the house, and by-and-by the young lady arrived. She said her name was Wên-chi, and that her admiration for her host's noble bearing had made her visit him, unknown to her mistress. "And gladly," added she, "would I be your handmaid for life." Our hero was delighted, and proposed to purchase her from the mistress she mentioned; and from this time she was in the habit of coming in every other day or so.

On one occasion it was raining hard, and, after hanging up her wet cloak upon a peg, she took off her shoes, and bade the young gentleman clean them for her. He noticed that they were newly embroidered with all the colors of the rainbow, but utterly spoilt by the soaking rain; and was just saying what a pity it was, when the young lady cried out, "I should never have asked you to do such menial work except to show my love for you." All this time the rain was falling fast outside, and Wên-chi now repeated the following line:—

"A nipping wind and chilly rain fill the river and the city."

"There," said she, "cap that." The young gentleman replied that he could not, as he did not even understand what it meant. "Oh, really," retorted the young lady, "if you're not more of a scholar than that, I shall begin to think very little of you." She then told him he had better practice making verses, and he promised he would do so.

By degrees Miss Wên-chi's frequent visits attracted the notice of the servants, as also of a brother-in-law named Sung, who was likewise a gentleman of position; and the latter begged our hero to be allowed to have a peep at her. He was told in reply that the young lady had strictly forbidden that any one should see her; however, he concealed himself in the servants' quarters, and when she arrived he looked at her through the window. Almost beside himself, he now opened the door; whereupon Wên-chi jumping up, vaulted over the wall and disappeared. Sung was really smitten with her, and went off to her mistress to try and arrange for her purchase; but when he mentioned Wên-chi's name, he was informed that they had once had such a girl, who had died several years previously.

In great amazement Sung went back and told his brother-in-law, and he now knew that his beloved Wên-chi was a disembodied spirit. So when she came again he asked her if it was so; to which she replied, "It is; but as you wanted a nice wife and I a handsome husband, I thought we should be a suitable pair. What matters it that one is a mortal and the other a spirit?" The young gentleman thoroughly coincided in her view of the case; and when his examination was over, and he was homeward bound, Wên-chi accompanied him, invisible to others and visible to him alone. Arriving at his parents' house, he installed her in the library; and the day she went to pay the customary bride's visit to her father and mother, he told his own mother the whole story. She and his father were greatly alarmed, and ordered him to have no more to do with her; but he would not listen to this, and then his parents tried by all kinds of devices to get rid of the girl, none of which met with any success.

One day our hero had left upon the table some written instructions for one of the servants, wherein he had made a number of mistakes in spelling, such as *paper* for *pepper*, *jinjer* for *ginger*, and so on; and when Wên-chi saw this, she wrote at the foot:—

"Paper for pepper do I see?
Jinjer for ginger can it be?
Of such a husband I'm afraid;
I'd rather be a servant-maid."

She then said to the young gentleman, "Imagining you to be a man of culture, I hid my blushes and sought you out the first. Alas, your qualifications are on the outside; should I not thus be a laughing-stock to all?" She then disappeared, at which the young gentleman was much hurt; but not knowing to what she alluded, he gave the instructions to his servant, and so made himself the butt of all who heard the story.

The Tiger Guest

A young man named Kung, a native of Min-chou, on his way to the examination at Hsi-ngan, rested awhile in an inn, and ordered some wine to drink. Just then a very tall and noble-looking stranger walked in, and, seating himself by the side of Kung, entered into conversation with him. Kung offered him a cup of wine, which the stranger did not refuse; saying, at the same time, that his name was Miao. But he was a rough, coarse fellow; and Kung, therefore, when the wine was finished, did not call for any more. Miao then rose, and observing that Kung did not appreciate a man of his capacity, went out into the market to buy some, returning shortly with a huge bowl full. Kung declined the proffered wine; but Miao, seizing his arm to persuade him, gripped it so painfully that Kung was forced to drink a few more cups, Miao himself swilling away as hard as he could go out of a soup-plate. "I am not good at entertaining people," cried Miao, at length; "pray go on or stop just as you please."

Kung accordingly put together his things and went off; but he had not gone more than a few miles when his horse was taken ill, and lay down in the road. While he was waiting there with all his heavy baggage, revolving in his mind what he should do, up came Mr. Miao; who, when he heard what was the matter, took off his coat and handed it to the servant, and lifting up the horse, carried it off on his back to the nearest inn, which was about six or seven miles distant. Arriving there he put the animal in the stable, and before long Kung and his servants arrived too. Kung was much astonished at Mr. Miao's feat; and, believing him to be superhuman, began to treat him with the utmost deference, ordering both wine and food to be procured for their refreshment. "My appetite," remarked Miao, "is one that you could not easily satisfy. Let us stick to wine." So they finished another stoup together, and then Miao got up and took his leave, saying, "It will be some time before your horse is well; I cannot wait for you." He then went away.

After the examination several friends of Kung's invited him to join them in a picnic to the Flowery Hill; and just as they were all feasting and laughing together, lo! Mr. Miao walked up. In one hand he held a large flagon, and in the other a ham, both of which he laid down on the ground before them. "Hearing," said he, "that you gentlemen were coming here, I have tacked myself on to you, like a fly to a horse's tail." Kung and his friends then rose and received him with the usual ceremonies, after which they all sat down promiscuously.

By-and-by, when the wine had gone round pretty freely, some one proposed capping verses; whereupon Miao cried out, "Oh, we're very jolly drinking like this; what's the use of making oneself uncomfortable?" The others, however, would not listen to him, and agreed that as a forfeit a huge goblet of wine should be drunk by any defaulter. "Let us rather make death the penalty," said Miao; to which they replied, laughing, that such a punishment was a trifle too severe; and then Miao retorted that if it was not to be death, even a rough fellow like himself might be able to join. A Mr. Chin, who was sitting at the top of the line, then began:—

"From the hill-top high, wide extends the gaze—"

upon which Miao immediately carried on with

"Redly gleams the sword o'er the shattered vase."

The next gentleman thought for a long time, during which Miao was helping himself to wine; and by-and-by they had all capped the verse, but so wretchedly that Miao called out, "Oh, come! if we aren't to be fined for these, we had better abstain from making any more." As none of them would agree to this, Miao could stand it no longer, and roared like a dragon till the hills and valleys echoed again. He then went down on his hands and knees, and jumped about like a lion, which utterly confused the poets, and put an end to their lucubrations.

The wine had now been round a good many times, and being half tipsy each began to repeat to the other the verses he had handed in at the recent examination, all at the same time indulging in any amount of mutual flattery. This so disgusted Miao that he drew Kung aside to have a game at "guess-fingers"; but as they went on droning away all the same, he at length cried out, "Do stop your rubbish, fit only for your own wives, and not for general company." The others were much abashed at this, and so angry were they at Miao's rudeness that they went on repeating all the louder. Miao then threw himself on the ground in a passion, and with a roar changed into a tiger, immediately springing upon the company, and killing them all except Kung and Mr. Chin. He then ran off roaring loudly.

Now this Mr. Chin succeeded in taking his master's degree; and three years afterward, happening to revisit the Flowery Hill, he beheld a Mr. Chi, one of those very gentlemen who had previously been killed by the tiger. In great alarm he was making off, when Chi seized his bridle and would not let him proceed. So he got down from his horse, and inquired what was the matter; to which Chi replied, "I am now the slave of Miao, and have to endure bitter toil for him. He must kill some one else before I can be set free. Three days hence a man, arrayed in the robes and cap of a scholar, should be eaten by the tiger at the foot of the Ts'ang-lung Hill. Do you on that day take some gentleman thither, and thus help your old friend." Chin was too frightened to say much, but promising that he would do so, rode away home.

He then began to consider the matter over with himself, and, regarding it as a plot, he determined to break his engagement, and let his friend remain the tiger's devil. He chanced, however, to repeat the story to a Mr. Chiang who was a relative of his, and one of the local scholars; and as this gentleman had a grudge against another scholar, named Yu, who had come out equal with him at the examination, he made up his mind to destroy him. So he invited Yu to accompany him on that day to the place in question, mentioning that he himself should appear in undress only. Yu could not make out the reason for this; but when he reached the spot there he found all kinds of wine and food ready for his entertainment.

Now that very day the Prefect had come to the hill; and being a friend of the Chiang family, and hearing that Chiang was below, sent for him to come up. Chiang did not dare to appear before him in undress, and borrowed Yu's clothes and hat; but he had no sooner got them on than out rushed the tiger and carried him away in its mouth.

The Sisters

His Excellency the Grand Secretary Mao came from an obscure family in the district of Yeh, his father being only a poor cow-herd. At the same place there resided a wealthy gentleman, named Chang, who owned a burial-ground in the neighborhood; and some one informed him that while passing by he had heard sounds of wrangling from within the grave, and voices saying, "Make haste and go away; do not disturb His Excellency's home." Chang did not much believe this; but subsequently he had several dreams in which he was told that the burial-ground in question really belonged to the Mao family, and that he had no right whatever to it. From this moment the affairs of his house began to go wrong; and at length he listened to the remonstrances of friends and removed his dead elsewhere.

One day Mao's father, the cow-herd, was out near this burial-ground, when, a storm of rain coming on, he took refuge in the now empty grave, while the rain came down harder than ever, and by-and-by flooded the whole place and drowned the old man. The Grand Secretary was then a mere boy, and his mother went off to Chang to beg a piece of ground wherein to bury her dead husband. When Chang heard her name he was greatly astonished; and on going to look at the spot where the old man was drowned, found that it was exactly at the proper place for the coffin. More than ever amazed, he gave orders that the body should be buried there in the old grave, and also bade Mao's mother bring her son to see him. When the funeral was over, she went with Mao to Mr. Chang's house, to thank him for his kindness; and so pleased was he with the boy that he kept him to be educated, ranking him as one of his own sons. He also said he would give him his eldest daughter as a wife, an offer which Mao's mother hardly dared accept; but Mrs. Chang said that the thing was settled and couldn't be altered, so then she was obliged to consent. The young lady, however, had a great contempt for Mao, and made no effort to disguise her feelings; and if any one spoke to her of him, she would put her fingers in her ears, declaring she would die sooner than marry the cow-boy.

On the day appointed for the wedding, the bridegroom arrived, and was feasted within, while outside the door a handsome chair was in waiting to convey away the bride, who all this time was standing crying in a corner, wiping her eyes with her sleeve, and absolutely refusing to dress. Just then the bridegroom sent in to say he was going, and the drums and trumpets struck up the wedding march, at which the bride's tears only fell the faster as her hair hung disheveled down her back. Her father managed to detain Mao awhile, and went in to urge his daughter to make haste, she weeping bitterly as if she did not hear what he was saying. He now got into a rage, which only made her cry the louder; and in the middle of it all a servant came to say the bridegroom wished to take his leave. The father ran out and said his daughter wasn't quite ready, begging Mao to wait a little longer; and then hurried back again to the bride. Thus they went on for some time, backward and forward, until at last things began to look serious, for the young lady obstinately refused to yield; and Mr. Chang was ready to commit suicide for want of anything better.

Just then his second daughter was standing by upbraiding her elder sister for her disobedience, when suddenly the latter turned round in a rage, and cried out, "So you are imitating the rest of them, you little minx; why don't you go and marry him yourself?"

"My father did not betroth me to Mr. Mao," answered she, "but if he had I should not require you to persuade me to accept him."

Her father was delighted with this reply, and at once went off and consulted with his wife as to whether they could venture to substitute the second for the elder; and then her mother came and said to her, "That bad girl there won't obey her parent's commands; we wish, therefore, to put you in her place: will you consent to this arrangement?" The younger sister readily agreed, saying that had they told her to marry a beggar she would not have dared to refuse, and that she had not such a low opinion of Mr. Mao as all that. Her father and mother rejoiced exceedingly at receiving this reply; and dressing her up in her sister's clothes, put her in the bridal chair and sent her off. She proved an excellent wife, and lived in harmony with her husband; but she was troubled with a disease of the hair, which caused Mr. Mao some annoyance. Later on, she told him how she had changed places with her sister, and this made him think more highly of her than before.

Soon after Mao took his bachelor's degree, and then set off to present himself as a candidate for the master's degree. On the way he passed by an inn, the landlord of which had dreamt the night before that a spirit appeared to him and said, "To-morrow Mr. Mao, first on the list, will come. Some day he will extricate you from a difficulty." Accordingly the landlord got up early, and took especial note of all guests who came from the eastward, until at last Mao himself arrived. The landlord was very glad to see him, and provided him with the best of everything, refusing to take any payment for it all, but telling what he had dreamt the night before.

Mao now began to give himself airs; and, reflecting that his wife's want of hair would make him look ridiculous, he determined that as soon as he attained to rank and power he would find another spouse. But alas! when the successful list of candidates was published, Mao's name was not among them; and he retraced his steps with a heavy heart, and by another road, so as to avoid meeting the innkeeper. Three years afterward he went up again, and the landlord received him with precisely the same attentions as on the previous occasion; upon which Mao said to him, "Your former words did not come true; I am now ashamed to put you to so much trouble."

"Ah," replied the landlord, "you meant to get rid of your wife, and the Ruler of the world below struck out your name. My dream couldn't have been false."

In great astonishment, Mao asked what he meant by these words; and then he learned that after his departure the landlord had had a second dream informing him of the above facts. Mao was much alarmed at what he heard, and remained as motionless as a wooden image, until the landlord said to him, "You, Sir, as a scholar, should have more self-respect, and you will certainly take the highest place." By-and-by when the list came out, Mao was the first of all; and almost simultaneously his wife's hair began to grow quite thick, making her much better-looking than she had hitherto been.

Now her elder sister had married a rich young fellow of good family, who lived in the neighborhood, which made the young lady more contemptuous than ever; but he was so extravagant and so idle that their property was soon gone, and they were positively in want of food. Hearing, too, of Mr. Mao's success at the examination, she was overwhelmed with shame and vexation, and avoided even meeting her sister in the street. Just then her husband died and left her destitute; and about the same time Mao took his doctor's degree, which so aggravated her feelings that, in a passion, she became a nun. Subsequently, when Mao rose to be a high officer of state, she sent a novice to his *yamên* to try and get a subscription out of him for the temple; and Mao's wife, who gave several pieces of silk and other things, secretly inserted a sum of money among them. The novice, not knowing this, reported what she had received to the elder sister, who cried out in a passion, "I wanted money to buy food with; of what use are these things to me?" So she bade the novice take them back; and when Mao and his wife saw her return, they suspected what had happened, and opening the parcel found the money still there. They now understood why the presents had been refused; and taking the money, Mao said to the novice, "If one hundred ounces of silver is too much luck for your mistress to secure, of course she could never have secured a high official, such as I am now, for her husband." He then took fifty ounces, and giving them to the novice, sent her away, adding, "Hand this to your mistress, I'm afraid more would be too much for her." The novice returned and repeated all that had been said; and then the elder sister sighed to think what a failure her life had been, and how she had rejected the worthy to accept the worthless. After this, the innkeeper got into trouble about a case of murder, and was imprisoned; but Mao exerted his influence, and obtained the man's pardon.

Foreign Priests

THE BUDDHIST PRIEST, T'I-K'UNG, RELATES THAT WHEN HE WAS AT CH'ING-CHOU HE saw two foreign priests of very extraordinary appearance. They wore rings in their ears, were dressed in yellow cloth, and had curly hair and beards. They said they had come from the countries of the west; and hearing that the Governor of the district was a devoted follower of Buddha, they went to visit him. The Governor sent a couple of servants to escort them to the monastery of the place, where the abbot, Ling-p'ei, did not receive them very cordially; but the secular manager, seeing that they were not ordinary individuals, entertained them and kept them there for the night. Some one asked if there were many strange men in the west, and what magical arts were practiced by the Lohans; whereupon one of them laughed, and putting forth his hand from his sleeve, showed a small pagoda, fully a foot in height, and beautifully carved, standing upon the palm.

Now very high up in the wall there was a niche; and the priest threw the pagoda up to it, when lo! it stood there firm and straight. After a few moments the pagoda began to incline to one side, and a glory, as from a relic of some saint, was diffused throughout the room. The other priest then bared his arms, and stretched out his left until it was five or six feet in length, at the same time shortening his right arm until it dwindled to nothing. He then stretched out the latter until it was as long as his left arm.

The Self-Punished Murderer

MR. LI TOOK HIS DOCTOR'S DEGREE LATE IN LIFE. ON THE 28TH OF THE 9TH MOON of the 4th year of K'ang Hsi, he killed his wife. The neighbors reported the murder to the officials, and the high authorities instructed the district magistrate to investigate the case. At this juncture Mr. Li was standing at the door of his residence; and snatching a butcher's knife from a stall hard by, he rushed into the Ch'êng-huang temple, where, mounting the theatrical stage, he threw himself on his knees, and spoke as follows:—"The spirit here will punish me. I am not to be prosecuted by evil men who, from party motives, confuse right and wrong. The spirit moves me to cut off an ear." Thereupon he cut off his left ear and threw it down from the stage. He then said the spirit was going to fine him a hand for cheating people out of their money; and he forthwith chopped off his left hand. Lastly, he cried out that he was to be punished severely for all his many crimes; and immediately cut his own throat. The

Viceroy subsequently received the Imperial permission to deprive him of his rank and bring him to trial; but he was then being punished by a higher power in the realms of darkness below.

The Master Thief

Before his rebellion, Prince Wu frequently told his soldiers that if any one of them could catch a tiger unaided he would give him a handsome pension and the title of the Tiger Daunter. In his camp there was a man named Pao-chu, as strong and agile as a monkey; and once when a new tower was being built, the wooden framework having only just been set up, Pao-chu walked along the eaves, and finally got up on to the very tip-top beam, where he ran backward and forward several times. He then jumped down, alighting safely on his feet.

Now Prince Wu had a favorite concubine, who was a skillful player on the guitar; and the nuts of the instrument she used were of warm jade, so that when played upon there was a general feeling of warmth throughout the room. The young lady was extremely careful of this treasure, and never produced it for any one to see unless on receipt of the Prince's written order. One night, in the middle of a banquet, a guest begged to be allowed to see this wonderful guitar; but the Prince, being in a lazy mood, said it should be exhibited to him on the following day. Pao-chu, who was standing by, then observed that he could get it without troubling the Prince to write an order. Some one was therefore sent off beforehand to instruct all the officials to be on the watch, and then the Prince told Pao-chu he might go; and after scaling numerous walls the latter found himself near the lady's room. Lamps were burning brightly within; the doors were bolted and barred, and it was impossible to effect an entrance. Under the verandah, however, was a cockatoo fast asleep on its perch; and Pao-chu first mewing several times like a cat, followed it up by imitating the voice of the bird, and cried out as though in distress, "The cat! the cat!" He then heard the concubine call to one of the slave girls, and bid her go rescue the cockatoo which was being killed; and, hiding himself in a dark corner, he saw a girl come forth with a light in her hand.

She had barely got outside the door when he rushed in, and there he saw the lady sitting with the guitar on a table before her. Seizing the instrument he turned and fled; upon which the concubine shrieked out, "Thieves! thieves!" And the guard, seeing a man making off with the guitar, at once started in pursuit. Arrows fell round Pao-chu like drops of rain, but he climbed up one of a number of huge ash trees growing there, and from its top leaped on to the top of the next, and so on, until he had reached the furthermost tree, when he jumped on to the roof of a house, and from that to another, more as if he were flying than anything else. In a few minutes he had disappeared, and before long presented himself suddenly at the banquet-table with the guitar in his hand, the entrance-gate having been securely barred all the time, and not a dog or a cock aroused.

A Flood

In the twenty-first year of K'ang Hsi there was a severe drought, not a green blade appearing in the parched ground all through the spring and well into the summer. On the 13th of the 6th moon a little rain fell, and people began to plant their rice. On the 18th there was a heavy fall, and beans were sown.

Now at a certain village there was an old man, who, noticing two bullocks fighting on the hills, told the villagers that a great flood was at hand, and forthwith removed with his family to another part of the country. The villagers all laughed at him; but before very long rain began to fall in torrents, lasting all through the night, until the water was several feet deep, and carrying away the houses. Among the others was a man who, neglecting to save his two children, with his wife assisted his aged mother to reach a place of safety, from which they looked down at their old home, now only an expanse of water, without hope of ever seeing the children again. When the flood had subsided, they went back, to find the whole place a complete ruin; but in their own house they discovered the two boys playing and laughing on the bed as if nothing had happened. Some one remarked that this was a reward for the filial piety of the parents. It happened on the 20th of the 6th moon.

Death by Laughing

A Mr. Sun Ching-hsia, a marshal of undergraduates, told me that in his village there was a certain man who had been killed by the rebels when they passed through the place. The man's head was left hanging down on his chest; and as soon as the rebels had gone, his servants secured the body and were about to bury it. Hearing, however, a sound of breathing, they looked more closely, and found that the windpipe was not wholly severed; and, setting his head in its proper place, they carried him back home. In twenty-four hours he began to moan; and by dint of carefully feeding him with a spoon, within six months he had quite recovered.

Some ten years afterward he was chatting with a few friends, when one of them made a joke which called forth loud applause from the others. Our hero, too, clapped his hands; but, as he was bending backward and forward with laughter, the seam on his neck split open, and down fell his head with a gush of blood. His friends now found that he was quite dead, and his father immediately commenced an action against the joker; but a sum of money was subscribed by those present and given to the father, who buried his son and stopped further proceedings.

Playing at Hanging

A NUMBER OF WILD YOUNG FELLOWS WERE ONE DAY OUT WALKING WHEN THEY SAW A young lady approach, riding on a pony. One of them said to the others, "I'll back myself to make that girl laugh," and a supper was at once staked by both sides on the result. Our hero then ran out in front of the pony, and kept on shouting "I'm going to die! I'm going to die!" at the same time pulling out from over the top of a wall a stalk of millet, to which he attached his own waistband, and tying the latter round his neck, made a pretense of hanging himself. The young lady did laugh as she passed by, to the great amusement of the assembled company; but as when she was already some distance off their friend did not move, the others laughed louder than ever. However, on going up to him they saw that his tongue protruded, and that his eyes were glazed; he was, in fact, quite dead. Was it not strange that a man should be able to hang himself on a millet stalk? It is a good warning against practical joking.

The Rat Wife

HSI SHAN WAS A NATIVE OF KAO-MI, AND A TRADER BY OCCUPATION. HE FREQUENTLY slept at a place called Mêng-i. One day he was delayed on the road by rain, and when he arrived at his usual quarters it was already late in the night. He knocked at all the doors, but no one answered; and he was walking backward and forward in the piazza when suddenly a door flew open and an old man came out. He invited the traveler to enter, an invitation to which Hsi Shan gladly responded; and, tying up his mule, he went in. The place was totally unfurnished; and the old man began by saying that it was only out of compassion that he had asked him in, as his house was not an inn. "There are only three or four of us," added he; "and my wife and daughter are fast asleep. We have some of yesterday's food, which I will get ready for you; you must not object to its being cold." He then went within, and shortly afterward returned with a low couch, which he placed on the ground, begging his guest to be seated, at the same time hurrying back for a low table, and soon for a number of other things, until at last Hsi Shan was quite uncomfortable, and entreated his host to rest himself awhile.

By-and-by a young lady came out, bringing some wine; upon which the old man said, "Oh, our A-ch'ien has got up." She was about sixteen or seventeen, a slender and pretty-looking girl; and as Hsi Shan had an unmarried brother, he began to think directly that she would do for him. So he inquired of the old man his name and address, to which the latter replied that his name was Ku, and that his children had all died save this one daughter. "I didn't like to wake her just now, but I suppose my wife told her to get up." Hsi Shan then asked the name of his son-in-law, and was informed that the young lady was not yet engaged,—at which he was secretly very much pleased. A tray of food was now brought in, evidently the remains from the day before; and when he had finished eating, Hsi Shan began respectfully to address the old man as follows:—

"I am only a poor wayfarer, but I shall never forget the kindness with which you have treated me. Let me presume upon it, and submit to your consideration a plan I have in my head. My younger brother, San-lang, is seventeen years old. He is a student, and by no means unsteady or dull. May I hope that you will unite our families together, and not think it presumption on my part?"

"I, too, am but a temporary sojourner," replied the old man, rejoicing; "and if you will only let me have a part of your house, I shall be very glad to come and live with you." Hsi Shan consented to this, and got up and thanked him for the promise of his daughter; upon which the old man set to work to make him comfortable for the night, and then went away. At cock-crow he was outside, calling his guest to come and have a wash; and when Hsi Shan had packed up ready to go, he offered to pay for his night's entertainment. This, however, the old man refused, saying, "I could hardly charge a stranger anything for a single meal; how much less could I take money from my intended son-in-law?"

They then separated, and in about a month Hsi Shan returned; but when he was a short distance from the village he met an old woman with a young lady, both dressed in deep mourning. As they approached he began to suspect it was A-ch'ien; and the young lady, after turning round to look at him, pulled the old woman's sleeve, and whispered something in her ear, which Hsi Shan himself did not hear. The old woman stopped immediately, and asked if she was addressing Mr. Hsi; and when informed that she was, she said mournfully, "Alas! my husband has been killed by the falling of a wall. We are going to bury him to-day. There is no one at home; but please wait here, and we will be back by-and-by." They then disappeared among the trees; and, returning after a short absence, they walked along together in the dusk of the evening. The old woman complained bitterly of their lonely and helpless state, and Hsi Shan himself was moved to compassion by the sight of her tears. She told him that the people of the neighborhood were a bad lot, and that if he thought of marrying the poor widow's daughter, he had better lose no time in doing so. Hsi Shan said he was willing; and when they reached the house the old woman, after lighting the lamp and setting food before him, proceeded to speak as follows:—

"Knowing, Sir, that you would shortly arrive, we sold all our grain except about twenty piculs. We cannot take this with us so far; but a mile or so to the north of the village, at the first house you come to, there lives a man named T'an Erh-ch'üan, who often buys grain from me. Don't think it too much trouble to oblige me by taking a sack with you on your mule and proceeding thither at once. Tell Mr. T'an that the old lady of the southern village has several piculs of grain which she wishes to sell in order to get money for a journey, and beg him to send some animals to carry it."

The old woman then gave him a sack of grain; and Hsi Shan, whipping up his mule, was soon at the place; and, knocking at the door, a great fat fellow came out, to whom he told his errand. Emptying the sack he had brought, he went back himself first; and before long a couple of men arrived leading five mules. The old woman took them into the granary, which was a cellar below ground, and Hsi Shan, going down himself, handed up the bags to the mother and daughter, who passed them on from one to the other. In a little while the men had got a load, with which they went off, returning altogether four times before all the grain was exhausted. They then paid the old woman, who kept one man and two mules, and, packing up her things, set off toward the east.

After traveling some seven miles day began to break; and by-and-by they reached a market town, where the old woman hired animals and sent back T'an's servant. When they arrived at Hsi Shan's home he related the whole story to his parents, who were very pleased at what had happened, and provided separate apartments for the old lady, at the same time engaging a fortune-teller to fix on a lucky day for A-ch'ien's marriage with their son San-lang. The old woman prepared a handsome trousseau; and as for A-ch'ien herself, she spoke but little, seldom losing her temper, and if any one addressed her she would only reply with a smile. She employed all her time in spinning, and thus became a general favorite with all alike. "Tell your brother," said she to San-lang, "that when he happens to pass our old residence he will do well not to make any mention of my mother and myself."

In three or four years' time the Hsi family had made plenty of money, and San-lang had taken his bachelor's degree, when one day Hsi Shan happened to pass a night with the people who lived next door to the house where he had met A-ch'ien. After telling them the story of his having had nowhere to sleep, and taking refuge with the old man and woman, his host said to him, "You must make a mistake, Sir; the house you allude to belongs to my uncle, but was abandoned three years ago in consequence of its being haunted. It has now been uninhabited for a long time. What old man and woman can have entertained you there?" Hsi Shan was very much astonished at this, but did not put much faith in what he heard; meanwhile his host continued, "For ten years no one dared enter the house; however, one day the back wall fell down, and my uncle, going to look at it, found, half-buried underneath the ruins, a large rat, almost as big as a cat. It was still moving, and my uncle went off to call for assistance, but when he got back the rat had disappeared. Everyone suspected some supernatural agency to be at work, though on returning to the spot ten days afterward nothing was to be either heard or seen; and about a year subsequently the place was inhabited once more."

Hsi Shan was more than ever amazed at what he now heard, and on reaching home told the family what had occurred; for he feared that his brother's wife was not a human being, and became rather anxious about him. San-lang himself continued to be much attached to A-ch'ien; but by-and-by the other members of the family let A-ch'ien perceive that they had suspicions about her. So one night she complained to San-lang, saying, "I have been a good wife to you for some years: now I have become an object of contempt. I pray you give me my divorce, and seek for yourself some worthier mate."

She then burst into a flood of tears; whereupon San-lang said, "You should know my feelings by this time. Ever since you entered the house the family has prospered; and that prosperity is entirely due to you. Who can say it is not so?"

"I know full well," replied A-ch'ien, "what you feel; still there are the others, and I do not wish to share the fate of an autumn fan."

At length San-lang succeeded in pacifying her; but Hsi Shan could not dismiss the subject from his thoughts, and gave out that he was going to get a first-rate mouser, with a view to testing A-ch'ien. She did not seem very frightened at this, though evidently ill at ease; and one night she told San-lang that her mother was not very well, and that he needn't come to bid her good night as usual. In the morning mother and daughter had disappeared; at which San-lang was greatly alarmed, and sent out to look for them in every direction. No traces of the fugitives could be discovered, and San-lang was overwhelmed with grief, unable either to eat or to sleep. His father and brother thought it was a lucky thing for him, and advised him to console himself with another wife. This, however, he refused to do; until, about a year afterward, nothing more having been heard of A-ch'ien, he could not resist their importunities any longer, and bought himself a concubine. But he never ceased to think of A-ch'ien; and some years later, when the prosperity of the family was on the wane, they all began to regret her loss.

Now San-lang had a step-brother, named Lan, who, when traveling to Chiao-chou on business, passed a night at the house of a relative named Lu. He noticed that during the night sounds of weeping and lamentation proceeded from their next-door neighbors, but he did not inquire the reason of it; however, on his way back he heard the same sounds, and then asked what was the cause of such demonstrations. Mr. Lu told him that a few years ago an old widow and her daughter had come there to live, and that the mother had died about a month previously, leaving her child quite alone in the world. Lan inquired what her name was, and Mr. Lu said it was Ku; "But," added he, "the door is closely barred, and as they never had any communication with the village, I know nothing of their antecedents."

"It's my sister-in-law," cried Lan, in amazement, and at once proceeded to knock at the door of the house. Some one came to the front door, and said, in a voice that betokened recent weeping, "Who's there? There are no men in this house." Lan looked through a crack, and saw that the young lady really was his sister-in-law; so he called out, "Sister, open the door. I am your step-brother A-sui."

A-ch'ien immediately opened the door and asked him in, and recounted to him the whole story of her troubles. "Your husband," said Lan, "is always thinking of you. For a trifling difference you need hardly have run away so far from him." He then proposed to hire a vehicle and take her home; but A-ch'ien replied, "I came hither with my mother to hide because I was held in contempt, and should make myself ridiculous by now returning thus. If I am to go back, my elder brother Hsi Shan must no longer live with us; otherwise, I will assuredly poison myself."

Lan then went home and told San-lang, who set off and traveled all night until he reached the place where A-ch'ien was. Husband and wife were overjoyed to meet again, and the following day San-lang notified the landlord of the house where A-ch'ien had been living. Now this landlord had long desired to secure A-ch'ien as a concubine for himself; and, after making no claim for rent for several years, he began to hint as much to her mother. The old lady, however, refused flatly; but shortly afterward she died, and then the landlord thought that he might be able to succeed. At this juncture San-lang arrived, and the landlord sought to hamper him by putting in his claim for rent; and, as San-lang was anything but well off at the moment, it really did annoy him very much. A-ch'ien here came to the rescue, showing San-lang a large quantity of grain she had in the house, and bidding him use it to settle accounts with the landlord. The latter declared he could not accept grain, but must be paid in silver; whereupon A-ch'ien sighed and said it was all her unfortunate self that had brought this upon them, at the same time telling San-lang of the landlord's former proposition. San-lang was very angry, and was about to take out a summons against him, when Mr. Lu interposed, and, by selling the grain in the neighborhood, managed to collect sufficient money to pay off the rent. San-lang and his wife then returned home; and the former, having explained the circumstances to his parents, separated his household from that of his brother.

A-ch'ien now proceeded to build, with her own money, a granary, which was a matter of some astonishment to the family, there not being a hundredweight of grain in the place. But in about a year the granary was full, and before very long San-lang was a rich man, Hsi Shan remaining as poor as before. Accordingly, A-ch'ien persuaded her husband's parents to come and live with them, and made frequent presents of money to the elder brother; so that her husband said, "Well, at any rate, you bear no malice." "Your brother's behavior," replied she, "was from his regard for you. Had it not been for him, you and I would never have met." After this there were no more supernatural manifestations.

The Man Who Was Thrown Down a Well

Mr. Tai, of An-ch'ing, was a wild fellow when young. One day as he was returning home tipsy, he met by the way a dead cousin of his named Chi; and having, in his drunken state, quite forgotten that his cousin was dead, he asked him where he was going. "I am already a disembodied spirit," replied Chi; "don't you remember?" Tai was a little disturbed at this; but, being under the influence of liquor, he was not frightened, and inquired of his cousin what he was doing in the realms below. "I am employed as scribe," said Chi, "in the court of the Great King." "Then you must know all about our happiness and misfortunes to come," cried Tai. "It is my business," answered his cousin, "so of course I know. But I see such an enormous mass that, unless of special reference to myself or family, I take no notice of any of it. Three days ago, by the way, I saw your name in the register." Tai immediately asked what there was about himself, and his cousin replied, "I will not deceive you; your name was put down for a dark and dismal hell." Tai was dreadfully alarmed, and at the same time sobered, and entreated his cousin to assist him in some way. "You may try," said Chi, "what merit will do for you as a means of mitigating your punishment; but the register of your sins is as thick as my finger, and nothing short of the most deserving acts will be of any avail. What can a poor fellow like myself do for you? Were you to perform one good act every day, you would not complete the necessary total under a year and more, and it is now too late for that. But henceforth amend your ways, and there may still be a chance of escape for you." When Tai heard these words he prostrated himself on the ground, imploring his cousin to help him; but, on raising his head, Chi had disappeared; he therefore returned sorrowfully home, and set to work to cleanse his heart and order his behavior.

Now Tai's next door neighbor had long suspected him of paying too much attention to his wife; and one day meeting Tai in the fields shortly after the events narrated above, he inveigled him into inspecting a dry well, and then pushed him down. The well was many feet deep, and the man felt certain that Tai was killed; however, in the middle of the night he came round, and sitting up at the bottom, he began to shout for assistance, but could not make any one hear him. On the following day, the neighbor, fearing that Tai might possibly have recovered consciousness, went to listen at the mouth of the well; and hearing him cry out for help, began to throw down a quantity of stones. Tai took refuge in a cave at the side, and did not dare utter another sound; but his enemy knew he was not dead, and forthwith filled the well almost up to the top with earth. In the cave it was as dark as pitch, exactly like the Infernal Regions; and not being able to get anything to eat or drink, Tai gave up all hopes of life. He crawled on his hands and knees further into the cave, but was prevented by water from going further than a few paces, and returned to take up his position at the old spot. At first he felt hungry; by-and-by, however, this sensation passed away; and then reflecting that there, at the bottom of a well, he co uld hardly perform any good action, he passed his time in calling loudly on the name of Buddha.

Before long he saw a number of Will-o'-the-Wisps flitting over the water and illuminating the gloom of the cave; and immediately prayed to them, saying, "O Will-o'-the-Wisps, I have heard that ye are the shades of wronged and injured people. I have not long to live, and am without hope of escape; still I would gladly relieve the monotony of my situation by exchanging a few words with you." Thereupon, all the Wills came flitting across the water to him; and among them was a man of about half the ordinary size. Tai asked him whence he came; to which he replied, "This is an old coal-mine. The proprietor, in working the coal, disturbed the position of some graves; and Mr. Lung-fei flooded the mine and drowned forty-three workmen. We are the shades of those men." He further said he did not know who Mr. Lung-fei was, except that he was secretary to the City God, and that in compassion for the misfortunes of the innocent workmen, he was in the habit of sending them a quantity of gruel every three or four days. "But the cold water," added he, "soaks into our bones, and there is but small chance of ever getting them removed. If, Sir, you some day return to the world above, I pray you fish up our decaying bones and bury them in some public burying-ground. You will thus earn for yourself boundless gratitude in the realms below."

Tai promised that if he had the luck to escape he would do as they wished; "but how," cried he, "situated as I am, can I ever hope to look again upon the light of day?" He then began to teach the Wills to say their prayers, making for them beads out of bits of mud, and repeating to them the liturgies of Buddha. He could not tell night from morning; he slept when he felt tired, and when he waked he sat up. Suddenly, he perceived in the distance the light of lamps, at which the shades all rejoiced, and said, "It is Mr. Lung-fei with our food." They then invited Tai to go with them; and when he said he couldn't because of the water, they bore him along over it so that he hardly seemed to walk. After twisting and turning about for nearly a quarter of a mile, he reached a place at which the Wills bade him walk by himself; and then he appeared to mount a flight of steps, at the top of which he found himself in an apartment lighted by a candle as thick round as one's arm. Not having seen the light of fire for some time, he was overjoyed and walked in; but observing an old man in a scholar's dress and cap seated in the post of honor, he stopped, not liking to advance further. But the old man had already caught sight of him, and asked him how he, a living man, had come there. Tai threw himself on the ground at his feet, and told him all; whereupon the old man cried out, "My great-grandson!" He then bade him get up; and offering him a seat, explained that his own name was Tai Ch'ien, and that he was otherwise known as Lung-fei. He said, moreover, that in days gone by a worthless grandson of his named T'ang, had associated himself with a lot of scoundrels and sunk a well near his grave, disturbing the peace of his everlasting night; and that therefore he had flooded the place with salt water and drowned them. He then inquired as to the general condition of the family at that time.

Now Tai was a descendant of one of five brothers, from the eldest of whom T'ang himself was also descended; and an influential man of the place had bribed T'ang to open a mine alongside the family grave. His brothers were afraid to interfere; and by-and-by the water rose and drowned all the workmen; whereupon actions for damages were commenced by the relatives of the deceased, and T'ang and his friend were reduced to poverty, and T'ang's descendants to absolute destitution. Tai was a son of one of T'ang's brothers, and having heard this story from his seniors, now repeated it to the old man. "How could they be otherwise than unfortunate," cried the latter, "with such an unfilial progenitor? But since you have come hither, you must on no account neglect your studies." The old man then provided him with food and wine, and spreading a volume of essays according to the old style before him, bade him study it most carefully. He also gave him themes for composition, and corrected his essays as if he had been his tutor. The candle remained always burning in the room, never needing to be snuffed and never decreasing. When he was tired he went to sleep, but he never knew day from night. The old man occasionally went out, leaving a boy to attend to his great-grandson's wants.

It seemed that several years passed away thus, but Tai had no troubles of any kind to annoy him. He had no other book except the volume of essays, one hundred in all, which he read through more than four thousand times. One day the old man said to him, "Your term of expiation is nearly completed, and you will be able to return to the world above. My grave is near the coal-mine, and the grosser breeze plays upon my bones. Remember to remove them to Tung-yüan." Tai promised he would see to this; and then the old man summoned all the shades together and instructed them to escort Tai back to the place where they had found him. The shades now bowed one after the other, and begged Tai to think of them as well, while Tai himself was quite at a loss to guess how he was going to get out.

Meanwhile, Tai's family had searched for him everywhere, and his mother had brought his case to the notice of the officials, thereby implicating a large number of persons, but without getting any trace of the missing man. Three or four years passed away and there was a change of magistrate; in consequence of which the search was relaxed, and Tai's wife, not being happy where she was, married another husband. Just then an inhabitant of the place set about repairing the old well and found Tai's body in the cave at the bottom. Touching it, he found it was not dead, and at once gave information to the family. Tai was promptly conveyed home, and within a day he could tell his own story.

Since he had been down the well, the neighbor who pushed him in had beaten his own wife to death; and his father-in-law having brought an action against him, he had been in confinement for more than a year while the case was being investigated. When released he was a mere bag of bones; and then hearing that Tai had come back to life, he was terribly alarmed and fled away. The family tried to persuade Tai to take proceedings against him, but this he would not do, alleging that what had befallen him was a proper punishment for his own bad behavior, and had nothing to do with the neighbor. Upon this, the said neighbor ventured to return; and when the water in the well had dried up, Tai hired men to go down and collect the bones, which he put in coffins and buried all together in one place. He next hunted up Mr. Lung-fei's name in the family tables of genealogy, and proceeded to sacrifice all kinds of nice things at his tomb. By-and-by the Literary Chancellor heard this strange story, and was also very pleased with Tai's compositions; accordingly, Tai passed successfully through his examinations, and, having taken his master's degree, returned home and reburied Mr. Lung-fei at Tung-yüan, repairing thither regularly every spring without fail.

The Virtuous Daughter-in-Law

An Ta-ch'êng was a Chung-ch'ing man. His father, who had gained the master's degree, died early; and his brother Erh-ch'êng was a mere boy. He himself had married a wife from the Ch'ên family, whose name was Shan-hu; and this young lady had much to put up with from the violent and malicious disposition of her husband's mother. However, she never complained; and every morning dressed herself up smart, and went in to pay her respects to the old lady. Once when Ta-ch'êng was ill, his mother abused Shan-hu for dressing so nicely; whereupon Shan-hu went back and changed her clothes; but even then Mrs. An was not satisfied, and began to tear her own hair with rage. Ta-ch'êng, who was a very filial son, at once gave his wife a beating, and this put an end to the scene.

From that moment his mother hated her more than ever, and although she was everything that a daughter-in-law could be, would never exchange a word with her. Ta-ch'êng then treated her in much the same way, that his mother might see he would have nothing to do with her; still the old lady wasn't pleased, and was always blaming Shan-hu for every trifle that occurred. "A wife," cried Ta-ch'êng "is taken to wait upon her mother-in-law. This state of things hardly looks like the wife doing her duty." So he bade Shan-hu begone, and sent an old maid-servant to see her home: but when Shan-hu got outside the village-gate, she burst into tears, and said, "How can a girl who has failed in her duties as a wife ever dare to look her parents in the face? I had better die." Thereupon she drew a pair of scissors and stabbed herself in the throat, covering herself immediately with blood. The servant prevented any further mischief, and supported her to the house of her husband's aunt, who was a widow living by herself, and who made Shan-hu stay with her. The servant went back and told Ta-ch'êng, and he bade her say nothing to any one, for fear his mother should hear of it.

In a few days Shan-hu's wound was healed, and Ta-ch'êng went off to ask his aunt to send her away. His aunt invited him in, but he declined, demanding loudly that Shan-hu should be turned out; and in a few moments Shan-hu herself came forth, and inquired what she had done. Ta-ch'êng said she had failed in her duty toward his mother; whereupon Shan-hu hung her head and made no answer, while tears of blood trickled from her eyes and stained her dress all over. Ta-ch'êng was much touched by this spectacle, and went away without saying any more; but before long his mother heard all about it, and, hurrying off to the aunt's, began abusing her roundly. This the aunt would not stand, and said it was all the fault of her own bad temper, adding, "The girl has already left you, and has nothing more to do with the family. Miss Ch'ên is staying with me, not your daughter-in-law; so you had better mind your own business." This made Mrs. An furious; but she was at a loss for an answer, and, seeing that the aunt was firm, she went off home abashed and in tears.

Shan-hu herself was very much upset, and determined to seek shelter elsewhere, finally taking up her abode with Mrs. An's elder sister, a lady of sixty odd years of age, whose son had died, leaving his wife and child to his mother's care. This Mrs. Yü was extremely fond of Shan-hu; and when she heard the facts of the case, said it was all her sister's horrid disposition, and proposed to send Shan-hu back. The latter, however, would not hear of this, and they continued to live together like mother and daughter; neither would Shan-hu accept the invitation of her two brothers to return home and marry some one else, but remained there with Mrs. Yü, earning enough to live upon by spinning and such work.

Ever since Shan-hu had been sent away, Ta-ch'êng's mother had been endeavoring to get him another wife; but the fame of her temper had spread far and wide, and no one would entertain her proposals. In three or four years Erh-ch'êng had grown up, and he was married first to a young lady named Tsang-ku, whose temper turned out to be something fearful, and far more ungovernable even than her mother-in-law's. When the latter only looked angry, Tsang-ku was already at the shrieking stage; and Erh-ch'êng, being of a very meek disposition, dared not side with either. Thus it came about that Mrs. An began to be in mortal fear of Tsang-ku; and whenever her daughter-in-law was in a rage she would try and turn off her anger with a smile. She seemed never to be able to please Tsang-ku, who in her turn worked her mother-in-law like a slave, Ta-ch'êng himself not venturing to interfere, but only assisting his mother in washing the dishes and sweeping the floor. Mother and son would often go to some secluded spot, and there in secret tell their griefs to one another; but before long Mrs. An was stretched upon a sick bed with nobody to attend to her except Ta-ch'êng. He watched her day and night without sleeping, until both eyes were red and inflamed; and then when he went to summon the younger son to take his place, Tsang-ku told him to leave the house. Ta-ch'êng now went off to inform Mrs. Yü, hoping that she would come and assist; and he had hardly finished his tale of woe before Shan-hu walked in. In great confusion at seeing her, he would have left immediately had not Shan-hu held out her arms across the door; whereupon he bolted underneath them and escaped. He did not dare tell his mother, and shortly afterward Mrs. Yü arrived, to the great joy of Ta-ch'êng's mother, who made her stay in the house.

Every day something nice was sent for Mrs. Yü, and even when she told the servants that there was no occasion for it, she having all she wanted at her sister's, the things still came as usual. However, she kept none of them for herself, but gave what came to the invalid, who gradually began to improve. Mrs. Yü's grandson also used to come by his mother's orders, and inquire after the sick lady's health, besides bringing a packet of cakes and so on for her.

"Ah, me!" cried Mrs. An, "what a good daughter-in-law you have got, to be sure. What have you done to her?"

"What sort of a person was the one you sent away?" asked her sister in reply.

"She wasn't as bad as some one I know of," said Mrs. An, "though not so good as yours."

"When she was here you had but little to do," replied Mrs. Yü; "and when you were angry she took no notice of it. How was she not as good?" Mrs. An then burst into tears, and saying how sorry she was, asked if Shan-hu had married again; to which Mrs. Yü replied that she did not know, but would make inquiries.

In a few more days the patient was quite well, and Mrs. Yü proposed to return; her sister, however, begged her to stay, and declared she should die if she didn't. Mrs. Yü then advised that Erh-ch'êng and his wife should live in a separate house, and Erh-ch'êng spoke about it to his wife; but she would not agree, and abused both Ta-ch'êng and his mother alike. It ended by Ta-ch'êng giving up a large share of the property, and ultimately Tsang-ku consented, and a deed of separation was drawn up. Mrs. Yü then went away, returning next day with a sedan-chair to carry her sister back; and no sooner had the latter put her foot inside Mrs. Yü's door, than she asked to see the daughter-in-law, whom she immediately began to praise very highly.

"Ah," said Mrs. Yü, "she's a good girl, with her little faults like the rest of us; but your daughter-in-law is just as good, though you are not aware of it."

"Alas!" replied her sister, "I must have been as senseless as a statue not to have seen what she was."

"I wonder what Shan-hu, whom you turned out of doors, says of you," rejoined Mrs. Yü.

"Why, swears at me, of course," answered Mrs. An. "If you examine yourself honestly and find nothing which should make people swear at you, is it at all likely you would be sworn at?" asked Mrs. Yü.

"Well, all people are fallible," replied the other, "and as I know she is not perfect, I conclude she would naturally swear at me."

"If a person has just cause for resentment, and yet does not indulge that resentment, such behavior should meet with a grateful acknowledgment; or if any one has just cause for leaving another and yet does not do so, such behavior should entitle them to kind treatment. Now, all the things that were sent when you were ill, and all the various little attentions, did not come from my daughter-in-law but from yours." Mrs. An was amazed at hearing this, and asked for some explanation; whereupon Mrs. Yü continued, "Shan-hu has been living here for a long time. Everything she sent to you was bought with money earned by her spinning, and that, too, continued late into the night." Mrs. An here burst into tears, and begged to be allowed to see Shan-hu, who came in at Mrs. Yü's summons, and threw herself on the ground at her mother-in-law's feet. Mrs. An was much abashed, and beat her head with shame; but Mrs. Yü made it all up between them, and they became mother and daughter as at first.

In about ten days they went home, and, as their property was not enough to support them, Ta-ch'êng had to work with his pen while his wife did the same with her needle. Erh-ch'êng was quite well off, but his brother would not apply to him, neither did he himself offer to help them. Tsang-ku, too, would have nothing to do with her sister-in-law, because she had been divorced; and Shan-hu in her turn, knowing what Tsang-ku's temper was, made no great efforts to be friendly. So the two brothers lived apart; and when Tsang-ku was in one of her outrageous moods, all the others would stop their ears, till at length there was only her husband and the servants upon whom to vent her spleen.

One day a maid-servant of hers committed suicide, and the father of the girl brought an action against Tsang-ku for having caused her death. Erh-ch'êng went off to the mandarin's to take her place as defendant, but only got a good beating for his pains, as the magistrate insisted that Tsang-ku herself should appear, and answer to the charge, in spite of all her friends could do. The consequence was she had her fingers squeezed until the flesh was entirely taken off; and the magistrate, being a grasping man, a very severe fine was inflicted as well. Erh-ch'êng had now to mortgage his property before he could raise enough money to get Tsang-ku released; but before long the mortgagee threatened to foreclose, and he was obliged to enter into negotiations for the sale of it to an old gentleman of the village named Jen.

Now Mr. Jen, knowing that half the property had belonged to Ta-ch'êng, said the deed of sale must be signed by the elder brother as well; however, when Ta-ch'êng reached his house, the old man cried out, "I am Mr. An, M.A., who is this Jen that he should buy my property?" Then, looking at Ta-ch'êng, he added, "The filial piety of you and your wife has obtained for me in the realms below this interview"; upon which Ta-ch'êng said, "O father, since you have this power, help my younger brother."

"The unfilial son and the vixenish daughter-in-law," said the old man, "deserve no pity. Go home and quickly buy back our ancestral property."

"We have barely enough to live upon," replied Ta-ch'êng; "where, then, shall we find the necessary money?"

"Beneath the crape myrtle-tree," answered his father, "you will find a store of silver, which you may take and use for this purpose."

Ta-ch'êng would have questioned him further, but the old gentleman said no more, recovering consciousness shortly afterward without knowing a word of what had happened.

Ta-ch'êng went back and told his brother, who did not altogether believe the story; Tsang-ku, however, hurried off with a number of men, and had soon dug a hole four or five feet deep, at the bottom of which they found a quantity of bricks and stones, but no gold. She then gave up the idea and returned home, Ta-ch'êng having meanwhile warned his mother and wife not to go near the place while she was digging.

When Tsang-ku left, Mrs. An went herself to have a look, and seeing only bricks and earth mingled together, she, too, retraced her steps. Shan-hu was the next to go, and she found the hole full of silver bullion; and then Ta-ch'êng repaired to the spot and saw that there was no mistake about it. Not thinking it right to apply this heir-loom to his own private use, he now summoned Erh-ch'êng to share it; and having obtained twice as much as was necessary to redeem the estate, the brothers returned to their homes. Erh-ch'êng and Tsang-ku opened their half together, when lo! the bag was full of tiles and rubbish. They at once suspected Ta-ch'êng of deceiving them, and Erh-ch'êng ran off to see how things were going at his brother's. He arrived just as Ta-ch'êng was spreading the silver on the table, and with his mother and wife rejoicing over their acquisition; and when he had told them what had occurred, Ta-ch'êng expressed much sympathy for him, and at once presented him with his own half of the treasure. Erh-ch'êng was delighted, and paid off the mortgage on the land, feeling very grateful to his brother for such kindness. Tsang-ku, however, declared it was a proof that Ta-ch'êng had been cheating him; "for how, otherwise," argued she, "can you understand a man sharing anything with another, and then resigning his own half?"

Erh-ch'êng himself did not know what to think of it; but next day the mortgagee sent to say that the money paid in was all imitation silver, and that he was about to lay the case before the authorities. Husband and wife were greatly alarmed at this, and Tsang-ku exclaimed, "Well, I never thought your brother was as bad as this. He's simply trying to take your life." Erh-ch'êng himself was in a terrible fright, and hurried off to the mortgagee to entreat for mercy; but as the latter was extremely angry and would hear of no compromise, Erh-ch'êng was obliged to make over the property to him to dispose of himself. The money was then returned, and when he got home he found that two lumps had been cut through, showing merely an outside layer of silver, about as thick as an onion-leaf, covering nothing but copper within. Tsang-ku and Erh-ch'êng then agreed to keep the broken pieces themselves, but send the rest back to Ta-ch'êng, with a message, saying that they were deeply indebted to him for all his kindness, and that they had ventured to retain two of the lumps of silver out of compliment to the giver; also that Ta-ch'êng might consider himself the owner of the mortgaged land, which he could redeem or not as he pleased. Ta-ch'êng, who did not perceive the intention in all this, refused to accept the land; however, Erh-ch'êng entreated him to do so, and at last he consented. When he came to weigh the money, he found it was five ounces short, and therefore bade Shan-hu pawn something from her jewel-box to make up the amount, with which he proceeded to pay off the mortgage. The mortgagee, suspecting it was the same money that had been offered him by Erh-ch'êng, cut the pieces in halves, and saw that it was all silver of the purest quality. Accordingly he accepted it in liquidation of his claim, and handed the mortgage back to Ta-ch'êng.

Meanwhile, Erh-ch'êng had been expecting some catastrophe; but when he found that the mortgaged land had been redeemed, he did not know what to make of it. Tsang-ku thought that at the time of the digging Ta-ch'êng had concealed the genuine silver, and immediately rushed off to his house, and began to revile them all round. Ta-ch'êng now understood why they had sent him back the money; and Shan-hu laughed and said, "The property is safe; why, then, this anger?" Thereupon she made Ta-ch'êng hand over the deeds to Tsang-ku.

One night after this Erh-ch'êng's father appeared to him in a dream, and reproached him, saying, "Unfilial son, unfraternal brother, your hour is at hand. Wherefore usurp rights that do not belong to you?" In the morning Erh-ch'êng told Tsang-ku of his dream, and proposed to return the property to his brother; but she only laughed at him for a fool. Just then the eldest of his two sons, a boy of seven, died of small-pox, and this frightened Tsang-ku so that she agreed to restore the deeds. Ta-ch'êng would not accept them; and now the second child, a boy of three, died also; whereupon Tsang-ku seized the deeds, and threw them into her brother-in-law's house. Spring was over, but the land was in a terribly neglected state; so Ta-ch'êng set to work and put it in order again. From this moment Tsang-ku was a changed woman toward her mother- and sister-in-law; and when, six months later, Mrs. An died, she was so grieved that she refused to take any nourishment. "Alas!" cried she, "that my mother-in-law has died thus early, and prevented me from waiting upon her. Heaven will not allow me to retrieve my past errors." Tsang-ku had thirteen children, but as none of them lived, they were obliged to adopt one of Ta-ch'êng's, who, with his wife, lived to a good old age, and had three sons, two of whom took their doctor's degree. People said this was a reward for filial piety and brotherly love.

Dr. Tsêng's Dream

There was a Fohkien gentleman named Tsêng, who had just taken his doctor's degree. One day he was out walking with several other recently-elected doctors, when they heard that at a temple hard by there lived an astrologer, and accordingly the party proceeded thither to get their fortunes told. They went in and sat down, and the astrologer made some very complimentary remarks to Tsêng, at which he fanned himself and smiled, saying, "Have I any chance of ever wearing the dragon robes and the jade girdle?" The astrologer immediately put on a serious face, and replied that he would be a Secretary of State during twenty years of national tranquility.

Thereupon Tsêng was much pleased, and began to give himself greater airs than ever. A slight rain coming on, they sought shelter in the priest's quarters, where they found an old bonze, with sunken eyes and a big nose, sitting upon a mat. He took no notice of the strangers, who, after having bowed to him, stretched themselves upon the couches to chat, not forgetting to congratulate Tsêng upon the destiny which had been foretold him. Tsêng, too, seemed to think the thing was a matter of certainty, and mentioned the names of several friends he intended to advance, among others the old family butler. Roars of laughter greeted this announcement, mingled with the patter-patter of the increasing rain outside.

Tsêng then curled himself up for a nap, when suddenly in walked two officials bearing a commission under the Great Seal appointing Tsêng to the Grand Secretariat. As soon as Tsêng understood their errand, he rushed off at once to pay his respects to the Emperor, who graciously detained him some time in conversation, and then issued instructions that the promotion and dismissal of all officers below the third grade should be vested in Tsêng alone. He was next presented with the dragon robes, the jade girdle, and a horse from the imperial stables, after which he performed the *ko-t'ow* before His Majesty and took his leave.

He then went home, but it was no longer the old home of his youth. Painted beams, carved pillars, and a general profusion of luxury and elegance, made him wonder where on earth he was; until, nervously stroking his beard, he ventured to call out in a low tone. Immediately the responses of numberless attendants echoed through the place like thunder. Presents of costly food were sent to him by all the grandees, and his gate was absolutely blocked up by the crowds of retainers who were constantly coming and going. When Privy Councillors came to see him, he would rush out in haste to receive them; when Under-Secretaries of State visited him, he made them a polite bow; but to all below these he would hardly vouchsafe a word. The Governor of Shansi sent him twelve singing-girls, two of whom, Ni-ni and Fairy, he made his favorites. All day long he had nothing to do but find amusement as best he could, until he bethought himself that formerly a man named Wang had often assisted him with money. Thereupon he memorialized the Throne and obtained official employment for him. Then he recollected that there was another man to whom he owed a long-standing grudge. He at once caused this man, who was in the Government service, to be impeached and stripped of his rank and dignities. Thus he squared accounts with both.

One day when out in his chair a drunken man bumped against one of his tablet-bearers. Tsêng had him seized and sent in to the mayor's *yamên*, where he died under the bamboo. Owners of land adjoining his would make him a present of the richest portions, fearing the consequences if they did not do so; and thus he became very wealthy, almost on a par with the State itself. By-and-by, Ni-ni and Fairy died, and Tsêng was overwhelmed with grief. Suddenly he remembered that in former years he had seen a beautiful girl whom he wished to purchase as a concubine, but want of money had then prevented him from carrying out his intention. Now there was no longer that difficulty; and accordingly he sent off two trusty servants to get the girl by force. In a short time she arrived, when he found that she had grown more beautiful than ever; and so his cup of happiness was full.

But years rolled on, and gradually his fellow-officials became estranged, Tsêng taking no notice of their behavior, until at last one of them impeached him to the Throne in a long and bitter memorial. Happily, however, the Emperor still regarded him with favor, and for some time kept the memorial by him unanswered. Then followed a joint memorial from the whole of the Privy Council, including those who had once thronged his doors, and had falsely called him their dear father. The Imperial rescript to this document was "Banishment to Yunnan," his son, who was Governor of P'ing-yang, being also implicated in his guilt. When Tsêng heard the news, he was overcome with fear; but an armed guard was already at his gate, and the lictors were forcing their way into his innermost apartments. They tore off his robe and official hat, and bound him and his wife with cords. Then they collected together in the hall his gold, his silver, and bank-notes, to the value of many hundred thousands of taels. His pearls, and jade, and precious stones filled many bushel baskets. His curtains, and screens, and beds, and other articles of furniture were brought out by thousands; while the swaddling-clothes of his infant boy and the shoes of his little girl were lying littered about the steps. It was a sad sight for Tsêng; but a worse blow was that of his concubine carried off almost lifeless before his eyes, himself not daring to utter a word. Then all the apartments, store-rooms, and treasuries were sealed up; and, with a volley of curses, the soldiers bade Tsêng begone, and proceeded to leave the place, dragging Tsêng with them. The husband and wife prayed that they might be allowed some old cart, but this favor was denied them. After about ten *li*, Tsêng's wife could barely walk, her feet being swollen and sore. Tsêng helped her along as best he could, but another ten *li* reduced him to a state of abject fatigue.

By-and-by they saw before them a great mountain, the summit of which was lost in the clouds; and, fearing they should be made to ascend it, Tsêng and his wife stood still and began to weep. The lictors, however, clamored round them, and would permit of no rest. The sun was rapidly sinking, and there was no place at hand where they could obtain shelter for the night. So they continued on their weary way until about half-way up the hill, when his wife's strength was quite exhausted, and she sat down by the roadside. Tsêng, too, halted to rest in spite of the soldiers and their abuse; but they had hardly stopped a moment before down came a band of robbers upon them, each with a sharp knife in his hand. The soldiers immediately took to their heels, and Tsêng fell on his knees before the robbers, saying, "I am a poor criminal going into banishment, and have nothing to give you. I pray you spare my life." But the robbers sternly replied, "We are all the victims of your crimes, and now we want your wicked head."

Then Tsêng began to revile them, saying, "Dogs! though I am under sentence of banishment, I am still an officer of the State." But the robbers cursed him again, flourishing a sword over his neck, and the next thing he heard was the noise of his own head as it fell with a thud to the ground. At the same instant two devils stepped forward and seized him each by one hand, compelling him to go with them.

After a little while they arrived at a great city where there was a hideously ugly king sitting upon a throne judging between good and evil. Tsêng crawled before him on his hands and knees to receive sentence, and the king, after turning over a few pages of his register, thundered out, "The punishment of a traitor who has brought misfortune on his country: the cauldron of boiling oil!" To this ten thousand devils responded with a cry like a clap of thunder, and one huge monster led Tsêng down alongside the cauldron, which was seven feet in height, and surrounded on all sides by blazing fuel, so that it was of a glowing red heat. Tsêng shrieked for mercy, but it was all up with him, for the devil seized him by the hair and the small of his back and pitched him headlong in. Down he fell with a splash, and rose and sank with the bubbling of the oil, which ate through his flesh into his very vitals. He longed to die, but death would not come to him.

After about half-an-hour's boiling, a devil took him out on a pitchfork and threw him down before the Infernal King, who again consulted his note-book, and said, "You relied on your position to treat others with contumely and injustice, for which you must suffer on the Sword-Hill." Again he was led away by devils to a large hill thickly studded with sharp swords, their points upward like the shoots of bamboo, with here and there the remains of many miserable wretches who had suffered before him. Tsêng again cried for mercy and crouched upon the ground; but a devil bored into him with a poisoned awl until he screamed with pain. He was then seized and flung up high into the air, falling down right on the sword points, to his most frightful agony. This was repeated several times until he was almost hacked to pieces.

He was then brought once more before the king, who asked what was the amount of his peculations while on earth. Immediately an accountant came forward with an abacus, and said that the whole sum was 3,210,000 taels, whereupon the king replied, "Let him drink that amount." Forthwith the devils piled up a great heap of gold and silver, and, when they had melted it in a huge crucible, began pouring it into Tsêng's mouth. The pain was excruciating as the molten metal ran down his throat into his vitals; but since in life he had never been able to get enough of the dross, it was determined he should feel no lack of it then. He was half-a-day drinking it, and then the king ordered him away to be born again as a woman in Kan-chou.

A few steps brought them to a huge frame, where on an iron axle revolved a mighty wheel many hundred *yojanas* in circumference, and shining with a brilliant light. The devils flogged Tsêng on to the wheel, and he shut his eyes as he stepped up. Then whiz—and away he went, feet foremost, round with the wheel, until he felt himself tumble off and a cold thrill ran through him, when he opened his eyes and found he was changed into a girl. He saw his father and mother in rags and tatters, and in one corner a beggar's bowl and a staff, and understood the calamity that had befallen him.

Day after day he begged about the streets, and his inside rumbled for want of food; he had no clothes to his back. At fourteen years of age he was sold to a gentleman as concubine; and then, though food and clothes were not wanting, he had to put up with the scoldings and floggings of the wife, who one day burned him with a hot iron. Luckily the gentleman took a fancy to him and treated him well, which kindness Tsêng repaid by an irreproachable fidelity.

It happened, however, that on one occasion when they were chatting together, burglars broke into the house and killed the gentleman, Tsêng having escaped by hiding himself under the bed. Thereupon he was immediately charged by the wife with murder, and on being taken before the authorities was sentenced to die the "lingering death." This sentence was at once carried out with tortures more horrible than any in all the Courts of Purgatory, in the middle of which Tsêng heard one of his companions call out, "Hullo, there! you've got the nightmare." Tsêng got up and rubbed his eyes, and his friends said, "It's quite late in the day, and we're all very hungry." But the old priest smiled, and asked him if the prophecy as to his future rank was true or not. Tsêng bowed and begged him to explain; whereupon the old priest said, "For those who cultivate virtue, a lily will grow up even in the fiery pit." Tsêng had gone thither full of pride and vainglory; he went home an altered man. From that day he thought no more of becoming a Secretary of State, but retired into the hills, and I know not what became of him after that.

The Country of the Cannibals

At Chiao-chou there lived a man named Hsü, who gained his living by trading across the sea. On one occasion he was carried far out of his course by a violent tempest, and reached a country of high hills and dense jungle, where, after making fast his boat and taking provisions with him, he landed, hoping to meet with some of the inhabitants. He then saw that the rocks were covered with large holes, like the cells of bees; and, hearing the sound of voices from within, he stopped in front of one of them and peeped in. To his infinite horror he beheld two hideous beings, with thick rows of horrid fangs, and eyes that glared like lamps, engaged in tearing to pieces and devouring some raw deer's flesh; and, turning round, he would have fled instantly from the spot, had not the cave-men already espied him; and, leaving their food, they seized him and dragged him in. Thereupon ensued a chattering between them, resembling the noise of birds or beasts, and they proceeded to pull off Hsü's clothes as if about to eat him; but Hsü, who was frightened almost to death, offered them the food he had in his wallet, which they ate up with great relish, and looked inside for more. Hsü waved his hand to show it was all finished, and then they angrily seized him again; at which he cried out, "I have a saucepan in my boat, and can cook you some."

The cave-men did not understand what he said; but, by dint of gesticulating freely, they at length seemed to have an idea of what he meant; and, having taken him down to the shore to fetch the saucepan, they returned with him to the cave, where he lighted a fire and cooked the remainder of the deer, with the flavor of which they appeared to be mightily pleased. At night they rolled a big stone to the mouth of the cave, fearing lest he should try to escape; and Hsü himself lay down at a distance from them in doubt as to whether his life would be spared. At daybreak the cave-men went out, leaving the entrance blocked, and by-and-by came back with a deer, which they gave to Hsü to cook. Hsü flayed the carcass, and from a remote corner of the cave took some water and prepared a large quantity, which was no sooner ready than several other cave-men arrived to join in the feast. When they had finished all there was, they made signs that Hsü's saucepan was too small; and three or four days afterward they brought him a large one of the same shape as those in common use amongst men, subsequently furnishing him with constant supplies of wolf and deer, of which they always invited him to partake. By degrees they began to treat him kindly, and not to shut him up when they went out; and Hsü, too, gradually learned to understand, and even to speak, a little of their language, which pleased them so much that they finally gave him a cave-woman for his wife. Hsü was horribly afraid of her; but, as she treated him with great consideration, always reserving tit-bits of food for him, they lived very happily together.

One day all the cave-people got up early in the morning, and, having adorned themselves with strings of fine pearls, they went forth as if to meet some honored guest, giving orders to Hsü to cook an extra quantity of meat that day. "It is the birthday of our King," said Hsü's wife to him; and then, running out, she informed the other cave-people that her husband had no pearls. So each gave five from his own string, and Hsü's wife added ten to these, making in all fifty, which she threaded on a hempen fiber and hung around his neck, each pearl being worth over an hundred ounces of silver. Then they went away, and as soon as Hsü had finished his cooking, his wife appeared and invited him to come and receive the King. So off they went to a huge cavern, covering about a mow of ground, in which was a huge stone, smoothed away at the top like a table, with stone seats at the four sides. At the upper end was a dais, over which was spread a leopard's skin, the other seats having only deer-skins; and within the cavern some twenty or thirty cave-men ranged themselves on the seats.

After a short interval a great wind began to stir up the dust, and they all rushed out to a creature very much resembling themselves, which hurried into the cave, and, squatting down cross-legged, cocked its head and looked about like a cormorant. The other cave-men then filed in and took up their positions right and left of the dais, where they stood gazing up at the King with their arms folded before them in the form of a cross. The King counted them one by one, and asked if they were all present; and when they replied in the affirmative, he looked at Hsü and inquired who he was. Thereupon Hsü's wife stepped forward and said he was her husband, and the others all loudly extolled his skill in cookery, two of them running out and bringing back some cooked meat, which they set before the King. His Majesty swallowed it by handfuls, and found it so nice that he gave orders to be supplied regularly; and then, turning to Hsü, he asked him why his string of beads was so short. "He has but recently arrived among us," replied the cave-men, "and hasn't got a complete set"; upon which the King drew ten pearls from the string round his own neck and bestowed them upon Hsü. Each was as big as the top of one's finger, and as round as a bullet; and Hsü's wife threaded them for him and hung them round his neck. Hsü himself crossed his arms and thanked the King in the language of the country, after which His Majesty went off in a gust of wind as rapidly as a bird can fly, and the cave-men sat down and finished what was left of the banquet.

Four years afterward Hsü's wife gave birth to a triplet of two boys and one girl, all of whom were ordinary human beings, and not at all like the mother; at which the other cave-people were delighted, and would often play with them and caress them. Three years passed away, and the children could walk about, after which their father taught them to speak his own tongue; and in their early babblings their human origin was manifested. The boys, as mere children, could climb about on the mountains as easily as though walking upon a level road; and between them and their father there grew up a mutual feeling of attachment.

One day the mother had gone out with the girl and one of the boys, and was absent for a long time. A strong north wind was blowing, and Hsü, filled with thoughts of his old home, led his other son down with him to the beach, where lay the boat in which he had formerly reached this country. He then proposed to the boy that they should go away together; and, having explained to him that they could not inform his mother, father and son stepped on board, and, after a voyage of only twenty-four hours, arrived safely at Chiao-chou. On reaching home Hsü found that his wife had married again; so he sold two of his pearls for an enormous sum of money, and set up a splendid establishment. His son was called Piao, and at fourteen or fifteen years of age the boy could lift a weight of three thousand catties (4,000 lbs.). He was extremely fond of athletics of all kinds, and thus attracted the notice of the Commander-in-Chief, who gave him a commission as sub-lieutenant. Just at that time there happened to be some trouble on the frontier, and young Piao, having covered himself with glory, was made a colonel at the age of eighteen.

About that time another merchant was driven by stress of weather to the country of the cave-men, and had hardly stepped ashore before he observed a young man whom he knew at once to be of Chinese origin. The young man asked him whence he came, and finally took him into a cave hid away in a dark valley and concealed by the dense jungle. There he bade him remain, and in a little while he returned with some deer's flesh, which he gave the merchant to eat, saying at the same time that his own father was a Chiao-chou man. The merchant now knew that the young man was Hsü's son, he himself being acquainted with Hsü as a trader in the same line of business.

"Why, he's an old friend of mine," cried the latter; "his other son is now a colonel." The young man did not know what was meant by a *colonel*, so the merchant told him it was the title of a Chinese mandarin.

"And what is a *mandarin*?" asked the youth.

"A mandarin," replied the merchant, "is one who goes out with a chair and horses; who at home sits upon a dais in the hall; whose summons is answered by a hundred voices; who is looked at only with sidelong eyes, and in whose presence all people stand aslant;—this is to be a mandarin."

The young man was deeply touched at this recital, and at length the merchant said to him, "Since your honored father is at Chiao-chou, why do you remain here?"

"Indeed," replied the youth, "I have often indulged the same feeling; but my mother is not a Chinese woman, and, apart from the difference of her language and appearance, I fear that if the other cave-people found it out they would do us some mischief." He then took his leave, being in rather a disturbed state of mind, and bade the merchant wait until the wind should prove favorable, when he promised to come and see him off, and charge him with a letter to his father and brother.

Six months the merchant remained in that cave, occasionally taking a peep at the cave-people passing backward and forward, but not daring to leave his retreat. As soon as the monsoon set in the young man arrived and urged him to hurry away, begging him, also, not to forget the letter to his father. So the merchant sailed away and soon reached Chiao-chou, where he visited the colonel and told him the whole story. Piao was much affected, and wished to go in search of those members of the family; but his father feared the dangers he would encounter, and advised him not to think of such a thing. However, Piao was not to be deterred; and having imparted his scheme to the commander-in-chief, he took with him two soldiers and set off.

Adverse winds prevailed at that time, and they beat about for half a moon, until they were out of sight of all land, could not see a foot before them, and had completely lost their reckoning. Just then a mighty sea arose and capsized their boat, tossing Piao into the water, where he floated about for some time at the will of the waves, until suddenly somebody dragged him out and carried him into a house. Then he saw that his rescuer was to all appearances a cave-man, and accordingly he addressed him in the cave-people's language, and told him whither he himself was bound. "It is my native place," replied the cave-man, in astonishment; "but you will excuse my saying that you are now 8,000 *li* out of your course. This is the way to the country of the Poisonous Dragons, and not your route at all." He then went off to find a boat for Piao, and, himself swimming in the water behind, pushed it along like an arrow from a bow, so quickly that by the next day they had traversed the whole distance. On the shore Piao observed a young man walking up and down and evidently watching him; and, knowing that no human beings dwelt there, he guessed at once that he was his brother. Approaching more closely, he saw that he was right; and, seizing the young man's hand, he asked after his mother and sister. On hearing that they were well, he would have gone directly to see them; but the younger one begged him not to do so, and ran away himself to fetch them.

Meanwhile, Piao turned to thank the cave-man who had brought him there, but he, too, had disappeared. In a few minutes his mother and sister arrived, and, on seeing Piao, they could not restrain their tears. Piao then laid his scheme before them, and when they said they feared people would ill-treat them, he replied, "In China I hold a high position, and people will not dare to show you disrespect." Thus they determined to go. The wind, however, was against them, and mother and son were at a loss what to do, when suddenly the sail bellied out toward the south, and a rustling sound was heard. "Heaven helps us, my mother!" cried Piao, full of joy; and, hurrying on board at once, in three days they had reached their destination. As they landed the people fled right and left in fear, Piao having divided his own clothes amongst the party; and when they arrived at the house, and his mother saw Hsü, she began to rate him soundly for running away without her. Hsü hastened to acknowledge his error, and then all the family and servants were introduced to her, each one being in mortal dread of such a singular personage.

Piao now bade his mother learn to talk Chinese, and gave her any quantity of fine clothes and rich meats, to the infinite delight of the old lady. She and her daughter both dressed in man's clothes, and by the end of a few months were able to understand what was said to them. The brother, named Pao, and the sister, Yeh, were both clever enough, and immensely strong into the bargain. Piao was ashamed that Pao could not read, and set to work to teach him; and the youngster was so quick that he learned the sacred books and histories by merely reading them once over. However, he would not enter upon a literary career, loving better to draw a strong bow or ride a spirited horse, and finally taking the highest military degree. He married the daughter of a post-captain; but his sister had some trouble in getting a husband, because of her being the child of a cave-woman. At length a sergeant, named Yüan, who was under her brother's command, was forced to take her as his wife. She could draw a hundred-catty bow, and shoot birds at a hundred paces without ever missing. Whenever Yüan went to battle she went with him; and his subsequent rise to high rank was chiefly due to her. At thirty-four years of age Pao got a command; and in his great battles his mother, clad in armor and grasping a spear, would fight by his side, to the terror of all their adversaries; and when he himself received the dignity of an hereditary title, he memorialized the Throne to grant his mother the title of "lady."

Foot-ball on the Tung-t'ing Lake

WANG SHIH-HSIU WAS A NATIVE OF LU-CHOU, AND SUCH A LUSTY FELLOW THAT HE COULD pick up a stone mortar. Father and son were both good foot-ball players; but when the former was about forty years of age he was drowned while crossing the Money Pool. So me eight or nine years later our hero happened to be on his way to Hunan; and anchoring in the Tung-t'ing lake, watched the moon rising in the east and illuminating the water into a bright sheet of light. While he was thus engaged, lo! from out of the lake emerged five men, bringing with them a large mat which they spread on the surface of the water so as to cover about six yards square. Wine and food were then arranged upon it, and Wang heard the sound of the dishes knocking together, but it was a dull, soft sound, not at all like that of ordinary crockery. Three of the men sat down on the mat and the other two waited upon them. One of the former was dressed in yellow, the other two in white, and each wore a black turban. Their demeanor as they sat there side by side was grave and dignified; in appearance they resembled three of the ancients, but by the fitful beams of the moon Wang was unable to see very clearly what they were like. The attendants wore black serge dresses, and one of them seemed to be a boy, while the other was many years older. Wang now heard the man in the yellow dress say, "This is truly a fine moonlight night for a drinking-bout";

to which one of his companions replied, "It quite reminds me of the night when Prince Kuang-li feasted at Pear-blossom Island." The three then pledged each other in bumping goblets, talking all the time in such a low tone that Wang could not hear what they were saying.

The boatmen kept themselves concealed, crouching down at the bottom of the boat; but Wang looked hard at the attendants, the elder of whom bore a striking resemblance to his father, though he spoke in quite a different tone of voice. When it was drawing toward midnight, one of them proposed a game at ball; and in a moment the boy disappeared in the water, to return immediately with a huge ball—quite an armful in fact—apparently full of quicksilver, and lustrous within and without. All now rose up, and the man in the yellow dress bade the old attendant join them in the game. The ball was kicked up some ten or fifteen feet in the air, and was quite dazzling in its brilliancy; but once, when it had gone up with a whish-h-h-h, it fell at some distance off, right in the very middle of Wang's boat. The occasion was irresistible, and Wang, exerting all his strength, kicked the ball with all his might. It seemed unusually light and soft to the touch, and his foot broke right through. Away went the ball to a good height, pouring forth a stream of light like a rainbow from the hole Wang had made, and making as it fell a curve like that of a comet rushing across the sky. Down it glided into the water, where it fizzed a moment and then went out.

"Ho, there!" cried out the players in anger, "what living creature is that who dares thus to interrupt our sport?"

"Well kicked—indeed!" said the old man, "that's a favorite drop-kick of my own." At this, one of the two in white clothes began to abuse him saying, "What! you old baggage, when we are all so annoyed in this manner, are you to come forward and make a joke of it? Go at once with the boy and bring back to us this practical joker, or your own back will have a taste of the stick." Wang was of course unable to flee; however, he was not a bit afraid, and grasping a sword stood there in the middle of the boat. In a moment, the old man and boy arrived, also armed, and then Wang knew that the former was really his father, and called out to him at once, "Father, I am your son." The old man was greatly alarmed, but father and son forgot their troubles in the joy of meeting once again.

Meanwhile, the boy went back, and Wang's father bade him hide, or they would all be lost. The words were hardly out of his mouth when the three men jumped on board the boat. Their faces were black as pitch, their eyes as big as pomegranates, and they at once proceeded to seize the old man. Wang struggled hard with them, and managing to get the boat free from her moorings, he seized his sword and cut off one of his adversaries' arms. The arm dropped down and the man in the yellow dress ran away; whereupon one of those in white rushed at Wang who immediately cut off his head, and he fell into the water with a splash, at which the third disappeared. Wang and his father were now anxious to get away, when suddenly a great mouth arose from the lake, as big and as deep as a well, and against which they could hear the noise of the water when it struck. This mouth blew forth a violent gust of wind, and in a moment the waves were mountains high and all the boats on the lake were tossing about. The boatmen were terrified, but Wang seized one of two huge stones there were on board for use as anchors, about 130 lbs. in weight, and threw it into the water, which immediately began to subside; and then he threw in the other one, upon which the wind dropped, and the lake became calm again. Wang thought his father was a disembodied spirit, but the old man said, "I never died. There were nineteen of us drowned in the river, all of whom were eaten by the fish-goblins except myself: I was saved because I could play foot-ball. Those you saw got into trouble with the Dragon King, and were sent here. They were all marine creatures, and the ball they were playing with was a fish-bladder." Father and son were overjoyed at meeting again, and at once proceeded on their way. In the morning they found in the boat a huge fin—the arm that Wang had cut off the night before.

The Thunder God

Lê Yün-hao and Hsia P'ing-tzŭ lived as boys in the same village, and when they grew up read with the same tutor, becoming the firmest of friends. Hsia was a clever fellow, and had acquired some reputation even at the early age of ten. Lê was not a bit envious, but rather looked up to him, and Hsia in return helped his friend very much with his studies, so that he, too, made considerable progress. This increased Hsia's fame, though try as he would he could never succeed at the public examinations, and by-and-by he sickened and died. His family was so poor they could not find money for his burial, whereupon Lê came forward and paid all expenses, besides taking care of his widow and children.

Every peck or bushel he would share with them, the widow trusting entirely to his support; and thus he acquired a good name in the village, though not being a rich man himself he soon ran through all his own property. "Alas!" cried he, "where talents like Hsia's failed, can I expect to succeed? Wealth and rank are matters of destiny, and my present career will only end by my dying like a dog in a ditch. I must try something else." So he gave up book-learning and went into trade, and in six months he had a trifle of money in hand.

One day when he was resting at an inn in Nanking, he saw a great big fellow walk in and seat himself at no great distance in a very melancholy mood. Lê asked him if he was hungry, and on receiving no answer, pushed some food over toward him. The stranger immediately set to feeding himself by handfuls, and in no time the whole had disappeared. Lê ordered another supply, but that was quickly disposed of in like manner; and then he told the landlord to bring a shoulder of pork and a quantity of boiled dumplings. Thus, after eating enough for half a dozen, his appetite was appeased and he turned to thank his benefactor, saying, "For three years I haven't had such a meal."

"And why should a fine fellow like you be in such a state of destitution?" inquired Lê; to which the other only replied, "The judgments of heaven may not be discussed."

Being asked where he lived, the stranger replied, "On land I have no home, on the water no boat; at dawn in the village, at night in the city."

Lê then prepared to depart; but his friend would not leave him, declaring that he was in imminent danger, and that he could not forget the late kindness Lê had shown him. So they went along together, and on the way Lê invited the other to eat with him; but this he refused, saying that he only took food occasionally. Lê marveled more than ever at this; and next day when they were on the river a great storm arose and capsized all their boats, Lê himself being thrown into the water with the others. Suddenly the gale abated and the stranger bore Lê on his back to another boat, plunging at once into the water and bringing back the lost vessel, upon which he placed Lê and bade him remain quietly there. He then returned once more, this time carrying in his arms a part of the cargo, which he replaced in the vessel, and so he went on until it was all restored. Lê thanked him, saying, "It was enough to save my life; but you have added to this the restoration of my goods." Nothing, in fact, had been lost, and now Lê began to regard the stranger as something more than human. The latter here wished to take his leave, but Lê pressed him so much to stay that at last he consented to remain. Then Lê remarked that after all he had lost a gold pin, and immediately the stranger plunged into the water again, rising at length to the surface with the missing article in his mouth, and presenting it to Lê with the remark that he was delighted to be able to fulfill his commands. The people on the river were all much astonished at what they saw; meanwhile Lê went home with his friend, and there they lived together, the big man only eating once in ten or twelve days, but then displaying an enormous appetite.

One day he spoke of going away, to which Lê would by no means consent; and as it was just then about to rain and thunder, he asked him to tell him what the clouds were like, and what thunder was, also how he could get up to the sky and have a look, so as to set his mind at rest on the subject. "Would you like to have a ramble among the clouds?" asked the stranger, as Lê was lying down to take a nap; on awaking from which he felt himself spinning along through the air, and not at all as if he was lying on a bed. Opening his eyes he saw he was among the clouds, and around him was a fleecy atmosphere. Jumping up in great alarm, he felt giddy as if he had been at sea, and underneath his feet he found a soft, yielding substance, unlike the earth. Above him were the stars, and this made him think he was dreaming; but looking up he saw that they were set in the sky like seeds in the cup of a lily, varying from the size of the biggest bowl to that of a small basin. On raising his hand he discovered that the large stars were all tightly fixed; but he managed to pick a small one, which he concealed in his sleeve; and then, parting the clouds beneath him, he looked through and saw the sea glittering like silver below. Large cities appeared no bigger than beans—just at this moment, however, he bethought himself that if his foot were to slip, what a tremendous fall he would have. He now beheld two dragons writhing their way along, and drawing a cart with a huge vat in it, each movement of their tails sounding like the crack of a bullock-driver's whip. The vat was full of water, and numbers of men were employed in ladling it out and sprinkling it on the clouds. These men were astonished at seeing Lê; however, a big fellow among them called out, "All right, he's my friend," and then they gave him a ladle to help them throw the water out.

Now it happened to be a very dry season, and when Lê got hold of the ladle he took good care to throw the water so that it should all fall on and around his own home. The stranger then told him that he was the God of Thunder, and that he had just returned from a three years' punishment inflicted on him in consequence of some neglect of his in the matter of rain. He added that they must now part; and taking the long rope which had been used as reins for the cart, bade Lê grip it tightly, that he might be let down to earth. Lê was afraid of this, but on being told there was no danger he did so, and in a moment whish-h-h-h-h—away he went and found himself safe and sound on *terra firma*. He discovered that he had descended outside his native village, and then the rope was drawn up into the clouds and he saw it no more. The drought had been excessive; for three or four miles round very little rain had fallen, though in Lê's own village the water-courses were all full. On reaching home he took the star out of his sleeve, and put it on the table. It was dull-looking like an ordinary stone; but at night it became very brilliant and lighted up the whole house. This made him value it highly, and he stored it carefully away, bringing it out only when he had guests, to light them at their wine. It was always thus dazzlingly bright, until one evening when his wife was sitting with him doing her hair, the star began to diminish in brilliancy, and to flit about like a fire-fly. Mrs. Lê sat gaping with astonishment, when all of a sudden it flitted into her mouth and ran down her throat. She tried to cough it up but couldn't, to the very great amazement of her husband. That night Lê dreamt that his old friend Hsia appeared before him and said, "I am the Shao-wei star. Your friendship is still cherished by me, and now you have brought me back from the sky. Truly our destinies are knitted together, and I will repay your kindness by becoming your son." Now Lê was thirty years of age but without sons; however, after this dream his wife bore him a male child, and they called his name Star. He was extraordinarily clever, and at sixteen years of age took his master's degree.

The Gambler's Talisman

A Taoist priest, called Han, lived at the T'ien-ch'i temple, in our district city. His knowledge of the black art was very extensive, and the neighbors all regarded him as an Immortal. My late father was on intimate terms with him, and whenever he went into the city invariably paid him a visit. One day, on such an occasion, he was proceeding thither in company with my late uncle, when suddenly they met Han on the road. Handing them the key of the door, he begged them to go on and wait awhile for him, promising to be there shortly himself. Following out these instructions they repaired to the temple, but on unlocking the door there was Han sitting inside—a feat which he subsequently performed several times.

Now a relative of mine, who was terribly given to gambling, also knew this priest, having been introduced to him by my father. And once this relative, meeting with a Buddhist priest from the T'ien-fo temple, addicted like himself to the vice of gambling, played with him until he had lost everything, even going so far as to pledge the whole of his property, which he lost in a single night. Happening to call in upon Han as he was going back, the latter noticed his exceedingly dejected appearance, and the rambling answers he gave, and asked him what was the matter. On hearing the story of his losses, Han only laughed, and said, "That's what always overtakes the gambler, sooner or later; if, however, you will break yourself of the habit, I will get your money back for you."

"Ah," cried the other, "if you will only do that, you may break my head with a pestle when you catch me gambling again."

So Han gave him a talismanic formula, written out on a piece of paper, to put in his girdle, bidding him only win back what he had lost, and not attempt to get a fraction more. He also handed him 1000 *cash*, on condition that this sum should be repaid from his winnings, and off went my relative delighted. The Buddhist, however, turned up his nose at the smallness of his means, and said it wasn't worth his while to stake so little; but at last he was persuaded into having one throw for the whole lot. They then began, the priest leading off with a fair throw, to which his opponent replied by a better; whereupon the priest doubled his stake, and my relative won again, going on and on until the latter's good luck had brought him back all that he had previously lost. He thought, however, that he couldn't do better than just win a few more strings of cash, and accordingly went on; but gradually his luck turned, and on looking into his girdle he found that the talisman was gone. In a great fright he jumped up, and went off with his winnings to the temple, where he reckoned up that after deducting Han's loan, and adding what he had lost toward the end, he had exactly the amount originally his. With shame in his face he turned to thank Han, mentioning at the same time the loss of the talisman; at which Han only laughed, and said, "That has got back before you. I told you not to be over-greedy, and as you didn't heed me, I took the talisman away."

The Husband Punished

Ching Hsing, of Wên-têng, was a young fellow of some literary reputation, who lived next door to a Mr. Ch'ên, their studios being separated only by a low wall. One evening Ch'ên was crossing a piece of waste ground when he heard a young girl crying among some pine-trees hard by. He approached, and saw a girdle hanging from one of the branches, as if its owner was just on the point of hanging herself. Ch'ên asked her what was the matter, and then she brushed away her tears, and said, "My mother has gone away and left me in charge of my brother-in-law; but he's a scamp, and won't continue to take care of me; and now there is nothing left for me but to die." Hereupon the girl began crying again, and Ch'ên untied the girdle and bade her go and find herself a husband; to which she said there was very little chance of that; and then Ch'ên offered to take her to his own home—an offer which she very gladly accepted.

Soon after they arrived, his neighbor Ching thought he heard a noise, and jumped over the wall to have a peep, when lo and behold! at the door of Ch'ên's house stood this young lady, who immediately ran away into the garden on seeing Ching. The two young men pursued her, but without success, and were obliged to return each to his own room, Ching being greatly astonished to find the same girl now standing at his door. On addressing the young lady, she told him that his neighbor's destiny was too poor a one for her, and that she came from Shantung, and that her name was Ch'i A-hsia. She finally agreed to take up her residence with Ching; but after a few days, finding that a great number of his friends were constantly calling, she declared it was too noisy a place for her, and that she would only visit him in the evening. This she continued to do for a few days, telling him in reply to his inquiries that her home was not very far off.

One evening, however, she remarked that their present *liaison* was not very creditable to either; that her father was a mandarin on the western frontier, and that she was about to set out with her mother to join him; begging him meanwhile to make a formal request for the celebration of their nuptials, in order to prevent them from being thus separated. She further said that they started in ten days or so, and then Ching began to reflect that if he married her she would have to take her place in the family, and that would make his first wife jealous; so he determined to get rid of the latter, and when she came in he began to abuse her right and left. His wife bore it as long as she could, but at length cried out it were better she should die; upon which Ching advised her not to bring trouble on them all like that, but to go back to her own home. He then drove her away, his wife asking all the time what she had done to be sent away like this after ten years of blameless life with him. Ching, however, paid no heed to her entreaties, and when he had got rid of her he set to work at once to get the house whitewashed and made generally clean, himself being on the tip-toe of expectation for the arrival of Miss A-hsia. But he waited and waited, and no A-hsia came; she seemed gone like a stone dropped into the sea.

Meanwhile emissaries came from his late wife's family begging him to take her back; and when he flatly refused, she married a gentleman of position named Hsia, whose property adjoined Ching's, and who had long been at feud with him in consequence, as is usual in such cases. This made Ching furious, but he still hoped that A-hsia would come, and tried to console himself in this way. Yet more than a year passed away and still no signs of her, until one day, at the festival of the Sea Spirits, he saw among the crowds of girls passing in and out one who very much resembled A-hsia. Ching moved toward her, following her as she threaded her way through the crowd as far as the temple gate, where he lost sight of her altogether, to his great mortification and regret. Another six months passed away, when one day he met a young lady dressed in red, accompanied by an old man-servant, and riding on a black mule. It was A-hsia. So he asked the old man the name of his young mistress, and learnt from him that she was the second wife of a gentleman named Chêng, having been married to him about a fortnight previously. Ching now thought she could not be A-hsia, but just then the young lady, hearing them talking, turned her head, and Ching saw that he was right. And now, finding that she had actually married another man, he was overwhelmed with rage, and cried out in a loud voice, "A-hsia! A-hsia! why did you break faith?"

The servant here objected to his mistress being thus addressed by a stranger, and was squaring up to Ching, when A-hsia bade him desist; and, raising her veil, replied, "And you, faithless one, how do you dare meet my gaze?"

"You are the faithless one," said Ching, "not I."

"To be faithless to your wife is worse than being faithless to me," rejoined A-hsia; "if you behaved like that to her, how should I have been treated at your hands? Because of the fair fame of your ancestors, and the honors gained by them, I was willing to ally myself with you; but now that you have discarded your wife, your thread of official advancement has been cut short in the realms below, and Mr. Ch'ên is to take the place that should have been yours at the head of the examination list. As for myself, I am now part of the Chêng family; think no more of me."

Ching hung his head and could make no reply; and A-hsia whipped up her mule and disappeared from his sight, leaving him to return home disconsolate. At the forthcoming examination, everything turned out as she had predicted; Mr. Ch'ên was at the top of the list, and he himself was thrown out. It was clear that his luck was gone. At forty he had no wife, and was so poor that he was glad to pick up a meal where he could.

One day he called on Mr. Chêng, who treated him well and kept him there for the night; and while there Chêng's second wife saw him, and asked her husband if his guest's name wasn't Ching.

"It is," said he, "how could you guess that?"

"Well," replied she, "before I married you, I took refuge in his house, and he was then very kind to me. Although he has now sunk low, yet his ancestors' influence on the family fortunes is not yet exhausted; besides he is an old acquaintance of yours, and you should try and do something for him."

Chêng consented, and having first given him a new suit of clothes, kept him in the house several days. At night a slave-girl came to him with twenty ounces of silver for him, and Mrs. Chêng, who was outside the window, said, "This is a trifling return for your past kindness to me. Go and get yourself a good wife. The family luck is not yet exhausted, but will descend to your sons and grandchildren. Do not behave like this again, and so shorten your term of life."

Ching thanked her and went home, using ten ounces of silver to procure a concubine from a neighboring family, who was very ugly and ill-tempered. However, she bore him a son, and he by-and-by graduated as doctor. Mr. Chêng became

Vice-President of the Board of Civil Office, and at his death A-hsia attended the funeral; but when they opened her chair on its return home, she was gone, and then people knew for the first time that she was not mortal flesh and blood. Alas! for the perversity of mankind, rejecting the old and craving for the new? And then when they come back to the familiar nest, the birds have all flown. Thus does heaven punish such people.

The Marriage Lottery

A certain laborer's son, named Ma T'ien-jung, lost his wife when he was only about twenty years of age, and was too poor to take another. One day when out hoeing in the fields, he beheld a nice-looking young lady leave the path and come tripping across the furrows toward him. Her face was well painted, and she had altogether such a refined look that Ma concluded she must have lost her way, and began to make some playful remarks in consequence. "You go along home," cried the young lady, "and I'll be with you by-and-by." Ma doubted this rather extraordinary promise, but she vowed and declared she would not break her word; and then Ma went off, telling her that his front door faced the north, etc., etc.

In the evening the young lady arrived, and then Ma saw that her hands and face were covered with fine hair, which made him suspect at once she was a fox. She did not deny the accusation; and accordingly Ma said to her, "If you really are one of those wonderful creatures you will be able to get me anything I want; and I should be much obliged if you would begin by giving me some money to relieve my poverty." The young lady said she would; and next evening when she came again, Ma asked her where the money was. "Dear me!" replied she, "I quite forgot it." When she was going away, Ma reminded her of what he wanted, but on the following evening she made precisely the same excuse, promising to bring it another day.

A few nights afterward Ma asked her once more for the money, and then she drew from her sleeve two pieces of silver, each weighing about five or six ounces. They were both of fine quality, with turned-up edges, and Ma was very pleased and stored them away in a cupboard. Some months after this, he happened to require some money for use, and took out these pieces; but the person to whom he showed them said they were only pewter, and easily bit off a portion of one of them with his teeth. Ma was much alarmed, and put the pieces away directly; taking the opportunity when evening came of abusing the young lady roundly. "It's all your bad luck," retorted she; "real gold would be too much for your inferior destiny." There was an end of that; but Ma went on to say, "I always heard that fox-girls were of surpassing beauty; how is it you are not?"

"Oh," replied the young lady, "we always adapt ourselves to our company. Now you haven't the luck of an ounce of silver to call your own; and what would you do, for instance, with a beautiful princess? My beauty may not be good enough for the aristocracy; but among your big-footed, burden-carrying rustics, why it may safely be called 'surpassing.'"

A few months passed away, and then one day the young lady came and gave Ma three ounces of silver, saying, "You have often asked me for money, but in consequence of your weak luck I have always refrained from giving you any. Now, however, your marriage is at hand, and I here give you the cost of a wife, which you may also regard as a parting gift from me." Ma replied that he wasn't engaged, to which the young lady answered that in a few days a go-between would visit him to arrange the affair.

"And what will she be like?" asked Ma.

"Why, as your aspirations are for 'surpassing' beauty," replied the young lady, "of course she will be possessed of surpassing beauty."

"I hardly expect that," said Ma; "at any rate three ounces of silver will not be enough to get a wife."

"Marriages," explained the young lady, "are made in the moon; mortals have nothing to do with them."

"And why must you be going away like this?" inquired Ma.

"Because," answered she, "we go on shilly-shallying from day to day, and month to month, and nothing ever comes of it. I had better get you another wife and have done with you." Then when morning came, she departed, giving Ma a pinch of yellow powder, saying, "In case you are ill after we are separated, this will cure you."

Next day, sure enough, a go-between did come, and Ma at once asked what the proposed bride was like; to which the former replied that she was very passable-looking. Four or five ounces of silver was fixed as the marriage present, Ma making no difficulty on that score, but declaring he must have a peep at the young lady. The go-between said she was a respectable girl, and would never allow herself to be seen; however it was arranged that they should go to the house together, and await a good opportunity. So off they went, Ma remaining outside while the go-between went in, returning in a little while to tell him it was all right. "A relative of mine lives in the same court, and just now I saw the young lady sitting in the hall. We have only got to pretend we are going to see my relative, and you will be able to get a glimpse of her." Ma consented, and they accordingly passed through the hall, where he saw the young lady sitting down with her head bent forward while some one was scratching her back. She seemed to be all that the go-between had said; but when they came to discuss the money, it appeared the young lady only wanted one or two ounces of silver, just to buy herself a few clothes, etc., at which Ma was delighted, and gave the go-between a present for her trouble, which just finished up the three ounces his fox-friend had provided. An auspicious day was chosen, and the young lady came over to his house; when lo! she was hump-backed and pigeon-breasted, with a short neck like a tortoise, and boat-shaped feet, full ten inches long. The meaning of his fox-friend's remarks then flashed upon him.

The Lo-ch'a Country and the Sea-market

Once upon a time there was a young man, named Ma Chün, who was also known as Lung-mei. He was the son of a trader, and a youth of surpassing beauty. His manners were courteous, and he loved nothing better than singing and playing. He used to associate with actors, and with an embroidered handkerchief round his head the effect was that of a beautiful woman. Hence he acquired the sobriquet of the Beauty. At fourteen years of age he graduated and began to make a name for himself; but his father, who was growing old and wished to retire from business, said to him, "My boy, book-learning will never fill your belly or put a coat on your back; you had much better stick to the old thing." Accordingly, Ma from that time occupied himself with scales and weights, with principle and interest, and such matters.

He made a voyage across the sea, and was carried away by a typhoon. After being tossed about for many days and nights he arrived at a country where the people were hideously ugly. When these people saw Ma they thought he was a devil and all ran screeching away. Ma was somewhat alarmed at this, but finding that it was they who were frightened at him, he quickly turned their fear to his own advantage. If he came across people eating and drinking he would rush upon them, and when they fled away for fear, he would regale himself upon what they had left. By-and-by he went to a village among the hills, and there the people had at any rate some facial resemblance to ordinary men. But they were all in rags and tatters like beggars. So Ma sat down to rest under a tree, and the villagers, not daring to come near him, contented themselves with looking at him from a distance. They soon found, however, that he did not want to eat them, and by degrees approached a little closer to him. Ma, smiling, began to talk; and although their language was different, yet he was able to make himself tolerably intelligible, and told them whence he had come.

The villagers were much pleased, and spread the news that the stranger was not a man-eater. Nevertheless, the very ugliest of all would only take a look and be off again; they would not come near him. Those who did go up to him were not very much unlike his own countrymen, the Chinese. They brought him plenty of food and wine. Ma asked them what they were afraid of. They replied, "We had heard from our forefathers that 26,000 *li* to the west there is a country called China. We had heard that the people of that land were the most extraordinary in appearance you can possibly imagine. Hitherto it has been hearsay; we can now believe it." He then asked them how it was they were so poor. They answered, "You see, in our country everything depends, not on literary talent, but on beauty. The most beautiful are made ministers of state; the next handsomest are made judges and magistrates; and the third class in looks are employed in the palace of the king. Thus these are enabled out of their pay to provide for their wives and families. But we, from our very birth, are regarded by our parents as inauspicious, and are left to perish, some of us being occasionally preserved by more humane parents to prevent the extinction of the family."

Ma asked the name of their country, and they told him it was Lo-ch'a. Also that the capital city was some 30 *li* to the north. He begged them to take him there, and next day at cock-crow he started thitherward in their company, arriving just about dawn. The walls of the city were made of black stone, as black as ink, and the city gate-houses were about 100 feet high. Red stones were used for tiles, and picking up a broken piece Ma found that it marked his finger-nail like vermilion. They arrived just when the Court was rising, and saw all the equipages of the officials. The village people pointed out one who they said was Prime Minister. His ears drooped forward in flaps; he had three nostrils, and his eye-lashes were just like bamboo screens hanging in front of his eyes. Then several came out on horseback, and they said these were the privy councillors. So they went on, telling him the rank of all the ugly uncouth fellows he saw. The lower they got down in the official scale the less hideous the officials were.

By-and-by Ma went back, the people in the streets marveling very much to see him, and tumbling helter-skelter one over another as if they had met a goblin. The villagers shouted out to re-assure them, and then they stood at a distance to look at him. When he got back, there was not a man, woman, or child in the whole nation but knew that there was a strange man at the village; and the gentry and officials became very desirous to see him. However, if he went to any of their houses the porter always slammed the door in his face, and the master, mistress, and family, in general, would only peep at, and speak to him through the cracks. Not a single one dared receive him face to face; but, finally, the village people, at a loss what to do, bethought themselves of a man who had been sent by a former king on official business among strange nations. "He," said they, "having seen many kinds of men, will not be afraid of you."

So they went to his house, where they were received in a very friendly way. He seemed to be about eighty or ninety years of age; his eye-balls protruded, and his beard curled up like a hedge-hog. He said, "In my youth I was sent by the king among many nations, but I never went to China. I am now one hundred and twenty years of age, and that I should be permitted to see a native of your country is a fact which it will be my duty to report to the Throne. For ten years and more I have not been to Court, but have remained here in seclusion; yet I will now make an effort on your behalf."

Then followed a banquet, and when the wine had already circulated pretty freely, some dozen singing girls came in and sang and danced before them. The girls all wore white embroidered turbans, and long scarlet robes which trailed on the ground. The words they uttered were unintelligible, and the tunes they played perfectly hideous. The host, however, seemed to enjoy it very much, and said to Ma, "Have you music in China?" He replied that they had, and the old man asked for a specimen. Ma hummed him a tune, beating time on the table, with which he was very much pleased, declaring that his guest had the voice of a phoenix and the notes of a dragon, such as he had never heard before.

The next day he presented a memorial to the Throne, and the king at once commanded Ma to appear before him. Several of the ministers, however, represented that his appearance was so hideous it might frighten His Majesty, and the king accordingly desisted from his intention. The old man returned and told Ma, being quite upset about it. They remained together some time until they had drunk themselves tipsy. Then Ma, seizing a sword, began to attitudinize, smearing his face all over with coal-dust. He acted the part of Chang Fei, at which his host was so delighted that he begged him to appear before the Prime Minister in the character of Chang Fei. Ma replied, "I don't mind a little amateur acting, but how can I play the hypocrite for my own personal advantage?" On being pressed he consented, and the old man prepared a great feast, and asked some of the high officials to be present, telling Ma to paint himself as before. When the guests had arrived, Ma was brought out to see them; whereupon they all exclaimed, "Ai-yah! how is it he was so ugly before and is now so beautiful?"

By-and-by, when they were all taking wine together, Ma began to sing them a most bewitching song, and they got so excited over it that next day they recommended him to the king. The king sent a special summons for him to appear, and asked him many questions about the government of China, to all of which Ma replied in detail, eliciting sighs of admiration from His Majesty. He was honored with a banquet in the royal guest-pavilion, and when the king had made himself tipsy he said to him, "I hear you are a very skillful musician. Will you be good enough to let me hear you?" Ma then got up and began to attitudinize, singing a plaintive air like the girls with the turbans. The king was charmed, and at once made him a privy councillor, giving him a private banquet, and bestowing other marks of royal favor.

As time went on his fellow-officials found out the secret of his painted face, and whenever he was among them they were always whispering together, besides which they avoided being near him as much as possible. Thus Ma was left to himself, and found his position anything but pleasant in consequence. So he memorialized the Throne, asking to be allowed to retire from office, but his request was refused. He then said his health was bad, and got three months' sick leave, during which he packed up his valuables and went back to the village. The villagers on his arrival went down on their knees to him, and he distributed gold and jewels among his old friends. They were very glad to see him, and said, "Your kindness shall be repaid when we go to the sea-market; we will bring you some pearls and things." Ma asked them where that was. They said it was at the bottom of the sea, where the mermaids kept their treasures, and that as many as twelve nations were accustomed to go thither to trade. Also that it was frequented by spirits, and that to get there it was necessary to pass through red vapors and great waves. "Dear Sir," they said, "do not yourself risk this great danger, but let us take your money and purchase these rare pearls for you. The season is now at hand." Ma asked them how they knew this. They said, "Whenever we see red birds flying backward and forward over the sea, we know that within seven days the market will open." He asked when they were going to start, that he might accompany them; but they begged him not to think of doing so. He replied, "I am a sailor: how can I be afraid of wind and waves?" Very soon after this people came with merchandise to forward, and so Ma packed up and went on board the vessel that was going.

This vessel held some tens of people, was flat-bottomed with a railing all round, and, rowed by ten men, it cut through the water like an arrow. After a voyage of three days they saw afar off faint outlines of towers and minarets, and crowds of trading vessels. They soon arrived at the city, the walls of which were made of bricks as long as a man's body, the tops of its buildings being lost in the Milky Way. Having made fast their boat they went in, and saw laid out in the market rare pearls and wondrous precious stones of dazzling beauty, such as are quite unknown among men. Then they saw a young man come forth riding upon a beautiful steed. The people of the market stood back to let him pass, saying he was the third son of the king; but when the Prince saw Ma, he exclaimed, "This is no foreigner," and immediately an attendant drew near and asked his name and country. Ma made a bow, and standing at one side told his name and family. The prince smiled, and said, "For you to have honored our country thus is no small piece of good luck." He then gave him a horse and begged him to follow. They went out of the city gate and down to the sea-shore, whereupon their horses plunged into the water. Ma was terribly frightened and screamed out; but the sea opened dry before them and formed a wall of water on either side.

In a little time they reached the king's palace, the beams of which were made of tortoise-shell and the tiles of fishes' scales. The four walls were of crystal, and dazzled the eye like mirrors. They got down off their horses and went in, and Ma was introduced to the king. The young prince said, "Sire, I have been to the market, and have got a gentleman from China." Whereupon Ma made obeisance before the king, who addressed him as follows:—"Sir, from a talented scholar like yourself I venture to ask for a few stanzas upon our sea-market. Pray do not refuse." Ma thereupon made a *kot'ow* and undertook the king's command. Using an ink-slab of crystal, a brush of dragon's beard, paper as white as snow, and ink scented like the larkspur, Ma immediately threw off some thousand odd verses, which he laid at the feet of the king. When His Majesty saw them, he said, "Sir, your genius does honor to these marine nations of ours." Then, summoning the members of the royal family, the king gave a great feast in the Colored Cloud pavilion; and, when the wine had circulated freely, seizing a great goblet in his hand, the king rose and said before all the guests, "It is a thousand pities, Sir, that you are not married. What say you to entering the bonds of wedlock?" Ma rose blushing, and stammered out his thanks; upon which the king looking round spoke a few words to the attendants, and in a few moments in came a bevy of court ladies supporting the king's daughter, whose ornaments went tinkle, tinkle, as she walked along. Immediately the nuptial drums and trumpets began to sound forth, and bride and bridegroom worshipped Heaven and Earth together. Stealing a glance Ma saw that the princess was endowed with a fairy-like loveliness. When the ceremony was over she retired, and by-and-by the wine-party broke up. Then came several beautifully-dressed waiting-maids, who with painted candles escorted Ma within. The bridal couch was made of coral adorned with eight kinds of precious stones, and the curtains were thickly hung with pearls as big as acorns. Next day at dawn a crowd of young slave-girls trooped into the room to offer their services; whereupon Ma got up and went off to Court to pay his respects to the king. He was then duly received as royal son-in-law and made an officer of state.

The fame of his poetical talents spread far and wide, and the kings of the various seas sent officers to congratulate him, vying with each other in their invitations to him.

Ma dressed himself in gorgeous clothes, and went forth riding on a superb steed, with a mounted body-guard all splendidly armed. There were musicians on horseback and musicians in chariots, and in three days he had visited every one of the marine kingdoms, making his name known in all directions. In the palace there was a jade tree, about as big round as a man could clasp. Its roots were as clear as glass, and up the middle ran, as it were, a stick of pale yellow. The branches were the size of one's arm; the leaves like white jade, as thick as a copper cash. The foliage was dense, and beneath its shade the ladies of the palace were wont to sit and sing. The flowers which covered the tree resembled grapes, and if a single petal fell to the earth it made a ringing sound. Taking one up, it would be found to be exactly like carved cornelian, very bright and pretty to look at. From time to time a wonderful bird came and sang there. Its feathers were of a golden hue, and its tail as long as its body. Its notes were like the tinkling of jade, very plaintive and touching to listen to. When Ma heard this bird sing, it called up in him recollections of his old home, and accordingly he said to the princess, "I have now been away from my own country for three years, separated from my father and mother. Thinking of them my tears flow and the perspiration runs down my back. Can you return with me?" His wife replied, "The way of immortals is not that of men. I am unable to do what you ask, but I cannot allow the feelings of husband and wife to break the tie of parent and child. Let us devise some plan." When Ma heard this he wept bitterly, and the princess sighed and said, "We cannot both stay or both go."

The next day the king said to him, "I hear that you are pining after your old home. Will to-morrow suit you for taking leave?" Ma thanked the king for his great kindness, which he declared he could never forget, and promised to return very shortly. That evening the princess and Ma talked over their wine of their approaching separation. Ma said they would soon meet again; but his wife averred that their married life was at an end. Then he wept afresh, but the princess said, "Like a filial son you are going home to your parents. In the meetings and separations of this life, a hundred years seem but a single day; why, then, should we give way to tears like children? I will be true to you; do you be faithful to me; and then, though separated, we shall be united in spirit, a happy pair. Is it necessary to live side by side in order to grow old together? If you break our contract your next marriage will not be a propitious one; but if loneliness overtakes you then choose a concubine. There is one point more of which I would speak, with reference to our married life. I am about to become a mother, and I pray you give me a name for your child." To this Ma replied, "If a girl I would have her called Lung-kung; if a boy, then name him Fu-hai." The princess asked for some token of remembrance, and Ma gave her a pair of jade lilies that he had got during his stay in the marine kingdom. She added, "On the 8th of the 4th moon, three years hence, when you once more steer your course for this country, I will give you up your child." She next packed a leather bag full of jewels and handed it to Ma, saying, "Take care of this; it will be a provision for many generations." When the day began to break a splendid farewell feast was given him by the king, and Ma bade them all adieu. The princess, in a car drawn by snow-white sheep, escorted him to the boundary of the marine kingdom, where he dismounted and stepped ashore. "Farewell!" cried the princess, as her returning car bore her rapidly away, and the sea, closing over her, snatched her from her husband's sight.

Ma returned to his home across the ocean. Some had thought him long since dead and gone; all marveled at his story. Happily his father and mother were yet alive, though his former wife had married another man; and so he understood why the princess had pledged him to constancy, for she already knew that this had taken place. His father wished him to take another wife, but he would not. He only took a concubine. Then, after the three years had passed away, he started across the sea on his return journey, when lo! he beheld, riding on the wave-crests and splashing about the water in playing, two young children. On going near, one of them seized hold of him and sprung into his arms; upon which the elder cried until he, too, was taken up. They were a boy and girl, both very lovely, and wearing embroidered caps adorned with jade lilies. On the back of one of them was a worked case, in which Ma found the following letter:—

"I presume my father and mother-in-law are well. Three years have passed away and destiny still keeps us apart. Across the great ocean, the letter-bird would find no path. I have been with you in my dreams until I am quite worn out. Does the blue sky look down upon any grief like mine? Yet Ch'ang-ngo lives solitary in the moon, and Chih Nü laments that she cannot cross the Silver River. Who am I that I should expect happiness to be mine? Truly this thought turns my tears into joy. Two months after your departure I had twins, who can already prattle away in the language of childhood, at one moment snatching a date, at another a pear. Had they no mother they would still live. These I now send to you, with the jade lilies you gave me in their hats, in token of the sender. When you take them upon your knee, think that I am standing by your side. I know that you have kept your promise to me, and I am happy. I shall take no second husband, even unto death. All thoughts of dress and finery are gone from me; my looking-glass sees no new fashions; my face has long been unpowdered, my eyebrows unblacked. You are my Ulysses, I am your Penelope; though not actually leading a married life, how can it be said that we are not husband and wife. Your father and mother will take their grandchildren upon their knees, though they have never set eyes upon the bride. Alas! there is something wrong in this. Next year your mother will enter upon the long night. I shall be there by the side of the grave as is becoming in her daughter-in-law. From this time forth our daughter will be well; later on she will be able to grasp her mother's hand. Our boy, when he grows up, may possibly be able to come to and fro. Adieu, dear husband, adieu, though I am leaving much unsaid."

Ma read the letter over and over again, his tears flowing all the time. His two children clung round his neck, and begged him to take them home. "Ah, my children," said he, "where is your home?" Then they all wept bitterly, and Ma, looking at the great ocean stretching away to meet the sky, lovely and pathless, embraced his children, and proceeded sorrowfully to return. Knowing, too, that his mother could not last long, he prepared everything necessary for the ceremony of interment, and planted a hundred young pine-trees at her grave.

The following year the old lady did die, and her coffin was borne to its last resting-place, when lo! there was the princess standing by the side of the grave. The lookers-on were much alarmed, but in a moment there was a flash of lightning, followed by a clap of thunder and a squall of rain, and she was gone. It was then noticed that many of the young pine-trees which had died were one and all brought to life. Subsequently, Fu-hai went in search of the mother for whom he pined so much, and after some days' absence returned. Lung-kung, being a girl, could not accompany him, but she mourned much in secret.

One dark day her mother entered and bid her dry her eyes, saying, "My child, you must get married. Why these tears?" She then gave her a tree of coral eight feet in height, some Baroos camphor, one hundred valuable pearls, and two boxes inlaid with gold and precious stones, as her dowry. Ma having found out she was there, rushed in and seizing her hand began to weep for joy, when suddenly a violent peal of thunder rent the building, and the princess had vanished.

The Fighting Cricket

During the reign of Hsüan Tê, cricket fighting was very much in vogue at court, levies of crickets being exacted from the people as a tax. On one occasion the magistrate of Hua-yin, wishing to make friends with the Governor, presented him with a cricket which, on being set to fight, displayed very remarkable powers; so much so that the Governor commanded the magistrate to supply him regularly with these insects. The latter, in his turn, ordered the beadles of his district to provide him with crickets; and then it became a practice for people who had nothing else to do to catch and rear them for this purpose. Thus the price of crickets rose very high; and when the beadle's runners came to exact even a single one, it was enough to ruin several families.

Now in the village of which we are speaking there lived a man named Ch'êng, a student who had often failed for his bachelor's degree; and, being a stupid sort of fellow, his name was sent in for the post of beadle. He did all he could to get out of it, but without success; and by the end of the year his small patrimony was gone. Just then came a call for crickets, and Ch'êng, not daring to make a like call upon his neighbors, was at his wits' end, and in his distress determined to commit suicide. "What's the use of that?" cried his wife. "You'd do better to go out and try to find some." So off went Ch'êng in the early morning, with a bamboo tube and a silk net, not returning till late at night; and he searched about in tumble-down walls, in bushes, under stones, and in holes, but without catching more than two or three, do what he would. Even those he did catch were weak creatures, and of no use at all, which made the magistrate fix a limit of time, the result of which was that in a few days Ch'êng got one hundred blows with the bamboo. This made him so sore that he was quite unable to go after the crickets any more, and, as he lay tossing and turning on the bed, he determined once again to put an end to his life.

About that time a hump-backed fortune-teller of great skill arrived at the village, and Ch'êng's wife, putting together a trifle of money, went off to seek his assistance. The door was literally blocked up—fair young girls and white-headed dames crowding in from all quarters. A room was darkened, and a bamboo screen hung at the door, an altar being arranged outside at which the fortune-seekers burned incense in a brazier, and prostrated themselves twice, while the soothsayer stood by the side, and, looking up into vacancy, prayed for a response. His lips opened and shut, but nobody heard what he said, all standing there in awe waiting for the answer. In a few moments a piece of paper was thrown from behind the screen, and the soothsayer said that the petitioner's desire would be accomplished in the way he wished. Ch'êng's wife now advanced, and, placing some money on the altar, burned her incense and prostrated herself in a similar manner. In a few moments the screen began to move, and a piece of paper was thrown down, on which there were no words, but only a picture. In the middle was a building like a temple, and behind this a small hill, at the foot of which were a number of curious stones, with the long, spiky feelers of innumerable crickets appearing from behind. Hard by was a frog, which seemed to be engaged in putting itself into various kinds of attitudes. The good woman had no idea what it all meant; but she noticed the crickets, and accordingly went off home to tell her husband. "Ah," said he, "this is to show me where to hunt for crickets"; and, on looking closely at the picture, he saw that the building very much resembled a temple to the east of their village. So he forced himself to get up, and, leaning on a stick, went out to seek crickets behind the temple. Rounding an old grave, he came upon a place where stones were lying scattered about as in the picture, and then he set himself to watch attentively. He might as well have been looking for a needle or a grain of mustard-seed; and by degrees he became quite exhausted, without finding anything, when suddenly an old frog jumped out. Ch'êng was a little startled, but immediately pursued the frog, which retreated into the bushes. He then saw one of the insects he wanted sitting at the root of a bramble; but on making a grab at it, the cricket ran into a hole, from which he was unable to move it until he poured in some water, when out the little creature came. It was a magnificent specimen, strong and handsome, with a fine tail, green neck, and golden wings; and, putting it in his basket, he returned home in high glee to receive the congratulations of his family. He would not have taken anything for this cricket, and proceeded to feed it up carefully in a bowl. Its belly was the color of a crab's, its back that of a sweet chestnut; and Ch'êng tended it most lovingly, waiting for the time when the magistrate should call upon him for a cricket.

Meanwhile, a son of Ch'êng's, aged nine, one day took the opportunity of his father being out to open the bowl. Instantaneously the cricket made a spring forward and was gone; and all efforts to catch it again were unavailing. At length the boy made a grab at it with his hand, but only succeeded in seizing one of its legs, which thereupon broke, and the little creature soon afterward died. Ch'êng's wife turned deadly pale when her son, with tears in his eyes, told her what had happened. "Oh! won't you catch it when your father comes home," said she; at which the boy ran away, crying bitterly. Soon after Ch'êng arrived, and when he heard his wife's story he felt as if he had been turned to ice, and went in search of his son, who, however, was nowhere to be found, until at length they discovered his body lying at the bottom of a well. Their anger was thus turned to grief, and death seemed as though it would be a pleasant relief to them as they sat facing each other in silence in their thatched and smokeless hut.

At evening they prepared to bury the boy; but, on touching the body, lo! he was still breathing. Overjoyed, they placed him upon the bed, and towards the middle of the night he came round; but a drop of bitterness was mingled in his parents' cup when they found that his reason had fled. His father, however, caught sight of the empty bowl in which he had kept the cricket, and ceased to think any more about his son, never once closing his eyes all night; and as day gradually broke, there he lay stiff and stark, until suddenly he heard the chirping of a cricket outside the house door.

Jumping up in a great hurry to see, there was his lost insect; but, on trying to catch it, away it hopped directly. At last he got it under his hand, though, when he came to close his fingers on it, there was nothing in them. So he went on, chasing it up and down, until finally it hopped into a corner of the wall; and then, looking carefully about, he espied it once more, no longer the same in appearance, but small, and of a dark red color. Ch'êng stood looking at it, without trying to catch such a worthless specimen, when all of a sudden the little creature hopped into his sleeve; and, on examining it more nearly, he saw that it really was a handsome insect, with well-formed head and neck, and forthwith took it indoors.

He was now anxious to try its prowess; and it so happened that a young fellow of the village, who had a fine cricket which used to win every bout it fought, and was so valuable to him that he wanted a high price for it, called on Ch'êng that very day. He laughed heartily at Ch'êng's champion, and, producing his own, placed it side by side, to the great disadvantage of the former. Ch'êng's countenance fell, and he no longer wished to back his cricket; however, the young fellow urged him, and he thought that there was no use in rearing a feeble insect, and that he had better sacrifice it for a laugh; so they put them together in a bowl. The little cricket lay quite still like a piece of wood, at which the young fellow roared again, and louder than ever when it did not move even though tickled with a pig's bristle. By dint of tickling it was roused at last, and then it fell upon its adversary with such fury, that in a moment the young fellow's cricket would have been killed outright had not its master interfered and stopped the fight. The little cricket then stood up and chirped to Ch'êng as a sign of victory; and Ch'êng, overjoyed, was just talking over the battle with the young fellow, when a cock caught sight of the insect, and ran up to eat it. Ch'êng was in a great state of alarm; but the cock luckily missed its aim, and the cricket hopped away, its enemy pursuing at full speed. In another moment it would have been snapped up, when, lo! to his great astonishment, Ch'êng saw his cricket seated on the cock's head, holding firmly on to its comb. He then put it into a cage, and by-and-by sent it to the magistrate, who, seeing what a small one he had provided, was very angry indeed. Ch'êng told the story of the cock, which the magistrate refused to believe, and set it to fight with other crickets, all of which it vanquished without exception. He then tried it with a cock, and as all turned out as Ch'êng had said, he gave him a present, and sent the cricket in to the Governor. The Governor put it into a golden cage, and forwarded it to the palace, accompanied by some remarks on its performances; and when there, it was found that of all the splendid collection of His Imperial Majesty, not one was worthy to be placed alongside of this one. It would dance in time to music, and thus became a great favorite, the Emperor in return bestowing magnificent gifts of horses and silks upon the Governor. The Governor did not forget whence he had obtained the cricket, and the magistrate also well rewarded Ch'êng by excusing him from the duties of beadle, and by instructing the Literary Chancellor to pass him for the first degree. A few months afterward Ch'êng's son recovered his intellect, and said that he had been a cricket, and had proved himself a very skillful fighter. The Governor, too, rewarded Ch'êng handsomely, and in a few years he was a rich man, with flocks, and herds, and houses, and acres, quite one of the wealthiest of mankind.

Taking Revenge

HSIANG KAO, OTHERWISE CALLED CH'U-TAN, WAS A T'AI-YÜAN MAN, AND DEEPLY attached to his half-brother Shêng. Shêng himself was desperately enamoured of a young lady named Po-ssŭ, who was also very fond of him: but the mother wanted too much money for her daughter. Now a rich young fellow named Chuang thought he should like to get Po-ssŭ for himself, and proposed to buy her as a concubine. "No, no," said Po-ssŭ to her mother, "I prefer being Shêng's wife to becoming Chuang's concubine." So her mother consented, and informed Shêng, who had only recently buried his first wife; at which he was delighted and made preparations to take her over to his own house.

When Chuang heard this he was infuriated against Shêng for thus depriving him of Po-ssŭ; and chancing to meet him out one day, set to and abused him roundly. Shêng answered him back, and then Chuang ordered his attendants to fall upon Shêng and beat him well, which they did, leaving him lifeless on the ground. When Hsiang heard what had taken place he ran out and found his brother lying dead upon the ground. Overcome with grief, he proceeded to the magistrate's, and accused Chuang of murder; but the latter bribed so heavily that nothing came of the accusation. This worked Hsiang to frenzy, and he determined to assassinate Chuang on the high road; with which intent he daily concealed himself, with a sharp knife about him, among the bushes on the hill-side, waiting for Chuang to pass.

By degrees, this plan of his became known far and wide, and accordingly Chuang never went out except with a strong body-guard, besides which he engaged at a high price the services of a very skillful archer, named Chiao T'ung, so that Hsiang had no means of carrying out his intention. However, he continued to lie in wait day after day, and on one occasion it began to rain heavily, and in a short time Hsiang was wet through to the skin. Then the wind got up, and a hailstorm followed, and by-and-by

Hsiang was quite numbed with the cold. On the top of the hill there was a small temple wherein lived a Taoist priest, whom Hsiang knew from the latter having occasionally begged alms in the village, and to whom he had often given a meal. This priest, seeing how wet he was, gave him some other clothes, and told him to put them on; but no sooner had he done so than he crouched down like a dog, and found that he had been changed into a tiger, and that the priest had vanished. It now occurred to him to seize this opportunity of revenging himself upon his enemy; and away he went to his old ambush, where lo and behold! he found his own body lying stiff and stark. Fearing lest it should become food for birds of prey, he guarded it carefully, until at length one day Chuang passed by. Out rushed the tiger and sprung upon Chuang, biting his head off, and swallowing it upon the spot; at which Chiao T'ung, the archer, turned round and shot the animal through the heart.

Just at that moment Hsiang awaked as though from a dream, but it was some time before he could crawl home, where he arrived to the great delight of his family, who didn't know what had become of him. Hsiang said not a word, lying quietly on the bed until some of his people came in to congratulate him on the death of his great enemy Chuang. Hsiang then cried out, "I was that tiger," and proceeded to relate the whole story, which thus got about until it reached the ears of Chuang's son, who immediately set to work to bring his father's murderer to justice. The magistrate, however, did not consider this wild story as sufficient evidence against him, and thereupon dismissed the case.

The Tipsy Turtle

At Lin-t'iao there lived a Mr. Fêng, whose other name the person who told me this story could not remember; he belonged to a good family, though now somewhat falling into decay. Now a certain man, who caught turtles, owed him some money which he could not pay, but whenever he captured any turtles he used to send one to Mr. Fêng. One day he took him an enormous creature, with a white spot on its forehead; but Fêng was so struck with something in its appearance, that he let it go again. A little while afterward he was returning home from his son-in-law's, and had reached the banks of the river, when in the dusk of the evening he saw a drunken man come rolling along, attended by two or three servants. No sooner did he perceive Fêng than he called out, "Who are you?" to which Fêng replied that he was a traveler. "And haven't you got a name?" shouted out the drunken man in a rage, "that you must call yourself a traveler?" To this Fêng made no reply, but tried to pass by; whereupon he found himself seized by the sleeve and unable to move. His adversary smelled horribly of wine, and at length Fêng asked him, saying, "And pray who are you?"

"Oh, I am the late magistrate at Nan-tu," answered he; "what do you want to know for?"

"A nice disgrace to society you are, too," cried Fêng; "however, I am glad to hear you are only *late* magistrate, for if you had been present magistrate there would be bad times in store for travelers." This made the drunken man furious, and he was proceeding to use violence, when Fêng cried out, "My name is So-and-so, and I'm not the man to stand this sort of thing from anybody."

No sooner had he uttered these words than the drunken man's rage was turned into joy, and, falling on his knees before Fêng, he said, "My benefactor! pray excuse my rudeness." Then getting up, he told his servants to go on ahead and get something ready; Fêng at first declining to go with him, but yielding on being pressed. Taking his hand, the drunken man led him along a short distance until they reached a village, where there was a very nice house and grounds, quite like the establishment of a person of position. As his friend was now getting sober, Fêng inquired what might be his name.

"Don't be frightened when I tell you," said the other; "I am the Eighth Prince of the T'iao river. I have just been out to take wine with a friend, and somehow I got tipsy; hence my bad behavior to you, which please forgive." Fêng now knew that he was not of mortal flesh and blood; but, seeing how kindly he himself was treated, he was not a bit afraid. A banquet followed, with plenty of wine, of which the Eighth Prince drank so freely that Fêng thought he would soon be worse than ever, and accordingly said he felt tipsy himself, and asked to be allowed to go to bed.

"Never fear," answered the Prince, who perceived Fêng's thoughts; "many drunkards will tell you that they cannot remember in the morning the extravagances of the previous night, but I tell you this is all nonsense, and that in nine cases out of ten those extravagances are committed wittingly and with malice prepense. Now, though I am not the same order of being as yourself, I should never venture to behave badly in your good presence; so pray do not leave me thus."

Fêng then sat down again and said to the Prince, "Since you are aware of this, why not change your ways?"

"Ah," replied the Prince, "when I was a magistrate I drank much more than I do now; but I got into disgrace with the Emperor and was banished here, since which time, ten years and more, I have tried to reform. Now, however, I am drawing near the wood, and being unable to move about much, the old vice has come upon me again; I have found it impossible to stop myself, but perhaps what you say may do me some good."

While they were thus talking, the sound of a distant bell broke upon their ears; and the Prince, getting up and seizing Fêng's hand, said, "We cannot remain together any longer; but I will give you something by which I may in part requite your kindness to me. It must not be kept for any great length of time; when you have attained your wishes, then I will receive it back again." Thereupon he spit out of his mouth a tiny man, no more than an inch high, and scratching Fêng's arm with his nails until Fêng felt as if the skin was gone, he quickly laid the little man upon the spot. When he let go, the latter had already sunk into the skin, and nothing was to be seen but a cicatrix well healed over. Fêng now asked what it all meant, but the Prince only laughed, and said, "It's time for you to go," and forthwith escorted him to the door. The prince here bade him adieu, and when he looked round, Prince, village, and house had all disappeared together, leaving behind a great turtle which waddled down into the water, and disappeared likewise.

He could now easily account for the Prince's present to him; and from this moment his sight became intensely keen. He could see precious stones lying in the bowels of the earth, and was able to look down as far as Hell itself; besides which he suddenly found that he knew the names of many things of which he had never heard before. From below his own bedroom he dug up many hundred ounces of pure silver, upon which he lived very comfortably; and once when a house was for sale, he perceived that in it lay concealed a vast quantity of gold, so he immediately bought it, and so became immensely rich in all kinds of valuables. He secured a mirror, on the back of which was a phoenix, surrounded by water and clouds, and portraits of the celebrated wives of the Emperor Shun, so beautifully executed that each hair of the head and eyebrows could easily be counted. If any woman's face came upon the mirror, there it remained indelibly fixed and not to be rubbed out; but if the same woman looked into the mirror again, dressed in a different dress, or if some other woman chanced to look in, then the former face would gradually fade away.

Now the third princess in Prince Su's family was very beautiful; and Fêng, who had long heard of her fame, concealed himself on the K'ung-tung hill, when he knew the Princess was going there. He waited until she alighted from her chair, and then getting the mirror full upon her, he walked off home. Laying it on the table, he saw therein a lovely girl in the act of raising her handkerchief, and with a sweet smile playing over her face; her lips seemed about to move, and a twinkle was discernible in her eyes. Delighted with this picture, he put the mirror very carefully away; but in about a year his wife had let the story leak out, and the Prince, hearing of it, threw Fêng into prison, and took possession of the mirror. Fêng was to be beheaded; however, he bribed one of the Prince's ladies to tell His Highness that if he would pardon him all the treasures of the earth might easily become his; whereas, on the other hand, his death could not possibly be of any advantage to the Prince. The Prince now thought of confiscating all his goods and banishing him; but the third princess observed, that as he had already seen her, were he to die ten times over it would not give her back her lost face, and that she had much better marry him. The Prince would not hear of this, whereupon his daughter shut herself up and refused all nourishment, at which the ladies of the palace were dreadfully alarmed, and reported it at once to the Prince. Fêng was accordingly liberated, and was informed of the determination of the Princess, which, however, he declined to fall in with, saying that he was not going thus to sacrifice the wife of his days of poverty, and would rather die than carry out such an order. He added that if His Highness would consent, he would purchase his liberty at the price of everything he had. The Prince was exceedingly angry at this, and seized Fêng again; and meanwhile one of the concubines got Fêng's wife into the palace, intending to poison her. Fêng's wife, however, brought her a beautiful present of a coral stand for a looking-glass, and was so agreeable in her conversation, that the concubine took a great fancy to her, and presented her to the Princess, who was equally pleased, and forthwith determined that they would both be Fêng's wives. When Fêng heard of this plan, he said to his wife, "With a Prince's daughter there can be no distinctions of first and second wife"; but Mrs. Fêng paid no heed to him, and immediately sent off to the Prince such an enormous quantity of valuables that it took a thousand men to carry them, and the Prince himself had never before heard of such treasures in his life. Fêng was now liberated once more, and solemnized his marriage with the Princess.

One night after this he dreamt that the Eighth Prince came to him and asked him to return his former present, saying that to keep it too long would be injurious to his chances of life. Fêng asked him to take a drink, but the Eighth Prince said that he had forsworn wine, acting under Fêng's advice, for three years. He then bit Fêng's arm, and the latter waked up with the pain to find that the cicatrix on his arm was no longer there.

The Magic Path

In the province of Kuangtung there lived a scholar named Kuo, who was one evening on his way home from a friend's, when he lost his way among the hills. He got into a thick jungle, where, after about an hour's wandering, he suddenly heard the sound of laughing and talking on the top of the hill. Hurrying up in the direction of the sound, he beheld some ten or a dozen persons sitting on the ground engaged in drinking. No sooner had they caught sight of Kuo than they all cried out, "Come along! just room for one more; you're in the nick of time." So Kuo sat down with the company, most of whom, he noticed, belonged to the literati, and began by asking them to direct him on his way home; but one of them cried out, "A nice sort of fellow you are, to be bothering about your way home, and paying no attention to the fine moon we have got to-night." The speaker then presented him with a goblet of wine of exquisite bouquet, which Kuo drank off at a draught, and another gentleman filled up again for him at once.

Now, Kuo was pretty good in that line, and being very thirsty withal from his long walk, tossed off bumper after bumper, to the great delight of his hosts, who were unanimous in voting him a jolly good fellow. He was, moreover, full of fun, and could imitate exactly the note of any kind of bird; so all of a sudden he began on the sly to twitter like a swallow, to the great astonishment of the others, who wondered how it was a swallow could be out so late. He then changed his note to that of a cuckoo, sitting there laughing and saying nothing, while his hosts were discussing the extraordinary sounds they had just heard. After a while he imitated a parrot, and cried, "Mr. Kuo is very drunk: you'd better see him home"; and then the sounds ceased, beginning again by-and-by, when at last the others found out who it was, and all burst out laughing. They screwed up their mouths and tried to whistle like Kuo, but none of them could do so; and soon one of them observed, "What a pity Madam Ch'ing isn't with us: we must rendezvous here again at mid-autumn, and you, Mr. Kuo, must be sure and come." Kuo said he would, whereupon another of his hosts got up and remarked that, as he had given them such an amusing entertainment, they would try to show him a few acrobatic feats. They all arose, and one of them planting his feet firmly, a second jumped up on to his shoulders, a third on to the second's shoulders, and a fourth on to his, until it was too high for the rest to jump up, and accordingly they began to climb as though it had been a ladder. When they were all up, and the topmost head seemed to touch the clouds, the whole column bent gradually down until it lay along the ground transformed into a path.

Kuo remained for some time in a state of considerable alarm, and then, setting out along this path, ultimately reached his own home. Some days afterward he revisited the spot, and saw the remains of a feast lying about on the ground, with dense bushes on all sides, but no sign of a path. At mid-autumn he thought of keeping his engagement; however, his friends persuaded him not to go.

The Faithless Widow

Mr. Niu was a Kiangsi man who traded in piece goods. He married a wife from the Chêng family, by whom he had two children, a boy and a girl. When thirty-three years of age he fell ill and died, his son Chung being then only twelve and his little girl eight or nine. His wife did not remain faithful to his memory, but, selling off all the property, pocketed the proceeds and married another man, leaving her two children almost in a state of destitution with their aunt, Niu's sister-in-law, an old lady of sixty, who had lived with them previously, and had now nowhere to seek a shelter. A few years later this aunt died, and the family fortunes began to sink even lower than before; Chung, however, was now grown up, and determined to carry on his father's trade, only he had no capital to start with. His sister marrying a rich trader named Mao, she begged her husband to lend Chung ten ounces of silver, which he did, and Chung immediately started for Nanking.

On the road he fell in with some bandits, who robbed him of all he had, and consequently he was unable to return; but one day when he was at a pawnshop he noticed that the master of the shop was wonderfully like his late father, and on going out and making inquiries he found that this pawnbroker bore precisely the same names. In great astonishment, he forthwith proceeded to frequent the place with no other object than to watch this man, who, on the other hand, took no notice of Chung; and by the end of three days, having satisfied himself that he really saw his own father, and yet not daring to disclose his own identity, he made application through one of the assistants, on the score of being himself a Kiangsi man, to be employed in the shop. Accordingly, an indenture was drawn up; and when the master noticed Chung's name and place of residence he started, and asked him whence he came. With tears in his eyes Chung addressed him by his father's name, and then the pawnbroker became lost in a deep reverie, by-and-by asking Chung how his mother was. Now Chung did not like to allude to his father's death, and turned the question by saying, "My father went away on business six years ago, and never came back; my mother married again and left us, and had it not been for my aunt our corpses would long ago have been cast out in the kennel."

Then the pawnbroker was much moved, and cried out, "I am your father!" seizing his son's hand and leading him within to see his step-mother. This lady was about twenty-two, and, having no children of her own, was delighted with Chung, and prepared a banquet for him in the inner apartments. Mr. Niu himself was, however, somewhat melancholy, and wished to return to his old home; but his wife, fearing that there would be no one to manage the business, persuaded him to remain; so he taught his son the trade, and in three months was able to leave it all to him. He then prepared for his journey, whereupon Chung informed his step-mother that his father was really dead, to which she replied in great consternation that she knew him only as a trader to the place, and that six years previously he had married her, which proved conclusively that he couldn't be dead. He then recounted the whole story, which was a perfect mystery to both of them; and twenty-four hours afterward in walked his father, leading a woman whose hair was all disheveled. Chung looked at her and saw that she was his own mother; and Niu took her by the ear and began to revile her, saying, "Why did you desert my children?" to which the wretched woman made no reply. He then bit her across the neck, at which she screamed to Chung for assistance, and he, not being able to bear the sight, stepped in between them. His father was more than ever enraged at this, when, lo! Chung's mother had disappeared. While they were still lost in astonishment at this strange scene, Mr. Niu's color changed; in another moment his empty clothes had dropped upon the ground, and he himself became a black vapor and also vanished from their sight. The step-mother and son were much overcome; they took Niu's clothes and buried them, and after that Chung continued his father's business and soon amassed great wealth. On returning to his native place he found that his mother had actually died on the very day of the above occurrence, and that his father had been seen by the whole family.

The Princess of the Tung-t'ing Lake

CH'ÊN PI-CHIAO WAS A PEKINGESE; AND BEING A POOR MAN HE ATTACHED HIMSELF AS secretary to the suite of a high military official named Chia. On one occasion, while anchored on the Tung-t'ing lake, they saw a dolphin floating on the surface of the water; and General Chia took his bow and shot at it, wounding the creature in the back. A fish was hanging on to its tail, and would not let go; so both were pulled out of the water together, and attached to the mast. There they lay gasping, the dolphin opening its mouth as if pleading for life, until at length young Ch'ên begged the General to let them go again; and then he himself half jokingly put a piece of plaster upon the dolphin's wound, and had the two thrown back into the water, where they were seen for some time afterwards diving and rising again to the surface.

About a year afterward, Ch'ên was once more crossing the Tung-t'ing lake on his way home, when the boat was upset in a squall, and he himself only saved by clinging to a bamboo crate, which finally, after floating about all night, caught in the overhanging branch of a tree, and thus enabled him to scramble on shore. By-and-by, another body floated in, and this turned out to be his servant; but on dragging him out, he found life was already extinct. In great distress, he sat himself down to rest, and saw beautiful green hills and waving willows, but not a single human being of whom he could ask the way. From early dawn till the morning was far advanced he remained in that state; and then, thinking he saw his servant's body move, he stretched out his hand to feel it, and before long the man threw up several quarts of water and recovered his consciousness. They now dried their clothes in the sun, and by noon these were fit to put on; at which period the pangs of hunger began to assail them, and accordingly they started over the hills in the hope of coming upon some habitation of man.

As they were walking along, an arrow whizzed past, and the next moment two young ladies dashed by on handsome palfreys. Each had a scarlet band round her head, with a bunch of pheasant's feathers stuck in her hair, and wore a purple riding-jacket with small sleeves, confined by a green embroidered girdle round the waist. One of them carried a cross-bow for shooting bullets, and the other had on her arm a dark-colored bow-and-arrow case. Reaching the brow of the hill, Ch'ên beheld a number of riders engaged in beating the surrounding cover, all of whom were beautiful girls and dressed exactly alike. Afraid to advance any further, he inquired of a youth who appeared to be in attendance, and the latter told him that it was a hunting party from the palace; and then, having supplied him with food from his wallet, he bade him retire quickly, adding that if he fell in with them he would assuredly be put to death. Thereupon Ch'ên hurried away; and descending the hill, turned into a copse where there was a building which he thought would in all probability be a monastery. On getting nearer, he saw that the place was surrounded by a wall, and between him and a half-open red-door was a brook spanned by a stone bridge leading up to it. Pulling back the door, he beheld within a number of ornamental buildings circling in the air like so many clouds, and for all the world resembling the Imperial pleasure-grounds; and thinking it must be the park of some official personage, he walked quietly in, enjoying the delicious fragrance of the flowers as he pushed aside the thick vegetation which obstructed his way.

After traversing a winding path fenced in by balustrades, Ch'ên reached a second enclosure, wherein were a quantity of tall willow-trees which swept the red eaves of the buildings with their branches. The note of some bird would set the petals of the flowers fluttering in the air, and the least wind would bring the seed-vessels down from the elm-trees above; and the effect upon the eye and heart of the beholder was something quite unknown in the world of mortals. Passing through a small kiosque, Ch'ên and his servant came upon a swing which seemed as though suspended from the clouds, while the ropes hung idly down in the utter stillness that prevailed. Thinking by this that they were approaching the ladies' apartments, Ch'ên would have turned back, but at that moment he heard sounds of horses' feet at the door, and what seemed to be the laughter of a bevy of girls. So he and his servant hid themselves in a bush; and by-and-by, as the sounds came nearer, he heard one of the young ladies say, "We've had but poor sport to-day"; whereupon another cried out, "If the princess hadn't shot that wild goose, we should have taken all this trouble for nothing."

Shortly after this, a number of girls dressed in red came in escorting a young lady, who went and sat down under the kiosque. She wore a hunting costume with tight sleeves, and was about fourteen or fifteen years old. Her hair looked like a cloud of mist at the back of her head, and her waist seemed as though a breath of wind might snap it—incomparable for beauty, even among the celebrities of old. Just then the attendants handed her some exquisitely fragrant tea, and stood glittering round her like a bank of beautiful embroidery. In a few moments the young lady arose and descended the kiosque; at which one of her attendants cried out, "Is your Highness too fatigued by riding to take a turn in the swing?" The princess replied that she was not; and immediately some supported her under the shoulders, while others seized her arms, and others again arranged her petticoats, and brought her the proper shoes. Thus they helped her into the swing, she herself stretching out her shining arms, and putting her feet into a suitable pair of slippers; and then—away she went, light as a flying-swallow, far up into the fleecy clouds. As soon as she had had enough, the attendants helped her out, and one of them exclaimed, "Truly, your Highness is a perfect angel!" At this the young lady laughed, and walked away, Ch'ên gazing after her in a state of semi-consciousness, until, at length, the voices died away, and he and his servant crept forth. Walking up and down near the swing, he suddenly espied a red handkerchief near the paling, which he knew had been dropped by one of the young ladies; and, thrusting it joyfully into his sleeve, he walked up and entered the kiosque. There, upon a table, lay writing materials, and taking out the handkerchief he indited upon it the following lines:—

"What form divine was just now sporting nigh?—
'Twas she, I trow of 'golden lily' fame;
Her charms the moon's fair denizens might shame,
Her fairy footsteps bear her to the sky."

Humming this stanza to himself, Ch'ên walked along seeking for the path by which he had entered; but every door was securely barred, and he knew not what to do. So he went back to the kiosque, when suddenly one of the young ladies appeared, and asked him in astonishment what he did there. "I have lost my way," replied Ch'ên; "I pray you lend me your assistance."

"Do you happen to have found a red handkerchief?" said the girl.

"I have, indeed," answered Ch'ên, "but I fear I have made it somewhat dirty"; and, suiting the action to the word, he drew it forth, and handed it to her.

"Wretched man!" cried the young lady, "you are undone. This is a handkerchief the princess is constantly using, and you have gone and scribbled all over it; what will become of you now?" Ch'ên was in a great fright, and begged the young lady to intercede for him; to which she replied, "It was bad enough that you should come here and spy about; however, being a scholar, and a man of refinement, I would have done my best for you; but after this, how am I to help you?" Off she then ran with the handkerchief, while Ch'ên remained behind in an agony of suspense, and longing for the wings of a bird to bear him away from his fate.

By-and-by, the young lady returned and congratulated him, saying, "There is some hope for you. The Princess read your verses several times over, and was not at all angry. You will probably be released; but, meanwhile, wait here, and don't climb the trees, or try to get through the walls, or you may not escape after all."

Evening was now drawing on, and Ch'ên knew not, for certain, what was about to happen; at the same time he was very empty, and, what with hunger and anxiety, death would have been almost a happy release. Before long, the young lady returned with a lamp in her hand, and followed by a slave-girl bearing wine and food, which she forthwith presented to Ch'ên. The latter asked if there was any news about himself; to which the young lady replied that she had just mentioned his case to the Princess who, not knowing what to do with him at that hour of the night, had given orders that he should at once be provided with food, "which, at any rate," added she, "is not bad news."

The whole night long Ch'ên walked up and down unable to take rest; and it was not till late in the morning that the young lady appeared with more food for him. Imploring her once more to intercede on his behalf, she told him that the Princess had not instructed them either to kill or to release him, and that it would not be fitting for such as herself to be bothering the Princess with suggestions. So there Ch'ên still remained until another day had almost gone, hoping for the welcome moment; and then the young lady rushed hurriedly in, saying, "You are lost! Some one has told the Queen, and she, in a fit of anger, threw the handkerchief on the ground, and made use of very violent language. Oh dear! oh dear! I'm sure something dreadful will happen."

Ch'ên threw himself on his knees, his face as pale as ashes, and begged to know what he should do; but at that moment sounds were heard outside, and the young lady waved her hand to him, and ran away. Immediately a crowd came pouring in through the door, with ropes ready to secure the object of their search; and among them was a slave-girl, who looked fixedly at our hero, and cried out, "Why, surely you are Mr. Ch'ên, aren't you?" at the same time stopping the others from binding him until she should have reported to the Queen. In a few minutes she came back, and said the Queen requested him to walk in; and in he went, through a number of doors, trembling all the time with fear, until he reached a hall, the screen before which was ornamented with green jade and silver. A beautiful girl drew aside the bamboo curtain at the door, and announced, "Mr. Ch'ên"; and he himself advanced, and fell down before a lady, who was sitting upon a dais at the other end, knocking his head upon the ground, and crying out, "Thy servant is from a far-off country; spare, oh! spare his life."

"Sir!" replied the Queen, rising hastily from her seat, and extending a hand to Ch'ên, "but for you, I should not be here to-day. Pray excuse the rudeness of my maids." Thereupon a splendid repast was served, and wine was poured out in chased goblets, to the no small astonishment of Ch'ên, who could not understand why he was treated thus. "Your kindness," observed the Queen, "in restoring me to life, I am quite unable to repay; however, as you have made my daughter the subject of your verse, the match is clearly ordained by fate, and I shall send her along to be your handmaid."

Ch'ên hardly knew what to make of this extraordinary accomplishment of his wishes, but the marriage was solemnized there and then; bands of music struck up wedding-airs, beautiful mats were laid down for them to walk upon, and the whole place was brilliantly lighted with a profusion of colored lamps. Then Ch'ên said to the Princess, "That a stray and unknown traveler like myself, guilty of spoiling your Highness's handkerchief, should have escaped the fate he deserved, was already more than could be expected; but now to receive you in marriage—this, indeed, far surpasses my wildest expectations."

"My mother," replied the Princess, "is married to the King of this lake, and is herself a daughter of the River Prince. Last year, when on her way to visit her parents, she happened to cross the lake, and was wounded by an arrow; but you saved her life, and gave her plaster for the wound. Our family, therefore, is grateful to you, and can never forget your good act. And do not regard me as of another species than yourself; the Dragon King has bestowed upon me the elixir of immortality, and this I will gladly share with you." Then Ch'ên knew that his wife was a spirit, and by-and-by he asked her how the slave-girl had recognized him; to which she replied, that the girl was the small fish which had been found hanging to the dolphin's tail. He then inquired why, as they didn't intend to kill him, he had been kept so long a prisoner. "I was charmed with your literary talent," answered the Princess, "but I did not venture to take the responsibility upon myself; and no one saw how I tossed and turned the livelong night."

"Dear friend," said Ch'ên; "but, come, tell me who was it that brought my food."

"A trusty waiting-maid of mine," replied the Princess; "her name is A-nien."

Ch'ên then asked how he could ever repay her, and the Princess told him there would be plenty of time to think of that; and when he inquired where the king, her father, was, she said he had gone off with the God of War to fight against Ch'ih-yu, and had not returned. A few days passed, and Ch'ên began to think his people at home would be anxious about him; so he sent off his servant with a letter to tell them he was safe and sound, at which they were all overjoyed, believing him to have been lost in the wreck of the boat, of which event news had already reached them. However, they were unable to send him any reply, and were considerably distressed as to how he would find his way home again. Six months afterward Ch'ên himself appeared, dressed in fine clothes, and riding on a splendid horse, with plenty of money, and valuable jewels in his pocket—evidently a man of wealth. From that time forth he kept up a magnificent establishment; and in seven or eight years had become the father of five children. Every day he kept open house, and if any one asked him about his adventures, he would readily tell them without reservation.

Now a friend of his, named Liang, whom he had known since they were boys together, and who, after holding an appointment for some years in Nan-fu, was crossing the Tung-t'ing Lake, on his way home, suddenly beheld an ornamental barge, with carved wood-work and red windows, passing over the foamy waves to the sound of music and singing from within. Just then a beautiful young lady leant out of one of the windows, which she had pushed open, and by her side Liang saw a young man sitting, in a *négligé* attitude, while two nice-looking girls stood by and shampooed him. Liang, at first, thought it must be the party of some high official, and wondered at the scarcity of attendants; but, on looking more closely at the young man, he saw it was no other than his old friend Ch'ên. Thereupon he began almost involuntarily to shout out to him; and when Ch'ên heard his own name, he stopped the rowers, and walked out toward the figure-head, beckoning Liang to cross over into his boat, where the remains of their feast was quickly cleared away, and fresh supplies of wine, and tea, and all kinds of costly foods spread out by handsome slave-girls.

"It's ten years since we met," said Liang, "and what a rich man you have become in the meantime."

"Well," replied Ch'ên, "do you think that so very extraordinary for a poor fellow like me?" Liang then asked him who was the lady with whom he was taking wine, and Ch'ên said she was his wife, which very much astonished Liang, who further inquired whither they were going. "Westward," answered Ch'ên, and prevented any further questions by giving a signal for the music, which effectually put a stop to all further conversation.

By-and-by, Liang found the wine getting into his head, and seized the opportunity to ask Ch'ên to make him a present of one of his beautiful slave-girls. "You are drunk, my friend," replied Ch'ên; "however, I will give you the price of one as a pledge of our old friendship." And, turning to a servant, he bade him present Liang with a splendid pearl, saying, "Now you can buy a Green Pearl; you see I am not stingy"; adding forthwith, "but I am pressed for time, and can stay no longer with my old friend." So he escorted Liang back to his boat, and, having let go the rope, proceeded on his way.

Now, when Liang reached home, and called at Ch'ên's house, whom should he see but Ch'ên himself drinking with a party of friends. "Why, I saw you only yesterday," cried Liang, "upon the Tung-t'ing. How quickly you have got back!" Ch'ên denied this, and then Liang repeated the whole story, at the conclusion of which, Ch'ên laughed, and said, "You must be mistaken. Do you imagine I can be in two places at once?" The company were all much astonished, and knew not what to make of it; and subsequently when Ch'ên, who died at the age of eighty, was being carried to his grave, the bearers thought the coffin seemed remarkably light, and on opening it to see, found that the body had disappeared.

The Princess Lily

At Chiao-chou there lived a man named Tou Hsün, otherwise known as Hsiao-hui. One day he had just dropped off to sleep when he beheld a man in serge clothes standing by the bedside, and apparently anxious to communicate something to him. Tou inquired his errand; to which the man replied that he was the bearer of an invitation from his master.

"And who is your master?" asked Tou.

"Oh, he doesn't live far off," replied the other; so away they went together, and after some time came to a place where there were innumerable white houses rising one above the other, and shaded by dense groves of lemon-trees. They threaded their way past countless doors, not at all similar to those usually used, and saw a great many official-looking men and women passing and repassing, each of whom called out to the man in serge, "Has Mr. Tou come?" to which he always replied in the affirmative.

Here a mandarin met them and escorted Tou into a palace, upon which the latter remarked, "This is really very kind of you; but I haven't the honor of knowing you, and I feel somewhat diffident about going in."

"Our Prince," answered his guide, "has long heard of you as a man of good family and excellent principles, and is very anxious to make your acquaintance."

"Who is your Prince?" inquired Tou.

"You'll see for yourself in a moment," said the other; and just then out came two girls with banners, and guided Tou through a great number of doors until they came to a throne, upon which sat the Prince. His Highness immediately descended to meet him, and made him take the seat of honor; after which ceremony exquisite viands of all kinds were spread out before them. Looking up, Tou noticed a scroll, on which was inscribed, *The Cassia Court*, and he was just beginning to feel puzzled as to what he should say next, when the Prince addressed him as follows:—

"The honor of having you for a neighbor is, as it were, a bond of affinity between us. Let us, then, give ourselves up to enjoyment, and put away suspicion and fear."

Tou murmured his acquiescence; and when the wine had gone round several times there arose from a distance the sound of pipes and singing, unaccompanied, however, by the usual drum, and very much subdued in volume. Thereupon the Prince looked about him and cried out, "We are about to set a verse for any of you gentlemen to cap; here you are:—'*Genius seeks the Cassia Court.*'"

While the courtiers were all engaged in thinking of some fit antithesis, Tou added, *"Refinement loves the Lily flower"*; upon which the Prince exclaimed, "How strange! Lily is my daughter's name; and, after such a coincidence, she must come in for you to see her."

In a few moments the tinkling of her ornaments and a delicious fragrance of musk announced the arrival of the Princess, who was between sixteen and seventeen and endowed with surpassing beauty. The Prince bade her make an obeisance to Tou, at the same time introducing her as his daughter Lily; and as soon as the ceremony was over the young lady moved away. Tou remained in a state of stupefaction, and, when the Prince proposed that they should pledge each other in another bumper, paid not the slightest attention to what he said. Then the Prince, perceiving what had distracted his guest's attention, remarked that he was anxious to find a consort for his daughter, but that unfortunately there was the difficulty of *species*, and he didn't know what to do; but again Tou took no notice of what the Prince was saying, until at length one of the bystanders plucked his sleeve, and asked him if he hadn't seen that the Prince wished to drink with him, and had just been addressing some remarks to him. Thereupon Tou started, and, recovering himself at once, rose from the table and apologized to the Prince for his rudeness, declaring that he had taken so much wine he didn't know what he was doing. "Besides," said he, "your Highness has doubtless business to transact; I will therefore take my leave."

"I am extremely pleased to have seen you," replied the Prince, "and only regret that you are in such a hurry to be gone. However, I won't detain you now; but, if you don't forget all about us, I shall be very glad to invite you here again." He then gave orders that Tou should be escorted home; and on the way one of the courtiers asked the latter why he had said nothing when the Prince had spoken of a consort for his daughter, as his Highness had evidently made the remark with an eye to securing Tou as his son-in-law. The latter was now sorry that he had missed his opportunity; meanwhile they reached his house, and he himself awoke. The sun had already set, and there he sat in the gloom thinking of what had happened. In the evening he put out his candle, hoping to continue his dream; but, alas! the thread was broken, and all he could do was to pour forth his repentance in sighs.

One night he was sleeping at a friend's house when suddenly an officer of the court walked in and summoned him to appear before the Prince; so up he jumped, and hurried off at once to the palace, where he prostrated himself before the throne. The Prince raised him and made him sit down, saying that since they had last met he had become aware that Tou would be willing to marry his daughter, and hoped that he might be allowed to offer her as a handmaid. Tou rose and thanked the Prince, who thereupon gave orders for a banquet to be prepared; and when they had finished their wine it was announced that the Princess had completed her toilet. Immediately a bevy of young ladies came in with the Princess in their midst, a red veil covering her head, and her tiny footsteps sounding like rippling water as they led her up to be introduced to Tou. When the ceremonies were concluded, Tou said to the Princess, "In your presence, Madam, it would be easy to forget even death itself; but, tell me, is not this all a dream?"

"And how can it be a dream," asked the Princess, "when you and I are here together?"

Next morning Tou amused himself by helping the Princess to paint her face, and then, seizing a girdle, began to measure the size of her waist and the length of her fingers and feet. "Are you crazy?" cried she, laughing; to which Tou replied, "I have been deceived so often by dreams, that I am now making a careful record. If such it turns out to be, I shall still have something as a souvenir of you."

While they were thus chatting a maid rushed into the room, shrieking out, "Alas, alas! a great monster has got into the palace: the Prince has fled into a side chamber: destruction is surely come upon us."

Tou was in a great fright when he heard this, and rushed off to see the Prince, who grasped his hand and, with tears in his eyes, begged him not to desert them. "Our relationship," cried he, "was cemented when Heaven sent this calamity upon us; and now my kingdom will be overthrown. What shall I do?"

Tou begged to know what was the matter; and then the Prince laid a despatch upon the table, telling Tou to open it and make himself acquainted with its contents. This despatch ran as follows:—

"The Grand Secretary of State, Black Wings, to His Royal Highness, announcing the arrival of an extraordinary monster, and advising the immediate removal of the Court in order to preserve the vitality of the empire. A report has just been received from the officer in charge of the Yellow Gate stating that, ever since the 6th of the 5th moon, a huge monster, 10,000 feet in length, has been lying coiled up outside the entrance to the palace, and that it has already devoured 13,800 and odd of your Highness's subjects, and is spreading desolation far and wide. On receipt of this information your servant proceeded to make a reconnaissance, and there beheld a venomous reptile with a head as big as a mountain and eyes like vast sheets of water. Every time it raised its head, whole buildings disappeared down its throat; and, on stretching itself out, walls and houses were alike laid in ruins. In all antiquity there is no record of such a scourge. The fate of our temples and ancestral halls is now a mere question of hours; we therefore pray your Royal Highness to depart at once with the Royal Family and seek somewhere else a happier abode."

When Tou had read this document his face turned ashy pale; and just then a messenger rushed in, shrieking out, "Here is the monster!" at which the whole Court burst into lamentations as if their last hour was at hand. The Prince was beside himself with fear; all he could do was to beg Tou to look to his own safety without regarding the wife through whom he was involved in their misfortunes. The Princess, however, who was standing by bitterly lamenting the fate that had fallen upon them, begged Tou not to desert her; and, after a moment's hesitation, he said he should be only too happy to place his own poor home at their immediate disposal if they would only deign to honor him.

"How can we talk of *deigning*," cried the Princess, "at such a moment as this? I pray you take us there as quickly as possible." So Tou gave her his arm, and in no time they had arrived at Tou's house, which the Princess at once pronounced to be a charming place of residence, and better even than their former kingdom. "But I must now ask you," said she to Tou, "to make some arrangement for my father and mother, that the old order of things may be continued here."

Tou at first offered objections to this; whereupon the Princess said that a man who would not help another in his hour of need was not much of a man, and immediately went off into a fit of hysterics, from which Tou was trying his best to recall her, when all of a sudden he awoke and found that it was all a dream. However, he still heard a buzzing in his ears which he knew was not made by any human being, and, on looking carefully about he discovered two or three bees which had settled on his pillow. He was very much astonished at this, and consulted with his friend, who was also greatly amazed at his strange story; and then the latter pointed out a number of other bees on various parts of his dress, none of which would go away even when brushed off. His friend now advised him to get a hive for them, which he did without delay; and immediately it was filled by a whole swarm of bees, which came flying from over the wall in great numbers. On tracing whence they had come, it was found that they belonged to an old gentleman who lived near, and who had kept bees for more than thirty years previously. Tou thereupon went and told him the story; and when the old gentleman examined his hive he found the bees all gone. On breaking it open he discovered a large snake inside of about ten feet in length, which he immediately killed, recognizing in it the "huge monster" of Tou's adventure. As for the bees, they remained with Tou, and increased in numbers every year.

The Donkey's Revenge

CHUNG CH'ING-YÜ WAS A SCHOLAR OF SOME REPUTATION, WHO LIVED IN MANCHURIA. When he went up for his master's degree, he heard that there was a Taoist priest at the capital who would tell people's fortunes, and was very anxious to see him; and at the conclusion of the second part of the examination, he accidentally met him at Pao-t'u-ch'üan. The priest was over sixty years of age, and had the usual white beard, flowing down over his breast. Around him stood a perfect wall of people inquiring their future fortunes, and to each the old man made a brief reply: but when he saw Chung among the crowd, he was overjoyed, and, seizing him by the hand, said, "Sir, your virtuous intentions command my esteem." He then led him up behind a screen, and asked if he did not wish to know what was to come; and when Chung replied in the affirmative, the priest informed him that his prospects were bad. "You may succeed in passing this examination," continued he, "but on returning covered with honor to your home, I fear that your mother will be no longer there."

Now Chung was a very filial son; and as soon as he heard these words, his tears began to flow, and he declared that he would go back without competing any further. The priest observed that if he let this chance slip, he could never hope for success; to which Chung replied that, on the other hand, if his mother were to die he could never hope to have her back again, and that even the rank of Viceroy would not repay him for her loss.

"Well," said the priest, "you and I were connected in a former existence, and I must do my best to help you now." So he took out a pill which he gave to Chung, and told him that if he sent it post-haste by some one to his mother, it would prolong her life for seven days, and thus he would be able to see her once again after the examination was over. Chung took the pill, and went off in very low spirits; but he soon reflected that the span of human life is a matter of destiny, and that every day he could spend at home would be one more day devoted to the service of his mother. Accordingly, he got ready to start at once, and, hiring a donkey, actually set out on his way back.

When he had gone about half-a-mile, the donkey turned round and ran home; and when he used his whip, the animal threw itself down on the ground. Chung got into a great perspiration, and his servant recommended him to remain where he was; but this he would not hear of, and hired another donkey, which served him exactly the same trick as the other one. The sun was now sinking behind the hills, and his servant advised his master to stay and finish his examination while he himself went back home before him. Chung had no alternative but to assent, and the next day he hurried through with his papers, starting immediately afterward, and not stopping at all on the way either to eat or to sleep. All night long he went on, and arrived to find his mother in a very critical state; however, when he gave her the pill she so far recovered that he was able to go in and see her. Grasping his hand, she begged him not to weep, telling him that she had just dreamt she had been down to the Infernal Regions, where the King of Hell had informed her with a gracious smile that her record was fairly clean, and that in view of the filial piety of her son she was to have twelve years more of life. Chung was rejoiced at this, and his mother was soon restored to her former health.

Before long the news arrived that Chung had passed his examination; upon which he bade adieu to his mother, and went off to the capital, where he bribed the eunuchs of the palace to communicate with his friend the Taoist priest. The latter was very much pleased, and came out to see him, whereupon Chung prostrated himself at his feet. "Ah," said the priest, "this success of yours, and the prolongation of your good mother's life, is all a reward for your virtuous conduct. What have I done in the matter?" Chung was very much astonished that the priest should already know what had happened; however, he now inquired as to his own future. "You will never rise to high rank," replied the priest, "but you will attain the years of an octogenarian. In a former state of existence you and I were once traveling together, when you threw a stone at a dog, and accidentally killed a frog. Now that frog has re-appeared in life as a donkey, and according to all principles of destiny you ought to suffer for what you did; but your filial piety has touched the Gods, a protecting star-influence has passed into your nativity sheet, and you will come to no harm. On the other hand, there is your wife; in her former state she was not as virtuous as she might have been, and her punishment in this life was to be widowed quite young; you, however, have secured the prolongation of your own term of years, and therefore I fear that before long your wife will pay the penalty of death." Chung was much grieved at hearing this; but after a while he asked the priest where his second wife to be was living. "At Chung-chou," replied the latter; "she is now fourteen years old." The priest then bade him adieu, telling him that if any mischance should befall him he was to hurry off toward the south-east.

About a year after this, Chung's wife did die; and his mother then desiring him to go and visit his uncle, who was a magistrate in Kiangsi, on which journey he would have to pass through Chung-chou, it seemed like a fulfilment of the old priest's prophecy. As he went along, he came to a village on the banks of a river, where a large crowd of people was gathered together round a theatrical performance which was going on there. Chung would have passed quietly by, had not a stray donkey followed so close behind him that he turned round and hit it over the ears. This startled the donkey so much that it ran off full gallop, and knocked a rich gentleman's child, who was sitting with its nurse on the bank, right into the water, before any one of the servants could lend a hand to save it. Immediately there was a great outcry against Chung, who gave his mule the rein and dashed away, mindful of the priest's warning, towards the south-east. After riding about seven miles, he reached a mountain village, where he saw an old man standing at the door of a house, and, jumping off his mule, made him a low bow. The old man asked him in, and inquired his name and whence he came; to which Chung replied by telling him the whole adventure.

"Never fear," said the old man; "you can stay here, while I send out to learn the position of affairs."

By the evening his messenger had returned, and then they knew for the first time that the child belonged to a wealthy family. The old man looked grave and said, "Had it been anybody else's child, I might have helped you; as it is I can do nothing." Chung was greatly alarmed at this; however, the old man told him to remain quietly there for the night, and see what turn matters might take. Chung was overwhelmed with anxiety, and did not sleep a wink; and next morning he heard that the constables were after him, and that it was death to any one who should conceal him. The old man changed countenance at this, and went inside, leaving Chung to his own reflections; but towards the middle of the night he came and knocked at Chung's door, and, sitting down, began to ask how old his wife was. Chung replied that he was a widower; at which the old man seemed rather pleased, and declared that in such case help would be forthcoming; "for," said he, "my sister's husband has taken the vows and become a priest, and my sister herself has died, leaving an orphan girl who has now no home; and if you would only marry her. . . ."

Chung was delighted, more especially as this would be both the fulfillment of the Taoist priest's prophecy, and a means of extricating himself from his present difficulty; at the same time, he declared he should be sorry to implicate his future father-in-law. "Never fear about that," replied the old man; "my sister's husband is pretty skillful in the black art. He has not mixed much with the world of late; but when you are married, you can discuss the matter with my niece."

So Chung married the young lady, who was sixteen years of age, and very beautiful; but whenever he looked at her he took occasion to sigh. At last she said, "I may be ugly; but you needn't be in such a hurry to let me know it"; whereupon Chung begged her pardon, and said he felt himself only too lucky to have met with such a divine creature; adding that he sighed because he feared some misfortune was coming on them which would separate them for ever. He then told her his story, and the young lady was very angry that she should have been drawn into such a difficulty without a word of warning. Chung fell on his knees, and said he had already consulted with her uncle, who was unable himself to do anything, much as he wished it. He continued that he was aware of her power; and then, pointing out that his alliance was not altogether beneath her, made all kinds of promises if she would only help him out of this trouble. The young lady was no longer able to refuse, but informed him that to apply to her father would entail certain disagreeable consequences, as he had retired from the world, and did not any more recognize her as his daughter.

That night they did not attempt to sleep, spending the interval in padding their knees with thick felt concealed beneath their clothes; and then they got into chairs and were carried off to the hills. After journeying some distance, they were compelled by the nature of the road to alight and walk; and it was only by a great effort that Chung succeeded at last in getting his wife to the top. At the door of the temple they sat down to rest, the powder and paint on the young lady's face having all mixed with the perspiration trickling down; but when Chung began to apologize for bringing her to this pass, she replied that it was a mere trifle compared with what was to come. By-and-by, they went inside; and threading their way to the wall beyond, found the young lady's father sitting in contemplation, his eyes closed, and a servant-boy standing by with a chowry. Everything was beautifully clean and nice, but before the dais were sharp stones scattered about as thick as the stars in the sky. The young lady did not venture to select a favorable spot; she fell on her knees at once, and Chung did likewise behind her. Then her father opened his eyes, shutting them again almost instantaneously; whereupon the young lady said, "For a long time I have not paid my respects to you. I am now married, and I have brought my husband to see you."

A long time passed away, and then her father opened his eyes and said, "You're giving a great deal of trouble," immediately relapsing into silence again. There the husband and wife remained until the stones seemed to pierce into their very bones; but after a while the father cried out, "Have you brought the donkey?" His daughter replied that they had not; whereupon they were told to go and fetch it at once, which they did, not knowing what the meaning of this order was.

After a few more days' kneeling, they suddenly heard that the murderer of the child had been caught and beheaded, and were just congratulating each other on the success of their scheme, when a servant came in with a stick in his hand, the top of which had been chopped off. "This stick," said the servant, "died instead of you. Bury it reverently, that the wrong done to the tree may be somewhat atoned for." Then Chung saw that at the place where the top of the stick had been chopped off there were traces of blood; he therefore buried it with the usual ceremony, and immediately set off with his wife, and returned to his own home.

The Wolf Dream

Mr. Pai was a native of Chi-li, and his eldest son was called Chia. The latter had been some two years holding an appointment as magistrate in the south; but because of the great distance between them, his family had heard nothing of him. One day a distant connection, named Ting, called at the house; and Mr. Pai, not having seen this gentleman for a long time, treated him with much cordiality. Now Ting was one of those persons who are occasionally employed by the Judge of the Infernal Regions to make arrests on earth; and, as they were chatting together, Mr. Pai questioned him about the realms below. Ting told him all kinds of strange things, but Pai did not believe them, answering only by a smile. Some days afterward, he had just lain down to sleep when Ting walked in and asked him to go for a stroll; so they went off together, and by-and-by reached the city.

"There," said Ting, pointing to a door, "lives your nephew," alluding to a son of Mr. Pai's elder sister, who was a magistrate in Honan; and when Pai expressed his doubts as to the accuracy of this statement, Ting led him in, when, lo and behold! there was his nephew, sitting in his court dressed in his official robes. Around him stood the guard, and it was impossible to get near him; but Ting remarked that his son's residence was not far off, and asked Pai if he would not like to see him too. The latter assenting, they walked along till they came to a large building, which Ting said was the place. However, there was a fierce wolf at the entrance, and Mr. Pai was afraid to go in. Ting bade him enter, and accordingly they walked in, when they found that all the employés of the place, some of whom were standing about and others lying down to sleep, were all wolves. The central pathway was piled up with whitening bones, and Mr. Pai began to feel horribly alarmed but Ting kept close to him all the time, and at length they got safely in. Pai's son, Chia, was just coming out; and when he saw his father accompanied by Ting, he was overjoyed, and, asking them to sit down, bade the attendants serve some refreshment. Thereupon a great big wolf brought in in his mouth the carcass of a dead man, and set it before them, at which Mr. Pai rose up in consternation, and asked his son what this meant.

"It's only a little refreshment for you, father," replied Chia; but this did not calm Mr. Pai's agitation, who would have retired precipitately, had it not been for the crowd of wolves which barred the path. Just as he was at a loss what to do, there was a general stampede among the animals which scurried away, some under the couches and some under the tables and chairs; and while he was wondering what the cause of this could be, in marched two knights in golden armor, who looked sternly at Chia, and, producing a black rope, proceeded to bind him hand and foot. Chia fell down before them, and was changed into a tiger with horrid fangs; and then one of the knights drew a glittering sword and would have cut off its head, had not the other cried out, "Not yet! not yet! that is for the fourth month next year. Let us now only take out its teeth." Immediately that knight produced a huge mallet, and, with a few blows, scattered the tiger's teeth all over the floor, the tiger roaring so loudly with pain as to shake the very hills, and frightening all the wits out of Mr. Pai—who woke up with a start. He found he had been dreaming, and at once sent off to invite Ting to come and see him; but Ting sent back to say he must beg to be excused.

Then Mr. Pai, pondering on what he had seen in his dream, despatched his second son with a letter to Chia, full of warnings and good advice; and lo! when his son arrived, he found that his elder brother had lost all his front teeth, these having been knocked out, as he averred, by a fall he had had from his horse when tipsy; and, on comparing dates, the day of that fall was found to coincide with the day of his father's dream. The younger brother was greatly amazed at this, and took out their father's letter, which he gave to Chia to read. The latter changed color, but immediately asked his brother what there was to be astonished at in the coincidence of a dream. And just at that time he was busily engaged in bribing his superiors to put him first on the list for promotion, so that he soon forgot all about the circumstance; while the younger, observing what harpies Chia's subordinates were, taking presents from one man and using their influence for another, in one unbroken stream of corruption, sought out his elder brother, and, with tears in his eyes, implored him to put some check upon their rapacity.

"My brother," replied Chia, "your life has been passed in an obscure village; you know nothing of our official routine. We are promoted or degraded at the will of our superiors, and not by the voice of the people. He, therefore, who gratifies his superiors is marked out for success; whereas he who consults the wishes of the people is unable to gratify his superiors as well."

Chia's brother saw that his advice was thrown away; he accordingly returned home and told his father all that had taken place. The old man was much affected, but there was nothing that he could do in the matter, so he devoted himself to assisting the poor, and such acts of charity, daily praying the Gods that the wicked son alone might suffer for his crimes, and not entail misery on his innocent wife and children. The next year it was reported that Chia had been recommended for a post in the Board of Civil Office, and friends crowded the father's door, offering their congratulations upon the happy event. But the old man sighed and took to his bed, pretending he was too unwell to receive visitors. Before long another message came, informing them that Chia had fallen in with bandits while on his way home, and that he and all his retinue had been killed. Then his father arose and said, "Verily the Gods are good unto me, for they have visited his sins upon himself alone"; and he immediately proceeded to burn incense and return thanks. Some of his friends would have persuaded him that the report was probably untrue; but the old man had no doubts as to its correctness, and made haste to get ready his son's grave.

But Chia was not yet dead. In the fatal fourth moon he had started on his journey and had fallen in with bandits, to whom he had offered all his money and valuables; upon which the latter cried out, "We have come to avenge the cruel wrongs of many hundreds of victims; do you imagine we want only *that*?" They then cut off his head, and the head of his wicked secretary, and the heads of several of his servants who had been foremost in carrying out his shameful orders, and were now accompanying him to the capital. They then divided the booty between them, and made off with all speed. Chia's soul remained near his body for some time, until at length a high mandarin passing by asked who it was that was lying there dead. One of his servants replied that he had been a magistrate at such and such a place, and that his name was Pai. "What!" said the mandarin, "the son of old Mr. Pai? It is hard that his father should live to see such sorrow as this. Put his head on again." Then a man stepped forward and placed Chia's head upon his shoulders again, when the mandarin interrupted him, saying, "A crooked-minded man should not have a straight body: put his head on sideways." By-and-by Chia's soul returned to its tenement; and when his wife and children arrived to take away the corpse, they found that he was still breathing. Carrying him home, they poured some nourishment down his throat, which he was able to swallow; but there he was at an out-of-the-way place, without the means of continuing his journey. It was some six months before his father heard the real state of the case, and then he sent off the second son to bring his brother home. Chia had indeed come to life again, but he was able to see down his own back, and was regarded ever afterward more as a monstrosity than as a man. Subsequently the nephew, whom old Mr. Pai had seen sitting in state surrounded by officials, actually became an Imperial Censor, so that every detail of the dream was thus strangely realized.

The Unjust Sentence

Mr. Chu was a native of Yang-ku, and, as a young man, was much given to playing tricks and talking in a loose kind of way. Having lost his wife, he went off to ask a certain old woman to arrange another match for him; and on the way, he chanced to fall in with a neighbor's wife who took his fancy very much. So he said in joke to the old woman, "Get me that stylish-looking, handsome lady, and I shall be quite satisfied."

"I'll see what I can do," replied the old woman, also joking, "if you will manage to kill her present husband"; upon which Chu laughed and said he certainly would do so.

Now about a month afterward, the said husband, who had gone out to collect some money due to him, was actually killed in a lonely spot; and the magistrate of the district immediately summoned the neighbors and beadle and held the usual inquest, but was unable to find any clue to the murderer. However, the old woman told the story of her conversation with Chu, and suspicion at once fell upon him. The constables came and arrested him; but he stoutly denied the charge; and the magistrate now began to suspect the wife of the murdered man. Accordingly, she was severely beaten and tortured in several ways until her strength failed her, and she falsely acknowledged her guilt. Chu was then examined, and he said, "This delicate woman could not bear the agony of your tortures; what she has stated is untrue; and, even should her wrong escape the notice of the Gods, for her to die in this way with a stain upon her name is more than I can endure. I will tell the whole truth. I killed the husband that I might secure the wife: she knew nothing at all about it." And when the magistrate asked for some proof, Chu said his bloody clothes would be evidence enough; but when they sent to search his house, no bloody clothes were forthcoming. He was then beaten till he fainted; yet when he came round he still stuck to what he had said. "It is my mother," cried he, "who will not sign the death-warrant of her son. Let me go myself and I will get the clothes." So he was escorted by a guard to his home, and there he explained to his mother that whether she gave up or withheld the clothes, it was all the same; that in either case he would have to die, and it was better to die early than late. Thereupon his mother wept bitterly, and going into the bedroom, brought out, after a short delay, the required clothes, which were taken at once to the magistrate's. There was now no doubt as to the truth of Chu's story; and as nothing occurred to change the magistrate's opinion, Chu was thrown into prison to await the day for his execution.

Meanwhile, as the magistrate was one day inspecting his gaol, suddenly a man appeared in the hall, who glared at him fiercely and roared out, "Dull-headed fool! unfit to be the guardian of the people's interests!"—whereupon the crowd of servants standing round rushed forward to seize him, but with one sweep of his arms he laid them all flat on the ground. The magistrate was frightened out of his wits, and tried to escape, but the man cried out to him, "I am one of Kuan Ti's lieutenants. If you move an inch you are lost." So the magistrate stood there, shaking from head to foot with fear, while his visitor continued, "The murderer is Kung Piao: Chu had nothing to do with it."

The lieutenant then fell down on the ground, and was to all appearance lifeless; however, after a while he recovered, his face having quite changed, and when they asked him his name, lo! it was Kung Piao. Under the application of the bamboo he confessed his guilt. Always an unprincipled man, he had heard that the murdered man was going out to collect money, and thinking he would be sure to bring it back with him, he had killed him, but had found nothing. Then when he learnt that Chu had acknowledged the crime as his own doing, he had rejoiced in secret at such a stroke of luck. How he had got into the magistrate's hall he was quite unable to say. The magistrate now called for some explanation of Chu's bloody clothes, which Chu himself was unable to give; but his mother, who was at once sent for, stated that she had cut her own arm to stain them, and when they examined her they found on her left arm the scar of a recent wound. The magistrate was lost in amazement at all this; unfortunately for him the reversal of his sentence cost him his appointment, and he died in poverty, unable to find his way home. As for Chu, the widow of the murdered man married him in the following year, out of gratitude for his noble behavior.

A Rip Van Winkle

The story runs that a Mr. Chia, after obtaining, with the assistance of a mysterious friend, his master's degree, became alive to the vanity of mere earthly honors, and determined to devote himself to the practice of Taoism, in the hope of obtaining the elixir of immortality.

So early one morning Chia and his friend, whose name was Lang, stole away together, without letting Chia's family know anything about it; and by-and-by they found themselves among the hills, in a vast cave where there was another world and another sky. An old man was sitting there in great state, and Lang presented Chia to him as his future master. "Why have you come so soon?" asked the old man; to which Lang replied, "My friend's determination is firmly fixed: I pray you receive him among you."

"Since you have come," said the old man, turning to Chia, "you must begin by putting away from you your earthly body."

Chia murmured his assent, and was then escorted by Lang to sleeping-chamber where he was provided with food, after which Lang went away. The room was beautifully clean: the doors had no panels and the windows no lattices; and all the furniture was one table and one couch. Chia took off his shoes and lay down, with the moon shining brightly into the room; and beginning soon to feel hungry, he tried one of the cakes on the table, which he found sweet and very satisfying. He thought Lang would be sure to come back, but there he remained hour after hour by himself, never hearing a sound. He noticed, however, that the room was fragrant with a delicious perfume; his viscera seemed to be removed from his body, by which his intellectual faculties were much increased; and every one of his veins and arteries could be easily counted.

Then suddenly he heard a sound like that of a cat scratching itself; and, looking out of the window, he beheld a tiger sitting under the verandah. He was horribly frightened for the moment, but immediately recalling the admonition of the old man, he collected himself and sat quietly down again. The tiger seemed to know that there was a man inside, for it entered the room directly afterward, and walking straight up to the couch sniffed at Chia's feet. Whereupon there was a noise outside, as if a fowl were having its legs tied, and the tiger ran away. Shortly afterward a beautiful young girl came in, suffusing an exquisite fragrance around; and going up to the couch where Chia was, she bent over him and whispered, "Here I am." Her breath was like the sweet odor of perfumes; but as Chia did not move, she whispered again, "Are you sleeping?" The voice sounded to Chia remarkably like that of his wife; however, he reflected that these were all probably nothing more than tests of his determination, so he closed his eyes firmly for a while. But by-and-by the young lady called him by his pet name, and then he opened his eyes wide to discover that she was no other than his own wife. On asking her how she had come there, she replied that Mr. Lang was afraid her husband would be lonely, and had sent an old woman to guide her to him.

Just then they heard the old man outside in a towering rage, and Chia's wife, not knowing where to conceal herself, jumped over a low wall near by and disappeared. In came the old man, and gave Lang a severe beating before Chia's face, bidding him at once to get rid of his visitor; so Lang led Chia away over the low wall, saying, "I knew how anxious you were to consummate your immortality, and accordingly I tried to hurry things on a bit; but now I see that your time has not yet come: hence this beating I have had. Good-by: we shall meet again some day." He then showed Chia the way to his home, and waving his hand bade him farewell. Chia looked down—for he was in the moon—and beheld the old familiar village and recollecting that his wife was not a good walker and would not have got very far, hurried on to overtake her.

Before long he was at his own door, but he noticed that the place was all tumble-down and in ruins, and not as it was when he went away. As for the people he saw, old and young alike, he did not recognize one of them; and recollecting the story of how Liu and Yüan came back from heaven, he was afraid to go in at the door. So he sat down and rested outside; and after a while an old man leaning on a staff came out, whereupon Chia asked him which was the house of Mr. Chia. "This is it," replied the old man; "you probably wish to hear the extraordinary story connected with the family? I know all about it. They say that Mr. Chia ran away just after he had taken his master's degree, when his son was only seven or eight years old; and that about seven years afterward the child's mother went into a deep sleep from which she did not awake. As long as her son was alive he changed his mother's clothes for her according to the seasons, but when he died, her grandsons fell into poverty, and had nothing but an old shanty to put the sleeping lady into. Last month she awaked, having been asleep for over a hundred years. People from far and near have been coming in great numbers to hear the strange story; of late, however, there have been rather fewer."

Chia was amazed when he heard all this, and, turning to the old man, said, "I am Chia Fêng-chih." This astonished the old man very much, and off he went to make the announcement to Chia's family. The eldest grandson was dead; and the second, a man of about fifty, refused to believe that such a young-looking man was really his grandfather; but in a few moments out came Chia's wife, and she recognized her husband at once. They then fell upon each other's necks and mingled their tears together.

[After which the story is drawn out to a considerable length, but is quite devoid of interest.]

The Three States of Existence

A CERTAIN MAN OF THE PROVINCE OF HUNAN COULD RECALL WHAT HAD HAPPENED TO him in three previous lives. In the first, he was a magistrate; and, on one occasion, when he had been nominated Assistant-Examiner, a candidate, named Hsing, was unsuccessful. Hsing went home dreadfully mortified, and soon after died; but his spirit appeared before the King of Purgatory, and read aloud the rejected essay, whereupon thousands of other shades, all of whom had suffered in a similar way, thronged around, and unanimously elected Hsing as their chief. The Examiner was immediately summoned to take his trial, and when he arrived the King asked him, saying, "As you are appointed to examine the various essays, how is it that you throw out the able and admit the worthless?"

"Sire," replied he, "the ultimate decision rests with the Grand Examiner; I only pass them on to him."

The King then issued a warrant for the apprehension of the Grand Examiner, and, as soon as he appeared, he was told what had just now been said against him; to which he answered, "I am only able to make a general estimate of the merits of the candidates. Valuable essays may be kept back from me by my Associate-Examiners, in which case I am powerless."

But the King cried out, "It's all very well for you two thus to throw the blame on each other; you are both guilty, and both of you must be bambooed according to law." This sentence was about to be carried into effect, when Hsing, who was not at all satisfied with its lack of severity, set up such a fearful screeching and howling, in which he was well supported by all the other hundreds and thousands of shades, that the King stopped short, and inquired what was the matter.

Thereupon Hsing informed His Majesty that the sentence was too light, and that the Examiners should both have their eyes gouged out, so as not to be able to read essays any more. The King would not consent to this, explaining to the noisy rabble that the Examiners did not purposely reject good essays, but only because they themselves were naturally wanting in capacity. The shades then begged that, at any rate, their hearts might be cut out, and to this the King was obliged to yield; so the Examiners were seized by the attendants, their garments stripped off, and their bodies ripped open with sharp knives. The blood poured out on the ground, and the victims screamed with pain; at which all the shades rejoiced exceedingly, and said, "Here we have been pent up, with no one to redress our wrongs; but now Mr. Hsing has come, our injuries are washed away." They then dispersed with great noise and hubbub.

As for our Associate-Examiner, after his heart had been cut out, he came to life again as the son of a poor man in Shensi; and when he was twenty years old he fell into the hands of the rebels, who were at that time giving great trouble to the country. By-and-by, a certain official was sent at the head of some soldiers to put down the insurrection, and he succeeded in capturing a large number of the rebels, among whom was our hero. The latter reflected that he himself was no rebel, and he was hoping that he would be able to obtain his release in consequence, when he noticed that the officer in charge was also a man of his own age, and, on looking more closely, he saw that it was his old enemy, Hsing. "Alas!" cried he, "such is destiny"; and so indeed it turned out, for all the other prisoners were forthwith released, and he alone was beheaded.

Once more his spirit stood before the King of Purgatory, this time with an accusation against Hsing. The King, however, would not summon Hsing at once, but said he should be allowed to complete his term of official life on earth; and it was not till thirty years afterward that Hsing appeared to answer to the charge. Then, because he had made light of the lives of his people, he was condemned to be born again as a brute-beast; and our hero, too, inasmuch as he had been known to beat his father and mother, was sentenced to a similar fate. The latter, fearing the future vengeance of Hsing, persuaded the King to give him the advantage of size; and, accordingly, orders were issued that he was to be born again as a big, and Hsing as a little, dog. The big dog came to life in a shop in Shun-t'ien Fu, and was one day lying down in the street, when a trader from the south arrived, bringing with him a little golden-haired dog, about the size of a wild cat, which, lo and behold! turned out to be Hsing. The other, thinking Hsing's size would render him an easy prey, seized him at once; but the little one caught him from underneath by the throat, and hung there firmly, like a bell. The big dog tried hard to shake him off, and the people of the shop did their best to separate them, but all was of no avail, and in a few moments both dogs were dead. Upon their spirits presenting themselves, as usual, before the King, each with its grievance against the other, the King cried out, "When will ye have done with your wrongs and your animosities? I will now settle the matter finally for you"; and immediately commanded that Hsing should become the other's son-in-law in the next world. The latter was then born at Ch'ing-yün, and when he was twenty-eight years of age took his master's degree. He had one daughter, a very pretty girl, whom many of his wealthy neighbors would have been glad to get for their sons; but he would not accept any of their offers. On one occasion, he happened to pass through the prefectural city just as the examination for bachelor's degree was over; and the candidate who had come out at the top of the list, though named Li, was no other than Mr. Hsing. So he led this man away, and took him to an inn, where he treated him with the utmost cordiality, finally arranging that, as Mr. Li was still unmarried, he should marry his pretty daughter. Everyone, of course, thought that this was done in admiration of Li's talents, ignorant that destiny had already decreed the union of the young couple. No sooner were they married than Li, proud of his own literary achievements, began to slight his father-in-law, and often passed many months without going near him; all of which the father-in-law bore very patiently, and when, at length, Li had repeatedly failed to get on any farther in his career, he even went so far as to set to work, by all manner of means, to secure his success; after which they lived happily together as father and son.

In the Infernal Regions

Hsi Fang-p'ing was a native of Tung-an. His father's name was Hsi Lien—a hasty-tempered man, who had quarreled with a neighbor named Yang. By-and-by Yang died: and some years afterward when Lien was on his death-bed, he cried out that Yang was bribing the devils in hell to torture him. His body then swelled up and turned red, and in a few moments he had breathed his last. His son wept bitterly, and refused all food, saying, "Alas! my poor father is now being maltreated by cruel devils;

I must go down and help to redress his wrongs." Thereupon he ceased speaking, and sat for a long time like one dazed, his soul having already quitted its tenement of clay. To himself he appeared to be outside the house, not knowing in what direction to go, so he inquired from one of the passers-by which was the way to the district city.

Before long he found himself there, and, directing his steps toward the prison, found his father lying outside in a very shocking state. When the latter beheld his son, he burst into tears, and declared that the gaolers had been bribed to beat him, which they did both day and night, until they had reduced him to his present sorry plight.

Then Fang-p'ing turned round in a great rage, and began to curse the gaolers. "Out upon you!" cried he; "if my father is guilty he should be punished according to law, and not at the will of a set of scoundrels like you." Thereupon he hurried away, and prepared a petition, which he took with him to present at the morning session of the City God; but his enemy, Yang, had meanwhile set to work, and bribed so effectually, that the City God dismissed his petition for want of corroborative evidence. Fang-p'ing was furious, but could do nothing; so he started at once for the prefectural city, where he managed to get his plaint received, though it was nearly a month before it came on for hearing, and then all he got was a reference back to the district city, where he was severely tortured, and escorted back to the door of his own home, for fear he should give further trouble. However, he did not go in, but stole away and proceeded to lay his complaint before one of the ten Judges of Purgatory; whereupon the two mandarins who had previously ill-used him, came forward and secretly offered him a thousand ounces of silver if he would withdraw the charge. This he positively refused to do; and some days subsequently the landlord of the inn, where he was staying, told him he had been a fool for his pains, and that he would now get neither money nor justice, the Judge himself having already been tampered with.

Fang-p'ing thought this was mere gossip, and would not believe it; but, when his case was called, the Judge utterly refused to hear the charge, and ordered him twenty blows with the bamboo, which were administered in spite of all his protestations. He then cried out, "Ah! it's all because I have no money to give you"; which so incensed the Judge, that he told the lictors to throw Fang-p'ing on the fire-bed. This was a great iron couch, with a roaring fire underneath, which made it red-hot; and upon that the devils cast Fang-p'ing, having first stripped off his clothes, pressing him down on it, until the fire ate into his very bones, though in spite of that he could not die. After a while the devils said he had had enough, and made him get off the iron bed, and put his clothes on again. He was just able to walk, and when he went back into court, the Judge asked him if he wanted to make any further complaints. "Alas!" cried he, "my wrongs are still unredressed, and I should only be lying were I to say I would complain no more."

The Judge then inquired what he had to complain of; to which Fang-p'ing replied that it was of the injustice of his recent punishment. This enraged the Judge so much that he ordered his attendants to saw Fang-p'ing in two. He was then led away by devils, to a place where he was thrust in between a couple of wooden boards, the ground on all sides being wet and sticky with blood. Just at that moment he was summoned to return before the Judge, who asked him if he was still of the same mind; and, on his replying in the affirmative, he was taken back again, and bound between the two boards. The saw was then applied, and as it went through his brain he experienced the most cruel agonies, which, however, he managed to endure without uttering a cry. "He's a tough customer," said one of the devils, as the saw made its way gradually through his chest; to which the other replied, "Truly, this is filial piety; and, as the poor fellow has done nothing, let us turn the saw a little out of the direct line, so as to avoid injuring his heart."

Fang-p'ing then felt the saw make a curve inside him, which caused him even more pain than before; and, in a few moments, he was cut through right down to the ground, and the two halves of his body fell apart, along with the boards to which they were tied, one on either side. The devils went back to report progress, and were then ordered to join Fang-p'ing together again, and bring him in. This they accordingly did,—the cut all down Fang-p'ing's body hurting him dreadfully, and feeling as if it would re-open every minute. But, as Fang-p'ing was unable to walk, one of the devils took out a cord and tied it round his waist, as a reward, he said, for his filial piety. The pain immediately ceased, and Fang-p'ing appeared once more before the Judge, this time promising that he would make no more complaints. The Judge now gave orders that he should be sent up to earth, and the devils, escorting him out of the north gate of the city, showed him his way home, and went away.

Fang-p'ing now saw that there was even less chance of securing justice in the Infernal Regions than upon the earth above; and, having no means of getting at the Great King to plead his case, he bethought himself of a certain upright and benevolent God, called Erh Lang, who was a relative of the Great King's, and him he determined to seek. So he turned about and took his way southward, but was immediately seized by some devils, sent out by the Judge to watch that he really went back to his home. These devils hurried him again into the Judge's presence, where he was received, contrary to his expectation, with great affability; the Judge himself praising his filial piety, but declaring that he need trouble no further in the matter, as his father had already been born again in a wealthy and illustrious family. "And upon you," added the Judge, "I now bestow a present of one thousand ounces of silver to take home with you, as well as the old age of a centenarian, with which I hope you will be satisfied." He then showed Fang-p'ing the stamped record of this, and sent him away in charge of the devils.

The latter now began to abuse him for giving them so much trouble, but Fang-p'ing turned sharply upon them, and threatened to take them back before the Judge. They were then silent, and marched along for about half-a-day, until at length they reached a village, where the devils invited Fang-p'ing into a house, the door of which was standing half-open. Fang-p'ing was just going in, when suddenly the devils gave him a shove from behind, and . . . there he was, born again on earth as a little girl. For three days he pined and cried, without taking any food, and then he died. But his spirit did not forget Erh Lang, and set out at once in search of that God. He had not gone far when he fell in with the retinue of some high personage, and one of the attendants seized him for getting in the way, and hurried him before his master. He was taken to a chariot, where he saw a handsome young man, sitting in great state; and thinking that now was his chance, he told the young man, who he imagined to be a high mandarin, all his sad story from beginning to end. His bonds were then loosed, and he went along with the young man until they reached a place where several officials came out to receive them; and to one of these he confided Fang-p'ing, who now learned that the young man was no other than God himself, the officials being the nine princes of heaven, and the one to whose care he was entrusted no other than Erh Lang. This last was very tall, and had a long white beard, not at all like the popular representation of a God; and when the other princes had gone, he took Fang-p'ing into a court-room, where he saw his father and their old enemy, Yang, besides all the lictors and others who had been mixed up in the case.

By-and-by, some criminals were brought in in cages, and these turned out to be the Judge, Prefect, and Magistrate. The trial was then commenced, the three wicked officers trembling and shaking in their shoes; and when he had heard the evidence, Erh Lang proceeded to pass sentence upon the prisoners, each of whom he sentenced, after enlarging upon the enormity of their several crimes, to be roasted, boiled, and otherwise put to most excruciating tortures. As for Fang-p'ing, he accorded him three extra decades of life, as a reward for his filial piety, and a copy of the sentence was put in his pocket. Father and son journeyed along together, and at length reached their home; that is to say, Fang-p'ing was the first to recover consciousness, and then bade the servants open his father's coffin, which they immediately did, and the old man at once came back to life. But when Fang-p'ing looked for his copy of the sentence, lo! it had disappeared. As for the Yang family, poverty soon overtook them, and all their lands passed into Fang-p'ing's hands; for as sure as any one else bought them, they became sterile forthwith, and would produce nothing; but Fang-p'ing and his father lived on happily, both reaching the age of ninety and odd years.

Singular Case of Ophthalmia

A Mr. Ku, of Chiang-nan, was stopping in an inn at Chi-hsia, when he was attacked by a very severe inflammation of the eyes. Day and night he lay on his bed groaning, no medicines being of any avail; and when he did get a little better, his recovery was accompanied by a singular phenomenon. Every time he closed his eyes, he beheld in front of him a number of large buildings, with all their doors wide open, and people passing and repassing in the background, none of whom he recognised by sight.

One day he had just sat down to have a good look, when, all of a sudden, he felt himself passing through the open doors. He went on through three court-yards without meeting any one; but, on looking into some rooms on either side, he saw a great number of young girls sitting, lying, and kneeling about on a red carpet, which was spread on the ground. Just then a man came out from behind the building, and, seeing Ku, said to him, "Ah, the Prince said there was a stranger at the door; I suppose you are the person he meant." He then asked Ku to walk in, which the latter was at first unwilling to do; however, he yielded to the man's instances, and accompanied him in, asking whose palace it was. His guide told him it belonged to the son of the Ninth Prince, and that he had arrived at the nick of time, for a number of friends and relatives had chosen this very day to come and congratulate the young gentleman on his recent recovery from a severe illness.

Meanwhile another person had come out to hurry them on, and they soon reached a spot where there was a pavilion facing the north, with an ornamental terrace and red balustrades, supported by nine pillars. Ascending the steps, they found the place full of visitors, and then espied a young man seated with his face to the north, whom they at once knew to be the Prince's son, and thereupon they prostrated themselves before him, the whole company rising as they did so. The young Prince made Ku sit down to the east of him, and caused wine to be served; after which some singing-girls came in and performed the Hua-fêng-chu. They had got to about the third scene, when, all of a sudden, Ku heard the landlord of the inn and his servant shouting out to him that dinner was ready, and was dreadfully afraid that the young Prince, too, had heard. No one, however, seemed to have noticed anything, so Ku begged to be excused a moment, as he wished to change his clothes, and immediately ran out. He then looked up, and saw the sun low in the west, and his servant standing by his bedside, whereupon he knew that he had never left the inn. He was much chagrined at this, and wished to go back as fast as he could; he, therefore, dismissed his servant, and on shutting his eyes once more, he found everything just as he had left it, except that where, on the first occasion, he had observed the young girls, there were none now to be seen, but only some disheveled hump-backed creatures, who cried out at him, and asked him what he meant by spying about there.

Ku didn't dare reply, but hurried past them as quickly as he could, and on to the pavilion of the young Prince. There he found him still sitting, but with a black beard over a foot in length; and the Prince was anxious to know where he had been, saying that seven scenes of the play were already over. He then seized a big goblet of wine, and made Ku drink it as a penalty, by which time the play was finished, and the list was handed up for a further selection. The "Marriage of P'êng Tsu" was selected, and then the singing-girls began to hand round the wine in cocoa-nuts big enough to hold about five quarts, which Ku declined, on the ground that he was suffering from weak eyes, and was consequently afraid to drink too much. "If your eyes are bad," cried the young Prince, "the Court physician is at hand, and can attend to you." Thereupon, one of the guests sitting to the east came forward, and opening Ku's eyes with his fingers, touched them with some white ointment, which he applied from the end of a jade pin. He then bade Ku close his eyes, and take a short nap; so the Prince had him conducted into a sleeping-room, where he found the bed so soft, and surrounded by such delicious perfume, that he soon fell into a deep slumber. By-and-by he was awaked by what appeared to be the clashing of cymbals, and fancied that the play was still going on; but on opening his eyes, he saw that it was only the inn-dog, which was licking an oilman's gong. His ophthalmia, however, was quite cured; and when he shut his eyes again he could see nothing.

Chou K'o-ch'ang and His Ghost

At Huai-shang there lived a graduate named Chou T'ien-i, who, though fifty years of age, had but one son, called K'o-ch'ang, whom he loved very dearly. This boy, when about thirteen or fourteen, was a handsome, well-favored fellow, strangely averse to study, and often playing truant from school, sometimes for the whole day, without any remonstrance on the part of his father. One day he went away and did not come back in the evening; neither, after a diligent search, could any traces of him be discovered. His father and mother were in despair, and hardly cared to live; but after a year and more had passed away, lo and behold! K'o-ch'ang returned, saying that he had been beguiled away by a Taoist priest, who, however, had not done him any harm, and that he had seized a moment while the priest was absent to escape and find his way home again.

His father was delighted, and asked him no more questions, but set to work to give him an education; and K'o-ch'ang was so much cleverer and more intelligent than he had been before, that by the following year he had taken his bachelor's degree and had made quite a name for himself. Immediately all the good families of the neighborhood wanted to secure him as a son-in-law. Among others proposed there was an extremely nice girl, the daughter of a gentleman named Chao, who had taken his doctor's degree, and K'o-ch'ang's father was very anxious that he should marry the young lady. The youth himself would not hear of it, but stuck to his books and took his master's degree, quite refusing to entertain any thought of marriage; and this so exasperated his mother that one day the good lady began to berate him soundly. K'o-ch'ang got up in a great rage and cried out, "I have long been wanting to get away, and have only remained for your sakes. I shall now say farewell, and leave Miss Chao for any one that likes to marry her." At this his mother tried to detain him, but in a moment he had fallen forward on the ground, and there was nothing left of him but his hat and clothes.

They were all dreadfully frightened, thinking that it must have been K'o-ch'ang's ghost who had been with them, and gave themselves up to weeping and lamentation; however, the very next day K'o-ch'ang arrived, accompanied by a retinue of horses and servants, his story being that he had formerly been kidnapped and sold to a wealthy trader, who, being then childless, had adopted him, but who, when he subsequently had a son born to him by his own wife, sent K'o-ch'ang back to his old home. And as soon as his father began to question him as to his studies, his utter dullness and want of knowledge soon made it clear that he was the real K'o-ch'ang of old; but he was already known as a man who had got his master's degree, (that is, the ghost of him had got it,) so it was determined in the family to keep the whole affair secret. This K'o-ch'ang was only too ready to espouse Miss Chao; and before a year had passed over their heads his wife had presented the old people with the much longed-for grandson.

The Spirits of the Po-yang Lake

An official, named Chai, was appointed to a post at Jao-chou, and on his way thither crossed the Po-yang lake. Happening to visit the shrine of the local spirits, he noticed a carved image of the patriotic Ting P'u-lang, and another of a namesake of his own, the latter occupying a very inferior position. "Come! come!" said Chai, "my patron saint shan't be put in the background like that"; so he moved the image into a more honorable place, and then went back on board his boat again. Soon after, a great wind struck the vessel, and carried away the mast and sails; at which the sailors, in great alarm, set to work to howl and cry. However, in a few moments they saw a small skiff come cutting through the waves, and before long they were all safely on board. The man who rowed it was strangely like the image in the shrine, the position of which Chai had changed; but they were hardly out of danger when the squall had passed over, and skiff and man had both vanished.

The Stream of Cash

A certain gentleman's servant was one day in his master's garden, when he beheld a stream of *cash* flowing by, two or three feet in breadth and of about the same depth. He immediately seized two large handfuls, and then threw himself down on the top of the stream in order to try and secure the rest. However, when he got up he found that it had all flowed away from under him, none being left except what he had got in his two hands.

The Injustice of Heaven

Mr. Hsü was a magistrate at Shantung. A certain upper chamber of his house was used as a store-room; but some creature managed so frequently to get in and make havoc among the stores, for which the servants were always being scolded, that at length some of the latter determined to keep watch. By-and-by they saw a huge spider as big as a peck measure, and hurried off to tell their master, who thought it so strange that he gave orders to the servants to feed the insect with cakes. It thus became very tame, and would always come forth when hungry, returning as soon as it had taken enough to eat.

Years passed away, and one day Mr. Hsü was consulting his archives, when suddenly the spider appeared and ran under the table. Thinking it was hungry, he bade his servants give it a cake; but the next moment he noticed two snakes, of about the thickness of a chop-stick, lying one on each side. The spider drew in its legs as if in mortal fear, and the snakes began to swell out until they were as big round as an egg; at which Mr. Hsü was greatly alarmed, and would have hurried away, when crash! went a peal of thunder, killing every person in the house. Mr. Hsü himself recovered consciousness after a little while, but only to see his wife and servants, seven persons in all, lying dead; and after a month's illness he, too, departed this life. Now Mr. Hsü was an upright, honorable man, who really had the interests of the people at heart. A subscription was accordingly raised to pay his funeral expenses, and on the day of his burial the air was rent for miles round with cries of weeping and lamentation.

The Sea-Serpent

A TRADER NAMED CHIA WAS VOYAGING ON THE SOUTH SEAS, WHEN ONE NIGHT IT suddenly became as light as day on board his ship. Jumping up to see what was the matter, he beheld a huge creature with its body half out of the water, towering up like a hill. Its eyes resembled two suns, and threw a light far and wide; and when the trader asked the boatmen what it was, there was not one who could say. They all crouched down and watched it; and by-and-by the monster gradually disappeared in the water again, leaving everything in darkness as before. And when they reached port, they found all the people talking about a strange phenomenon of a great light that had appeared in the night, the time of which coincided exactly with the strange scene they themselves had witnessed.

The Magic Mirror

". . . BUT IF YOU WOULD REALLY LIKE TO HAVE SOMETHING THAT HAS BELONGED TO me," said Fêng-hsien to Liu, "you shall." Whereupon she took out a mirror and gave it to him, saying, "Whenever you want to see me, you must look for me in your books; otherwise I shall not be visible";—and in a moment she had vanished.

Liu went home very melancholy at heart; but when he looked in the mirror, there was Fêng-hsien, standing with her back to him, gazing, as it were, at some one who was going away, and about a hundred paces from her. He then bethought himself of her injunctions, and settled down to his studies, refusing to receive any visitors; and a few days subsequently, when he happened to look in the mirror, there was Fêng-hsien, with her face turned towards him, and smiling in every feature.

After this, he was always taking out the mirror to look at her; however, in about a month his good resolutions began to disappear, and he once more went out to enjoy himself and waste his time as before. When he returned home and looked in the mirror, Fêng-hsien seemed to be crying bitterly; and the day after, when he looked at her again, she had her back turned toward him as on the day he received the mirror. He now knew that it was because he had neglected his studies, and forthwith set to work again with all diligence, until in a month's time she had turned round once again.

Henceforward, whenever anything interrupted his progress, Fêng-hsien's countenance became sad; but whenever he was getting on well, her sadness was changed to smiles. Night and morning Liu would look at the mirror, regarding it quite in the light of a revered preceptor; and in three years' time he took his degree in triumph. "Now," cried he, "I shall be able to look Fêng-hsien in the face." And there, sure enough, she was, with her delicately-penciled arched eye-brows, and her teeth just showing between her lips, as happy-looking as she could be, when, all of a sudden, she seemed to speak, and Liu heard her say, "A pretty pair we make, I must allow"—and the next moment Fêng-hsien stood by his side.

Courage Tested

Mr. Tung was a Hsü-chou man, very fond of playing broad-sword, and a light-hearted, devil-may-care fellow, who was often involving himself in trouble. One day he fell in with a traveler who was riding on a mule and going the same way as himself; whereupon they entered into conversation, and began to talk to each other about feats of strength and so on. The traveler said his name was T'ung, and that he belonged to Liao-yang; that he had been twenty years away from home, and had just returned from beyond the sea. "And I venture to say," cried Tung, "that in your wanderings on the Four Seas you have seen a great many people; but have you seen any supernaturally clever ones?" T'ung asked him to what he alluded; and then Tung explained what his own particular hobby was, adding how much he would like to learn from them any tricks in the art of broad-sword.

"Supernaturals," replied the traveler, "are to be found everywhere. It needs but that a man should be a loyal subject and a filial son for him to know all that the supernaturals know."

"Right you are, indeed!" cried Tung, as he drew a short sword from his belt, and, tapping the blade with his fingers, began to accompany it with a song. He then cut down a tree that was by the wayside, to show T'ung how sharp it was; at which T'ung smoothed his beard and smiled, begging to be allowed to have a look at the weapon. Tung handed it to him, and, when he had turned it over two or three times, he said, "This is a very inferior piece of steel; now, though I know nothing about broad-sword myself, I have a weapon which is really of some use." He then drew from beneath his coat a sword of a foot or so in length, and with it he began to pare pieces off Tung's sword, which seemed as soft as a melon, and which he cut quite away like a horse's hoof. Tung was greatly astonished, and borrowed the other's sword to examine it, returning it after carefully wiping the blade. He then invited T'ung to his house, and made him stay the night; and, after begging him to explain the mystery of his sword, began to nurse his leg and sit listening respectfully without saying a word.

It was already pretty late, when suddenly there was a sound of scuffling next door, where Tung's father lived; and, on putting his ear to the wall, he heard an angry voice saying, "Tell your son to come here at once, and then I will spare you." This was followed by other sounds of beating and a continued groaning, in a voice which Tung knew to be his father's. He therefore seized a spear, and was about to rush forth, but T'ung held him back, saying, "You'll be killed for a certainty if you go. Let us think of some other plan." Tung asked what plan he could suggest; to which the other replied, "The robbers are killing your father: there is no help for you; but as you have no brothers, just go and tell your wife and children what your last wishes are, while I try and rouse the servants." Tung agreed to this, and ran in to tell his wife, who clung to him and implored him not to go, until at length all his courage had ebbed away, and he went upstairs with her to get his bow and arrows ready to resist the robbers' attack.

At that juncture he heard the voice of his friend T'ung, outside on the eaves of the house, saying, with a laugh, "All right; the robbers have gone"; but on lighting a candle, he could see nothing of him. He then stole out to the front door, where he met his father with a lantern in his hand, coming in from a party at a neighbor's house; and the whole court-yard was covered with the ashes of burnt grass, whereby he knew that T'ung the traveler was himself a supernatural.

The Disembodied Friend

Mr. Ch'ên, M.A., of Shun-t'ien Fu, when a boy of sixteen, went to school at a Buddhist temple. There were a great many scholars besides himself, and, among others, one named Ch'u, who said he came from Shantung. This Ch'u was a very hard-working fellow; he never seemed to be idle, and actually slept in the schoolroom, not going home at all. Ch'ên became much attached to him, and one day asked him why he never went away. "Well, you see," replied Ch'u, "my people are very poor, and can hardly afford to pay for my schooling; but, by dint of working half the night, two of my days are equal to three of anybody else's." Thereupon Ch'ên said he would bring his own bed to the school, and that they would sleep there together; to which Ch'u replied that the teaching they got wasn't worth much, and that they would do better by putting themselves under a certain old scholar named Lü. This they were easily able to do, as the arrangement at the temple was monthly, and at the end of each month anyone was free to go or to come. So off they went to this Mr. Lü, a man of considerable literary attainments, who had found himself in Shun-t'ien Fu without a cash in his pocket, and was accordingly obliged to take pupils. He was delighted at getting two additions to his number and, Ch'u showing himself an apt scholar, the two soon became very great friends, sleeping in the same room and eating at the same table. At the end of the month Ch'u asked for leave of absence, and, to the astonishment of all, ten days elapsed without anything being heard of him.

It then chanced that Ch'ên went to the T'ien-ning temple, and there he saw Ch'u under one of the verandahs, occupied in cutting wood for lucifer-matches. The latter was much disconcerted by the arrival of Ch'ên, who asked him why he had given up his studies; so the latter took him aside, and explained that he was so poor as to be obliged to work half a month to scrape together funds enough for his next month's schooling. "You come along back with me," cried Ch'ên, on hearing this, "I will arrange for the payment," which Ch'u immediately consented to do on condition that Ch'ên would keep the whole thing a profound secret.

Now Ch'ên's father was a wealthy tradesman, and from his till Ch'ên abstracted money wherewith to pay for Ch'u; and by-and-by, when his father found him out, he confessed why he had done so. Thereupon Ch'ên's father called him a fool, and would not let him resume his studies; at which Ch'u was much hurt, and would have left the school too, but that old Mr. Lü discovered what had taken place, and gave him the money to return to Ch'ên's father, keeping him still at the school, and treating him quite like his own son. So Ch'ên studied no more, but whenever he met Ch'u he always asked him to join in some refreshment at a restaurant, Ch'u invariably refusing, but yielding at length to his entreaties, being himself loth to break off their old acquaintanceship.

Thus two years passed away, when Ch'ên's father died, and Ch'ên went back to his books under the guidance of old Mr. Lü, who was very glad to see such determination. Of course Ch'ên was now far behind Ch'u; and in about six months Lü's son arrived, having begged his way in search of his father, so Mr. Lü gave up his school and returned home with a purse which his pupils had made up for him, Ch'u adding nothing thereto but his tears. At parting, Mr. Lü advised Ch'ên to take Ch'u as his tutor, and this he did, establishing him comfortably in the house with him. The examination was very shortly to commence, and Ch'ên felt convinced that he should not get through; but Ch'u said he thought he should be able to manage the matter for him.

On the appointed day he introduced Ch'ên to a gentleman who he said was a cousin of his, named Liu, and asked Ch'ên to accompany this cousin, which Ch'ên was just proceeding to do when Ch'u pulled him back from behind, and he would have fallen down but that the cousin pulled him up again, and then, after having scrutinized his appearance, carried him off to his own house. There being no ladies there, Ch'ên was put into the inner apartments; and a few days afterward Liu said to him, "A great many people will be at the gardens to-day; let us go and amuse ourselves awhile, and afterward I will send you home again." He then gave orders that a servant should proceed on ahead with tea and wine, and by-and-by they themselves went, and were soon in the thick of the fête. Crossing over a bridge, they saw beneath an old willow tree a little painted skiff, and were soon on board, engaged in freely passing round the wine. However, finding this a little dull, Liu bade his servant go and see if Miss Li, the famous singing-girl, was at home; and in a few minutes the servant returned bringing Miss Li with him. Ch'ên had met her before, and so they at once exchanged greetings, while Liu begged her to be good enough to favor them with a song. Miss Li, who seemed laboring under a fit of melancholy, forthwith began a funeral dirge; at which Ch'ên was not much pleased, and observed that such a theme was hardly suitable to the occasion. With a forced smile, Miss Li changed her key, and gave them a love-song; whereupon Ch'ên seized her hand, and said, "There 's that song of the Huan-sha river, which you sang once before; I have read it over several times, but have quite forgotten the words." Then Miss Li began—

"Eyes overflowing with tears, she sits gazing into her glass,
Lifting the bamboo screen, one of her comrades approaches;
She bends her head and seems intent on her bow-like slippers,
And forces her eyebrows to arch themselves into a smile.
With her scarlet sleeve she wipes the tears from her perfumed cheek,
In fear and trembling lest they should guess the thoughts that o'erwhelm her."

Ch'ên repeated this over several times, until at length the skiff stopped, and they passed through a long verandah, where a great many verses had been inscribed on the walls, to which Ch'ên at once proceeded to add a stanza of his own. Evening was now coming on, and Liu remarked that the candidates would be just about leaving the examination-hall; so he escorted him back to his own home, and there left him. The room was dark, and there was no one with him; but by-and-by the servants ushered in some one whom at first he took to be Ch'u. However, he soon saw that it was not Ch'u, and in another moment the stranger had fallen against him and knocked him down. "Master's fainted!" cried the servants, as they ran to pick him up; and then Ch'ên discovered that the one who had fallen down was really no other than himself. On getting up, he saw Ch'u standing by his side; and when they had sent away the servants the latter said, "Don't be alarmed: I am nothing more than a disembodied spirit. My time for re-appearing on earth is long overdue, but I could not forget your great kindness to me, and accordingly I have remained under this form in order to assist in the accomplishment of your wishes. The three bouts are over, and your ambition will be gratified."

Ch'ên then inquired if Ch'u could assist him in like manner for his doctor's degree; to which the latter replied, "Alas! the luck descending to you from your ancestors is not equal to that. They were a niggardly lot, and unfit for the posthumous honors you would thus confer on them." Ch'ên next asked him whither he was going; and Ch'u replied that he hoped, through the agency of his cousin, who was a clerk in Purgatory, to be born again in old Mr. Lü's family. They then bade each other adieu; and, when morning came, Ch'ên set off to call on Miss Li, the singing-girl; but on reaching her house he found that she had been dead some days. He walked on to the gardens, and there he saw traces of verses that had been written on the walls, and evidently rubbed out, so as to be hardly decipherable. In a moment it flashed across him that the verses and their composers belonged to the other world. Toward evening Ch'u re-appeared in high spirits, saying that he had succeeded in his design, and had come to wish Ch'ên a long farewell. Holding out his open palms, he requested Ch'ên to write the word *Ch'u* on each; and then, after refusing to take a parting cup, he went away, telling Ch'ên that the examination-list would soon be out, and that they would meet again before long. Ch'ên brushed away his tears and escorted him to the door, where a man, who had been waiting for him, laid his hand on Ch'u's head and pressed it downward until Ch'u was perfectly flat. The man then put him in a sack and carried him off on his back.

A few days afterward the list came out, and, to his great joy, Ch'ên found his name among the successful candidates; whereupon he immediately started off to visit his old tutor, Mr. Lü. Now Mr. Lü's wife had had no children for ten years, being about fifty years of age, when suddenly she gave birth to a son, who was born with both fists doubled up so that no one could open them. On his arrival Ch'ên begged to see the child, and declared that inside its hands would be found written the word Ch'u. Old Mr. Lü laughed at this; but no sooner had the child set eyes on Ch'ên than both its fists opened spontaneously, and there was the word as Ch'ên had said. The story was soon told, and Ch'ên went home, after making a handsome present to the family; and later on, when Mr. Lü went up for his doctor's degree and stayed at Ch'ên's house, his son was thirteen years old, and had already matriculated as a candidate for literary honors.

The Cloth Merchant

A CERTAIN CLOTH MERCHANT WENT TO CH'ING-CHOU, WHERE HE HAPPENED TO stroll into an old temple, all tumble-down and in ruins. He was lamenting over this sad state of things, when a priest who stood by observed that a devout believer like himself could hardly do better than put the place into repair, and thus obtain favor in the eyes of Buddha. This the merchant consented to do; whereupon the priest invited him to walk into the private quarters of the temple, and treated him with much courtesy; but he went on to propose that our friend the merchant should also undertake the general ornamentation of the place both inside and out. The latter declared he could not afford the expense, and the priest began to get very angry, and urged him so strongly that at last the merchant, in terror, promised to give all the money he had. After this he was preparing to go away, but the priest detained him, saying, "You haven't given the money of your own free will, and consequently you'll be owing me a grudge: I can't do better than make an end of you at once." Thereupon he seized a knife, and refused to listen to all the cloth merchant's entreaties, until at length the latter asked to be allowed to hang himself, to which the priest consented; and, showing him into a dark room, told him to make haste about it.

At this juncture, a Tartar-General happened to pass by the temple; and from a distance, through a breach in the old wall, he saw a damsel in a red dress pass into the priest's quarters. This roused his suspicions, and dismounting from his horse, he entered the temple and searched high and low, but without discovering anything. The dark room above-mentioned was locked and double-barred, and the priest refused to open it, saying the place was haunted. The General in a rage burst open the door, and there beheld the cloth merchant hanging from a beam. He cut him down at once, and in a short time he was brought round and told the General the whole story. They then searched for the damsel, but she was nowhere to be found, having been nothing more than a divine manifestation. The General cut off the priest's head and restored the cloth merchant's property to him, after which the latter put the temple in thorough repair and kept it well supplied with lights and incense ever afterward.

A Strange Companion

Han Kung-fu, of Yü-ch'êng, told me that he was one day traveling along a road with a man of his village, named P'êng, when all of a sudden the latter disappeared, leaving his mule to jog along with an empty saddle. At the same moment, Mr. Han heard his voice calling for assistance, and apparently proceeding from inside one of the panniers strapped across the mule's back; and on looking closely, there indeed he was in one of the panniers, which, however, did not seem to be at all displaced by his weight. On trying to get him out the mouth of the pannier closed itself tightly; and it was only when he cut it open with a knife that he saw P'êng curled up in it like a dog. He then helped him out, and asked him how he managed to get in; but this he was unable to say. It further appeared that his family was under fox influence, many strange things of this kind having happened before.

Spiritualistic Séances

It is customary in Shantung, when any one is sick, for the womenfolk to engage an old sorceress or medium, who strums on a tambourine and performs certain mysterious antics. This custom obtains even more in the capital, where young ladies of the best families frequently organize such *séances* among themselves. On a table in the hall they spread out a profusion of wine and meat, and burn huge candles which make the place as light as day. Then the sorceress, shortening her skirts, stands on one leg and performs the *shang-yang*, while two of the others support her, one on each side. All this time she is chattering unintelligible sentences, something between a song and a prayer, the words being confused but uttered in a sort of tune; while the hall resounds with the thunder of drums, enough to stun a person, with which her vaticinations are mixed up and lost. By-and-by her head begins to droop, and her eyes to look aslant; and but for her two supporters she would inevitably fall to the ground. Suddenly she stretches forth her neck and bounds several feet into the air, upon which the other women regard her in terror, saying, "The spirits have come to eat"; and immediately all the candles are blown out and everything is in total darkness. Thus they remain for about a quarter of an hour, afraid to speak a word, which in any case would not be heard through the din, until at length the sorceress calls out the personal name of the head of the family and some others; whereupon they immediately relight the candles and hurry up to ask if the reply of the spirits is favorable or otherwise. They then see that every scrap of the food and every drop of the wine has disappeared. Meanwhile, they watch the old woman's expression, whereby they can tell if the spirits are well disposed; and each one asks her some question, to which she as promptly replies. Should there be any unbelievers among the party, the spirits are at once aware of their presence; and the old sorceress, pointing her finger at such a one, cries out, "Disrespectful mocker! where are your trousers?" upon which the mocker alluded to looks down, and lo! her trousers are gone—gone to the top of a tree in the court-yard, where they will subsequently be found.

Manchu women and girls, especially, are firm believers in spiritualism. On the slightest provocation they consult their medium, who comes into the room gorgeously dressed, and riding on an imitation horse or tiger. In her hand she holds a long spear, with which she mounts the couch and postures in an extraordinary manner, the animal she rides snorting or roaring fiercely all the time. Some call her Kuan Ti, others Chang Fei, and others again Chou Kung, from her terribly martial aspect, which strikes fear into all beholders. And should any daring fellow try to peep in while the *séance* is going on, out of the window darts the spear, transfixes his hat, and draws it off his head into the room, while women and girls, young and old, hop round one after the other like geese, on one leg, without seeming to get the least fatigued.

The Mysterious Head

Several traders who were lodging at an inn in Peking, occupied a room which was divided from the adjoining apartment by a partition of boards from which a piece was missing, leaving an aperture about as big as a basin. Suddenly a girl's head appeared through the opening, with very pretty features and nicely dressed hair; and the next moment an arm, as white as polished jade. The traders were much alarmed, and, thinking it was the work of devils, tried to seize the head, which, however, was quickly drawn in again out of their reach. This happened a second time, and then, as they could see no body belonging to the head, one of them took a knife in his hand and crept up against the partition underneath the hole. In a little while the head re-appeared, when he made a chop at it and cut it off, the blood spurting out all over the floor and wall. The traders hurried off to tell the landlord, who immediately reported the matter to the authorities, taking the head with him, and the traders were forthwith arrested and examined; but the magistrate could make nothing of the case, and, as no one appeared for the prosecution, the accused, after about six months' incarceration, were accordingly released, and orders were given for the girl's head to be buried.

The Spirit of the Hills

A man named Li, of I-tu, was once crossing the hills when he came upon a number of persons sitting on the ground engaged in drinking. As soon as they saw Li they begged him to join them, and vied with each other in filling his cup. Meanwhile, he looked about him and noticed that the various trays and dishes contained all kinds of costly food; the wine only seemed to him a little rough on the palate. In the middle of their fun up came a stranger with a face about three feet long and a very tall hat; whereupon the others were very much alarmed, and cried out, "The hill spirit! the hill spirit!" running away in all directions as fast as they could go. Li hid himself in a hole in the ground; and when by-and-by he peeped out to see what had happened, the wine and food had disappeared, and there was nothing there but a few dirty potsherds and some pieces of broken tiles with efts and lizards crawling over them.

Ingratitude Punished

K'u Ta-yu was a native of the Yang district, and managed to get a military appointment under the command of Tsu Shu-shun. The latter treated him most kindly, and finally sent him as Major-General of some troops by which he was then trying to establish the dynasty of the usurping Chows. K'u soon perceived that the game was lost, and immediately turned his forces upon Tsu Shu-shun, whom he succeeded in capturing, after Tsu had been wounded in the hand, and whom he at once forwarded as a prisoner to headquarters. That night he dreamed that the Judge of Purgatory appeared to him, and, reproaching him with his base ingratitude, bade the devil-lictors seize him and scald his feet in a cauldron of boiling oil. K'u then woke up with a start, and found that his feet were very sore and painful; and in a short time they swelled up, and his toes dropped off. Fever set in, and in his agony he shrieked out, "Ungrateful wretch that I was indeed," and fell back and expired.

Smelling Essays

NOW AS SUNG AND WANG WANDERED ABOUT THE TEMPLE THEY CAME UPON AN OLD blind priest sitting under the verandah, engaged in selling medicines and prescribing for patients. "Ah!" cried Sung, "there is an extraordinary man who is well versed in the arts of composition"; and immediately he sent back to get the essay they had just been reading, in order to obtain the old priest's opinion as to its merits. At the same moment up came their friend from Yü-hang, and all three went along together. Wang began by addressing him as "Professor"; whereupon the priest, who thought the stranger had come to consult him as a doctor, inquired what might be the disease from which he was suffering. Wang then explained what his mission was; upon which the priest smiled and said, "Who's been telling you this nonsense? How can a man with no eyes discuss with you the merits of your compositions?" Wang replied by asking him to let his ears do duty for his eyes; but the priest answered that he would hardly have patience to sit out Wang's three sections, amounting perhaps to some two thousand and more words. "However," added he, "if you like to burn it, I'll try what I can do with my nose."

Wang complied, and burned the first section there and then; and the old priest, snuffing up the smoke, declared that it wasn't such a bad effort, and finally gave it as his opinion that Wang would probably succeed at the examination. The young scholar from Yü-hang didn't believe that the old priest could really tell anything by these means, and forthwith proceeded to burn an essay by one of the old masters; but the priest no sooner smelt the smoke than he cried out, "Beautiful indeed! beautiful indeed! I do enjoy this. The light of genius and truth is evident here." The Yü-hang scholar was greatly astonished at this, and began to burn an essay of his own; whereupon the priest said, "I had had but a taste of that one; why change so soon to another?"

"The first paragraph," replied the young man, "was by a friend; the rest is my own composition." No sooner had he uttered these words than the old priest began to retch violently, and begged that he might have no more, as he was sure it would make him sick. The Yü-hang scholar was much abashed at this, and went away; but in a few days the list came out and his name was among the successful ones, while Wang's was not. He at once hurried off to tell the old priest, who, when he heard the news, sighed and said, "I may be blind with my eyes but I am not so with my nose, which I fear is the case with the examiners. Besides," added he, "I was talking to you about composition: I said nothing about *destiny*."

His Father's Ghost

A MAN NAMED T'IEN TZŬCH'ÊNG, OF CHIANG-NING, WAS CROSSING THE TUNG-T'ING lake, when the boat was capsized, and he was drowned. His son, Liang-ssŭ, who, toward the close of the Ming dynasty, took the highest degree, was then a baby in arms; and his wife, hearing the bad news, swallowed poison forthwith, and left the child to the care of his grandmother. When Liang-ssŭ grew up, he was appointed magistrate in Hu-pei, where he remained about a year. He was then transferred to Hu-nan, on military service; but, on reaching the Tung-t'ing lake, his feelings overpowered him, and he returned to plead inability as an excuse for not taking up his post. Accordingly, he was degraded to the rank of Assistant-Magistrate, which he at first declined, but was finally compelled to accept; and thenceforward gave himself up to roaming about on the lakes and streams of the surrounding country, without paying much attention to his official duties.

One night he had anchored his boat alongside the bank of a river, when suddenly the cadence of a sweetly-played flageolet broke upon his ear; so he strolled along by the light of the moon in the direction of the music, until, after a few minutes' walking, he reached a cottage standing by itself, with a few citron-trees round it, and brilliantly-lighted inside. Approaching a window, he peeped in, and saw three persons sitting at a table, engaged in drinking. In the place of honor was a graduate of about thirty years of age; an old man played the host, and at the side sat a much younger man playing on the flageolet. When he had finished, the old man clapped his hands in admiration; but the graduate turned away with a sigh, as if he had not heard a note. "Come now, Mr. Lu," cried the old man, addressing the latter, "kindly favor us with one of your songs, which, I know, must be worth hearing." The graduate then began to sing as follows:—

"Over the river the wind blows cold on lonely me:
Each flow'ret trampled under foot, all verdure gone.
At home a thousand *li* away, I cannot be;
So toward the Bridge my spirit nightly wanders on."

The above was given in such melancholy tones that the old man smiled and said, "Mr. Lu, these must be experiences of your own," and, immediately filling a goblet, added, "I can do nothing like that; but if you will let me, I will give you a song to help us on with our wine." He then sung a verse from "Li T'ai-poh," and put them all in a lively humor again; after which the young man said he would just go outside and see how high the moon was, which he did, and observing Liang-ssŭ outside, clapped his hands, and cried out to his companions, "There is a man at the window, who has seen all we have been doing." He then led Liang-ssŭ in; whereupon the other two rose, and begged him to be seated, and to join them in their wine. The wine, however, was cold, and he therefore declined; but the young man at once perceived his reason, and proceeded to warm some for him.

Liang-ssŭ now ordered his servant to go and buy some more, but this his host would not permit him to do. They next inquired Liang-ssŭ's name, and whence he came, and then the old man said, "Why, then, you are the father and mother of the district in which I live. My name is River: I am an old resident here. This young man is a Mr. Tu, of Kiang-si; and this gentleman," added he, pointing to the graduate, "is Mr. Rushten, a fellow-provincial of yours." Mr. Rushten looked at Liang-ssŭ in rather a contemptuous way, and without taking much notice of him; whereupon Liang-ssŭ asked him whereabouts he lived in Chiang-ning, observing that it was strange he himself should never have heard of such an accomplished gentleman. "Alas!" replied Rushten, "it is many a long day since I left my home, and I know nothing even of my own family. Alas, indeed!" These words were uttered in so mournful a tone of voice that the old man broke in with, "Come, come, now! talking like this, instead of drinking when we're all so jolly together; this will never do." He then drained a bumper himself, and said, "I propose a game of forfeits. We'll throw with three dice; and whoever throws so that the spots on one die equal those on the other two shall give us a verse with a corresponding classical allusion in it." He then threw himself, and turned up an ace, a two, and a three; whereupon he sang the following lines:—

"An ace and a deuce on one side, just equal a three on the other:
For Fan a chicken was boiled, though three years had passed,
by Chang's mother.
Thus friends love to meet!"

Then the young musician threw, and turned up two twos and a four; whereupon he exclaimed, "Don't laugh at the feeble allusion of an unlearned fellow like me:—

"Two deuces are equal to a four:
Four men united their valor in the old city.
Thus brothers love to meet!"

Mr. Rushten followed with two aces and a two, and recited these lines:—

> "Two aces are equal to a two:
> Lu-hsiang stretched out his two arms and embraced his father.
> Thus father and son love to meet!"

Liang then threw, and turned up the same as Mr. Rushten; whereupon he said:—

> "Two aces are equal to a two:
> Mao-jung regaled Lin-tsung with two baskets.
> Thus host and guest love to meet!"

When the *partie* was over Liang-ssŭ rose to go, but Mr. Rushten said, "Dear me! why are you in such a hurry; we haven't had a moment to speak of the old place. Please stay: I was just going to ask you a few questions." So Liang-ssŭ sat down again, and Mr. Rushten proceeded. "I had an old friend," said he, "who was drowned in the Tung-t'ing lake. He bore the same name as yourself; was he a relative?"

"He was my father," replied Liang-ssŭ; "how did you know him?"

"We were friends as boys together; and when he was drowned, I recovered and buried his body by the river-side." Liang-ssŭ here burst into tears, and thanked Mr. Rushten very warmly, begging him to point out his father's grave.

"Come again to-morrow," said Mr. Rushten, "and I will show it to you. You could easily find it yourself. It is close by here, and has ten stalks of water-rush growing on it."

Liang-ssŭ now took his leave, and went back to his boat, but he could not sleep for thinking of what Mr. Rushten had told him; and at length, without waiting for the dawn, he set out to look for the grave. To his great astonishment, the house where he had spent the previous evening had disappeared; but hunting about in the direction indicated by Mr. Rushten, he found a grave with ten water-rushes growing on it, precisely as Mr. Rushten had described. It then flashed across him that Mr. Rushten's name had a special meaning, and that he had been holding converse with none other than the disembodied spirit of his own father. And, on inquiring of the people of the place, he learned that twenty years before a benevolent old gentleman, named Kao, had been in the habit of collecting the bodies of persons found drowned, and burying them in that spot. Liang then opened the grave, and carried off his father's remains to his own home, where his grandmother, to whom he described Mr. Rushten's appearance, confirmed the suspicion he himself had formed. It also turned out that the young musician was a cousin of his, who had been drowned when nineteen years of age; and then he recollected that the boy's father had subsequently gone to Kiang-si, and that his mother had died there, and had been buried at the Bamboo Bridge, to which Mr. Rushten had alluded in his song. But he did not know who the old man was.

The Boat-Girl Bride

WANG KULI-NGAN WAS A YOUNG MAN OF GOOD FAMILY. IT HAPPENED ONCE WHEN HE was traveling southward, and had moored his boat to the bank, that he saw in another boat close by a young boat-girl embroidering shoes. He was much struck by her beauty, and continued gazing at her for some time, though she took not the slightest notice of him. By-and-by he began singing—

"The Lo-yang lady lives over the way:
[Fifteen years is her age I should say]."

to attract her attention, and then she seemed to perceive that he was addressing himself to her; but, after just raising her head and glancing at him, she resumed her embroidery as before. Wang then threw a piece of silver toward her, which fell on her skirt; however she merely picked it up, and flung it on to the bank, as if she had not seen what it was, so Wang put it back in his pocket again. He followed up by throwing her a gold bracelet, to which she paid no attention whatever, never taking her eyes off her work. A few minutes after her father appeared, much to the dismay of Wang, who was afraid he would see the bracelet; but the young girl quietly placed her feet over it, and concealed it from his sight. The boatman let go the painter, and away they went down stream, leaving Wang sitting there, not knowing what to do next. And, having recently lost his wife, he regretted that he had not seized this opportunity to make another match; the more so, as when he came to ask the other boat-people of the place, no one knew anything about them.

So Wang got into his own boat, and started off in pursuit; but evening came on, and, as he could see nothing of them, he was obliged to turn back and proceed in the direction where business was taking him. When he had finished that, he returned, making inquiries all the way along, but without hearing anything about the object of his search. On arriving at home, he was unable either to eat or to sleep, so much did this affair occupy his mind; and about a year afterward he went south again, bought a boat, and lived in it as his home, watching carefully every single vessel that passed either up or down, until at last there was hardly one he didn't know by sight. But all this time the boat he was looking for never reappeared.

Some six months passed away thus, and then, having exhausted all his funds, he was obliged to go home, where he remained in a state of general inaptitude for anything. One night he dreamed that he entered a village on the river-bank, and that, after passing several houses, he saw one with a door toward the south, and a palisade of bamboos inside. Thinking it was a garden, he walked in and beheld a beautiful magnolia, covered with blossoms, which reminded him of the line—

"And Judas-tree in flower before her door."

A few steps farther on was a neat bamboo hedge, on the other side of which, toward the north, he found a small house, with three columns, the door of which was locked; and another, toward the south, with its window shaded by the broad leaves of a plaintain-tree. The door was barred by a clothes-horse, on which was hanging an embroidered petticoat; and, on seeing this, Wang stepped back, knowing that he had got to the ladies' quarters; but his presence had already been noticed inside, and, in another moment, out came his heroine of the boat. Overjoyed at seeing her, he was on the point of grasping her hand, when suddenly the girl's father arrived, and, in his consternation, Wang waked up, and found that it was all a dream. Every incident of it, however, remained clear and distinct in his mind, and he took care to say nothing about it to anybody, for fear of destroying its reality.

Another year passed away, and he went again to Chinkiang, where lived an official, named Hsü, who was an old friend of the family, and who invited Wang to come and take a cup of wine with him. On his way thither, Wang lost his way, but at length reached a village which seemed familiar to him, and which he soon found, by the door with the magnolia inside, to be identical, in every particular, with the village of his dream. He went in through the doorway, and there was everything as he had seen it in his dream, even to the boat-girl herself. She jumped up on his arrival, and, shutting the door in his face, asked what his business was there. Wang inquired if she had forgotten about the bracelet, and went on to tell her how long he had been searching for her, and how, at last, she had been revealed to him in a dream. The girl then begged to know his name and family; and when she heard who he was, she asked what a gentleman like himself could want with a poor boat-girl like her, as he must have a wife of his own. "But for you," replied Wang, "I should, indeed, have been married long ago." Upon which the girl told him if that was really the case, he had better apply to her parents, "although," added she, "they have already refused a great many offers for me. The bracelet you gave me is here, but my father and mother are just now away from home; they will be back shortly. You go away now and engage a match-maker, when I dare say it will be all right if the proper formalities are observed."

Wang then retired, the girl calling after him to remember that her name was Mêng Yün, and her father's Mêng Chiang-li. He proceeded at once on his way to Mr. Hsü's, and after that sought out his intended father-in-law, telling him who he was, and offering him at the same time one hundred ounces of silver, as betrothal-money for his daughter. "She is already promised," replied the old man; upon which Wang declared he had been making careful inquiries, and had heard, on all sides, that the young lady was not engaged, winding up by begging to know what objection there was to his suit. "I have just promised her," answered her father, "and I cannot possibly break my word"; so Wang went away, deeply mortified, not knowing whether to believe it or not.

That night he tossed about a good deal; and next morning, braving the ridicule with which he imagined his friend would view his wished-for alliance with a boat-girl, he went off to Mr. Hsü, and told him all about it. "Why didn't you consult me before?" cried Mr. Hsü; "her father is a connection of mine." Wang then went on to give fuller particulars, which his friend interrupted by saying, "Chang-li is indeed poor, but he has never been a boatman. Are you sure you are not making a mistake?"

He then sent off his elder son to make inquiries; and to him the girl's father said, "Poor I am, but I don't *sell* my daughter. Your friend imagined that I should be tempted by the sight of his money to forego the usual ceremonies, and so I won't have anything to do with him. But if your father desires this match, and everything is in proper order, I will just go in and consult with my daughter, and see if she is willing." He then retired for a few minutes, and when he came back he raised his hands in congratulation, saying, "Everything is as you wish"; whereupon a day was fixed, and the young man went home to report to his father. Wang now sent off betrothal presents, with the usual formalities, and took up his abode with his friend, Mr. Hsü, until the marriage was solemnized, three days after which he bade adieu to his father-in-law, and started on his way northward. In the evening, as they were sitting on the boat together, Wang said to his wife, "When I first met you near this spot, I fancied you were not of the ordinary boating-class. Where were you then going?"

"I was going to visit my uncle," she replied. "We are not a wealthy family, you know, but we don't want anything through an improper channel; and I couldn't help smiling at the great eyes you were making at me, all the time trying to tempt me with money. But when I heard you speak, I knew at once you were a man of refinement, though I guessed you were a bit of a rake; and so I hid your bracelet, and saved you from the wrath of my father."

"And yet," replied Wang, "you have fallen into my snare after all"; adding, after a little pressure, "for I can't conceal from you much longer the fact that I have already a wife, belonging to a high official family."

This she did not believe, until he began to affirm it seriously; and then she jumped up and ran out of the cabin. Wang followed at once, but, before he could reach her, she was already in the river; whereupon he shouted out to boats to come to their assistance, causing quite a commotion all round about; but nothing was to be seen in the river, save only the reflection of the stars shining brightly on the water. All night long Wang went sorrowfully up and down, and offered a high reward for the body, which, however, was not forthcoming. So he went home in despair, and then, fearing lest his father-in-law should come to visit his daughter, he started on a visit to a connection of his, who had an appointment in Honan.

In the course of a year or two, when on his homeward journey, he chanced to be detained by bad weather at a roadside inn of rather cleaner appearance than usual. Within he saw an old woman playing with a child, which, as soon as he entered, held out its arms to him to be taken. Wang took the child on his knee, and there it remained, refusing to go back to its nurse; and, when the rain had stopped, and Wang was getting ready to go, the child cried out, "Pa-pa gone!" The nurse told it to hold its tongue, and, at the same moment, out from behind the screen came Wang's long-lost wife. "You bad fellow," said she, "what am I to do with this?" pointing to the child; and then Wang knew that the boy was his own son. He was much affected, and swore by the sun that the words he had uttered had been uttered in jest, and by-and-by his wife's anger was soothed. She then explained how she had been picked up by a passing boat, the occupant of which was the owner of the house they were in, a man of sixty years of age, who had no children of his own, and who kindly adopted her. She also told him how she had had several offers of marriage, all of which she had refused, and how her child was born, and that she had called him Chi-shêng, and that he was then a year old. Wang now unpacked his baggage again, and went in to see the old gentleman and his wife, whom he treated as if they had actually been his wife's parents. A few days afterward they set off together toward Wang's home, where they found his wife's real father awaiting them.

He had been there more than two months, and had been considerably disconcerted by the mysterious remarks of Wang's servants; but the arrival of his daughter and her husband made things all smooth again, and when they told him what had happened, he understood the demeanour of the servants which had seemed so strange to him at first.

The Two Brides

Now Chi-shêng, or Wang Sun, was one of the cleverest young fellows in the district; and his father and mother, who had foreseen his ability from the time when, as a baby in long clothes, he distinguished them from other people, loved him very dearly. He grew up into a handsome lad; at eight or nine he could compose elegantly, and by fourteen he had already entered his name as a candidate for the first degree, after which his marriage became a question for consideration.

Now his father's younger sister, Erh-niang, had married a gentleman named Chêng Tzŭ-ch'iao, and they had a daughter called Kuei-hsiu, who was extremely pretty, and with whom Chi-shêng fell deeply in love, being soon unable either to eat or to sleep. His parents became extremely uneasy about him, and inquired what it was that ailed him; and when he told them, they at once sent off a match-maker to Mr. Chêng. The latter, however, was rather a stickler for the proprieties, and replied that the near relationship precluded him from accepting the offer. Thereupon Chi-shêng became dangerously ill, and his mother, not knowing what to do, secretly tried to persuade Erh-niang to let her daughter come over to their house; but Mr. Chêng heard of it, and was so angry that Chi-shêng's father and mother gave up all hope of arranging the match.

At that time there was a gentleman named Chang living near by, who had five daughters, all very pretty, but the youngest, called Wu-k'o, was singularly beautiful, far surpassing her four sisters. She was not betrothed to any one, when one day, as she was on her way to worship at the family tombs, she chanced to see Chi-shêng, and at her return home spoke about him to her mother. Her mother guessed what her meaning was, and arranged with a match-maker, named Mrs. Yü, to call upon Chi-shêng's parents. This she did precisely at the time when Chi-shêng was so ill, and forthwith told his mother that her son's complaint was one she, Mrs. Yü, was quite competent to cure; going on to tell her about Miss Wu-k'o and the proposed marriage, at which the good lady was delighted, and sent her in to talk about it to Chi-shêng himself.

"Alas!" cried he, when he had heard Mrs. Yü's story, "you are bringing me the wrong medicine for my complaint."

"All depends upon the efficacy of the medicine," replied Mrs. Yü; "if the medicine is good, it matters not what is the name of the doctor who administers the draught; while to set your heart on a particular person, and to lie there and die because that person doesn't come, is surely foolish in the extreme."

"Ah," rejoined Chi-shêng, "there's no medicine under heaven that will do me any good."

Mrs. Yü told him his experience was limited, and proceeded to expatiate by speaking and gesticulating on the beauty and liveliness of Wu-k'o. But all Chi-shêng said was that she was not what he wanted, and, turning round his face to the wall, would listen to no more about her. So Mrs. Yü was obliged to go away, and Chi-shêng became worse and worse every day, until suddenly one of the maids came in and informed him that the young lady herself was at the door. Immediately he jumped up and ran out, and lo! there before him stood a beautiful girl, whom, however he soon discovered not to be Kuei-hsiu. She wore a light yellow robe with a fine silk jacket and an embroidered petticoat, from beneath which her two little feet peeped out; and altogether she more resembled a fairy than anything else. Chi-shêng inquired her name; to which she replied that it was Wu-k'o, adding that she couldn't understand his devoted attachment to Kuei-hsiu, as if there was nobody else in the world. Chi-shêng apologized, saying that he had never before seen any one so beautiful as Kuei-hsiu, but that he was now aware of his mistake. He then swore everlasting fidelity to her, and was just grasping her hand, when he awoke and found his mother rubbing him. It was a dream, but so accurately defined in all its details that he began to think if Wu-k'o was really such as he had seen her, there would be no further need to try for his impracticable cousin.

So he communicated his dream to his mother; and she, only too delighted to notice this change of feeling, offered to go to Wu-k'o's house herself; but Chi-shêng would not hear of this, and arranged with an old woman who knew the family to find some pretext for going there, and to report to him what Wu-k'o was like. When she arrived Wu-k'o was ill in bed, and lay with her head propped up by pillows, looking very pretty indeed. The old woman approached the couch and asked what was the matter; to which Wu-k'o made no reply, her fingers fidgetting all the time with her waistband.

"She's been behaving badly to her father and mother," cried the latter, who was in the room; "there's many a one has offered to marry her, but she says she'll have none but Chi-shêng: and then when I scold her a bit, she takes on and won't touch her food for days."

"Madam," said the old woman, "if you could get that young man for your daughter they would make a truly pretty pair; and as for him, if he could only see Miss Wu-k'o, I'm afraid it would be too much for him. What do you think of my going there and getting them to make proposals?"

"No, thank you," replied Wu-k'o; "I would rather not risk his refusal"; upon which the old woman declared she would succeed, and hurried off to tell Chi-shêng, who was delighted to find from her report that Wu-k'o was exactly as he had seen her in his dream, though he didn't trust implicitly in all the old woman said.

By-and-by, when he began to get a little better, he consulted with the old woman as to how he could see Wu-k'o with his own eyes; and, after some little difficulty, it was arranged that Chi-shêng should hide himself in a room from which he would be able to see her as she crossed the yard supported by a maid, which she did every day at a certain hour. This Chi-shêng proceeded to do, and in a little while out she came, accompanied by the old woman as well, who instantly drew her attention either to the clouds or the trees, in order that she should walk more leisurely. Thus Chi-shêng had a good look at her, and saw that she was truly the young lady of his dream. He could hardly contain himself for joy; and when the old woman arrived and asked if she would do instead of Kuei-hsiu, he thanked her very warmly and returned to his own home. There he told his father and mother, who sent off a match-maker to arrange the preliminaries; but the latter came back and told them that Wu-k'o was already betrothed. This was a terrible blow for Chi-shêng, who was soon as ill as ever, and offered no reply to his father and mother when they charged him with having made a mistake. For several months he ate nothing but a bowl of rice-gruel a-day, and he became as emaciated as a fowl, when all of a sudden the old woman walked in and asked him what was the matter.

"Foolish boy," said she, when he had told her all; "before you wouldn't have her, and do you imagine she is bound to have you now? But I'll see if I can't help you; for were she the Emperor's own daughter, I should still find some way of getting her." Chi-shêng asked what he should do, and she then told him to send a servant with a letter next day to Wu-k'o's house, to which his father at first objected for fear of another repulse; but the old woman assured him that Wu-k'o's parents had since repented, besides which no written contract had as yet been made; "and you know the proverb," added she, "that those who are first at the fire will get their dinner first."

So Chi-shêng's father agreed, and two servants were accordingly sent, their mission proving a complete success. Chi-shêng now rapidly recovered his health, and thought no more of Kuei-hsiu, who, when she heard of the intended match, became in her turn very seriously ill, to the great anger of her father, who said she might die for all he cared, but to the great sorrow of her mother, who was extremely fond of her daughter. The latter even went so far as to propose to Mr. Chang that Kuei-hsiu should go as second wife, at which he was so enraged that he declared he would wash his hands of the girl altogether. The mother then found out when Chi-shêng's wedding was to take place; and, borrowing a chair and attendants from her brother under pretense of going to visit him, put Kuei-hsiu inside and sent her off to her uncle's house. As she arrived at the door, the servants spread a carpet for her to walk on, and the band struck up the wedding march. Chi-shêng went out to see what it was all about, and there met a young lady in a bridal veil, from whom he would have escaped had not her servants surrounded them, and, before he knew what he was doing, he was making her the usual salutation of a bridegroom. They then went in together, and, to his further astonishment, he found that the young lady was Kuei-hsiu; and, being now unable to go and meet Wu-k'o, a message was sent to her father, telling him what had occurred. He, too, got into a great rage, and vowed he would break off the match; but Wu-k'o herself said she would go all the same, her rival having only got the start of her in point of time. And go she did; and the two wives, instead of quarrelling, as was expected, lived very happily together like sisters, and wore each other's clothes and shoes without distinction, Kuei-hsiu taking the place of an elder sister as being somewhat older than Wu-k'o.

One day, after these events, Chi-shêng asked Wu-k'o why she had refused his offer; to which she replied that it was merely to pay him out for having previously refused her father's proposal.

"Before you had seen me, your head was full of Kuei-hsiu; but after you had seen me, your thoughts were somewhat divided; and I wanted to know how I compared with her, and whether you would fall ill on my account as you had on hers, that we mightn't quarrel about our looks."

"It was a cruel revenge," said Chi-shêng; "but how should I ever have got a sight of you had it not been for the old woman?"

"What had she to do with it?" replied Wu-k'o; "I knew you were behind the door all the time. When I was ill I dreamt that I went to your house and saw you, but I looked upon it only as a dream until I heard that you had dreamt that I had actually been there, and then I knew that my spirit must have been with you." Chi-shêng now related to her the particulars of his vision, which coincided exactly with her own; and thus, strangely enough, had the matrimonial alliances of both father and son been brought about by dreams.

A Supernatural Wife

A CERTAIN MR. CHAO, OF CH'ANG-SHAN, LODGED IN A FAMILY OF THE NAME OF T'AI. He was very badly off, and, falling sick, was brought almost to death's door. One day they moved him into the verandah, that it might be cooler for him; and, when he awoke from a nap, lo! a beautiful girl was standing by his side. "I am come to be your wife," said the girl, in answer to his question as to who she was; to which he replied that a poor fellow like himself did not look for such luck as that; adding that, being then on his death-bed, he would not have much occasion for the services of a wife. The girl said she could cure him; but he told her he very much doubted that; "And even," continued he, "should you have any good prescription, I have not the means of getting it made up."

"I don't want medicine to cure you with," rejoined the girl, proceeding at once to rub his back and sides with her hand, which seemed to him like a ball of fire. He soon began to feel much better, and asked the young lady what her name was, in order, as he said, that he might remember her in his prayers. "I am a spirit," replied she; "and you, when alive under the Han dynasty as Ch'u Sui-liang, were a benefactor of my family. Your kindness being engraven on my heart, I have at length succeeded in my search for you, and am able in some measure to requite you."

Chao was dreadfully ashamed of his poverty-stricken state, and afraid that his dirty room would spoil the young lady's dress; but she made him show her in, and accordingly he took her into his apartment, where there were neither chairs to sit upon, nor signs of anything to eat, saying, "You might, indeed, be able to put up with all this; but you see my larder is empty, and I have absolutely no means of supporting a wife."

"Don't be alarmed about that," cried she; and in another moment he saw a couch covered with costly robes, the walls papered with a silver-flecked paper, and chairs and tables appear, the latter laden with all kinds of wine and exquisite viands. They then began to enjoy themselves, and lived together as husband and wife, many people coming to witness these strange things, and being all cordially received by the young lady, who in her turn always accompanied Mr. Chao when he went out to dinner anywhere.

One day there was an unprincipled young graduate among the company, which she seemed immediately to become aware of; and, after calling him several bad names, she struck him on the side of the head, causing his head to fly out of the window while his body remained inside; and there he was, stuck fast, unable to move either way, until the others interceded for him and he was released. After some time visitors became too numerous, and if she refused to see them they turned their anger against her husband. At length, as they were sitting together drinking with some friends at the Tuan-yang festival, a white rabbit ran in, whereupon the girl jumped up and said, "The doctor has come for me"; then, turning to the rabbit, she added, "You go on: I'll follow you." So the rabbit went away, and then she ordered them to get a ladder and place it against a high tree in the back yard, the top of the ladder overtopping the tree. The young lady went up first and Chao close behind her; after which she called out to anybody who wished to join them to make haste up. None ventured to do so with the exception of a serving-boy belonging to the house, who followed after Chao; and thus they went up, up, up, up, until they disappeared in the clouds and were seen no more. However, when the bystanders came to look at the ladder, they found it was only an old door-frame with the panels knocked out; and when they went into Mr. Chao's room, it was the same old, dirty, unfurnished room as before. So they determined to find out all about it from the serving-boy when he came back; but this he never did.

Bribery and Corruption

AT PAO-TING FU THERE LIVED A YOUNG MAN, WHO HAVING PURCHASED THE LOWEST degree was about to proceed to Peking, in the hope of obtaining, by the aid of a little bribery, an appointment as District Magistrate. His boxes were all ready packed, when he was taken suddenly ill and was confined to his bed for more than a month.

One day the servant entered and announced a visitor; whereupon our sick man jumped up and ran to the door as if there was nothing the matter with him. The visitor was elegantly dressed like a man of some position in society; and, after bowing thrice, he walked into the house, explaining that he was Kung-sun Hsia, tutor to the Eleventh Prince, and that he had heard our Mr. So-and-so wished to arrange for the purchase of a magistracy. "If that is really so," added he, "would you not do better to buy a prefecture?" So-and-so thanked him warmly, but said his funds would not be sufficient; upon which Mr. Kung-sun declared he should be delighted to assist him with half the purchase-money, which he could repay after taking up the post. He went on to say that being on intimate terms with the various provincial Governors the thing could be easily managed for about five thousand taels; and also that at that very moment Chên-ting Fu being vacant, it would be as well to make an early effort to get the appointment. So-and-so pointed out that this place was in his native province; but Kung-sun only laughed at his objection, and reminded him that money could obliterate all distinctions of that kind. This did not seem quite satisfactory; however, Kung-sun told him not to be alarmed, as the post of which he was speaking was below in the infernal regions. "The fact is," said he, "that your term of life has expired, and that your name is already on the death list; by these means you will take your place in the world below as a man of official position. Farewell! in three days we shall meet again." He then went to the door and mounted his horse and rode away.

So-and-so now opened his eyes and spoke a few parting words to his wife and children, bidding them take money from his strong-room and go buy large quantities of paper ingots, which they immediately did, quite exhausting all the shops. This was piled in the court-yard with paper images of men, devils, horses, etc., and burning went on day and night until the ashes formed quite a hill. In three days Kung-sun returned, bringing with him the money; upon which So-and-so hurried off to the Board of Civil Office, where he had an interview with the high officials, who, after asking his name, warned him to be a pure and upright officer, and then calling him up to the table handed him his letter of appointment. So-and-so bowed and took his leave; but recollecting at once that his purchased degree would not carry much weight with it in the eyes of his subordinates, he sent off to buy elaborate chairs and a number of horses for his retinue, at the same time despatching several devil lictors to fetch his favorite wife in a beautifully adorned sedan-chair.

All arrangements were just completed when some of the Chên-ting staff came to meet the new Prefect, others awaiting him all along the line of road, about half a mile in length. He was immensely gratified at this reception, when all of a sudden the gongs before him ceased to sound and the banners were lowered to the ground. He had hardly time to ask what was the matter before he saw those of his servants who were on horseback jump hastily to the ground and dwindle down to about a foot in height, while their horses shrunk to the size of foxes or racoons. One of the attendants near his chariot cried out in alarm, "Here's Kuan Ti!" and then he, too, jumped out in a fright, and saw in the distance Kuan Ti himself slowly approaching them, followed by four or five retainers on horseback. His great beard covered the lower half of his face, quite unlike ordinary mortals; his aspect was terrible to behold, and his eyes reached nearly to his ears. "Who is this?" roared he to his servants; and they immediately informed him that it was the new Prefect of Chên-ting. "What!" cried he; "a petty fellow like that to have a retinue like this?" Whereupon So-and-so's flesh began to creep with fear, and in a few moments he found that he too had shrunk to the size of a little boy of six or seven.

Kuan Ti bade his attendants bring the new Prefect with them, and went into a building at the roadside, where he took up his seat facing the south and calling for writing materials told So-and-so to write down his name and address. When this was handed to him he flew into a towering passion, and said, "The scribbly scrawl of a placeman, indeed! Can such a one be entrusted with the welfare of the people? Look me up the record of his good works." A man then advanced, and whispered something in a low tone; upon which Kuan Ti exclaimed in a loud voice, "The crime of the briber is comparatively trifling; the heavy guilt lies with those who sell official posts for money."

So-and-so was now seized by angels in golden armor, and two of them tore off his cap and robes, and administered to him fifty blows with the bamboo until hardly any flesh remained on his bones. He was then thrust outside the door, and lo! his carriages and horses had disappeared, and he himself was lying, unable to walk for pain, at no great distance from his own house. However, his body seemed as light as a leaf, and in a day and a night he managed to crawl home. When he arrived, he awoke as it were from a dream, and found himself groaning upon the bed; and to the inquiries of his family he only replied that he felt dreadfully sore. Now he really had been dead for seven days; and when he came round thus, he immediately asked for A-lien, which was the name of his favorite wife. But the very day before, while chatting with the other members of the family, A-lien had suddenly cried out that her husband was made Prefect of Chên-ting, and that his lictors had come to escort her thither. Accordingly she retired to dress herself in her best clothes, and, when ready to start, she fell back and expired. Hearing this sad story, So-and-so began to mourn and beat his breast, and he would not allow her to be buried at once, in the hope that she might yet come round; but this she never did. Meanwhile So-and-so got slowly better, and by the end of six months was able to walk again. He would often exclaim, "The ruin of my career and the punishment I received—all this I could have endured; but the loss of my dear A-lien is more than I can bear."

A Chinese Jonah

A MAN NAMED SUN PI-CHÊN WAS CROSSING THE RIVER WHEN A GREAT THUNDER-squall broke upon the vessel and caused her to toss about fearfully, to the great terror of all the passengers. Just then, an angel in golden armor appeared standing upon the clouds above them, holding in his hand a scroll inscribed with certain characters, also written in gold, which the people on the vessel easily made out to be three in number, namely *Sun Pi-chên*. So, turning at once to their fellow-traveler, they said to him, "You have evidently incurred the displeasure of Heaven; get into a boat by yourself, and do not involve us in your punishment." And without giving him time to reply whether he would do so or not, they hurried him over the side into a small boat and set him adrift; but when Sun Pi-chên looked back, lo! the vessel itself had capsized.

Chang Pu-liang

A CERTAIN TRADER WHO WAS TRAVELING IN THE PROVINCE OF CHIH-LI, BEING overtaken by a storm of rain and hail, took shelter among some standing crops by the way-side. There he heard a voice from heaven, saying, "These are Chang Pu-liang's fields; do not injure his crops." The trader began to wonder who this Chang Pu-liang could be, and how, if he was *pu liang* (not virtuous), he came to be under divine protection; so when the storm was over and he had reached the neighboring village, he made enquiries on the subject, and told the people there what he had heard. The villagers then informed him that Chang Pu-liang was a very wealthy farmer, who was accustomed every spring to make loans of grain to the poor of the district, and who was not too particular about getting back the exact amount he had lent,—taking, in fact, whatever they brought him without discussion; hence the sobriquet of *pu liang* "no measure" (*i.e.*, the man who doesn't measure the repayments of his loans). After that, they all proceeded in a body to the fields, where it was discovered that vast damage had been done to the crops generally, with the exception of Chang Pu-liang's, which had escaped uninjured.

The Dutch Carpet

FORMERLY, WHEN THE DUTCH WERE PERMITTED TO TRADE WITH CHINA, THE OFFICER in command of the coast defenses would not allow them, on account of their great numbers, to come ashore. The Dutch begged very hard for the grant of a piece of land such as a carpet would cover; and the officer above-mentioned, thinking that this could not be very large, acceded to their request. A carpet was accordingly laid down, big enough for about two people to stand on; but by dint of stretching, it was soon enough for four or five; and so they went on, stretching and stretching, until at last it covered about an acre, and by-and-by, with the help of their knives, they had filched a piece of ground several miles in extent.

Carrying a Corpse

A WOODSMAN WHO HAD BEEN TO MARKET WAS RETURNING HOME WITH HIS POLE across his shoulder, when suddenly he felt it become very heavy at the end behind him, and looking round he saw attached to it the headless trunk of a man. In great alarm, he got his pole quit of the burden and struck about him right and left, whereupon the body disappeared. He then hurried on to the next village, and when he arrived there in the dusk of the evening, he found several men holding lights to the ground as if looking for something. On asking what was the matter, they told him that while sitting together a man's head had fallen from the sky into their midst; that they had noticed the hair and beard were all draggled, but in a moment the head had vanished. The woodsman then related what had happened to himself; and thus one whole man was accounted for, though no one could tell whence he came. Subsequently, another man was carrying a basket when some one saw a man's head in it, and called out to him; whereupon he dropped the basket in a fright, and the head rolled away and disappeared.

A Taoist Devotee

CHÜ YAO-JU WAS A CH'ING-CHOU MAN, WHO, WHEN HIS WIFE DIED, LEFT HIS HOME and became a priest. Some years afterward he returned, dressed in the Taoist garb, and carrying his praying-mat over his shoulder; and after staying one night he wanted to go away again. His friends, however, would not give him back his cassock and staff; so at length he pretended to take a stroll outside the village, and when there, his clothes and other belongings came flying out of the house after him, and he got safely away.

Justice for Rebels

DURING THE REIGN OF SHUN CHIH, OF THE PEOPLE OF T'ÊNG-I, SEVEN IN TEN WERE opposed to the Manchu dynasty. The officials dared not touch them; and subsequently, when the country became more settled, the magistrates used to distinguish them from the others by always deciding any cases in their favor: for they feared lest these men should revert to their old opposition. And thus it came about that one litigant would begin by declaring himself to have been a "rebel," while his adversary would follow up by showing such statement to be false; so that before any case could be heard on its actual merits, it was necessary to determine the status both of plaintiff and defendant, whereby infinite labor was entailed upon the Registrars.

Now it chanced that the *yamên* of one of the officials was haunted by a fox, and the official's daughter was bewitched by it. Her father, therefore, engaged the services of a magician, who succeeded in capturing the animal and putting it into a bottle; but just as he was going to commit it to the flames, the fox cried out from inside the bottle, "I'm a rebel!" at which the bystanders were unable to suppress their laughter.

Killing a Serpent

AT KU-CHI ISLAND IN THE EASTERN SEA, THERE WERE CAMELLIAS OF ALL COLORS WHICH bloomed throughout the year. No one, however, lived there, and very few people ever visited the spot. One day, a young man of Têng-chou, named Chang, who was fond of hunting and adventure, hearing of the beauties of the place, put together some wine and food, and rowed himself across in a small open boat. The flowers were just then even finer than usual, and their perfume was diffused for a mile or so around; while many of the trees he saw were several armfuls in circumference. So he roamed about and gave himself up to enjoyment of the scene; and by-and-by he opened a flask of wine, regretting very much that he had no companion to share it with him, when all of a sudden a most beautiful young girl, with extremely bright eyes and dressed in red, stepped down from one of the camellias before him. "Dear me!" said she on seeing Mr. Chang; "I expected to be alone here, and was not aware that the place was already occupied."

Chang was somewhat alarmed at this apparition, and asked the young lady whence she came; to which she replied that her name was Chiao-ch'ang, and that she had accompanied thither a Mr. Hai, who had gone off for a stroll and had left her to await his return. Thereupon Chang begged her to join him in a cup of wine, which she very willingly did, and they were just beginning to enjoy themselves when a sound of rushing wind was heard and the trees and plants bent beneath it. "Here's Mr. Hai!" cried the young lady; and jumping quickly up, disappeared in a moment.

The horrified Chang now beheld a huge serpent coming out of the bushes near by, and immediately ran behind a large tree for shelter, hoping the reptile would not see him. But the serpent advanced and enveloped both Chang and the tree in its great folds, binding Chang's arms down to his sides so as to prevent him from moving them; and then raising its head, darted out its tongue and bit the poor man's nose, causing the blood to flow freely out. This blood it was quietly sucking up, when Chang, who thought that his last hour had come, remembered that he had in his pocket some fox poison; and managing to insert a couple of fingers, he drew out the packet, broke the paper, and let the powder lie in the palm of his hand. He next leaned his hand over the serpent's coils in such a way that the blood from his nose dripped into his hand, and when it was nearly full the serpent actually did begin to drink it. And in a few moments the grip was relaxed; the serpent struck the ground heavily with its tail, and dashed away up against another tree, which was broken in half, and then stretched itself out and died. Chang was a long time unable to rise, but at length he got up and carried the serpent off with him. He was very ill for more than a month afterward, and even suspected the young lady of being a serpent, too, in disguise.

The Resuscitated Corpse

A CERTAIN OLD MAN LIVED AT TS'AI-TIEN, IN THE YANG-HSIN DISTRICT. THE VILLAGE was some miles from the district city, and he and his son kept a roadside inn where travelers could pass the night. One day, as it was getting dusk, four strangers presented themselves and asked for a night's lodging; to which the landlord replied that every bed was already occupied. The four men declared it was impossible for them to go back, and urged him to take them in somehow; and at length the landlord said he could give them a place to sleep in if they were not too particular,—which the strangers immediately assured him they were not. The fact was that the old man's daughter-in-law had just died, and that her body was lying in the women's quarters, waiting for the coffin, which his son had gone away to buy.

So the landlord led them round thither, and walking in, placed a lamp on the table. At the further end of the room lay the corpse, decked out with paper robes, etc., in the usual way; and in the foremost section were sleeping-couches for four people. The travellers were tired, and, throwing themselves on the beds, were soon snoring loudly, with the exception of one of them, who was not quite off when suddenly he heard a creaking of the trestles on which the dead body was laid out, and, opening his eyes, he saw by the light of the lamp in front of the corpse that the girl was raising the coverings from her and preparing to get down. In another moment she was on the floor and advancing toward the sleepers. Her face was of a light yellow hue, and she had a silk kerchief round her head; and when she reached the beds she blew on the other three travelers, whereupon the fourth, in a great fright, stealthily drew up the bed-clothes over his face, and held his breath to listen. He heard her breathe on him as she had done on the others, and then heard her go back again and get under the paper robes, which rustled distinctly as she did so.

He now put out his head to take a peep, and saw that she was lying down as before; whereupon, not daring to make any noise, he stretched forth his foot and kicked his companions, who, however, showed no signs of moving. He now determined to put on his clothes and make a bolt for it; but he had hardly begun to do so before he heard the creaking sound again, which sent him back under the bed-clothes as fast as he could go. Again the girl came to him, and breathing several times on him, went away to lie down as before, as he could tell by the noise of the trestles. He then put his hand very gently out of bed, and, seizing his trousers, got quickly into them, jumped up with a bound, and rushed out of the place as fast as his legs would carry him. The corpse, too, jumped up; but by this time the traveler had already drawn the bolt, and was outside the door, running along and shrieking at the top of his voice, with the corpse following close behind. No one seemed to hear him, and he was afraid to knock at the door of the inn for fear they should not let him in in time; so he made for the highway to the city, and after awhile he saw a monastery by the roadside, and, hearing the "wooden fish," he ran up and thumped with all his might at the gate. The priest, however, did not know what to make of it, and would not open to him; and as the corpse was only a few yards off, he could do nothing but run behind a tree which stood close by, and there shelter himself, dodging to the right as the corpse dodged to the left, and so on. This infuriated the dead girl to madness; and at length, as tired and panting they stood watching each other on opposite sides of the tree, the corpse made a rush forward with one arm on each side in the hope of thus grabbing its victim. The traveler, however, fell backward and escaped, while the corpse remained rigidly embracing the tree.

By-and-by the priest, who had been listening from the inside, hearing no sounds for some time, came out and found the traveler lying senseless on the ground; whereupon he had him carried into the monastery, and by morning they had got him round again. After giving him a little broth to drink, he related the whole story; and then in the early dawn they went out to examine the tree, where they found the girl fixed tightly to the tree. The news being sent to the magistrate, that functionary attended at once in person, and gave orders to remove the body; but this they were at first unable to do, the girl's fingers having penetrated into the bark so far that her nails were not to be seen. At length they got her away, and then a messenger was despatched to the inn, already in a state of great commotion over the three travelers, who had been found dead in their beds. The old man accordingly sent to fetch his daughter-in-law; and the surviving traveler petitioned the magistrate, saying, "Four of us left home, but only one will go back. Give me something that I may show to my fellow-townsmen." So the magistrate gave him a certificate and sent him home again.

The Fisherman and His Friend

In the northern parts of Tzŭ-chou there lived a man named Hsü, a fisherman by trade. Every night when he went to fish he would carry some wine with him, and drink and fish by turns, always taking care to pour out a libation on the ground, accompanied by the following invocation:—"Drink too, ye drowned spirits of the river!" Such was his regular custom; and it was also noticeable that, even on occasions when the other fishermen caught nothing, he always got a full basket. One night, as he was sitting drinking by himself, a young man suddenly appeared and began walking up and down near him. Hsü offered him a cup of wine, which was readily accepted, and they remained chatting together throughout the night, Hsü meanwhile not catching a single fish. However, just as he was giving up all hope of doing anything, the young man rose and said he would go a little way down the stream and beat them up toward Hsü, which he accordingly did, returning in a few minutes and warning him to be on the look-out.

Hsü now heard a noise like that of a shoal coming up the stream, and, casting his net, made a splendid haul,—all that he caught being over a foot in length. Greatly delighted, he now prepared to go home, first offering his companion a share of the fish, which the latter declined, saying that he had often received kindnesses from Mr. Hsü, and that he would be only too happy to help him regularly in the same manner if Mr. Hsü would accept his assistance. The latter replied that he did not recollect ever meeting him before, and that he should be much obliged for any aid the young man might choose to afford him; regretting, at the same time, his inability to make him any adequate return. He then asked the young man his name and surname; and the young man said his surname was Wang, adding that Hsü might address him when they met as Wang Liu-lang, he having no other name. Thereupon they parted, and the next day Hsü sold his fish and bought some more wine, with which he repaired as usual to the river bank. There he found his companion already awaiting him, and they spent the night together in precisely the same way as the preceding one, the young man beating up the fish for him as before. This went on for some months, until at length one evening the young man, with many expressions of his thanks and his regrets, told Hsü that they were about to part for ever. Much alarmed by the melancholy tone in which his friend had communicated this news, Hsü was on the point of asking for an explanation, when the young man stopped him, and himself proceeded as follows:—

"The friendship that has grown up between us is truly surprising; and, now that we shall meet no more, there is no harm in telling you the whole truth. I am a disembodied spirit—the soul of one who was drowned in this river when tipsy. I have been here many years, and your former success in fishing was due to the fact that I used secretly to beat up the fish toward you, in return for the libations you were accustomed to pour out. To-morrow my time is up: my substitute will arrive, and I shall be born again in the world of mortals. We have but this one evening left, and I therefore take advantage of it to express my feelings to you."

On hearing these words, Hsü was at first very much alarmed; however, he had grown so accustomed to his friend's society, that his fears soon passed away; and, filling up a goblet, he said, with a sigh, "Liu-lang, old fellow, drink this up, and away with melancholy. It's hard to lose you; but I'm glad enough for your sake, and won't think of my own sorrow." He then inquired of Liu-lang who was to be his substitute; to which the latter replied, "Come to the river-bank to-morrow afternoon and you'll see a woman drowned: she is the one." Just then the village cocks began to crow, and, with tears in their eyes, the two friends bade each other farewell.

Next day Hsü waited on the river bank to see if anything would happen, and lo! a woman carrying a child in her arms came along. When close to the edge of the river, she stumbled and fell into the water, managing, however, to throw the child safely on to the bank, where it lay kicking and sprawling and crying at the top of its voice. The woman herself sank and rose several times, until at last she succeeded in clutching hold of the bank and pulled herself, dripping, out; and then, after resting awhile, she picked up the child and went on her way. All this time Hsü had been in a great state of excitement, and was on the point of running to help the woman out of the water; but he remembered that she was to be the substitute of his friend, and accordingly restrained himself from doing so. Then when he saw the woman get out by herself, he began to suspect that Liu-lang's words had not been fulfilled. That night he went to fish as usual, and before long the young man arrived and said, "We meet once again: there is no need now to speak of separation." Hsü asked him how it was so; to which he replied, "The woman you saw had already taken my place, but I could not bear to hear the child cry, and I saw that my one life would be purchased at the expense of their two lives, wherefore I let her go, and now I cannot say when I shall have another chance. The union of our destinies may not yet be worked out."

"Alas!" sighed Hsü, "this noble conduct of yours is enough to move God Almighty."

After this the two friends went on much as they had done before, until one day Liu-lang again said he had come to bid Hsü farewell. Hsü thought he had found another substitute, but Liu-lang told him that his former behavior had so pleased Almighty

Heaven, that he had been appointed guardian angel of Wu-chên, in the Chao-yüan district, and that on the following morning he would start for his new post. "And if you do not forget the days of our friendship," added he, "I pray you come and see me, in spite of the long journey."

"Truly," replied Hsü, "you well deserved to be made a God; but the paths of Gods and men lie in different directions, and even if the distance were nothing, how should I manage to meet you again?"

"Don't be afraid on that score," said Liu-lang, "but come"; and then he went away, and Hsü returned home. The latter immediately began to prepare for the journey, which caused his wife to laugh at him and say, "Supposing you do find such a place at the end of that long journey, you won't be able to hold a conversation with a clay image." Hsü, however, paid no attention to her remarks, and traveled straight to Chao-yüan, where he learned from the inhabitants that there really was a village called Wu-chên, whither he forthwith proceeded and took up his abode at an inn. He then inquired of the landlord where the village temple was; to which the latter replied by asking him somewhat hurriedly if he was speaking to Mr. Hsü. Hsü informed him that his name was Hsü, asking in reply how he came to know it; whereupon the landlord further inquired if his native place was not Tzŭ-chou. Hsü told him it was, and again asked him how he knew all this; to which the landlord made no answer, but rushed out of the room; and in a few moments the place was crowded with old and young, men, women, and children, all come to visit Hsü. They then told him that a few nights before they had seen their guardian deity in a vision, and he had informed them that Mr. Hsü would shortly arrive, and had bidden them to provide him with traveling expenses, etc. Hsü was very much astonished at this, and went off at once to the shrine, where he invoked his friend as follows:—

"Ever since we parted I have had you daily and nightly in my thoughts; and now that I have fulfilled my promise of coming to see you, I have to thank you for the orders you have issued to the people of the place. As for me, I have nothing to offer you but a cup of wine, which I pray you accept as though we were drinking together on the river-bank."

He then burned a quantity of paper money, when lo! a wind suddenly arose, which, after whirling round and round behind the shrine, soon dropped, and all was still. That night Hsü dreamed that his friend came to him, dressed in his official cap and robes, and very different in appearance from what he used to be, and thanked him, saying, "It is truly kind of you to visit me thus: I only regret that my position makes me unable to meet you face to face, and that though near we are still so far. The people here will give you a trifle, which pray accept for my sake; and when you go away, I will see you a short way on your journey."

A few days afterward Hsü prepared to start, in spite of the numerous invitations to stay which poured in upon him from all sides; and then the inhabitants loaded him with presents of all kinds, and escorted him out of the village. There a whirlwind arose and accompanied him several miles, when he turned round and invoked his friend thus:—

"Liu-lang, take care of your valued person. Do not trouble yourself to come any farther. Your noble heart will ensure happiness to this district, and there is no occasion for me to give a word of advice to my old friend."

By-and-by the whirlwind ceased, and the villagers, who were much astonished, returned to their own homes. Hsü, too, traveled homeward, and being now a man of some means, ceased to work any more as a fisherman. And whenever he met a Chao-yüan man he would ask him about that guardian angel, being always informed in reply that he was a most beneficent God. Some say the place was Shih-k'êng-chuang, in Chang-ch'in: I can't say which it was myself.

The Priest's Warning

A MAN NAMED CHANG DIED SUDDENLY, AND WAS ESCORTED AT ONCE BY DEVIL-LICTORS into the presence of the King of Purgatory. His Majesty turned to Chang's record of good and evil, and then, in great anger, told the lictors they had brought the wrong man, and bade them take him back again. As they left the judgment-hall, Chang persuaded his escort to let him have a look at Purgatory; and, accordingly, the devils conducted him through the nine sections, pointing out to him the Knife Hill, the Sword Tree, and other objects of interest. By-and-by, they reached a place where there was a Buddhist priest, hanging suspended in the air head downward, by a rope through a hole in his leg. He was shrieking with pain, and longing for death; and when Chang approached, lo! he saw that it was his own brother. In great distress, he asked his guides the reason of this punishment; and they informed him that the priest was suffering thus for collecting subscriptions on behalf of his order, and then privately squandering the proceeds in gambling and debauchery. "Nor," added they, "will he escape this torment unless he repents him of his misdeeds." When Chang came round, he thought his brother was already dead, and hurried off to the Hsing-fu monastery, to which the latter belonged. As he went in at the door, he heard a loud shrieking; and, on proceeding to his brother's room, he found him laid up with a very bad abscess in his leg, the leg itself being tied up above him to the wall, this being, as his brother informed him, the only bearable position in which he could lie. Chang now told him what he had seen in Purgatory, at which the priest was so terrified, that he at once gave up taking wine and meat, and devoted himself entirely to religious exercises. In a fortnight he was well, and was known ever afterward as a most exemplary priest.

Metempsychosis

MR. LIN, WHO TOOK HIS MASTER'S DEGREE IN THE SAME YEAR AS THE LATE MR. WÊN Pi, could remember what had happened to him in his previous state of existence, and once told the whole story, as follows:—

I was originally of a good family, but, after leading a very dissolute life, I died at the age of sixty-two. On being conducted into the presence of the King of Purgatory, he received me civilly, bade me be seated, and offered me a cup of tea. I noticed, however, that the tea in His Majesty's cup was clear and limpid, while that in my own was muddy, like the lees of wine. It then flashed across me that this was the potion which was given to all disembodied spirits to render them oblivious of the past: and, accordingly, when the King was looking the other way, I seized the opportunity of pouring it under the table, pretending afterward that I had drunk it all up. My record of good and evil was now presented for inspection, and when the King saw what it was, he flew into a great passion, and ordered the attendant devils to drag me away, and send me back to earth as a horse. I was immediately seized and bound, and the devils carried me off to a house, the door-sill of which was so high I could not step over it. While I was trying to do so, the devils behind lashed me with all their might, causing me such pain that I made a great spring, and—lo and behold! I was a horse in a stable.

"The mare has got a nice colt," I then heard a man call out; but, although I was perfectly aware of all that was passing, I could say nothing myself. Hunger now came upon me, and I was glad to be suckled by the mare; and by the end of four or five years I had grown into a fine strong horse, dreadfully afraid of the whip, and running away at the very sight of it. When my master rode me, it was always with a saddle-cloth, and at a leisurely pace, which was bearable enough; but when the servants mounted me barebacked, and dug their heels into me, the pain struck into my vitals; and at length I refused all food, and in three days I died. Reappearing before the King of Purgatory, His Majesty was enraged to find that I had thus tried to shirk working out my time; and, flaying me forthwith, condemned me to go back again as a dog. And when I did not move, the devils came behind me and lashed me until I ran away from them into the open country, where, thinking I had better die right off, I jumped over a cliff, and lay at the bottom unable to move. I then saw that I was among a litter of puppies, and that an old bitch was licking and suckling me by turns; whereby I knew that I was once more among mortals. In this hateful form I continued for some time, longing to kill myself, and yet fearing to incur the penalty of shirking.

At length, I purposely bit my master in the leg, and tore him badly; whereupon he had me destroyed, and I was taken again into the presence of the King, who was so displeased with my vicious behavior that he condemned me to become a snake, and shut me up in a dark room, where I could see nothing. After a while I managed to climb up the wall, bore a hole in the roof, and escape; and immediately I found myself lying in the grass, a veritable snake. Then I registered a vow that I would harm no living thing, and I lived for some years, feeding upon berries and such like, ever remembering neither to take my own life, nor by injuring any one to incite them to take it, but longing all the while for the happy release, which did not come to me. One day, as I was sleeping in the grass, I heard the noise of a passing cart, and, on trying to get across the road out of its way, I was caught by the wheel, and cut in two. The King was astonished to see me back so soon, but I humbly told my story, and, in pity for the innocent creature that loses its life, he pardoned me, and permitted me to be born again at my appointed time as a human being.

Such was Mr. Lin's story. He could speak as soon as he came into the world; and could repeat anything he had once read. In the year 1621 he took his master's degree, and was never tired of telling people to put saddle-cloths on their horses, and recollect that the pain of being gripped by the knees is even worse than the lash itself.

The Forty Strings of Cash

MR. JUSTICE WANG HAD A STEWARD, WHO WAS POSSESSED OF CONSIDERABLE MEANS. One night the latter dreamt that a man rushed in and said to him, "To-day you must repay me those forty strings of cash." The steward asked who he was; to which the man made no answer, but hurried past him into the women's apartments. When the steward awoke, he found that his wife had been delivered of a son; and, knowing at once that retribution was at hand, he set aside forty strings of cash to be spent solely in food, clothes, medicines, and so on, for the baby. By the time the child was between three and four years old, the steward found that of the forty strings only about seven hundred cash remained; and when the wet-nurse, who happened to be standing by, brought the child and dandled it in her arms before him, he looked at it and said, "The forty strings are all but repaid; it is time you were off again." Thereupon the child changed color; its head fell back, and its eyes stared fixedly, and, when they tried to revive it, lo! respiration had already ceased. The father then took the balance of the forty strings, and with it defrayed the child's funeral expenses—truly a warning to people to be sure and pay their debts.

Formerly, an old childless man consulted a great many Buddhist priests on the subject. One of them said to him, "If you owe no one anything, and no one owes you anything, how can you expect to have children? A good son is the repayment of a former debt; a bad son is a dunning creditor, at whose birth there is no rejoicing, at whose death no lamentations."

Saving Life

A CERTAIN GENTLEMAN OF SHÊN-YU, WHO HAD TAKEN THE HIGHEST DEGREE, COULD remember himself in a previous state of existence. He said he had formerly been a scholar, and had died in middle life; and that when he appeared before the Judge of Purgatory, there stood the cauldrons, the boiling oil, and other apparatus of torture, exactly as we read about them on earth. In the eastern corner of the hall were a number of frames from which hung the skins of sheep, dogs, oxen, horses, etc.; and when anybody was condemned to re-appear in life under any one of these forms, his skin was stripped off and a skin was taken from the proper frame and fixed on to his body. The gentleman of whom I am writing heard himself sentenced to become a sheep; and the attendant devils had already clothed him in a sheep's-skin in the manner above described, when the clerk of the record informed the Judge that the criminal before him had once saved another man's life. The Judge consulted his books, and forthwith cried out, "I pardon him; for although his sins have been many, this one act has redeemed them all." The devils then tried to take off the sheep's-skin, but it was so tightly stuck on him that they couldn't move it. However, after great efforts, and causing the gentleman most excruciating agony, they managed to tear it off bit by bit, though not quite so cleanly as one might have wished. In fact, a piece as big as the palm of a man's hand was left near his shoulder; and when he was born again into the world, there was a great patch of hair on his back, which grew again as fast as it was cut off.

The Salt Smuggler

WANG SHIH, OF KAO-WAN, A PETTY SALT HUCKSTER, WAS INORDINATELY FOND OF gambling. One night he was arrested by two men, whom he took for lictors of the Salt Gabelle; and, flinging down what salt he had with him, he tried to make his escape. He found, however, that his legs would not move with him, and he was forthwith seized and bound. "We are not sent by the Salt Commissioner," cried his captors, in reply to an entreaty to set him free; "we are the devil-constables of Purgatory." Wang was horribly frightened at this, and begged the devils to let him bid farewell to his wife and children; but this they refused to do, saying, "You aren't going to die; you are only wanted for a little job there is down below." Wang asked what the job was; to which the devils replied, "A new Judge has come into office, and, finding the river and the eighteen hells choked up with the bodies of sinners, he has determined to employ three classes of mortals to clean them out. These are thieves, unlicensed founders, and unlicensed dealers in salt, and, for the dirtiest work of all, he is going to take musicians."

Wang accompanied the devils until at length they reached a city, where he was brought before the Judge, who was sitting in his Judgment-hall. On turning up his record in the books, one of the devils explained that the prisoner had been arrested for unlicensed trading; whereupon the Judge became very angry, and said, "Those who drive an illicit trade in salt, not only defraud the State of its proper revenue, but also prey upon the livelihood of the people. Those, however, whom the greedy officials and corrupt traders of to-day denounce as unlicensed traders, are among the most virtuous of mankind—needy unfortunates who struggle to save a few cash in the purchase of their pint of salt. Are they your unlicensed traders?" The Judge then bade the lictors buy four pecks of salt, and send it to Wang's house for him, together with that which had been found upon him; and, at the same time, he gave Wang an iron scourge, and told him to superintend the works at the river. So Wang followed the devils, and found the river swarming with people like ants in an ant-hill. The water was turbid and red, the stench from it being almost unbearable, while those who were employed in cleaning it out were working there naked. Sometimes they would sink down in the horrid mass of decaying bodies: sometimes they would get lazy, and then the iron scourge was applied to their backs. The assistant-superintendents had small scented balls, which they held in their mouths. Wang himself approached the bank, and saw the licensed salt-merchant of Kao-wan in the midst of it all, and thrashed him well with his scourge, until he was afraid he would never come up again. This went on for three days and three nights, by which time half the workmen were dead, and the work completed; whereupon the same two devils escorted him home again, and then he waked up.

As a matter of fact, Wang had gone out to sell some salt, and had not come back. Next morning, when his wife opened the house door, she found two bags of salt in the court-yard; and, as her husband did not return, she sent off some people to search for him, and they discovered him lying senseless by the wayside. He was immediately conveyed home, where, after a little time, he recovered consciousness, and related what had taken place. Strange to say, the licensed salt-merchant had fallen down in a fit on the previous evening, and had only just recovered; and Wang, hearing that his body was covered with sores—the result of the beating with the iron scourge—went off to his house to see him; however, directly the wretched man set eyes on Wang, he hastily covered himself up with the bed-clothes, forgetting that they were no longer at the infernal river. He did not recover from his injuries for a year, after which he retired from trade.

Collecting Subscriptions

The Frog-God frequently employs a magician to deliver its oracles to those who have faith. Should the magician declare that the God is pleased, happiness is sure to follow; but if he says the God is angry, women and children sit sorrowfully about, and neglect even their meals. Such is the customary belief, and it is probably not altogether devoid of foundation.

There was a certain wealthy merchant, named Chou, who was a very stingy man. Once, when some repairs were necessary to the temple of the God of War, and rich and poor were subscribing as much as each could afford, he alone gave nothing. By-and-by the works were stopped for want of funds, and the committee of management were at a loss what to do next. It happened that just then there was a festival in honor of the Frog-God, at which the magician suddenly cried out, "General Chou has given orders for a further subscription. Bring forth the books." The people all shouting assent to this, the magician went on to say, "Those who have already subscribed will not be compelled to do so again; those who have not subscribed must give according to their means." Thereupon various persons began to put down their names, and when this was finished, the magician examined the books. He then asked if Mr. Chou was present; and the latter, who was skulking behind, in dread lest he should be detected by the God, had no alternative but to come to the front. "Put yourself down for one hundred taels," said the magician to him; and when Chou hesitated, he cried out to him in anger, "You could give two hundred for your own bad purposes: how much more should you do so in a good cause?" alluding to a scandalous intrigue of Chou's, the consequences of which he had averted by payment of the sum mentioned. This put our friend to the blush, and he was obliged to enter his name for one hundred taels, at which his wife was very angry, and said the magician was a rogue, and whenever he came to collect the money he was put off with some excuse.

Shortly afterward, Chou was one day going to sleep, when he heard a noise outside his house, like the blowing of an ox, and beheld a huge frog walking leisurely through the front door, which was just big enough to let it pass. Once inside, the creature laid itself down to sleep, with its head on the threshold, to the great horror of all the inmates; upon which Chou observed that it had probably come to collect his subscription, and burning some incense, he vowed that he would pay down thirty taels on the spot, and send the balance later on. The frog, however, did not move, so Chou promised fifty, and then there was a slight decrease in the frog's size. Another twenty brought it down to the size of a peck measure; and when Chou said the full amount should be paid on the spot, the frog became suddenly no larger than one's fist, and disappeared through a hole in the wall. Chou immediately sent off fifty taels, at which all the other subscribers were much astonished, not knowing what had taken place. A few days afterward the magician said Chou still owed fifty taels, and that he had better send it in soon; so Chou forwarded ten more, hoping now to have done with the matter. However, as he and his wife were one day sitting down to dinner, the frog reappeared, and glaring with anger, took up a position on the bed, which creaked under it, as though unable to bear the weight. Putting its head on the pillow, the frog went off to sleep, its body gradually swelling up until it was as big as a buffalo, and nearly filled the room, causing Chou to send off the balance of his subscription without a moment's delay. There was now no diminution in the size of the frog's body; and by-and-by crowds of small frogs came hopping in, boring through the walls, jumping on the bed, catching flies on the cooking-stove, and dying in the saucepans, until the place was quite unbearable. Three days passed thus, and then Chou sought out the magician, and asked him what was to be done. The latter said he could manage it, and began by vowing on behalf of Chou twenty more taels' subscription. At this the frog raised its head, and a further increase caused it to move one foot; and by the time a hundred taels was reached, the frog was walking out of the door. At the door, however, it stopped, and lay down once more, which the magician explained by saying, that immediate payment was required; so Chou handed over the amount at once, and the frog, shrinking down to its usual size, mingled with its companions, and departed with them.

The repairs to the temple were accordingly completed, but for "lighting the eyes," and the attendant festivities, some further subscriptions were wanted. Suddenly, the magician, pointing at the managers, cried out, "There is money short; of fifteen men, two of you are defaulters." At this, all declared they had given what they could afford; but the magician went on to say, "It is not a question of what you can afford; you have misappropriated the funds that should not have been touched, and misfortune would come upon you, but that, in return for your exertions, I shall endeavor to avert it from you. The magician himself is not without taint. Let him set you a good example." Thereupon, the magician rushed into his house, and brought out all the money he had, saying, "I stole eight taels myself, which I will now refund." He then weighed what silver he had, and finding that it only amounted to a little over six taels, he made one of the bystanders take a note of the difference. Then the others came forward and paid up, each what he had misappropriated from the public fund. All this time the magician had been in a divine ecstasy, not knowing what he was saying; and when he came round, and was told what had happened, his shame knew no bounds, so he pawned some of his clothes, and paid in the balance of his own debt. As to the two defaulters who did not pay, one of them was ill for a month and more; while the other had a bad attack of boils.

Taoist Miracles

At Chi-nan Fu there lived a certain priest: I cannot say whence he came, or what was his name. Winter and summer alike he wore but one unlined robe, and a yellow girdle about his waist, with neither shirt nor trousers. He combed his hair with a broken comb, holding the ends in his mouth, like the strings of a hat. By day he wandered about the market-place; at night he slept in the street, and to a distance of several feet round where he lay, the ice and snow would melt. When he first arrived at Chi-nan he used to perform miracles, and the people vied with each other in making him presents. One day a disreputable young fellow gave him a quantity of wine, and begged him in return to divulge the secret of his power; and when the priest refused, the young man watched him get into the river to bathe, and then ran off with his clothes. The priest called out to him to bring them back, promising that he would do as the young man required; but the latter, distrusting the priest's good faith, refused to do so; whereupon the priest's girdle was forthwith changed into a snake, several spans in circumference, which coiled itself round its master's head, and glared and hissed terribly. The young man now fell on his knees, and humbly prayed the priest to save his life; at which the priest put his girdle on again, and a snake that had appeared to be his girdle, wriggled away and disappeared.

The priest's fame was thus firmly established, and the gentry and officials of the place were constantly inviting him to join them in their festive parties. By-and-by the priest said he was going to invite his entertainers to a return feast; and at the appointed time each one of them found on his table a formal invitation to a banquet at the Water Pavilion, but no one knew who had brought the letters. However, they all went, and were met at the door by the priest, in his usual garb; and when they got inside, the place was all desolate and bare, with no banquet ready. "I'm afraid I shall be obliged to ask you gentlemen to let me use your attendants," said the priest to his guests; "I am a poor man, and keep no servants myself." To this all readily consented; whereupon the priest drew a double door upon the wall, and rapped upon it with his knuckles. Somebody answered from within, and immediately the door was thrown open, and a splendid array of handsome chairs, and tables loaded with exquisite viands and costly wines, burst upon the gaze of the astonished guests. The priest bade the attendants receive all these things from the door, and bring them outside, cautioning them on no account to speak with the people inside; and thus a most luxurious entertainment was provided to the great amazement of all present.

Now this Pavilion stood upon the bank of a small lake, and every year, at the proper season, it was literally covered with lilies; but, at the time of this feast, the weather was cold, and the surface of the lake was of a smoky green color. "It's a pity," said one of the guests, "that the lilies are not out"—a sentiment in which the others very cordially agreed, when suddenly a servant came running in to say that, at that moment, the lake was a perfect mass of lilies. Every one jumped up directly, and ran to look out of the window, and, lo! it was so; and in another minute the fragrant perfume of the flowers was borne toward them by the breeze. Hardly knowing what to make of this strange sight, they sent off some servants, in a boat, to gather a few of the lilies, but they soon returned empty-handed, saying, that the flowers seemed to shift their position as fast as they rowed toward them; at which the priest laughed, and said, "These are but the lilies of your imagination, and have no real existence." And later on, when the wine was finished, the flowers began to droop and fade; and by-and-by a breeze from the north carried off every sign of them, leaving the lake as it had been before.

A certain Taot'ai, at Chi-nan, was much taken with this priest, and gave him rooms at his yamên. One day, he had some friends to dinner, and set before them some very choice old wine that he had, and of which he only brought out a small quantity at a time, not wishing to get through it too rapidly. The guests, however, liked it so much that they asked for more; upon which the Taot'ai said, "he was very sorry, but it was all finished." The priest smiled at this, and said, "I can give the gentlemen some, if they will oblige me by accepting it"; and immediately inserted the wine-kettle in his sleeve, bringing it out again directly, and pouring out for the guests. This wine tasted exactly like the choice wine they had just been drinking, and the priest gave them all as much of it as they wanted, which made the Taot'ai suspect that something was wrong; so, after the dinner, he went into his cellar to look at his own stock, when he found the jars closely tied down, with unbroken seals, but one and all empty. In a great rage, he caused the priest to be arrested for sorcery, and proceeded to have him bambooed; but no sooner had the bamboo touched the priest than the Taot'ai himself felt a sting of pain, which increased at every blow; and, in a few moments, there was the priest writhing and shrieking under every cut, while the Taot'ai was sitting in a pool of blood. Accordingly, the punishment was soon stopped, and the priest was commanded to leave Chi-nan, which he did, and I know not whither he went. He was subsequently seen at Nanking, dressed precisely as of old; but on being spoken to, he only smiled and made no reply.

Arrival of Buddhist Priests

Two Buddhist priests having arrived from the West, one went to the Wu-t'ai hill, while the other hung up his staff at T'ai-shan. Their clothes, complexions, language, and features, were very different from those of our country. They further said they had crossed the Fiery Mountains, from the peaks of which smoke was always issuing as from the chimney of a furnace; that they could only travel after rain, and that excessive caution was necessary to avoid displacing any stone and thus giving a vent to the flames. They also stated that they had passed through the River of Sand, in the middle of which was a crystal hill with perpendicular sides and perfectly transparent; and that there was a defile just broad enough to admit a single cart, its entrance guarded by two dragons with crossed horns. Those who wished to pass prostrated themselves before these dragons, and on receiving permission to enter, the horns opened and let them through. The dragons were of a white color, and their scales and bristles seemed to be of crystal. Eighteen winters and summers these priests had been on the road; and of twelve who started from the west together, only two reached China. These two said that in their country four of our mountains are held in great esteem, namely, T'ai,

Hua, Wu-t'ai, and Lo-chia. The people there also think that China is paved with yellow gold, that Kuan-yin and Wên-shu are still alive, and that they have only come here to be sure of their Buddhahood and of immortal life. Hearing these words it struck me that this was precisely what our own people say and think about the West; and that if travelers from each country could only meet half way and tell each other the true state of affairs, there would be some hearty laughter on both sides, and a saving of much unnecessary trouble.

The Stolen Eyes

When His Excellency Mr. T'ang, of our village, was quite a child, a relative of his took him to a temple to see the usual theatrical performances. He was a clever little fellow, afraid of nothing and nobody; and when he saw one of the clay images in the vestibule staring at him with its great glass eyes, the temptation was irresistible; and, secretly gouging them out with his finger, he carried them off with him. When they reached home, his relative was taken suddenly ill and remained for a long time speechless; at length, jumping up he cried out several times in a voice of thunder, "Why did you gouge out my eyes?" His family did not know what to make of this, until little T'ang told them what he had done; they then immediately began to pray to the possessed man, saying, "A mere child, unconscious of the wickedness of his act, took away in his fun thy sacred eyes. They shall be reverently replaced." Thereupon the voice exclaimed, "In that case, I shall go away"; and he had hardly spoken before T'ang's relative fell flat upon the ground and lay there in a state of insensibility for some time. When he recovered, they asked him concerning what he had said; but he remembered nothing of it. The eyes were then forthwith restored to their original sockets.

The Invisible Priest

Mr. Han was a gentleman of good family, on very intimate terms with a skillful Taoist priest and magician named Tan, who, when sitting amongst other guests, would suddenly become invisible. Mr. Han was extremely anxious to learn this art, but Tan refused all his entreaties, "Not," as he said, "because I want to keep the secret for myself, but simply as a matter of principle. To teach the superior man would be well enough; others, however, would avail themselves of such knowledge to plunder their neighbors. There is no fear that you would do this, though even you might be tempted in certain ways." Mr. Han, finding all his efforts unavailing, flew into a great passion, and secretly arranged with his servants that they should give the magician a sound beating; and, in order to prevent his escape through the power of making himself invisible, he had his threshing-floor covered with a fine ash-dust, so that at any rate his footsteps would be seen and the servants could strike just above them. He then inveigled Tan to the appointed spot, which he had no sooner reached than Han's servants began to belabor him on all sides with leathern thongs. Tan immediately became invisible, but his footprints were clearly seen as he moved about hither and thither to avoid the blows, and the servants went on striking above them until finally he succeeded in getting away.

Mr. Han then went home, and subsequently Tan reappeared and told the servants that he could stay there no longer, adding that before he went he intended to give them all a feast in return for many things they had done for him. And diving into his sleeve he brought forth a quantity of delicious meats and wines which he spread out upon the table, begging them to sit down and enjoy themselves. The servants did so, and one and all of them got drunk and insensible; upon which Tan picked each of them up and stowed them away in his sleeve. When Mr. Han heard of this, he begged Tan to perform some other trick; so Tan drew upon the wall a city, and knocking at the gate with his hand it was instantly thrown open. He then put inside it his wallet and clothes, and stepping through the gateway himself, waved his hand and bade Mr. Han farewell. The city gates were now closed, and Tan vanished from their sight. It was said that he appeared again in Ch'ing-chou, where he taught little boys to paint a circle on their hands, and, by dabbing this on to another person's face or clothes, to imprint the circle on the place thus struck without a trace of it being left behind upon the hand.

The Censor in Purgatory

JUST BEYOND FÊNG-TU THERE IS A FATHOMLESS CAVE WHICH IS REPUTED TO BE THE entrance to Purgatory. All the implements of torture employed therein are of human manufacture; old, worn-out gyves and fetters being occasionally found at the mouth of the cave, and as regularly replaced by new ones, which disappear the same night, and for which the magistrate of the district makes a formal charge in his accounts.

Under the Ming dynasty, there was a certain Censor, named Hua, whose duties brought him to this place; and hearing the story of the cave, he said he did not believe it, but would penetrate into it and see for himself. People tried to dissuade him from such an enterprise; however, he paid no heed to their remonstrances, and entered the cave with a lighted candle in his hand, followed by two attendants. They had proceeded about half a mile, when suddenly the candle was violently extinguished, and Mr. Hua saw before him a broad flight of steps leading up to the Ten Courts, or Judgment-halls, in each of which a judge was sitting with his robes and tablets all complete. On the eastern side there was one vacant place; and when the judges saw Mr. Hua, they hastened down the steps to meet him, and each one cried out, "So you have come at last, have you? I hope you have been quite well since last we met." Mr. Hua asked what the place was; to which they replied that it was the Court of Purgatory, and then Mr. Hua in a great fright was about to take his leave, when the judges stopped him, saying, "No, no, Sir! that is your seat there; how can you imagine you are to go back again?" Thereupon Mr. Hua was overwhelmed with fear, and begged and implored the judges to forgive him; but the latter declared they could not interfere with the decrees of fate, and taking down the register of Life and Death they showed him that it had been ordained that on such a day of such a month his living body would pass into the realms of darkness. When Mr. Hua read these words he shivered and shook as if iced water was being poured down his back, and thinking of his old mother and his young children, his tears began to flow. At that juncture an angel in golden armor appeared, holding in his hand a document written on yellow silk, before which the judges all performed a respectful obeisance.

They then unfolded and read the document, which was nothing more or less than a general pardon from the Almighty for the suffering sinners in Purgatory, by virtue of which Mr. Hua's fate would be set aside, and he would be enabled to return once more to the light of day. Thereupon the judges congratulated him upon his release, and started him on his way home; but he had not got more than a few steps of the way before he found himself plunged in total darkness. He was just beginning to despair, when forth from the gloom came a God with a red face and a long beard, rays of light shooting out from his body and illuminating the darkness around. Mr. Hua made up to him at once, and begged to know how he could get out of the cave; to which the God curtly replied, "Repeat the *sûtras* of Buddha!" and vanished instantly from his sight. Now Mr. Hua had forgotten almost all the *sûtras* he had ever known; however, he remembered a little of the diamond *sûtra*, and, clasping his hands in an attitude of prayer, he began to repeat it aloud. No sooner had he done this than a faint streak of light glimmered through the darkness, and revealed to him the direction of the path; but the next moment he was at a loss how to go on and the light forthwith disappeared. He then set himself to think hard what the next verse was, and as fast as he recollected and could go on repeating, so fast did the light reappear to guide him on his way, until at length he emerged once more from the mouth of the cave. As to the fate of the two servants who accompanied him it is needless to inquire.

Mr. Willow and the Locusts

During the Ming dynasty a plague of locusts visited Ch'ing-yen, and was advancing rapidly toward the I district, when the magistrate of that place, in great tribulation at the pending disaster, retired one day to sleep behind the screen in his office. There he dreamt that a young graduate, named Willow, wearing a tall hat and a green robe, and of very commanding stature, came to see him, and declared that he could tell the magistrate how to get rid of the locusts. "To-morrow," said he, "on the south-west road, you will see a woman riding on a large jennet: she is the Spirit of the Locusts; ask her, and she will help you." The magistrate thought this strange advice; however, he got everything ready, and waited, as he had been told, at the road-side. By-and-by, along came a woman with her hair tied up in a knot, and a serge cape over her shoulders, riding slowly northward on an old mule; whereupon the magistrate burned some sticks of incense, and, seizing the mule's bridle, humbly presented a goblet of wine. The woman asked him what he wanted; to which he replied, "Lady, I implore you to save my small magistracy from the dreadful ravages of your locusts." "Oho!" said the woman, "that scoundrel, Willow, has been letting the cat out of the bag, has he? He shall suffer for it: I won't touch your crops." She then drank three cups of wine, and vanished out of sight. Subsequently, when the locusts did come, they flew high in the air, and did not settle on the crops; but they stripped the leaves off every willow-tree far and wide; and then the magistrate awaked to the fact that the graduate of his dream was the Spirit of the Willows. Some said that this happy result was owing to the magistrate's care for the welfare of his people.

Mr. Tung, or Virtue Rewarded

At Ch'ing-chow there lived a Mr. Tung, President of one of the Six Boards, whose domestic regulations were so strict that the men and women servants were not allowed to speak to each other. One day he caught a slave-girl laughing and talking with one of his attendants, and gave them both a sound rating. That night he retired to sleep, accompanied by his *valet-de-chambre*, in his library, the door of which, as it was very hot weather, was left wide open. When the night was far advanced, the valet was awaked by a noise at his master's bed: and, opening his eyes, he saw, by the light of the moon, the attendant above-mentioned pass out of the door with something in his hand. Recognizing the man as one of the family, he thought nothing of the occurrence, but turned round and went to sleep again. Soon after, however, he was again aroused by the noise of footsteps tramping heavily across the room, and, looking up, he beheld a huge being with a red face and a long beard, very like the God of War, carrying a man's head. Horribly frightened, he crawled under the bed, and then he heard sounds above him as of clothes being shaken out, and as if some one was being shampooed. In a few moments, the boots tramped once more across the room and went away; and then he gradually put out his head, and, seeing the dawn beginning to peep through the window, he stretched out his hand to reach his clothes. These he found to be soaked through and through, and, on applying his hand to his nose, he smelt the smell of blood. He now called out loudly to his master, who jumped up at once; and, by the light of a candle, they saw that the bed clothes and pillows were alike steeped in blood. Just then some constables knocked at the door, and when Mr. Tung went out to see who it was, the constables were all astonishment; "for," said they, "a few minutes ago a man rushed wildly up to our yamên, and said he had killed his master; and, as he himself was covered with blood, he was arrested, and turned out to be a servant of yours. He also declared that he had buried your head alongside the temple of the God of War; and when we went to look, there, indeed, was a freshly-dug hole, but the head was gone."

Mr. Tung was amazed at all this story, and, on proceeding to the magistrate's *yamên*, he discovered that the man in charge was the attendant whom he had scolded the day before. Thereupon, the criminal was severely bambooed and released; and then Mr. Tung, who was unwilling to make an enemy of a man of this stamp, gave him the girl to wife. However, a few nights afterward the people who lived next door to the newly-married couple heard a terrific crash in their house, and, rushing in to see what was the matter, found that husband and wife, and the bedstead as well, had been cut clean in two as if by a sword. The ways of the God are many, indeed, but few more extraordinary than this.

The Dead Priest

A CERTAIN TAOIST PRIEST, OVERTAKEN IN HIS WANDERINGS BY THE SHADES OF evening, sought refuge in a small Buddhist monastery. The monk's apartment was, however, locked; so he threw his mat down in the vestibule of the shrine, and seated himself upon it. In the middle of the night, when all was still, he heard a sound of some one opening the door behind him; and looking round, he saw a Buddhist priest, covered with blood from head to foot, who did not seem to notice that anybody else was present. Accordingly, he himself pretended not to be aware of what was going on; and then he saw the other priest enter the shrine, mount the altar, and remain there some time embracing Buddha's head, and laughing by turns. When morning came, he found the monk's room still locked; and, suspecting something was wrong, he walked to a neighboring village, where he told the people what he had seen. Thereupon the villagers went back with him, and broke open the door, and there before them lay the priest weltering in his blood, having evidently been killed by robbers, who had stripped the place bare. Anxious now to find out what had made the disembodied spirit of the priest laugh in the way it had been seen to do, they proceeded to inspect the head of the Buddha on the altar; and, at the back of it, they noticed a small mark, scraping through which they discovered a sum of over thirty ounces of silver. This sum was forthwith used for defraying the funeral expenses of the murdered man.

The Flying Cow

A certain man, who had bought a fine cow, dreamt the same night that wings grew out of the animal's back, and that it had flown away. Regarding this as an omen of some pending misfortune, he led the cow off to market again, and sold it at a ruinous loss. Wrapping up in a cloth the silver he received, he slung it over his back, and was half way home, when he saw a falcon eating part of a hare. Approaching the bird, he found it was quite tame, and accordingly tied it by the leg to one of the corners of the cloth, in which his money was. The falcon fluttered about a good deal, trying to escape; and, by-and-by, the man's hold being for a moment relaxed, away went the bird, cloth, money, and all. "It was destiny," said the man every time he told the story; ignorant as he was, first, that no faith should be put in dreams; and, secondly, that people shouldn't take things they see by the wayside. Quadrupeds don't usually fly.

The "Mirror-and-Listen" Trick

At I-tu there lived a family of the name of Chêng. The two sons were both distinguished scholars, but the elder was early known to fame, and, consequently, the favorite with his parents, who also extended their preference to his wife. The younger brother was a trifle wild, which displeased his father and mother very much, and made them regard his wife, too, with anything but a friendly eye. The latter reproached her husband for being the cause of this, and asked him why he, being a man like his brother, could not vindicate the slights that were put upon her. This piqued him; and, setting to work in good earnest, he soon gained a fair reputation, though still not equal to his brother's.

That year the two went up for the highest degree; and, on New Year's Eve, the wife of the younger, very anxious for the success of her husband, secretly tried the "mirror-and-listen" trick. She saw two men pushing each other in jest, and heard them say, "You go and get cool," which remark she was quite unable to interpret for good or for bad, so she thought no more about the matter. After the examination, the two brothers returned home; and one day, when the weather was extremely hot, and their two wives were hard at work in the cook-house, preparing food for their field-laborers, a messenger rode up in hot haste to announce that the elder brother had passed. Thereupon his mother went into the cook-house, and, calling to her daughter-in-law, said, "Your husband has passed; *you go and get cool*." Rage and grief now filled the breast of the second son's wife, who, with tears in her eyes, continued her task of cooking, when suddenly another messenger rushed in to say, that the second son had passed, too. At this, his wife flung down her frying-pan, and cried out, "Now I'll *go and get cool*"; and as in the heat of her excitement she uttered these words, the recollection of her trial of the "mirror-and-listen" trick flashed upon her, and she knew that the words of that evening had been fulfilled.

The Cattle Plague

CH'ÊN HUA-FÊNG, OF MÊNG-SHAN, OVERPOWERED BY THE GREAT HEAT, WENT AND lay down under a tree, when suddenly up came a man with a thick comforter round his neck, who also sat down on a stone in the shade, and began fanning himself as hard as he could, the perspiration all the time running off him like a waterfall. Ch'ên rose and said to him with a smile, "If Sir, you were to remove that comforter, you would be cool enough without the help of a fan." "It would be easy enough," replied the stranger, "to take off my comforter; but the difficulty would be in getting it on again." He then went on to converse generally upon other matters, in a manner which betokened considerable refinement; and by-and-by he exclaimed, "What I should like now is just a draught of iced wine to cool the twelve joints of my esophagus."

"Come along, then," cried Ch'ên, "my house is close by, and I shall be happy to give you what you want."

So off they went together; and Ch'ên set before them some capital wine, which he produced from a cave, cold enough to numb their teeth. The stranger was delighted, and remained there drinking until late in the evening, when, all at once, it began to rain. Ch'ên lighted a lamp; and he and his guest, who now took off the comforter, sat talking together in *dishabille*. Every now and again the former thought he saw a light coming from the back of the stranger's head; and when at length he had gone off into a tipsy sleep,

Ch'ên took the light to examine more closely. He found behind the ears a large cavity, partitioned by a number of membranes, and looking like a lattice, with a thin skin hanging down in front of each, the spaces being apparently empty. In great astonishment Ch'ên took a hair-pin, and inserted it into one of these places, when pff! out flew something like a tiny cow, which broke through the window, and was gone. This frightened Ch'ên, and he determined to play no more tricks; just then, however, the stranger waked up.

"Alas!" cried he, "you have been at my head, and have let out the Cattle Plague. What is to be done, now?" Ch'ên asked what he meant: upon which the stranger said, "There is no object in further concealment. I will tell you all. I am the Angel of Pestilence for the six kinds of domestic animals. That form which you have let out attacks oxen, and I fear that, for miles round, few will escape alive."

Now Ch'ên himself was a cattle-farmer, and when he heard this was dreadfully alarmed, and implored the stranger to tell him what to do. "What to do!" replied he; "why, I shall not escape punishment myself; how can I tell you what to do. However, you will find powdered *K'u-ts'an* an efficacious remedy, that is if you don't keep it a secret for your private use."

The stranger then departed, first of all piling up a quantity of earth in a niche in the wall, a handful of which, he told Ch'ên, given to each animal, might prove of some avail. Before long the plague did break out; and Ch'ên, who was desirous of making a little money by it, told the remedy to no one, with the exception of his younger brother. The latter tried it on his own beasts with great success; while, on the other hand, those belonging to Ch'ên himself died off, to the number of fifty head, leaving him only four or five old cows, which showed every sign of soon sharing the same fate. In his distress, Ch'ên suddenly bethought himself of the earth in the niche; and, as a last resource, gave some to the sick animals. By the next morning they were quite well, and then he knew that his secrecy about the remedy had caused it to have no effect. From that moment his stock went on increasing, and in a few years he had as many as ever.

The Marriage of the Virgin Goddess

At Kuei-chi there is a shrine to the Plum Virgin, who was formerly a young lady named Ma, and lived at Tung-wan. Her betrothed husband dying before the wedding, she swore she would never marry, and at thirty years of age she died. Her kinsfolk built a shrine to her memory, and gave her the title of the Plum Virgin. Some years afterward, a Mr. Chin, on his way to the examination, happened to pass by the shrine; and entering in, he walked up and down thinking very much of the young lady in whose honor it had been erected. That night he dreamt that a servant came to summon him into the presence of the Goddess; and that, in obedience to her command, he went and found her waiting for him just outside the shrine. "I am deeply grateful to you, Sir," said the Goddess, on his approach, "for giving me so large a share of your thoughts; and I intend to repay you by becoming your humble handmaid." Mr. Chin bowed an assent; and then the Goddess escorted him back, saying, "When your place is ready, I will come and fetch you." On waking in the morning, Mr. Chin was not over pleased with his dream; however that very night every one of the villagers dreamt that the Goddess appeared and said she was going to marry Mr. Chin, bidding them at once prepare an image of him. This the village elders, out of respect for their Goddess, positively refused to do; until at length they all began to fall ill, and then they made a clay image of Mr. Chin, and placed it on the left of the Goddess. Mr. Chin now told his wife that the Plum Virgin had come for him; and, putting on his official cap and robes, he straightway died. Thereupon his wife was very angry; and, going to the shrine, she first abused the Goddess, and then, getting on the altar, slapped her face well. The Goddess is now called Chin's virgin wife.

The Wine Insect

A Mr. Lin of Ch'ang-shan was extremely fat, and so fond of wine that he would often finish a pitcher by himself. However, he owned about fifty acres of land, half of which was covered with millet, and being well off, he did not consider that his drinking would bring him into trouble. One day a foreign Buddhist priest saw him, and remarked that he appeared to be suffering from some extraordinary complaint. Mr. Lin said nothing was the matter with him; whereupon the priest asked him if he often got drunk. Lin acknowledged that he did; and the priest told him that he was afflicted by the wine insect. "Dear me!" cried Lin, in great alarm, "do you think you could cure me?" The priest declared there would be no difficulty in doing so; but when Lin asked him what drugs he intended to use, the priest said he should not use any at all. He then made Lin lie down in the sun; and tying his hands and feet together, he placed a stoup of good wine about half a foot from his head. By-and-by, Lin felt a deadly thirst coming on; and the flavor of the wine passing through his nostrils, seemed to set his vitals on fire. Just then he ex perienced a tickling sensation in his throat, and something ran out of his mouth and jumped into the wine. On being released from his bonds, he saw that it was an insect about three inches in length, which wriggled about in the wine like a tadpole, and had mouth and eyes all complete. Lin was overjoyed, and offered money to the priest, who refused to take it, saying, all he wanted was the insect, which he explained to Lin was the essence of wine, and which, on being stirred up in water, would turn it into wine. Lin tried this, and found it was so; and ever afterward he detested the sight of wine. He subsequently became very thin, and so poor that he had hardly enough to eat and drink.

The Faithful Dog

A certain man of Lu-ngan, whose father had been cast into prison, and was brought almost to death's door, scraped together one hundred ounces of silver, and set out for the city to try and arrange for his parent's release. Jumping on a mule, he saw that a black dog, belonging to the family, was following him. He tried in vain to make the dog remain at home; and when, after traveling for some miles, he got off his mule to rest awhile, he picked up a large stone and threw it at the dog, which then ran off. However, he was no sooner on the road again, than up came the dog, and tried to stop the mule by holding on to its tail. His master beat it off with the whip; whereupon the dog ran barking loudly in front of the mule, and seemed to be using every means in its power to cause his master to stop. The latter thought this a very inauspicious omen, and turning upon the animal in a rage, drove it away out of sight. He now went on to the city; but when, in the dusk of the evening, he arrived there, he found that about half his money was gone. In a terrible state of mind he tossed about all night; then, all of a sudden, it flashed across him that the strange behavior of the dog might possibly have some meaning; so getting up very early, he left the city as soon as the gates were open, and though, from the number of passers-by, he never expected to find his money again, he went on until he reached the spot where he had got off his mule the day before. There he saw his dog lying dead upon the ground, its hair having apparently been wetted through with perspiration; and, lifting up the body by one of its ears, he found his lost silver. Full of gratitude, he bought a coffin and buried the dead animal; and the people now call the place the Grave of the Faithful Dog.

An Earthquake

In 1668 there was a very severe earthquake. I myself was staying at Chi-hsia, and happened to be that night sitting over a kettle of wine with my cousin Li Tu. All of a sudden we heard a noise like thunder, traveling from the south-east in a north-westerly direction. We were much astonished at this, and quite unable to account for the noise; in another moment the table began to rock, and the wine-cups were upset; the beams and supports of the house snapped here and there with a crash, and we looked at each other in fear and trembling. By-and-by we knew that it was an earthquake; and, rushing out, we saw houses and other buildings, as it were, fall down and get up again; and, amidst the sounds of crushing walls, we heard the shrieks of women and children, the whole mass being like a great seething cauldron. Men were giddy and could not stand, but rolled about on the ground; the river overflowed its banks; cocks crowed, and dogs barked from one end of the city to the other. In a little while the quaking began to subside; and then might be seen men and women running half naked about the streets, all anxious to tell their own experiences, and forgetting that they had on little or no clothing. I subsequently heard that a well was closed up and rendered useless by this earthquake; that a house was turned completely round, so as to face the opposite direction; that the Chi-hsia hill was riven open, and that the waters of the I river flowed in and made a lake of an acre and more. Truly such an earthquake as this is of rare occurrence.

Making Animals

THE TRICKS FOR BEWITCHING PEOPLE ARE MANY. SOMETIMES DRUGS ARE PUT IN THEIR food, and when they eat they become dazed, and follow the person who has bewitched them. This is commonly called *ta hsü pa*; in Kiang-nan it is known as *ch'ê hsü*. Little children are most frequently bewitched in this way. There is also what is called "making animals," which is better known on the south side of the River.

One day a man arrived at an inn in Yang-chow, leading with him five donkeys. Tying them up near the stable, he told the landlord he would be back in a few minutes, and bade him give his donkeys no water. He had not been gone long before the donkeys, which were standing out in the glare of the sun, began to kick about, and make a noise; whereupon the landlord untied them, and was going to put them in the shade, when suddenly they espied water, and made a rush to get at it. So the landlord let them drink; and no sooner had the water touched their lips than they rolled on the ground, and changed into women. In great astonishment, the landlord asked them whence they came; but their tongues were tied, and they could not answer, so he hid them in his private apartments, and at that moment their owner returned, bringing with him five sheep. The latter immediately asked the landlord where his donkeys were; to which the landlord replied by offering him some wine, saying, the donkeys would be brought to him directly. He then went out and gave the sheep some water, on drinking which they were all changed into boys. Accordingly, he communicated with the authorities, and the stranger was arrested and forthwith beheaded.

Cruelty Avenged

A CERTAIN MAGISTRATE CAUSED A PETTY OIL-VENDOR, WHO WAS BROUGHT BEFORE HIM for some trifling misdemeanor, and whose statements were very confused, to be bambooed to death. The former subsequently rose to high rank; and having amassed considerable wealth, set about building himself a fine house. On the day when the great beam was to be fixed in its place, among the friends and relatives who arrived to offer their congratulations, he was horrified to see the oilman walk in. At the same instant one of the servants came rushing up to announce to him the birth of a son; whereupon, he mournfully remarked, "The house not yet finished, and its destroyer already here." The bystanders thought he was joking, for they had not seen what he had seen. However, when that boy grew up, by his frivolity and extravagance he quite ruined his father. He was finally obliged himself to go into service; and spent all his earnings in oil, which he swallowed in large quantities.

The Wei-ch'i Devil

A CERTAIN GENERAL, WHO HAD RESIGNED HIS COMMAND, AND HAD RETIRED TO HIS own home, was very fond of roaming about and amusing himself with wine and *wei-ch'i*. One day—it was the 9th of the 9th moon, when everybody goes up high—as he was playing with some friends, a stranger walked up, and watched the game intently for some time without going away. He was a miserable-looking creature, with a very ragged coat, but nevertheless possessed of a refined and courteous air. The general begged him to be seated, an offer which he accepted, being all the time extremely deferential in his manner. "I suppose you are pretty good at this," said the general, pointing to the board; "try a bout with one of my friends here."

The stranger made a great many apologies in reply, but finally accepted, and played a game in which, apparently to his great disappointment, he was beaten. He played another with the same result; and now, refusing all offers of wine, he seemed to think of nothing but how to get some one to play with him. Thus he went on until the afternoon was well advanced; when suddenly, just as he was in the middle of a most exciting game, which depended on a single place, he rushed forward, and throwing himself at the feet of the general, loudly implored his protection. The general did not know what to make of this; however, he raised him up, and said, "It's only a game: why get so excited?" To this the stranger replied by begging the general not to let his gardener seize him; and when the general asked what gardener he meant, he said the man's name was Ma-ch'êng.

Now this Ma-ch'êng was often employed as a lictor by the Ruler of Purgatory, and would sometimes remain away as much as ten days, serving the warrants of death; accordingly, the general sent off to inquire about him, and found that he had been in a trance for two days. His master cried out that he had better not behave rudely to his guest, but at that very moment the stranger sunk down to the ground, and was gone. The general was lost in astonishment; however, he now knew that the man was a disembodied spirit, and on the next day, when Ma-ch'êng came round, he asked him for full particulars.

"The gentleman was a native of Hu-hsiang," replied the gardener, "who was passionately addicted to *wei-ch'i*, and had lost a great deal of money by it. His father, being much grieved at his behavior, confined him to the house; but he was always getting out, and indulging the fatal passion, and at last his father died of a broken heart. In consequence of this, the Ruler of Purgatory curtailed his term of life, and condemned him to become a hungry devil, in which state he has already passed seven years. And now that the Phoenix Tower is completed, an order has been issued for the literati to present themselves, and compose an inscription to be cut on stone, as a memorial thereof, by which means they would secure their own salvation as a reward. Many of the shades failing to arrive at the appointed time, God was very angry with the Ruler of Purgatory, and the latter sent off me, and others who are employed in the same way, to hunt up the defaulters. But as you, Sir, bade me treat the gentleman with respect, I did not venture to bind him."

The general inquired what had become of the stranger; to which the gardener replied, "He is now a mere menial in Purgatory, and can never be born again."

"Alas!" cried his master, "thus it is that men are ruined by any inordinate passion."

The Fortune-Hunter Punished

A CERTAIN MAN'S UNCLE HAD NO CHILDREN, AND THE NEPHEW, WITH AN EYE TO HIS uncle's property, volunteered to become his adopted son. When the uncle died all the property passed accordingly to his nephew, who thereupon broke faith as to his part of the contract. He did the same with another uncle, and thus united three properties in his own person, whereby he became the richest man of the neighborhood. Suddenly he fell ill, and seemed to go out of his mind; for he cried out, "So you wish to live in wealth, do you?" and immediately seizing a sharp knife, he began hacking away at his own body until he had strewed the floor with pieces of flesh. He then exclaimed, "You cut off other people's posterity and expect to have posterity yourself, do you?" and forthwith he ripped himself open and died. Shortly afterward his son, too, died, and the property fell into the hands of strangers. Is not this a retribution to be dreaded?

Life Prolonged

A CERTAIN CLOTH MERCHANT OF CH'ANG-CH'ING WAS STOPPING AT T'AI-NGAN, WHEN he heard of a magician who was said to be very skilled in casting nativities. So he went off at once to consult him; but the magician would not undertake the task, saying, "Your destiny is bad: you had better hurry home." At this the merchant was dreadfully frightened, and, packing up his wares, set off towards Ch'ang-ch'ing. On the way he fell in with a man in short clothes, like a constable; and the two soon struck up a friendly intimacy, taking their meals together.

By-and-by the merchant asked the stranger what his business was; and the latter told him he was going to Ch'ang-ch'ing to serve summonses, producing at the same time a document and showing it to the merchant, who, on looking closely, saw a list of names, at the head of which was his own. In great astonishment he inquired what he had done that he should be arrested thus; to which his companion replied, "I am not a living being: I am a lictor in the employ of the infernal authorities, and I presume your term of life has expired." The merchant burst into tears and implored the lictor to spare him, which the latter declared was impossible; "but," added he, "there are a great many names down, and it will take me some time to get through them: you go off home and settle up your affairs, and, as a slight return for your friendship, I'll call for you last." A few minutes afterward they reached a stream where the bridge was in ruins, and people could only cross with great difficulty; at which the lictor remarked, "You are now on the road to death, and not a single cash can you carry away with you. Repair this bridge and benefit the public; and thus from a great outlay you may possibly yourself derive some small advantage."

The merchant said he would do so; and when he got home, he bade his wife and children prepare for his coming dissolution, and at the same time set men to work and made the bridge sound and strong again. Some time elapsed, but no lictor arrived; and his suspicions began to be aroused, when one day the latter walked in and said, "I reported that affair of the bridge to the Municipal God, who communicated it to the Ruler of Purgatory; and for that good act your span of life has been lengthened, and your name struck out of the list. I have now come to announce this to you." The merchant was profuse in his thanks; and the next time he went to T'ai-ngan, he burnt a quantity of paper ingots, and made offerings and libations to the lictor, out of gratitude for what he had done. Suddenly the lictor himself appeared, and cried out, "Do you wish to ruin me? Happily my new master has only just taken up his post, and he has not noticed this, or where should I be?" The lictor then escorted the merchant some distance; and, at parting, bade him never return by that road, but, if he had any business at T'ai-ngan, to go thither by a roundabout way.

The Clay Image

On the river I there lived a man named Ma, who married a wife from the Wang family, with whom he was very happy in his domestic life. Ma, however, died young; and his wife's parents were unwilling that their daughter should remain a widow, but she resisted all their importunities, and declared firmly she would never marry again. "It is a noble resolve of yours, I allow," argued her mother; "but you are still a mere girl, and you have no children. Besides, I notice that people who start with such rigid determinations always end by doing something discreditable, and therefore you had better get married as soon as you can, which is no more than is done every day." The girl swore she would rather die than consent, and accordingly her mother had no alternative but to let her alone. She then ordered a clay image to be made, exactly resembling her late husband; and whenever she took her own meals, she would set meat and wine before it, precisely as if her husband had been there.

One night she was on the point of retiring to rest, when suddenly she saw the clay image stretch itself and step down from the table, increasing all the while in height, until it was as tall as a man, and neither more nor less than her own husband. In great alarm she called out to her mother, but the image stopped her, saying, "Don't do that! I am but showing my gratitude for your affectionate care of me, and it is chill and uncomfortable in the realms below. Such devotion as yours casts its light back on generations gone by; and now I, who was cut off in my prime because my father did evil, and was condemned to be without an heir, have been permitted, in consequence of your virtuous conduct, to visit you once again, that our ancestral line may yet remain unbroken." Every morning at cock-crow her husband resumed his usual form and size as the clay image; and after a time he told her that their hour of separation had come, upon which husband and wife bade each other an eternal farewell. By-and-by the widow, to the great astonishment of her mother, bore a son, which caused no small amusement among the neighbors who heard the story; and, as the girl herself had no proof of what she stated to be the case, a certain beadle of the place, who had an old grudge against her husband, went off and informed the magistrate of what had occurred. After some investigation, the magistrate exclaimed, "I have heard that the children of disembodied spirits have no shadow; and that those who have shadows are not genuine." Thereupon they took Ma's child into the sunshine, and lo! there was but a very faint shadow, like a thin vapor. The magistrate then drew blood from the child, and smeared it on the clay image; upon which the blood at once soaked in and left no stain. Another clay image being produced and the same experiment tried, the blood remained on the surface so that it could be wiped away. The girl's story was thus acknowledged to be true; and when the child grew up, and in every feature was the counterpart of Ma, there was no longer any room for suspicion.

Dishonesty Punished

AT CHIAO-CHOU THERE LIVED A MAN NAMED LIU HSI-CH'UAN, WHO WAS STEWARD TO His excellency Mr. Fa. When already over forty a son was born to him, whom he loved very dearly, and quite spoiled by always letting him have his own way. When the boy grew up he led a dissolute, extravagant life, and ran through all his father's property. By-and-by he fell sick, and then he declared that nothing would cure him but a slice off a fat old favorite mule they had; upon which his father had another and more worthless animal killed; but his son found out he was being tricked, and, after abusing his father soundly, his symptoms became more and more alarming. The mule was accordingly killed, and some of it was served up to the sick man; however, he only just tasted it and sent the rest away. From that time he got gradually worse and worse, and finally died, to the great grief of his father, who would gladly have died too.

Three or four years afterward, as some of the villagers were worshipping on Mount Tai, they saw a man riding on a mule, the very image of Mr. Liu's dead son; and, on approaching more closely, they saw that it was actually he. Jumping from his mule, he made them a salutation, and then they began to chat with him on various subjects, always carefully avoiding that one of his own death. They asked him what he was doing there; to which he replied that he was only roaming about, and inquired of them in his turn at what inn they were staying; "For," added he, "I have an engagement just now, but I will visit you to-morrow."

So they told him the name of the inn, and took their leave, not expecting to see him again. However, the next day he came, and, tying his mule to a post outside, went in to see them. "Your father," observed one of the villagers, "is always thinking about you. Why do you not go and pay him a visit?" The young man asked to whom he was alluding; and, at the mention of his father's name, he changed color and said, "If he is anxious to see me, kindly tell him that on the 7th of the 4th moon I will await him here."

He then went away, and the villagers returned and told Mr. Liu all that had taken place. At the appointed time the latter was very desirous of going to see his son; but his master dissuaded him, saying that he thought from what he knew of his son that the interview might possibly not turn out as he would desire; "Although," added he, "if you are bent upon going, I should be sorry to stand in your way. Let me, however, counsel you to conceal yourself in a cupboard, and thus, by observing what takes place, you will know better how to act, and avoid running into any danger." This he accordingly did, and, when his son came, Mr. Fa received him at the inn as before.

"Where's Mr. Liu?" cried the son.

"Oh, he hasn't come," replied Mr. Fa. "The old beast! What does he mean by that?" exclaimed his son; whereupon Mr. Fa asked him what *he* meant by cursing his own father.

"My father!" shrieked the son; "why he's nothing more to me than a former rascally partner in trade, who cheated me out of all my money, and for which I have since avenged myself on him. What sort of a father is that, I should like to know?" He then went out of the door; and his father crept out of the cupboard from which, with the perspiration streaming down him and hardly daring to breathe, he had heard all that had passed, and sorrowfully wended his way home again.

The Mad Priest

A CERTAIN MAD PRIEST, WHOSE NAME I DO NOT KNOW, LIVED IN A TEMPLE ON THE hills. He would sing and cry by turns, without any apparent reason; and once somebody saw him boiling a stone for his dinner. At the autumn festival of the 9th day of the 9th moon, an official of the district went up in that direction for the usual picnic, taking with him his chair and his red umbrellas. After luncheon he was passing by the temple, and had hardly reached the door, when out rushed the priest, barefooted and ragged, and himself opening a yellow umbrella, cried out as the attendants of a mandarin do when ordering the people to stand back. He then approached the official, and made as though he were jesting at him; at which the latter was extremely indignant, and bade his servants drive the priest away. The priest moved off with the servants after him, and in another moment had thrown down his yellow umbrella, which split into a number of pieces, each piece changing immediately into a falcon, and flying about in all directions. The umbrella handle became a huge serpent, with red scales and glaring eyes; and then the party would have turned and fled, but that one of them declared it was only an optical delusion, and that the creature couldn't do any hurt. The speaker accordingly seized a knife and rushed at the serpent, which forthwith opened its mouth and swallowed its assailant whole. In a terrible fright the servants crowded round their master and hurried him away, not stopping to draw breath until they were fully a mile off. By-and-by several of them stealthily returned to see what was going on; and, on entering the temple, they found that both priest and serpent had disappeared. But from an old ash-tree hard by they heard a sound proceeding,— a sound, as it were, of a donkey panting; and at first they were afraid to go near, though after a while they ventured to peep through a hole in the tree, which was an old hollow trunk; and there, jammed hard and fast with his head downward, was the rash assailant of the serpent. It being quite impossible to drag him out, they began at once to cut the tree away; but by the time they had set him free he was already perfectly unconscious. However, he ultimately came round and was carried home; but from this day the priest was never seen again.

Feasting the Ruler of Purgatory

AT CHING-HAI THERE LIVED A YOUNG MAN, NAMED SHAO, WHOSE FAMILY WAS VERY poor. On the occasion of his mother completing her cycle, he arranged a quantity of meat-offerings and wine on a table in the court-yard, and proceeded to invoke the Gods in the usual manner; but when he rose from his knees, lo and behold! all the meat and wine had disappeared. His mother thought this was a bad omen, and that she was not destined to enjoy a long life; however, she said nothing on the subject to her son, who was himself quite at a loss to account for what had happened. A short time afterward the Literary Chancellor arrived; and young Chao, scraping together what funds he could, went off to present himself as a candidate. On the road he met with a man who gave him such a cordial invitation to his house that he willingly accepted; and the stranger led him to a stately mansion, with towers and terraces rising one above the other as far as the eye could reach. In one of the apartments was a king, sitting upon a throne, who received Shao in a very friendly manner; and, after regaling him with an excellent banquet, said, "I have to thank you for the food and drink you gave my servants that day we passed your house."

Shao was greatly astonished at this remark, when the King proceeded, "I am the Ruler of Purgatory. Don't you recollect sacrificing on your mother's birthday?" The King then bestowed on Shao a packet of silver, saying, "Pray accept this in return for your kindness." Shao thanked him and retired; and in another moment the palace and its occupants had one and all vanished from his sight, leaving him alone in the midst of some tall trees. On opening his packet he found it to contain five ounces of pure gold; and, after defraying the expenses of his examination, half was still left, which he carried home and gave to his mother.

The Picture Horse

A certain Mr. Ts'ui, of Lin-ch'ing, was too poor to keep his garden walls in repair, and used often to find a strange horse lying down on the grass inside. It was a black horse marked with white, and having a scrubby tail, which looked as if the end had been burned off; and, though always driven away, would still return to the same spot. Now Mr. Ts'ui had a friend, who was holding an appointment in Shansi; and though he had frequently felt desirous of paying him a visit, he had no means of traveling so far. Accordingly, he one day caught the strange horse and, putting a saddle on its back, rode away, telling his servant that if the owner of the horse should appear, he was to inform him where the animal was to be found. The horse started off at a very rapid pace, and, in a short time, they were thirty or forty miles from home; but at night it did not seem to care for its food, so the next day Mr. Ts'ui, who thought perhaps illness might be the cause, held the horse in, and would not let it gallop so fast. However, the animal did not seem to approve of this, and kicked and foamed until at length Mr. Ts'ui let it go at the same old pace; and by mid-day he had reached his destination.

As he rode into the town, the people were astonished to hear of the marvelous journey just accomplished, and the Prince sent to say he should like to buy the horse. Mr. Ts'ui, fearing that the real owner might come forward, was compelled to refuse this offer; but when, after six months had elapsed, no inquiries had been made, he agreed to accept eight hundred ounces of silver, and handed over the horse to the Prince. He then bought himself a good mule, and returned home. Subsequently, the Prince had occasion to use the horse for some important business at Lin-ch'ing; and when there it took the opportunity to run away. The officer in charge pursued it right up to the house of a Mr. Tsêng, who lived next door to Mr. Ts'ui, and saw it run in and disappear. Thereupon he called upon Mr. Tsêng to restore it to him; and, on the latter declaring he had never even seen the animal, the officer walked into his private apartments, where he found, hanging on the wall, a picture of a horse, by Tzŭ-ang, exactly like the one he was in search of, and with part of the tail burnt away by a joss-stick. It was now clear that the Prince's horse was a supernatural creature; but the officer, being afraid to go back without it, would have prosecuted Mr. Tsêng, had not Ts'ui, whose eight hundred ounces of silver had since increased to something like ten thousand, stepped in and paid back the original purchase-money. Mr. Tsêng was exceedingly grateful to him for this act of kindness, ignorant, as he was, of the previous sale of the horse by Ts'ui to the Prince.

The Butterfly's Revenge

MR. WANG, OF CH'ANG-SHAN, WAS IN THE HABIT, WHEN A DISTRICT MAGISTRATE, OF commuting the fines and penalties of the Penal Code, inflicted on the various prisoners, for a corresponding number of butterflies. These he would let go all at once in the court, rejoicing to see them fluttering hither and thither, like so many tinsel snippings borne about by the breeze. One night he dreamt that a young lady, dressed in gay-colored clothes, appeared to him and said, "Your cruel practice has brought many of my sisters to an untimely end, and now you shall pay the penalty of thus gratifying your tastes." The young lady then changed into a butterfly and flew away. Next day, the magistrate was sitting alone, over a cup of wine, when it was announced to him that the censor was at the door; and out he ran at once to receive His Excellency, with a white flower, that some of his women had put in his official hat, still sticking there. His Excellency was very angry at what he deemed a piece of disrespect to himself; and, after severely censuring Mr. Wang, turned round and went away. Thenceforward no more penalties were commuted for butterflies.

The Doctor

A CERTAIN POOR MAN, NAMED CHANG, WHO LIVED AT I, FELL IN ONE DAY WITH A Taoist priest. The latter was highly skilled in the science of physiognomy; and, after looking at Chang's features, said to him, "You would make your fortune as a doctor."

"Alas!" replied Chang, "I can barely read and write; how then could I follow such a calling as that?"

"And where, you simple fellow," asked the priest, "is the necessity for a doctor to be a scholar? You just try, that's all."

Thereupon Chang returned home; and, being very poor, he simply collected a few of the commonest prescriptions, and set up a small stall with a handful of fishes' teeth and some dry honeycomb from a wasp's nest, hoping thus to earn, by his tongue, enough to keep body and soul together, to which, however, no one paid any particular attention. Now it chanced that just then the Governor of Ch'ing-chou was suffering from a bad cough, and had given orders to his subordinates to send to him the most skillful doctors in their respective districts; and the magistrate of I, which was an out-of-the-way mountainous district, being unable to lay his hands on any one whom he could send in, gave orders to the beadle to do the best he could under the circumstances. Accordingly, Chang was nominated by the people, and the magistrate put his name down to go in to the Governor. When Chang heard of his appointment, he happened to be suffering himself from a bad attack of bronchitis, which he was quite unable to cure, and he begged, therefore, to be excused; but the magistrate would not hear of this, and forwarded him at once in charge of some constables.

While crossing the hills, he became very thirsty, and went into a village to ask for a drink of water; but water there was worth its weight in jade, and no one would give him any. By-and-by he saw an old woman washing a quantity of vegetables in a scanty supply of water which was, consequently, very thick and muddy; and, being unable to bear his thirst any longer, he obtained this and drank it up. Shortly afterward he found that his cough was quite cured, and then it occurred to him that he had hit upon a capital remedy. When he reached the city, he learned that a great many doctors had already tried their hand upon the patient, but without success; so asking for a private room in which to prepare his medicines, he obtained from the town some bunches of bishop-wort, and proceeded to wash them as the old woman had done. He then took the dirty water, and gave a dose of it to the Governor, who was immediately and permanently relieved. The patient was overjoyed; and, besides making Chang a handsome present, gave him a certificate written in golden characters, in consequence of which his fame spread far and wide; and of the numerous cases he subsequently undertook, in not a single instance did he fail to effect a cure.

One day, however, a patient came to him, complaining of a violent chill; and Chang, who happened to be tipsy at the time, treated him by mistake for remittent fever. When he got sober, he became aware of what he had done; but he said nothing to anybody about it, and three days afterward the same patient waited upon him with all kinds of presents to thank him for a rapid recovery. Such cases as this were by no means rare with him; and soon he got so rich that he would not attend when summoned to visit a sick person, unless the summons was accompanied by a heavy fee and a comfortable chair to ride in.

Snow in Summer

On the 6th day of the 7th moon of the year Ting-Hai (1647) there was a heavy fall of snow at Soochow. The people were in a great state of consternation at this, and went off to the temple of the Great Prince to pray. Then the spirit moved one of them to say, "You now address me as *Your Honor*. Make it *Your Excellency*, and, though I am but a lesser deity, it may be well worth your while to do so." Thereupon the people began to use the latter term, and the snow stopped at once; from which I infer that flattery is just as pleasant to divine as to mortal ears.

Planchette

AT CH'ANG-SHAN THERE LIVED A MAN, NAMED WANG JUI-T'ING, WHO UNDERSTOOD the art of planchette. He called himself a disciple of Lü Tung-pin, and some one said he was probably that worthy's crane. At his *séances* the subjects were always literary—essays, poetry, and so on. The well-known scholar, Li Chih, thought very highly of him, and availed himself of his aid on more than one occasion; so that by degrees the literati generally also patronized him. His responses to questions of doubt or difficulty were remarkable for their reasonableness; matters of mere good or bad fortune he did not care to enter into.

In 1631, just after the examination at Chi-nan, a number of the candidates requested Mr. Wang to tell them how they would stand on the list; and, after having examined their essays, he proceeded to pass his opinion on their merits. Among the rest there happened to be one who was very intimate with another candidate, not present, whose name was Li Pien; and who, being an enthusiastic student and a deep thinker, was confidently expected to appear among the successful few. Accordingly, the friend submitted Mr. Li's essay for inspection; and in a few minutes two characters appeared on the sand—namely, "Number one." After a short interval this sentence followed:—

"The decision given just now had reference to Mr. Li's essay simply as an essay. Mr. Li's destiny is darkly obscured, and he will suffer accordingly. It is strange, indeed, that a man's literary powers and his destiny should thus be out of harmony. Surely the Examiner will judge of him by his essay;—but stay: I will go and see how matters stand."

Another pause ensued, and then these words were written down:—

"I have been over to the Examiner's *yamên*, and have found a pretty state of things going on; instead of reading the candidates' papers himself, he has handed them over to his clerks, some half-dozen illiterate fellows who purchased their own degrees, and who, in their previous existence, had no status whatever,—'hungry devils' begging their bread in all directions; and who, after eight hundred years passed in the murky gloom of the infernal regions, have lost all discrimination, like men long buried in a cave and suddenly transferred to the light of day. Among them may be one or two who have risen above their former selves, but the odds are against an essay falling into the hands of one of these."

The young men then begged to know if there was any method by which such an evil might be counteracted; to which the planchette replied that there was, but, as it was universally understood, there was no occasion for asking the question. Thereupon they went off and told Mr. Li, who was so much distressed at the prediction that he submitted his essay to His Excellency Sun Tzŭ-mei, one of the finest scholars of the day. This gentleman examined it, and was so pleased with its literary merit that he told Li he was quite sure to pass, and the latter thought no more about the planchette prophecy. However, when the list came out, there he was down in the fourth class; and this so much disconcerted His Excellency Mr. Sun, that he went carefully through the essay again for fear lest any blemishes might have escaped his attention. Then he cried out, "Well, I have always thought this Examiner to be a scholar; he can never have made such a mistake as this; it must be the fault of some of his drunken assistants, who don't know the mere rudiments of composition." This fulfilment of the prophecy raised Mr. Wang very high in the estimation of the candidates, who forthwith went and burned incense and invoked the spirit of the planchette, which at once replied in the following terms:—

"Let not Mr. Li be disheartened by temporary failure. Let him rather strive to improve himself still further, and next year he may be among the first on the list."

Li carried out these injunctions; and after a time the story reached the ears of the Examiner, who gratified Li by making a public acknowledgment that there had been some miscarriage of justice at the examination; and the following year he was passed high up on the list.

Friendship with Foxes

A CERTAIN MAN HAD AN ENORMOUS STACK OF STRAW, AS BIG AS A HILL, IN WHICH HIS servants, taking what was daily required for use, had made quite a hole. In this hole a fox fixed his abode, and would often show himself to the master of the house under the form of an old man. One day the latter invited the master to walk into the cave, which he at first declined, but accepted on being pressed by the fox; and when he got inside, lo! he saw a long suite of handsome apartments. They then sat down, and exquisitely perfumed tea and wine were brought; but the place was so gloomy that there was no difference between night and day.

By-and-by, the entertainment being over, the guest took his leave; and on looking back the beautiful rooms and their contents had all disappeared. The old man himself was in the habit of going away in the evening and returning with the first streaks of morning; and as no one was able to follow him, the master of the house asked him one day whither he went. To this he replied that a friend invited him to take wine; and then the master begged to be allowed to accompany him, a proposal to which the old man very reluctantly consented. However, he seized the master by the arm, and away they went as though riding on the wings of the wind; and, in about the time it takes to cook a pot of millet, they reached a city, and walked into a restaurant, where there were a number of people drinking together and making a great noise.

The old man led his companion to a gallery above, from which they could look down on the feasters below; and he himself went down and brought away from the tables all kinds of nice food and wine, without appearing to be seen or noticed by any of the company. After awhile a man dressed in red garments came forward and laid upon the table some dishes of cumquats; and the master at once requested the old man to go down and get him some of these. "Ah," replied the latter, "that is an upright man: I cannot approach him." Thereupon the master said to himself, "By thus seeking the companionship of a fox, I then am deflected from the true course. Henceforth I, too, will be an upright man."

No sooner had he formed this resolution, than he suddenly lost all control over his body, and fell from the gallery down among the revelers below. These gentlemen were much astonished by his unexpected descent; and he himself, looking up, saw there was no gallery to the house, but only a large beam upon which he had been sitting. He now detailed the whole of the circumstances, and those present made up a purse for him to pay his travelling expenses; for he was at Yü-t'ai—one thousand *li* from home.

The Great Rat

During the reign of the Emperor Wan Li, the palace was troubled by the presence of a huge rat, quite as big as a cat, which ate up all the cats that were set to catch it. Just then it chanced that among the tribute offerings sent by some foreign State was a lion-cat, as white as snow. This cat was accordingly put into the room where the rat usually appeared; and, the door being closely shut, a secret watch was kept. By-and-by the rat came out of its hole and rushed at the cat, which turned and fled, finally jumping up on the table. The rat followed, upon which the cat jumped down; and thus they went on up and down for some time. Those who were watching said the cat was afraid and of no use; however, in a little while the rat began to jump less briskly, and soon after squatted down out of breath. Then the cat rushed at it, and, seizing the rat by the back of the neck, shook and shook while its victim squeaked and squeaked, until life was extinct. Thus they knew the cat was not afraid, but merely waited for its adversary to be fatigued, fleeing when pursued and itself pursuing the fleeing rat. Truly, many a bad swordsman may be compared with that rat!

Wolves

I

A certain village butcher, who had bought some meat at market and was returning home in the evening, suddenly came across a wolf, which followed him closely, its mouth watering at the sight of what he was carrying. The butcher drew his knife and drove the animal off; and then reflecting that his meat was the attraction, he determined to hang it up in a tree and fetch it the next morning. This he accordingly did, and the wolf followed him no further; but when he went at daylight to recover his property, he saw something hanging up in the tree resembling a human corpse. It turned out to be the wolf, which, in its efforts to get at the meat, had been caught on the meat-hook like a fish; and as the skin of a wolf was just then worth ten ounces of silver, the butcher found himself possessed of quite a little capital. Here we have a laughable instance of the result of "climbing trees to catch fish."

II

A butcher, while traveling along at night, was sore pressed by a wolf, and took refuge in an old mat shed which had been put up for the watchman of the crops. There he lay, while the wolf sniffed at him from outside, and at length thrust in one of its paws from underneath. This the butcher seized hold of at once, and held it firmly, so that the wolf couldn't stir; and then, having no other weapon at hand, he took a small knife he had with him and slit the skin underneath the wolf's paw. He now proceeded to blow into it, as butchers blow into pork; and after vigorously blowing for some time, he found that the wolf had ceased to struggle; upon which he went outside and saw the animal lying on the ground, swelled up to the size of a cow, and unable to bend its legs or close its open mouth. Thereupon he threw it across his shoulders and carried it off home. However, such a feat as this could only be accomplished by a butcher.

Singular Verdict

A servant in the employ of a Mr. Sun was sleeping alone one night, when all on a sudden he was arrested and carried before the tribunal of the Ruler of Purgatory. "This is not the right man," cried his Majesty, and immediately sent him back. However, after this the servant was afraid to sleep on that bed again, and took up his quarters elsewhere. But another servant, named Kuo Ngan, seeing the vacant place, went and occupied it. A third servant, named Li Lu, who had an old standing grudge against the first, stole up to the bed that same night with a knife in his hand, and killed Kuo Ngan in mistake for his enemy. Kuo's father at once brought the case before the magistrate of the place, pleading that the murdered man was his only son on whom he depended for his living; and the magistrate decided that Kuo was to take Li Lu in the place of his dead son, much to the discomfiture of the old man. Truly the descent of the first servant into Purgatory was not so marvelous as the magistrate's decision!

The Grateful Dog

A CERTAIN TRADER WHO HAD BEEN DOING BUSINESS AT WU-HU AND WAS RETURNING home with the large profits he had made, saw on the river bank a butcher tying up a dog. He bought the animal for much more than its value, and carried it along with him in his boat. Now the boatman had formerly been a bandit; and, tempted by his passenger's wealth, ran the boat among the rushes, and, drawing a knife, prepared to slay him. The trader begged the man to leave him a whole skin; so the boatman wrapped him up in a carpet and threw him into the river. The dog, on seeing what was done, whined piteously, and jumping into the river, seized the bundle with his teeth and did its best to keep the trader above water until at length a shallow spot was reached. The animal then succeeded by continuous barking in attracting the attention of some people on the bank, and they hauled the bundle out of the river, and released the trader who was still alive. The latter asked to be taken back to Wu-hu where he might look out for the robber boatman; but just as he was about to start, lo! the dog was missing. The trader was much distressed at this; and after spending some days at Wu-hu without being able to find, among the forest of masts collected there, the particular boat he wanted, he was on the point of returning home with a friend, when suddenly the dog re-appeared and seemed by its barking to invite its master to follow in a certain direction. This the trader did, until at length the dog jumped on a boat and seized one of the boatmen by the leg. No beating could make the animal let go; and on looking closely at the man, the trader saw he was the identical boatman who had robbed and tried to murder him. He had changed his clothes and also his boat, so that at first he was not recognizable; he was now, however, arrested, and the whole of the money was found in his boat. To think that a dog could show gratitude like that! Truly there are not a few persons who would be put to shame by that faithful animal.

The Great Test

BEFORE MR. YANG TA-HUNG WAS KNOWN TO FAME, HE HAD ALREADY ACQUIRED SOME reputation as a scholar in his own part of the country, and felt convinced himself that his was to be no mean destiny. When the list of successful candidates at the examination was brought to where he lived, he was in the middle of dinner, and rushed out with his mouth full to ask if his name was there or not; and on hearing that it was not, he experienced such a revulsion of feeling that what he then swallowed stuck fast like a lump in his chest and made him very ill. His friends tried to appease him by advising him to try at the further examination of the rejected, and when he urged that he had no money, they subscribed ten ounces of silver and started him on his way.

That night he dreamt that a man appeared to him and said, "Ahead of you there is one who can cure your complaint: beseech him to aid you." The man then added—

"A tune on the flute 'neath the riverside willow:
Oh, show no regret when 'tis cast to the billow!"

Next day, Mr. Yang actually met a Taoist priest sitting beneath a willow tree; and, making him a bow, asked him to prescribe for his malady. "You have come to the wrong person," replied the priest, smiling; "I cannot cure diseases; but had you asked me for a tune on the flute, I could have possibly helped you." Then Mr. Yang knew that his dream was being fulfilled; and going down on his knees offered the priest all the money he had. The priest took it, but immediately threw it into the river, at which Mr. Yang, thinking how hardly he had come by this money, was moved to express his regret. "Aha!" cried the priest at this; "so you are not indifferent, eh? You'll find your money all safe on the bank." There indeed Mr. Yang found it, at which he was so much astonished that he addressed the priest as though he had been an angel. "I am no angel," said the priest, "but here comes one"; whereupon Mr. Yang looked behind him, and the priest seized the opportunity to give him a slap on the back, crying out at the same time, "You worldly-minded fellow!" This blow brought up the lump of food that had stuck in his chest, and he felt better at once; but when he looked round the priest had disappeared.

The Alchemist

At Ch'ang-ngan there lived a scholar named Chia Tzŭ-lung, who one day noticed a very refined-looking stranger; and, on making inquiries about him, learnt that he was a Mr. Chên, who had taken lodgings hard by. Accordingly, next day Chia called and sent in his card, but did not see Chên, who happened to be out at the time. The same thing occurred thrice; and at length Chia engaged some one to watch and let him know when Mr. Chên was at home. However, even then the latter would not come forth to receive his guest, and Chia had to go in and rout him out. The two now entered into conversation, and soon became mutually charmed with each other; and by-and-by Chia sent off a servant to bring wine from a neighboring wine-shop.

Mr. Chên proved himself a pleasant boon companion, and when the wine was nearly finished, he went to a box, and took from it some wine-cups and a large and beautiful jade tankard, into the latter of which he poured a single cup of wine, and lo! it was filled to the brim. They then proceeded to help themselves from the tankard; but however much they took out, the contents never seemed to diminish. Chia was astonished at this, and begged Mr. Chên to tell him how it was done. "Ah," replied Mr. Chên, "I tried to avoid making your acquaintance solely because of your one bad quality—avarice. The art I practice is a secret known to the Immortals only: how can I divulge it to you?"

"You do me wrong," rejoined Chia, "in thus attributing avarice to me. The avaricious, indeed, are always poor."

Mr. Chên laughed, and they separated for that day; but from that time they were constantly together, and all ceremony was laid aside between them. Whenever Chia wanted money, Mr. Chên would bring out a black stone, and, muttering a charm, would rub it on a tile or a brick, which was forthwith changed into a lump of silver. This silver he would give to Chia, and it was always just as much as he actually required, neither more nor less; and if ever the latter asked for more, Mr. Chên would rally him on the subject of avarice. Finally, Chia determined to try and get possession of this stone; and one day, when Mr. Chên was sleeping off the fumes of a drinking-bout, he tried to extract it from his clothes. However, Chên detected him at once, and declared that they could be friends no more, and next day he left the place altogether.

About a year afterward Chia was one day wandering by the river-bank, when he saw a handsome-looking stone, marvelously like that in the possession of Mr. Chên; and he picked it up at once and carried it home with him. A few days passed away, and suddenly Mr. Chên presented himself at Chia's house, and explained that the stone in question possessed the property of changing anything into gold, and had been bestowed upon him long before by a certain Taoist priest, whom he had followed as a disciple. "Alas!" added he, "I got tipsy and lost it; but divination told me where it was, and if you will now restore it to me, I shall take care to repay your kindness."

"You have divined rightly," replied Chia; "the stone is with me; but recollect, if you please, that the indigent Kuan Chung shared the wealth of his friend Pao Shu."

At this hint Mr. Chên said he would give Chia one hundred ounces of silver; to which the latter replied that one hundred ounces was a fair offer, but that he would far sooner have Mr. Chên teach him the formula to utter when rubbing the stone on anything, so as just to try the thing once himself. Mr. Chên was afraid to do this; whereupon Chia cried out, "You are an Immortal yourself; you must know well enough that I would never deceive a friend."

So Mr. Chên was prevailed upon to teach him the formula, and then Chia would have tried the art upon the immense stone washing-block which was lying near at hand, had not Mr. Chên seized his arm and begged him not to do any thing so outrageous. Chia then picked up half a brick and laid it on the washing-block, saying to Mr. Chên, "This little piece is not too much, surely?" Accordingly, Mr. Chên relaxed his hold and let Chia proceed; which he did by promptly ignoring the half brick and quickly rubbing the stone on the washing-block. Mr. Chên turned pale when he saw him do this, and made a dash forward to get hold of the stone; but it was too late, the washing-block was already a solid mass of silver, and Chia quietly handed him back the stone.

"Alas! alas!" cried Mr. Chên, in despair, "what is to be done now? For having thus irregularly conferred wealth upon a mortal, Heaven will surely punish me. Oh, if you would save me, give away one hundred coffins and one hundred suits of wadded clothes."

"My friend," replied Chia, "my object in getting money was not to hoard it up like a miser."

Mr. Chên was delighted at this; and during the next three years Chia engaged in trade, taking care to be all the time fulfilling his promise to Mr. Chên. At the expiration of that time Mr. Chên himself reappeared, and, grasping Chia's hand, said to him, "Trustworthy and noble friend, when we last parted the Spirit of Happiness impeached me before God, and my name was erased from the list of angels. But now that you have carried out my request, that sentence has accordingly been rescinded. Go on as you have begun, without ceasing."

Chia asked Mr. Chên what office he filled in heaven; to which the latter replied that he was only a fox, who, by a sinless life, had finally attained to that clear perception of the Truth which leads to immortality. Wine was then brought, and the two friends enjoyed themselves together as of old; and even when Chia had passed the age of ninety years, that fox still used to visit him from time to time.

Raising the Dead

Mr. T'ang P'ing, who took the highest degree in the year 1661, was suffering from a protracted illness, when suddenly he felt, as it were, a warm glow rising from his extremities upward. By the time it had reached his knees, his feet were perfectly numb and without sensation; and before long his knees and the lower part of his body were similarly affected. Gradually this glow worked its way up until it attacked the heart, and then some painful moments ensued. Every single incident of Mr. T'ang's life from his boyhood upward, no matter how trivial, seemed to surge through his mind, borne along on the tide of his heart's blood. At the revival of any virtuous act of his, he experienced a delicious feeling of peace and calm; but when any wicked deed passed before his mind, a painful disturbance took place within him, like oil boiling and fretting in a cauldron. He was quite unable to describe the pangs he suffered; however, he mentioned that he could recollect having stolen, when only seven or eight years old, some young birds from their nest, and having killed them; and for this alone, he said, boiling blood rushed through his heart during the space of an ordinary mealtime. Then when all the acts of his life had passed one after another in panorama before him, the warm glow proceeded up his throat, and, entering the brain, issued out at the top of his head like smoke from a chimney.

By-and-by Mr. T'ang's soul escaped from his body by the same aperture, and wandered far away, forgetting all about the tenement it had left behind. Just at that moment a huge giant came along, and, seizing the soul, thrust it into his sleeve, where it remained cramped and confined, huddled up with a crowd of others, until existence was almost unbearable. Suddenly Mr. T'ang reflected that Buddha alone could save him from this horrible state, and forthwith he began to call upon his holy name. At the third or fourth invocation he fell out of the giant's sleeve, whereupon the latter picked him up and put him back; but this happened several times, and at length the giant, wearied of picking him up, let him lie where he was. The soul lay there for some time, not knowing in which direction to proceed; however, it soon recollected that the land of Buddha was in the west, and westward accordingly it began to shape its course. In a little while the soul came upon a Buddhist priest sitting by the roadside, and, hastening forward, respectfully inquired of him which was the right way. "The record of life and death for scholars," replied the priest, "is in the hands of Wên-ch'ang and Confucius; any application must receive the consent of both."

The priest then directed Mr. T'ang on his way, and the latter journeyed along until he reached a Confucian temple, in which the Sage was sitting with his face to the south. On hearing his business, Confucius referred him on to Wên-ch'ang; and, proceeding onward in the direction indicated, Mr. T'ang by-and-by arrived at what seemed to be the palace of a king, within which sat Wên-ch'ang, precisely as we depict him on earth.

"You are an upright man," replied the God, in reply to Mr. T'ang's prayer, "and are certainly entitled to a longer span of life; but by this time your mortal body has become decomposed, and unless you can secure the assistance of P'u-sa, I can give you no aid."

So Mr. T'ang set off once more, and hurried along until he came to a magnificent shrine standing in a thick grove of tall bamboos; and, entering in, he stood in the presence of the God, on whose head was the *ushnisha*, whose golden face was round like the full moon, and at whose side was a green willow-branch bending gracefully over the lip of a vase. Humbly Mr. T'ang prostrated himself on the ground, and repeated what Wên-ch'ang had said to him; but P'u-sa seemed to think it would be impossible to grant his request, until one of the Lohans who stood by cried out, "O God, Thou canst perform this miracle: take earth and make his flesh; take a sprig of willow and make his bones." Thereupon P'u-sa broke off a piece from the willow-branch in the vase beside him; and, pouring a little of the water upon the ground, he made clay, and, casting the whole over Mr. T'ang's soul, bade an attendant lead the body back to the place where his coffin was. At that instant Mr. T'ang's family heard a groan proceeding from within his coffin, and, on rushing to it and helping out the lately-deceased man, they found he had quite recovered. He had then been dead seven days.

Fêng-Shui

At I-chow there lived a high official named Sung, whose family were all ardent supporters of Fêng-Shui; so much so, that even the women-folk read books on the subject, and understood the principles of the science. When Mr. Sung died, his two sons set up separate establishments, and each invited to his own house geomancers from far and near, who had any reputation in their art, to select a spot for the dead man's grave. By degrees, they had collected together as many as a hundred a-piece, and every day they would scour the country round, each at the head of his own particular regiment.

After about a month of this work, both sides had fixed upon a suitable position for the grave; and the geomancers engaged by one brother, declared that if their spot was selected he would certainly some day be made a marquis, while the other brother was similarly informed, by his geomancers, that by adopting their choice he would infallibly rise to the rank of Secretary of State. Thus, neither brother would give way to the other, but each set about making the grave in his own particular place,—pitching marquees, and arranging banners, and making all necessary preparations for the funeral. Then when the coffin arrived at the point where roads branched off to the two graves, the two brothers, each leading on his own little army of geomancers, bore down upon it with a view to gaining possession of the corpse. From morn till dewy eve the battle raged; and as neither gained any advantage over the other, the mourners and friends, who had come to witness the ceremony of burial, stole away one by one; and the coolies, who were carrying the coffin, after changing the poles from one shoulder to another until they were quite worn out, put the body down by the roadside, and went off home. It then became necessary to make some protection for the coffin against the wind and rain; whereupon the elder brother immediately set about building a hut close by, in which he purposed leaving some of his attendants to keep guard; but he had no sooner begun than the younger brother followed his example; and when the elder built a second and third, the younger also built a second and third; and as this went on for the space of three whole years, by the end of that time the place had become quite a little village.

By-and-by, both brothers died, one directly after the other; and then their two wives determined to cast to the winds the decision of each party of geomancers. Accordingly, they went together to the two spots in question; and after inspecting them carefully, declared that neither was suitable. The next step was to jointly engage another set of geomancers, who submitted for their approval several different spots, and ten days had hardly passed away before the two women had agreed upon the position for their father-in-law's grave, which, as the wife of the younger brother prophesied, would surely give to the family a high military degree. So the body was buried, and within three years Mr. Sung's eldest grandson, who had entered as a military cadet, actually took the corresponding degree to a literary master of arts.

The Lingering Death

There was a man in our village who led an exceedingly disreputable life. One morning when he got up rather early, two men appeared, and led him away to the market-place, where he saw a butcher hanging up half a pig. As they approached, the two men shoved him with all their might against the dead animal, and lo! his own flesh began to blend with the pork before him, while his conductors hurried off in an opposite direction. By-and-by the butcher wanted to sell a piece of his meat; and seizing a knife, began to cut off the quantity required. At every touch of the blade our disreputable friend experienced a severe pang, which penetrated into his very marrow; and when, at length, an old man came and haggled over the weight given him, crying out for a little bit more fat, or an extra portion of lean, then, as the butcher sliced away the pork ounce by ounce, the pain was unendurable in the extreme. By about nine o'clock the pork was all sold, and our hero went home, whereupon his family asked him what he meant by staying in bed so late. He then narrated all that had taken place, and on making inquiries, they found that the pork-butcher had only just come home; besides which our friend was able to tell him every pound of meat he had sold, and every slice he had cut off. Fancy a man being put to the lingering death like this before breakfast!

Dreaming Honors

WANG TZŬNGAN WAS A TUNG-CH'ANG MAN, AND A SCHOLAR OF SOME REPUTE, but unfortunate at the public examinations. On one occasion, after having been up for his master's degree, his anxiety was very great; and when the time for the publication of the list drew near, he drank himself gloriously tipsy, and went and lay down on the bed. In a few moments a man rushed in, and cried out, "Sir! you have passed!" whereupon Wang jumped up, and said, "Give him ten strings of cash."

Wang's wife, seeing he was drunk, and wishing to keep him quiet, replied, "You go on sleeping: I've given him the money."

So Wang lay down again, but before long in came another man who informed Wang that his name was among the successful candidates for the highest degree.

"Why, I haven't been up for it yet"; said Wang, "how can I have passed?"

"What! you don't mean to say you have forgotten the examination?" answered the man; and then Wang got up once more, and gave orders to present the informant with ten strings of cash.

"All right," replied his wife; "you go on sleeping: I've given him the money."

Another short interval, and in burst a third messenger to say that Wang had been elected a member of the National Academy, and that two official servants had come to escort him thither. Sure enough there were the two servants bowing at the bedside, and accordingly Wang directed that they should be served with wine and meat, which his wife, smiling at his drunken nonsense, declared had been already done. Wang now bethought him that he should go out and receive the congratulations of the neighbors, and roared out several times to his official servants; but without receiving any answer.

"Go to sleep," said his wife, "and wait till I have fetched them"; and after awhile the servants actually came in; whereupon Wang stamped and swore at them for being such idiots as to go away.

"What! you wretched scoundrel," cried the servants, "are you cursing us in earnest, when we are only joking with you!"

At this Wang's rage knew no bounds, and he set upon the men, and gave them a sound beating, knocking the hat of one off on to the ground. In the *mêlée*, he himself tumbled over, and his wife ran in to pick him up, saying, "Shame upon you, for getting so drunk as this!"

"I was only punishing the servants as they deserved," replied Wang; "why do you call me drunk?"

"Do you mean the old woman who cooks our rice and boils the water for your foot-bath," asked his wife, smiling, "that you talk of servants to wait upon your poverty-stricken carcass?"

At this sally all the women burst out in a roar of laughter; and Wang, who was just beginning to get sober, waked up as if from a dream, and knew that there was no reality in all that had taken place. However, he recollected the spot where the servant's hat had fallen off, and on going thither to look for it, lo! he beheld a tiny official hat, no larger than a wine-cup, lying there behind the door. They were all much astonished at this, and Wang himself cried out, "Formerly people were thus tricked by devils; and now foxes are playing the fool with me!"

The She-Wolf and the Herd-Boys

TWO HERD-BOYS WENT UP AMONG THE HILLS AND FOUND A WOLF'S LAIR WITH TWO little wolves in it. Seizing each of them one, they forthwith climbed two trees which stood there, at a distance of forty or fifty paces apart. Before long the old wolf came back, and, finding her cubs gone, was in a great state of distress. Just then, one of the herd-boys pinched his cub and made it squeak; whereupon the mother ran angrily toward the tree whence the sound proceeded, and tried to climb up it. At this juncture, the boy in the other tree pinched the other cub, and thereby diverted the wolf's attention in that direction. But no sooner had she reached the foot of the second tree, than the boy who had first pinched his cub did so again, and away ran the old wolf back to the tree in which her other young one was. Thus they went on time after time, until the mother was dead tired, and lay down exhausted on the ground. Then, when after some time she showed no signs of moving, the herd-boys crept stealthily down, and found that the wolf was already stiff and cold. And truly, it is better to meet a blustering foe with his hand upon his sword-hilt, by retiring within doors, and leaving him to fret his violence away unopposed; for such is but the behavior of brute beasts, of which men thus take advantage.

Adulteration Punished

AT CHIN-LING THERE LIVED A SELLER OF SPIRITS, WHO WAS IN THE HABIT OF adulterating his liquor with water and a certain drug, the effect of which was that even a few cups would make the strongest-headed man as drunk as a jelly-fish. Thus his shop acquired a reputation for having a good article on sale, and by degrees he became a rich man.

One morning, on getting up, he found a fox lying drunk alongside of the spirit vat; and tying its legs together, he was about to fetch a knife, when suddenly the fox waked up, and began pleading for its life, promising in return to do anything the spirit-merchant might require. The latter then released the animal, which instantly changed into the form of a human being. Now, at that very time, the wife of a neighbor was suffering under fox influence, and this recently-transformed animal confessed to the spirit-merchant that it was he who had been troubling her. Thereupon the spirit-merchant, who knew the lady in question to be a celebrated beauty, begged his fox friend to secretly introduce him to her. After raising some objections, the fox at length consented, and conducted the spirit-merchant to a cave, where he gave him a suit of serge clothes, which he said had belonged to his late brother, and in which he told him he could easily go. The merchant put them on, and returned home, when to his great delight he observed that no one could see him, but that if he changed into his ordinary clothes everybody could see him as before. Accordingly he set off with the fox for his neighbor's house; and, when they arrived, the first thing they beheld was a charm on the wall, like a great wriggling dragon. At this the fox was greatly alarmed, and said, "That scoundrel of a priest! I can't go any farther." He then ran off home, leaving the spirit-merchant to proceed by himself. The latter walked quietly in to find that the dragon on the wall was a real one, and preparing to fly at him, so he too turned, and ran away as fast as his legs could carry him. The fact was that the family had engaged a priest to drive away the fox influence; and he, not being able to go at the moment himself, gave them this charm to stick up on the wall.

The following day the priest himself came, and, arranging an altar, proceeded to exorcise the fox. All the villagers crowded round to see, and among others was the spirit-merchant, who, in the middle of the ceremony, suddenly changed color, and hurried out of the front door, where he fell on the ground in the shape of a fox, having his clothes still hanging about his arms and legs. The bystanders would have killed him on the spot, but his wife begged them to spare him; and the priest let her take the fox home, where in a few days it died.

A Chinese Solomon

In our district there lived two men, named Hu Ch'êng and Fêng Ngan, between whom there existed an old feud. The former, however, was the stronger of the two; and accordingly Fêng disguised his feelings under a specious appearance of friendship, though Hu never placed much faith in his professions. One day they were drinking together, and being both of them rather the worse for liquor, they began to brag of the various exploits they had achieved. "What care I for poverty," cried Hu, "when I can lay a hundred ounces of silver on the table at a moment's notice?"

Now Fêng was well aware of the state of Hu's affairs, and did not hesitate to scout such pretensions, until Hu further informed him in perfect seriousness that the day before he had met a merchant traveling with a large sum of money and had tumbled him down a dry well by the wayside; in confirmation of which he produced several hundred ounces of silver, which really belonged to a brother-in-law on whose behalf he was managing some negotiation for the purchase of land. When they separated, Fêng went off and gave information to the magistrate of the place, who summoned Hu to answer to the charge. Hu then told the actual facts of the case, and his brother-in-law and the owner of the land in question corroborated his statement. However, on examining the dry well by letting a man down with a rope round him, lo! there was a headless corpse lying at the bottom. Hu was horrified at this, and called Heaven to witness that he was innocent; whereupon the magistrate ordered him twenty or thirty blows on the mouth for lying in the presence of such irrefragable proof, and cast him into the condemned cell, where he lay loaded with chains. Orders were issued that the corpse was not to be removed, and a notification was made to the people, calling upon the relatives of the deceased to come forward and claim the body.

Next day a woman appeared, and said deceased was her husband; that his name was Ho, and that he was proceeding on business with a large sum of money about him when he was killed by Hu. The magistrate observed that possibly the body in the well might not be that of her husband, to which the woman replied that she felt sure it was; and accordingly the corpse was brought up and examined, when the woman's story was found to be correct. She herself did not go near the body, but stood at a little distance making the most doleful lamentations; until at length the magistrate said, "We have got the murderer, but the body is not complete; you go home and wait until the head has been discovered, when life shall be given for life."

He then summoned Hu before him, and told him to produce the head by the next day under penalty of severe torture; but Hu only wandered about with the guard sent in charge of him, crying and lamenting his fate, but finding nothing. The instruments of torture were then produced, and preparations were made as if for torturing Hu; however, they were not applied, and finally the magistrate sent him back to prison, saying, "I suppose that in your hurry you didn't notice where you dropped the head." The woman was then brought before him again; and on learning that her relatives consisted only of one uncle, the magistrate remarked, "A young woman like you, left alone in the world, will hardly be able to earn a livelihood. [Here she burst into tears and implored the magistrate's pity.] The punishment of the guilty man has been already decided upon, but until we get the head, the case cannot be closed. As soon as it is closed, the best thing you can do is to marry again. A young woman like yourself should not be in and out of a police-court."

The woman thanked the magistrate and retired; and the latter issued a notice to the people, calling upon them to make a search for the head. On the following day, a man named Wang, a fellow villager of the deceased, reported that he had found the missing head; and his report proving to be true, he was rewarded with 1,000 *cash*. The magistrate now summoned the woman's uncle above-mentioned, and told him that the case was complete, but that as it involved such an important matter as the life of a human being, there would necessarily be some delay in closing it for good and all. "Meanwhile," added the magistrate, "your niece is a young woman and has no children; persuade her to marry again and so keep herself out of these troubles, and never mind what people may say."

The uncle at first refused to do this; upon which the magistrate was obliged to threaten him until he was ultimately forced to consent. At this, the woman appeared before the magistrate to thank him for what he had done; whereupon the latter gave out that any person who was willing to take the woman to wife was to present himself at his yamên. Immediately afterward an application was made—by the very man who had found the head. The magistrate then sent for the woman and asked her if she could say who was the real murderer; to which she replied that Hu Chêng had done the deed. "No!" cried the magistrate; "it was not he. It was you and this man here. [Here both began loudly to protest their innocence.] I have long known this; but, fearing to leave the smallest loophole for escape, I have tarried thus long in elucidating the circumstances. How [to the woman], before the corpse was removed from the well, were you so certain that it was your husband's body? *Because you already knew he was dead.* And does a trader who has several hundred ounces of silver about him dress as shabbily as your husband was dressed? And you, [to the man], how did you manage to find the head so readily? *Because you were in a hurry to marry the woman.*" The two culprits stood there as pale as death, unable to utter a word in their defense; and on the application of torture both confessed the crime. For this man, the woman's paramour, had killed her husband, curiously enough, about the time of Hu Chêng's braggart joke. Hu was accordingly released, but Fêng suffered the penalty of a false accuser; he was severely bambooed, and banished for three years. The case was thus brought to a close without the wrongful punishment of a single person.

The Roc

TWO HERONS BUILT THEIR NESTS UNDER ONE OF THE ORNAMENTS ON THE ROOF OF A temple at Tientsin. The accumulated dust of years in the shrine below concealed a huge serpent, having the diameter of a washing-basin; and whenever the heron's young were ready to fly, the reptile proceeded to the nest and swallowed every one of them, to the great distress of the bereaved parents. This took place three years consecutively, and people thought the birds would build there no more. However, the following year they came again; and when the time was drawing nigh for their young ones to take wing, away they flew, and remained absent for nearly three days. On their return, they went straight to the nest, and began amidst much noisy chattering to feed their young ones as usual. Just then the serpent crawled up to reach his prey; and as he was nearing the nest the parent-birds flew out and screamed loudly in mid-air. Immediately, there was heard a mighty flapping of wings, and darkness came over the face of the earth, which the astonished spectators now perceived to be caused by a huge bird obscuring the light of the sun. Down it swooped with the speed of wind or falling rain, and, striking the serpent with its talons, tore its head off at a blow, bringing down at the same time several feet of the masonry of the temple. Then it flew away, the herons accompanying it as though escorting a guest. The nest too had come down, and of the two young birds one was killed by the fall; the other was taken by the priests and put in the bell tower, whither the old birds returned to feed it until thoroughly fledged, when it spread its wings and was gone.

The Faithful Gander

A sportsman of Tientsin, having snared a wild goose, was followed to his home by the gander, which flew round and round him in great distress, and only went away at nightfall. Next day, when the sportsman went out, there was the bird again; and at length it alighted quite close to his feet. He was on the point of seizing it when suddenly it stretched out its neck and disgorged a piece of pure gold; whereupon, the sportsman, understanding what the bird meant, cried out, "I see! this is to ransom your mate, eh?" Accordingly, he at once released the goose, and the two birds flew away with many expressions of their mutual joy, leaving to the sportsman nearly three ounces of pure gold. Can, then, mere birds have such feelings as these? Of all sorrows there is no sorrow like separation from those we love; and it seems that the same holds good even of dumb animals.

The Elephants and the Lion

A huntsman of Kuang-si, who was out on the hills with his bow and arrows, lay down to rest awhile, and unwittingly fell fast asleep. As he was slumbering, an elephant came up, and, coiling his trunk around the man, carried him off. The latter gave himself up for dead; but before long the elephant had deposited him at the foot of a tall tree, and had summoned a whole herd of comrades, who crowded about the huntsman as though asking his assistance. The elephant who had brought him went and lay down under the tree, and first looked up into its branches and then looked down at the man, apparently requesting him to get up into the tree. So the latter jumped on the elephant's back and then clambered up to the topmost branch, not knowing what he was expected to do next. By-and-by a lion arrived, and from among the frightened herd chose out a fat elephant, which he seemed as though about to devour. The others remained there trembling, not daring to run away, but looking wistfully up into the tree. Thereupon the huntsman drew an arrow from his quiver and shot the lion dead, at which all the elephants below made him a grateful obeisance. He then descended, when the elephant lay down again and invited him to mount by pulling at his clothes with its trunk. This he did, and was carried to a place where the animal scratched the ground with its foot, and revealed to him a vast number of old tusks. He jumped down and collected them in a bundle, after which the elephant conveyed him to a spot whence he easily found his way home.

The Hidden Treasure

Li Yüeh-shêng was the second son of a rich old man who used to bury his money, and who was known to his fellow-townsmen as "Old Crocks." One day the father fell sick, and summoned his sons to divide the property between them. He gave four-fifths to the elder and only one-fifth to the younger, saying to the latter, "It is not that I love your brother more than I love you: I have other money stored away, and when you are alone I will hand that over to you."

A few days afterward the old man grew worse, and Yüeh-shêng, afraid that his father might die at any moment, seized an opportunity of seeing him alone to ask about the money that he himself was to receive. "Ah," replied the dying man, "the sum of our joys and of our sorrows is determined by fate. You are now happy in the possession of a virtuous wife, and have no right to an increase of wealth." For, as a matter of fact, this second son was married to a lady from the Ch'ê family whose virtue equaled that of any of the heroines of history: hence his father's remark. Yüeh-shêng, however, was not satisfied, and implored to be allowed to have the money; and at length the old man got angry and said, "You are only just turned twenty; you have known none of the trials of life, and were I to give a thousand ounces of gold, it would soon be all spent. Go! and, until you have drunk the cup of bitterness to its dregs, expect no money from me."

Now Yüeh-shêng was a filial son, and when his father spoke thus he did not venture to say any more, and hoped for his speedy recovery that he might have a chance of coaxing him to comply with his request. But the old man got worse and worse, and at length died; whereupon the elder brother took no trouble about the funeral ceremonies, leaving it all to the younger, who, being an open-handed fellow, made no difficulties about the expense. The latter was also fond of seeing a great deal of company at his house, and his wife often had to get three or four meals a-day ready for guests; and, as her husband did very little toward looking after his affairs, and was further sponged upon by all the needy ones of the neighborhood, they were soon reduced to a state of poverty. The elder brother helped them to keep body and soul together, but he died shortly afterward, and this resource was cut off from them.

Then, by dint of borrowing in the spring and repaying in the autumn, they still managed to exist, until at last it came to parting with their land, and they were left actually destitute. At that juncture their eldest son died, followed soon after by his mother; and Yüeh-shêng was left almost by himself in the world. He now married the widow of a sheep-dealer, who had a little capital; and she was very strict with him, and wouldn't let him waste time and money with his friends. One night his father appeared to him and said, "My son, you have drained your cup of bitterness to the dregs. You shall now have the money. I will bring it to you." When Yüeh-shêng woke up, he thought it was merely a poor man's dream; but the next day, while laying the foundations of a wall, he did come upon a quantity of gold. And then he knew what his father had meant by "when you are alone"; for of those about him at that time, more than half were gone.

The Boatmen of Lao-lung

When His Excellency Chu was Viceroy of Kuangtung, there were constant complaints from the traders of mysterious disappearances; sometimes as many as three or four of them disappearing at once and never being seen or heard of again. At length the number of such cases, filed of course against some person or persons unknown, multiplied to such an extent that they were simply put on record, and but little notice was further taken of them by the local officials. Thus, when His Excellency entered upon his duties, he found more than a hundred plaints of the kind, besides innumerable cases in which the missing man's relatives lived at a distance and had not instituted proceedings. The mystery so preyed upon the new Viceroy's mind that he lost all appetite for food; and when, finally, all the inquiries he had set on foot resulted in no clue to an elucidation of these strange disappearances, then His Excellency proceeded to wash and purify himself, and, having notified the Municipal God, he took to fasting and sleeping in his study alone. While he was in ecstasy, lo! an official entered, holding a tablet in his hand, and said that he had come from the Municipal temple with the following instructions to the Viceroy:—

"Snow on the whiskers descending:
Live clouds falling from heaven:
Wood in water buoyed up:
In the wall an opening effected."

The official then retired, and the Viceroy waked up; but it was only after a night of tossing and turning that he hit upon what seemed to him the solution of the enigma. "The first line," argued he, "must signify *old* (*lao* in Chinese); the second refers to the *dragon* (*lung* in Chinese); the third is clearly a *boat*; and the fourth a *door* here taken in its secondary sense—*man*." Now, to the east of the province, not far from the pass by which traders from the north connect their line of trade with the southern seas, there was actually a ferry known as the Old Dragon (*Lao-lung*); and thither the Viceroy immediately despatched a force to arrest those employed in carrying people backward and forward. More than fifty men were caught, and they all confessed at once without the application of torture. In fact, they were bandits under the guise of boatmen; and after beguiling passengers on board, they would either drug them or burn stupefying incense until they were senseless, finally cutting them open and putting a large stone inside to make the body sink. Such was the horrible story, the discovery of which brought throngs to the Viceroy's door to serenade him in terms of gratitude and praise.

The Pious Surgeon

A CERTAIN VETERINARY SURGEON, NAMED HOU, WAS CARRYING FOOD TO HIS FIELD laborers, when suddenly a whirlwind arose in his path. Hou seized a spoon and poured out a libation of gruel, whereupon the wind immediately dropped. On another occasion, he was wandering about the municipal temple when he noticed an image of Liu Ch'üan presenting the melon, in whose eye was a great splotch of dirt. "Dear me, Sir Liu!" cried Hou, "who has been ill-using you like this?" He then scraped away the dirt with his finger-nail, and passed on.

Some years afterward, as he was lying down very ill, two lictors walked in and carried him off to a *yamên*, where they insisted on his bribing them heavily. Hou was at his wits' end what to do; but just at that moment a personage dressed in green robes came forth, who was greatly astonished at seeing him there, and asked what it all meant. Our hero at once explained; whereupon the man in green turned upon the lictors and abused them for not showing proper respect to Mr. Hou. Meanwhile a drum sounded like the roll of thunder, and the man in green told Hou that it was for the morning session, and that he would have to attend. Leading Hou within he put him in his proper place, and, promising to inquire into the charge against him, went forward and whispered a few words to one of the clerks.

"Oh," said the latter, advancing and making a bow to the veterinary surgeon, "yours is a trifling matter. We shall merely have to confront you with a horse, and then you can go home again."

Shortly afterward, Hou's case was called; upon which he went forward and knelt down, as did also a horse which was prosecuting him. The judge now informed Hou that he was accused by the horse of having caused its death by medicines, and asked him if he pleaded guilty or not guilty.

"My lord," replied Hou, "the prosecutor was attacked by the cattle-plague, for which I treated him accordingly; and he actually recovered from the disease, though he died on the following day. Am I to be held responsible for that?"

The horse now proceeded to tell his story; and after the usual cross-examination and cries for justice, the judge gave orders to look up the horse's term of life in the Book of Fate. Therein it appeared that the animal's destiny had doomed it to death on the very day on which it had died; whereupon the judge cried out, "Your term of years had already expired; why bring this false charge? Away with you!" and turning to Hou, the judge added, "You are a worthy man, and may be permitted to live."

The lictors were accordingly instructed to escort him back, and with them went out both the clerk and the man in green clothes, who bade the lictors take every possible care of Hou by the way.

"You gentlemen are very kind," said Hou, "but I haven't the honor of your acquaintance, and should be glad to know to whom I am so much indebted."

"Three years ago," replied the man in green, "I was traveling in your neighborhood, and was suffering very much from thirst, which you relieved for me by a few spoonfuls of gruel. I have not forgotten that act."

"And my name," observed the other, "is Liu Ch'üan. You once took a splotch of dirt out of my eye that was troubling me very much. I am only sorry that the wine and food we have down here is unsuitable to offer you. Farewell."

Hou now understood all that had happened, and went off home with the two lictors where he would have regaled them with some refreshment, but they refused to take even a cup of tea. He then waked up and found that he had been dead for two days. From this time forth he led a more virtuous life than ever, always pouring out libations to Liu Ch'üan at all the festivals of the year. Thus he reached the age of eighty, a hale and hearty man, still able to sit in the saddle; until one day he met Liu Ch'üan riding on horseback, as if about to make a long journey. After a little friendly conversation, the latter said to him, "Your time is up, and the warrant for your arrest is already issued; but I have ordered the constables to delay awhile, and you can now spend three days in preparing for death, at the expiration of which I will come and fetch you. I have purchased a small appointment for you in the realms below, by which you will be more comfortable." So Hou went home and told his wife and children; and after collecting his friends and relatives, and making all necessary preparations, on the evening of the fourth day he cried out, "Liu Ch'üan has come!" and, getting into his coffin, lay down and died.

Another Solomon

At T'ai-yüan there lived a middle-aged woman with her widowed daughter-in-law. The former was on terms of too great intimacy with a notably bad character of the neighborhood; and the latter, who objected very strongly to this, did her best to keep the man from the house. The elder woman accordingly tried to send the other back to her family, but she would not go; and at length things came to such a pass that the mother-in-law actually went to the mandarin of the place and charged her daughter-in-law with the offence she herself was committing. When the mandarin inquired the name of the man concerned, she said she had only seen him in the dark and didn't know who he was, referring him for information to the accused. The latter, on being summoned, gave the man's name, but retorted the charge on her mother-in-law; and when the man was confronted with them, he promptly declared both their stories to be false. The mandarin, however, said there was a *primâ facie* case against him, and ordered him to be severely beaten, whereupon he confessed that it was the daughter-in-law whom he went to visit. This the woman herself flatly denied, even under torture; and on being released, appealed to a higher court, with a very similar result. Thus the case dragged on, until a Mr. Sun, who was well-known for his judicial acumen, was appointed district magistrate at that place. Calling the parties before him, he bade his lictors prepare stones and knives, at which they were much exercised in their minds, the severest tortures allowed by law being merely gyves and fetters. However, everything was got ready, and the next day Mr. Sun proceeded with his investigation. After hearing all that each one of the three had to say, he delivered the following judgment:—

"The case is a simple one; for although I cannot say which of you two women is the guilty one, there is no doubt about the man, who has evidently been the means of bringing discredit on a virtuous family. Take those stones and knives there and put him to death. I will be responsible."

Thereupon the two women began to stone the man, especially the younger one, who seized the biggest stones she could see and threw them at him with all the might of her pent-up anger; while the mother-in-law chose small stones and struck him on non-vital parts. So with the knives: the daughter-in-law would have killed him at the first blow, had not the mandarin stopped her, and said, "Hold! I now know who is the guilty woman." The mother-in-law was then tortured until she confessed, and the case was thus terminated.

The Incorrupt Official

MR. WU, SUB-PREFECT OF CHI-NAN, WAS AN UPRIGHT MAN, AND WOULD HAVE no share in the bribery and corruption which was extensively carried on, and at which the higher authorities connived, and in the proceeds of which they actually shared. The Prefect tried to bully him into adopting a similar plan, and went so far as to abuse him in violent language; upon which Mr. Wu fired up and exclaimed, "Though I am but a subordinate official, you should impeach me for anything you have against me in the regular way; you have not the right to abuse me thus. Die I may, but I will never consent to degrade my office and turn aside the course of justice for the sake of filthy lucre." At this outbreak the Prefect changed his tone, and tried to soothe him. . . . [How dare people accuse the age of being corrupt, when it is themselves who will not walk in the straight path.] One day after this a certain fox-medium came to the Prefect's *yamên* just as a feast was in full swing, and was thus addressed by a guest:—

"You who pretend to know everything, say how many officials there are in this Prefecture."

"*One*," replied the medium; at which the company laughed heartily, until the medium continued, "There are really seventy-two holders of office, but Mr. Sub-prefect Wu is the only one who can justly be called an official."

Chinese Folk Tales

The Infamous Chow Sin and the Beautiful T'a Ki

It is related by the early writers that the infamous King Chow Sin, on one occasion, paid a visit to the temple of a famous female spirit named Lu O. This honored goddess was the daughter of a spirit that lived in a very remote period still further back and was distinguished for the purity of her life and for the extraordinary powers she possessed. It is believed that she was present at the creation of all things, and when Panku made the great division between the firmament and the earth and the former was in danger of collapsing, she used her power to prop it up, so that it has remained in its place until the present day. Her fame rests mainly upon the high character she had acquired for a chaste and virtuous life, that even in those early days exercised such a charm over her worshippers.

In this temple there was a beautiful statue of Lu O. Chow Sin was so charmed and entranced with her beauty that he immediately experienced a passionate longing that she should become one of the royal concubines. Unfortunately for himself he expressed this desire in the presence of some of his great ministers who accompanied him, and the virtuous Lu O was so indignant at the insult that the king had offered her, that she determined to avenge herself by the most condign punishment upon the exalted offender. She accordingly summoned to her presence one of the chiefs among the demons, and gave him instructions to set in motion all his forces and all the great army of gnomes under his control for the utter destruction of the king, as well as his dynasty and all the members of the Imperial family and clan. "Do not spare this royal voluptuary," she said, "and stay not your hand until the wrong he had done me be avenged in the disgrace and ruin of all those that bear his name."

When he returned to his palace, Chow Sin still raved about the marvelous beauty of Lu O, and expressed his sorrow that it was impossible for him to have her enrolled among the members of his harem, but, since it was impossible for him to obtain her, he would wish inquiries to be made throughout his empire to see if there were not among the beauties of China some one more distinguished than the rest who could adequately fill the place of the goddess Lu O. The ministers of the crown advised that a royal edict should be promulgated throughout the country forbidding the betrothal of any more maidens until the emperor had been given the opportunity of selecting from among the most beautiful of them the ones that might be deemed suitable to be included in the number of his concubines.

As such a procedure had never been adopted in the past, there was considerable discussion as to whether such a thing could be carried out without danger to the stability of the throne. The situation for the moment was saved by the intervention of the Prime Minister Iu Hui, who nourished a deep grudge against one of the viceroys, who was of a bold and independent character and who had grievously offended him by refusing to pay court to him when his duties called him to the capital. The last time he had been there this viceroy had treated him with scant courtesy and had absolutely refused to make him the ordinary presents by which the high officials propitiated him, so that he vowed to take vengeance whenever a good opportunity offered.

The time had now come when Iu thought he could wound him in a way that would bring him the greatest possible distress. Approaching the emperor he said, "Your Majesty is desirous of finding a lady in China that would equal the famous goddess Lu O in the beauty of her person. Such a lady exists, and if common fame is to be believed, never in the annals of the past has any woman been possessed of such charms as she is credited with. No royal edict js required to demand the attendance of the beauties of China at your court, for this lovely girl is the daughter of one of your viceroys, and you have but to command her father to bring her to your palace, and you will never more desire to have Lu O as one of the members of your harem."

By giving this advice to the emperor, Iu Hui believed that he was inflicting a deadly wound upon the viceroy in question, for he was firmly of the conviction that if his royal master acted upon his suggestion, the final result would be the disgrace and death of the bold and independent ruler of one of the provinces of the empire. Su Heu, for so he was named, possessed a large amount of sterling and original character. He was deeply beloved by all the people, high and low and rich and poor, within the province over which he ruled, for he meted out justice to all alike, no matter what their position in life might be.

He had one daughter of whom he was inordinately proud, and good reason he had to be so. She was an exceedingly beautiful girl, the loveliest, perhaps, that had ever been born within the broad and extensive limits of the Flowery Kingdom. His very life seemed bound up in T'a Ki. There was nothing in the world so precious to him as this beloved daughter, and all his wealth and power combined seemed as nothing in his eyes when compared with this beautiful creature, who repaid his love with the most tender and devoted affection. Iu Hui knew that in bringing her to the Imperial notice he was going to injure Su Heu in a manner that would leave its deepest sting upon his heart, while at the same time the destruction of himself and his entire family would be certainly accomplished.

No sooner had the glowing description of T'a Ki been given to the dissolute and depraved emperor, than he gave immediate orders to the prime minister to send out a dispatch, post haste, to Su Heu, requiring his attendance at once in the capital, together with that of his beautiful daugther T'a Ki, who, it was declared, was to have the honor of becoming one of his august Majesty's concubines.

In Hui's schemes of vengeance were most admirably devised and produced the exact results that his cunning mind had foreseen, but he little dreamed of the dire and tragic consequences that were to come to himself and his royal master in the near future, and that he was but a pawn in the hand of fate in the game of life that was being played, when the wrongs that had been committed by Chow Sin would be terribly avenged by the wiping out of his dynasty and the destruction of all those who had helped him in the misgovernment of the country.

The receipt of the Imperial rescript, filled Su Heu with the greatest consternation. To most men it would have been the source of satisfaction and delight. To have a daughter of such distinguished beauty in the royal harem, who might possibly one day become queen meant that honors and power and wealth would be lavished upon her family and that it would become one of the powerful ones of the state.

Su Heu, however, was made of nobler materials than to be willing to have his fortunes built on the degradation of his beloved daughter.

Without one moment's hesitation, he replied to the royal demand by absolutely refusing to comply with it. "Your Majesty," he said, "has done me the honor of asking for my daughter to become one of your concubines. I am not worthy of it. Besides, she is very dear to me, and I cannot endure the thought of losing her companionship, which I should assuredly do were she to become a member of your harem. In the whole of your kingdom there are many beautiful girls that would deem it an honor to be selected by your Majesty, and whose parents would only be too glad to be allied to you by the gift of their daughters. Send out a royal proclamation expressing your wish and you will assuredly have a noble collection of the beauties of the empire from which to make your selection. As for my daughter, I positively refuse to allow her to go to the capital."

The king was enraged beyond measure at what he considered the rebellious language of his viceroy and he determined to give him such a lesson in obedience that he would never dare transgress again. He accordingly raised a large army and sent it under skillful generals against Su Heu, with the order to bring him and his daughter T'a Ki with all haste into his presence. The doughty viceroy was not, however, to be so easily conquered as he had imagined. The first symptoms of rebellion against this dissolute and unprincipled monarch had already begun to spread throughout the kingdom, and men's minds were concerned at the carnival of vice and misgovernment that was being carried on in the capital.

Ere the royal forces had reached the territories of Su Heu, the whole of his province had risen in arms for his defense and in the battles that took place the king's troops were defeated with great slaughter and were compelled to retreat. Chow Sin, instead of being discouraged by the repulses that the royal army had suffered, became more determined in his purpose that the beautiful T'a Ki should be surrendered to him. He therefore collected another army, larger and better equipped than the one that he had sent before, with orders that, if necessary, the whole of the revolted province should be laid waste by fire and sword, its inhabitants utterly exterminated, and Su Heu brought in chains to the capital, there to expiate his offenses by the most terrible death that the imagination of man could conceive.

The royal army was led by the finest generals of the country and the bravest troops had been selected from the other provinces in order that success should this time be obtained over the rebellious viceroy, but the men were lacking in enthusiasm and their feeling was rather in favor of the enemy they were about to attack than for the sovereign whose orders they were obeying. Chow Sin was a tyrant who was despised and hated because of his vices and his crimes, while Su Heu was a hero, who was fighting for his home and for the honor and safety of his beloved daughter. Another great battle was fought and once more the soldiers of the king suffered a tremendous defeat.

This process was repeated several times, when Wun Wang, the viceroy of Shansi, who was a friend of Su Heu and who dreaded the effect of his rebellion upon the rest of the empire, wrote him an urgent letter beseeching him to submit to the royal demand and give the king his daughter. "You cannot hope," he said, "with the power of your one province successfully to resist the forces of the whole kingdom. In the end you will have to submit and a vengeance will be wreaked upon you and your whole clan, as well as upon the whole of your people. The other viceroys of the kingdom have stood aloof as long as possible from this contest, but ere long they will be compelled by the orders of the king to marshal their forces against you, and you are wise enough to see that when that takes place you will inevitably be crushed before the overwhelmingly large number of troops that can be brought against you."

These wise and weighty words of Wun Wang made a deep impression upon Su Heu. He accordingly sent in his submission to the king and informed him that upon a certain day he would proceed to the capital in order to obtain his forgiveness, and that his daughter T'a Ki would accompany him, and that he would place her at the disposal of his Majesty to do with her whatever he thought best. Hostilities upon this at once ceased and preparations were made by the sorrowful viceroy for the surrender of his beloved daughter.

On a certain day, in accordance with a prescribed program that he had drawn up for himself, Su Heu with considerable misgivings as to the future, set forth with T'a Ki on his journey to the capital. His heart was rent with agony about her. He had done his very utmost to deliver her from the fate that lay before her, but he had been worsted in the contest and to save her was absolutely beyond his power. Another source of anxiety was the character of Chow Sin. He was a man of absolutely no moral character and he might feel that, when once he had got possession of T'a Ki, he would revenge himself upon her father for his rebellion by putting him to an ignominious death. It may, therefore, be imagined with what sorrowful feelings both father and daughter left their home to go on a journey that caused the hearts of both of them to be filled with so many doleful forebodings. Little did either of them dream that a great and tragic change was to take place before they reached the end of it, that would involve the most serious consequence both to T'a Ki and the very empire itself.

The long and painful traveling had nearly come to an end, and they had reached the last resting-place that lay between them and the capital. On the morrow they would be there, and they then would both be within the grip of the infamous Chow Sin. It may easily be imagined what a sorrowful evening they spent with each other, and the hearts of both must have been almost on the point of breaking as they thought of the separation that would take place next day, when their lives would for ever be divided, the one from the other, and the old familiar ties with which they had been bound to each other in the past would be severed, never again to be reunited.

T'a Ki had retired to her room only a few minutes when the demon who had been commissioned by the insulted goddess to avenge her wrongs upon Chow Sin entered the apartment and put her to death. He then by his necromantic powers entered the body of the dead maiden, which, animated by this new spirit, had all the semblance of the beautiful girl that but a few minutes previously had been alive and full of health. To all outward appearance she was the same lovely and modest girl who had everywhere won golden opinions not simply for the beauty of her person, but also for the refined and tender spirit that had made her life so charming to all who had any acquaintance with her.

On the morrow morning when Su Heu met his daughter, and they had started on the final stage of their journey to the capital, he had not the remotest suspicion that he was not talking to T'a Ki, but to a malign demon who had murdered her, and who was filled with the maddest schemes that ever took possession even of so degraded a being's brain, for the destruction of a royal family.

Su Heu had no idea that any change had taken place in his daughter. The one that had assumed her role acted her part so perfectly that there was nothing in her demeanor that could cause him for a moment to suspect that he was being imposed upon. Her person was the same, and the voice and manner and little ways of T'a Ki were so faithfully reproduced, that it never entered into the heart of anyone to question her identity.

When the party reached the capital and were led into the presence of the king, he was so enamored with the beauty of T'a Ki that he seemed to come at once under her spell. There was full reason for this, for not only was the woman before him the most beautiful one in the kingdom, but she had also the power by the black arts that were at her control to influence Chow Sin's mind in a way that no merely human being could ever hope to succeed in doing. He was so delighted indeed that he accorded a most gracious reception to Su Heu, and gave him complete forgiveness for his disobedience to him and for his daring to resist the forces he had sent against him when he refused to comply with his demands.

A very short time had elapsed before Chow Sin came completely under the control of T'a Ki, whose influence over him was always for evil. This was entirely in accordance with the plan that had been designed for the destruction of himself and his whole family. Instead of restraining him, she invented new methods by which he should shock the kingdom through his disgraceful irregularities both in his government and in his own personal conduct. The court had always been a highly immoral one, but, since the arrival of the new favorite, it had gone beyond anything that had ever disgraced it in the past in its shameful profligacy and utter disregard for the opinion of the nation.

Signs of uneasiness began to be manifested throughout the kingdom, so outraged became the public sentiment at the conduct of Chow Sin and T'a Ki, and a general feeling prevailed that unless there was a change there would be a revolution that would end in the destruction of the dynasty. Some of the more faithful of his councillors remonstrated with the king, but they were promptly put to death in a most cruel and savage way by the express orders of this infamous woman. Some of the leading vassals of the empire who had complained of the dissolute extravagance of the sovereign were put to death by new and ingenious methods that had been specially devised by T'a Ki. One of these was called the "roasting punishment." This consisted of a tube of copper covered with grease, which was placed above a pit that was filled with burning charcoal. The victims were compelled to walk along this slippery bridge, until they fell into the fiery furnace below.

The condition of things at length became so intolerable that viceroys and nobles and dukes and earls, to the number of eight hundred, combined their forces and rebelled. Prince Wu became their commander-in-chief, because of his military ability and also because of the nobility of his character. After a good many skirmishes with the royal forces a great battle was fought when Prince Wu gained a decided victory. Chow Sin was captured and put to death. T'a Ki was also among the prisoners, but tradition has it that her beauty was so great that no one could be found to deal the final blow that was to deprive her of life. Several were appointed to execute her, but there seemed a power of enchantment about her that, no sooner did anyone come near her, than their arms dropped paralyzed, so potent were the powers that her charms exercised. At length an aged councillor of Prince Wu, covering his face with a thick cloth so that he might not see her face stepped forward and with one mighty thrust of his sword laid the enchantress low.

The Love Adventures of the Fox Fairy, Prince Hu

Once upon a time in the early and romantic days of China's history, there lived in the province of Shensi a wealthy scholar who was noted throughout the district in which he lived for his great literary attainments. His abilities had been of such a high order that he had actually been able to take his third degree of "Advanced Scholar," and consequently his name was known far and wide as that of a rising and distinguished man.

Mr. Lin, for so this scholar was named, was one of those men of genius. As he was a man of very considerable means he was in no hurry to accept the many high official posts that were offered him by the Government. His ambition, indeed, led him to desire to shine in the world of letters, and at the time that he appears upon the scene, he was engaged in the preparation of a great work on the classics, that, if it were only successful, would forever link his name with that of Confucius and Mencius, and thus secure immortal honor to himself and his clan.

It became necessary for him in the prosecution of his plans to engage a scholar to assist him in carrying out some of the details, for which he himself had no leisure. Such a man would be very difficult to obtain. Any ordinary hack would not serve his purpose. He must be a born student, who would be able to enter into the spirit of his great enterprise, and he must also have been a great reader so that he would have at his finger ends any reference which might have to be made to any of the authorities that it might be desirable to quote.

One day a servant informed Mr. Lin that a gentleman had called to see him and was now waiting for him in the reception room. His card showed that his name was Hu, and the fact that he had one to send in indicated that he was a man that probably belonged to the scholar class. Mr. Lin, at the first glance at the stranger, was very much prepossessed in his favor. He was a fine, handsome man of about thirty years of age. He had a most intelligent-looking countenance and a refined air about him that unmistakably showed that he was a gentleman.

It did not take Mr. Lin long to discover that he was exceedingly well read, for there was not a book mentioned that he had not mastered its contents so fully that he could describe with great accuracy the subjects that were treated in it. While they were engaged in a most brilliant conversation, he experienced an intense longing to be able to secure his services to assist him in the literary work on which he was engaged.

After a time Mr. Hu himself broached the subject, and said that he had heard that Mr. Lin was in search of a person to assist him on some book that he was preparing for the press, and as he had been on the look-out for some employment, he would be very pleased if he would consent to accept him as an assistant. This proposition was received with the greatest pleasure and after a short conversation in which the terms were discussed and settled, Mr. Hu became an inmate in the house of Mr. Lin.

Further acquaintance with this remarkable stranger only added to Mr. Lin's delight that he had been able to obtain such a thoroughly good man to assist him in the great enterprise that he hoped would place him among the distinguished scholars of China. He was a man of unwearied perseverance. He never seemed to tire, no matter how long the day might be, or how arduous the toil needed to elucidate some knotty point that had arisen in the discussion of some important question in Mr. Lin's great work.

He was a person also of the most profound erudition and scholarship. It soon became apparent, indeed, that he had at his finger ends all the best works that had appeared in any age in the history of the past, and could quote them with accuracy and effect whenever it was necessary to do so. He was, in point of fact, a perfect encyclopedia in himself and endowed with a memory so perfect that he could utilize everything he had read without having continually to refer to the books themselves for the information he wished to use.

The one only unsatisfactory thing about Mr. Lin was the mystery that surrounded him. No information could be got from him as to where he came from, or where his family resided, or in what part of China he was born. On these subjects Hu was as silent as the grave, and not a word was breathed about them to a single member of the new home in which he was living. He seemed, indeed, not to have a single relative in existence, for no letters ever reached him from anywhere, and no reference was ever made of any kindred that belonged to him in any other part of China.

This state of things naturally produced suspicion in the minds of every one associated with him in the large patriarchal-like family of Mr. Lin. As he was a very wealthy man and belonged to a very powerful clan it numbered fully a hundred people that lived together within the same compound and that acknowledged him as their head. Besides the large array of servants that were necessary to do the work of so great an establishment, there were dependents of various grades and kinds who were employed in the more honorable service of waiting on Mr. Lin and of thus adding to his dignity and his prestige among the great families in the region around.

The position of Hu being one of great responsibility and honor, he naturally became the subject of observation to all the numerous members of this great household, and very frequently, in leisure moments, men would discuss among themselves this strange character who had so mysteriously and without any warning come as a resident among them. There was no disputing but that he was a very remarkable man. He was more handsome than any one they had ever seen. He was a genius of so high an order that even their own master who had obtained with high honors the third degree of "The Advanced Man," confessed that he was far inferior to him in the matter of scholarship.

But who was he? That was a question they would like answered. They knew absolutely nothing about his antecedents. Although so profoundly learned he had never gone up for any of the triennial examinations and had never got even "The Embroidered Ability," the first of the degrees that is given to the successful undergraduate in this flowery land of China. This was a most decidedly mysterious thing, for the aim and passion of every scholar's life is to have his name enrolled among the successful aspirants after literary fame and to be classed among the thinkers of the empire.

As time went by and still the household was left to wonder and surmise about this gifted and handsome scholar, certain things began to happen that intensified the suspicions that people had entertained concerning him. It seemed to some of the more acute and observant that he was the possessor of supernatural powers, for they had seen on several occasions how completely he had control over matter. Stone walls that are a serious impediment to ordinary mortals suddenly dissolved into thin air when he came to pass through them, and just as speedily assumed their solid form the moment he had disappeared.

It was his custom to go out every evening just as the shadows were gathering thickly over the earth and were blotting out the narrow pathways along which men had then to travel. The gate-keeper would occasionally warn him that the roads were bad and that it would be wiser for him to remain within doors. He would answer with a merry laugh that his eyes were good and that he had no fear of falling, as he knew the country well, and besides he would add, "I must go out for a turn in the fresh air. I have been poring over those ancient books the livelong day, and I shall be getting as dry and as musty as they if I do not let some of the fresh breezes of heaven blow away the cobwebs that have been weaving themselves in my brain."

Sometimes by accident the door-keeper would be awake in the early hours of the morning when Hu would come stealing through the darkness. He would then give a cheery response to the greeting of the old man, and pass on to his room through the little side door that was always on the latch for late-comers. More often than not, however, he would sleep through the night and, though the great gates were safely barred and locked, he would find when he peeped at the dawn of day into Hu's bedroom that he was lying fast asleep, as though he had not been out the whole night.

On one occasion a great storm was raging, the blinding flashes of lightning were lighting up with lurid gleams the darkness that lay upon the earth, and the rain was being driven in torrents by the storm, when the door-keeper, who had been standing just within the shelter of his doorway, caught sight of Hu, in one of the vivid flashes, as he came silently along toward the main entrance. His instinct had been to rush out and open the door for him, but while he was hesitating he saw, to his amazement, that he had passed through the great gates as easily as though they had been flung wide open before him, and that, in a moment, he had vanished through the great stone wall of the mansion and had disappeared within the building.

It may be as well to explain here that Hu was a fairy, and that he had transformed himself into a man in order that he might gain the daughter of Mr. Lin for his wife. He had on several occasions caught sight of her, and he had been so struck with her beauty that he had fallen deeply in love with her.

The plan of turning himself into a scholar and of living in the same family had suggested itself to his mind as the best way of ingratiating himself with the father and of becoming acquainted with the daughter. The scheme, however, had been but partially successful, for though he was a general favorite, and every one admired his noble presence and looked up to him with profound respect for the marvelous abilities with which he was endowed, there was a feeling that he belonged to another race and that, therefore, there could be no common sympathies between him and ordinary mortals.

Even Mr. Lin, who looked upon him as a perfect treasure, and who valued him for the part he played in the production of his great work, had an uneasy feeling that he must be on his guard against him. The weird stories of his passing through walls, and of his careering over the country on the darkest nights, and of his coming like a flash unhurt through storm and tempest had left their impression on his mind, and he was beginning to wonder whether it was quite safe to have a man with such supernatural powers dwelling with him under the same roof.

One morning Hu was missing, and not a trace was left behind to say whither he had vanished. Some declared that he had disappeared in a flash of lightning. Others were quite as certain that he had transformed himself into a heron, and that he had joined a flock of these graceful birds that had been seen the previous evening flying with swift and speedy flight into the distant sky.

About a week after the mysterious disappearance of Hu, a stranger, riding a magnificent mule, rode up to the mansion of Mr. Lin, and requested to have a private interview with him on a question that was quite private and that could be communicated only to the master of the house. He was a very striking looking man and at once engaged the attention of the servants and dependents, whose duty it was to receive visitors and to see to their courteous reception until they were ushered into the presence of Mr. Lin.

He was tall and dignified and his bearing was that of one who had been accustomed to mingle in the very highest society. He was about fifty years of age, and his face indicated that he was a man of thought and of good breeding. After the compliments of the day had been passed, he informed Mr. Lin that he had come as an envoy from Mr. Hu to enter into negotiations with him with regard to his daughter whom he wished to have as his wife. As this proposal did not at all harmonize with the views that Mr. Lin had for his daughter, he endeavored to parry it by declaring that she was already engaged, and that, while he was deeply sensible of the honor that had been done him by Hu, for whom he had the profoundest respect, he was sorry to say that she had been already promised to another and therefore it was impossible for him to entertain the idea that had been presented to him.

The envoy, in as polite and refined a way as it was possible to be expressed, soon let Mr. Lin know that he knew perfectly well that the daughter never had been betrothed to anyone, and that his statement that she was merely evaded the question, and was anything but an answer to the demand that he had made for an alliance.

At this Mr. Lin, who was a proud and haughty man, began to lose his temper, and finally declared that he did not wish to have Hu as a son-in-law, and he, therefore, begged to decline to discuss the subject any further. The middleman politely asked him to state his objections so that he might report to his master, who, he declared, was desperately in love with his daughter. "You cannot possibly refuse this alliance," he said, "on the ground that he is not equal in rank to you. In point of fact, in this respect he is your superior, for he is of royal blood and comes of a race of kings."

"His rank does not concern me at all," Mr. Lin warmly replied; "Mr. Hu belongs to a different race from myself and therefore I decidedly refuse to allow my daughter to be married to him."

After some further conversation, in which high words were used, the envoy became so irritated that he used some insulting language to Mr. Lin, who promptly called some servants and had him ejected from the house. This was an indignity so great that the envoy fled away in the greatest haste, apparently forgetting all about the magnificent black mule on which he had ridden when he came to the interview that had ended so disastrously.

While they were standing round gazing at this beautiful animal, to the amazement of everyone a most mysterious change began to pass over it. The exquisitely molded limbs that everyone was admiring because of their grace and symmetry slowly stiffened and became rigid. Almost the next instant, its whole frame seemed to collapse till all that was left of it was a good-sized cricket, that with its shrill and strident cry hopped away out of sight under some bushes that were growing near by.

Mr. Lin, who had always felt sure that Hu was a disguised fairy, now became convinced that his suspicions had been correct, and he felt that he must make immediate preparations to meet the attack that Hu would make upon him for the insulting way in which he had treated his envoy. Accordingly, that very same evening he sent round to the members of his clan and urged that every available man that could be spared should hasten without any delay to his assistance, and help him to meet the foe that he knew by instinct was already collecting his forces to avenge himself for the insults that had been offered him.

Well, indeed, was it for Mr. Lin that he so promptly took these precautionary measures, for early next day, while everyone was at his post waiting for the coming of the enemy, a large detachment of the fairy army was seen advancing in their direction. Some were on horseback and others on foot, and they were armed with spears, javelins, and long bows, while some grasped swords that gleamed in the sun as the men brandished them. They rushed on with a shout and a tread that seemed to shake the very ground beneath them.

The first effort of the fairies was to set the house on fire, but all their attempts were frustrated by the bravery of Mr. Lin's men. These fought with the most desperate courage, for they realized that their own lives and those of the women and children who were hiding terror-stricken within the building would all be sacrificed the moment they allowed the enemy to vanquish them. This thought, instead of bringing despair, nerved their arms in the gigantic struggle that was carried on for hours.

After a time the fairy host began to show symptoms of wavering, and upon a given signal the men rushed forth from the building and made a furious onslaught upon the broken ranks of the fairies. Unable to withstand the fury of the assailants the whole body fled from the field and left it in possession of the victors. The serious nature of the struggle was seen by the number of arms that lay scattered in all directions wherever the fairies had made a stand. The men were struck with the appearance of these, for they all had such a slight and unwarlike aspect, and, moreover, they were white and glistening. When they came to examine them a roar of amusement burst from the lips of every one, for it was discovered that the weapons' of the beaten foe consisted of stalks of millet that, in the hands of the fairies and under their enchantment, had been able to do such valiant deeds in the battle that had just taken place.

On the morrow, the fighting was renewed by the fairies, only this time the tactics they employed took a different form from the regular system they had adopted on the previous day. On this occasion they were careful to keep whatever men they had in reserve completely out of view from Lin's forces that he had ar ranged with excellent military judgment in the prospect of another attack, which he fully expected. As the men looked out from their loopholes and from behind the stone walls that had been hurriedly strengthened, they could not see a single horseman nor a solitary foot-soldier amongst the trees that bounded their view. Everything was as silent as though a state of war in which men were fighting for their very lives had no existence in all this region.

All at once, as though a bolt had been hurled from the blue, there descended from the sky with the speed of a thunderbolt a man of immense size. He was fully fifteen feet in height and broad in proportion. He was a beau-ideal warrior in appearance, and quite fitted to terrify any ordinary opponent that might have the hardihood to stand up against him. In his right hand he carried an enormous two-edged sword, that he kept whirling about with the rapidity of lightning, and which flashed and gleamed in the sun as its rays fell upon its ample blade.

The leaders of the fairies had got the impression that this huge giant with a sword that no man could wield but himself would so terrify Lin's men that they would fly in dismay before him, but in this they were entirely mistaken. With a courage that had been immensely stimulated by the victory they had just obtained, they boldly stood their ground, and fiercely attacked him with all the weapons at their command. Showers of stones were hurled at him, spears were flung with unerring precision at his huge body, and arrows were shot by men who had been trained in the use of the bow, all with such deadly effect that ere long the great flaming sword fell from the hands of this fairy Goliath, and he himself dropped lifeless to the ground.

A rush was made by a number of the besieged to the spot where this gigantic body lay, when to their utter amazement they discovered that there was nothing human about it, but that it was composed of grass, and that the sword that lay by its side was simply a huge banana leaf that by the magic power of the fairies had been changed into the mighty weapon it seemed to be.

Miscellaneous fighting went on for some considerable time without any very decided advantage on either side. Lin had increased the number of his fighting men, until his home had rather the look of a garrisoned castle than that of the dwelling place of a wealthy citizen. The fairies, too, had gathered in increasing numbers, but with all their maneuvering they had not been able to make any impression on the sturdy forces that were holding their own manfully against them.

The struggle was at length ended in a very dramatic way, and in a manner very satisfactory to both sides. One day an unusually large detachment of the fairies had assembled and were marching in battle array straight for the forces that Lin had led out to be ready to join in battle against the enemy. On this occasion Hu himself was seen leading his men, and as he drew near Lin, in a loud voice, addressed him and asked him how it was that he was showing such bitter hostility to him.

"I have never given you any cause," he said, "for the hatred you seem to cherish against me and mine. When you were a member of my household, I treated you with the greatest courtesy, and all my dealings with you were of a most friendly character. Why then should you lead your soldiers against me to endeavor to destroy me? What is it that has turned your heart against me?"

Hu seemed deeply affected by this appeal to himself, for with a wave of his hand his soldiers marched back and disappeared behind the trees that lay beyond, while he himself advanced alone up to where Lin was standing in front of his men, and seizing him by the hand begged to be forgiven for his conduct toward him.

Lin, who was of a not less generous nature than Hu, and at heart was really fond of his talented opponent, led him into the house and explained to him that his objection to his marrying his daughter was not to him personally. "I should have been quite prepared," he said, "to have given her to you in marriage, had you been of the same race as myself I always suspected, however, that you were a fairy, and that as you lived upon the mountains and led a wandering and uncertain life my daughter would not have been able to endure the hardships that such a life would have entailed upon her; so I was compelled to refuse. In order to convince you that I have no personal animosity against you and no dislike to an alliance with you, I propose now that if you have a marriageable sister I shall be most pleased to have her betrothed to my son, with whom you are fully acquainted, and whom you know to be a man of such excellent conduct that you could well entrust her happiness to him."

Hu was delighted beyond measure with this proposal, as it showed the real esteem in which he was held by Mr. Lin, and, besides, he was most anxious to be allied with so distinguished a family as Lin's was. He accordingly informed Lin that the union of the two houses that he had just suggested was one that could easily be carried out, for he had a sister in fairyland who would be a beau-ideal wife for his son. In the course of a comparatively brief conversation, all the preliminaries for the proposed marriage were discussed and agreed to, and a day was settled when the fairy bride should be brought from her distant home to become a member of Mr. Lin's family.

The arrival of this beautiful girl was the occasion of unbounded delight both to Mr. Lin and also to her distinguished brother, who afterward turned out to be a prince amongst the fairies and was one who stood high among the magnates in fairyland. Everyone was charmed, not merely with the loveliness of her face, but also with her modest and unassuming disposition, and soon every heart in her new home was bound to her by the strongest ties of love and devotion. The marriage ceremonies were on a grander scale than anyone had ever witnessed or had ever dreamt of. Even a royal princess never had such a magnificent display of beautiful robes, costly jewels, and rare wedding presents as were seen that day when the fairy bride became the wife of Mr. Lin's son. The precious gifts that had been bestowed upon her by her mysterious friends in the land of the spirits were enough of themselves to enrich her and her husband for many a long year to come. That the marriage in these circumstances was an unusually happy one need hardly be told. Long years of prosperity ensued. The young wife was so contented with her lot that she never longed to go back to the life from which she had come, and numerous descendants of hers are still to be found who claim with becoming pride that they can trace their ancestry back to her.

Yu Kong the Athlete

Once upon a time, in a certain city in the north of China that was famous for the number of young bloods and men of fiery mettle that it contained, there lived a young man of the name of Yu Kong. He was noted throughout the town as a wrestler with whom few would dare to compete. He was a man of great strength and he had so persistently trained himself by a severe discipline that he knew how to use it to the greatest advantage in his contests with other well-known athletes.

He had also learned the art of fencing and could wield the broad sword with a science that made him a dangerous rival for anyone to try their skill upon. He was proficient too in his knowledge of the bow and arrow and he rarely ever missed the "moon" as the center of the target is called, in the great shooting matches, when men gathered from far and near to carry away the victor's laurels. So proficient was he in every athletic art that he entered the examination hall to compete for B.A. and came out successfully amongst the very first in the list of those who had satisfied the examiners.

Yu Kong was a bold and generous-minded young fellow. His physical training had developed his muscles and put every organ into such healthy and harmonious working that he was saved from all dyspeptic ailments and could consequently take a broader and more generous view of life in general. He was, moreover, of a naturally happy-minded disposition and more inclined to have faith in his fellowmen than to be perpetually entertaining suspicions of them. The result was that he was a most popular man with everyone who knew him, and even many who were not personally acquainted with him, when they heard his name mentioned, showed by the pleased smile that lit up their countenance that they had heard his praise sung and were inclined to think well of him.

While Yu Kong was so popular with his fellowmen, it unfortunately happened that he had incurred the hatred of one of the evil spirits whose aim and purpose seems to be the infliction of pain and disaster upon mankind. His very generosity and large-heartedness had signaled him out as the very one from among all the crowds in that great city who ought to be doomed to destruction. His death would not merely afflict his friends and those who loved him with sorrow; it would also be the means of depriving his comrades and acquaintances of a true and steadfast friend and of thus diminishing the sum of human happiness.

In order to carry out his malevolent purposes, this gnome assumed a human form, and as an inexorable fate, that controls the actions even of the demons, would not permit him to take that of some high-minded or benevolent individual, he decided to become a fortune-teller.

This he did, and taking a small room in one of the most crowded streets in the city he gave out that he was a great wizard who had come from the wild and dreary steppes of the far north, where the spirits amidst the storms and wild commotions of nature learned the secrets that concerned the lives of men in every grade of society.

Many of these had been imparted to him, he declared, and he was now prepared to divulge them, for a consideration, to those who might consult him. He had power, he said, to look into the future and predict coming disaster; he could read the "Book of Life and Death" that was in the possession of the king of the "Land of Shadows" and tell how long each one had to live before his majesty sent his messengers to call him into his kingdom. This "Book of Life and Death" is a register that is kept by the king of the "Land of Shadows" of every human being, and tells when each was born, and how long each one has to live.

People flocked to consult him, and, being a demon with more than human knowledge, he produced a sensation by the knowledge he seemed to have of the secrets in the lives of those who came to have their minds relieved from the many perplexities that were troubling them. Things that were supposed to be known only to the members of the family were spoken of by this wonderful wizard as though he were perfectly familiar with them. Coming troubles too were averted by his advice, and sinister influences that were about to bring calamities upon homes were averted by a single wave of his hand that seemed to bring terror into the hearts of the malign spirits that peopled the air.

In a short time he would have made his fortune, so popular had he become, but his purpose was not to gain wealth but to inflict sorrow upon the one man that he hated with an undying hatred. What, indeed, was the use of money to him? He could not carry it into the boundless air spaces where he had his home, neither could it buy him the ease of soul that in his wildest flights of power he never could induce to visit him. It was Yu Kong that he wanted within his grasp, and all the riches of the city, though they were poured into his lap, would not have been sufficient to compensate him were Yu to escape his vengeance.

At length the time arrived when it seemed as though Yu Kong were going to fall within his clutches. One day his servant was attacked with a most dangerous fever that resisted all the medicines that the Chinese doctors were wont to prescribe for such, and Yu Kong, who was of a kindly disposition and tender-hearted, felt greatly distressed at the sufferings that the man was enduring. He spared no expense in procuring the services of the most eminent doctors of the town, but their unanimous decision was that this was no common complaint, but was due to the presence of a malign spirit that was evidently determined upon his destruction, and they all advised that he should consult the famous wizard that had taken up his abode in the town.

For some time he was unwilling to do this, as he was a man of liberal views and had not as much faith in necromancers as the common folk usually had. As the sickness of his servant, however, grew in intensity and the medical profession declared that they could do nothing for him, he decided at last that he would go and see this famous fortune-teller, who seemed from all reports to have a marvelous knowledge of what was going on in the unseen world.

The delight of the wizard when he saw Yu Kong enter his doors was unbounded and without waiting for him to tell the reason why he had sought him, he said "Oh! you have come to me about your servant who has been very ill." Yu Kong was taken aback and demanded how he knew that the man had been sick.

"Oh! that is a very simple question," he replied, "it has been no difficult matter for me to discover that. There is one thing far more important than that for you to know and that is within three days you will be a dead man."

"How do you dare to say that to me?" angrily demanded Yu Kong.

"I say it," replied the wizard, "because I have penetrated the secrets of those who have the disposal of men's lives within their hands and I know that before three days have passed you will have ceased to live. Not that you need really die after all," he continued, "for I have the power of frustrating the designs even of the great and terrible king of the 'Land of Shadows,' and if you will consent to agree to my terms, I will guarantee that no harm shall come to you, but that your life shall be prolonged to old age."

Instead of being mollified by this statement of the wizard, Yu Kong became highly incensed. "Why should I agree to make terms with you?" he said. "I am well and strong and in robust and vigorous health. You evidently want to impose upon me to satisfy your own evil purposes. You are a cheat and I defy you to do me any injury."

With these words he set off home and gathering a few choice friends together he rehearsed to them all that had happened to him with the wizard. These strongly advised him not to incur the hatred of such a powerful man, but to come to terms at once with him and thus avert the disaster that they were afraid would fall upon him.

Yu Kong absolutely refused to do this. He was a brave and high-spirited man, and, moreover, he was under the strong conviction that the fortune-teller was a rogue and that for some sinister purpose he wished to get him within his toils. He told his friends, therefore, that he was determined to fight him and that he felt convinced he would come out the conqueror.

Two days went by without any sign from the wizard. Yu Kong, however, though he was every moment on his guard felt that the critical time would be on the third day, and he accordingly made all his preparations for the struggle that he was persuaded would take place. He chose from an armorer's shop the finest and sharpest sword that was in stock. With this in his hand he sat in his room, the windows all thrown wide open, waiting for the supreme moment when the wizard would begin to use his enchantments against him.

The hours went slowly by, and midnight was near at hand, after which the peril that had been predicted would cease to threaten him. All at once as a drowsy fit was coming over him, the room was darkened with a mighty shadow and a figure of monstrous proportions and fierce and horrible aspect came with a clash and a roar into his room.

Any person of less fine metal than Yu Kong would have succumbed with terror before such a terrible apparition. It seemed, however, only to inspire his courage, and with a bound he was instantly on his feet, and with the swiftness of lightning he was slashing in all directions at the hideous figure that grinned down upon him. So rapid and so mighty were the strokes that the unsightly form that seemed to fill the room became paralyzed in its movements and a mightier lunge than usual struck it a fatal blow and it fell to the ground. On examination, Yu Kong found that the thing he had been fighting was a paper figure of an unearthly and ghastly-looking aspect, that was enough to strike terror into the bravest heart.

He had hardly recovered his composure when the room was again invaded by a warrior-like form, spear in hand, that appeared frightful enough to have come from the lowest depths of the infernal regions. With a roar of thunder that was intended to paralyze every faculty of Yu Kong, he rushed upon him believing that an easy victory awaited him.

He little dreamed, however, of the heroic spirit that dweltt in the heart of his opponent. Every thrust of the spear was met by the gleaming sword that flashed more quickly than the deadly weapon that was aimed at his heart. His fencing powers that had been developed by years of severe training now stood him in good stead, and before many minutes had passed not only had he parried every blow, but the chance came when he thrust his steel into the body of the monster, and with a groan that shook the room it fell to the ground.

On examining its body, that descended with a crash to the floor, he found that it was a grinning ogre made of clay, through which his trusty sword had pierced to the heart and laid it low.

Yu Kong felt satisfied with the two signal victories he had obtained, for he recognized that behind these apparently harmless figures there had lain a world of infernal machinations, and that the arch conspirator had but barely escaped the most serious injury by hastily dropping the outward form that he had assumed to conceal his personality. He was convinced, however, that the battle was not yet over, and that a fiercer struggle would have to be fought before he could be delivered from the peril that threatened him.

This conviction was a true one, for before many minutes had elapsed a huge figure, with broadsword in one hand and a gigantic spear in the other, with an appalling shriek, leaped into the room. Yu Kong, instead of being terrified as most mortals would have been, only found his courage rise and the spirit of battle rush mightily through every vein in his body. He felt that the crisis of his life had now come and it was a question of a few minutes whether he would succumb before this terrible monster, or whether he would come out conqueror in one of the greatest contests that had ever been waged with the demons of the upper air.

It was well that Yu Kong had a brave and heroic heart and that years of strenuous practice had given him such a complete control of the broadsword that he wielded. The foe was no petty master of the art, such as he had often met in the examination lists, but was one that knew every trick and turn by which an opponent was to be foiled. The very fact, however, that he had chosen to appear with a weapon in each hand was the cause of his final downfall. Yu Kong, sure of foot and with an eagle eye, anticipated every stroke that was made against him, and in one unguarded moment of his enemy he was able to thrust his sword into the body of the grim monster, which at once fell with a tremendous crash on the floor, and the great and mortal fight was at an end.

The famous fortune-teller suddenly disappeared from the town and not a vestige was ever seen of him afterward. Persons curious to pry into the future sought in vain to find him, and strange did it appear that a man so well versed in the black art should vanish from the public gaze just at the moment when riches were to be poured into his lap. In time the story leaked out and then Yu Kong became the popular hero whose valiant deeds from that time to this have traveled down the centuries.

Li, the Man with the Iron Staff

Of all the fairies that figure in the national life of the Chinese there is none that stands out more prominently or more distinctly in the public eye than Li, the Man with the Iron Staff. The pictures that are given of Li generally represent him as a man of medium height. He is lame in one leg, and as he limps along he is assisted in his painful walk by an iron staff, upon which he leans, and which is supposed to have a special virtue in conveying blessings upon those who have gained the favorable notice of this distinguished fairy.

On his back he has strapped a large hollow gourd that has been dried in the sun, and which seems to be a convenient receptacle for the doles of cold boiled rice and the little odds and ends of food that are given to the beggarmen as they stand whining at the door. It really, however, contains a preparation of the famous elixir of life that men in all ages have been anxious to discover, but which has hitherto eluded the keenest investigations that the most thoughtful and earnest minds have made to find out its secret.

One day Li appeared in the city of Shanghai, bent on trying to discover whether there was anyone in that busy center of trade that was ready for the purifying and transforming process by which he would finally become a dweller in the Western Heaven. In order to prevent anyone having a suspicion of who he was, Li appeared in the streets of Shanghai in the disguise of a beggar. He seemed to be a man who was utterly forlorn and destitute. His hair was uncombed and straggled in wild disorder over his forehead and down the back of his head. His clothes were filthy in the extreme and had been so worn to tatters that it seemed that a strong gust of wind would scatter them as leaves before the breath of the storm. His crippled leg and his ungainly motions, as he strove with the aid of his iron staff to hobble over the rough uneven roads, seemed to add intensity to the general air of wretchedness that hung over the man.

The disguise was so complete that no one ever dreamt of supposing that he was anything but a stray member of the beggars' camp on the outskirts of the town, who had wandered into the crowded thoroughfare to excite the compassion of the kind-hearted by the sight of his extreme poverty. If anyone had thought but for a moment of looking into his eyes he would have seen a flash in them that never gleamed in any mortal ones before nor since, and would have begun to suspect the genuineness of this wretched specimen of humanity, but no one did.

He seemed to be strolling along aimlessly, but his piercing gaze was narrowly scanning the faces of the people who passed before him, in order to see if there were not some one who had aspirations after a better life, upon whom he could begin the transforming process that would fit him in time to become a glorified member of the Western Heaven. Moving slowly along he came in front of a large house, where a middle-aged, benevolent-looking gentleman stood at his own door looking up and down the street.

No sooner did he catch sight of Li than a wave of compassion surged through his heart and a feeling of profound pity stirred his soul to its very depths. Little did he imagine that this was the famous fairy with the iron staff whose praises had been sung by great writers during the past centuries, and whose wonderful deeds had been the theme of many a ballad that had stirred the thought and excited the imagination of the lovers of romance throughout the empire.

He was moved with a genuine human sympathy for the wretched object who was hobbling along the street, and calling Li to him he expressed his concern that he should be in such dire distress and that, as he evidently had no home where he could live and no friends to assist him, he invited him to come and stay a few days with him promising to do all he could to make his life more bearable for a short time.

Li, who was charmed with the spirit of the man, and who saw in him a possible convert who might be developed into a fairy, gladly accepted his offer and became an inmate of his home. That the gentleman was sincere in his desire to serve the beggarman was evident from the way in which he treated him. He had every stitch of his clothes taken off him and buried, while garments that belonged to himself were given him in exchange. A barber was called in who washed and dressed his head and a small room was given him which was put entirely at his disposal, where he could rest and enjoy himself.

The transformation in Li was, as might have been expected, immense, and his benefactor was agreeably surprised to find that he was a man of rare intelligence who was anxious to discuss with him subjects that had been the theme of sages and great scholars in the early days of Chinese history. The great object of his guest, he found out before long, was to induce him to abandon his home and the property that belonged to him, and go with him in pursuit of a higher life that would end in his becoming immortal.

The gentleman was of a kind and generous disposition and was willing to go out of his way to assist those who were unfortunate in life, but he was not prepared for such a revolutionary movement as that. He told Li that he was quite content with his present life. He had his wife and children and sufficient means to surround himself with most of the comforts of this world, and he had no desire to give up a certainty for what might turn out to be only a visionary and romantic dream.

Li saw that his host, while far ahead of the most of his fellowmen in the homely virtues, did not possess that heroic spirit that would qualify him to be a leader of men in the endeavor to emancipate them from the pains and sorrows of this world. He accordingly determined not to press the matter any further, but to go elsewhere in the search for some one who might be of a kindred spirit with himself.

He accordingly informed his host of his intention of proceeding on his begging journey, as he was not suited by temperament for a settled life such as he was enjoying now. "I had hoped," he said, "that I should have had you for a companion, and that in our travels we might be able to learn some of the secrets from the land of the fairies that would uplift our lives beyond the common lot of men and secure us from pain and sorrow. I see, however, that you are not prepared for self-denial and that you are content with your present conditions, so I must continue my travels alone.

"I want to prove to you, however, before I leave, that I am indeed most grateful to you for all the attentions you have shown me. You took me, a poor beggar, from the streets and your whole family has treated me with honor and respect. I am profoundly thankful to you for your courtesy and liberality and I would like to repay you, in some little way, so that you may understand that I do appreciate your goodness to me. I want to inform you that there is a time of peril coming to you and your home. Mongol soldiers will come to Shanghai before very long, who will ravage and plunder and leave you homeless and desolate. I would strongly advise that you make immediate preparations for departure to some safer locality, and do not return until the foreign invaders have been driven from the soil of China. This will happen before very many years have elapsed. Leave everything except what you can conveniently carry with you, but delay not, for the danger is imminent.

"As I know that you will be reduced to very indigent circumstances, I wish to make you a present of my beggar's staff. Take the greatest care of it. Whatever you lose, be sure that you do not lose that, for it contains a fortune that will enrich you and your posterity for many future generations. After you return to your home again you must set up a medicine shop and the concoctions you make must all be stirred with my staff. The result will be that all your prescriptions will turn out well. Your name will become famous even in distant parts of the empire, and your medicines stirred with my staff will be the means of salvation to many a poor suffering mortal."

The next day, with mutual regrets, Li bade good-by to the family that had treated him so generously.

The man was not inclined to accept Li's suggestion about a hasty flight to another region. He thought that he was only a superior kind of beggar and could not possibly have any knowledge of future events. How could he, a man he had picked up from the streets in rags and tatters, have any minute acquaintance with the movements of the Mongol invaders? He refused to place any credence in the predictions and still continued to remain in his home.

One morning he was greatly startled with the flying rumors that disturbed the composure of the inhabitants of Shanghai. Men came flying in from the outlying districts with faces full of terror, and with stories of the barbarities that an approaching army of the Mongols were committing. Neither life nor property was safe from the brutal soldiers, who slaughtered the people without any discrimination of age or sex. He had but just time to pick up a few things that could he carried, when he and his family had to flee for their lives into another county, where some of his relatives were living.

He was very careful, however, that among the things that he managed to convey with him was the beggar's staff. His opinion of its former owner had greatly risen, since he began to believe that perhaps after all the iron stick that had been left as a legacy with him contained within it the fortune that was in future years to enrich him and his family.

A few years went by when the owner of the beggar's gift returned with his family to Shanghai. Everything that he had formerly possessed he found had disappeared. His fields, lying waste and covered with weeds and desolation, were the only things that were left of all his possessions, and these for fully another year would be practically of no value to him. He was penniless and he might have starved, only he clung to the hope that the beggar's staff, which he had preserved with the utmost care during his exile from home, would in some mysterious way bring him the fortune that his beggar guest had promised him.

Remembering that eccentric man's instructions, he at once opened a small drug shop in one of the by-streets in Shanghai. He had no capital to rent a more pretentious shop or to lay in a large stock of medicines. All that he could do was to buy half-a-dozen or so of simples that were used by the common people for bruises, sores, and cuts. His whole collection did not cost him more than a shilling, yet it was not on these that he was relying, but on the magic staff that by an alchemy of its own was going to convert these herbs that had been gathered from the hillside, and that now constituted his entire pharmacopoeia, into silver dollars and ingots and finally into broad lands and magnificent houses.

For some time it seemed as though no trade was ever going to be done in that wretched, miserable-looking little shop. People passed by it with a smile of scorn upon their faces. A few dried and withered looking grasses, and a bunch or two of antiquated leaves were the only things visible to the public. The man that professed to be able to salve the wounds and bruises of a whole district with such a meager stock as was exhibited in this out-of-the-way shop must be an adventurer with no means and no medical knowledge to entitle him to the patronage or respect of those who might need his services.

Li's staff was placed in a secure place in an inner room, ready to be used at a moment's notice, but it seemed to have no power to attract customers, nor to influence the destiny of the man who was trusting to its unseen magic for his very existence. If things did not soon take a turn he would have to buy a beggar's wallet and, grasping the stick that had been left him as an emblem of good luck, beg his way from place to place.

At last, one day, when hope had almost fled from the man's heart, an incident took place that proved to be the turn in the tide that was to lead to fortune. A countryman, with a heavy load that he had slung on a bamboo that rested on his shoulder, slipped and fell right in front of the mean- looking drug shop. After the passers-by had helped the poor man to his feet it was found that he was suffering from a deep cut in one of his knees from which the blood was slowly oozing, and that the skin on one of his arms was badly grazed. Immediate help was needed to stanch the blood and bind up the wounds from which he was suffering.

The shopkeeper was appealed to and was asked whether he had any medicine that could give immediate relief in a case like this. With a brave face, but with a beating heart, he declared that he had a salve that he could prepare in a few seconds that would work a cure before their very eyes, for it would not only ease the pain, but it would also enable the countryman to continue his journey without experiencing any inconvenience from his fall. A smile of incredulity wreathed the broad and spacious countenances of the Celestials as the man brought out a curiously-shaped iron staff, with which he stirred the ingredients of the mixture that was to work so marvelous a cure.

Never had any concoctor of drugs been known to use such a weird and strange fantastic instrument as this and, consequently, the excitement was great as with deft and facile hand he got ready to relieve the sufferer. This, however, was small when compared with the wonder and amazement that filled every heart when the balsam was applied to the deep gash in the knee. As if by magic the gaping wound slowly but perceptibly united till only a thin and narrow ridge marked the line where the flesh had been torn. The bruise on the arm which was raw where the skin had been abraded, no sooner felt the touch of the ointment than every trace of the accident had disappeared and a fine, healthy cuticle spread over the scar, so that, to an inexperienced eye, it would have been difficult to have told where the man had suffered from his fall.

The news of this remarkable cure spread like lightning throughout the town. Every man that was present in that narrow street that day became a herald, wherever he went, to proclaim the advent of a doctor more famous than any of the great men that had been deified in former ages, because of their skill in curing the diseases of mankind. Every time the story was told it was magnified. The teller seemed to think a reflected glory would fall upon himself the more marvelous it was and so imagination was let loose to add to the fame of the druggist.

From this time the business of the little shop in the obscure street never suffered an eclipse. Men with bruises and wounds and huge glaring ulcers, so common amongst the laboring classes, came with their ailments and found speedy relief. But it was especially in cases of rheumatism that the owner of the beggar's staff became famous, for no one could produce such ointment as he and none could ease the pains like that which had been stirred with the magic stick. In course of time the fame of this wonder-working medicine grew and orders from all parts of the country came for it. Many have tried to imitate it, but the magic power of the staff is wanting, and so it remains without a rival ever since the first day it was used, when the countryman fell and wounded himself, until the present day.

Wong Sing; or, How the Fortunes of a Royal Family Were Restored by a Fairy

WONG SING WAS DESCENDED FROM A FALLEN ROYAL FAMILY THOUGH NO ONE WOULD have known it. He hid himself in an obscure village where the life and bustle of the outside world were absolutely unknown, and all ambition to rise out of his miserable surroundings seemed to have been crushed out of his heart. Unfortunately he was not a man with a strong character, and his marriage helped to drag him down and prevent him from ever dreaming that there was any place for him in life higher than the one he now occupied.

His home was a little shanty by the roadside, and as is invariably the case with the very poor in China, it was the very picture of discomfort and despair. The furniture was of the poorest and the cheapest kind that could be bought, but the most distressing feature about this wretched home was the dust and dirt that lay on everything in it. Cobwebs, spun by great bloated spiders that blinked from smoke-dyed rafters above, hung in tatters in the air, and waved and tossed with every sudden gust of wind that with a mad spirit of fun flashed in at the open door.

There was a grimy feeling in the air, for dust had invaded the home and had taken possession of every nook and corner in it. The utterly untidy look and the disheveled hair and the thread-bare clothes of his wife as she moved about the house, seemed to be absolutely in harmony with the grimy, unlovely aspect of his miserable home. But the time had come at last when the fortunes of this fallen family were to be restored, and if not with the old regal splendor, at least with a magnificence that Wong Sing never had dreamed of in his happiest moments of any inspiration that may have stirred the depths of his heart.

One day, as he wandered about in his usual listless way, with the gray shadows of his life resting upon him, he saw gleaming in the long grass a long golden hairpin such as wealthy women use as ornaments for their hair. Picking it up he discovered that it was of rare and beautiful workmanship, and strange to say had the royal arms of his dynasty engraved upon it. This was a mystery to him. However could such a relic of a mighty house have got into this obscure village, where the wives and daughters of the farmers could only afford to buy the cheapest hairpins with which to keep their long black tresses from falling in disorder down their shoulders. Full of perplexity, he put the precious relic in his breast pocket and walked slowly on, trying to think out how such an extraordinary event could have happened as that which had just taken place.

All at once his thoughts were diverted by the appearance of an elderly lady coming along the pathway toward him. She had an exceedingly striking appearance, so much so that he felt himself powerfully attracted toward her. Her eyes were black and piercing and had such an intelligent look about them that they at once commanded the attention of Wong Sing. Although her dress was very plain, there was a dignity about her carriage and the pose of her figure that made her seem as though she belonged to some aristocratic home, and that by some strange accident or other she had lost her road and was wandering about in this unfrequented and out-of-the-way village.

As she drew near to Wong Sing, she addressed him in a very courteous, lady-like manner, and told him that she was in considerable trouble as she had unfortunately lost a very valuable hairpin that she had dropped on the road somewhere in the neighborhood of where they were standing.

"May I ask whether you have seen anything of it?" she asked Wong, looking at him with those bright eyes of hers as though they would pierce his very soul.

"Oh! yes," he replied, "I presume I have the very one you have lost," and, putting his hand into the pocket where he had placed it, he drew forth the hairpin and handed it to her.

"You are indeed an honest man," she cried, "and I thank you with all my heart for restoring to me something that I highly cherish not simply because of its intrinsic value, but also because of the tender associations connected with it."

"May I ask," said Wong, "how it is that you happen to have a gold ornament in your possession that has engraved upon it the royal arms of the dynasty that used to reign over China?"

"Oh! I can easily explain that," she said, and her eyes flashed and a look of pride overspread her countenance. "This hairpin originally belonged to my husband, who was a descendant of that Royal House, and years ago when we were married he gave it to me as a wedding gift. He has now been dead for many years, but I still remember his love for me, and I felt exceedingly distressed to-day when I found I had lost his present to me, and of course I am very grateful to you for restoring it to me."

"It appears to me," said Wong, "that you and I are relatives, for I too am a descendant of the Royal Family to which you say your husband belonged. I would like exceedingly to ask you to come with me to my home, but I know that I could not entertain you as you deserve. The house is so wretched and uncleanly, and we are so exceedingly poor that I fear you would turn away in disgust from us because of our forlorn and miserable circumstances."

"Oh! you must not say that," the lady quickly replied; "that you have fallen into poverty is not a thing to be ashamed of, for I know by your conduct to-day that you are still an honorable man. I am determined now that I have discovered a relative not to lose sight of him, and besides who knows but that I may be able to give you such advice and assistance as may be of service in lifting you out of the position into which you, the heir of kings, has unfortunately descended!"

When they reached Wong's house, the lady seemed shocked at the sight that met her gaze. It was not simply that she saw signs of extreme poverty such as marked the lowest ebb to which any family could fall. She perceived something that was to her infinitely more distressing, and that was the untidy, slovenly and absolutely neglected air that reigned throughout the house. Mrs. Wong might have been a beggar woman just recently imported from the nearest beggar camp. Her face was grimy with accumulated dirt, her hair unkempt, and her clothes, untouched by water for many a long day, were worn and patched and repatched until but a shadow of the original cloth lingered amidst the various bits that held the vanishing dress from entirely disappearing.

She was determined, however, that Mrs, Wong should never know anything of her thoughts, so with eyes dancing with pleasure and with a smile upon her face that seemed to fill the room as though sunbeams had flashed through it, she said, "Do you know that I have just discovered from your husband that we are relatives, and that we all belong to the same Royal House that once ruled China, and that if we had our rights you would not be living in this poor home, but would be grandees of the Empire and housed in a palace in the Capital? I am so delighted that I have been able to meet with those who are so near akin to me, and, in order that we may get to know each other well, I propose that I shall come and live with you and get thoroughly acquainted with you."

Mrs. Wong gazed with wonder and amazement upon the lady who thus addressed her. She did not know what to make of her. That she was far superior in rank to herself or anyone in the neighborhood was evident from the natural dignity and grace with which she bore herself. There was also an elegance of manner about her that showed that she had been accustomed to mingle in refined society. That she should condescend even to visit them in a home so poor and squalid was a marvel, but that she should propose to take up her abode with them and actually live in these mean and humble surroundings was something too much for her to believe.

As she stood with a dazed and perplexed look upon her countenance, the lady, who had a grace and charm of manner that won the heart of Mrs. Wong, began to suggest that various improvements might be made in the home that would render it more pleasant and attractive. As she said that extreme poverty was the main cause for the forlorn condition of the family, she gave Wong some money and directed him to go out at once and buy certain articles that were essential for immediate use. Then with a broom in hand she attacked the accumulations of dust and refuse that had lain undisturbed about the floor and on the furniture with such vigor that Mrs. Wong became inspired with her spirit and wielded the feather-duster with such effect that ere long the rooms, though they still had an air of destitution about them, presented a clean and cheerful look such as they had never had since the day when they left the builders' hands.

The fairy, for such the strange lady was, soon worked such wonders in the home that it could hardly be recognized. A regular campaign of cleanliness was organized. The walls were whitewashed and made as white as lime could make them. The cobweb streamers that had hung fluttering from the rafters had disappeared and so too had the huge spiders that had spun them. The grimy look that the dust-laden air and the indolent slatternly ways of Mrs. Wong had given to everything in the home had entirely vanished and now there was a sense of freshness and purity, as though one were on a mountain top and the fresh breezes of heaven were blowing around one.

But the most remarkable change was in Mrs. Wong. The old rags in which she had been content to be clothed had been discarded, and dresses of the very latest fashion and of the very best materials that the shops contained had been got for her by the mysterious stranger, who seemed to have an unlimited supply of money at her command.

With the clean and healthy surroundings and white walls that showed not a speck of dirt upon them, and her own person dressed in clothes that made her feel as though she were living in fairy-land, there gradually came back the sense of womanhood that had been lost in her.

The fairy, with her delicate and refined sense of what was highest and best in woman, knew that until she had touched and developed this in Mrs. Wong her efforts to raise the family ideal would be attended with no success. She, accordingly, did everything in her power to make the dawning self-respect, that was touching her life with a new ambition, one of the forces that would lift her up from the mean and wretched condition into which she had fallen.

The most exquisite little bits of jewelry would find their way, in some mysterious manner that utterly perplexed Mrs. Wong, into her bedroom. Hairpins enameled with the delicate blue feathers of the kingfisher that had once skimmed along the rivers and up and down the banks of the streams in the land where the fairies have their home, earrings of rare and ingenious workmanship, and bracelets made of jadestone in hues that no one had ever seen before, would appear in her dressing case, without any apparent reason, when she opened it in the morning to perform her toilette. In time she became so changed a character that it would have been impossible to have recognized in the refined and well-dressed lady, the wretched miserable-looking woman whom the fairy had found in such a degraded condition when she came from fairyland on her errand of mercy.

But it was not simply with Mrs. Wong that this fairy with the beautiful spirit had a difficulty in changing and transforming the character. Her husband, in some respects, was even a more difficult problem to solve than his wife. His many years of indolence had eaten into his very soul and had taken all ambition out of him. He was stubborn and obstinate and therefore the fairy had to be extremely cautious in her endeavors to arouse a manly, independent spirit within him.

By degrees she got him interested in making money, and supplied him with funds to start several little ventures, and though they were failures because of his want of enterprise, they had the effect of developing within him a more ambitious view of life, that made him desirous of rising out of the mean position that he occupied in the poor and insignificant village in which he lived.

At length the fairy saw that the time had at last arrived when it was safe for her to put into operation a scheme that she had devised for the making of his fortune. At that particular time there was a perfect craze among nearly all classes for quail fighting. The quail, it may be explained, is a timid, delicate-looking bird, and one would never dream that so shy-looking a little thing would have the fighting element so strongly within so frail and feeble-looking a body as it possesses.

Rumor had brought the report to the village where Wong lived that a certain Prince of the Blood had got a collection of quails that were famous for their fighting powers, and that they had managed to defeat every bird that had been brought into the arena against them. So sure, indeed, was he of their prowess, that he had issued challenges to all those who possessed quails and invited them to come to the palace and try issues with his famous fighters.

This was precisely the chance the fairy desired. Coming in one morning with a graceful, delicate looking quail in her hand, she informed Mr. Wong that she was going to make him a present of it, and she advised him to proceed at once to the Capital that lay a few miles away and try his fortune against the birds that belonged to the Prince.

"There is no quail in all China," she said, "that can beat this one. It is a modest-looking little thing, and does not seem to have much fighting power in it, but it is bound to beat every rival that dares to stand up before it, and it is going to bring you great good fortune. I have given it the name 'Pearl,' so now you can start with it as soon as you like for the Capital, where it will secure you both honor and the beginning of great wealth."

Full of a new ambition that now stirred his soul, Mr. Wong reached the city and found that the one subject of conversation wherever he went was the great quail tournament that was expected to take place on the morrow. The Prince had once more sent his challenges abroad and invited quail holders to appear and contest for the mastery with the famous birds that he possessed.

A vast concourse was assembled in the grounds where the tournament was to take place, and men from many districts were there with their favorite birds, each one anxious to carry off the palm of victory and to secure the honor and the renown that would come to the one that remained the victor in the great contest that was about to be fought.

The Prince, with a magnificent retinue, arrived with but two of his most famous quails. He was so sure that these would be certain to defeat any birds that might be brought forward that he did not think it necessary to bring a large number.

The first that he put into the enclosure where the fighting was to take place was a beautiful quail named "Summer Dawn." One after another of the birds were put in to fight with this, but after a more or less prolonged struggle every quail fled in dismay into any corner where it could crouch and hide itself, while "Summer Dawn" remained the acknowledged master of the field.

All this time Mr. Wong had been filled with doubt and uncertainty, and was wondering within himself whether the bird that he held in his hand, and whose timid-looking eyes seemed to be looking up to him would be able to stand up against birds that had been trained to fight, and whose confidence had been gained by victory in many a well-fought contest.

Just then the voice of the Prince was heard calling upon any one who wished to be a competitor to come forward without delay. His bird had beaten every other one that had been pitted against it and the lists would be closed unless another entry was speedily made.

With a hurried, impetuous movement Mr. Wong stepped forward and placed his timid little "Pearl" within the enclosure, right in front of the victorious "Summer Dawn," and standing aside he watched with beating heart to see what would be the result of this, to him, most momentous contest. The fairy had told him that his fortunes were to be made to-day, and that wealth and honors would pour into his home from the victory that "Pearl" would achieve for him in this great tournament.

Every one shrugged his shoulders at the sight of "Pearl" and numerous were the prophecies that it would soon share the fate of the other quails that had fled before the prowess of "Summer Dawn." No sooner, however, had it got into a fighting attitude than its whole demeanor seemed to undergo a marvelous change. A fire flashed through the dove-like eyes that showed that a warrior spirit burned within its breast, and the manful way in which it stood up to "Summer Dawn" and resisted every assault that was made upon it showed that it was not going to be defeated without a struggle. Attack and counter-attack were made in rapid succession and the crowd became excited and even the Prince began to have a fear that his famous fighting bird had at last fairly met its match. The fighting went on for about a quarter of an hour when "Summer Dawn" fled from the contest and "Pearl" stood triumphant in the ring alone.

The Prince was distressed at the disgrace that had come upon his bird, but he was determined that the honors of the day should not be carried off by an unknown stranger that no one had ever heard of before until that day. He accordingly brought forward the other quail that he had in reserve, and which because of its great strength he had named "Ironbeak."

It was indeed a powerful looking bird for it was larger in the body and longer in the legs than the ordinary run of quails, and as it stood towering over "Pearl" it suggested the idea of a crane to many of those that looked upon the two birds. As to which would be the victor there was no question in the minds of the excited crowd that waited with breathless attention to watch the great battle that was now going to be fought. That "Pearl" would never be able to withstand the onslaughts of "Ironbeak" was the almost unanimous conviction of those who were present.

The fight began with a great deal of cautious sparring on both sides. "Ironbeak" would have rushed matters, but the steady way in which "Pearl" met every maneuver to put him at a disadvantage seemed to make him more careful in his tactics. If "Pearl" was smaller in body, he was certainly not inferior to him in courage or in the spirit with which he met every attack that was made upon him.

For a whole hour the momentous struggle went on. There were times when "Pearl," overborne by the heavier weight of his antagonist, seemed as though he would be compelled to flee, but each time, with as brave a front as ever, he stood facing "Ironbeak," and with an unsubdued mien he received his blows and paid them back again with interest. The contest seemed as if it would never end excepting with the death of these two brave fighters, when, after one brief and furious struggle more severe than any that had taken place before, "Ironbeak" was seen to fly and "Pearl" was left the acknowledged victor in this famous tournament.

Mr. Wong now became the hero of the moment, for men crowded round him to see the wonderful bird that once more lay nestling in the grip of his right hand. He was about to leave for his lodgings when he was stopped by the Prince, who besought him to sell it to him. At first he refused but a final offer of a sum equal to about two hundred pounds induced him to consent, and in a moment he became a comparatively rich man.

"Pearl" after all had brought him wealth, for with the money he had received for it he entered into business which succeeded so well that in time he became possessed of considerable property.

One day the lady who had worked such a transformation in the home told Mrs. Wong that she felt that the time had come when she must leave her. "You do not need my help any longer. Your home is a prosperous one and you are surrounded with everything that your heart can desire." Mrs. Wong was distressed when she heard this, and she used every argument she could think of to induce her to reconsider the matter and still remain with them a loved and honored friend, but she would make no promise in the matter.

Next day when the family rose, no trace of her could be found and they never saw her face again. She had completely vanished. Up to this time they had never suspected that she was a fairy. They had often marveled at her wonderful powers of mind and the ability she displayed in any of the common affairs of life.

They had been greatly struck, too, with her high-toned morality and with the lofty ideals that she believed every man should set before him. The perfectly miraculous change, moreover, that she had effected in their family came as a crowning reason that she must have possessed supernatural powers, and that, therefore, she was a fairy that with a benign intention had come into their lives to restore the fallen fortunes of their home.

The Stirring Adventures of the Scholar Wang

In a certain city in the Hunan province there lived a scholar with the name of Wang. He was exceedingly clever, and in all the literary examinations in which he had competed he had shown himself to be a man of brilliant parts, for he had usually come out first among the thousands that entered the examination cells at the same time that he did. True to the character of the men of the province, he was masterful and imperious in his treatment of his fellow men. He could brook no reproof, and if any one dared to oppose him he would break out into the wildest passion and use the most abominable language toward the person who thus had the hardihood to speak his mind to him.

One day, as Wang was sauntering along in the suburbs of the town, he met a man that proved to be a Taoist priest. He was really a fairy, but he had taken this particular form in which to disguise himself. No sooner did he see Wang than without any ceremony he came up to him and addressing him in a brusque and off-hand manner, he said, "You have a very fine gentlemanly appearance, but you have no sense of propriety and you never know how to treat people with the respect that is due to them. You are also a man of a powerful intellect and you have abilities far beyond the average, but you are so abominably conceited and have such a high opinion of yourself, that men who know you intimately have the most profound contempt for you. I want to tell you a secret that you seem to have lost and that is, you were once a fairy, but even in heaven you were so disgustingly proud that you were expelled from it, and reduced to the condition of a mere man. I can tell you further that you will have to go through ages of self-denial and suffering before you can travel back to the happiness of Heaven, and be once more admitted to the company of the immortals that live there."

Wang was taken aback at the almost insolent manner of the priest, but there was something about him that prevented him from indulging in the violent passion that would have been evoked if any one else had dared to address him as this stranger had done. Pretending not to notice the insulting way in which he had been spoken to, he replied, "You know very well that there are no such things as fairies, and that they exist only in the imagination of the credulous and the uneducated. I appeal to you," he said, "whether you have ever seen one of those mysterious beings, or have ever met with any one who has actually come to such close acquaintanceship with one that he could verily aver that what he saw was not a delusion but a real living fairy?"

The priest, looking upon him with an amused smile, said, "If you are willing to come with me, I will let you see quite a number of fairies, so large, indeed, that you will never doubt again as to their existence, and you shall live with them long enough to know that they are not mere creations of the fancy, but real living beings just as beautiful in life and character as the popular belief has declared them to be."

Still skeptical, but moved by the evident faith of the priest in the existence of fairies, Wang replied, "Very good, let me have but sufficient evidence of the truth of what you assert, and then I shall become a convert to your opinions, but in the meantime I prefer to have my own thoughts in the matter, which are decidedly not the same as yours."

"Well, come with me," the priest said, "and I will soon disperse all your doubts," and putting forth the stick that he had his hand, he asked him to get astride of it. "Shut your eyes now," he commanded, "and for your very life's sake do not dare to open them until I give you permission." At the word "Ascend," Wang found himself rising with incredible swiftness from the earth. The stick that he bestrode he found had grown to such dimensions that he could sit on it with perfect ease as though he had been on horseback. Putting his hands down to feel what kind of an animal he was riding on, he realized by the scales that met his touch that he was sitting on the back of a dragon.

He knew now that he must be in the hands of a great wizard who had power to perform the most wonderful miracles. A man that could command the services of the mysterious dragon to carry out his behests must be one with unlimited resources at his disposal, since the very spirits that all men stand in awe of were compelled to perform the most menial services that he required from them. Swifter than the swiftest arrow that ever flew from the full-drawn bow, Wang darted through the air. At one time he felt himself passing through clouds that seemed to eclipse the sun and to fill the air with darkness, and then emerging into the dazzling light he felt himself instinctively putting up his hands to shade his closed eyes from the brilliance that shone upon them. Onward he sped with amazing swiftness far away up beyond the sounds of earth, through the mysterious tracts where no human footsteps had ever trodden, and where the wing of the eagle in its highest flight had never carried the monarch of the air.

By and by Wang become conscious that he was not alone, and that the superior force of the man, whom at first he had deemed to be but a common Taoist priest upon whom he had looked down with the semi-contempt with which such men were usually regarded, was really controlling and directing the movements of the dragon he was bestriding. This in some degree gave him confidence. For some time after they had started on their adventurous flight, he had been filled with a nervous dread lest he should find himself being flung headlong into the mighty abyss below, where he would be dashed into a thousand pieces. After a time a feeling of exhilaration took possession of him and fear of death seemed to vanish from his heart. Instead, there surged through him a spirit of adventure, that would have led him, had he had full control of himself and his movements, into madder and more dangerous excursions than the wildest flights of imagination that ever coursed through the human brain could have suggested to him.

Suddenly, while entranced with the new sensations that were now filling his heart, the voice of the priest was heard exclaiming, "We have arrived," and in an instant the dragon, as though it had been shot, fell like a meteor from the sky, and Wang in a few seconds, with his heart in his mouth, found himself in an instant once more on *terra firma*. Opening his eyes he saw that he was standing in front of a magnificent palace the like of which he had never seen before. It seemed to be built of rubies and sapphires, and all manner of precious stones, and as the sun shone upon them they reflected back his glory in all the colors of the rainbow, but in such harmony and beautiful proportion that the eyes seemed to be rested as they gazed upon the marvelous sight of this wondrous building.

Wang found to his astonishment that the dragon had vanished, and that the priest had discarded the peculiar dress of his class and was dressed in the richest garments, such as no king or royal prince on earth had ever donned. Leading the way he led Wang into the spacious grounds that surrounded the palace, and here fresh wonders filled his mind with the utmost astonishment and delight. The gardens were laid out with the most exquisite taste and abounded in flowers whose fragrance and beauty far excelled anything that he had ever seen or heard of. They were adapted, moreover, for giving the very highest enjoyment. Summer-houses garlanded with trailing vines, cozy corners where a perfect retreat could be obtained, and green sward where the fairies could dance in the moonlight, were some of the charming features that he caught a glimpse of as they slowly wended their way to the mansion that glittered in the distance and seemed like a beautiful gem set in a frame that appeared to be aiming at eclipsing the splendor of the thing it was meant to show off.

At last, after many a winding and turning, where all sense of weariness was lost in the delights that came from unexpected beauties that flashed upon them from these fairy grounds, they reached the building toward which they had been walking for more than an hour. Here they were met by an old man of a most venerable and pleasing aspect. He seemed to Wang to personify the conception that painters had delighted to conceive as the beau-ideal image of the typical fairy, that with a benevolent heart and a face full of tenderness was accustomed to mingle in human life for the purpose of alleviating the sorrows of mankind.

He greeted Wang's companion with the most effusive delight and it soon became evident from their conversation that these two were fairies who stood high in this magic world, and had attained to an eminence that showed what exalted beings they were. Seeing Wang in the ex-priest's company, though simply a mere mortal, the old man seemed to put himself out to show him honor and respect, and invited him in the most courteous manner to come in and be seated, assuring Wang that he would be delighted to have him as his guest as long as it was his pleasure to remain with him.

They passed through great halls, decorated by an art so beautiful and so subtle that every sense seemed to be charmed as the eye rested upon the wonderful creations of fancy and of genius that had turned them into veritable halls of delight. Everything that could minister to the intellect and to the imagination had been collected and arranged with an idea to produce the highest effect upon the mind of the beholder.

Passing through a magnificent suite of rooms, they at last came to one that was evidently considered the living room, and here the old gentleman introduced Wang to his two daughters, who were evidently awaiting their arrival. They were both of them exceedingly beautiful women and of that graceful type of form and face that has always been associated in the minds of mortals in all lands with the typical fairy. One of these was named "Phoenix Clouds," and she was so exquisitely lovely and had such a charming and winning manner with her that Wang almost immediately lost his heart to her.

After some little conversation, the fairy that had conducted Wang to this beautiful spot in fairyland declared that the latter had expressed his utter disbelief in the existence of fairies, and he had therefore brought him here to give him ocular demonstration that his unbelief was absolutely without any sufficient reason. "I propose," he said, "that we have a grand feast and that we invite a great number of fairies from West, East, North and South to meet our guest, when he will get sufficient evidence of their existence that he will never be able to doubt again as long as he lives."

With many good-natured smiles this proposal was agreed to. A day was set, and messages to far-off fairy regions were sent by a telegraphy that far surpassed anything that had ever been thought of or invented by the profoundest brains of mortal man, for in some mysterious way the intimation of the intended feast was carried to every expected guest in the course of a few minutes.

On the appointed day and punctual to the very hour the fairy visitors began to flock in from every quarter. Some came floating on clouds through which the sun had flashed his golden colors, till they seemed reclining on a royal throne. Another company came dashing through the great expanse on cranes, while immediately after a number followed on the mythical phoenix, and still more on various kinds of strange and fanciful-looking birds that were known only in those fairy regions of the world.

By the time they had all arrived, hundreds of fairies, both male and female, had assembled for the coming feast, which was spread on a great lawn, shaded by magnificent trees, with the scent and perfume of flowers filling the air with their sweetness. Whatever conceptions men may have of the nature and disposition of these mysterious beings that are supposed to have such an influence on human life, there was one thing revealed that day to Wang that gave him new thoughts about them, such as had never entered his mind before. He found that with all their supernatural powers they were in some respects as human as himself, and that laughter and fun and pleasant conversation were as much enjoyed as they would have been had the gathering been one composed simply of men and women, who had assembled together to celebrate some festal occasion.

The only difference he could see was that there was more refinement and more courtesy shown to each other than would have marked a human assemblage that had met for purposes of festivity. There were smiling faces and bright laughing eyes that sparkled with amusement, and there were flashes of humor and delightful repartee, but no frown ever gathered upon the face of anyone at some remark that had been uttered, and no voice was raised in displeasure. It seemed, indeed, as though they had all set out to entertain each other, and all selfish motives had been banished from the heart of everyone.

At the conclusion of the feast, some time was spent in wandering among the spacious gardens, and in enjoying the beautiful flowers and inhaling the odors that exhaled a subtle fragrance of their own, such as can be found only in fairyland, where the dust of earth has never been able to soil with its touch the absolute beauty of these wonderful creations. Then an hour or two were spent in music, so new to Wang that his soul was touched by the exquisite harmonies that came with such ease and with such perfect taste from the strange instruments that the fairy fingers touched into life. After that preparations were made for the departure of the visitors to their various homes. This was a most interesting process, and Wang looked upon what was a very commonplace thing to the fairies with the keenest enjoyment. Those who had come on clouds, as above described, floated with the most perfect grace higher and higher towards the sun, until catching sight of fleecy, errant vapor, that seemed to have wandered from some snow-capped mountain, they seated themselves on it and were soon wafted out of sight.

All at once there was a rush, the sound of wings was heard, and a flock of beautiful white herons gracefully wheeled over the heads of the assembly. In an instant a number of the fairies with a light and airy movement rose from where they were standing, and the next moment the graceful birds were winging their way through a bright and cloudless sky, until they became but mere specks in the far-off heavens and then were slowly lost to sight.

Hardly had the herons started on their romantic journey, when the shadows of another flight of birds fell upon the waiting guests and, looking up, Wang saw they were phoenix that had come to carry their masters and mistresses back to their far-off homes.

Scarcely had a minute elapsed, when these birds, with a stronger wing and more daring flight than those of the herons, were soaring away in a clear and unclouded sky.

After the last of the fairy visitors had taken his flight and the home had assumed its normal condition, the fairy that had brought Wang asked him if he were now satisfied that the fairies were not the creation of fancy but were beings that really had an existence. Wang assured him in tones of perfect conviction that his skepticism had entirely vanished and that he would never doubt again as long as he lived. When it was suggested that they should return to earth again Wang, whose heart had been completely captivated by Phoenix Clouds, made so many excuses to remain that it was finally settled that the other should go on in advance alone, while he should remain to study more fully the life and habits of the fairies. The result was that in the course of a few months Phoenix Clouds was married to him and it was settled that he should take up his permanent abode in his new home.

For nearly two years Wang lived a most happy life in the fairy home, and his heart was more and more knit to Phoenix Clouds, when there came a longing over him to see his old father whom he had left behind him in the family homestead in the land of the mortals. He had often thought of him before, but never with such an intense desire to see him and to learn how he was at the present moment. On consulting his wife she became seriously alarmed, for she loved Wang with the same passionate devotion that he had for her. Since the time when he had taken up his abode amongst the fairies his character had immensely improved. The proud and imperious manners that had once distinguished him had vanished, and now he had become so gentle and modest under the new influence amongst which he had lived, that even the fairies felt attracted toward him, so loving and gentle was his whole bearing and demeanor.

Phoenix Clouds at first declared that it was possible for him to return to earth, but he would never be able to see her again. She belonged to fairyland, she said, and she did not see how she could accompany him to earth and live there like one of the ordinary mortals. On consultation, however, with some of the more experienced fairies who sympathized with her desire not to be separated from her husband, they declared that if Wang promised to return with his fairy wife after the death of his father the thing could be done. Wang, of course, gladly gave his consent to this, for he could as little brook the idea of separation as could his wife. The preparations were at once entered upon for the journey to earth, and for their departure from a home where Wang had spent the happiest days of his life.

On the morning of his departure Phoenix Clouds' sister came to him and said that she had a small present to make him which he was to take with him, and which he was to preserve with the utmost care. As his happiness and that of his wife, while he was a dweller on earth, would largely depend upon it, he must understand, she said, that it was of the very first importance that no harm should come to it while they were on their journey to his father's home.

On examining this wonderful present, he found that it was a miniature house, the very facsimile of the one in which they were at present living. He was surprised at its beauty and the infinite care with which every detail in their present home had been reproduced. Not only were the halls and the rooms the same in number, but the furniture in them, down to its smallest article, was exactly similar. Only fairy hands could have produced within such a small compass the magnificent mansion with all its equipments with such fidelity as was done in this beautiful little model that could easily be laid upon the palm of the hand. "When you arrive at your native home," she said, "select some spot outside the village, and place this present of mine on it and you will see what will happen."

Stepping into a carriage that stood waiting outside the great entrance for them, Wang and his beautiful wife found themselves in a moment traveling at what seemed lightning speed far away beyond the sight of earth, where nothing but the sunlight shone around them, and where not even a cloud could be seen, so far had they soared above the highest point to which these ever float. In a very short space of time the carriage in which they were sitting began to take a downward course, and soon they were traveling among dense masses of clouds, which offered, however, not the slightest impediment to their onward speed. Then the mountains seemed to start like solitary islands out of a sea of mist and in a moment the whole landscape of plains and hills stretched out beneath them, and as in a flash they found themselves on the outskirts of the village where the family of Wang had always resided.

Remembering the parting words of Phoenix Clouds' sister, Wang had most carefully kept the beautiful model of their home in fairyland in his hand during the whole of the journey, and now, walking a short way from where they had landed, he laid it carefully on the edge of the plain that gradually sloped up in the direction of a neighboring hill. No sooner had it touched the ground than it immediately became transformed into a magnificent mansion, the very counterpart of the one in fairyland, with everything in it precisely the same as that they had left only a few minutes ago. The only things they missed were the friends that were so dear to them, and the exhilarating air that made life so joyous, and that was so in keeping with the immortals that breathed it.

Wang went almost immediately in search of his father. He found that great sorrows had come upon him since he had last seen him. The little money he had possessed had all vanished and the ancestral home was falling into decay. He was, indeed, in the direst poverty and the son had returned only just in time to save him from great suffering. He at once took him to his own home, where he was tended with the most loving care by Phoenix Clouds, and everything was done to make his last days happy.

For two years he lived a most gloriously happy existence, every want being met and every thought and desire of his heart being more than satisfied. At the end of that time he died and was buried with a magnificence that none of his ancestors had ever had the fortune to experience.

Next morning when men came out to have a glance at the great mansion that had been the wonder and the admiration of all those who had had the good fortune to behold it, it had completely vanished and not a single trace remained of it. The beautiful gardens, that had been the delight of great crowds that had been allowed to wander amongst them unreproved by Wang or his fairy wife, had completely disappeared and the ground was the wild, uncultivated common that it was before the mysterious model had been placed upon it two years ago by Wang. Many were the speculations of the country folks around as to what had become of him and his princely home, but no satisfactory explanation was ever given by anyone, and to this day the stories prevalent in that region about that wonderful building and of the lavish hospitality shown by its owners are told with glistening eyes and bated breath by the sons and daughters of those who had actually seen with their own eyes the wonders of those two eventful years.

The Mysterious Peach

Our story tells of two light-hearted fairies, whose hearts beat with such tender sympathy and compassion for the men and women of the Celestial Empire, that they determined to descend to earth and perform such wonderful feats of magic that men would forget in their wonder and astonishment any griefs that might be gnawing at their hearts.

In order to remove any suspicion in the minds of men as to their true character, they determined to assume the role of jugglers, and one elected to be the father and the other to be the son. They were of the common type that one meets at country fairs, or in the busy towns, where no sooner do they take their stand in some open space than, as if drawn by a magnet, a crowd speedily gathers around them and stands with wondering eyes gazing upon their feats of legerdemain. These men, though rough and uneducated and belonging to the commoner classes of society, are usually shrewd and intelligent, with a marvelous power in the use of their hands, a faculty of speech that gives them a persuasive oratory that bends the hearts of their audience to believe the deceptive stories with which they try to beguile them.

On a certain day in early spring, just about the time of the Feast of Tombs, two common-looking jugglers were seen wending their way towards a large city at which it was known there were to be a series of rejoicings, and crowds from all the country round would join with the inhabitants of the town in the festivities that were to be celebrated on a very large and liberal scale. Their clothes were of the common homely blue cotton in which the masses of this Empire like to array themselves. They were evidently the worse for the hard service they had seen, for rents here and patches there showed that wear and tear were beginning to tell seriously upon them.

They had a worn look too about them that seemed to have made them careless about their appearance, for their hair was unkempt and it was evident that many a day had passed since any water had made acquaintance with their faces. The were typical specimens of a light-hearted Bohemian set of men, who with a restless spirit within them refuse to settle down to any of the ordinary avocations of men, but prefer to lead a roving life and gather excitement from the applause of the crowds that they entertain with their tricks.

Little did the people that walked side by side with them on the great thoroughfares that led to the city dream that the common-looking men that they regarded with a kind of good-natured contempt were citizens of the Western Heaven, who, in compassion for the grayness and dreariness of human life, had come down to earth to put a little laughter into men's hearts, and in the fun and merriment they could give them for an hour or two make them forget the weariness that dwelt in their hearts.

By and by the great city was reached, and what a scene of animation and excitement it presented. It seemed as though the spirit of the day had infected everyone and had banished the idea of work from every heart. There was no spread of bunting as is usual on such festal occasions in the West, and no flags run up from public buildings or from the merchant firms, to testify to the general hilarity that was making the entire population throb with one great spirit of enjoyment.

The farmer lads from the surrounding farms and villages seemed to be wandering aimlessly about, with open mouths and wide, staring eyes, gazing at the wonderful sights that the streets displayed. They wanted nothing more; they were content with simply that. They had got away from the monotonous, endless toil that is never broken into by the coming of the Sunday, and simply to do nothing but to feel that they can let go the everlasting grip of the hoe and wander about at their own sweet will is a thing that brings to them the most exquisite enjoyment.

Our two jugglers, without dallying by the way either to look at the exciting dramas that were being enacted, or to indulge in any of the savory preparations of which the itinerant kitchens were sending forth their odors to tempt the lovers of good eating, made their way straight to the *yamên*, where they knew crowds would be attracted; for on this special festal occasion, the mandarins were bound by custom and by law to take an active part in guiding and directing the festivities of the day.

The *yamên*, it may be explained, is the official court and residence of the resident mandarin who has rule over the town and also over the district in which it is situated. In cases of the higher mandarins it is large and imposing, and is really the only public building in a city that is worthy of being looked at. A Chinese town is signally deficient in such, for besides it and the temples of the idols there are no public buildings worthy of the name. Town halls, infirmaries, hospitals, national galleries, spacious buildings where public meetings can be held, are still in the dim and distant future, and are only the dream of those that believe that China one day will become as great an empire as any of those that exist in the West.

When they got to the *yamên* they found that thousands had gathered in the vacant space in front and in the spacious courts that led up to the inner sanctum where all official business was ordinarily transacted. The solemn and dignified air that usually rested over a place that was supposed to be the abode of justice, but where in reality the gravest wrongs were perpetrated under the name of law, had vanished, and an air of joyousness and frivolity filled the lofty courts with an atmosphere that must have seemed to them like an utter desecration of the imperial uses for which they had been built.

It was indeed a great occasion, for the mandarins were dressed in their richest robes, while the soldiers in attendance were attired in scarlet uniforms, that stood out in striking contrast against the universal blue of the crowds around. Bands of music too, were in attendance, which now and again, as if under the spell of the joyousness of the day, broke into sudden flights of music that made every face beam with delight, as they heard the screams and wails that remind one forcibly of a Highland bagpipe, not played on a hillside, but in some narrow street where its echoes have no room to escape.

The jugglers, who were there with a certain well-defined purpose, pressed their way through the laughing good-natured masses that were waiting to see what new forms of amusement would be suggested by the mandarins for their entertainment. Suddenly a man dressed in black came to them with a message from the great man and asked them what pieces of jugglery they could perform that would be entertaining for the crowds waiting to be amused.

"Tell their excellencies," they said, "we can do things more wonderful than jugglers ever performed throughout the length and breadth of China. We are no common performers, for we can make the living die and we can bring back the dead from their graves; there is nothing in fact that we cannot accomplish. Just ask the mandarins what they would like us to do and we will instantly proceed to carry out their wishes."

The messenger was amused at the high-flown talk of these wretched-looking jugglers and smiling he returned to the mandarins and reported what they had commissioned him to tell them. They were so entertained at what they considered the humor of the men that they laughed outright, and entering into the joke, they said "Will you go once more and tell them we do not wish them to murder any one, neither will we tax their powers by asking them to bring back anyone from the Land of Shadows, but we should just like them to do us the small but easy favor of producing a peach that shall be equal to those that nature will give us in the course of a few months."

When this message reached the jugglers, the father pretended to be very much put out at what he considered the unreasonable request of the mandarins. "How is it possible for me," he said, "to produce a peach at this season of the year? Last winter's snow is still on the ground, and the time for the peach trees to blossom is still in the distance. How am I to be expected to produce something that nature itself cannot accomplish? It is most unreasonable of their excellencies to ask of me to do what they must know no human being has ever been known to attempt."

By this time the news of the trick that the mandarins had requested the jugglers to perform had spread with wonderful rapidity throughout the waiting crowds, and some were laughing, some were discussing the possibilities of the case, and some were laying wagers that these common-looking men could never do such a wonderful thing as to produce a rich, ripe peach while the snow was on the ground and while the transforming power of the peach trees still lay dormant within them. All was excitement and expectation and every eye was fastened upon them, wondering what magic power they could possess that would enable them to work such a miracle as had been demanded of them by the mandarins.

When the father had finished his complaint, the son, turning to him, said, "You must remember that you have already promised them to do whatever they liked to demand from you, and if you refuse to produce a peach for them they will call you a braggart and you will lose your reputation."

The father pretended to be troubled at the unreasonable request that had been made of him, but finally he said, "It is true that the earth at the present moment cannot produce a single peach, but I know that in Heaven in a certain garden there are the most lovely peaches that ever the eye looked on. To get one of these, I shall have to ascend the sky and steal one."

"But how are you going to get there?" asked the son. "Have you a ladder that will reach beyond the clouds and that will take you up to the land where you say the beautiful garden is where the peaches are growing?"

"Oh! that is very simple matter," replied the father, and going to his box where he kept the juggling apparatus, he took out a delicate coil of silken rope that he unwound with the greatest possible care. This he did most ostentatiously in the sight of the crowd, who by this time were being wrought up to a high pitch of excitement at the idea of a man actually climbing up into heaven to bring down a peach from those sublime regions to be handled and tasted by men on earth.

After unwinding the silken coils for some considerable time without apparently coming any nearer to the end of them, the juggler seized hold of the loose end and with a deft and masterly cast he flung it toward the sky, where, with a graceful spiral motion, it ascended swiftly through the air until it disappeared in a rift in the clouds and was lost to view. After a time the uncoiling of the silken rope stopped and the juggler announced that connection had been securely made with the Western Heaven.

This, of course, filled the crowd with the most exalted idea of the wonder-working power of these two common-looking men. There was no deception in the miracle that had been wrought, for the silken rope was there plainly before their eyes, and it could be seen stretching in one unbroken line till lost from the keenest vision in the heights that stretched away toward the blue sky.

But the wonders that remained to be accomplished were far to transcend in importance anything that had yet been done. As soon as the connection was made with the unseen world, the father said to the son, "I am not as nimble as you are, so I think you had better climb the silken ladder and bring down the peach for the mandarins." The son, however, pretended to be afraid, and he said, "Supposing the rope were to break when I had got half-way up, my body would be dashed into a thousand pieces, so that you would not be able to recognize me."

The father assured him that that was an impossibility and urged him to start on his journey without delay, otherwise the patience of the crowd would be exhausted. "You can catch hold of the knots that are on the silken rope, so that you will be kept from slipping, and, besides, you may be assured that when you return their excellencies will be so impressed by the wonders you have performed that they will certainly make you a present of enough money to buy yourself a wife. Now go on like a good son and let these people see how clever you are."

With a bound that electrified the whole of the spectators, he made a spring on to the rope, and in a moment was mounting the long slender-looking thread that reached away into the sky. Exclamations of wonder burst from every lip as the young man, apparently with the greatest ease, and skimming like a bird in the air, ascended higher and higher till his form was lost in the great expanse above.

Every eye was now turned toward the rift in the cloud into which the young juggler had vanished, and speculations were rife as to whether he would ever be seen again, and how he could possibly descend the thin slender rope by which he had climbed into the unknown land beyond. The more observant of them, watching the attitude of the father, observed that one hand was held out in an attitude as though he were waiting to catch a ball. There was a look too of eager expectation on his face that showed that he believed that his son would accomplish his mission and bring down the promised peach from the famous garden in the Western Heaven. While he was looking with straining eyes into the fleecy clouds that moved gently along before the lightest of zephyrs, suddenly a black speck was seen descending with the speed of a meteor until it lay in the hand of the juggler.

The excitement was now beyond all control, and the people crowded round him to look at the peach that lay safely within his grasp. Extricating himself from the multitude, he struggled forward to where the mandarins were seated and handed them the mysterious peach that had come from the unknown land beyond the clouds.

They were almost too afraid to touch it lest there should be some magic about it that would work some terrible mischief upon them. Taking heart, however, as the juggler assured them that this was a fairy peach that would ensure them from sickness and would even confer upon them the gift of immortality, they ventured at last to taste it, when to their delight the most exquisite aroma filled the *yamên* with its fragrance, and they declared that never had the most luscious fruit that the gardens of earth had produced been so delicious as this wonderful peach that the juggler had given them.

The latter meanwhile had returned to his station and was gazing with an anxious look into the place in the sky where his son had disappeared. All at once the silken rope fell in coils at his feet, but no sign could be traced of him anywhere in the wide expanse of heaven.

The father's heart now seemed to be torn with anguish. "Miserable me," he exclaimed, "I have lost my son. The owner of the peach garden has discovered the theft and in revenge he has murdered him, and I shall never see him again." He wrung his hands as though he were in the utmost despair, and his distress was so extreme that everyone around him was moved to pity as they listened to his expressions of grief for the loss of his son.

In the midst of these lamentations, which were uttered in a wild and wailing tone, a most weird and tragic incident occurred to give emphasis to the heart-rending sorrow of the juggler. Suddenly from the blue there appeared an object descending with a motion that was as rapid as a cannon ball that had been projected from above. On it came till it fell directly at the feet of the man who was convulsed with sorrow. With a cry of horror he picked it up, when it was discovered that it was the head of his son. Almost immediately after a leg came hurtling through the air, until bit by bit the whole of the dismembered body lay at the father's feet. Weeping and sobbing he picked them all up and packed them carefully in his juggler's box, until he could buy a coffin and have them buried.

The man kept bemoaning the sad fate that had caused him to lose his son, and appealed to the mandarins and the crowd to subscribe sufficient funds to enable him to give him a decent burial. The call to the people was responded to most liberally, and soon his bag, into which he had put the donations, was filled with the cash that were poured upon him. Stepping up to the box in which the mangled remains of his son had been carefully packed, and tapping on it a number of times, he said, in a loud voice, "Son, will you not come out and thank the people for the generous way in which they have subscribed to give you a royal funeral?" At once, to the amazement and delight of the large numbers who had witnessed the performance, the box-lid was slowly uplifted, and lo, and behold! the son was seen standing smiling and bowing to the wondering crowd.

The rebound from the distress that they had all felt for the supposed death of the young man was so great that the wildest joy filled the hearts both of the officials and of the assembled crowds. Everybody moreover had been filled with amazement at the wonderful performance that they had witnessed that day, and so when they beheld him in perfect health, as though nothing had happened to him, the public feeling expressed itself in demonstrations of gladness and un- bounded joy. Every man was talking with his neighbor and speaking in admiration of the marvelous skill of the jugglers, when all at once it was discovered that the two men had mysteriously vanished and not left a single trace behind them. No one had seen them leave the *yamên*, but suddenly and without a word they and their boxes and the juggling apparatus had dissolved into the thin air. Everybody then knew that no common conjurors had been there that day entertaining the people, and that the tricks that had so astonished the assembled crowds could only have been performed by the fairies.

Several weeks went by and a marvelous change had come over the mandarins that had partaken of the fairy peach. The juggler had told them that the eating of it would confer immortality upon them. This they treated as a joke that was uttered at random by a man who was endeavoring to astonish his audience by the bravery of his words. As the days went by a subtle transformation, however, came over them that changed their whole thoughts about life. They were no longer anxious to amass money, and they utterly repudiated the idea of accepting bribes to influence their decisions in public matters. They had been previously famous for their rapacity and the shameless way in which they perverted justice. Their fame for integrity spread with marvelous rapidity throughout the district over which they ruled, and men spoke of them as the embodiment of the ancient sages of China. One day a great storm gathered over the city. The heavens were black with dense clouds that trailed along the earth and turned everything into midnight. The lightnings flashed and the thunders reverberated with terrific grandeur till every heart ceased almost to beat. It seemed as though it was some great occasion in which the powers of nature were called forth to give a fitting coloring to some momentous event that deserved more than a passing recognition.

When the sun shone forth once more, and the mist and clouds had vanished from the earth, it was discovered that these mandarins whose names were beginning to be household words in every home had suddenly and mysteriously disappeared in the midst of a flash of lightning that had startled and terrified the city, and that no trace of them could ever be discovered by any of their sorrowing friends and relatives.

The Strange Adventures of the Scholar Siu

Once upon a time there lived in the wild and mountainous region of Shansi a scholar of the name of Siu. Though still a young man he had gained the first of the four degrees that China is prepared to bestow upon the students of the empire, and he had shown such exceptional ability in the papers that he had written that the Imperial Examiner gave him a title that showed he had passed with honors.

In addition to the reputation that Siu had obtained for his literary ability, he had won the reverence and respect of the whole country side for his filial devotion to his widowed mother. There was no sacrifice that he was not willing to endure for her, and no self-denial that he was not prepared to undergo for her sake. His fame had traveled far and had even reached the land of the fairies, who were so moved by the stories that were told them about him that it was determined that whenever the occasion arose they would show their appreciation of his virtues by some special favor that they would bestow upon him.

The opportunity was not long in coming. One day Siu fell ill, and his disease seemed such a serious one that his mother's heart was wrung with agony as she witnessed the sufferings he had to endure.

As he lay tossing about on his bed one day, a man suddenly appeared at his bedroom door and with a polite bow and a most gracious smile invited Siu to get up and go with him. "I have brought a horse with me," he said, "for you to ride upon, and he stands outside waiting to carry you to the place to which I have to lead you."

Mr. Siu was greatly struck with the appearance of his mysterious visitor. He had a most gracious, but imposing manner with him, and he was dressed in robes such as only the highest mandarins are accustomed to wear. What impressed the sick man most, however, was the tender, winning way he had with him and the look of concern that he had upon his face as he gazed into the eyes of Siu and saw how he was suffering.

Little did the latter realize that the man that stood at the door with such a benevolent face was a fairy, who had come from the pearly gates of bliss to reward him by a signal piece of service for his loving devotion to his mother.

Siu excused himself from accepting the invitation of the unknown, by saying that he was too ill to think of taking a journey then, and that it was impossible for him even to lift, himself from his bed. The stranger, who had a masterful though perfectly courteous manner, still pressed him to get up and at once start with him. After a most vigorous but exceedingly painful effort, Siu managed to get out of bed and crawl to the door where he found a white horse fully caparisoned waiting for him.

The moment he got on the horse's back he seemed relieved from his disease, the pain and weariness from which he had been suffering entirely vanished, and life seemed to open up to him new possibilities. There was one thing that greatly astonished him as they rode along and that was that the roads and the scenery through which they passed were entirely strange and unknown to him. It seemed indeed that from the moment he left his home he was wandering in fairy land, for the scenes among which he had spent his life had vanished completely from his gaze.

After traveling for some time they came to what seemed to him like a royal city, the capital of an empire, for the walls were massive and lofty, like those that surround Peking, and there was a grandeur and a repose about them that showed that personages of exalted rank had their dwellings within them. Passing through one of the spacious gates, his guide led him by devious ways and along great thoroughfares, crowded with restless, throbbing crowds until at last they entered what was really the palace of the reigning king. Entering through the great gates, where shadowy-looking guards kept ward and watch, he was led through courtyard after courtyard into a magnificent pavilion, where about a dozen men splendidly attired were sitting in solemn silence as though they had been awaiting his arrival. The central and most commanding figure of them all Siu recognized from the pictures that he had often seen as being the dread King of the Land of Shadows, who ruled with despotic power over the region of the dead.

Siu had no doubt whatever that the imposing personage who acted as President of this venerable assembly was really the ruler of the underworld, and while he was debating in his own mind what this strange meeting portended, he was informed by the King that he was about to undergo an examination in order to test his ability and show what position he was qualified to fill in his kingdom.

He was then directed to a table close by on which were pens and ink and paper, and at which a solitary figure sat as though he too were to go through the same process that was demanded of him. Hardly was he seated when the Prince gave out the subject of the essay they were to write upon. It consisted of eight characters and was enigmatical enough to have been given by the Delphic Oracle. Freely translated the words meant "One man, two men; with high purpose, with no high purpose."

The two men sat down to try and discover the hidden meaning that the examiners had wrapped up in this cryptic sentence. Siu's mind was a philosophical one, and it soon flashed upon him that these words contained a profound teaching that lay at the root of all human actions.

The "one man" referred to the individual himself with his doubts and fears and with his wide world of thought. "Two men" included every other man outside of his own life, his neighbor in fact, with whom he was knit by bonds that could never be broken.

"With high purpose" pointed to the man who had a purpose in life, and kept that as the ideal from which he never willingly departed. The mistakes he might make or the errors of judgment into which he might fall could be easily condoned, because men felt that in pursuing the noble aims by which he hoped to enrich the world, those were but evidences of the frailty of human nature.

"With no high purpose" designated the ordinary run of men who take life as it is, and who have no intention of helping anyone but themselves. If they do anything that turns out to be really good and serviceable they deserve no credit for it, for it is not through pain and suffering that they have achieved it but by an accident.

When Siu handed his paper to the King, murmurs of admiration expressed the delight which he and the officials about him felt at the beautiful thoughts that gleamed like gems throughout it. Faces beamed with smiles, and eager whispered conferences were held among these great mandarins, and finally the Prince said to Siu, "We are profoundly impressed with the beauty of the essay you have just written and the exquisite thoughts you have expressed in it, and I have determined at once to appoint you to a high post in the province of Honan to which you will at once proceed."

These words were no sooner uttered than Siu as with a flash of lightning realized for the first time that he was no longer in the land of the living, but that he was really in that Land of Shadows and that he was face to face with the great King that was so feared by mortals. He was so paralyzed with the thought that his heart sank within him, and for a time he felt himself absolutely unable to utter a single word.

Recovering himself he besought His Majesty to listen to his humble petition. "I have an old mother," he said, "in my home, who is seventy years of age, whose heart will be bowed down with sorrow at my loss. Let me return to her, I beseech you, that I may comfort and care for her as long as she lives, and when death comes and I have offered the proper sacrifices to her spirit at the grave then I shall willingly come back and carry out the gracious plan you have so generously arranged for me."

The King looked down with compassion upon Siu and turning to one of the high mandarins by his side he said to him, "Bring me the Book of Life and Death that I may see how long the old lady has yet to live."

In a few minutes he returned and turning over its pages it was found that it was recorded that her life had yet nine years to run.

"Your prayer is granted," said the Prince to Siu, "and your companion here will take your place until your mother's death, when I shall again summon you to undertake the duties to which I have appointed you."

These words that filled the heart of Siu with profound satisfaction and delight had hardly been uttered when Yen Lo, with his attendant ministers rising from their seats, informed him that he was now at liberty to return to the life of the world that he had so recently left, and that until his mother died there would be no call upon him to appear again in the Land of Shadows.

Approaching the scholar who had been examined at the same time that he was, and who was to occupy his position until the time had elapsed when he was to take it up himself, he got into conversation with him and he found that he was a man of generous and enlightened views. He seemed dull, however, and depressed because Yen Lo had not given him a release and permitted him to return to his home in the land of sunshine as he had done to Siu. He talked of his friends from whom he had been torn, and he grieved that he should never again see the faces of those whom he loved so dearly.

As they were conversing, they, unconsciously as it were, strolled away from the great hall where the examination had been held. Siu indeed felt impelled by an impulse that he could not account for to be moving, although he had no definite purpose as to the direction toward which his steps should take.

Passing through several great rooms that lay in gloom and shadow, and descending magnificent flights of stone steps, they at last came to the palace gates through which they emerged into the streets of the city. Here the crowds were as dense and the thoroughfares just as narrow as could be found in the sunlit empire of the upper world. Siu noticed, however, that a gloom seemed to rest upon everything. No smiles lit up the faces of any of those that he met and no sound of laughter broke upon the air, nor did a single note of music anywhere dispel the universal air of melancholy that pervaded this solemn-looking city.

Drawn as it were by an unseen hand, they found themselves winding and turning down the intricate streets of this sunless city until at last they came to the huge and massive gates that led into the country that lay beyond the battlements that guarded the town. Coming up to these, Siu's companion stopped him and declared that he was not permitted to go any further with him, and in a few parting words he besought Siu when he returned to earth to visit his friends and tell them how he was and what were Yen Lo's plans for him in the future.

No sooner had he got outside the gates than he was surprised to find the stranger who had led him from his sick bed into the Land of Shadows waiting for him, and with the same winning smile and tender, gracious manner that had before won his confidence he informed him that he was going to conduct him back again to his home. Mounting the horses that had evidently been waiting for his arrival, they proceeded on their journey, through the same kind of scenery that had charmed and delighted him when he traveled through it before.

As they advanced on their way, Siu was conscious of a growing exhilaration that filled his heart with a pleasure that he had not known since he left his home. The atmosphere seemed too to grow brighter, and the gloom and shadows that permeated everything he had looked upon in Hades became tinged with a light that was never found in the Land of Shadows. Suddenly in the far-off horizon there gleamed such golden flames that the whole landscape was touched with their glory, and in an instant his courteous companion had vanished from his side, and the sights and scenes through which he had passed slowly melted into oblivion, and like a dream at the opening day had completely crept out of his memory as though they had never existed.

Siu's mother was sitting in her room desolate, and her heart was torn with anguish for the loss of her son. Her only hope and stay in life had gone out of it. He had been dead about twenty-four hours and had been laid in his coffin, but the lid had not yet been nailed down. All at once she heard a strange sound in the room where her son lay.

Rushing in she found to her amazement and delight that the son she had been mourning for as dead was alive and sitting up in his coffin. With tears, that gleamed like dewdrops through which the morning's rays were flashing, she expressed out of the fullness of her heart the joy she felt that he had in some miraculous way been brought back to life again, and that now they would be once more happy together as they had been in the days of the past.

It was some time before Siu could quite take in the whole situation. His journey to the Land of Shadows and his strange experience there had passed completely from his memory, so that he had no recollection of what had happened during the last twenty-four hours. He knew indeed that he had been very ill, but he never dreamed that he had died, and with a puzzled, anxious look, he asked his mother how he happened to be in a coffin, and what meant all these preparations for a funeral.

She explained that his severe sickness had seemed to terminate in death. The doctor had testified that he had presented all the appearance of one who had been bereft of life. They had consequently made all preparations for his funeral, and had he not so wonderfully recovered from the deep swoon into which he had fallen, he would in a few hours have been carried to the hillside and buried amongst his kindred who had departed this life.

"But let us not talk of that now," she said, with a beaming face and with eyes alight with pleasure. "We shall talk no more of death, for you seem to have recovered in a most remarkable way from the deadly disease, that we thought had carried you off."

Nine years went by and at last the mother died and was laid in her grave on the hillside. Siu with true filial devotion saw that everything was done that would minister to her comfort in the Dark World, and the offerings were made at her tomb that would prevent her being a hungry, wandering ghost in that gloomy land.

Full of sorrow at his loss, and sad and discontented in the home that seemed so desolate now that his mother was gone, Siu lay down to rest.

In the gray twilight of the next morning a stranger happened to pass by his home, and was astonished to see a wonderful procession of horses and high officials and attendants slowly wind away from the home of the scholar.

Next morning people awaited the coming forth of Siu from his room, but they waited in vain, for when they entered they found that his spirit had left him and that he lay calm and silent in death. The neighbors thought that it was sorrow for the death of his mother that had killed him. They little dreamed that it was a message from the Ruler of Hades that had summoned him away.

The Romantic Story of the Phoenix Fairy

Once upon a time in the famous province of Shensi, a region where the earliest traditions of the Chinese race have their origin, and where the men of to-day find the most stirring stories of the birth of this great Empire, there lived a young man of the name of Liu. His home was in the county of "Peace and Joy," and there the wonderful events that we are about to relate took place.

Liu was a remarkably good-looking young fellow and was endowed with abilities that were far beyond the common. It is related of him that when he was a lad of only fifteen years of age, he went in for his examinations for B.A. and though he was so young and could hardly have been expected to pass where several thousands of scholars were competing with him, he yet came out at almost the very head of the favored few that were happy enough to obtain the coveted degree.

He was a natural born genius, but as is often the case with very original characters, he was apt to be uncertain and unstable in his ways. He had been left an orphan while quite young and had fallen into very irregular and indolent habits, such as threatened to wreck his life and prevent him from attaining to the high position that nature intended he should occupy, through the profuse gifts with which she had endowed him.

Fortunately there was a kindly fairy who saw that the magnificent abilities that he possessed were being wasted, and he determined that he would do his very utmost to deliver him from the evil habits and turn him into a distinguished member of society.

By careful observation he saw that the young man was not radically bad, but rather, because there was no one who had authority to give him advice, he was drifting into habits that would lead to further deterioration of character. Our story will tell of the ingenious method that this kind-hearted being took to save Liu from the errors into which he had fallen.

One evening he had been invited by a friend to take supper with him, when he suddenly remembered that when he left home he had forgotten to put out the light. Fearful lest some accident should happen and that the house might be burned, he begged to be excused for a short time while he went and saw for himself that everything was all right. As he drew near to his dwelling, he saw that the light was burning brightly within, and, as he came close up to it, he heard the sound of persons talking to each other in a low voice as though they were discussing some matter that they did not wish anyone else to hear.

His first impression was that the people next door had something to do with this, for their character was not above suspicion, and he had long been fearful that there was something very morally wrong about them; or it flashed upon his mind that the voices he heard might be those of the fox fairies. As Liu had absolutely no fear of these mysterious beings, and indeed was anxious to meet one face to face, he rushed incontinently into his house, when to his amazement he saw a young man of singularly prepossessing appearance, and with a refined and scholarly air, sitting in his bedroom. No sooner did the stranger catch sight of Liu, than he became apparently paralyzed with fear, and making a rush for a side door disappeared through it, and vanished from sight.

Looking around the room, Liu discovered that he had in his hurry forgotten to take away with him one or two of his upper garments. These were of most curious workmanship and of materials such as he had never seen before. Evidently the fingers that had wrought the figures on these articles of dress were no human ones, neither had the stuff of which they had been made ever been woven in the looms of earth.

That the owner of them was a fairy, Liu had now no manner of doubt, for on examining them minutely he discovered to his amazement that one of them, a long gown, was of most delicate texture and as light as gossamer, and rendered the person invisible that had it on. Testing this point to see if it were true, he found that when he put it on he became absolutely invisible and that he could move about with the lightness and rapidity of a bird.

Carefully folding this up he put it safely away for future emergencies. He had hardly done so when a young man came into the room where he was sitting, and in a very humble tone and with a modest demeanor begged Liu to restore him the things that a friend of his had left behind him.

"Can you describe the things, that you say were left here?" Liu asked him.

"Certainly, I can," he replied, and he at once gave a minute description of the articles he came to claim. Liu, who knew the extreme value of the property claimed, for some time refused to deliver them up.

"I do not think that I shall consent to let you have them at all," he at last said.

"What right has anyone to come into my house when I am away, and take possession of it as though it were his own? I cannot conceive what motive the man had whose clothes you wish me to give up to you, and so I must be careful how I act in a case like this, lest others might take advantage of my good nature and come in when I am away and carry off some of my property."

The young man seemed greatly distressed at this decision of Liu, and begged and entreated that he should consent to reconsider it, for it was of the utmost importance to the owner of the clothes that he should be able to recover them. He offered that if Liu would grant his request he would provide a grand feast for him, where he would be regaled with all the delicacies of the season, and where eatables that had never been found on the tables of monarchs, and fairy peaches from the gardens in the Western Heaven, and flowers that never bloomed on earth, would grace the feast that would be spread for him and his friends.

Liu refused to consider this tempting proposal, and the young man then offered to give him a large sum of money that would be sufficient to enrich him for life, but he once more declined to be tempted even by this most seductive offer.

Leaving Liu for a moment, he went out, but returning almost in a moment, he said, "I have another proposition to make to you, which I hope this time you will be induced to listen to. If you will give me the things I ask for," he continued. "I will prepare a most beautiful bride for you, that shall be more comely and charming than any maiden that has ever been seen in all this region."

"Who is the lady you refer to," eagerly asked Liu, "and tell me more particularly what she is like."

"The maiden I shall bestow upon you," said the young man, "is named the Phoenix Fairy because of her grace of manner, and the beauty of her person. In all the annals of China there has never been any one of the celebrated beauties that have surpassed her in any of the charms with which she is endowed. Even Mo Hi and T'a Ki, whom poets and painters like to take as the ideals of every womanly grace and beauty, were in no way superior to the Phoenix Fairy who shall be yours, if you will only hand over to me the articles I am anxious to recover."

"I willingly agree to your proposal," said Liu, "and when you have produced the lady, I shall with pleasure hand you over the things that are in my keeping."

"I pray you not to make such terms with me. You must trust me; it would be quite impossible for me to produce the lady on the instant, but that she will come to you without delay you may be assuredly certain. The things I want from you are, for certain urgent reasons, needed at once, and so I beg of you let me have them now, and so relieve the anxiety of the person who had the misfortune to leave them behind when he fled from your room."

Seeing the real distress of the young man, and believing that the contract would be faithfully carried out, he consented to hand over the fairy possessions and believe that in due time his bride would appear.

Several days went by without the appearance of the lady that had been promised him, and he began to be suspicious that he had been deceived when, one evening as he was sitting in his study, the door was suddenly opened, and two men appeared in the doorway, leading in a young girl, who was strikingly beautiful, and who far surpassed the vision that his mind had conjured up when he had been promised a bride in exchange for the fairy garments that he had got in such an unexpected manner.

All the pictures that the most famous artists had drawn of the most celebrated beauties of the past seemed but tame and common placed beside this maiden, who, with a modest look, and with a person exquisitely molded and fashioned by nature in her brightest artistic attempts, stood in front of him.

"This is the lady," one of the men that accompanied her said, "who was promised to you a few days ago. She is yours, and you need not attempt to investigate into her parentage or from what land she comes. Be assured that the prize you have won is a rare one, for in all the world there is not a fairer nor more noble character than the girl that comes of her own free will to be your wife."

That the union was an exceedingly happy one was proved by the fact that the deepest and profoundest love sprung up in the hearts of them both for each other. It was an ideal marriage, and never in the romance of fiction, or in the fervid imagination of the poet, had such a pure and exalted love as that which existed between Phoenix Fairy and Liu been ever imagined or conceived.

Some months went by of extreme happiness to both, but the great purpose for which the fairies had interfered in the case was as far as ever from being accomplished. Liu instead of being impelled to a nobler and more strenuous life, led even a more easy and a less ambitious one than he had been accustomed to. There had been many times when he had been spurred to a noble exertion and had shown that he possessed abilities of a very high order. Since his marriage, however, to "Phoenix Fairy" it had seemed as though he had abandoned every noble aim in life, and settled down to be contented with the ordinary and humdrum routine that men with common minds so naturally fall into.

Something heroic, consequently, had to be done to save him, and the one to do that was his fairy wife, who mortal though he was, loved him with as passionate a love as ever woman felt for man in any time of the world's history. In playing her part she would have to take her share of suffering, but to emancipate her husband, and to arouse ambitions within him that would lead him to a higher plane than that on which he was now living, was a task that she alone could perform.

One morning, with a shadow on her face. Phoenix Fairy approached her husband and in a sad and mournful voice informed him that she would be compelled to leave him for a time, how long she could not say, but there were imperative reasons why she had to be separated from him. She could not reveal these to him now, but the day would come when she trusted they could be told him, and then he would see that they were such as would appeal to his judgment as being eminently wise and proper. The next moment she had vanished from his presence, and no trace could be found as to where she had gone.

Liu was in a terrible state of despondency, and it seemed for a long time as though the heroic measures that Phoenix Fairy had adopted to arouse her husband to a wider conception of his duties as a man would be an entire failure. Instead of trying to relieve the intense sorrow of mind that oppressed him, by taking up his studies that had been neglected so long, he became moody and silent.

For days together he spent his time in brooding over his loss. There was nothing in life that seemed to influence him, and his books lay in his study untouched by him, as though they had lost all their power over him.

The weeks went by but they seemed to bring no consolation to Liu, and it appeared as though he would sink permanently into an indolent misanthropic mood, from which it would be difficult to arouse him. Phoenix Fairy, who had been watching him all the time with a heart full of intense love, saw at last that it was time to intervene in order to save him from having his life completely wrecked.

One day Liu was climbing the mountain path that led to a famous temple when he saw a lady riding on a horse coming down the road towards him. She was closely veiled, but as she came up to him she lifted it slightly, and then to his unutterable joy he discovered that it was his wife, that he had begun to despair of ever seeing again. Phoenix Fairy, for it was she, at once dismounted, and sitting with her husband under the shadow of a huge tree, she spoke to him about the need there was to exert himself, and not to allow himself to fall into habits that would disqualify him for taking his proper place in the world.

Liu excused himself for his recent conduct by explaining that her disappearance had affected him with such a profound melancholy that he had found it simply impossible to overcome it, and he feared that if she saw no way to accomplish her return home, his hopes of happiness would be so blighted that he would never feel any incentive to work again.

Phoenix Fairy, with words of tenderness and love, endeavored to console him, and she reminded him that the length of their separation depended entirely upon himself. "The fates had so decided it," she said, "that unless he rose to the position that he might do by a strenuous use of the abilities with which heaven had endowed him, he would lose her for ever."

"This," she continued, "would be as great a sorrow for me as it could possibly be for you, and so I beseech you, by the love you bear for me, to dismiss your melancholy thoughts and give your heart to work in a way that you have never done in all your life before. Remember that your fortunes lie within your own grasp, but the only way in which you can seize them is by your books that you have neglected for so long a time."

"In order, however, to stimulate you to a new exertion," she said, "I will give you a picture of myself, that you can look upon whenever you get weary and want to see me. It will be such a living, striking one that when you look upon it, it will be as though I were standing before you, and I were a living reality with whom you could hold converse."

Saying this, she put into his hands a gold case, which she told him contained her portrait, so portrayed that, while he could see her figure distinctly, her face would never be visible to him unless he had been working hard at his studies. If he, therefore, loved her as he said he did, he could always through the medium of hard work enjoy a most realistic sight of her whenever he desired.

In a moment, as on one or two former occasions she vanished from his sight, and he was once more left with his heart full of heaviness and despair. By and by, he opened the case that Phoenix Fairy had given him and began to examine the picture of her that it contained. It was a rare product of the artist's genius; indeed, he felt convinced that it was no human hand that had drawn that beautiful figure, that stood out from the paper as though it had been a living being.

While he gazed upon it, he felt his heart throb with excitement as he saw what a perfect image he had of his beloved wife. She was in miniature, it is true, but there was such an air of reality about her, that a sense of companionship sprang up within him.

He fancied that he could see her breathing, for her form rose and fell just as a living, breathing person's would have done. The pose that she took was the one she naturally had on ordinary occasions, and her dress was the one that he admired the most of all among the various kinds in which she used to array herself.

The only disappointing thing about this exquisite reproduction of his wife was the fact that her face was turned away from him, and all that he was allowed to see was a back view of her. Long and eagerly did he look at the picture, hoping every moment that she would turn round and cast one of her lovely smiles upon him, but in vain. A view of her face, she had declared, could only be obtained through constant persistent work, and, as he saw her standing with her back to him, he realized that his only chance of happiness was by a steady application to his studies.

As soon as he reached his home, he hurried away to his sanctum, and collecting his books he laid out a plan of reading that meant severe toil and labor. He felt that if ever he was to gain possession of his wife again, he must be prepared to endure the greatest self-denial, and that the days of idleness in which he had so long indulged had passed away never again to be repeated until he had gained the very highest honors that the state could give him.

Placing the picture of Phoenix Fairy before him, where his eye could catch it whenever he lifted his head from his books, he began the study of those famous classics of China that were to be the means by which his beloved wife was to be restored to him.

After he had been studying hard for some months and had mastered some of the books upon which he would be examined by the imperial examiner in the course of a few months, he was one day immensely delighted to find that the figure of his wife in the picture had slightly turned round, and he could distinctly see her face smiling upon him. It was a side face it is true, but it was just enough to enable him to catch the beautiful expression that had always exercised such a charm over him, and to let him know that she was in a supremely happy mood because he was carrying out her desires in sedulously giving himself up to study.

His work once more assumed a different aspect from what it had done before this delightful change in the position of the figure had taken place. He had been highly comforted and inspired by the thought that a living image of his wife was close beside him, and that the atmosphere of her presence filled the room that would otherwise have been dreary indeed without her.

Now, however, a new feeling of delight filled his heart. The old musty books took on a new coloring, and the crabbed old-world works that seemed to lie with a look of defiance and mystery on their pages appeared to peer into his face with a facetious air, as though they were going to put some side-splitting conundrum to him.

After he returned with his new honors, a still further improvement took place in the attitude of the picture of Phoenix Fairy. The face was so far turned that he now could catch the whole of it, and he could see the love that beamed out of her eyes, and the smile of happiness that suffused her beautiful face.

During the year of study that Liu had to go through before taking his final degree, the sweet face of his wife was the one source of inspiration to him, and sometimes, when the labor became so irksome that he fain would have given it up for a time and taken a long holiday, the shadow that came over it, and the look of pain that quenched the smile, always prompted him to new exertions and to a more determined purpose to further strenuous effort. Then indeed he got his reward, for the look of affection deepened, and the eyes flashed, and the smile became the sunniest that ever lit up any human countenance.

Often in the long nights during the midnight hours when drowsiness crept over him, and a feeling of utter weariness seemed to put despair into his heart, would there come a voice from the picture encouraging him to persevere and telling that the toil and sorrow would soon be over, and then they would be reunited and life would be one long dream of happiness, never to be broken again by any separation.

Never had a pure woman's love acted with such magic power as did that of Phoenix Fairy. She had played a truly fairy part in the way in which she had changed an erratic genius into a first-rate scholar, with a mind and a purpose that were to fit him to take a high place among the rulers of his country.

In the final examination Liu excelled all his previous efforts, and came out at the head of all the scholars that had entered for examination in the Imperial Academy for that year. He entered the lists with fear and trembling and his courage would have utterly failed him had it not been for the magic influence that his fairy wife exercised over him in this supreme moment of his life.

Opening the case to have a last look at her, before he started for the Imperial Palace where the Dragon Emperor was to meet the candidates, with a start of surprise he noticed that the figure had turned quite round, and that now she was facing him. Her smiles, always beautiful, seemed ten times more so at this moment when his heart was so full of anxious fears. Tones too, distinct and audible, came from her lips, telling him that his long trial was over, and that to-day the greatest triumph in a scholar's life would be gained by him, and that he would come out the first of all the men that entered and gain the coveted title *chungyuan*.

No scholar can enter for the Hanlin examination unless he has successfully passed three previous ones. The men, therefore, that come up are the very pick of all the scholars in the empire. In this final competition, the man that comes out first is crowned with the title of *chungyuan*, and he becomes the famous man of the year. His name is flashed throughout the length and breadth of the land by telegraph, by couriers, and by the thousand mysterious ways that the Chinese have of transmitting news to the remotest corners of the empire, and it is posted up in all the literary guilds, and in almost every school and private study of the students and scholars of the eighteen provinces.

The prophecies of his beloved wife had come true, and when his name was posted up as the chungyuan of the year he felt that, now that he stood upon the highest rung of the ladder of fame, it was entirely due to her influence that his life had not turned out a failure instead of a brilliant success. Opening the case to look at the beautiful face of Phoenix Fairy, he started back in amazement to find that the figure had vanished and only an empty frame stared him in the face.

While he was perplexed and in distress a light touch on his arm caused him to look around and there, standing close by him, was his wife. "Our sorrows are over now" she said; "we have both suffered. You have had to endure toil and weariness of study, while I have had to bear the misery I felt in being separated from you. Now that is all over and we never need be parted from each other again."

From that time the lives of both ran smoothly. Liu rose to high office in the service of the Government, where he was distinguished not only for his executive ability, but also for the honesty and purity with which he carried out his official duties.

Mr. Tang, the Filial Son

In one of the hilly regions in the famous province of Hunan, there lived a farmer who, with his only son Tang, cultivated the few fields that had come down to him from his fathers. The farm was a very unproductive one, for it was situated on the slope of a hill, and the soil was thin, and continued crops of stones, that constantly recurred no matter how often they were picked up and cast on the road side, were the only ones that he was perfectly sure of gathering in at almost any season of the year.

The wonderful fertility of these fields in producing stones had been the marvel of all those who for generations had tilled them. Successive owners had diligently cleared the land, as they thought, of these indigestible products, but the next time they came to put the seed in, they found to their dismay that a fresh growth had arisen to usurp the place that the more legitimate crops were intended to occupy.

In addition to the trouble arising from the poor and scanty soil there was also the uncertainty of the weather to contend with. When the rains from heaven were abundant, just enough to meet the actual wants of the home could then be dragged out of the unwilling fields, but when these failed and the great, red-hot sun licked up every drop of moisture out of them with his fiery tongue, then famine would come sometimes and stare into the miserable shanty on the hill-side where father and son lived out their lonely, wretched lives.

Tang and his father were the only ones now left together. The mother had died and so had a sister and a brother. The stress of poverty had been too severe and food had been too scant, and the struggle with the fields that would have yielded enough for the support of the home if only the skies would have sent down a constant supply of rain, was so hard, that one after another laid themselves down in the bare and poverty-stricken cottage, and left the husband and son to work out the problem of how to keep body and soul together.

At last the father laid down his hoe for the last time, and Tang was left alone and solitary in the home where all the voices had ceased except his own, and the only sound that now could be heard were the cries of bitterness and agony that were wrung from his soul, at the loss of one whom he loved with all the passion of his heart.

The scene in the home of Tang was indeed a sad and a pitiful one. The hovel consisted of one large room about fifteen feet square. In two corners of it were two apologies for beds. They consisted simply of coarse planks laid on trestles, on the top of which was strewed some rice straw to disguise the hardness of the boards. An old cotton quilt lay tossed on each one, black with age and worn and tattered, showing the hard service they had both seen since years ago they were brought home from the nearest market town. The only articles of furniture in the room besides these were a rough, square table, two or three chairs, and the same number of stools. The floor was earthen and seemed rarely to have been swept, for dust and dirt abounded in every direction, but especially in the corners, where useless things were thrown with the indifference of the Chinese to neatness and tidiness. There was an utter absence of everything like comfort, and no attempt had been made by the dwellers in this wretched abode to add in the slightest degree to the home feeling of the place.

And now the father lay dead, worn out with the incessant toil that was necessary to meet the daily wants of the home and by the meager fare that had been gradually sapping his system, bringing on premature decay. The son, Tang, was a fine specimen of the young manhood of China. He was a well-formed, handsome-looking fellow and would have attracted the attention of even the most casual observer. He was, moreover, of a generous, loving disposition and had gained the admiration of the other dwellers on the hillside, who had been touched by his unselfishness and by his readiness to oblige whenever anyone was in need of his services.

He was now in the greatest distress of mind at the death of his father, to whom he had always been devotedly attached. He could not bear to think that every member of the home had been taken away, and that he should be left alone in the dreary cottage with none to speak to him or to comfort him. The idea of getting married was entirely out of the question, for he had not a cash with which to bless himself, and as for getting the hundred dollars that would be required to pay for the dowry of the bride, that sum was as much beyond the power of his obtaining as the moon would be if he had had any designs upon it.

The pressing difficulty, however, just now was the question of how he should bury his father. There was not a coin in the house, and without a certain amount of cash he could not go to the coffin shop in the adjacent market town and hope to get a coffin in which to lay the dead. He could not buy on trust, for he had no property that could be held as a guarantee that the cost of the coffin would ever be paid in the future. He did not dare to attempt to borrow from his neighbors, for they were all in nearly the same predicament as himself. Money was scarce. They had a certain amount of corn and potatoes that they had gathered from their fields for home consumption; but cash, the current coin of the realm, was conspicuous by its absence, in all the farmers' houses where Tang would have had a chance of borrowing enough to provide for the funeral of his father.

In this dilemma he thought of an expedient that showed the noble character of the man, and also the profoundly filial spirit with which he was animated.

Closing the door of the cottage where his father lay, he proceeded to a large and thriving mansion, where a rich man lived. Seeking an interview with him, he told him his story and offered, if he would advance him enough to bury his father, to become his slave for life, and faithfully work for him as long as he lived.

Fortunately the wealthy man was endowed with a generous spirit and was touched by the devotion of the young fellow who stood with a modest and yet manly air before him. He was also influenced by the fact that for a mere nominal sum he would secure the services of a hardy worker and one who, humanly speaking, would be able to serve him for many a long year to come. Moved by this double motive the rich man agreed to advance the money that would be enough to bury the old man in one of his own fields and to secure him a roughly-cut stone to place at the head of the grave so that his name might be remembered in the future when, perhaps, the son had passed away from the earth, and the neighbors had lost all memory of his existence.

A document was drawn up stating, in legal phraseology, that Tang had sold himself to be a life-long slave to so-and-so; that his identity might never be questioned, his hand blackened with Indian ink was impressed upon the paper, so that in case of any possible dispute hereafter he himself should stand as witness against himself The amount that had been agreed upon was handed over to Tang, who gave his father a royal burial.

The first duty that was set to the enslaved son was the task of looking after the extensive gardens, which were famous throughout the entire region. In this work, for which Tang had never had any special training, he disclosed such taste and such ingenuity in the cultivation of the beautiful flowers with which the rich man had stocked his grounds, that the owner of them was filled with delight that he had obtained such a genius as his own property and that he need never fear that he should be deprived of him in the future.

In the meantime, the conduct of Tang in his willingness to deprive himself of his liberty, in order to secure that his father should receive an honorable burial, had excited the wildest admiration wherever the story had been told. It turned out, however, eventually that it was a theme that had been discussed far beyond the limits of human life, and that the fairies were as much enamored of this splendid exhibition of filial piety as the mortals around him had been, and even more so.

A number of them felt so strongly on the subject that they decided that they should do something practical to show their appreciation of his conduct, and they met in council to deliberate what steps should be taken. It was considered that as Tang was now a slave it was highly improbable that he would ever have the means of purchasing a wife, or that if his master out of pity provided him with one she would be a woman of low degree, and quite unfit to mate with a man of such distinguished virtue as Tang. It was accordingly decided that one of their number named Flower should descend to earth and become his wife. This she at once consented to do, and she began her preparations to leave her home in the Western Heaven and to take upon herself the form and appearance of an earthly being.

One day Tang was busy among his flowers, when he was astonished to see a young lady walking leisurely from flower to flower and plucking the most beautiful ones she could find among them. Approaching her with great deference, he very gently and politely informed her that these flowers belonged to his master, who, he had no doubt, would be highly pleased to let her have as many as she wished if she would only apply to him. He was very strict, he said, about people plucking them without his consent, and if she would only allow him to conduct her into his presence, he was quite sure that he would give her permission to take her choice among the finest specimens in the whole of the gardens.

This she consented to do, and Tang led her up to the great house, where they were met at the door by the only daughter of the rich man, who started with amazement when she beheld a young lady magnificently dressed and of a most refined appearance, and more beautiful than any woman that she had ever beheld in all her life. She invited her to come in and, taking her into a private room, she looked at this mysterious stranger for an explanation of her visit.

Flower at once proceeded to explain that she was a fairy and that she had just arrived from the Western Heaven on a commission that she had been deputed to carry out. The girl, whose name was Pearl, opened her eyes wide with wonder when she realized that the beautiful woman in front of her was one of those mysterious beings that people often talk about, but who are rarely visible to mortal eyes. She listened with rapt attention as Flower explained how the fairy world had been greatly moved by Tang's self-sacrifice, and how, in order to reward him for his noble devotion to his father, they had agreed that she should be deputed to descend to the earth and become his wife. "I hope," she said, "that you will use your influence with your father to get him to consent to this arrangement, for not only will Tang be benefited by it, but your home will feel the effect of my presence, and prosperity will fill every heart with contentment."

The romance of the affair had a powerful attraction for Pearl, who, quite independent of any advantage that was likely to come to the home, was strongly inclined to go in heartily for the scheme of the fairies. There was an air of mystery, too, about the whole business. The idea of having a real fairy living together with them, with all the possibilities of strange adventures and miraculous exhibitions of power, had a fascination for her that at once enlisted her sympathies and her hearty co-operation.

When the rich man was consulted in the matter, and after he had seen Flower and had grasped the idea that she laid before him, he gave his most hearty consent, and in a few days the marriage was carried out amidst the greatest possible rejoicings and with feastings to which half the country side were invited. If Tang had been his son he could not have been more lavish in his expenditure, and everyone felt that, while he had been willing to sacrifice much in selling himself into slavery, he had certainly been amply rewarded in the royal entertainment that had been got up for him, and in the possession of a wife to whom there was no equal for beauty in all the country side.

At the end of a year a little son was born to Flower that seemed to make the happiness of the home complete, for a more perfect wife than she could not be found anywhere. Her self-denial in leaving the Western Heaven and living under human conditions had been loyally carried out by her, but now that she could leave a son with Tang to perpetuate his name and to make him feel that he was not alone in the world, she considered that her work was done, and that she was quite at liberty to drop her role as a mortal and resume the position she had voluntarily abandoned at the request of her fellow immortals.

One day, handing over the little infant to Tang, she said, "I am now going to return to the Western Heaven, for I consider that the special service I was commissioned to perform has been accomplished. I am a fairy as you have always known and, though for a time I have taken the form of a woman and have striven to do my duty to you as a wife, my home is far off and I must hasten back to it. I would advise you now to marry one of your own kind who will keep your home after I am gone, and who will care for your little son. Pearl is deeply in love with you and would make you an excellent wife. Her father, I think, would have no objections to your becoming his son-in-law, and so I advise you to marry her. As for me you will never see me again," and even as she was uttering these last words, her form became shadowy and indistinct, and when Tang would have put out his hand to detain her she was gone, and every trace of her had vanished.

As the fairy had discovered, Pearl, from the very first day in which Tang had come into their home, had lost her heart to him, and now that the astounding news had flashed through the house that the fairy had disappeared never to return, her heart bounded with delight, and a great hope sprang up in it that after all she might be able to be wedded to him. Chinese propriety, however, forbade that she should utter a thought on this delicate subject, for in this land of China the settling of marriage is left to the friends, while the young man and the girl must be content to stand by speechless while arrangements that are to affect the whole of their lives are left to other hands to arrange.

The female members of the household had, however, long seen Pearl's ill-disguised affection for Tang, and they all believed that a marriage between the two would be the most admirable thing possible. Tang was of such a generous, manly spirit that he had gained the affection of the whole household. It is true he was a slave and socially far below the position that Pearl occupied. Still, he was not an ordinary slave who had been bought in the market and who had the low, debased feelings that such men usually have. His being a bondservant was the source of the highest honor to him, and his having become so was the theme of admiration among the dwellers in the Western Heaven. He had a son, too, that was born of a fairy and any woman that could claim the privilege of calling him her son would indeed be a happy one, for honors and wealth were sure to be showered upon the house to which he belonged. With these feelings in the minds of all in the home, the marriage of Pearl with our hero was a thing that was easily accomplished. No delay was needed, for there was no mourning required for a dead wife, and etiquette was not called in to decide how long the bereaved husband should remain single before he took another partner to preside over his household.

And now once more, the home of the rich man resounded with the sounds of laughter and rejoicing. The marriage festivities were on an unusually splendid scale. A year ago they were considered to be specially fine, but now they surpassed anything one had ever dreamed of before. Of course, there was a reason for this. Last year it was the marriage of a dependent, but now, it was the bringing of a distinguished son-in-law into the family, who had been honored by the notice of a heavenly visitor and whose name and virtues would shed luster upon the home for many a generation yet to come.

The years went slowly by and the son of the fairy when he was old enough was sent to school. There happened just then to be a famous scholar who had settled in the neighborhood, to whom the young lad was sent, in order to study the intricacies of the Chinese language, and to be initiated into the mysteries of the great books that every student has to master if would hope to attain to eminence in the empire. From the first, the lad showed that he was possessed of unusual abilities. He was a perfect genius in the way he absorbed learning and in the original thought he showed in grasping subjects that only men of unusually profound judgment would ever endeavor to grapple with. The result was that in the literary examinations he passed with the highest honors, and there was every promise that he would ultimately attain to the very highest positions in the gift of the state.

His teacher was so delighted with the success of his pupil that he confided his own history to him. He said, "You have never known that I am a fairy that has voluntarily come to earth in order to serve mankind. The fairies, you must know, have the good of the world laid upon them, and wherever they can see an opportunity of benefiting men they eagerly seize upon it, even though it may be at the cost of pain and suffering to themselves.

"The fairies are not the light-hearted creatures that they are often supposed to be, simply flying about on the mountain slopes, or careering through valleys, and always planning amusements for themselves. Happy times they have in abundance, but it is mainly in their efforts to benefit the human race that they find their highest sources of enjoyment. It is for this reason that there are so many scattered throughout the world at the present moment, all engaged in the noble effort to alleviate the sorrows of men, or to stimulate them to nobler and more unselfish lives than they could possibly live by any efforts of their own. It is this too that explains why your mother consented to come and live as a wife to your father, not simply that she might comfort him in his sorrow for the loss of his father, but that she might by her self-sacrifice induce others to imitate his noble example in love and devotion to their parents. My object too, in living here for years is to instill in the hearts of the youth of this neighborhood a love for learning such as shall give them noble ideas and qualify them to become leaders of thought in the government of their country."

The young scholar was deeply moved by the revelation that this distinguished teacher had just made to him, and he felt his heart drawn to him not only because he had so successfully led him along the road of scholarship but also because he realized that they were of a kindred race, and had things in common that not merely mortal man could dare to aspire to. He expressed his delight at the wonderful news he had given him, and he asked him if he would assist him in the one great purpose of his life and that was to discover where his mother was. Latterly he had had an intense longing to see her, but he could think of no plan by which this purpose could be accomplished.

The teacher replied that he had a number of books in his possession that he thought by a reckoning that was familiar to him, the secret of where she was and what form she had assumed would be revealed to him. A few days later, he called the young student into his study, and he said to him, "I have worked out the problem you gave me the other day, and I have found that Flower is now in the neighborhood of a certain lake not far from here, and that she has taken the shape of a crane. I advise you at once to go to the border of the lake and watch the passage of these birds. You will soon observe that seven of these fly in a flock and keep company with each other. They are all fairies and one of them is your mother. You will recognize her from the others, by the fact that she has one of her wings drooping, as though she had been wounded. She flies low too and as she passes by try and seize her. If you succeed in doing this she will not attempt to escape, but will reveal herself to you."

Full of joy and believing that he would soon have the inexpressible pleasure of seeing the mother whom he had long desired to behold, he hastened to the lake and took up his abode in a small cottage on the shore. After dawn he saw the white wings of a flock of cranes gleaming in the sun. They were flying in his direction, and breathless with nervous anxiety he soon saw that there were just seven, the number that his teacher had taught him to expect. One of them to his great joy had a drooping wing, and as it was flying low over his head he managed to grasp hold of it, at the same time crying out with a passionate voice, "Mother! Mother! Mother!" In an instant the crane was changed into a beautiful woman, with the form and features that had often been described to him by his father and by those who knew her years ago when she lived as the wife of Tang in the home in which he had been reared.

With a tender and loving voice she said, "My son, I may not stay with you, our destinies lie in different directions. You must work out your life on earth by a noble and strenuous manhood. I have passed through all the stages by which men become emancipated from the evils that press upon humanity, and now my energies must be devoted to assist in uplifting men and women who have within them the ambition to live a nobler life. I shall never, therefore, see you again after to-day, and do not attempt to seek me, for the search will be in vain."

She then gave him a golden gourd, telling him it would act as a talisman and save him from any great misfortune that might threaten him. He was to be sure, however, to remember that the charm would work only so long as he kept his noble ideal before him, for its virtues would cease to exist the moment that he allowed the passions of his heart to influence and master him.

"Here is another one," she said, "that I also give you that you are to present to your teacher. He may possibly close his door and refuse you admittance when he knows that you are coming with it, for he is a fairy and he would understand while you were on your way the purpose for which you were coming."

With a look of ineffable sweetness, and one that lingered in his memory as long as he lived, the fairy mother vanished and not a trace of her was seen either in the air where she might have flown as a crane, or along the shore where everything was visible for miles.

Hastening away to fulfill his mission to the teacher, he found, when he arrived at his house, that the door was fast closed and bolted, and though he knocked loudly and long their seemed to be no one inside to open it. Seeing a little side window open he threw his gourd among the books that were the precious possession of his teacher, and that were lying about in all directions just as he was accustomed to have them when he was studying. No sooner had it touched them than an explosion took place and every book in the room was instantly in flames. Among them were the magic manuscripts by which it was possible to discover where his mother was. These in a few minutes were a mass of cinders, and so all possibility of discovering any trace of her whereabouts was entirely lost for ever.

This was precisely what Flower intended should be the case when she gave the golden gourd to her son with the minute directions as to how he was to employ it. His teacher mourned over the loss of his books, and he assured his pupil that not even he with all his knowledge of magic could ever again assist him in his search for his mother. The young man accepted this as final, and from this time he applied himself with such intensity to his studies that he rose to supreme eminence in the empire and was appointed to some of the highest posts in the service of the Government.

Soat-Lip and the Youthful Fairy

THE HERO OF THIS STORY WAS A CHINESE SCHOLAR WHO HAD HIS HOME IN THE northern portion of the empire. His family was of a poor and humble origin but Soat-Lip was a man of a charming disposition. Though he had risen from this lowly rank, there was a native refinement about him that was not solely the result of his studies, but was inherent in the very texture of the man. That a finer strain ran through him was manifest from the fact that he was a poet of no mean order. His thoughts and his vivid imagination were constantly carrying him beyond the dull gray fact of life around him, and he had caught visions of a world into which ordinary mortals had never dreamed of treading.

He had made many friends, mainly because of his naturally sweet and generous character, but none of these had been able to deliver him from the grinding poverty that rested upon him and his home, and there seemed no way by which he could be delivered from the constant anxieties with which an inability to meet the necessities of his home daily oppressed him.

If he had only been a little more enterprising he could have easily made his way, for he was a scholar of no mean ability, and there were many rich men in the neighborhood who would have been willing to have secured his services as tutor to their sons. He was of a shy, diffident disposition, however, and he shrank either from thrusting himself forward or from leaving his home, where he could indulge in the luxury of wandering in imagination into the regions of fancy and romance, and where he could catch fleeting visions of wondrous scenes that no mortal eye had ever gazed upon.

At last there came a change in the fortunes of his life that was to break in upon dreary monotony of a struggle for existence. One day a letter arrived from a distant province from an old student friend who was a county magistrate in an important city there, urgently inviting him to come and pay him a visit. He told him that he had long desired to see him, and, besides, he hoped from his official position in the county that he would soon find means of procuring some employment for him that would deliver him from all want in the future. In order to show that this invitation was not a mere matter of form but a real evidence of his affection for him, he sent him an order on one of the native banks for a good round sum to meet the expenses of his long journey across the country.

Soat-Lip was delighted with this proof of the friendship of his companion with whom he had spent many a pleasant day when they were studying together for their degree. It seemed indeed as though the clouds had at last lifted from his life and a new inspiration had been given to his thoughts. The only trouble was his mother, whose heart was struck with a chill as she thought of the hundreds of miles that would separate her from her beloved son, and of the possibility that she might never see him again. She would have much preferred to have gone on as they had been doing, even though the life they had been leading was one of great privation, rather than be parted from the one human being in whom it might be said that her whole soul was entirely wrapped up.

The son, though he loved his mother dearly, and did not wish to be parted from her, felt that the chance in his life had come to him at last, and that his friend the mandarin would soon find some opening for him where he would be able to make enough money to enable him to support his mother in a better way than he had been able to do in the past, and he reasoned with himself that it would be highly culpable in him if he neglected to take advantage of it.

Accordingly, after making preparations for the long journey that lay before him, and after having made full inquiries as to the route by which he should travel, he one fine morning with a sad and sorrowful heart bade good-by to his mother, and turned his face in the direction of the region where his friend lived.

The latter had been so generous in supplying him with funds for his journey that he found he would not require them all, and so he was able to leave a nice little sum with his mother, to enable her to carry on until he could send her more from the distant home to which he was going.

After several weeks traveling Soat-Lip at length arrived in safety at his journey's end, and to his consternation and his horror he found, when he entered the *yamên* expecting a hearty greeting from his friend, that he had died a week or two ago and a new man had been appointed in his place.

Soat-Lip was stunned with this intelligence, for he found himself stranded in this far-off city with absolutely no means at his command. He had been so certain of being received and cared for by his friend that he had spent all the money that had been so generously sent him, and he was left with only enough cash in his pocket to meet the necessary expenses for food and lodging for the next week or so.

To a man of his easy-going temperament this was a trial that seemed for the moment as if it would crush him. In monetary matters he had never been accustomed to think for himself. His mother had done all this for him, but now he could not turn to her for consolation, for he was separated from her by hundreds of miles, and he had not a single friend amidst the teeming crowds that jostled him on the streets that he could appeal to for assistance.

In this dilemma, the latent powers of the man, that had hitherto remained dormant within him, seemed to start into life. He must do something at once or in a few days he would be starving. He had never had such an urgent question as this to deal with before, for his mother, who was a woman of great resources of mind, had seen to it that the difficulties of housekeeping should never be laid upon him.

Wandering in the outskirts of the town and deeply engrossed with the thought as to how he should get employment, he came to the doors of a great temple where men and women were coming and going, evidently worshippers of the great god Tai Shen, that was enshrined within, and whose reported powers of protecting people in all the emergencies of life had drawn great numbers from far and near to its shrine.

Sauntering idly through its courts, and watching the worshippers who, with a business-like air, were burning their incense and tossing their divining rods in the air, Soat-Lip walked aimlessly around, his mind absorbed with the one perplexing question as to how he could get into some position where he could earn enough to keep body and soul together.

Soat-Lip was a pleasant, gentlemanly-looking young fellow, and had a face that won the attention even of the casual observer. An elderly priest with his shaven head and slate-colored robe, who was moving about amongst the worshippers, observed him and touched by the magnetism of his person was led to study him more carefully.

He noticed that there was an anxious, worried look about him that seemed to make him oblivious to everything around him. He walked up and down amidst the groups that had collected to worship, but he saw nothing of what was going on, so absorbed was he in his own thoughts.

Coming up to him he remarked that he was evidently a stranger and had come to this place from a far-off region. They soon got into conversation and the young man, drawn by the sympathy of the priest, told him his story, and related how he had been stranded in this town without money and without friends, and without the means of returning to his home in a distant province. He was so distressed with this thought, he continued, that he had no eyes to see anything or thoughts to consider aught but his own miserable condition.

The priest, really sorry for the scholar, suggested that he might come and stay with him in the temple and do some copying for him. He could not give him any salary, he said, for the temple was too poor to allow of that, but he could give him his board and lodging as long as he liked to remain with him, or until he could get some remunerative employment that would relieve him of his present anxiety. Soat-Lip was overjoyed at the proposal, and the priest, leading him to the rear of the temple, showed him a little room that he said he might consider his own as long as he might think it necessary to be a guest.

Several months went by and Soat-Lip was exceedingly happy as far as his immediate wants were concerned, but he was greatly distressed about his mother. She was very poor and would have to earn her living, for he knew that by this time the money he had left with her would be nearly expended. He saw no way of earning enough to enable him to make the long return journey that would have taken him home, and so many a sorrowful hour he spent in bemoaning the unhappy fate that prevented him from easing the lot of one whom he loved so dearly.

One beautiful morning in winter, when the snow lay thickly on the ground and the whole landscape sparkled under the rays of the sun that rode in an unclouded sky, Soat-Lip went for a walk through the country, tempted by the beauty of the scenery and anxious to dispel the gloomy thoughts that oppressed his mind, when he thought of his unlucky fortune and his inability to do anything for his mother.

Wandering carelessly along he passed through a small hamlet and was much struck by one house in it. While he was looking at it, a young man with a most handsome and winning countenance came to the door, and, seeing him, courteously invited him to come in and rest awhile. Little did Soat-Lip dream that from this moment his fortunes were about to be changed, and that the shadows that had rested upon them for so long in the past were to be for ever lifted.

He found to his amazement when he entered the house that it differed very much from the ordinary run of dwellings, and was furnished in a style that only the very wealthiest in the land could have afforded. The walls were hung with the most exquisite draperies of silk and satin, while pictures by the most famous artists, which must have cost a great deal of money, gave the impression that the owner of the house must be a man possessed of a very considerable fortune. There were signs too that he was a man of culture, for, as was quite unusual even in the house of the literati of China, books lay about conspicuously as though reading was a constant habit in this home. They were elaborately got up too, and were of the rarest and most expensive editions.

Soat-Lip, being a scholar, was greatly interested in this, and his eyes kindled with delight as he took up one volume after another with which he was familiar. There was one, however, among them that he had never seen nor even heard of before. Looking at the title he saw it was called "The Story of the Land of Fairies." It was lavishly illustrated with pictures of that unknown country, and the figures of fairies in every imaginable position and grouping crowded its pages. Turning to the young man, he said, "What a remarkable book this is, and how did you manage to get such a rare and fascinating edition."

The young man seemed to evade answering this question and politely asked Soat-Lip to be seated while they sipped the tea that a little slave girl had just brought in. Sitting and enjoying the delicious aroma of the fragrant Bohea they were drinking, their hearts seemed all the more drawn to each other, and before long Soat-Lip found himself telling the story of his life to this stranger that he had known only a few brief moments.

His young host showed such extreme sympathy in his strikingly beautiful face that he seemed compelled to confide in him his troubles and to tell him what distress of mind he was in at the present moment in being so far away from his home, without any hopes of earning enough to enable him to make the long journey that lay between him and his mother.

After Soat-Lip had concluded his story, the young man, who had shown the most lively concern both by his attitude and by the emotions that swept over his very speaking countenance, said "But why do you not open a school? With your abilities and scholarship there are no reasons why you should not be able in the course of a year or so to lay up enough to enable you to return to your home. If you do not think it too much beneath you, take me as your pupil and come and live with us, and I guarantee that all your troubles will be at an end, and we will care for you as though you belonged to our own family.

"I must explain to you," he continued, "that my name is Hong Hu, and that we originally came from the province of Shensi, where our home is. In consequence of a great misfortune we removed from there and for the time being we have taken up our residence here. My father is an old man, and I am sure will be ready to fall in with the plan I have suggested to you, for he has long wished to engage a scholar like yourself to continue my education, which through our troubles has been very much interrupted."

In a few minutes a white-haired old gentleman, full of dignity but with a most loving, gracious manner entered the room and began to thank Soat-Lip for his condescension in promising to teach his son, and he insisted that he should at once take up his abode with them and feel that he was no longer amongst strangers, but that he was really adopted into their family, where he should receive the same treatment as though he were one of his sons.

In such an abode of bliss Soat-Lip began to be pleasantly conscious that the burden that had so long oppressed him had rolled as it were off his shoulders; and now that he had the funds to send to the relief of his mother, he felt that life had assumed a totally different aspect.

In such happy circumstances did the education of Hong Hu commence. Soat-Lip found that he was a man of extraordinary mental powers, and that the mastery of the Chinese literature in which scholars were educated at that time presented no difficulties whatsoever to him. He never wearied in the fervent devotion to his teacher that he had manifested from the very beginning, and he never lost any of his affection for him. Not only had he enriched him with considerable presents of money, but he had also arranged a marriage for him with a beautiful cousin of his.

Soat-Lip was exceedingly happy in his new home, when one day Hong Hu came to him with a clouded face, and told him that he was going to leave this locality for ever, for circumstances had arisen that made it expedient for him to remove to a distant region, and that this would also involve his separation from him for an indefinite period.

"I should advise you," said he, "to return to your mother together with your wife, while I take the way that fate shall lead me. You need not, however, be troubled by any fear of the long, weary road that lies between you and her. I wish you, therefore, to hurry up your preparations for departure as speedily as possible, for there are serious troubles before me and my family that I must as a matter of life and death avoid at all costs."

On the morrow, when everything had been packed up and had been laid in the open courtyard ready to be removed, Hong Hu, calling to Soat-Lip, asked him to come out with his wife. "You are now going to your mother," he said, "but will require a great deal of nerve to carry out the orders I have to give you. I want you, however, to have perfect faith in me, and no harm can possibly happen to you, but if you should disregard the directions I am going to give you, your life will be sacrificed and you will never see your ancestral home again. As for your wife, I have no fear, as she belongs to the same race as myself, and many a journey has she taken more perilous than the one you are going to make to-day."

Taking hold of the hands of each of them he sternly gave the command that on no account were they to open their eyes for an instant, for that would cause disaster and death to Soat-Lip at least. Having seen that this order was faithfully obeyed, in a loud, imperious voice he cried "Ascend," and in an instant like a flash of lightning that has gleamed across the sky they were rushing through space and, borne up by billows of air, were traveling at a rate that made it difficult for him to breathe.

Terrified by the danger that had been threatened him if he dared to look out for an instant upon the weird scene through which they were being shot, Soat-Lip had sufficient command over his nerves not to lose his presence of mind, and hardly had he time to realize the supreme danger in which he was placed, when the same commanding voice exclaimed "We have arrived," and feeling the touch of earth under his feet, he opened his eyes and found himself with his wife and all his belongings in the courtyard of his old home. Hong Hu, however, had vanished and not a trace of him was to be seen, though Soat-Lip made anxious search for him in all the region around about.

The delight of the mother may easily be imagined when she saw her son, whom she had long mourned, actually standing in her presence with his beautiful wife, shy and nervous-looking, as though doubtful of the reception she was going to receive from her mother-in-law. Any fears, however, that the young wife might have entertained were soon dissipated by the warmth of the greeting that was given her, and by the tender look of love that was flashed upon her and her husband by the delighted mother.

Soat-Lip now, having ample means at his command, devoted all his leisure time to the prosecution of his studies. He was so successful in these that he took his degree of Master of Arts with honors, and in time was appointed a mandarin. Honors and wealth seemed continually to be thrust upon him, and now the only regret in his life was that his dear friend Hong Hu, to whom he traced all his prosperity, had so completely vanished out of his life that there was no trace left by which he could ascertain whither Hong had disappeared.

Walking along the road one day he saw a man on horseback approaching him. There was something so familiar about his appearance that he was startled, and waiting for his coming up he discovered to his great joy that it was the long lost Hong Hu, for whom he had mourned for several years.

While he was expressing his delight and his unbounded joy at once more meeting with him. Hong Hu, with fear and terror printed on his countenance, told him in hasty words that he and his whole family were in the most deadly peril. "We are fairies, as you know ere this," he said, "and certain demons who have a grudge against us have plotted to destroy us, and unless you come to our assistance we shall all perish."

Soat-Lip declared that his life and all that he had were at Hong's disposal and that he had but to show him how he could serve him, and he would shed the last drop of his blood to prove his devotion. Dismounting from his horse, Hong Hu expressed his thanks and told him that in a few minutes his courage would be put to a severe test, for his enemies were already on their way to endeavor to destroy him "and with his death your whole family will become their victims, and every member of it, including even your wife, who is one of our clan, will be exterminated."

"Take this sword," he said, "and hold it high in the air and strike whatever comes near you. Only swerve not and show no fear, for to do that would mean death to yourself as well as to us."

He had hardly done speaking, when the sky became suddenly darkened with dense masses of clouds that seemed to be flying in terror before some great tornado that was blowing behind them. The lightning flashed and the thunders crashed on high as though the world were coming to an end, when all at once, out of the commotion and from amidst the horrible darkness that prevailed, there seemed to rush out a figure darker than the gloom from which it emerged. It made straight for Soat-Lip as though it would overwhelm him and crush him out of existence.

Forwarned by Hong Hu, he held his ground with unflinching bravery, and striking out with his sword he felt a terrible shock that flung both Hong Hu and himself to the ground. When he came to himself once more, he found his friend lying on the ground, pale and stricken and apparently lifeless, but after a little he sat up and examining himself he found that beyond the shock of the onslaught of his inveterate foes he had received no damage whatsoever.

The sky too by this time was serene and clear, and the sun as though in congratulation of their escape was filling the heavens with his beams, and was causing the hills and the wide-spreading landscape to be filled with a glory that seemed to make them belong to a fairy world rather than this.

Hong Hu soon parted with Soat-Lip, telling him that his destiny lay elsewhere and that probably he should never see him again, and thanking him warmly for the service he had rendered him. From this time forward happiness and prosperity were the lot of the latter and for many years he lived a happy life with his fairy wife, his only regret being that he could not have the company of his well-beloved friend and benefactor Hong Hu as well.

The King of the Nine Mountains

In the county of Eternal Spring in the province of the Western Mountains, there lived in early days a scholar of the name of Li. He was a wealthy man, for considerable property had been handed down to him from his forefathers. He was, moreover, a man of more than average ability and had so far distinguished himself that, in the examination for B.A., he had easily come out the very first in the list of those who had been able to obtain this coveted degree.

Li was a man, however, of a mean and sordid disposition, and instead of keeping up the family reputation by a wise and liberal use of his money he was so miserly that he allowed the ancestral mansion to fall into ruins, while he occupied a miserable shanty on the borders of the land which had been left him by his fathers. His spirit too was contemptible and he was wanting in that large and liberal way of looking at men and things that a mind cultured such as his was, and imbued with the noble sentiments that he had learned in the works of the sages, should have been able to do.

One day an old man came to him and said he was going to remove into his neighborhood, and as it was difficult to obtain a house that would be suitable, he proposed renting the old family home from him, and offered to pay him a hundred taels annually for the use of it.

Li at first declined the offer and explained that the house he spoke of was really in a most dilapidated condition and quite unfit for anyone to live in. After some little further conversation, during which the old man informed him that he knew all about the condition of the house, but that he was still prepared to rent it for the sum he had mentioned, Li finally agreed, though he had his suspicions that everything was not all right, and that the old gentleman had some motive for taking a house that was positively uninhabitable.

The next day, the villagers were greatly excited by seeing a splendid procession of horses and carriages that passed along the main street. There were young men riding on the horses and what appeared to be the families were seated in the carriages. There was something very much out of the ordinary in the appearance of this striking cavalcade. There was an air of distinction about them that proclaimed them to belong to society that was far superior to any that existed in that part of the country.

The young men sat on their horses with a dignity that would have suited them had they been Princes of the Blood, while the women, both young and old, looked as though they had recently come out of a palace. The horses too were of a breed that evidently betokened a high lineage. They were sleek and well fed, and they champed their bits and tossed their heads in the air, and seemed to realize that they were different from the scarecrows that were working in the fields, and which appeared to cast sidelong glances of envy at them as they pranced by.

In wonder and amazement the villagers hastily collected to see this remarkable sight. The women gathered in knots to gaze upon it, and mothers picking up their babies stood at their doors, and with a strange look in their eyes and mouths wide open with astonishment they remained spell-bound while the grand possession moved by. A number of men impelled by curiosity followed close in the rear to see where it was going to, and people could hardly believe their eyes when they saw it proceed steadily on till it entered the old ruined house that had been rented from the scholar Li. Without any stoppage, and without the faltering of a step, the horses with their riders, and the carriages with their brilliant occupants, as well as the numerous attendants that followed on foot, behind, entered within the gray and ruined walls, just as though they had passed through the noble archway of some great castle, and were being received with all due ceremony in the spacious courtyard by the Governor.

The sight was so amazing that the crowd ran in the wildest excitement to the shanty where Li lived and asked him who these grand people were that has just entered in such style and with such magnificence the ruined home of his fathers. He was mightily astonished when he was told what a splendid procession of equipages had just disappeared within its walls. "I never heard a sound," he declared, "of horses' feet and was quite unaware that anything whatever had been taking place such as you are talking about."

It was then remembered by the knowing ones, which in their amazement at the time they had not noticed, that no sound had proceeded from the horses' feet and no crunching of the gravel on the roads had been produced over it, and so, of course, it was impossible that Li should have heard the sounds that on ordinary occasions would have aroused the deepest sleeper from his slumbers.

Hurrying out with the crowd that had been growing all the time, in the direction of the dilapidated house, he pointed out to them that they must certainly be mistaken, for no signs of horses' hoofs could be detected on the soft grass of the grounds outside the house, and no carriage ruts had made a single indentation in the loamy soil of which they were composed. When they reached the old forsaken home and rushed in with wonder in their eyes to look for the procession that only a minute or two before had swept by in such proud array, they could not find a single trace of it.

The old house had evidently never been disturbed. The rank grass still grew about the main entrance and forced its long green leaves through the crevices of the great slabs of stone with which the courtyard was paved. Climbing vines crawled up the walls and seemed to be playing hide-and-seek through the stone windows that gave a dim light to the rooms within. Great bloated spiders, that spun their long trailing webs and let them fly like streamers from the blackened rafters, reveled in their undisturbed possession of the gloomy chambers. If would seem indeed as though nature had taken up her abode where men should have lived, and with her usual industry was working out her plans and filling the house with signs of her handiwork.

By-and-by the crowd dispersed, sullen and discontented, for the scholar had jeered at them because of their folly and declared that they had all been dreaming and that the horse-men and the carriages and the gay troupes of men and women existed only in their imaginations. This was hard to bear, for the whole village had seen them, and it was impossible to be conceived that so many people in broad daylight should have with one consent declared that they had seen something which after all had no existence in fact.

There was no denying that the old house into which a number of people had seen the splendid cavalcade enter and disappear from their gaze was absolutely empty when they entered in search of them. There were no signs that the place had been disturbed by any visitors, but was in precisely the same condition that it had been in for several years.

A week or two later after this strange occurrence, the old gentleman who had rented the house from Li paid him a visit and asked him if he would not do him the honor of making a call upon him. "I have been rather remiss," he said, "in doing my duty to you. I have really been so busy in repairing and enlarging the house that I could not possibly come earlier. The building you know was in a very dilapidated condition and required a vast amount of renovating to make it habitable for my large family. All the necessary work, however, I am glad to say, has been completely finished, and I shall be happy if you will come and take pot luck with us to-morrow at noon, when my son who has come of age, and for whom we are making a party, will be happy to entertain you."

On the next day at the appointed time Mr. Li made his way toward his old ancestral home, wondering how it was going to be transformed, so that it should be made fit to become the residence of a wealthy family. As he drew near he was astonished at the amazing change that in some mysterious way had been effected in it. He had never seen any signs of builders or masons about it, and no workmen were known to have been engaged to rebuild and beautify the tumble-down, old building, and yet here was a mansion that was suited for a mandarin of high rank.

Everything was as new looking as though it had only been furnished yesterday. Li could hardly believe his eyes as he looked upon the magnificent pile that rose in such stately grandeur before him, and all this had been accomplished in the course of a few days. It was, however, when he entered the building that his astonishment reached its extreme limit. He found that everything that art or money could supply existed in the greatest luxuriance within its walls. In the outer courtyard there were the rarest flowers that China could produce in full bloom, and ready to catch the attention of the visitor, both by their beauty and by the exquisite fragrance that they diffused throughout the house. Every room, too, seemed a perfect museum of the choicest collection that some connoisseur had gathered from all parts of the empire to beautify and adorn the home. There were scrolls hanging on the walls painted by the most famous artists, depicting some of the famous historical scenes that happened in the distant past. There were also the choicest vases made in the potteries of Kingtehchen, with that beautiful blue color that only the workmen there know how to produce. There were also tables and chairs of the famous ebony wood that the Cantonese workmen make with such patience and matchless skill.

Turn where he would his eye was riveted on some special gem that had been brought from a distant province to add to the luxuriance of the rooms. Silken fans from Soochow, embroidered in the most delicate colors, and satin screens from Hangchow that artistic hands had covered with five-clawed Dragons and with figures of fairies, gave a lightness and a grace to the rooms in which they were placed. Then there were jade stones of the purest green, worth the ransom of a king, placed promiscuously about as though they were the commonest stones that could be picked up for a trifle in some jeweler's shop, and here and there were delicate lacquer trays, with willow trees of feathery branches that seemed to be bending to a summer's breeze, on which were placed tiny cups that would hold but a mouthful, and delicate brown tea-pots resting beside them, ready to draw out the fragrance of the tea such as no commoner ones would have done.

The reception that Li received was a right hearty and royal one. The eldest son, whose birthday was being celebrated, came to the door to receive him, and with courtly grace he led him into the guest chamber and placed him in the seat of honor. He was astonished to find what a large household it was that was occupying the old deserted mansion where his father once had lived. Servants dressed in uniform flitted about in considerable numbers carrying out the orders of their superiors. Occasionally he could hear the merry, silver laugh of young women and the footsteps of little children gamboling about in the spacious passages. From a rough estimate of the persons he caught glimpses of and the different voices that he heard, he calculated that there could not be fewer than fifty or sixty people, old and young, that made up the membership of this wonderful household.

After some time spent in conversation, a servant came and announced that dinner was ready. Li was led to the seat of honor and was treated with the most marked politeness and respect. It is needless to say that the feast that had been prepared was such as he had never seen in all his life before. He had read indeed of royal dinners, and how the delicacies of China as well as those of lands that lay beyond the control of the Dragon Throne had been brought together to grace the table of the Emperor. The accounts seemed as though they had been written by some romancer, who had let fling his imagination in order to excite the wonder of his readers.

Here, however, the very things that he had imagined belonged to dreamland were actually set before him and he was partaking of them. As each course was brought on by the silent-footed servants, he was more and more amazed at the rareness of the delicacies that these well-trained men laid with such deftness on the table. There were shark's fins that had once cleaved in the waters of the Formosa Channel, and there was *bêche-de-mer*, crisp and appetizing to the taste, that had grown on the reefs in the Southern Pacific. There were ducks, too, that had been specially fed until they had grown so fat that some time before they had been killed they had not been able to move, but were given their food and water by persons engaged for this purpose. Dish after dish came and each contained a surprise that made the mouth water and stimulated the appetite for further gastronomic efforts. There were lily seeds boiled in sweetened, fragrant waters, and pigeon eggs floating unbroken in a delicious soup in which they had been prepared for the table. The one article in the menu, however, that aroused the most attention was the birds' nest soup. The nests had been collected by adventurous hunters in the island of Borneo from huge caves in which the swallows build their nests. They are considered a great delicacy simply because of their rarity, as in themselves they are exceedingly insipid and flavorless.

At last, after thirty courses had tested the powers of the guests, the final dish that concludes every great feast was brought in, and then they knew that their banquet would soon be at an end. This consisted of bowls of rice, without which no feast would be considered to be complete. It was amusing to watch the eagerness with which each one fingered his chopsticks and applied himself with gleaming eyes to the huge white-grained rice that lay like a snow-capped hill in the basin before him. It would have seemed from the energy with which it was attacked that the four long hours that had been spent in disposing of the delicacies that had composed the feast had been utterly misspent, and now at length some proper food was being eaten that would appease the hunger that had been growing upon them.

One would naturally have concluded that such generous treatment as had been accorded to Li would have filled his heart with feelings of gratitude and respect, but that was not so. The sight of all the rare and precious treasures that adorned the house, and the royal feast that had been set out with a luxuriance that would have honored a king, seemed to inflame within him the wildest and the meanest of passions, and he made a solemn vow that he would set fire to this beautiful mansion and if possible burn every soul within it. He accordingly went to the nearest market town and ordered a vast quantity of sulfur and other deadly combustibles, and had them secretly bestowed away out of sight in various parts of the building.

When his deadly and murderous plans had been completed, he managed one day with the help of some men that he had let into the secret to set fire to the house. The wind was blowing a gale at the time, and this, aided by the fiery materials that a touch of fire would send into a blaze, soon wrapped the place in sheets of flame, that in their wild fury seemed to mount up to the very heavens. There was no possibility of any escape from the burning building for those who were inside it. The screams and cries from the wretched inmates were pitiable in the extreme, but Li looked on with perfect complacency, for he considered that it was not men of his own flesh and blood that were being destroyed. He therefore allowed the fire to burn on until the house had been destroyed and apparently every soul in it had been burned to death.

The next day the old gentleman who had rented the house from him and who had been away from home when the tragedy took place came and upbraided him for his cruelty in destroying the members of his family. "You had no real cause of quarrel with me," he said, "I never injured you in any way, and I paid you a liberal rent for the house that was falling to pieces and which you could not by any possibility make any use of as a dwelling-place for your own household. Why then plan so deliberately for the destruction of so numerous a family as mine was? I can only assure you that I shall inflict a terrible revenge upon you, and as you have brought desolation and sorrow upon those whom I loved better than life, so in like manner the day is not far distant when not only you shall miserably perish, but the whole of your clan, young and old, shall be swept off the face of the earth." With these ominous words the old man instantly vanished from his presence, and though Li made vigorous efforts to trace him, in order that he might wreak his vengeance on him for the threats he had uttered, no traces of him could ever be discovered, though the most diligent investigations were made as to his whereabouts.

A whole year went by and still the sorrows threatened by the old man had not fallen upon the scholar. It seemed, indeed, as though additional prosperity had been thrust upon him. His investments had all turned out exceedingly well, and he found that his wealth had been materially increased so that he was one of the richest men in all the country side. His lands too had been unusually productive. The rains had fallen with great regularity and the crops had been better than they had been for at least ten years. Everything that he touched seemed to prosper with him, and the weird denunciations of coming calamity, that had been hurled against him by the man whom he had so terribly injured, began slowly to fade away from his recollection.

Just about that time the region in which he lived began to be disturbed by frequent insurrections amongst the people, and bands of lawless men gathered in various quarters to organize armed opposition to the Government. The spirit of disaffection spread so rapidly that before many weeks had passed more than forty thousand men were in arms and were ready to assume the offensive against the local authorities.

Li was in great distress, for he had extensive property, and he was afraid that if the disturbances spread and the Government did not take immediate steps to suppress the rebellion he might possibly lose all that he had and his family suffer extermination as well. Just at this particular time, it was rumored that a famous wizard had taken up his abode in the nearest market town, and it was said by those who had consulted him that his knowledge of the future and his power to pry into the secrets of the other world far excelled anything that had ever appeared in China.

Li, anxious to know what the coming days had in store for him, got into his sedan-chair and, accompanied by his private secretary and a retinue suitable to the position he held in society, he started off for the office of the famous soothsayer in the hopes that he might disclose some way in which he might avert the disasters that he feared were coming upon him.

When he entered he was surprised to find a man in the very prime of life, with a face full of intelligence, and to judge by appearance with a mind of a far higher order than that possessed by an ordinary fortune-teller. Ordering his attendants to remain outside and gently closing the door behind him, he came up to Li and in a low, mysterious voice, he whispered, "I have been waiting for you. I knew," he continued, "by certain signs that you were coming to consult me, and I began at once to work out your horoscope before you arrived. I have been greatly moved by the momentous changes that I see are going speedily to happen in your life. Do you know," he murmured in a low tone, "that I have discovered by occult art that you are the real heir to the crown and that you should be sitting on the Dragon Throne instead of the man that now occupies it?"

Li was so utterly astonished at the wonderful communication made to him by the wizard that for some time he sat with blanched face and an astounded look in his eyes, gazing at the wizard, unable to utter a single word. He did not at once, however, reject the suggestion as one that was too dangerous for a subject to entertain. The idea began to filter through his mind that, if this statement were true, there was no reason why he should not consider the question of claiming his rights and becoming emperor of the Chinese empire. He was an exceedingly ambitious man and his vanity led him to believe that he was quite capable of administering the affairs of the nation as well as the ruler that now governed the empire.

The wizard, who had been watching him narrowly and could read into his very soul, strongly advised him to take advantage of the present disturbed state of society and assert his rights. "I have a great deal of influence," he said, "with the leaders of the revolutionary movement that is now going on in this region, and if you will consent to be influenced by my advice, I will see them and get them to acknowledge you as the rightful heir to the throne."

After a long discussion as to the feasibility of his succeeding in his treason against the dynasty, he was finally convinced by the eloquence of the fortune-teller that there was no possibility of any failure in the scheme that was laid before him, and so he threw himself heart and soul into the contest that he believed would end in placing him on the Dragon Throne.

The first thing he did was to appoint the wizard, who had impressed upon him the idea that he was a man of extraordinary ability, to be his military adviser, with full powers to negotiate with the rebel lieutenants and to have his name published as the leader in the revolution against the reigning family. These, of course, were delighted with the proposition, for the movement had hitherto been very desultory and very largely disconnected. With the accession of a man of Li's wealth and standing in society a prestige was at once given to the rebellion, and numbers hastened to join the various standards who had hitherto held aloof because they had no confidence in the men that were the leading spirits in the insurrection.

From the moment that Li consented to the advice of the wizard he threw himself heart and soul into the movement, and all his resources were freely expended in buying arms and munitions of war for the great army that he had under his command. So thoroughly equipped were his men that the imperial troops that appeared in the field were on several occasions defeated with great slaughter. This so added to the reputation of Li and the wizard who had been subsequently made commander-in-chief of all the rebel forces, that new recruits were daily coming in and enrolling themselves under the banners.

The Government in the meanwhile had been making prodigious efforts to put such an army into the field that they would be able at one fell blow to crush out the rebellion. In this they had succeeded and the royal forces were advancing by forced marches in the direction of the rebels. On the evening before the great battle was to be fought that was fraught with such mighty issues, the commander-in-chief of the latter sought the tent of Li and begged an interview with him. When he was admitted, the former was struck with consternation when, in the general of his troops, he recognized the old man that had formerly rented his house from him. A sense of coming disaster paralyzed him with terror, for he remembered the threat that had been made that he would revenge himself upon Li for the wanton destruction of his family.

"I see you have recognized me," he said, as he stood within the tent door, and looked with a world of passion in his eyes upon the cowering man before him. "I told you a year ago that I would fearfully revenge the grievous wrong you worked upon me and upon my home. The idea of vengeance has never left my mind, and I have planned it so that I have left no possibility of escape for you. This rebellion has been fostered by me, that I might involve you and every member of your family in ruin. Your fortune has already been spent to the last cash, and to-morrow's battle will see the triumph of the imperial forces, and the scattering of the soldiers upon whom you are relying for victory. You knew that I and the members of my family were fairies, and yet you dared to measure yourself against us." With these words the old man vanished, and Li was left to the despair that had been gradually creeping over his heart as in fateful language he heard the denunciations of the man he had wronged.

On the morrow confusion and disorder reigned throughout the rebel camp. The commander-in-chief who carried the plan of the battle in his brain was nowhere to be found, and none of the generals and officers knew what disposition of the men should be made to meet the attack of the foe. The imperialists carried everything before them and in the course of a few hours the rebels were flying in disorder over the face of the country. Li was taken prisoner and every member of his own and wife's clan, men and women and children, were ruthlessly exterminated, until there was not a single person left to bear the name of the man that had dared to conspire against the Government. The vengeance of the fairy had indeed been complete.

The Fairy Scholar

Once upon a time in the early days of Chinese history a certain fairy, intent upon the purpose of alleviating the pains and sorrows of human life, left his home in the Heaven and descended into one of the northern provinces of the empire, where he wandered about in search of those whose state of mind and aspirations after a higher life would induce them to listen to the high and mighty themes about which he had to discourse.

Unlike Li, of the Iron Staff, who thought that a mean and lowly role would help him best to discover who were the men that would be willing to relinquish all that this life could give them in their passionate desire to obtain the joys and immortality of the Western Heaven, he decided to appear as a scholar, deeply learned in the lore of China, and whose scholarship should cause him to stand pre-eminent above all the famous literary men whose names were known throughout the empire. He hoped by this method to attract to himself all the thinkers of the region in which he should fix his home, and from some of them he hoped to gain converts who should finally be converted into fairies.

He accordingly took up his abode in a country market town within easy distance of a large and flourishing city that was distinguished not only for the extensive trade that it carried on with the far West, but also for the large number of scholars and thinkers that had their residence in it.

Before long men began to talk in whispers of the strange and mysterious scholar that had appeared among them. He was a man of royal bearing and of a dignity that would have suited the great sage Confucius himself, but he was gracious and condescending withal and no touch of the pride that disfigures the character of the learned in China marred the symmetry of his life.

That he was a man of profound learning was a most undoubted fact. There was not a classic that had been written during any period of China's history that he was not perfectly familiar with. He knew not only the text and the commentaries that had been written upon them, but on the obscure passages that had puzzled the greatest scholars who had attempted to elucidate them, he could throw a flood of light that seemed to dissipate at once the mystery in which they had been enshrouded.

It appeared indeed as though he had entered into the mind and purpose of each writer to such an extent that he knew perfectly what they had intended to say, and he so unloosed the tangle in the sentences that were obscuring the meaning, that under his vivid explanations the most profound sentences became as plain as the sun at noon-day.

All the Confucianist guilds for miles around discussed the virtues of this great scholar when they assembled at various times to deal with literary questions. It seemed to them that a new era was going to dawn upon China, and that the sacred books of the nation would be placed upon a higher pinnacle than they had ever been since the days when they left the hands of the great sages and scholars who composed them.

These high expectations were doomed to disappointment through a weakness that is inherent in human nature, but which one never dreamed of as existing in fairyland. This distinguished fairy, who had come down specially to this world from the Heaven in order to emancipate men from the trammels of earth, fell in love with a mortal.

It seemed that not very far from where he lived there dwelt a family who had a daughter of surprising loveliness. She possessed the ideal features. There was not one that outshone this beautiful village maiden, either in the perfection of her form or in the exquisite charms that gave such a fascination to her countenance.

The fairy scholar, calling at her home one day, happened to catch a glimpse of her as she was disappearing behind the screen that shuts off the women's apartments from the outside world. It was but a fleeting glance he caught of her, but Cupid had taken advantage of that one swift look to send his arrow straight through the heart, and love from that moment took possession of his soul.

He was as passionately and as profoundly moved as any human being had ever been in all the world, and with the same impetuosity that impels mortals, he took steps to secure the lady he had seen as his wife. Calling a middle woman, instructions were given her to see the mother of the lady he had fallen in love with. He intimated at the same time that money was no object and that he would readily give whatever sum they demanded, while a present that would make her heart jump for joy would be given to her for her own personal use, if she succeeded in bringing the marriage about.

Having gained the heart of this woman by such unusual and liberal promises, the negotiations, as may be imagined, proceeded rapidly and smoothly. The family of Rosebud, the name of their beautiful daughter, were in very moderate circumstances and the large sum that they were told they might ask for her was the source of extreme satisfaction to them all. But in addition to this there was the exalted position of the suitor to be considered. The honor that would come to them from being allied with such a learned scholar would add greatly to their dignity, and would give them a standing in society that they could never have hoped to attain.

It was true that the proposed son-in-law seemed in some respects to be hardly suited for Rosebud, who was a bright laughing girl and full of fun from morning till night. He, on the other hand, was staid and dignified as became a master of learning such as he was, and he might not be well pleased when he found that his wife's temperament differed so much from his own.

This was the only thing that gave the parents of Rosebud any anxiety about the future. All the arrangements for the marriage were hurried on, and one day, when the sun was shining with his brightest rays in the heavens, the bridal chair with its gorgeous crimson, and with bands of music filling the air with festal notes, carried the beautiful bride to the home of the bridegroom.

The marriage seemed to be an exceedingly happy one. The scholar was absorbed in his devotion to his wife, and it would seem for the time being he had completely forgotten the high position he occupied as a member of the Western Heaven and that he was willing to forfeit his immortality for the sake of the beautiful mortal that had captured his heart. If Rosebud had only been enamored with him as much as he was with her, the tragedy that ere long wrecked their home would never have occurred.

After living together very happily for a year or two, the scholar, one beautiful spring morning, went out for a walk among the fields that lay outside the market town. As he was wandering listlessly about listening to the song of the birds and marking how the trees were putting on their summer dress, he was much struck by the conduct of a woman who was standing in front of a newly-made grave, that was a little off the road. He observed that she had a palm leaf fan in her hand with which she was vigorously fanning the undried mortar with which the grave was plastered.

Coming up to her, the scholar said, "I hope you will excuse me, but I really should like to know what you mean by fanning this tomb. I have never seen anyone do anything of the kind before, and I am greatly interested to know why you should be doing it?"

The woman replied, "I will explain to you and then you will see that l have a good reason for doing what must seem to be a very extraordinary act to you. A few days ago my husband died, and his last request of me was that I should not marry again until at least his grave had had time to dry. I have been anxious to carry out his dying wish, but I am very poor and he left me no means to enable me to support myself, and so I am hastening the drying of the tomb so that I may the sooner arrange for getting another husband who will care for me and my children."

When the scholar reached his home he told the story of the woman to his wife, and he was high in her praise because she had been so faithful to the promise she has made to her dying husband. "If she had not been a woman of a good deal of principle," he said, "she might easily have arranged to get married again without anyone being the wiser."

"To my mind," Rosebud replied, "the woman was perfectly disgusting, and I have no words to express my contempt for her. The idea of her being so anxious to get married before her husband is barely cold in his grave! Why, the thought is most revolting to any right-minded woman. She ought to have struggled on for a longer time, and then, when every plan had been exhausted and when out of sheer necessity she was compelled to think of another husband, one would have felt less contempt for her than one cannot help feeling now for such shameless and heartless conduct.

"If it had been my case," she continued, "I would never have dreamed of ever getting married again, but I should have remained a widow as long as I lived. I cannot understand what you see to admire in such a disgraceful specimen of womanhood, for I think her conduct is most unseemly and unwomanly."

In order to test this last statement of his wife, the scholar determined to put into practice a scheme that had flashed through his mind while she was speaking. It was a cruel one and showed that he had no true sense of love, and that in spite of all his professions of devotion he was perfectly heartless and that, in carrying out what might appear to him to be a practical joke, he was going to prove that his wife's honor and reputation were things that were absolutely indifferent to him.

The conception we have of a Chinese fairy is very much lowered by the conduct of this man, for his five hundred years spent in gradually obliterating the meaner passions of the heart, and in filling it with the loftiest virtues, had evidently been in vain, for in his conduct to the woman he married he showed himself to be influenced by motives that would have disgraced any high-minded citizen of the empire.

Two or three days after this conversation, the family was thrown into the wildest confusion by the scholar being attacked very suddenly with a mortal disease, that was so rapid in its action that in the course of a few hours he had ceased to breathe. Rosebud was reduced to despair and refused to be comforted. The neighbors gathered round her and endeavored to soothe her, but her sorrow was too profound and the sense of her loss too overpowering to allow her to be influenced by anything they could say. She could only weep and sob and make loud lamentations such as the Chinese are wont to indulge in when death enters a home.

Still, in spite of pain and sorrow, the serious business of the home had to be attended to. The scholar lay stiff and stark in a room whither the body had been conveyed, and arrangements must be made for his burial. An old servant who had been employed as a kind of major-domo in the family called in the coffin-maker who, from his stock, returned in an hour or two with a coffin into which the departed scholar was put by his men.

Chinese coffins are all of one general plan and are made to meet every contingency that may possibly occur. Some are larger and some are smaller, but one look of the experienced eye of the coffin-maker enables him to select the one he has in stock that will be suitable on any given occasion. They are all made roomy and ample in their proportions, for the Chinese who can afford it dearly like to clothe the dead in a large number of clothes, which they believe they carry with them into the Land of Shadows and wear there. In consequence of this belief, the coffins that are generally used are so large and heavy that when they are being conveyed to the grave as many as a dozen sturdy coolies are required to carry them to their last resting-place.

And now the home was in gloom and sadness. The master of the house was dead and lying in his coffin. Rosebud was in despair, and her maidservants, moved with pity for her in her distress, wandered about the house like ghosts, speaking in whispers to each other, and not daring even to smile lest they should intensify the sorrow of their mistress, who had gained their hearts by her gentleness and by the loving way in which she had been accustomed to treat them.

Things were now in this sad condition when the major-domo came to announce to his mistress that a visitor had arrived from a long distance, who, having heard of the great fame of her husband, had traveled many hundreds of miles in order to see so famous a scholar, and to be instructed by him in some of the more profound subjects that modern thinkers were anxious to have explained. He said he had told him that her husband had mysteriously passed away within the last few days and therefore it would be impossible for him to see him.

The visitor expressed his great grief at the news that had been given him, but begged for an interview with his widow, that he might explain to her his own disappointment and the loss that the nation had sustained in the death of such an illustrious savant.

At first Rosebud absolutely refused to see the stranger. She was a young woman, she said, and had only recently been made a widow, and it was entirely contrary to the rules of etiquette that she should be seen by any man, excepting he was a member of her own family.

The servant suggested that this was an exceptional case, that ought not to be ruled by the ordinary precedents that regulated persons in their intercourse with each other. This gentleman had traveled hundreds of miles in order to visit her celebrated husband, and it would be cruel, he thought, to send him back without giving him an opportunity of expressing his disappointment at not being able to see the widow of the illustrious scholar, whose fame had traveled throughout the length and breadth of China.

After considerable discussion and arguments on the part of the major-domo, Rosebud at last very reluctantly gave her consent to have an interview with the stranger, and escorted by two of her handmaidens she entered the room where the visitor was awaiting her.

She was rather startled to find herself confronted by a young man not quite thirty years of ago, whose face was most prepossessing, for it united in it all the elements that make up the beau-ideal countenance that painters and poets have liked to depict. It was such a one as would make an impression upon a woman, for while it was a strong one, it had an element of comeliness and gentleness that gave it a peculiar fascination of its own.

In the address that he made to Rosebud he was the perfect gentleman, and he told his story in such a modest, sympathetic way that she found her heart moved with a strange flutter that her dead husband had never caused her to feel.

After he had explained how disappointed he had felt when he reached her home and found that the man he had long expected to meet had passed into the Land of Shadows, he begged leave to express his profound sympathy with her and his hopes that she would not sorrow too much for the one that was gone. With a graceful bow, and with a smile that made her heart beat quickly, he withdrew from the apartment, and she could not help but feel that with his departure something had vanished out of her life and left her poorer than she was before.

Hardly had he gone than her manager appeared and suggested that her visitor having nowhere to stay and being an absolute stranger in the place should be invited to occupy one of the many rooms in the house for the few days he was resting before he returned to his distant home.

Rosebud at first demurred to this on the ground that it would cause a scandal, but her objections were all the more easily overruled since her heart, almost unconsciously to herself, was in favor of the suggestion. He was accordingly installed in one of the best rooms of the house, and from that moment it may be said that the famous beauty was doomed to lose her heart to this strange visitor, who had in such a brief space of time exercised such a powerful fascination over her.

Love grew fast and furious in the hearts both of Rosebud and the unknown visitor that she had admitted to her home so easily, simply because his personality had exercised such a powerful influence over her. In a day or two neither of them made any pretense of concealing their sentiments for each other. They were in fact madly in love with each other and as there was no reason now why they should not get married, a near day was settled when they should become husband and wife.

On the day appointed a number of guests were invited and a marriage feast was prepared and all was festivity and rejoicing. The house was filled with laughter and sounds of music filled the air, when all in a moment and without an instant's warning the bridegroom fell to the ground in a dead faint. Every effort was made to restore him but without any result. He lay as though life was extinct, for there was no evidence of breath or pulsation and not the least sign of vitality could be discovered in him.

Rosebud was in the greatest distress and appealed to her major-domo to know what ought to be done. The doctor had been called in, but he seemed helpless and could do nothing except shake his head and put on a serious look. He said this was a most dangerous case, and he feared very much that it must end fatally. On one occasion, indeed, he declared, he had seen a case very similar to this, which finally recovered, but the remedy employed was a very heroic one, though it was perfectly successful and in the end the man was brought to life again.

"What was the plan you saw adopted," asked the bride in an agonized tone of voice, "and why should we not resort to it now so that my husband should be saved from dying before my very eyes?"

"Well it seems a very horrible thing to tell you," he said, "but the doctor who was attending the case, and who was a very distinguished man in his profession, declared that the only thing that could save the man was that a dead body should be opened and the heart taken out and the juices from it put within the lips of the man who lay insensible. There happened at the time to be a son lying dead in his coffin in the house, and it was decided that if his body could be utilized to save his father's life it would be a most meritorious and filial act that would redound to his credit in the other world, and would doubtless influence the Prince of the Land of Shadows to treat him with special kindness and consideration. The body was accordingly opened and, the treatment recommended by the doctor having been carried out, the father was in a very short time completely restored to health.

"Now, it seems to me," he continued, "though it is terrible even to suggest such a thing, that we have the possibility of a cure for this young man in this very house. Your former husband's body lies still unburied in the next room. His life is extinct, of that we are most sure, then why not try a remedy that I am assured was used with perfect success and thus save the man you love from certain death?"

The poor bride of only a few hours' duration was so overwhelmed with sorrow and her mind so bewildered with the sudden tragedy that had driven the sun out of her life and filled it instead with shadows that she had no idea what was the proper thing for her to do. Her heart was so filled with love, moreover, that in her anxiety to save the man who had captured her very soul, she was ready for the wildest and most daring of actions, not thinking how society might look upon them or how they might misjudge her for what she had done.

Seizing an axe she rushed into the room where the coffin of her dead husband lay, and hacking and hewing at it she soon was able to raise the lid that covered his remains. Tearing this away, what was her horror to see the man who was supposed to be dead slowly rise from his recumbent posture. Rubbing his eyes as though he was just awaking from a profound slumber, he said, "What a long time I have been asleep! why did you not wake me before this?"

Poor Rosebud was so thunderstruck with what seemed to her a resurrection from the dead that she dropped her hatchet on the floor, and ran with all her might to see what was happening to the man who had fainted in the next room. When she got there, there was not a sign or trace of him to be found anywhere. He had absolutely vanished.

It then dawned upon her mind that a practical joke had been played upon her, and that the man that had been acting as her lover and whom she married that day was really her husband who had been testing her statement to him, that she would never dream of marrying another in case she were left a widow.

The feeling of shame that crept over her when she realized this was so overpowering that she felt she could never meet her husband again, and so, rushing out of the house, he threw herself into the well and in its depths hid for ever the intolerable sense of misery that was worse for her to bear than even death itself.

Phoenix, the Beautiful Fox Fairy

In one of the northern provinces, there existed at the time this story opens a famous city named Kaifeng. It lay on the great road that joined the eastern and western extremities of the empire, and every day it was thronged with passengers that traveled along from the moment that the dawn threw its pale, dim light on it, until the evening shadows gathered so thickly that it became lost in the night.

And what a diversity of human kind it was that made up the motley groups that from one year's end to the next filled it with their echoes, as with the foot of fate they moved along this weary endless road. There were high mandarins in gorgeous sedan-chairs with retinues in long gowns and tasseled hats that swung by with a mighty domineering air, as though the world were made for them.

Scattered thickly along it as far as the eye could reach were the coolies and porters and carriers, the men that do the rough work of the empire. And jostling up alongside of these were farmers carrying their produce to the market, strings of mules and camels laden with merchandise for the West, beggarmen with sores on their legs and bodies, their private stock-in-trade to enable them to draw on the pockets of the benevolent, play-actors and mountebanks, shaven priests, and almost every variety of human life that makes up the four hundred millions of this densely populated country.

The city, through which the restless, moving crowds had to pass in their onward march east and west, was a magnificent walled town. It had once been the capital of the empire, and it showed its royal character by its massive walls and lofty battlements, and for many miles they formed a pleasant and imposing picture as the travelers caught sight of them in their approach to this famous emporium.

The roads, too, were amongst the finest in all the northern provinces, for they bound the east and the west in one long line of communication.

For long distances they wound their way over fertile plains and across the foothills of a range of mountains, and then dipping once more to the lowlands they came close to the edge of a noble river that brought trade and life and excitement to the city of more than a million inhabitants that had built their homes in and around the walls of this bygone metropolis.

The spaces occupied by the city were wide and extensive. Outside the crowded streets, where the business of the town was carried on and where shops and warehouses were densely packed side by side in a fashion that could exist only in an Oriental city, there were wide and ample spaces where fields were cultivated and flower gardens supplied the rarest flowers that could be grown for the toilette of rich and poor in the city, and where kitchen gardens produced a great variety of vegetables for the markets that abounded in the busy streets of the great city.

There were also extensive open spaces on which magnificent mansions had been built, and where, surrounded by trees and shady walks and picturesque representations of hill and dale and springing fountains, the wealthy inhabitants, undisturbed by the sounds of the city, could enjoy the quiet and repose of a country life.

No wonder that this ancient city, with the many romances that time had woven around it and the mysteries that gathered about the fallen fortunes of many a noble house that had fallen into decay, should have become the chosen rendezvous of the kindly fairies, who, though long since emancipated from human conditions, still retained a kindly feeling toward the race of man from which they had sprung. But besides the fairies there were gathered the spirits and elves that delighted in the storm and in darkness, and in playing mad pranks that often times had more of wild and boisterous fun than ill-will or mischief in them. There also were to be seen by those who had done some signal service to them, the fox fairies, who were keenly alive to any favor that might be rendered them by man, and who always endeavored to repay in no niggardly way any kindly action that might have been done to them. The story that is now being told will fully bear out this statement.

In one of the aristocratic quarters of the city, where the rich built their mansions and where the sounds of the mart never broke in upon the delicious stillness of the place, there was an old dwelling house that had an air of antiquity and grandeur resting upon it. It was situated within its own grounds, which were very extensive, and winding paths embowered amidst trees and rare shrubs, and summer pavilions peeping out at unexpected points showed the artistic tastes of those who had planned and laid them out.

Unfortunately, the glories of the place had considerably waned, for evil times had fallen upon the family that owned it, and poverty had laid its cold and chilly hand upon them. In order to cut down expenses, fully half the building had been closed, and the rooms that had once resounded with sounds of human life were now desolate and forsaken.

In course of time the family that occupied the other half began to be unpleasantly conscious of strange and weird sounds that proceeded from the part of the building that had been closed up. Banging of doors that were known to be barred and bolted, and long-drawn mournful sighs that seemed to proceed from persons in the bitterest agony filled them with creepy sensations that made life a burden to them.

Occasionally too, about midnight, the sound of voices could be heard above the howling of the storm that were so wild and unearthly that everyone's heart stood still with terror, and sleep was banished from their eyes. The tension at last became so severe that it was determined to abandon the house. This was accordingly done and only an old caretaker was left in it, who was so poor that he dared to risk the unseen dangers that the spirits might bring upon him rather than endure the evils that poverty was certain to visit him with.

In the same city there lived the nephew of the owner of the haunted dwelling. He was a young fellow, a little over twenty, and was noted for his tenderness of heart toward dumb animals. He could not endure to see any of them hurt, much less killed, and many a fox had he saved when in the hunting expeditions the hounds had been on the point of tearing it to pieces, and had set it free again.

Unconsciously to himself he had on several occasions rescued not simply a poor terrified fox but a fairy in disguise. That he did not dream of this at the time was not because he did not believe in the popular superstition that the fox could at pleasure transform itself into a human being and then again return to the old shape and habits of its race whenever it pleased. He was as deeply imbued with it and had as great faith in it as the most unlearned in the country round had.

There is no doubt but that the well-known cunning of the fox and its fertility in inventing disguises by which it escapes the hands of its pursuers have seemed to the superstitious and rustic minds of the country people of this land, who on the whole are densely ignorant and uneducated, to prove that it has supernatural powers. The many instances, too, to which the credulous can point where foxes have been known to personate human beings has helped to perpetuate the belief which, like the legends and solar myths of ancient times, took such a vivid hold upon the imagination of peoples of various countries for many centuries.

His reputation for tender-heartedness had spread among the fairies, and the story of his goodness in delivering so many of their race had been repeated from one to another until his name became a familiar one among them, and many a vow was made that one day they would repay him a thousand-fold for his deeds of kindness to them.

In addition to this loving quality of mercy for the hunted fox, Ping was a man of high courage, to whom fear was entirely unknown. The ordinary dread of ghosts and fairies that was so prevalent, never influenced him in the slightest degree, and his great desire had been to investigate the mystery of the strange beings that haunted his uncle's house and that had driven him and his family in mortal terror from it.

He accordingly arranged with the old man that had been left in charge of the building to come and call him whenever there were any signs that fairies were h aving any of their nocturnal goings-on, as he would like to visit them and make their acquaintance.

On the very next night, just about midnight, the old man hurried into Ping's home, and with eyes full of wonder and a voice trembling with excitement informed him that the unused rooms were brilliantly lighted up, and voices, gentle and subdued, could be heard as though a family had met for an evening entertainment.

Ping, without a moment's hesitation, hurried out of the house and with hasty footsteps made his way along the narrow, ill-paved streets, only fearful lest the fairies should have vanished before he could get to them. The night was an ideal one for an adventure. It was intensely dark, for there was no moon and the flying clouds had blotted out the stars. Everything had a weird and uncanny look about it. The houses could be just dimly seen through the gloom like giant specters crouching by the wayside, while the trees enlarged and distorted by the intense gloom in which they were shrouded, seemed like ghostly, shadowy figures that had wandered from the other world to terrify the mortals in this.

When they reached the house Ping noticed that the rooms that had long been closed up were ablaze with a most brilliant light, that from their midnight setting of darkness seemed to shine and sparkle with a radiance such as no human being had ever seen before. A gentle hum of voices traveled across the courtyard and broke in upon the stillness of the night.

Ping, without any hesitation, advanced up to the room from whence the sounds came and, looking through a crack in the door, he saw a party of four sitting round a table where they seemed to be enjoying themselves in a quiet and luxurious manner.

Two of the people that he saw were middle-aged, evidently husband and wife, who had a refined and elegant look about their faces that showed them to be no common people. There was also a young man about the same age as Ping, scholarly in his manner, and with an air of high breeding that plainly indicated that he came from a high family. The fourth was a young girl of about nineteen, who seemed from the instant he saw her to exercise a wonderful fascination over Ping. She was not only exceedingly beautiful, but there was a sprightliness and a charm about her countenance that added to the grace that nature had bestowed upon her.

Without any ceremony Ping flung wide open the door and entered upon the astonished company. The elderly gentleman rose from his seat and indignantly asked him how he had ventured to intrude himself upon them.

"I am not the intruder," replied Ping, "this house belongs to my uncle and if anyone is an intruder it is you."

The gentleman gave him a long, keen glance and then a pleasant smile softened down the angry lines upon his face, and in a most courteous manner he asked him to be seated and to join in their evening meal. Nothing loth, Ping sat down and soon found himself at home with this mysterious family.

The one attraction for him, however, in this pleasant and refined company was the beautiful daughter, Phoenix, who with the very first sight he had caught of her had captured his heart and made him her slave for ever. The charm of the evening and the keen enjoyment that came to him every moment during the hours that he spent in the company of his newly-made friends were entirely due to the attraction that this lovely girl had for him.

Ping before long discovered to his intense satisfaction by certain signs and tokens that nature exhibits, no matter what the race or clime may be, that the beautiful Phoenix was as much attracted by him as he had been to her, and when he left for home, as the dark clouds in the east began to be tinged with the first hues of dawn, the last thing that lingered in his memory was the flash of her beautiful eyes, and the tender look that rested upon her face, as she thus eloquently expressed her love for him.

Next day Ping, in the expectation of once more meeting with Phoenix, came to make a return call upon the family who had entertained him so royally, but every vestige of them had vanished. The exquisite scrolls that had adorned the walls, the ebony table, the gold and silver ornaments, the jade stones, and the blue enameled ware of priceless value, had all disappeared, and nothing was left but the dingy, musty-looking rooms that had been allowed to go to ruin by their owner.

Ping was in despair, for he was afraid that Phoenix was lost to him for ever. He had no means of tracing her, and as he was now convinced that she was a fairy he was quite hopeless that any quest of his would ever bring him to the land where she lived.

So deeply, however, was he in love that he determined to take up his residence in the haunted rooms, in the hope that the fairies might one day return and then he would meet with his beloved.

Weeks and months went by, but no traces of his lost love ever appeared to gladden his heart, and he began to feel that he would never have the happiness of meeting her again.

One day, sitting in the old room where he had first met her, and with his thoughts wandering away in imagination into the unreal world where the fairies are supposed to pass their time, there suddenly lighted upon a branch of a tree that hung down gracefully, close to the open window near which he sat, a bird with most exquisite plumage. Never had he beheld anything so graceful nor colors so charmingly intermixed as those he now beheld.

As he grazed with admiring wonder upon this beautiful bird which seemed to be absolutely without any fear of him it began to trill a song with the sweetest music that he had ever heard in his life. As he listened, entranced with the full, rich notes that came from the singer's throat, it suddenly dawned upon him that there was a story in this music that was meant for him.

He caught the name of Phoenix distinctly and he found that embedded in the beautiful notes that the bird trilled out there was a message from her that filled his heart with the most perfect happiness. She had never forgotten him, he was told, but fate had been against their meeting. The time, however, would soon come when they should see each other again, though in the meanwhile she would have to pass through a great peril from which she would be delivered by him.

Some weeks after this Ping was out watching a hunting party. They were in pursuit of a fox that had given them a long run over the hills and through the woods, and it seemed as though it would give them the slip, so fleet of foot had it been and with such cunning had it managed to elude the dogs.

As he stood looking for some sign of the hunters, he suddenly heard the sound of the excited baying of the dogs, and the voices of men urging them on in their pursuit of the fox. All at once there flashed out from some undergrowth near by the very animal they were after. It seemed utterly exhausted and worn out with its long run, and there was no question but that it would soon fall a prey to the dogs, whose short, impatient yelps showed that they were conscious that the fox could only hold out a very little longer.

Ping's heart was moved with pity at the pitiable condition of the animal, when to his utter astonishment instead of avoiding him it rushed up to him and lay breathless and panting at his feet.

With the instinct of compassion that he had always had for animals in distress he picked it up in his arms and hurried home with it as fast as his feet could carry him. Laying it down on a couch in his room, he began to think what he could do to relieve the utter exhaustion of the animal, when he was startled to see the figure of the fox change into that of his beloved and beautiful Phoenix.

His delight and his happiness knew no bounds when he found that the woman he had loved with such devoted affection, and who had seemed to be utterly lost to him, was actually here with him and that he had been the means of rescuing her from a cruel and miserable death.

As they were deeply in love with each other, and Phoenix declared that she would never more revert to her old fox life, they were speedily married and their union brought great happiness to them both. The whole of the fox fairy tribe joined in showering down prosperity upon the happy couple, riches flowed into the home and the grim shadow of poverty that had long rested upon it was replaced by sunshine and gladness.

The old mansion that had fallen into such decay was restored to its ancient magnificence. The garden, that had been turned into a wilderness through long neglect, became beautiful once more under the skillful touch of men who had learned the secrets of nature, and who knew how to draw forth the beauties that she refuses to disclose except to those who are in sympathy with her. The deserted rooms of the old decayed house now resounded with the pleasant sounds of human life that banished dullness from them. No longer could they be employed by the wandering fairies in which to hold their midnight revels, for they were now tenanted by troops of relatives that gathered round Ping to share in the good fortune that these mysterious beings had sent him. His name and his house become famous, not only in the city of Kaifeng, but also throughout the province, and many looked with envy upon him for the good fortune that had enabled him to enlist the sympathies and the goodwill of such powerful friends as the fairies had proved themselves to be.

The Scholar Hai, and the Fairy Songster, Lady Kwey

Once upon a time, in the famous province of Shansi ("Western Mountains") there lived a graduate of the empire who had greatly distinguished himself in his studies. Although he was only a little over twenty years of age, he had been selected out of the thousands of competitors that had gone up with him for their examinations for the proud title that every one of them longed to possess, and that was the first degree that is bestowed upon the successful aspirant for literary honors.

Although he had obtained his degree his ambition had been by no means satisfied. It had indeed only been whetted for further triumphs in the future, and in imagination at least he saw himself coming successfully out of three examinations that still lay before him, until he had come out first in the final one in Peking, where the emperor himself was the examiner. He would then have the distinction of being the first scholar in the empire for the year and his name would be in every school and college, and in the homes of the scholars throughout the length and breadth of the land, as one of the heroes in literature who was to stand out as an example and model for all the students in the empire.

In order to carry out his purpose more thoroughly, Hai took a room in a temple among the hills, where, excepting for the occasional chanting of the priests, and the visits of the souls anxious for some revelation from the idols of the destiny that was in store for them, the profoundest stillness reigned. It was not that he hoped for any inspiration from the hills that towered around, or from the running stream that sang its way along the wooded ravines to the plain below. The voice of spring sounded among those silent heights, the trees budded, and the flowers broke into blossom at its echoes, but for Hai there was no music in it that touched a responsive chord in his heart.

It seemed indeed as though nature in her wildest or her gentlest moods had no power to touch his heart, so absorbed was he in the one eternal grind of mastering those weird and old-world hieroglyphs in which the masters of thought had in ancient times enshrined the ideas that they left as a painful legacy to their posterity. His one passion was to get the very language of the ancient writers so inwoven into his brain, that when the Imperial Chancellor came round to examine the students of his district he would be so able to recall every phrase and every sentence, that his vast learning would gain him the coveted degree that was to bring him fame and honor in the service of his country.

Hai's voice could be heard at all hours of the day and even of the night, as with the scholar's well-known intoning of the pages before him he endeavored to impress upon his memory not only each grotesque picture that made up a word but also the ideas that each one contained. It was very wonderful that he had the bodily capacity to go on day after day and week after week at a work that made such demands upon his strength. Not only did he study every hour of the day and night that he was not sleeping or eating, but he also refused to stay his unceasing vigilance even during the recognized holidays, when the most strenuous scholars have always felt it incumbent upon them to cease for a time their exhausting studies.

Such intensity of purpose and such a worthy ambition to excel in the world of letters not only excited the admiration of those who knew him, but in some mysterious way the thing became known in the land of fairies, and its inhabitants, who have an abiding love for mankind, became so interested in him that they determined that they would do something to add to the happiness of this solitary man whose life was so nobly spent in the acquisition of learning. Not only would they help him in the furtherance of the plans he was pursuing with such unremitting labor for a brilliant future, but they would also try and secure for him some of the home comforts without which the lot of man, even with all the honors that the world can thrust upon him, can never be an ideal one.

One of their number was accordingly specially deputed to carry out the intention of the fairies. He without any delay hastened away from the Western Heaven and flying with the swiftness of lightning he reached the solitary temple among the hills after the darkness of night had fallen upon them. Glancing at one of the side rooms he saw the glimmer of a single wick that could be dimly discerned amidst the pall of night, and at the same time he could hear the monotonous and unmusical chanting of the scholar as he ran along the tones that each one of the intricate little figures called characters claims to be recognized by.

Walking through the large room in which the idols were enshrined, and guided in the darkness by the clear voice of the chanter, the fairy from the invisible world slowly crept his way to the room from which the sounds proceeded. Tapping gently at the door, the sounds at once ceased and Hai, opening the door, looked with surprise at seeing the rare and unusual sight of a visitor at that hour of the evening. Inviting him to come in and sit down, he was greatly impressed with his appearance and instinctively felt himself attracted to him. There was an air of dignity about him that made Hai feel that he was in the presence of a man of no ordinary character. His face, too, was a strong one, but so marked with tenderness and good nature that it seemed to invite confidence and trust in anyone that looked upon it.

After conversing together for some little time, the visitor suggested that as it was a festal time of the year he should put away his books and that they should have a pleasant evening together. "I can sing a little," he said, "and if you have anything of a voice you could take a part, and we would make this dreary old temple echo with merry sounds such as have never wandered through its desolate halls during the long years of its existence."

Hai, who had a soul that was full of music, felt a thrill of delight flash through his heart as he heard the cheery words of this pleasant stranger. For a moment the incubus of his long weary studies seemed to drop away from him, as he gladly consented to the proposition that chimed in so well with his own inclinations.

"Before we begin our musical evening," the stranger said, "I may tell you of a liberty I have taken and for which I hope you will excuse me. I knew that in this forlorn and out-of-the-way place it would not be possible to engage a singing girl to accompany us with her musical instrument or to entertain us with her singing, and so I have brought one with me. I left her at the door of the temple and with your leave I will bring her in to help us in our evening entertainment."

As he said this he hastily left the room, but returned in a minute or two leading a young girl of about seventeen or eighteen with him, who was holding a guitar in her hand. Hai was struck with amazement, for he had never in all his life seen such a beautiful woman as this. She was tall and graceful as the bending willow, while her face was more lovely than the pictures he had seen of the famous beauties that had been renowned in the history of the empire. As he looked at her, he became convinced that she was a fairy, for no woman that he had ever met had combined in her person such grace and dignity as this girl that stood before them with the air of a princess in her bearing.

The singing girl in China is one who is often met with in jovial parties of young fellows who wish to spend a merry time together. They are not usually of a high character, but, unfortunately, they have no choice in the selection of this doubtful profession, and are certainly much to be pitied for the position in which they find themselves. They are women that have been sold by their parents when they were young girls to persons who make it their business to provide singing girls for private or public entertainments.

They are trained very carefully in the use of certain musical instruments, and they are taught the popular songs both of the past and of the present day, which they sing to the accompaniment of one of the instruments they have learned. They are a source of great profit to their masters. It is hardly needful to say that the girl introduced by the visitor to Hai was a fairy in disguise who, with the intention of adding somewhat to the joys of human life and of helping to disperse some of the shadows that hang so heavily over it, had transformed herself into a singing girl and with her magnificent voice was charming the companies she was called upon to entertain.

"May I ask," Hai said to the visitor, "where you have brought this lady from, for I was not aware that in the whole of this region there existed any singing girls, or any place where one could be engaged."

"Oh!" replied the man with a smile, "I knew, when I was coming to see you this evening, and when I had determined that for a few hours at least your mind should be relieved from the drudgery of your incessant study of these heart-breaking books, that there was no artiste that I could engage to help us to spend the time pleasantly. And so, as I was passing over 'The Western Lake,' I bethought me of a famous singer who lived on its shore, and I induced her to come along with me."

"The Western Lake!" cried Hai in amazement, "but that is a thousand miles from here. However can you say that you and this fairy lady have traveled so far in the course of an afternoon and that you made such a journey just to give me some extra pleasure?"

After the interchange of a few pleasant words, and the expression of deep gratitude on the part of Hai, the courteous visitor proposed that they should now proceed with their singing. Out of an inner garment he drew a beautifully shaped flute upon which he blew a few notes to test it, while the fair musician whose name was Lady Kwey, and who had remained silent while the conversation was going on, tuned her guitar with her long graceful fingers and waited for the moment to begin the concert.

Hai, who was well trained in the music of the Chinese, was simply entranced with the beautiful voice of the Lady Kwey. Never before had he heard such sweet notes coming from any human throat as those that echoed round his room, that had hitherto resounded only with the echoes of the mechanical tones of the characters that he had been intoning for so many dreary months during the past year.

It seemed as though a new spirit was born within him, as he listened to the strains she sang and the tender sentiments of the ancient songs and ballads that she rendered with such exquisite feeling. He soon began to feel that there was something more in his heart than mere admiration for a well-trained artiste, and that love that he had never felt for any woman before had burst upon his soul with a new revelation of sweetness and power.

While these pleasant thoughts were beginning to burn within his heart, he still could not get over the thought that these delightful visitors who had turned the dreariness of his room into an earthly paradise were not human, but had come from a far-off land where the footsteps of mankind had never trodden. The fact that they had come that afternoon from the Western Lake that was situated far away in the western portion of the empire was proof positive of this. The beauty of the Lady Kwey and the exquisite charm with which she rendered the pieces she had sung made such an impression upon his heart that, whether human or not, or whether they were fairies from the Heaven, it mattered not, he had fallen deeply and madly in love with her, and it seemed as though the world would for ever be a dull and dreary place without her.

While these thoughts were passing rapidly through his mind his visitor said to him, "How exquisitely the moon is shining to-night. See how the hills around are bathed in its silver light. It would seem as though all nature were gazing with upturned face at her, as she rides through the sky, and the spell of her beauty is so strong upon the world that it lies in solemn stillness drinking in the inspiration and the poetry that are poured upon it from an unclouded sky. But if you want to see the full magnificence," he continued, "of the full moon shining in her unclouded glory, you must go to the Western Lake, and on such a night as this watch the moonbeams as they play upon its surface, and see how the moon makes for herself a silver path right across its waters along which the fairies may pass to and fro. Will you not come with us and look at this wonderful sight and see the glory of the moon on that romantic lake?"

Hai, who by this time was deeply in love with the fair singer, and who would have been willing to travel the wide world over in her company, signified his delight at the proposal, but expressed his wonder as to how they could travel a thousand miles during the short hours of a winter's night.

"Oh! as far as that is concerned," the stranger smilingly replied, "you need have no concern whatever. A thousand miles is no more to me than it would be for you to go to your next door neighbor. The question now to be thought of is how would you like to travel. Would you like to make the journey by horse or by boat, for you can have your choice of either mode of locomotion? For myself I advise the boat and, if you agree, I shall at once summon one from the Milky Way that shall carry us with the speed of lightning to the distant lake."

Hai, by this time, was so overcome with amazement that he could do nothing but simply acquiesce in whatever the stranger proposed. The latter then, with a wave of his hand, pointed toward the sky in which the full-orbed moon was riding with great brilliance and majesty, when a fleecy cloud was seen suddenly to appear and, quick as thought, it came traveling through the air to where Hai and the two visitors were standing, and in a moment was floating at their side.

The shape of this boat from the Milky Way was of the most exquisite design and workmanship, and Hai looked upon it with the utmost wonder and astonishment. Its shape was that of an open fan, while the rowers, who sat in silence waiting the orders of the mysterious visitor, seemed to be a collection of the most graceful and beautiful wings such as were far beyond the conception of any human mind to devise.

Taking their seats, at a motion of the visitor's hand, the boat shot up with inconceivable rapidity into the sky. So high, indeed, did they go that all sight of the earth was lost, and the stars gleamed in the firmament while the figure of the "Woman in the Moon" came out so brilliantly distinct that the outlines that are so dim and hazy from the earth became clear and well defined as they soared up into infinite space.

The travelers seemed scarcely to have started on their journey when the boat began to descend, the mountains came into view, and the lights of earth flashed like far-off stars. In a moment they found themselves resting on the surface of the famed Western Lake. The scene was indeed a most beautiful one. Hundreds of boats were moving about on the moonlit waters, while the sound of music came traveling over the silver flood with a beauty and a harmony that filled the heart with the most exquisite pleasure.

For hours the mysterious rowers with the gentlest motion of their wings propelled the boat in and out among the merry craft that lingered on the lake, enjoying the sights and sounds that seemed more beautiful than they would have done had the sun been shining in his strength. After a time, another boat drew up alongside of them, and the occupants said they had come to carry the Lady Kwey to the shore. Hai, who had become more and more enamored of the beautiful singer, used every persuasion that he was capable of to prevent her departure. He was a fine handsome-looking young fellow, and he had such a look of culture and of high breeding that he had evidently made a deep impression upon the heart of Lady Kwey.

When he found it impossible to detain her from the friends who had come for her his heart seemed to be filled with despair, and with eyes filled with love and looking upon her with the tenderest affection, he asked her when it would be possible for him to see her again.

"If you really love me," she replied, "you will easily find me out, if you inquire for Lady Kwey, for I am known everywhere, and anyone will direct you to where I live."

Just at this point the mysterious visitor intervened, and asking Hai for his pocket handkerchief he handed it to the Lady Kwey, and said, "This will be received by her as an evidence that she is pledged to you, and any time within the next three years that you come to claim her as your wife, she will be ready to give herself to you." The young girl signified her consent to this. She then passed into the boat that had come to carry her off and in a short time it was lost in the shadows that lined the shore.

As the night wore on and the moon sank lower and lower in the western sky, the visitor suggested that they should now go ashore, as the special beauty of the moonlit lake would disappear before the coming of the sun. No sooner had they reached the bank of the lake than the boat shot up with incredible swiftness into the air and in an instant was out of sight, leaving them gazing at its flight.

As they were sauntering along the shore, and the early dawn was revealing the mountains that lay like sleeping giants in the near distance, all at once a most beautiful horse, fully caparisoned, came out of the shadows that lay in the distance, and approaching Hai stood in front of him as though it wished him to mount. No sooner had he got upon its back, than his companion vanished out of his sight, and no trace could be found of him, though Hai made the most anxious search for him.

Hai was now in great anxiety as to what course he should take. He was an immense distance from his own home, and there was not a single person with whom he was acquainted in this entire region. He was, moreover, entirely without friends, and how he was to get back to the mountain temple in the distant province without them was a thought that filled his heart with dismay. While he was mentally discussing this very important question, he suddenly noticed a small bundle that was tied securely to the front of his saddle. Wondering what it could be, he opened it, when to his extreme joy, he found it contained silver ingots to the value of several hundreds of taels, which had been generously provided by the mysterious visitor who had shown such marvelous powers during the past night.

Relieved of all anxiety by this pleasant discovery that he had made, Hai turned his horse's head in the direction of his home. This animal he found to be a perfect treasure that never failed him once during the long journey of several weeks that had to be traveled before he reached the temple where he had been living. It never tired and it never attempted to escape from him. It traveled up the sides of great mountain paths that led to the plains on the other side. The great rivers that lay in the way it crossed at a single bound, no matter how wide they might be. The journey with such an animal was an exquisite pleasure trip, and when they reached the well-known gates, a feeling came over Hai that he wished it could have been extended for some weeks more.

Ever since the eventful night in which he had parted with the Lady Kwey, Hai had never once forgotten her. His love indeed seemed to have become intensified, and the thought that he had probably lost her for ever added but to the sorrow that filled his heart, and his longing to see her once more. It was useless to endeavor to search for her, for she had vanished so completely that she had left absolutely no trace of her existence. He would have gone to the world's end to find her if only the slightest clue could have been given him as to where she was to be found.

His only solace now were his studies, which he pursued with even more intensity and devotion than he had ever done, but life was never the same to him since the beautiful singer had touched his heart with a new sensation of love. After two years of most strenuous labor at his books, during which he had gained fresh literary honors,

Hai's longing to behold the Lady Kwey was at length gratified. Having been invited to a great feast in the house of a relative, he was informed that one of the attractions in connection with it would be the presence of a famous singing girl whose voice was such a magnificent one that her praises were sung by all those who had had the privilege of hearing her sing.

Hai was greatly interested in this, though it did not occur to him to connect her with the one who had been in his thoughts ever since he had parted from her. As soon, however, as she entered the room his heart gave a great bound of delight when he recognized her as the woman to whom he had lost his heart, and whom he had given up all hope of ever seeing again. His joy was enhanced by the fact that he saw that she had not forgotten him, but that a wave of color flashed across her face when she caught sight of him.

Addressing her at the close of the entertainment he discovered that her love for him was just as strong as was his for her. This simplified matters considerably, and arrangements were made for their speedy marriage. It was a profoundly happy one and Hai and his fairy bride became famous for the devotion they showed to each other, and for the distinguished honors that were showered upon their home during the passing years.

Mr. Wang and the Taoist Abbot

THE YOUNG MR. WANG WAS THE SON OF A MAN WHO WAS NOTED FOR HIS WEALTH AND also because of the fact that he was the fortunate father of twelve sons. This latter fact had given him a reputation that made him the envy of many a home in the region in which he lived.

The seventh boy in Mr. Wang's family was possessed of a fine imagination, and fairy stories had for him a fascination and an attraction that never failed to fill his mind with the utmost delight. As he grew up he devoured all the books he could buy or lay his hands upon that described the life and doings of that mysterious class of beings that to childhood of whatever nationality has always possessed an unfailing interest. As he advanced in years his passion for the marvelous only seemed to intensify, and his desire to be possessed with the power that would enable him to execute the wonderful feats that the fairies could perform grew stronger and stronger within him.

Not far from where he lived, there was a famous Taoist monastery in which dwelt a number of priests, the heads of which though they had the appearance of ordinary mortals, were yet in reality fairies who, for the sake of working out certain benevolent purposes for the benefit of mankind, had assumed the appearance of Taoist priests in order the better to carry out their beneficent designs.

The guise that these kindly beings had taken upon themselves in order to hide their secret from men was the very best that could have been adopted by them. The priests of the Taoist church have always been credited with having extraordinary powers over all kinds of spiritual forces. They are supposed to be able to control the countless spirits, both good and bad, that are continually roaming through the illimitable spaces that bound this earth of ours. They possess potent spells, and mysterious charms and high-sounding incantations with which they can terrify the invisible foes that would bring ruin on human life, and thus cause them to fly in terror to some far-off scene, where their intended victims need never fear them again.

For example, a certain district is troubled with an outbreak of cholera. This is not put down to bad drains and shocking insanitary conditions as it ought to be, but to the workings of malign spirits who have a deadly hatred against the people residing in it. Money is collected and a certain number of Taoist priests are engaged to drive away the evil forces and bring back health and happiness to the terror-stricken inhabitants.

Besides incantations, actual force is employed to terrify the spirits, and men with rusty swords are seen flying about, slashing at the air and cutting at the invisible foes. These, it is believed, are so frightened that they fly in the utmost alarm and seek refuge in other parts where the priests have no power to pursue them.

Anxious to be initiated into the mysteries of the unseen, by which he would gain powers that would make him supreme against all the chances and changes of this mortal life, Wang one day started for a visit to the mountain monastery.

He was a young man of large ambitions and a vivid imagination, but without that earnestness or stability of character that might have led to a realization of some of the visions that flashed through his brain. As he ascended the hill, he saw the plain lying like a great garden stretching away from the foot of the mountain, and his thoughts seemed to catch the inspiration that the pure air of those lofty heights imparted to them. He was now going to enter upon a career, he believed, that would satisfy the longings that he had felt for many a year, and his mind was full of contentment.

After winding his way up the lofty sides of the mountain and through miniature ravines that were hidden away amidst giant boulders that far-off centuries had thrown with careless and yet artistic hands into poses of solemn grandeur, he finally landed on a terrace embowered amidst great pine trees and lofty cedars, whose birthdays had long been lost in the mists of the past. Nestling beneath the shadow of these rose the walls of the famous monastery whose name was known far beyond the province in which it was situated.

As Wang entered the great doors that ever stood open, he saw a venerable looking priest sitting cross-legged on a cushion. He was the abbot of the monastery, and though to all appearance he was simply a man of exalted position in the Taoist church, he was in reality a fairy from the Western Heaven, who had consented to become man in order that he might be able to use his influence in uplifting and blessing any of the human race with whom he might come into contact. He at once recognized Wang as a man full of visionary and impractical ideas about fairies, and he determined that he would, if possible, teach him a few lessons that would dissipate the nonsense that was filling his brain and would make him more qualified to fulfill the common duties of every-day life.

No sooner did Wang catch sight of the priest than he approached him with a profound obeisance and told him that he had traveled up the mountain side in order that he might solicit the privilege of becoming his disciple and of learning from him the mysteries of the Taoist religion. The abbot received him in a most gracious manner, but expressed a doubt whether he would be able to stand the hard discipline through which he would have to pass before he could hope to grasp the mysterious power that would give him control over forces more subtle and potent than any that exist among men.

"You must remember," he said, "that you have been brought up in a home where almost every wish and desire of your heart has been granted you. You have never known the grip of poverty, for your father is a rich man, and the pain and sorrow through which men become refined have never darkened your life or strengthened your moral fibers. If you will take my advice," he continued, "you will return to your home after you have rested with us awhile, and you will find, if you are willing to go through as many hardships as those that await you here, that a new power will be given you that will prove more serviceable to you than any supernatural or magical influence that you may fancy you will acquire by your residence among us."

The young man was enthusiastic and his mind was too dazzled with the brilliant prospect which his imagination painted in such bright colors to accept this homely and common-sense advice. He protested, on the other hand, that he was prepared for any test that they might decide to put him to, and that, however hard it might be, he would willingly submit to it.

In the dim twilight early next morning, the abbot presented him with an axe and told him off with a number of others to go on to the hill side and cut firewood for the use of the dwellers in the monastery. It was with a joyous and gladsome heart and with jokes and laughter that sent their echoes along the ravines and steep mountain cliffs, he accompanied the merry band that sought out the sprouting pine trees, or cut off the branches of the older ones, while the sunbeams began to slide down the western side of the great range, and to cast his long streams of light across the landscape that stretched far away into the distance.

Wang now felt even in this humble occupation that he was taking his first step that would ultimately lead him into the fairy-land where he would be initiated into the mysteries that would give him mastery over the spirits, and enable him to acquire powers that would elevate him above the pains and sorrows of life.

Day after day went on, but there was no change in the monotonous labor that had been assigned to him on the morning when he was supposed to commence his novitiate. Every day at dawn he had to start out with his companions and begin the weary march among the boulders and sheltered spots where the storms that swept these great towering heights could not touch the tender pines that hid themselves within them. For the first few days the novelty and the romance enabled him to look upon this work as a most delightful one. The bracing air, the healthy exercise, and the sense of exhilaration that filled his whole frame as he looked over the wide expanse of hills and plains that met his vision gave him an exquisite feeling of happiness. But as the time went on, he began to tire of what he felt was a drudgery that had always been left in his home to the laborers that his father had employed to do such rough work.

His hands, moreover, that had never been accustomed to such toil, began to be blistered, so that it was a positive pain for him to grasp the axe or attempt to cut the firewood that was needed for the cooking of the food of the large numbers that resided in the monastery. He became so discontented with his lot that he began to have serious thoughts of returning home and abandoning all attempts to get initiated into the secrets of the fairy world.

The abbot, who had been watching him with a kindly interest, and who saw how his plans for awakening him to a common-sense view of life were beginning to succeed, determined now to complete the cure and to send him home with all his fantastic views completely knocked out of his brain.

Returning from the mountain side with his burden of firewood that he had gathered with such labor, the fairy abbot invited him to come and spend an hour or two with him in the company of some friends, who had come from a distance specially to visit him. After changing his dress, Wang found, when he came at the appointed time into the large reception hall, that a considerable number of the novitiates had also been invited, and that two distinguished-looking men whom he had never seen before were seated talking to the abbot.

In a very short time the light began to fade, for the sun had set some time before, and Wang was expecting that at any moment the servants would be called to bring in lights. Instead of this, the abbot cut with a pair of scissors a piece of white paper into a round globular shape, and throwing it with a dexterous flick of his fingers on to the wall, in an instant the large room was lighted up with what seemed a full moon, only the light was so brilliant that for the moment it appeared as though the sun had been brought back again from its westward course and was once more illumining the world.

The conversation that was now carried on between the abbot and his two distinguished guests was of such a lofty and exalted character that the young priests sat spell-bound as they listened in amazement to the high and noble themes that were being discussed by them. So entranced were they that they forgot the passage of time and became absorbed in the mysteries that were being talked about as though they were of the commonest and most ordinary character, though they were indeed such as are never heard in the language of mortals.

All at once one of the guests said to the abbot, "You have given us the moon with which the room is so beautifully illumined, could you not by the same power bring to us the woman that lives in it, so that she might entertain us for a short time?" With a smile upon his face, the abbot seized a chopstick that was lying on the table by which he was sitting and threw it deftly at the moon that was shining on the wall, when instantly a diminutive figure of an exceedingly beautiful woman was seen to appear in the very center of the shining orb. As every one looked on in wonder and amazement, the exquisite figure grew larger until it assumed the proportions of an ordinary woman, only with so fair a face and such perfect symmetrical outlines as are never seen on earth.

Stepping down out of the moon, she first of all sang some beautiful songs that gave intense pleasure to the hearers, for her voice was like the mellow, sweet notes of a flute that lingered on the air, and filled it with a delightful harmony. She then began to dance, and her motions were so full of grace that every pose she made filled the onlookers with the greatest admiration. Finally she made one surpassing graceful bound into the air, and landing on to the table she was transformed again into the original chopstick, that lay quivering and trembling close to the hand of the fairy abbot.

Wang, after this wonderful evening in which he had seen the miracles that he had often dreamed about actually performed in his very presence, determined to banish the thought of going home that had filled his heart before, and to remain on, in the hope that before long he would not be required to fulfill the menial duties that he had thus far been given to perform.

The days, however, went on just as they had done when he first entered the monastery. Every morning he was compelled to shoulder his axe, and wander about in search of the stunted pines, that only a diligent scrutiny could now discover in out of the way places and in sheltered spots on the mountain side.

After a month of this, he again sought the abbot and informed him that he had decided to return to his family, for it seemed to him that he was making no progress in the knowledge that he had come so far to learn. He could not see, he said, how the cutting down of firewood on these barren hills was going to help him to gain an insight into the mysteries of the spirits, or to help him to perform the wonders that would make him superior to his fellowmen. "I thought my life in this famous monastery was going to be one of study instead of manual labor. I have never spent such a laborious time in all my life as I have done during these past two months, and I would ask permission from you to let me go back to my home."

The venerable priest replied with a smile that he quite approved of this decision. He had evidently come, he said, to the temple with an entirely wrong conception of how men were to gain an entry amongst the spirits so as to acquire the mysterious powers they possessed. It was only by high virtues, and patient self-denial, and intense love for man that the secrets of the Western Heaven were ever revealed to mortal man. "I have tested you for two months with a very simple form of labor, yet you have broken down, and you have shown that your sole motive for desiring to gain miraculous powers was simply a vain desire to penetrate into mysteries that can never be revealed but to those who have gained such a lofty character by the utter abnegation of self that it would be safe to entrust to them the powers that come to those who would know how to use them aright. It will be well for you," he continued, "to return to your family and, casting aside your wild and visionary views, try to carry out the duties of life in the best manner you can."

Wang was terribly disappointed at this outspoken and homely advice of the abbot. He was naturally of a vain and frivolous nature, with a vast amount of self-conceit, and he could not comprehend how the possession of control over spirits and the material forces of nature had anything what- ever to do with personal character.

"I am sorry to hear you say this," he said, "as I was always under the impression that the whole thing consisted of certain secrets that might be revealed to any one, and that as you possessed them you could easily initiate me into them so that I should have powers that would free me from the limitations of time and sense, and enable me to perform such wonderful things as I saw you accomplish a month ago. As you do not seem willing to do this may I beg of you before I leave that you will give me one little atom of power such as I have seen you exercise occasionally when you have been moving about in the monastery? What I mean is this, I have observed that walls seem to have no influence in impeding you when you are moving about, but that you walk through them as though they did not exist. Give me," he continued, "the ability to do just this one thing, so that when I return home, I may have something to show my friends that will prevent them from laughing at me."

The abbot who seemed highly amused, said smilingly, "Very well, I shall grant your request, though remember that to be able always to accomplish even such a trifling thing as that you will require to live a virtuous life, and to have your mind endowed with noble ideals. You see the wall before you. Go straight on and walk through it, as though there were nothing in your way."

Wang started forth delighted, but his steps began to falter as he drew near to it and saw no sign of its yielding before him. "Go on," said the man, "for not a stone will move till you are close up to it. Push on and only have faith, for before that everything must give way." Inspired by these words Wang made a sudden movement forward and, dashing full speed at the wall, he found it open up before him, and, turning back to look at it, after he had passed through, he saw that the breach had automatically closed up behind him and that the wall now stood between him and the venerable abbot, who stood smiling on the other side of it.

Next morning at dawn he bade good-by to the monastery and began his descent of the mountain. Hours went by as he painfully picked his way down the stone steps that had been constructed centuries before. They had now become so smooth through the tread of countless feet that had traveled up and down them in the weary pilgrimages of men and women to the monastery, who had hoped to get relief from the burdens of life that oppressed them, that it was no simple matter to keep his footing on them. In some places, too, the slabs that formed the footway had been dislocated by the heavy rains that had sent their streams tearing down in torrents over them, and by the winter storms that had tried to wrench them from their places.

At length, however, the strain upon his muscles in the long descent was over and he finally stood upon the plain, while the great mountain, now bathed in the midday sun, stood up in magnificent splendor, with its brow seeming to touch the sky, and with the proud air of a monarch as it cast its glance far over the distant landscapes over which it seemed to rule.

Wang was received back by his family with the greatest delight. They had long been distressed at what they considered his folly in his endeavor to penetrate into the secrets of the spiritual world, and they had hoped that something would happen to him on the mountain that would give him a saner view of life and drive the nonsense out of his head. They little dreamed that it was the wisdom of the wise old abbot, the fairy in disguise from the far-off Heaven, that was really going to cure him of the ideas that fancy had wrought into his brain, and which no amount of argument had hitherto been able to expel from his thoughts.

After the congratulations upon his safe return were over, and smiling faces showed how hearty was the delight that filled every heart at seeing him once more in their midst, some one laughingly asked him whether his visit to the famous shrine had been the means of initiating him into the mysteries of the world of spirits. Had he got control over these mysterious beings? Could he turn the roving elves out of the haunted houses, and could he prevent them from wandering about during the midnight hours and prevent them from casting a spell over people's dwellings? They would all be so pleased if he would but give them some display of the magic art that the famous abbot in the mountain monastery was credited with possessing.

Wang replied that his stay had been too short to enable him to acquire all the knowledge he had desired, but still it had not been entirely in vain, and he would now proceed to give them a demonstration of a power that had been bestowed upon him that was denied to ordinary mortals.

Leading the company out from the room in which they had all been sitting into the open courtyard in front, he pointed to the high, enclosing wall and asked them to take particular notice of it. It was high and substantially built of granite blocks, and was well in keeping with the ancestral building which in a certain sense it was supposed to protect. "Be silent now and watch," he said, "and mark the ease with which I shall pass through it, as though it were made of the lightest vapor."

They all laughed at this, and gathering in two groups on each side of him, they looked on with amused faces and with sparkling eyes, eagerly expecting the proof Wang was going to give them of his supernatural power. "Behold now," he called out in a loud voice, and with head lowered he made a sudden bolt and rushed with all his speed at the wall. Instead, however, of passing through it with the ease he had predicted, his head came with a violent shock against the stone work and in an instant he was lying senseless on the ground.

For a long time he lay in danger of his life. Concussion of the brain ensued and it was with difficulty that he finally emerged from the serious condition into which he had been thrown. When he did, the fantastic notions that he had previously held had all vanished, and never again was he heard to express any desire to make incursions into the land of the spirits.

The King of the Snakes

In the land of the snakes, where human beings are never allowed to enter because of their known hostility and their desire to kill every serpent that they come near to, a numerous race of these despised reptiles live a life of their own. They have their own laws by which they regulate their conduct to each other. They have also codes of honor, which exercise an ennobling influence upon serpent society generally, and they have well defined legislation with regard to right and wrong, that tends to encourage what is good and to repress what is evil. The highly intelligent and subtle character of this snake community has tended to produce a more refined and civilized condition of society than what is found in any of the other lower orders of creation.

In consequence of this, it has been found that some of the more advanced among the serpents have become dissatisfied with their inferior condition and have had ambitious longings to emerge from their mean and lowly state and to be transformed into men. A notable instance of this was seen in the one who is the hero of our present story.

This serpent, by his superior wisdom as well as his noble birth, had been elected king, and he ruled his subjects with such justice and impartiality that he was exceedingly popular in every class of snake society. He was not content, however, with the power that this gave him, nor did he rest satisfied until he had discovered a method by which he could assume the human shape, while he retained all the characteristics of his own original nature. He was able at will to change from one to the other, so that he could govern in his own kingdom just as he had always done, while he could enjoy the pleasures of the world of man, whenever he felt inclined to do so.

The role that this Prince of the Snakes elected to adopt was that of a country gentleman, and, as he had a large amount of money at his command, he bought a small estate and had it laid out in the most beautiful way that the highest art could suggest. His gardens were especially famous, for not only had large sums been expended upon them, but they also contained the finest flowers that China produced, while at the same time there were specimens amongst them that had never before bloomed in the Flowery Kingdom. These had been brought by the ingenuity of the King of the

Snakes from his own dominions, and because of their rarity were regarded by visitors with special pleasure and admiration.

One day in strolling round his gardens, he observed an old man busily going from flower bed to flower bed picking the choicest flowers he could find in each. Approaching him, he said, "Old man, how is it that you take the liberty of coming into my garden, and plucking my flowers?"

"I pluck them," he replied, "for my four daughters, who have a passionate fondness for flowers of every description."

"How many daughters have you?" the prince asked, "and will you describe them to me?"

"I have four, and they are all at home with me, for I am so fond of them that I have not found it in my heart to be willing to arrange for their marriage, though I have had many offers from the parents around, who are anxious to have wives for their sons. The eldest is the least well favored of them all. She is pockmarked, but she is a woman of a great deal of character, and with a strong and active mind; the second is round-faced like a drum; the third has a face shaped like a duck's egg; while the fourth, who is the prettiest of the lot, has features that resemble a typical hen's egg."

The king, with admirable eye for the beautiful, though originally he was nothing but a snake, declared to the astonished old man that he had made up his mind that he would have the fourth daughter for his wife, and that unless she came to his mansion, that was situated some distance away in the country within ten days, he would send vast numbers of serpents, both large and small, that would proceed to devour him and all his family.

Deeply impressed with this threat, for he seems to have been unusually impressed with the personality of this strong man that addressed him, he went home and took to his bed. His eldest daughter by and by came to him and asked him what was the matter. He explained to her that if one of his daughters was not given in marriage to a certain rich man, whose gardens he had visited that day, a plague of snakes would visit him that would devour him. He then asked her if she would not be willing to do something to rescue her father from the impending destruction by consenting to be married to this man.

This young lady had very decided opinions of her own, and had evidently been allowed too much of her own way in the years gone by. The young lady promptly replied that she should on no account agree to any such proposal as had just been made to her, and that it was better that her father should be devoured by snakes than that she should be compelled to live with a man that, from his very nature, would most certainly be unkind to her. The old man, greatly distressed at the unfilial conduct of his eldest daughter, and the cruel answer she had given to his appeal, asked the second and third, successively, if they would not come to his assistance, but they both peremptorily refused to do anything for him, and they declared plainly that whether he lived or died was no concern of theirs.

The fourth daughter whose name was "Almond Blossom" was the most beautiful among the four daughters. Her face was not only of the typical contour so admired by the Chinese, but its attraction was also increased by the beauty of her soul that seemed to shine throughout her features and to add a grace and a dignity to them.

She was of a very gentle, loving disposition and her unconscious aim in life had always been to forget herself and to add to the happiness of those around her. Under the imperious rule of the eldest sister she had been very much coerced and kept down in the home, but this had never seemed to quench the loving, tender feeling that beat so warmly within her heart for her and for the other members of the family.

When her father appealed to her to know if she would be willing to sacrifice herself for him, she at once timidly and with the teardrops glistening within her eyelids, eagerly responded to his request. "Better that I should die than that my father should suffer," she answered in loving accents, and the old father then realized what a noble daughter he had in Almond Blossom.

But the devotion that had touched to its very depths the heart of her old father had produced an impression that was not likely to be forgotten far beyond the vicinity of her own home. The fairies, who are always on the look out for noble deeds amongst the dwellers on earth, heard the loving words of Almond Blossom to her father, in which she expressed her willingness to die in his stead, and they were moved with the profoundest admiration for the sacrifice she was prepared to make for him.

"We know," said one of the leaders in the fairyland, "that the action of this noble woman will be attended with great peril to her life and, unless we are prepared to succor her, she will not be able to survive the machinations of her enemies, and so she will miserably perish. I am going, therefore, to commission one of you to descend to the far-off earth, and attend her wherever she goes, and foil every attempt against her life."

Hardly had he done speaking than one of the brightest fairies that had listened to the story of Almond Blossom, seated on a dew drop through which the colors of the rainbow glistened, was flying through the air with the speed of a sunbeam to the village where our heroine lived.

The time specified by the Snake King for the delivery of his bride had almost elapsed, when on the morning of the tenth day a mean-looking sedan-chair, quite different from the gorgeous bridal ones that custom demands should be used for conveying the bride, drew up at the door of Almond Blossom's home and was set down in front of it. The men that carried it had a most disreputable look about them. They said they had been sent by their master to bring the fourth daughter of the family to his home, and they would be glad if matters could be hurried up as they had a considerable way to travel, and they were anxious to get back as quickly as possible.

The sight of the mean-looking bridal chair, and of the decidedly inferior character of the coolies that were to carry her, gave Almond Blossom a feeling of alarm which she found it difficult to suppress, but not for one single moment did she dream of endeavoring to escape from the sacrifice that she believed lay before her. Dressing herself in the best of the dresses that she possessed, she came to bid a final adieu to her beloved father, when, with a heart full of sorrow, he asked her how he could discover where she lived, so that at the proper time he might come and visit her in her new home. "My heart goes with you," he said, "and ere long I shall want to come and see how you are getting on. I shall have no peace of mind indeed until I can assure myself that you are happy, and that your husband loves you and is trying to make your life a joyous and contented one."

His daughter, who was sincerely and devotedly attached to him, replied that she would be just as anxious to see him again as he was to see her, and that she would take with her in her chair a good supply of hemp seed and small beans that she would drop every now and again along the road they traveled, and by the aid of these he would be able to trace her to her new home.

Saying this she stepped into the chair that had come for her and, suppressing her feelings and hiding the emotion that filled her heart so long as her father was looking upon her, was swiftly borne away by her mysterious bearers, who really belonged to the race of snakes. In a turning of the road she was soon lost sight of by her disconsolate father.

After the proper time allowed by etiquette, the old father, who had perpetually thought about his daughter and wondered as to her fate, set out with a heart full of doubt and anxiety to visit her. After proceeding a few yards from his home, with his eyes fixed on the ground, he suddenly to his great joy discovered the seeds that his beloved daughter had dropped, in order to guide him in his search of her. There was no break in the line of these loving mementoes of one who, while believing she was going to her destruction, could still think with such tender care of the one for whom she was giving her life.

After many a mile had been traveled, the trail suddenly diverged from the main road and led through a beautiful country, diversified with trees and running streams and wild flowers. Gradually it began to take the aspect of a park that had been laid out in connection with some nobleman's mansion, for rare and valuable trees were seen growing, and flowers full of perfume filled the air with their fragrance. The whole seemed more like some fairy scene that had been transferred from fairyland than any earthly one that his eyes had ever rested upon.

The old man began to doubt whether he was not trespassing on some great man's property, and he would have retreated had not his eye caught sight of the beans that his daughter had dropped to guide him to her. At length, after winding his way for some time among the most lovely gardens, he found himself in the presence of a most extensive range of buildings, that evidently belonged to some man who was immensely wealthy.

The old father was perplexed. This surely could not be the house of his daughter, who had left him in such a mean conveyance as her husband had sent to bring her home. He was once more feeling uneasy and thinking he ought to retrace his steps when his eye just then caught the tiny symbols of his daughter's affection lying plentifully on the ground, as though to dispel any doubts that might exist in his mind about this being the right place.

All hesitation now vanished from his mind, and, advancing to the main entrance, he inquired of a servant who seemed to be in charge of the door if his mistress was in. Gazing steadily at the poor common-looking old man, as though in doubt as to whether he should not drive him off the premises, he asked him, with a patronizing air, what it mattered to him whether his mistress was in or not. Just at that moment, and before he could answer the question that had been put to him, his daughter, who was passing through one of the spacious courtyards, caught sight of him and rushed toward him with her face beaming with smiles.

Seizing hold of his hand she led him into an inner apartment, all the while testifying to her extreme delight in once more seeing him, and in having him with her. Here she described what had happened to her on the eventful day when she bade him good-by as she then thought forever. All her fears had been falsified the moment she saw her husband, for he had received her with the most loving and tender courtesy and by his subsequent devotion to her he had completely won her heart. "I am only sorry," she continued, "that you will not be able to meet him on this visit, for he has gone on a long journey that will prevent him from getting back for several weeks."

"But you must come and see my house," she said, and wandering from room to room of this spacious mansion, the old father's eyes opened in astonishment at the magnificent things with which they were all adorned. There was a lavishness in the way each one had been furnished that would seem more befitting an emperor's palace than the home of a commoner. The old man had never seen such splendid things before and was lost in wonder as the glories of each room burst upon his astonished gaze. Amidst all his delight, however, there was one thing that gave him unbounded satisfaction, and that was that the beloved daughter who had been prepared to sacrifice her life for him was happy, and that her filial devotion had been rewarded by heaven with such a home as she now possessed.

After spending a few days with Almond Blossom, he returned to his home, laden with the most costly presents of silks and satins that his daughter had pressed upon him. The astonishment of his daughters was very great when their father rehearsed to them all the glories of the palace in which he declared their youngest sister was now living, and envy, cruel and bitter, entered into the heart of the eldest sister when she remembered that all that had been offered to her but had been rejected. For the moment she comforted herself with the fiction that her father was exaggerating the glories of her sister's home, and that it was not nearly so grand as he had represented it to be. She would, however, test the matter for herself, and pay a visit to this palatial mansion, and see whether it was really as magnificent as he had described it to them.

Burning with impatience, and jealous that her sister, on whom she had always looked with a kind of contempt because of her want of spirit, should be the mistress of an establishment so regal and so magnificent as that described by her father, the very next day she started to verify with her own eyes the marvelous stories that she had been told of Blossom's home. As she drew near to the house she began to feel a kind of awe creeping over her, for the accounts given by her father of her sister's residence were far from giving an adequate picture of its grandeur and magnificence. She was a woman of determination, however, and she was not going to allow the purpose she had already formed in her mind to be thwarted by any craven fears that might come over her.

Coming up boldly to the great entrance, she demanded of the men in charge that she should be taken to her sister, whom she said she had come to visit. This statement brought forth a most ready obedience and in a moment or two she found herself in the presence of Blossom. The latter, with her charming disposition and absolutely unsuspicious nature, received her with the greatest demonstrations of joy and affection. She made her sit down and tell how she had been, and all the family news, while her eyes glistened with delight as she heard about what was going on in her old home.

After some time the elder sister suggested that she would like very much to be shown over the house, of which she had received such a graphic description, she said, from her father, and of the wonderful things it contained. She was longing, she declared, to see them for herself, and to be gratified by their marvels. After wandering about among the spacious halls that were adorned by exquisite scrolls that the most famous artists of China and of snake land had painted, and through the numerous rooms that abounded in this great mansion, they came out into a large courtyard around which some of them had been built. Here were collected specimens of the rarest flowers, some of them so fragrant that they filled the air with their perfume.

In the center of this extensive court was a large well, which Blossom explained had been dug more than a hundred years ago and which was looked upon with a great deal of superstition by the people around. It was believed that spirits had their abode within its depths, for sounds that did not seem earthly were being made day and night within its dark recesses that could only be the result of either fairies or gnomes that had their dwelling down there. The water was never used, she continued, for men were afraid of disturbing the mysterious beings whose inarticulate sounds could be constantly heard from above.

While Blossom was telling her story with an innocent face and with a heart full of faith in the reality of the invisible beings that she believed had possession of the well, her sister's mind was rapidly working out the plan by which she might dispose of her, and establish herself as her successor in this magnificent home. Suddenly the opportunity came, for while Blossom was bending over the well and peering into the depths below, her sister gave her a violent push that precipitated her into it, and with a cry of despair she vanished out of sight into the hidden abyss below.

Everything had favored this murderous act. Not a soul was around to witness it. The servants were far away in another part of the building, and they two were the only ones that were in this large wing of the house. There was no possibility of discovery and what was needed now was a bold front and an assumption of perfect innocence and there was no reason why anyone should ever know of the terrible crime that had been committed that day. She little dreamed of the invisible forces that were already at work to avenge the wrong that she had committed, or how the fairy that had been specially sent down from the Heaven had already rescued Blossom from a violent death, and had her in safe keeping until she could restore her to her husband, when in due time he returned from his visit to the kingdom of the snakes.

After resting for a considerable time, she called one of the servants and asked him if she knew where his mistress was. "I left her some time ago," she explained, "and she was to follow me immediately; will you please call her and tell her I would be glad to see her."

The man went slowly away, but by-and-by he returned with a most anxious look on his face and declared that he could not find a trace of her. Search was then made by all the servants in the house, until every room and corner in the building had been examined, but no sign could be seen of her anywhere.

Great was the excitement throughout the whole of the establishment, for Blossom had been beloved by every member in it, both high and low. Messengers were at once dispatched to the neighboring villages and along the high road to make inquiries as to whether anyone had seen her, but after hours of anxious searching they returned without any light being thrown upon the mysterious disappearance of their beloved mistress.

On the morrow a strange but beautiful-looking bird flew out of the well, down which Blossom had been hurled, and alighting upon a branch of a tree that grew in the courtyard, began to sing in a most melodious but mournful manner. As the sister sat and listened to the melody, she was startled to find that mingled with the bird-like notes of the songster there was something exceedingly human about them. As she listened she discovered to her horror that the bird was singing the story of the crime she had committed, and that if any of the servants had been about they would have found out how it was that Blossom had disappeared. Mad with fear she made a sudden rush upon the singer and seizing it she twisted its neck and threw it outside the house. Marvelous to say, the next morning, when she glanced at the spot where she had thrown the bird, she found that a clump of most beautiful bamboos had grown up on the very spot where it had been cast.

While she was looking with wonder upon the graceful trees as they bent before the morning breeze, her heart almost stood still when she found that the sounds that came from the agitated bamboos were articulate, and in low and plaintive language they were rehearsing minutely the scene at the well, when Blossom had been violently pushed into it.

Seizing an axe she speedily cut down the tell-tale bamboos, hoping that now the story of her crime would be for ever forgotten, but she soon found to her sorrow that wickedness is not so easily covered up, and that heaven has ways that men never dream of by which it reveals the secrets of those who have committed wrong. Besides, the fairy who had Blossom in hiding was still planning for her restoration to her home and for the condign punishment of her unnatural sister.

Some of the servants gathering up the bamboos that had been cut down were so struck by the peculiar shape and coloring of them that they did not dare to burn them as they would have done the ordinary common specimens.

They were so beautiful that they thought them worthy of preservation, for they were of a kind that had never been seen before in that region. The stem instead of being round was square, while the color was not the usual pale yellow, but was jet black. With the utilitarian ideas of the Chinese, they determined that they should not be wasted, so calling in an itinerant worker in bamboo they commissioned him to make them into chairs that they might present them to their master when he returned from his journey. This he did the very day on which they were finished.

His first inquiry when he entered his home was for his wife. The servants had only the sorrowful tale to tell that on a certain day she had mysteriously disappeared and though they had searched the whole country round not a single trace of her could be found.

The sister coming in at the moment, with every appearance of distress on her countenance, corroborated their statements and described how she had left Blossom for a moment to go into the next room, and how from that time to the present she had vanished so completely that they could never discover what had become of her.

And now a most remarkable miracle was performed. While they were all standing round listening to the story of the last speaker, and a profound gloom rested upon the face of the master, suddenly one of the chairs underwent a wonderful transformation, for it seemed to dissolve before their very eyes and from it arose the figure of Blossom. She told the story of how her sister had attempted to destroy her, and how a good fairy had rescued her from drowning and had kept her in safety until the return of her husband, when she need no longer fear the plots that might be made against her life. The King of the Snakes was so enraged at the wickedness of the sister that he had her executed. No one seemed to regret her death; indeed, when the tale was told it seemed to every one who heard it, that it was a just retribution for the cruel design she had conceived and carried out for the murder of Blossom.

How an Expectant Prime Minister Was Cured of His Ambition by the Ingenious Device of a Fairy

In a certain city that lay not many miles away from the capital of this great empire of China, there lived a young man into whose heart there had come the wildest spirit of ambition. The thought of rising to the highest honors that the State could confer influenced him in all his waking moments and even tinged his dreams with romantic visions that but added to the great passion of his life.

He was a man of more than ordinary ability and he was vain enough to believe that there was no position that the gods could give him that he was not competent to fill. In many respects he was of a lovable, generous nature, and could he but have been delivered from this unhappy disposition that overshadowed the many excellent qualities that he really possessed he would have made a very useful member of society.

The fairies, who take such an interest in the affairs of mankind, seemed distressed that such a promising young fellow should have his prospects blighted by an infirmity that in the end would ruin his life, and determined to interfere to save him, so one of their number was deputed to fly with all speed from Heaven down to earth to rescue him from the sorrow that they knew would inevitably come upon him.

One day, Chan, with a number of youthful companions, was rambling on the outskirts of the town, when they came to a monastery, embowered amidst huge boulders and shadowed by great pine trees that had been planted a century ago. Some one suddenly remarked that just now there was a famous physiognomist living in it who had wonderful power in discovering men's fortunes from the conformation of their face and from the lines that nature with some subtle intention had carved upon them.

Chan no sooner heard this than, impelled by a desire to know what fate had in store for him in the future, he rushed off in search of this fortune-teller, who, he hoped, might possibly be able to tell him how his life was going to turn out.

He found him sitting in one of the courtyards under an umbrella-shaped awning to keep the sun from shining on him, with pictures of various kinds of faces that he had grouped around to illustrate his theories and to impress the imagination of those who came to consult him.

After looking long and steadily at Chan, as though he would read into his very soul, he said, as he leisurely fanned himself with his broad palm-leaf fan, "You are one of the favorites of fortune. I see good luck stamped upon every feature of your face just as though heaven had written your destiny on every line in it. The days are not far distant when you will become the greatest mandarin in the State, and when the emperor will shower upon you honors that will make you immensely wealthy and cause your name to be a household word in the home of every scholar in the land."

Chan, overjoyed with the words of the physiognomist, broke out into expressions of delight. "Is it true, indeed," he asked, "that I shall be a mandarin of such a high degree that all these honors and emoluments that you predict for me will ever really come into my life?" "You may rest assured," the fortune-teller answered, "that every word that I have uttered shall be fulfilled in ampler measure than I have language to express. I can plainly see by signs that are to me most certain and infallible that you will become Prime Minister and for twenty years of continued peace you will be the highest subject in the State."

Just at this moment a heavy shower of rain began to fall, and Chan, having gladly paid a generous fee to the fortune-teller, fled with all haste into a room that was occupied by one of the priests connected with the monastery.

Here seated on a hassock, he saw a venerable-looking bonze who was so absorbed in meditation that the entrance of Chan made no impression upon him. His appearance was a very striking one, and was very different from that of the ordinary, illiterate, coarse-looking priests that are usually found in the temples and monasteries throughout the country.

He had the refined and delicate look of the true recluse, who, dissatisfied with life, had dedicated himself to the service of the gods in the hope that by contemplation and by a long course of self-denial he might finally have the happiness of being absorbed into Nirvana, where neither joy nor sorrow would ever disturb the infinite rest of the soul.

Chan looked at him and would have been glad to have conversed with him, for so elated was he with the brilliant prospects that had been promised him by the fortune-teller that he felt as if he could not contain the good news within his own breast. No sign, however, came from the man that he was conscious of his presence, so absorbed was he in the thoughts and visions of a world that only the eye of the seer can ever hope to behold. Little did he dream that this was a fairy that had traveled from the far-off fairyland to work out his deliverance and that even at that very moment when he seemed so oblivious of his presence, he was thinking out the mode by which the purpose for which he had come to earth could be best accomplished.

Chan sat down somewhat impatiently to wait for the passing away of the rain, when almost immediately a fit of drowsiness that he seemed to have no power to control gradually crept over him. He tried to resist this, but without success, and seeing a couch near by he stretched himself out upon it, and in an instant he was sound asleep.

And then began a series of visions so wonderful and so amazing that his heart was filled with the intensest delight. While he was pondering in his mind what all this meant, he suddenly saw two men in official robes drawing near to him, whom he at once recognized as messengers from the emperor. They presented him with a document which they told him was a royal edict, commanding his immediate attendance at palace, as his presence was required there to discuss certain affairs of State of great importance that His Majesty was unwilling to have transacted before he had consulted him upon them.

Chan was delighted. The predictions of the fortune-teller were evidently coming true faster than ever he had dared to dream they would. With hasty footsteps he followed the imperial messengers, and finally he was ushered into the presence of the Son of Heaven by the high officials, with the most profound reverence and respect.

His fears as to how he would be received were soon driven from his heart when he had been ushered with all the quaint and dignified ceremony of an Eastern Court into the presence of the emperor, especially when, with unaffected simplicity, he had caused him to sit by his side and had treated him as though he had been one of the high mandarins with whom he was daily wont to converse on the great affairs of the kingdom.

After they had been discussing these for a considerable time His Majesty, turning to Chan, said, "I have come to the conclusion that you are the most suitable man that I could find to become my Prime Minister, and I accordingly appoint you to that office from this very moment. I am so satisfied with your ability to undertake the responsible duties connected with this important position that I shall at once issue an edict to that effect, so that there may be no unnecessary delay in your attending the great Council meetings that are held every morning before the dawn has come upon the world. In order to show you the confidence that I have in your honor and discretion, of the nine grades of officials that are employed in ruling the people of my empire, with the exception of the three highest, I shall hand over to you to appoint and dispose of as may seem best to you. I know I can do this with safety, for your wisdom and your purity of character are sufficient guarantees to me that in conferring such large and unusual power upon you I shall but be benefiting the State. And now as you are leaving let me bestow upon you as a token of my esteem a parting gift. The value is not great, but it will remind you of our meeting to-day and of the new tie that binds you and me for years to come, I hope. It is a horse of rare beauty that has been sent me from the far West, and when men see you riding on it they will recognize it as one that I have often used myself and so will all the more be inclined to pay you honor."

Chan returned home amazed and delighted, and with his brain full of visions of what the coming years would bring him. He was still young, but with one great bound he had landed on the highest pinnacle of glory, and now everything that heart could wish to possess lay within his grasp.

When he reached his home his mind became perplexed at the mysterious change that had come over it. The old home where he and his fathers had lived was now radiant with the newest and the brightest colors that the most skilled painters could lay upon it. They were all of a regal tone and such as well befitted the mansion of a high Minister of State.

It was, however, when he had entered inside that his mind was struck with wonder at the strange transformation that had been effected upon everything that he saw. It seemed, indeed, as though the rarest treasures of the kingdom had been sought out, and with fairy hands had been transported to it, and had been placed with such deft and cunning hand that their glories shone out with the most conspicuous result. There were ebony chairs and tables from Canton, but of so rare and delicate carving, and with such quaint and difficult designs, that only the master artists of the nation could ever have executed them. There were scrolls, too, that adorned the walls, made of various colored silks that had been woven in the looms of Soochow and Hangchow, of such delicate hues and tints that the eye rested upon them with the most exquisite pleasure. Scattered too, about the rooms, with apparent carelessness, as though they were of but little value, were vases and dishes from the potteries in Kiangsi, with the famous hallmarks and the exquisite colors that made each of them almost worth a king's ransom.

All this was very astonishing to Chan, but there were further surprises still in store, far greater than any that had yet happened to him. Calling for one of his servants, he was thunderstruck by half a dozen men, dressed in long robes and with an official air as though they might have been small mandarins, hurrying in, and in a submissive tone of voice, begging to know what service was required of them.

Hardly had he pulled himself together and remembered that he was no longer the commoner Chan, but the Prime Minister of China, when a commotion was heard in the outer courtyard and the voices of coolies filled the air with their noisy clamor. Asking one of these stately servants, that he felt almost afraid to address, so grand did he seem to him, what was the meaning of this he was informed with a profound obeisance that they were porters that were bringing presents to him from a powerful mandarin in the city, who in this substantial manner wished to congratulate him on the honors that had been conferred upon him by His Majesty.

His old life he soon found had been completely displaced by the larger one, that never even in his moments of highest ambition had flashed upon his imagination. When he went out on any public business it seemed indeed that the eyes of all the world were upon him to pay him reverence. The common people bowed low their heads as he rode by, and fled with haste to the road-sides, while the center of the street was left deserted for him and his retinue.

Even the mandarins of lower grade manifested the utmost obsequiousness when they accidentally met him by the way. Some bowed almost to the ground, others knelt on the roadway, while some again who hoped to obtain preferment took off their shoes, unworthy they would have him think to stand in any other guise before him.

The years went by and Chan's power grew and strengthened with the lapse of time. His intellect was naturally powerful and the science of statesmanship was one that had a special attraction for him, and so it came to pass that the conduct of imperial matters fell into his hands. Unfortunately his avarice grew apace with the extension of his influence. The privilege of disposing of offices throughout the empire which the emperor had bestowed upon him when he made him Prime Minister had exercised a most baneful effect upon him.

The piling up of wealth became at last the one ambition of his soul. Anyone or anything that stood in his way in regard to this one dominant feature in his life was swept relentlessly from his path. If some noble had possessions that he may have held, while some doubtful point of law existed with regard to his title, he was soon robbed by Chan of everything he had. And woe be to the man that dared to stand up for his rights, for as the judges were afraid to offend so great a man by doing justice, he and his whole family were condemned to death as traitors to their country.

At last his exactions and his tyranny became so intolerable that a movement was made to impeach him before the emperor. A mandarin in high official position accordingly drew up a list of the offences of which he was guilty and presented them.

In this petition it was shown that he had latterly neglected the affairs of the kingdom, he was utterly reckless in the amassing of money, and he had caused large numbers of people to be put to death without any sufficient reason, but simply because they had been obnoxious to him for some reason or other. For all the crimes he had committed both against the kingdom and against the lives and property of His Majesty's subjects, the emperor was besought to deprive him of all his offices and have him put to death.

Chan was in mortal terror when this petition was presented to the Cabinet Council over which the Son of Heaven presided, and when the long list of his crimes was duly read before the members that composed it. Fortunately for him the emperor happened to be in an easy mood at the time, and he rather made light of the charges that were brought against him, fancying for the moment that they were a plot got up by some enemy of the Prime Minister to get him ousted from his position in order that he might step into his place.

The failure of this attempt to bring Chan to justice caused widespread alarm and consternation amongst the nobles and high mandarins in the capital, for they feared the vengeance he might exact upon all whom he might suspect of being privy to this attempt to cause his overthrow. They accordingly combined their forces, and as a united body they drew up an indictment even stronger and more forcible than the former one, and giving ample and convincing proof that all the crimes laid to his charge were absolutely true.

This time the king became convinced that the matter was more serious than he had formerly deemed possible. The character of the men and the number of those who had signed the accusation were a sufficient guarantee that the charges brought against the Prime Minister must have some foundation in fact. After a careful examination of these, he came to the conclusion that Chan was guilty, and he accordingly issued an edict depriving him of his office and banishing him to the province of Yünnan, while at the same time the whole of his property was confiscated to the State.

Immediately following upon the issue of this decree, a whole regiment of soldiers was dispatched to the home of the disgraced minister, and took possession of everything it contained. There were found to be millions worth of property in it, for the jewelry and precious jade stones that had been accumulating for many years were in themselves enough to make the man that owned them a millionaire.

No pity was shown to the man that but yesterday was the most powerful subject in the empire. He and his wife and his sons and daughters were all seized, bound with ropes and treated with the utmost indignity. As the home was being dismantled and the heaps of precious things were ruthlessly carried off amid the scoffing and laughter of the soldiers, Chan and his family were in the utmost distress. Not a kindly word was said to any one of them, but insults were heaped upon them, and reproaches and maledictions that were even worse to bear than the loss of all the property that had been the cause of all the disasters that had come upon them.

After the house had been cleared of every article that had made one of the most luxurious mansions in the empire, and the doors had been sealed with the imperial seal showing that the building was now the property of the State, the villainous-looking runners that had been deputed to carry out the sentence of banishment to the far-off province of Yunnan, with rough and brutal hands seized upon the fallen minister. They then fastened a rope about his neck, lest he might attempt to escape, and gathering close around him in order to prevent the possibility of a rescue they dragged him out on the long and weary journey that lay before him before he could reach his destination in the west.

The misery of that moment when he was thus ignominiously driven through the streets of the capital, a miserable criminal, where once his power had been supreme, was the bitterest experience of his life. Those streets that for many years had been witnesses of his glory, when the crowds used to gather to behold the pomp and splendor that he displayed as he rode through them to the palace of the emperor, now saw him degraded and fallen, dragged along by sordid hands, the object of contempt, with no eyes filled with tears at his fate, and no thought of pity amongst those that looked upon this spectacle of fallen greatness.

Mile after mile he was hurried along the road ready to drop through fatigue. He begged and entreated that even the roughest conveyance might be given him, so that he could rest his weary limbs. He pleaded that he had never been accustomed to walk and that unless some little sympathy were shown him he would most certainly perish on the road, and die in their very hands.

He spoke, however, to men whose souls had been so hardened by duties that had tended to obliterate the finest feelings of the heart, that the only impression that his piteous appeal had upon them was to tighten the rope that bound their victim, and to rush on with increased speed along the doleful way.

At length they came to the foot of a pass that led over a high range of hills, and, as Chan looked up and saw the narrow pathways winding up higher and higher away up among the mountains, his heart sank within him. "It is quite impossible," he said, "that I can climb those steep and rugged heights, for my strength is almost exhausted. Have pity on me, and let us rest here for the night and to-morrow, after I have been refreshed with sleep, we may then continue our journey with some hope that I may be able to scale the many ranges of hills that lie between us and the plains beyond."

The only reply to this most sad and touching speech was a violent dash forward to mount the stone stairway. Every step that Chan took caused him unutterable pain and weariness, so utterly exhausted had he become by the cruel strain that had been put upon him since he left his home. The thought too of his wife and children, left to the tender mercies of the world, and of his own wrecked fortunes, added bitterness to the forlorn condition in which he found himself, and his heart was like to break with the accumulated sorrows that in one unhappy day had fallen upon him and his house.

The day was drawing to a close when the highest ridge of this lofty pass could be dimly seen in the distance. The shadows had already fallen deep and heavy on the valleys below, and the fading light of day was getting blurred and misty on the higher points on which the setting sun was shedding his parting gift to the world.

Just at this moment the party entered a pine grove and, in the involved and winding paths that were rendered in- distinct by the gloom shed upon them by the trees, they found it difficult to advance. They had not only to pick their way among the stones that formed the ancient road- way, that the feet of countless travelers had worn smooth and which the storms of rain had torn from their places, but they had also to see that their prisoner did not escape them during the growing darkness that was falling upon them.

They were just emerging out of the gloom of this miniature forest, and were congratulating themselves that they would soon reach the rest house that had been built for the use of travelers on the crest of the pass, when the confused noise of many voices was heard in front of them. Everyone stopped in alarm, for the sounds were not those of peaceful travelers, but of the robbers that were known to infest these hills. By and by a band of men could be seen flying wildly toward them, each of whom had a sword in his hand which he brandished in the air, at the same time uttering the most savage imprecations and threats of murder.

"Robbers!" the runners cried, and in an instant everyone had fled in the utmost terror, leaving Chan standing on the road, a solitary figure to meet the excited thieves that were rushing upon him.

When they came up to him, he fell upon his knees and besought for mercy. "Have pity upon me," he cried, "and spare my life. I have nothing in the world to give you, for the riches that I once possessed have all been taken from me, and now I own only the clothes in which you see me dressed."

"We want nothing from you but your life," one that seemed to be a leader shouted in a loud excited voice. "Do you know who we are?" he asked in a threatening voice. "We are not robbers as you suppose. Look well at us. Can you not recognize us? We are the spirits of the men that you plundered and hounded to death when you were Prime Minister, and we are here now to avenge the wrongs that brought destruction upon us and our homes, and therefore you must die." With that a dozen swords gleamed in the air and in a moment were sheathed in his body, and the unfortunate minister was left dead upon the road.

The avenging spirits now seized upon the soul of the murdered man, and, flying with a speed that far surpassed the lightning's flash, they soon arrived at the palace of Yen-lo, the dread ruler of the Land of Shadows. Here the keepers of the doors led them into the presence of the king, who was then engaged in deciding the cases of a number of wretched-looking spirits that stood trembling before him. When it came to Chan's turn to be tried, the stern ruler called for the book in which the actions of men were recorded. Turning over page after page he at last came to the chapter on which the life of Chan was minutely detailed.

No sooner had he read a few lines of that, than he seemed convulsed with anger. "This man," he said, "has always acted as a traitor to his king and his country, and is therefore deserving of the severest punishment that I can mete out to him. Here, Lictors!" he cried, "carry him away at once and let him stew for half-an-hour in the great oil cauldron."

In an instant a dozen attendant spirits had seized upon Chan and had dragged him along in the direction of where smoke was rising in thick volumes from what seemed to be a blazing furnace. When he came closer to it, he saw that fires were raging underneath and all around a huge cauldron filled with oil that was kept continually on the boil by the constant supply of fuel that dark, forbidding-looking spirits kept heaping on the fires below.

When Chan saw this his mind was filled with such terror that he cried out in perfect agony, and putting forth all his strength he endeavored to loosen the grip that the spirits had upon him and to make his escape, but all in vain. Before he knew where he was he had been pitched headlong into the boiling oil and was suffering such tortures as he had never deemed it possible that any human being could endure and yet live. His cries now were pitiable in the extreme. He wanted to die he said. The oil got down his throat, and into his very bones so that he seemed to be on fire, and he cried for mercy, but compassion was a thing that had long died out of the hearts of those who were carrying out the orders of the dread Yen-lo. After a time Chan was forked out of the boiling oil, by long prongs that stuck into his flesh, and once more he was hurried with indecent haste before the judgment seat.

"I see by the books," the great judge thundered out, "that you were the cause of the death of many of the inhabitants of the Celestial Empire; that you were never known to spare an enemy, and that men called upon you for mercy, but you always turned a deaf ear to them. I adjudge, therefore, that you be carried away and that you be impaled upon the knives that stand ready for such criminals as you are on the Knife Mountain."

Once more Chan felt himself caught up with incredible swiftness and in what seemed but a few seconds he saw the Knife Mountain looming up above him. It was one mass of knives, that were stuck in at all possible angles, so that whoever fell upon them could not escape the deadly thrust that these cruel instruments of torture were intended to give. While he was gazing at this awful spectacle, that almost froze his blood and filled his heart with the wildest terror, he felt himself suddenly flung into the air and a moment after he fell upon the cruel knives.

The agony he had to endure seemed even more intense than what he had suffered from the boiling oil. Again he wanted to die but could not. He dared not move, he scarcely dared to breathe. Happily he was soon relieved from this and once more he was flying through the air in the grip of the evil spirits and placed in front of Yen-lo.

"I find," this latter said, "that when you were Prime Minister you sold the offices of the Crown and that you made an enormous fortune out of these sales, though you knew they were illegal and hurtful to the purity of justice and to the welfare of the kingdom." "Take the counting board," he said, to a man with a bushy beard that stood by, "and reckon up the full amount that this man received during the years in which he held the highest office in the State."

In a few seconds this grim accountant had added up the various sums that had been received by Chan, when they were found to amount to three hundred and twenty million taels. "I adjudge," said the grim ruler with the suspicion of a twinkle in his eye, "that he shall this instant be made to swallow this vast sum that he so unrighteously accumulated when he was on earth."

Without a moment's delay a band of spirits went out to the Mountain of Gold that loomed up near by and dug up just the amount that Chan had gained. This they melted in a furnace, and laying him on his back, they poured the molten stream down his throat, causing him the most unutterable pains and agonies that the human frame seemed capable of enduring.

Once more the wretched, tortured Prime Minister stood in the presence of the judge. The final sentence came sharp and crisp from his lips. "The prisoner," he said, "shall now return to earth, and there in the new life that I have assigned to him, he shall work out the punishment that I have already meted out to him in this Land of Shadows. His crimes have been too great to be lightly forgiven, and even in the new birth a nemesis must follow him. He shall be born a woman of such low and humble rank, that, unless some germ of virtue enters his heart and so uplifts him, he shall learn the bitterness of poverty that shall crowd his life with sorrow and despair."

Scarcely were these words uttered when the figure of Yen-lo began to grow shadowy and the forms of his tormentors became attenuated, while the scenes, where he had suffered such excruciating torments, lost their identity in a hazy mist, and everything vanished from his sight. His first stage of suffering had passed away, and now as a woman he was to go on in the expiation of his crimes, until by a life of self-sacrifice he could show that he had repented and had proved himself worthy of being again placed in the higher ranks of society.

When Chan was old enough to realize that he was reincarnated, he found himself or rather herself, for he was now a girl, in an exceedingly poor home that was so scantily furnished that the whole of the furniture consisted of not more than a half a dozen indispensable articles. She found, too, that her mother was a beggar woman, and in course of time her little daughter was compelled to go with her on her begging expeditions.

This wretched kind of existence lasted till she was sixteen, when her mother sold her to a man in a respectable position of life as a concubine. Here her fortunes began to mend. She was no longer the squalid beggar, clothed in rags, and living on the miserable doles of the charitable. Her life now seemed secure against all want, for she was well dressed and had abundance of good food. There was an additional reason too why her heart began to rejoice and that was the love of her husband. Although by no means pretty, there was something in her manner and her native ability that made her most attractive to him, and so on every occasion he treated her with the greatest kindness and love.

The one drawback to all this new enjoyment upon which she had entered was the hatred of the wife. She was intensely jealous of her and adopted every means in her power to make her life miserable. The tenderness, however, with which her husband treated her, and the comforts that had come to her since she had been able to abandon the beggar's role enabled her to bear with tolerable patience the ill-treatment of her rival.

A new and beautiful life had dawned upon her, and it seemed that now at last her sorrows and troubles were gone forever, and only sunshine would flash upon her path in the years that were before her. The decrees of fate, however, were not so easily to be evaded. The grim judge of the Land of Shadows had foretold that infinite sorrows would be her lot, until the crimes of her previous existence had been expiated. Ere many months had passed she was to find how fatally true was this prediction.

One evening she was sitting with her husband and quietly chatting with him, when the door was suddenly burst open and two men entered with long knives in their hands. Rushing furiously at her husband, the men attacked him with these deadly weapons and in a few seconds he was lying dead upon the floor. The robbers, gathering up what valuables they could hastily collect, fled from the room and the poor woman who had been too terrified to utter a sound before, now with loud outcries called for assistance from the rest of the family.

The first to arrive was the unfortunate man's wife, who at once accused the concubine of being the cause of his death. She was in league with confederates outside, she declared, and together they had planned this daring act of murder and robbery. Word was at once sent to the nearest mandarin who ordered his soldiers to apprehend the poor young woman.

The judicial investigations that followed seemed to prove her guilt and she was finally condemned to death. When she heard this decision she was so over-mastered with the sense of injustice that had been done her that she shrieked with horror. And in a moment the girl had vanished from the stage and, lo and behold, it was discovered that it was Chan that had made the outcry that had filled the room with notes of horror.

His companions gathered round him, anxious to know what had caused the awful shriek that had been wrung from him. "What is the matter?" they asked him.

"You must have had a terribly bad dream to make you cry out in the way you have just done. What a fright you have given us. You must have thought someone was murdering you to get up such a yell as just now exploded from you. What has happened to you?"

Dazed and confused with the memory of the awful scenes that he had just been passing through, Chan for some time could give no reply to the eager questions that were pressed upon him by his comrades. Looking round he caught the look of the priest that was fastened upon him. It was full of sympathy and his eyes glistened with pleasure as he asked Chan if he still wished to be a Prime Minister.

A sudden terror fell upon the newly-awakened sleeper, and a dim conviction seemed to creep over him that in some way or other he had conjured up the visions that had been passing with such realistic power before him while in the land of dreams.

"No," he replied, "I never shall dream again of holding so high an office in the State. The perils, as you have shown me, are too great and the responsibilities too heavy for any common man like me to dare to incur them. But tell me I pray you, how I should spend my life so that I may get the greatest good out of it?"

The priest, with a beaming countenance, replied, "If you really desire to make the most of life you must spend it in the practice of virtue. The meaner thoughts and ambitions by which most men are swayed always end fatally for those who are controlled by them. But when I speak of virtue, never forget the chiefest of them all is the one that the ancient sage has put at the head of the five ideals that he has declared shall remain as long as human life exists, and that is kindness to one's fellowmen. No virtue can be carried out and no supreme happiness can come to any man unless the love of men is deeply rooted within his very soul."

As the fairy uttered these exquisite words, his form seemed gradually to dissolve in mist, and Chan looked with eager eyes at the spot where, but a moment ago, he had been sitting, but no trace could he see of him. He had completely vanished from sight.

CHINESE FAIRY TALES

Nursery Fairy Tales

Women's Words Part Flesh and Blood

Once upon a time there were two brothers, who lived in the same house. And the big brother listened to his wife's words, and because of them fell out with the little one. Summer had begun, and the time for sowing the high-growing millet had come. The little brother had no grain, and asked the big one to loan him some, and the big one ordered his wife to give it to him. But she took the grain, put it in a large pot and cooked it until it was done. Then she gave it to the little fellow. He knew nothing about it, and went and sowed his field with it. Yet, since the grain had been cooked, it did not sprout. Only a single grain of seed had not been cooked; so only a single sprout shot up. The little brother was hard-working and industrious by nature, and hence he watered and hoed the sprout all day long. And the sprout grew mightily, like a tree, and an ear of millet sprang up out of it like a canopy, large enough to shade half an acre of ground. In the fall the ear was ripe. Then the little brother took his ax and chopped it down. But no sooner had the ear fallen to the ground, than an enormous Roc came rushing down, took the ear in his beak and flew away. The little brother ran after him as far as the shore of the sea.

Then the bird turned and spoke to him like a human being, as follows: "You should not seek to harm me! What is this one ear worth to you? East of the sea is the isle of gold and silver. I will carry you across. There you may take whatever you want, and become very rich."

The little brother was satisfied, and climbed on the bird's back, and the latter told him to close his eyes. So he only heard the air whistling past his ears, as though he were driving through a strong wind, and beneath him the roar and surge of flood and waves. Suddenly the bird settled on a rock: "Here we are!" he said.

Then the little brother opened his eyes and looked about him: and on all sides he saw nothing but the radiance and shimmer of all sorts of white and yellow objects. He took about a dozen of the little things and hid them in his breast.

"Have you enough?" asked the Roc.

"Yes, I have enough," he replied.

"That is well," answered the bird. "Moderation protects one from harm."

Then he once more took him up, and carried him back again.

When the little brother reached home, he bought himself a good piece of ground in the course of time, and became quite well to do.

But his brother was jealous of him, and said to him, harshly: "Where did you manage to steal the money?"

So the little one told him the whole truth of the matter. Then the big brother went home and took counsel with his wife.

"Nothing easier," said his wife. "I will just cook grain again and keep back one seedling so that it is not done. Then you shall sow it, and we will see what happens."

No sooner said than done. And sure enough, a single sprout shot up, and sure enough, the sprout bore a single ear of millet, and when harvest time came around, the Roc again appeared and carried it off in his beak. The big brother was pleased, and ran after him, and the Roc said the same thing he had said before, and carried the big brother to the island. There the big brother saw the gold and silver heaped up everywhere. The largest pieces were like hills, the small ones were like bricks, and the real tiny ones were like grains of sand. They blinded his eyes. He only regretted that he knew of no way by which he could move mountains. So he bent down and picked up as many pieces as possible.

The Roc said: "Now you have enough. You will overtax your strength."

"Have patience but a little while longer," said the big brother. "Do not be in such a hurry! I must get a few more pieces!"

And thus time passed.

The Roc again urged him to make haste: "The sun will appear in a moment," said he, "and the sun is so hot it burns human beings up."

"Wait just a little while longer," said the big brother. But that very moment a red disk broke through the clouds with tremendous power. The Roc flew into the sea, stretched out both his wings, and beat the water with them in order to escape the heat. But the big brother was shriveled up by the sun.

The Three Rhymsters

Once there were three daughters in a family. The oldest one married a physician, the second one married a magistrate; but the third, who was more than usually intelligent and a clever talker, married a farmer.

Now it chanced, once upon a time, that their parents were celebrating a birthday. So the three daughters came, together with their husbands, to wish them long life and happiness. The parents-in-law prepared a meal for their three sons-in-law, and put the birthday wine on the table. But the oldest son-in-law, who knew that the third one had not attended school, wanted to embarrass him.

"It is far too tiresome," said he, "just to sit here drinking: let us have a drinking game. Each one of us must invent a verse, one that rimes and makes sense, on the words, 'in the sky, on the earth, at the table, in the room,' and whoever cannot do so, must empty three glasses as a punishment."

All the company were satisfied. Only the third son-in-law felt embarrassed and insisted on leaving. But the guests would not let him go, and obliged him to keep his seat.

Then the oldest son-in-law began: "I will make a start with my verse. Here it is:

"In the sky the phonix proudly flies,
On the earth the lambkin tamely lies,
At the table through an ancient book I wade,
In the room I softly call the maid."

The second one continued: "And I say:

"In the sky the turtle-dove flies round,
On the earth the ox paws up the ground,
At the table one studies the deeds of yore,
In the room the maid she sweeps the floor."

But the third son-in-law stuttered, and found nothing to say. And when all of them insisted, he broke out in rough tones of voice:

"In the sky—flies a leaden bullet,
On the earth—stalks a tiger-beast,
On the table—lies a pair of scissors,
In the room—I call the stable-boy."

The other two sons-in-law clapped their hands and began to laugh loudly.

"Why the four lines do not rhymme at all," said they, "and, besides they do not make sense. A leaden bullet is no bird, the stable-boy does his work outside, would you call him into the room? Nonsense, nonsense! Drink!"

Yet before they had finished speaking, the third daughter raised the curtain of the women's room, and stepped out. She was angry, yet she could not suppress a smile.

"How so do our lines not make sense?" said she. "Listen a moment, and I'll explain them to you: In the sky our leaden bullet will shoot your phoenix and your turtle-dove. On the earth our tiger-beast will devour your sheep and your ox. On the table our pair of scissors will cut up all your old books. And finally, in the room—well, the stable-boy can marry your maid!"

Then the oldest son-in-law said: "Well scolded! Sister-in-law, you know how to talk! If you were a man you would have had your degree long ago. And, as a punishment, we will empty our three glasses."

How Greed for a Trifling Thing Led a Man to Lose a Great One

ONCE UPON A TIME THERE WAS AN OLD WOMAN, WHO HAD TWO SONS. BUT HER OLDER son did not love his parents, and left his mother and brother. The younger one served her so faithfully, however, that all the people spoke of his filial affection.

One day it happened that there was a theatrical performance given outside the village. The younger son started to carry his mother there on his back, so that she might look on. But there was a ravine before the village, and he slipped and fell down in the middle of it. And his mother was killed by the rolling stones, and her blood and flesh were sprinkled about everywhere. The son stroked his mother's corpse, and wept bitterly. He was about to kill himself when, suddenly, he saw a priest standing before him.

The latter said: "Have no fear, for I can bring your mother back to life again!" And as he said so, he stooped, gathered up her flesh and bones, and laid them together as they should be. Then he breathed upon them, and at once the mother was alive again. This made the son very happy, and he thanked the priest on his knees. Yet on a sharp point of rock he still saw a bit of his mother's flesh hanging, a bit about an inch long.

"That should not be left hanging there either," said he, and hid it in his breast.

"In truth, you love your mother as a son should," said the priest. Then he bade the son give him the bit of flesh, kneaded a manikin out of it, breathed upon it, and in a minute there it stood, a really fine-looking little boy.

"His name is Small Profit," said he, turning to the son, "and you may call him brother. You are poor and have not the wherewithal with which to nourish your mother. If you need something, Small Profit can get it for you."

The son thanked him once more, then took his mother on his back again, and his new little brother by the hand, and went home. And when he said to Small Profit:

"Bring meat and wine!" then meat and wine were at hand at once, and steaming rice was already cooking in the pot. And when he said to Small Profit: "Bring money and cloth!" then his purse filled itself with money, and the chests were heaped up with cloth to the brim. Whatever he asked for that he received. Thus, in the course of time, they came to be very well off indeed.

But his older brother envied him greatly. And when there was another theatrical performance in the village, he took his mother on his back—by force—and went to it. And when he reached the ravine, he slipped purposely, and let his mother fall into the depths, only intent to see that she really was shattered into fragments. And sure enough his mother had such a bad fall that her limbs and trunk were strewn around in all directions. He then climbed down, took his mother's head in his hands, and pretended to weep.

And at once the priest was on hand again, and said: "I can wake the dead to life again, and surround white bones with flesh and blood!"

Then he did as he had done before, and the mother came to life again. But the older brother already had hidden one of her ribs on purpose. He now pulled it out and said to the priest: "Here is a bone left. What shall I do with it?"

The priest took the bone, enclosed it in lime and earth, breathed upon it, as he had done the other time, and it became a little man, resembling Small Profit, but larger in stature.

"His name is Great Duty," he told his older brother, "if you stick to him he will always lend you a hand."

The son took his mother back again, and Great Duty walked beside him.

When he came to their courtyard door, he saw his younger brother coming out, holding Small Profit in his arms.

"Where are you going?" he said to him.

His brother answered: "Small Profit is a divine being, who does not wish to dwell for all time among men. He wants to fly back to the heavens, and so I am escorting him."

"Give Small Profit to me! Don't let him get away!" cried the older brother.

Yet, before he had ended his speech, Small Profit was rising in the air. The older brother then quickly let his mother drop on the ground, and stretched out his hand to catch Small Profit. But he did not succeed, and now Great Duty, too, rose from the ground, took Small Profit's hand, and together they ascended to the clouds and disappeared.

Then the older brother stamped on the ground, and said with a sigh: "Alas, I have lost my Great Duty because I was too greedy for that Small Profit!"

Who Was the Sinner?

Once upon a time there were ten farmers, who were crossing a field together. They were surprised by a heavy thunder-storm, and took refuge in a half-ruined temple. But the thunder drew ever nearer, and so great was the tumult that the air trembled about them, while the lightning flew around the temple in a continuous circle. The farmers were greatly frightened, and thought that there must be a sinner among them, whom the lightning would strike. In order to find out who it might be, they agreed to hang their straw hats up before the door, and he whose hat was blown away was to yield himself up to his fate.

No sooner were the hats outside, than one of them was blown away, and the rest thrust its unfortunate owner out of doors without pity. But as soon as he had left the temple the lightning ceased circling around, and struck it with a crash.

The one whom the rest had thrust out, had been the only righteous one among them, and for his sake the lightning had spared the temple. So the other nine had to pay for their hard-heartedness with their lives.

The Magic Cask

Once upon a time there was a man who dug up a big, earthenware cask in his field. So he took it home with him and told his wife to clean it out. But when his wife started brushing the inside of the cask, the cask suddenly began to fill itself with brushes. No matter how many were taken out, others kept on taking their place. So the man sold the brushes, and the family managed to live quite comfortably.

Once a coin fell into the cask by mistake. At once the brushes disappeared and the cask began to fill itself with money. So now the family became rich; for they could take as much money out of the cask as ever they wished.

Now the man had an old grandfather at home, who was weak and shaky. Since there was nothing else he could do, his grandson set him to work shoveling money out of the cask, and when the old grandfather grew weary and could not keep on, he would fall into a rage, and shout at him angrily, telling him he was lazy and did not want to work. One day, however, the old man's strength gave out, and he fell into the cask and died. At once the money disappeared, and the whole cask began to fill itself with dead grandfathers. Then the man had to pull them all out and have them buried, and for this purpose he had to use up again all the money he had received. And when he was through, the cask broke, and he was just as poor as before.

The Favorite of Fortune and the Child of Ill Luck

ONCE UPON A TIME THERE WAS A PROUD PRINCE WHO HAD A DAUGHTER. BUT THE daughter was a child of ill luck. When it came time for her to marry, she had all her suitors assemble before her father's palace. She was going to throw down a ball of red silk among them, and whoever caught it was to be her husband. Now there were many princes and counts gathered before the castle, and in their midst there was also a beggar. And the princess could see dragons crawling into his ears and crawling out again from his nostrils, for he was a child of luck. So she threw the ball to the beggar and he caught it.

Her father asked angrily: "Why did you throw the ball into the beggar's hands?"

"He is a favorite of Fortune," said the princess, "I will marry him, and then, perhaps, I will share in his good luck."

But her father would not hear of it, and since she insisted, he drove her from the castle in his rage. So the princess had to go off with the beggar. She dwelt with him in a little hut, and had to hunt for herbs and roots, and cook them herself, so that they might have something to eat; and often they both went hungry.

One day her husband said to her: "I will set out and seek my fortune. And when I have found it, I will come back again and fetch you." The princess was willing, and he went away, and was gone for eighteen years. Meanwhile the princess lived in want and affliction, for her father remained hard and merciless. If her mother had not secretly given her food and money, no doubt she would have starved to death during all that time.

But the beggar found his fortune, and at length became emperor. He returned and stood before his wife. She however, no longer recognized him: She only knew that he was the powerful emperor.

He asked her how she was getting along.

"Why do you ask me how I am getting along?" she replied. "I am too far beneath your notice."

"And who may your husband be!"

"My husband was a beggar. He went away to seek his fortune. That was eighteen years ago, and he has not yet returned."

"And what have you done during all those long years?"

"I have been waiting for him to return."

"Do you wish to marry some one else, seeing that he has been missing so long?"

"No, I will remain his wife until I die."

When the emperor saw how faithful his wife was, he told her who he was, had her clothed in magnificent garments, and took her with him to his imperial palace. And there they lived in splendor and happiness.

After a few days the emperor said to his wife: "We spend every day in festivities, as though every day were New Year."

"And why should we not celebrate," answered his wife, "since we have now become emperor and empress?"

Yet his wife was a child of ill luck. When she had been empress no more than eighteen days, she fell sick and died. But her husband lived for many a long year.

The Bird with Nine Heads

LONG, LONG AGO, THERE ONCE LIVED A KING AND A QUEEN WHO HAD A DAUGHTER. One day, when the daughter went walking in the garden, a tremendous storm suddenly came up and carried her away with it. Now the storm had come from the bird with nine heads, who had robbed the princess, and brought her to his cave. The king did not know whither his daughter had disappeared, so he had proclaimed throughout the land: "Whoever brings back the princess may have her for his bride!"

Now a youth had seen the bird as he was carrying the princess to his cave. This cave, though, was in the middle of a sheer wall of rock. One could not climb up to it from below, nor could one climb down to it from above. And as the youth was walking around the rock, another youth came along and asked him what he was doing there. So the first youth told him that the bird with nine heads had carried off the king's daughter, and had brought her up to his cave. The other chap knew what he had to do. He called together his friends, and they lowered the youth to the cave in a basket. And when he went into the cave, he saw the king's daughter sitting there, and washing the wound of the bird with nine heads; for the hound of heaven had bitten off his tenth head, and his wound was still bleeding. The princess, however, motioned to the youth to hide, and he did so. When the king's daughter had washed his wound and bandaged it, the bird with nine heads felt so comfortable, that one after another, all his nine heads fell asleep. Then the youth stepped forth from his hiding-place, and cut off his nine heads with a sword. But the king's daughter said: "It would be best if you were hauled up first, and I came after."

"No," said the youth. "I will wait below here, until you are in safety." At first the king's daughter was not willing; yet at last she allowed herself to be persuaded, and climbed into the basket. But before she did so, she took a long pin from her hair, broke it into two halves and gave him one and kept the other. She also divided her silken kerchief with him, and told him to take good care of both her gifts. But when the other man had drawn up the king's daughter, he took her along with him, and left the youth in the cave, in spite of all his calling and pleading.

The youth now took a walk about the cave. There he saw a number of maidens, all of whom had been carried off by the bird with nine heads, and who had perished there of hunger. And on the wall hung a fish, nailed against it with four nails. When he touched the fish, the latter turned into a handsome youth, who thanked him for delivering him, and they agreed to regard each other as brothers. Soon the first youth grew very hungry. He stepped out in front of the cave to search for food, but only stones were lying there. Then, suddenly, he saw a great dragon, who was licking a stone. The youth imitated him, and before long his hunger had disappeared. He next asked the dragon how he could get away from the cave, and the dragon nodded his head in the direction of his tail, as much as to say he should seat himself upon it. So he climbed up, and in the twinkling of an eye he was down on the ground, and the dragon had disappeared. He then went on until he found a tortoise-shell full of beautiful pearls. But they were magic pearls, for if you flung them into the fire, the fire ceased to burn and if you flung them into the water, the water divided and you could walk through the midst of it. The youth took the pearls out of the tortoise-shell, and put them in his pocket. Not long after he reached the sea-shore. Here he flung a pearl into the sea, and at once the waters divided and he could see the sea-dragon. The sea-dragon cried: "Who is disturbing me here in my own kingdom?" The youth answered: "I found pearls in a tortoise-shell, and have flung one into the sea, and now the waters have divided for me."

"If that is the case," said the dragon, "then come into the sea with me and we will live there together." Then the youth recognized him for the same dragon whom he had seen in the cave. And with him was the youth with whom he had formed a bond of brotherhood: He was the dragon's son.

"Since you have saved my son and become his brother, I am your father," said the old dragon. And he entertained him hospitably with food and wine.

One day his friend said to him: "My father is sure to want to reward you. But accept no money, nor any jewels from him, but only the little gourd flask over yonder. With it you can conjure up whatever you wish."

And, sure enough, the old dragon asked him what he wanted by way of a reward, and the youth answered: "I want no money, nor any jewels. All I want is the little gourd flask over yonder."

At first the dragon did not wish to give it up, but at last he did let him have it, after all. And then the youth left the dragon's castle.

When he set his foot on dry land again he felt hungry. At once a table stood before him, covered with a fine and plenteous meal. He ate and drank. After he had gone on a while, he felt weary. And there stood an ass, waiting for him, on which he mounted. After he had ridden for a while, the ass's gait seemed too uneven, and along came a wagon, into which he climbed. But the wagon shook him up too, greatly, and he thought: "If I only had a litter! That would suit me better." No more had he thought so, than the litter came along, and he seated himself in it. And the bearers carried him to the city in which dwelt the king, the queen and their daughter.

When the other youth had brought back the king's daughter, it was decided to hold the wedding. But the king's daughter was not willing, and said: "He is not the right man. My deliverer will come and bring with him half of the long pin for my hair, and half my silken kerchief as a token." But when the youth did not appear for so long a time, and the other one pressed the king, the king grew impatient and said: "The wedding shall take place to-morrow!" Then the king's daughter went sadly through the streets of the city, and searched and searched in the hope of finding her deliverer. And this was on the very day that the litter arrived. The king's daughter saw the half of her silken handkerchief in the youth's hand, and filled with joy, she led him to her father. There he had to show his half of the long pin, which fitted the other exactly, and then the king was convinced that he was the right, true deliverer. The false bridegroom was now punished, the wedding celebrated, and they lived in peace and happiness till the end of their days.

The Cave of the Beasts

Once upon a time there was a family in which there were seven daughters. One day when the father went out to gather wood, he found seven wild duck eggs. He brought them home, but did not think of giving any to his children, intending to eat them himself, with his wife. In the evening the oldest daughter woke up, and asked her mother what she was cooking. The mother said: "I am cooking wild duck eggs. I will give you one, but you must not let your sisters know." And so she gave her one. Then the second daughter woke up, and asked her mother what she was cooking. She said: "Wild duck eggs. If you will not tell your sisters, I'll give you one." And so it went. At last the daughters had eaten all the eggs, and there were none left.

In the morning the father was very angry with the children, and said: "Who wants to go along to grandmother?" But he intended to lead the children into the mountains, and let the wolves devour them there. The older daughters suspected this, and said: "We are not going along!" But the two younger ones said: "We will go with you." And so they drove off with their father. After they had driven a good ways, they asked: "Will we soon get to grandmother's house?" "Right away," said their father. And when they had reached the mountains he told them: "Wait here. I will drive into the village ahead of you, and tell grandmother that you are coming." And then he drove off with the donkey-cart. They waited and waited, but their father did not come. At last they decided that their father would not come back to fetch them, and that he had left them alone in the mountains. So they went further and further into the hills seeking a shelter for the night. Then they spied a great stone. This they selected for a pillow, and rolled it over to the place where they were going to lie down to sleep. And then they saw that the stone was the door to a cave. There was a light in the cave, and they went into it. The light they had seen came from the many precious stones and jewels of every sort in the cave, which belonged to a wolf and a fox. They had a number of jars of precious stones and pearls that shone by night. The girls said: "What a lovely cave this is! We will lie right down and go to bed." For there stood two golden beds with gold-embroidered covers. So they lay down and fell asleep. During the night the wolf and fox came home. And the wolf said: "I smell human flesh!" But the fox replied: "Oh, nonsense! There are no human beings who can enter our cave. We lock it up too well for that." The wolf said: "Very well, then let us lie down in our beds and sleep." But the fox answered: "Let us curl up in the kettles on the hearth. They still hold a little warmth from the fire." The one kettle was of gold and the other of silver, and they curled up in them.

When the girls rose early in the morning, they saw the wolf and the fox lying there, and were much frightened. And they put the covers on the kettles and heaped a number of big stones on them, so that the wolf and the fox could not get out again. Then they made a fire. The wolf and the fox said: "Oh, how nice and warm it is this morning! How does that happen?" But at length it grew too hot for them. Then they noticed that the two girls had kindled a fire and they cried: "Let us out! We will give you lots of precious stones, and lots of gold, and will do you no harm!" But the girls would not listen to them, and kept on making a bigger fire. So that was the end of the wolf and the fox in the kettles.

Then the girls lived happily for a number of days in the cave. But their father was seized with a longing for his daughters, and he went into the mountains to look for them. And he sat right down on the stone in front of the cave to rest, and tapped his pipe against it to empty the ashes. Then the girls within called out: "Who is knocking at our door?" And the father said: "Are those not my daughters' voices?" While the daughters replied: "Is that not our father's voice?" Then they pushed aside the stone and saw that it was their father, and their father was glad to see them once more. He was much surprised to think that they should have chanced on this cave full of precious stones, and they told him the whole story. Then their father fetched people to help him carry home the jewels. And when they got home, his wife wondered where he had obtained all these treasures. So the father and daughters told her everything, and they became a very wealthy family, and lived happily to the end of their days.

The Panther

Once upon a time there was a widow who had two daughters and a little son. And one day the mother said to her daughters: "Take good care of the house, for I am going to see grandmother, together with your little brother!" So the daughters promised her they would do so, and their mother went off. On her way a panther met her, and asked where she were going.

She said: "I am going with my child to see my mother."

"Will you not rest a bit?" asked the panther.

"No," said she, "it is already late, and it is a long road to where my mother lives."

But the panther did not cease urging her, and finally she gave in and sat down by the road side.

"I will comb your hair a bit," said the panther. And the woman allowed the panther to comb her hair. But as he passed his claws through her hair, he tore off a bit of her skin and devoured it.

"Stop!" cried the woman, "the way you comb my hair hurts!"

But the panther tore off a much larger piece of skin. Now the woman wanted to call for help, but the panther seized and devoured her. Then he turned on her little son and killed him too, put on the woman's clothes, and laid the child's bones, which he had not yet devoured, in her basket. After that he went to the woman's home, where her two daughters were, and called in at the door: "Open the door, daughters! Mother has come home!" But they looked out through a crack and said: "Our mother's eyes are not so large as yours!"

Then the panther said: "I have been to grandmother's house, and saw her hens laying eggs. That pleases me, and is the reason why my eyes have grown so large."

"Our mother had no spots in her face such as you have."

"Grandmother had no spare bed, so I had to sleep on the peas, and they pressed themselves into my face."

"Our mother's feet are not so large as yours."

"Stupid things! That comes from walking such a distance. Come, open the door quickly!"

Then the daughters said to each other: "It must be our mother," and they opened the door. But when the panther came in, they saw it was not really their mother after all.

At evening, when the daughters were already in bed, the panther was still gnawing the bones he had brought with him.

Then the daughters asked: "Mother, what are you eating?"

"I'm eating beets," was the answer.

Then the daughters said: "Oh, mother, give us some of your beets, too! We are so hungry!"

"No," was the reply, "I will not give you any. Now be quiet and go to sleep."

But the daughters kept on begging until the false mother gave them a little finger. And then they saw that it was their little brother's finger, and they said to each other: "We must make haste to escape else he will eat us as well." And with that they ran out of the door, climbed up into a tree in the yard, and called down to the false mother: "Come out! We can see our neighbor's son celebrating his wedding!" But it was the middle of the night.

Then the mother came out, and when she saw that they were sitting in the tree, she called out angrily: "Why, I'm not able to climb!"

The daughters said: "Get into a basket and throw us the rope and we will draw you up!"

The mother did as they said. But when the basket was half-way up, they began to swing it back and forth, and bump it against the tree. Then the false mother had to turn into a panther again, lest she fall down. And the panther leaped out of the basket, and ran away.

Gradually daylight came. The daughters climbed down, seated themselves on the doorstep, and cried for their mother. And a needle-vender came by and asked them why they were crying.

"A panther has devoured our mother and our brother," said the girls. "He has gone now, but he is sure to return and devour us as well."

Then the needle-vendor gave them a pair of needles, and said: "Stick these needles in the cushion of the arm chair, with the points up." The girls thanked him and went on crying.

Soon a scorpion-catcher came by; and he asked them why they were crying. "A panther has devoured our mother and brother," said the girls. "He has gone now, but he is sure to return and devour us as well."

The man gave them a scorpion and said: "Put it behind the hearth in the kitchen." The girls thanked him and went on crying.

Then an egg-seller came by and asked them why they were crying. "A panther has devoured our mother and our brother," said the girls. "He has gone now, but he is sure to return and devour us as well."

So he gave them an egg and said: "Lay it beneath the ashes in the hearth." The girls thanked him and went on crying.

Then a dealer in turtles came by, and they told him their tale. He gave them a turtle and said: "Put it in the water-barrel in the yard." And then a man came by who sold wooden clubs. He asked them why they were crying. And they told him the whole story. Then he gave them two wooden clubs and said: "Hang them up over the door to the street." The girls thanked him and did as the men had told them.

In the evening the panther came home. He sat down in the armchair in the room. Then the needles in the cushion stuck into him. So he ran into the kitchen to light the fire and see what had jabbed him so; and then it was that the scorpion hooked his sting into his hand. And when at last the fire was burning, the egg burst and spurted into one of his eyes, which was blinded. So he ran out into the yard and dipped his hand into the water-barrel, in order to cool it; and then the turtle bit it off. And when in his pain he ran out through the door into the street, the wooden clubs fell on his head and that was the end of him.

The Great Flood

Once upon a time there was a widow, who had a child. And the child was a kind-hearted boy of whom every one was fond. One day he said to his mother: "All the other children have a grandmother, but I have none. And that makes me feel very sad!"

"We will hunt up a grandmother for you," said his mother. Now it once happened that an old beggar-woman came to the house, who was very old and feeble. And when the child saw her, he said to her: "You shall be my grandmother!" And he went to his mother and said: "There is a beggar-woman outside, whom I want for my grandmother!" And his mother was willing and called her into the house; though the old woman was very dirty. So the boy said to his mother: "Come, let us wash grandmother!" And they washed the woman. But she had a great many burrs in her hair, so they picked them all out and put them in a jar, and they filled the whole jar. Then the grandmother said: "Do not throw them away, but bury them in the garden. And you must not dig them up again before the great flood comes."

"When is the great flood coming?" asked the boy.

"When the eyes of the two stone lions in front of the prison grow red, then the great flood will come," said the grandmother.

So the boy went to look at the lions, but their eyes were not yet red. And the grandmother also said to him: "Make a little wooden ship and keep it in a little box." And this the boy did. And he ran to the prison every day and looked at the lions, much to the astonishment of the people in the street.

One day, as he passed the chicken-butcher's shop, the butcher asked him why he was always running to the lions. And the boy said: "When the lions' eyes grow red then the great flood will come." But the butcher laughed at him. And the following morning, quite early, he took some chicken-blood and rubbed it on the lions' eyes. When the boy saw that the lions' eyes were red he ran swiftly home, and told his mother and grandmother. And then his grandmother said: "Dig up the jar quickly, and take the little ship out of its box." And when they dug up the jar, it was filled with the purest pearls and the little ship grew larger and larger, like a real ship. Then the grandmother said: "Take the jar with you and get into the ship. And when the great flood comes, then you may save all the animals that are driven into it; but human beings, with their black heads, you are not to save." So they climbed into the ship, and the grandmother suddenly disappeared.

Now it began to rain, and the rain kept falling more and more heavily from the heavens. Finally there were no longer any single drops falling, but just one big sheet of water which flooded everything.

Then a dog came drifting along, and they saved him in their ship. Soon after came a pair of mice, with their little ones, loudly squeaking in their fear. And these they also saved. The water was already rising to the roofs of the houses, and on one roof stood a cat, arching her back and mewing pitifully. They took the cat into the ship, too. Yet the flood increased and rose to the tops of the trees. And in one tree sat a raven, beating his wings and cawing loudly. And him, too, they took in. Finally a swarm of bees came flying their way. The little creatures were quite wet, and could hardly fly. So they took in the bees on their ship. At last a man with black hair floated by on the waves. The boy said: "Mother, let us save him, too!" But the mother did not want to do so. "Did not grandmother tell us that we must save no black-headed human beings?" But the boy answered: "We will save the man in spite of that. I feel sorry for him, and cannot bear to see him drifting along in the water." So they also saved the man.

Gradually the water subsided. Then they got out of their ship, and parted from the man and the beasts. And the ship grew small again and they put it away in its box.

But the man was filled with a desire for the pearls. He went to the judge and entered a complaint against the boy and his mother, and they were both thrown into jail. Then the mice came, and dug a hole in the wall. And the dog came through the hole and brought them meat, and the cat brought them bread, so they did not have to hunger in their prison. But the raven flew off and returned with a letter for the judge. The letter had been written by a god, and it said: "I wandered about in the world of men disguised as a beggar woman. And this boy and his mother took me in. The boy treated me like his own grandmother, and did not shrink from washing me when I was dirty. Because of this I saved them out of the great flood by means of which I destroyed the sinful city wherein they dwelt. Do you, O judge, free them, or misfortune shall be your portion!"

So the judge had them brought before him, and asked what they had done, and how they had made their way through the flood. Then they told him everything, and what they said agreed with the god's letter. So the judge punished their accuser, and set them both at liberty.

When the boy had grown up he came to a city of many people, and it was said that the princess intended to take a husband. But in order to find the right man, she had veiled herself, and seated herself in a litter, and she had had the litter, together with many others, carried into the market place. In every litter sat a veiled woman, and the princess was in their midst. And whoever hit upon the right litter, he was to get the princess for his bride. So the youth went there, too, and when he reached the market place, he saw the bees whom he had saved from the great flood, all swarming about a certain litter. Up he stepped to it, and sure enough, the princess was sitting in it. And then their wedding was celebrated, and they lived happily ever afterward.

The Fox and the Tiger

Once a fox met a tiger. The latter bared his teeth, stretched out his claws, and was about to devour him. But the fox spoke and said: "My dear sir, you must not think that you are the only king of beasts. Your courage does not compare with my own. Let us walk together, and do you keep behind me. And if men catch sight of me and do not fear me, then you may devour me." The tiger was willing, and so the fox led him along a broad highway. But the travelers, when they saw the tiger in the distance, were all frightened and ran away.

Then the fox said: "How about it? I went in advance, and the men saw me and had not as yet seen you."

And thereupon the tiger drew in his tail and ran away himself.

The tiger had remarked quite well that the men were afraid of the fox, but he had not noticed that the fox had borrowed the terror he inspired from him.

The Tiger's Decoy

That the fox borrowed the terror he inspired from the tiger is more than a simile; but that the tiger has his decoy is something we read about in the story books, and grandfathers talk about a good deal, too. So there must be some truth in it. It is said that when a tiger devours a human being, the latter's spirit cannot free itself, and that the tiger then uses it for a decoy. When he goes out to seek his prey, the spirit of the man he has devoured must go before him, to hide him, so that people cannot see him. And the spirit is apt to change itself into a beautiful girl, or a lump of gold or a bolt of silk. All sorts of deceptions are used to lure folk into the mountain gorges. Then the tiger comes along and devours his victim, and the new spirit must serve as his decoy. The old spirit's time of service is over and it may go. And so it continues, turn by turn. Probably that is why they say of people who are forced to yield themselves up to cunning and powerful men, in order that others may be harmed: "They are the tiger's decoys!"

The Fox and the Raven

The fox knows how to flatter, and how to play many cunning tricks. Once upon a time he saw a raven, who alighted on a tree with a piece of meat in his beak. The fox seated himself beneath the tree, looked up at him, and began to praise him.

"Your color," he began, "is pure black. This proves to me that you possess all the wisdom of Laotzse, who knows how to shroud his learning in darkness. The manner in which you manage to feed your mother shows that your filial affection equals that which the Master Dsong had for his parents. Your voice is rough and strong. It proves that you have the courage with which King Hiang once drove his foes to flight by the mere sound of his voice. In truth, you are the king of birds!"

The raven, hearing this, was filled with joy and said: "I thank you! I thank you!"

And before he knew it, the meat fell to earth from his opened beak.

The fox caught it up, devoured it and then said, laughing: "Make note of this, my dear sir: if some one praises you without occasion, he is sure to have a reason for doing so."

Why Dog and Cat Are Enemies

Once upon a time there was a man and his wife and they had a ring of gold. It was a lucky ring, and whoever owned it always had enough to live on. But this they did not know, and hence sold the ring for a small sum. But no sooner was the ring gone than they began to grow poorer and poorer, and at last did not know when they would get their next meal. They had a dog and a cat, and these had to go hungry as well. Then the two animals took counsel together as to how they might restore to their owners their former good fortune. At length the dog hit upon an idea.

"They must have the ring back again," he said to the cat.

The cat answered: "The ring has been carefully locked up in the chest, where no one can get at it."

"You must catch a mouse," said the dog, "and the mouse must gnaw a hole in the chest and fetch out the ring. And if she does not want to, say that you will bite her to death, and you will see that she will do it."

This advice pleased the cat, and she caught a mouse. Then she wanted to go to the house in which stood the chest, and the dog came after. They came to a broad river. And since the cat could not swim, the dog took her on his back and swam across with her. Then the cat carried the mouse to the house in which the chest stood. The mouse gnawed a hole in the chest, and fetched out the ring. The cat put the ring in her mouth and went back to the river, where the dog was waiting for her, and swam across with her. Then they started out together for home, in order to bring the lucky ring to their master and mistress. But the dog could only run along the ground; when there was a house in the way he always had to go around it. The cat, however, quickly climbed over the roof, and so she reached home long before the dog, and brought the ring to her master.

Then her master said to his wife: "What a good creature the cat is! We will always give her enough to eat and care for her as though she were our own child!"

But when the dog came home they beat him and scolded him, because he had not helped to bring home the ring again. And the cat sat by the fireplace, purred and said never a word. Then the dog grew angry at the cat, because she had robbed him of his reward, and when he saw her he chased her and tried to seize her.

And ever since that day cat and dog are enemies.

LEGENDS OF THE GODS

How the Five Ancients Became Men

BEFORE THE EARTH WAS SEPARATED FROM THE HEAVENS, ALL THERE WAS WAS A GREAT ball of watery vapor called chaos. And at that time the spirits of the five elemental powers took shape, and became the five Ancients. The first was called the Yellow Ancient, and he was the ruler of the earth. The second was called the Red Lord, and he was the ruler of the fire. The third was called the Dark Lord, and he was the ruler of the water. The fourth was known as the Wood Prince, and he was the ruler of the wood. The fifth was called the Mother of Metals, and ruled over them. These five Ancients set all their primal spirit into motion, so that water and earth sank down. The heavens floated upward, and the earth grew firm in the depths. Then they allowed the waters to gather into rivers and seas, and hills and plains made their appearance. So the heavens opened and the earth was divided. And there were sun, moon and all the stars, wind, clouds, rain, and dew. The Yellow Ancient set earth's purest power spinning in a circle, and added the effect of fire and water thereto. Then there came forth grasses and trees, birds and beasts, and the tribes of the serpents and insects, fishes and turtles. The Wood Prince and the Mother of Metals combined light and darkness, and thus created the human race as men and women. And thus the world gradually came to be.

At that time there was one who was known as the True Prince of the Jasper Castle. He had acquired the art of sorcery through the cultivation of magic. The five Ancients begged him to rule as the supreme god. He dwelt above the three and thirty heavens, and the Jasper Castle, of white jade with golden gates, was his. Before him stood the stewards of the eight-and-twenty houses of the moon, and the gods of the thunders and the Great Bear, and in addition a class of baneful gods whose influence was evil and deadly. They all aided the True Prince of the Jasper Castle to rule over the thousand tribes under the heavens, and to deal out life and death, fortune and misfortune. The Lord of the Jasper Castle is now known as the Great God, the White Jade Ruler.

The five Ancients withdrew after they had done their work, and thereafter lived in quiet purity. The Red Lord dwells in the South as the god of fire. The Dark Lord dwells in the North, as the mighty master of the somber polar skies. He lived in a castle of liquid crystal. In later ages he sent Confucius down upon earth as a saint. Hence this saint is known as the Son of Crystal. The Wood Prince dwells in the East. He is honored as the Green Lord, and watches over the coming into being of all creatures. In him lives the power of spring and he is the god of love. The Mother of Metals dwells in the West, by the sea of Jasper, and is also known as the Queen-Mother of the West. She leads the rounds of the fairies, and watches over change and growth. The Yellow Ancient dwells in the middle. He is always going about in the world, in order to save and to help those in any distress. The first time he came to earth he was the Yellow Lord, who taught mankind all sorts of arts. In his later years he fathomed the meaning of the world on the Ethereal Mount, and flew up to the radiant sun. Under the rule of the Dschou dynasty he was born again as Li Oerl, and when he was born his hair and beard were white, for which reason he was called Laotsze, "Old Child." He wrote the book of "Meaning and Life" and spread his teachings through the world. He is honored as the head of Taoism. At the beginning of the reign of the Han dynasty, he again appeared as the Old Man of the River (Ho Schang Gung). He spread the teachings of Tao abroad mightily, so that from that time on Taoism flourished greatly. These doctrines are known to this day as the teachings of the Yellow Ancient. There is also a saying: "First Laotsze was, then the heavens were." And that must mean that Laotsze was that very same Yellow Ancient of primal days.

The Herd Boy and the Weaving Maiden

THE HERD BOY WAS THE CHILD OF POOR PEOPLE. WHEN HE WAS TWELVE YEARS OLD, he took service with a farmer to herd his cow. After a few years the cow had grown large and fat, and her hair shone like yellow gold. She must have been a cow of the gods.

One day while he had her out at pasture in the mountains, she suddenly began to speak to the Herd Boy in a human voice, as follows: "This is the Seventh Day. Now the White Jade Ruler has nine daughters, who bathe this day in the Sea of Heaven. The seventh daughter is beautiful and wise beyond all measure. She spins the cloud-silk for the King and Queen of Heaven, and presides over the weaving which maidens do on earth. It is for this reason she is called the Weaving Maiden. And if you go and take away her clothes while she bathes, you may become her husband and gain immortality."

"But she is up in Heaven," said the Herd Boy, "and how can I get there?"

"I will carry you there," answered the yellow cow.

So the Herd Boy climbed on the cow's back. In a moment clouds began to stream out of her hoofs, and she rose into the air. About his ears there was a whistling like the sound of the wind, and they flew along as swiftly as lightning. Suddenly the cow stopped.

"Now we are here," said she.

Then round about him the Herd Boy saw forests of chrysophrase and trees of jade. The grass was of jasper and the flowers of coral. In the midst of all this splendor lay a great, four-square sea, covering some five-hundred acres. Its green waves rose and fell, and fishes with golden scales were swimming about in it. In addition there were countless magic birds who winged above it and sang. Even in the distance the Herd Boy could see the nine maidens in the water. They had all laid down their clothes on the shore.

"Take the red clothes, quickly," said the cow, "and hide away with them in the forest, and though she ask you for them never so sweetly do not give them back to her until she has promised to become your wife."

Then the Herd Boy hastily got down from the cow's back, seized the red clothes and ran away. At the same moment the nine maidens noticed him and were much frightened.

"O youth, whence do you come, that you dare to take our clothes?" they cried. "Put them down again quickly!"

But the Herd Boy did not let what they said trouble him; but crouched down behind one of the jade trees. Then eight of the maidens hastily came ashore and drew on their clothes.

"Our seventh sister," said they, "whom Heaven has destined to be yours, has come to you. We will leave her alone with you."

The Weaving Maiden was still crouching in the water.

But the Herd Boy stood before her and laughed.

"If you will promise to be my wife," said he, "then I will give you your clothes."

But this did not suit the Weaving Maiden.

"I am a daughter of the Ruler of the Gods," said she, "and may not marry without his command. Give back my clothes to me quickly, or else my father will punish you!"

Then the yellow cow said: "You have been destined for each other by fate, and I will be glad to arrange your marriage, and your father, the Ruler of the Gods, will make no objection. Of that I am sure."

The Weaving Maiden replied: "You are an unreasoning animal! How could you arrange our marriage?"

The cow said: "Do you see that old willow-tree there on the shore? Just give it a trial and ask it. If the willow tree speaks, then Heaven wishes your union."

And the Weaving Maiden asked the willow.

The willow replied in a human voice:

> "This is the Seventh day,
> The Herd Boy his court to the Weaver doth pay!"

and the Weaving Maiden was satisfied with the verdict. The Herd Boy laid down her clothes, and went on ahead. The Weaving Maiden drew them on and followed him. And thus they became man and wife.

But after seven days she took leave of him.

"The Ruler of Heaven has ordered me to look after my weaving," said she. "If I delay too long I fear that he will punish me. Yet, although we have to part now, we will meet again in spite of it."

When she had said these words she really went away. The Herd Boy ran after her. But when he was quite near she took one of the long needles from her hair and drew a line with it right across the sky, and this line turned into the Silver River. And thus they now stand, separated by the River, and watch for one another.

And since that time they meet once every year, on the eve of the Seventh Day. When that time comes, then all the crows in the world of men come flying and form a bridge over which the Weaving Maiden crosses the Silver River. And on that day you will not see a single crow in the trees, from morning to night, no doubt because of the reason I have mentioned. And besides, a fine rain often falls on the evening of the Seventh Day. Then the women and old grandmothers say to one another: "Those are the tears which the Herd Boy and the Weaving Maiden shed at parting!" And for this reason the Seventh Day is a rain festival.

To the west of the Silver River is the constellation of the Weaving Maiden, consisting of three stars. And directly in front of it are three other stars in the form of a triangle. It is said that once the Herd Boy was angry because the Weaving Maiden had not wished to cross the Silver River, and had thrown his yoke at her, which fell down just in front of her feet. East of the Silver River is the Herd Boy's constellation, consisting of six stars. To one side of it are countless little stars which form a constellation pointed at both ends and somewhat broader in the middle. It is said that the Weaving Maiden in turn threw her spindle at the Herd Boy; but that she did not hit him, the spindle falling down to one side of him.

Yang Oerlang

THE SECOND DAUGHTER OF THE RULER OF HEAVEN ONCE CAME DOWN UPON THE earth and secretly became the wife of a mortal man named Yang. And when she returned to Heaven she was blessed with a son. But the Ruler of Heaven was very angry at this desecration of the heavenly halls. He banished her to earth and covered her with the Wu-I hills. Her son, however, Oerlang by name, the nephew of the Ruler of Heaven, was extraordinarily gifted by nature. By the time he was full grown he had learned the magic art of being able to control eight times nine transformations. He could make himself invisible, or could assume the shape of birds and beasts, grasses, flowers, snakes and fishes, as he chose. He also knew how to empty out seas and remove mountains from one place to another. So he went to the Wu-I hills and rescued his mother, whom he took on his back and carried away. They stopped to rest on a flat ledge of rock.

Then the mother said: "I am very thirsty!"

Oerlang climbed down into the valley in order to fetch her water, and some time passed before he returned. When he did his mother was no longer there. He searched eagerly, but on the rock lay only her skin and bones, and a few blood-stains. Now you must know that at that time there were still ten suns in the heavens, glowing and burning like fire. The Daughter of Heaven, it is true, was divine by nature; yet because she had incurred the anger of her father and had been banished to earth, her magic powers had failed her. Then, too, she had been imprisoned so long beneath the hills in the dark that, coming out suddenly into the sunlight, she had been devoured by its blinding radiance.

When Oerlang thought of his mother's sad end, his heart ached. He took two mountains on his shoulders, pursued the suns and crushed them to death between the mountains. And whenever he had crushed another sun-disk, he picked up a fresh mountain. In this way he had already slain nine of the ten suns, and there was but one left. And as Oerlang pursued him relentlessly, he hid himself in his distress beneath the leaves of the portulacca plant. But there was a rainworm close by who betrayed his hiding-place, and kept repeating: "There he is! There he is!"

Oerlang was about to seize him, when a messenger from the Ruler of the Heaven suddenly descended from the skies with a command: "Sky, air and earth need the sunshine. You must allow this one sun to live, so that all created beings may live. Yet, because you rescued your mother, and showed yourself to be a good son, you shall be a god, and be my bodyguard in the Highest Heaven, and shall rule over good and evil in the mortal world, and have power over devils and demons." When Oerlang received this command he ascended to Heaven.

Then the sun-disk came out again from beneath the portulacca leaves, and out of gratitude, since the plant had saved him, he bestowed upon it the gift of a free-blooming nature, and ordained that it never need fear the sunshine. To this very day one may see on the lower side of the portulacca leaves quite delicate little white pearls. They are the sunshine that remained hanging to the leaves when the sun hid under them. But the sun pursues the rainworm, when he ventures forth out of the ground, and dries him up as a punishment for his treachery.

Since that time Yang Oerlang has been honored as a god. He has oblique, sharply marked eyebrows, and holds a double-bladed, three-pointed sword in his hand. Two servants stand beside him, with a falcon and a hound; for Yang Oerlang is a great hunter. The falcon is the falcon of the gods, and the hound is the hound of the gods. When brute creatures gain possession of magic powers or demons oppress men, he subdues them by means of the falcon and hound.

Notscha

The oldest daughter of the Ruler of Heaven had married the great general Li Dsing. Her sons were named Gintscha, Mutscha and Notscha. But when Notscha was given her, she dreamed at night that a Taoist priest came into her chamber and said: "Swiftly receive the Heavenly Son!" And straightway a radiant pearl glowed within her. And she was so frightened at her dream that she awoke. And when Notscha came into the world, it seemed as though a ball of flesh were turning in circles like a wheel, and the whole room was filled with strange fragrances and a crimson light.

Li Dsing was much frightened, and thought it was an apparition. He clove the circling ball with his sword, and out of it leaped a small boy whose whole body glowed with a crimson radiance. But his face was delicately shaped and white as snow. About his right arm he wore a golden armlet and around his thighs was wound a length of crimson silk, whose glittering shine dazzled the eyes. When Li Dsing saw the child he took pity on him and did not slay him, while his wife began to love the boy dearly.

When three days had passed, all his friends came to wish him joy. They were just sitting at the festival meal when a Taoist priest entered and said: "I am the Great One. This boy is the bright Pearl of the Beginning of Things, bestowed upon you as your son. Yet the boy is wild and unruly, and will kill many men. Therefore I will take him as my pupil to gentle his savage ways." Li Dsing bowed his thanks and the Great One disappeared.

When Notscha was seven years old he once ran away from home. He came to the river of nine bends, whose green waters flowed along between two rows of weeping-willows. The day was hot, and Notscha entered the water to cool himself. He unbound his crimson silk cloth and whisked it about in the water to wash it. But while Notscha sat there and whisked about his scarf in the water, it shook the castle of the Dragon-King of the Eastern Sea to its very foundations. So the Dragon-King sent out a Triton, terrible to look upon, who was to find out what was the matter. When the Triton saw the boy he began to scold. But the latter merely looked up and said: "What a strange-looking beast you are, and you can actually talk!" Then the Triton grew enraged, leaped up and struck at Notscha with his ax. But the latter avoided the blow, and threw his golden armlet at him. The armlet struck the Triton on the head and he sank down dead.

Notscha laughed and said: "And there he has gone and made my armlet bloody!" And he once more sat down on a stone, in order to wash his armlet. Then the crystal castle of the dragon began to tremble as though it were about to fall apart. And a watchman also came and reported that the Triton had been slain by a boy. So the Dragon-King sent out his son to capture the boy. And the son seated himself on the water-cleaving beast, and came up with a thunder of great waves of water. Notscha straightened up and said: "That is a big wave!" Suddenly he saw a creature rise out of the waves, on whose back sat an armed man who cried in a loud voice: "Who has slain my Triton?" Notscha answered: "The Triton wanted to slay me so I killed him. What difference does it make?" Then the dragon assailed him with his halberd. But Notscha said: "Tell me who you are before we fight." "I am the son of the Dragon-King," was the reply. "And I am Notscha, the son of General Li Dsing. You must not rouse my anger with your violence, or I will skin you, together with that old mud-fish, your father!" Then the dragon grew wild with rage, and came storming along furiously. But Notscha cast his crimson cloth into the air, so that it flashed like a ball of fire, and cast the dragon-youth from his breast. Then Notscha took his golden armlet and struck him on the forehead with it, so that he had to reveal himself in his true form as a golden dragon, and fall down dead.

Notscha laughed and said: "I have heard tell that dragon-sinews make good cords. I will draw one out and bring it to my father, and he can tie his armor together with it." And with that he drew out the dragon's back sinew and took it home.

In the meantime the Dragon-King, full of fury, had hastened to Notscha's father Li Dsing and demanded that Notscha be delivered up to him. But Li Dsing replied: "You must be mistaken, for my boy is only seven years old and incapable of committing such misdeeds." While they were still quarreling Notscha came running up and cried: "Father, I'm bringing along a dragon's sinew for you, so that you may bind up your armor with it!" Now the dragon broke out into tears and furious scolding. He threatened to report Li Dsing to the Ruler of the Heaven, and took himself off, snorting with rage.

Li Dsing grew very much excited, told his wife what had happened, and both began to weep. Notscha, however, came to them and said: "Why do you weep? I will just go to my master, the Great One, and he will know what is to be done." And no sooner had he said the words than he had disappeared. He came into his master's presence and told him the whole tale. The latter said: "You must get ahead of the dragon, and prevent him from accusing you in Heaven!" Then he did some magic, and Notscha found himself set down by the gate of Heaven, where he waited for the dragon. It was still early in the morning; the gate of Heaven had not yet been opened, nor was the watchman at his post. But the dragon was already climbing up. Notscha, whom his master's magic had rendered invisible, threw the dragon to the ground with his armlet, and began to pitch into him. The dragon scolded and screamed. "There the old worm flounders about," said Notscha, "and does not care how hard he is beaten! I will scratch off some of his scales." And with these words he began to tear open the dragon's festal garments, and rip off some of the scales beneath his left arm, so that the red blood dripped out. Then the dragon could no longer stand the pain and begged for mercy. But first he had to promise Notscha that he would not complain of him, before the latter would let him go. And then the dragon had to turn himself into a little green snake, which Notscha put into his sleeve and took back home with him. But no sooner had he drawn the little snake from his sleeve than it assumed human shape. The dragon then swore that he would punish Li Dsing in a terrible manner, and disappeared in a flash of lightning.

Li Dsing was now angry with his son in earnest. Therefore Notscha's mother sent him to the rear of the house to keep out of his father's sight. Notscha disappeared and went to his master, in order to ask him what he should do when the dragon returned. His master advised him and Notscha went back home. And all the Dragon Kings of the four seas were assembled, and had bound his parents, with cries and tumult, in order to punish them. Notscha ran up and cried with a loud voice: "I will take the punishment for whatever I have done! My parents are blameless! What is the punishment you wish to lay upon me?" "Life for life!" said the dragon. "Very well then, I will destroy myself!" And so he did and the dragons went off satisfied; while Notscha's mother buried him with many tears.

But the spiritual part of Notscha, his soul, fluttered about in the air, and was driven by the wind to the cave of the Great One. He took it in and said to it: "You must appear to your mother! Forty miles distant from your home rises a green mountain cliff. On this cliff she must build a shrine for you. And after you have enjoyed the incense of human adoration for three years, you shall once more have a human body." Notscha appeared to his mother in a dream, and gave her the whole message, and she awoke in tears. But Li Dsing grew angry when she told him about it. "It serves the accursed boy right that he is dead! It is because you are always thinking of him that he appears to you in dreams. You must pay no attention to him." The woman said no more, but thenceforward he appeared to her daily, as soon as she closed her eyes, and grew more and more urgent in his demand. Finally all that was left for her to do was to erect a temple for Notscha without Li Dsing's knowledge.

And Notscha performed great miracles in his temple. All prayers made in it were granted. And from far away people streamed to it to burn incense in his honor.

Thus half a year passed. Then Li Dsing, on the occasion of a great military drill, once came by the cliff in question, and saw the people crowding thickly about the hill like a swarm of ants. Li Dsing inquired what there were to see upon the hill. "It is a new god, who performs so many miracles that people come from far and near to honor him." "What sort of a god is he?" asked Li Dsing. They did not dare conceal from him who the god was. Then Li Dsing grew angry. He spurred his horse up the hill and, sure enough, over the door of the temple was written: "Notscha's Shrine." And within it was the likeness of Notscha, just as he had appeared while living. Li Dsing said: "While you were alive you brought misfortune to your parents. Now that you are dead you deceive the people. It is disgusting!" With these words he drew forth his whip, beat Notscha's idolatrous likeness to pieces with it, had the temple burned down, and the worshipers mildly reproved. Then he returned home.

Now Notscha had been absent in the spirit upon that day. When he returned he found his temple destroyed; and the spirit of the hill gave him the details. Notscha hurried to his master and related with tears what had befallen him. The latter was roused and said: "It is Li Dsing's fault. After you had given back your body to your parents, you were no further concern of his. Why should he withdraw from you the enjoyment of the incense?" Then the Great One made a body of lotus-plants, gave it the gift of life, and enclosed the soul of Notscha within it. This done he called out in a loud voice: "Arise!" A drawing of breath was heard, and Notscha leaped up once more in the shape of a small boy. He flung himself down before his master and thanked him. The latter bestowed upon him the magic of the fiery lance, and Notscha thenceforward had two whirling wheels beneath his feet: The wheel of the wind and the wheel of fire. With these he could rise up and down in the air. The master also gave him a bag of panther-skin in which to keep his armlet and his silken cloth.

Now Notscha had determined to punish Li Dsing. Taking advantage of a moment when he was not watched, he went away, thundering along on his rolling wheels to Li Dsing's dwelling. The latter was unable to withstand him and fled. He was almost exhausted when his second son, Mutscha, the disciple of the holy Pu Hain, came to his aid from the Cave of the White Crane. A violent quarrel took place between the brothers; they began to fight, and Mutscha was overcome; while Notscha once more rushed in pursuit of Li Dsing. At the height of his extremity, however, the holy Wen Dschu of the Hill of the Five Dragons, the master of Gintscha, Li Dsing's oldest son, stepped forth and hid Li Dsing in his cave. Notscha, in a rage, insisted that he be delivered up to him; but Wen Dschu said: "Elsewhere you may indulge your wild nature to your heart's content, but not in this place."

And when Notscha in the excess of his rage turned his fiery lance upon him, Wen Dschu stepped back a pace, shook the seven-petaled lotus from his sleeve, and threw it into the air. A whirlwind arose, clouds and mists obscured the sight, and sand and earth were flung up from the ground. Then the whirlwind collapsed with a great crash. Notscha fainted, and when he regained consciousness found himself bound to a golden column with three thongs of gold, so that he could no longer move. Wen Dschu now called Gintscha to him and ordered him to give his unruly brother a good thrashing. And this he did, while Notscha, obliged to stand it, stood grinding his teeth. In his extremity he saw the Great One floating by, and called out to him: "Save me, O Master!" But the latter did not notice him; instead he entered the cave and thanked Wen Dschu for the severe lesson which he had given Notscha. Finally they called Notscha in to them and ordered him to be reconciled to his father. Then they dismissed them both and seated themselves to play chess. But no sooner was Notscha free than he again fell into a rage, and renewed his pursuit of his father. He had again overtaken Li Dsing when still another saint came forward to defend the latter. This time it was the old Buddha of the Radiance of the Light. When Notscha attempted to battle with him he raised his arm, and a pagoda shaped itself out of red, whirling clouds and closed around Notscha. Then Radiance of Light placed both his hands on the pagoda and a fire arose within it which burned Notscha so that he cried loudly for mercy. Then he had to promise to beg his father's forgiveness and always to obey him in the future. Not till he had promised all this did the Buddha let him out of the pagoda again. And he gave the pagoda to Li Dsing; and taught him a magic saying which would give him the mastery over Notscha. It is for this reason that Li Dsing is called the Pagoda-bearing King of Heaven.

Later on Li Dsing and his three sons, Gintscha, Mutscha and Notscha, aided King Wu of the Dschou dynasty to destroy the tyrant Dschou-Sin.

None could withstand their might. Only once did a sorcerer succeed in wounding Notscha in the left arm. Any other would have died of the wound. But the Great One carried him into his cave, healed his wound and gave him three goblets of the wine of the gods to drink, and three fire-dates to eat. When Notscha had eaten and drunk he suddenly heard a crash at his left side and another arm grew out from it. He could not speak and his eyes stood out from their sockets with horror. But it went on as it had begun: six more arms grew out of his body and two more heads, so that finally he had three heads and eight arms. He called out to his Master: "What does all this mean?" But the latter only laughed and said: "All is as it should be. Thus equipped you will really be strong!" Then he taught him a magic incantation by means of which he could make his arms and heads visible or invisible as he chose. When the tyrant Dschou-Sin had been destroyed, Li Dsing and his three sons, while still on earth, were taken up into heaven and seated among the gods.

The Lady of the Moon

In the days of the Emperor Yau lived a prince by the name of Hou I, who was a mighty hero and a good archer. Once ten suns rose together in the sky, and shone so brightly and burned so fiercely that the people on earth could not endure them. So the Emperor ordered Hou I to shoot at them. And Hou I shot nine of them down from the sky. Besides his bow, Hou I also had a horse which ran so swiftly that even the wind could not catch up with it. He mounted it to go a-hunting, and the horse ran away and could not be stopped. So Hou I came to Kunlun Mountain and met the Queen-Mother of the Jasper Sea. And she gave him the herb of immortality. He took it home with him and hid it in his room. But his wife who was named Tschang O, once ate some of it on the sly when he was not at home, and she immediately floated up to the clouds. When she reached the moon, she ran into the castle there, and has lived there ever since as the Lady of the Moon.

On a night in mid-autumn, an emperor of the Tang dynasty once sat at wine with two sorcerers. And one of them took his bamboo staff and cast it into the air, where it turned into a heavenly bridge, on which the three climbed up to the moon together. There they saw a great castle on which was inscribed: "The Spreading Halls of Crystal Cold." Beside it stood a cassia tree which blossomed and gave forth a fragrance filling all the air. And in the tree sat a man who was chopping off the smaller boughs with an ax. One of the sorcerers said: "That is the man in the moon. The cassia tree grows so luxuriantly that in the course of time it would overshadow all the moon's radiance. Therefore it has to be cut down once in every thousand years." Then they entered the spreading halls. The silver stories of the castle towered one above the other, and its walls and columns were all formed of liquid crystal. In the walls were cages and ponds, where fishes and birds moved as though alive. The whole moon-world seemed made of glass. While they were still looking about them on all sides the Lady of the Moon stepped up to them, clad in a white mantle and a rainbow-colored gown. She smiled and said to the emperor: "You are a prince of the mundane world of dust. Great is your fortune, since you have been able to find your way here!" And she called for her attendants, who came flying up on white birds, and sang and danced beneath the cassia tree. A pure clear music floated through the air. Beside the tree stood a mortar made of white marble, in which a jasper rabbit ground up herbs. That was the dark half of the moon. When the dance had ended, the emperor returned to earth again with the sorcerers. And he had the songs which he had heard on the moon written down and sung to the accompaniment of flutes of jasper in his pear-tree garden.

The Morning Star and the Evening Star

Once upon a time there were two stars, sons of the Golden King of the Heavens. The one was named Tschen and the other Shen. One day they quarreled, and Tschen struck Shen a terrible blow. Thereupon both stars made a vow that they would never again look upon each other. So Tschen only appears in the evening, and Shen only appears in the morning, and not until Tschen has disappeared is Shen again to be seen. And that is why people say: "When two brothers do not live peaceably with one another they are like Tschen and Shen."

The Girl with the Horse's Head; or, The Silkworm Goddess

IN THE DIM AGES OF THE PAST THERE ONCE WAS AN OLD MAN WHO WENT ON A JOURNEY. No one remained at home save his only daughter and a white stallion. The daughter fed the horse day by day, but she was lonely and yearned for her father.

So it happened that one day she said in jest to the horse: "If you will bring back my father to me then I will marry you!"

No sooner had the horse heard her say this, than he broke loose and ran away. He ran until he came to the place where her father was. When her father saw the horse, he was pleasantly surprised, caught him and seated himself on his back. And the horse turned back the way he had come, neighing without a pause.

"What can be the matter with the horse?" thought the father. "Something must have surely gone wrong at home!" So he dropped the reins and rode back. And he fed the horse liberally because he had been so intelligent; but the horse ate nothing, and when he saw the girl, he struck out at her with his hoofs and tried to bite her. This surprised the father; he questioned his daughter, and she told him the truth, just as it had occurred.

"You must not say a word about it to any one," spoke her father, "or else people will talk about us."

And he took down his crossbow, shot the horse, and hung up his skin in the yard to dry. Then he went on his travels again.

One day his daughter went out walking with the daughter of a neighbor. When they entered the yard, she pushed the horse-hide with her foot and said: "What an unreasonable animal you were—wanting to marry a human being! What happened to you served you right!"

But before she had finished her speech, the horse-hide moved, rose up, wrapped itself about the girl and ran off.

Horrified, her companion ran home to her father and told him what had happened. The neighbors looked for the girl everywhere, but she could not be found.

At last, some days afterward, they saw the girl hanging from the branches of a tree, still wrapped in the horse-hide; and gradually she turned into a silkworm and wove a cocoon. And the threads which she spun were strong and thick. Her girl friend then took down the cocoon and let her slip out of it; and then she spun the silk and sold it at a large profit.

But the girl's relatives longed for her greatly. So one day the girl appeared riding in the clouds on her horse, followed by a great company and said: "In heaven I have been assigned to the task of watching over the growing of silkworms. You must yearn for me no longer!" And thereupon they built temples to her in her native land, and every year, at the silkworm season, sacrifices are offered to her and her protection is implored. And the Silkworm Goddess is also known as the girl with the Horse's Head.

The Queen of Heaven

THE QUEEN OF HEAVEN, WHO IS ALSO KNOWN AS THE HOLY MOTHER, WAS IN MORTAL life a maiden of Fukien, named Lin. She was pure, reverential and pious in her ways and died at the age of seventeen. She shows her power on the seas and for this reason the seamen worship her. When they are unexpectedly attacked by wind and waves, they call on her and she is always ready to hear their pleas.

There are many seamen in Fukien, and every year people are lost at sea. And because of this, most likely, the Queen of Heaven took pity on the distress of her people during her lifetime on earth. And since her thoughts are uninterruptedly turned toward aiding the drowning in their distress, she now appears frequently on the seas.

In every ship that sails a picture of the Queen of Heaven hangs in the cabin, and three paper talismans are also kept on shipboard. On the first she is painted with crown and scepter, on the second as a maiden in ordinary dress, and on the third she is pictured with flowing hair, barefoot, standing with a sword in her hand. When the ship is in danger the first talisman is burned, and help comes. But if this is of no avail, then the second and finally the third picture is burned. And if no help comes then there is nothing more to be done.

When seamen lose their course among wind and waves and darkling clouds, they pray devoutly to the Queen of Heaven. Then a red lantern appears on the face of the waters. And if they follow the lantern they will win safe out of all danger. The Queen of Heaven may often be seen standing in the skies, dividing the wind with her sword. When she does this the wind departs for the North and South, and the waves grow smooth.

A wooden wand is always kept before her holy picture in the cabin. It often happens that the fish-dragons play in the seas. They are two giant fish who spout up water against one another till the sun in the sky is obscured, and the seas are shrouded in profound darkness. And often, in the distance, one may see a bright opening in the darkness. If the ship holds a course straight for this opening it will win through, and is suddenly floating in calm waters again. Looking back, one may see the two fishes still spouting water, and the ship will have passed directly beneath their jaws. But a storm is always near when the fish dragons swim; therefore it is well to burn paper or wool so that the dragons do not draw the ship down into the depths. Or the Master of the Wand may burn incense before the wand in the cabin. Then he must take the wand and swing it over the water three times, in a circle. If he does so the dragons will draw in their tails and disappear.

When the ashes in the censer fly up into the air without any cause, and are scattered about, it is a sign that great danger is threatening.

Nearly two-hundred years ago an army was fitted out to subdue the island of Formosa. The captain's banner had been dedicated with the blood of a white horse. Suddenly the Queen of Heaven appeared at the tip of the banner-staff. In another moment she had disappeared, but the invasion was successful.

On another occasion, in the days of Kien Lung, the minister Dschou Ling was ordered to install a new king in the Liu-Kiu Islands. When the fleet was sailing by south of Korea, a storm arose, and his ship was driven toward the Black Whirlpool. The water had the color of ink, sun and moon lost their radiance, and the word was passed about that the ship had been caught in the Black Whirlpool, from which no living man had ever returned. The seaman and travelers awaited their end with lamentations. Suddenly an untold number of lights, like red lanterns, appeared on the surface of the water. Then the seamen were overjoyed and prayed in the cabins. "Our lives are saved!" they cried, "the Holy Mother has come to our aid!" And truly, a beautiful maiden with golden earrings appeared. She waved her hand in the air and the winds became still and the waves grew even. And it seemed as though the ship were being drawn along by a mighty hand. It moved plashing through the waves, and suddenly it was beyond the limits of the Black Whirlpool.

Dschou Ling on his return told of this happening, and begged that temples be erected in honor of the Queen of Heaven, and that she be included in the list of the gods. And the emperor granted his prayer.

Since then temples of the Queen of Heaven are to be found in all sea-port towns, and her birthday is celebrated on the eighth day of the fourth month with spectacles and sacrifices.

The Fire-God

LONG BEFORE THE TIME OF FU HI, DSCHU YUNG, THE MAGIC WELDER, WAS THE RULER of men. He discovered the use of fire, and succeeding generations learned from him to cook their food. Hence his descendants were intrusted with the preservation of fire, while he himself was made the Fire-God. He is a personification of the Red

Lord, who showed himself at the beginning of the world as one of the Five Ancients. The Fire-God is worshiped as the Lord of the Holy Southern Mountain. In the skies the Fiery Star, the southern quarter of the heavens and the Red Bird belong to his domain. When there is danger of fire the Fiery Star glows with a peculiar radiance. When countless numbers of fire-crows fly into a house, a fire is sure to break out in it.

In the land of the four rivers there dwelt a man who was very rich. One day he got into his wagon and set out on a long journey. And he met a girl, dressed in red, who begged him to take her with him. He allowed her to get into the wagon, and drove along for half-a-day without even looking in her direction. Then the girl got out again and said in farewell: "You are truly a good and honest man, and for that reason I must tell you the truth. I am the Fire-God. To-morrow a fire will break out in your house. Hurry home at once to arrange your affairs and save what you can!" Frightened, the man faced his horses about and drove home as fast as he could. All that he possessed in the way of treasures, clothes and jewels, he removed from the house. And, when he was about to lie down to sleep, a fire broke out on the hearth which could not be quenched until the whole building had collapsed in dust and ashes. Yet, thanks to the Fire-God, the man had saved all his movable belongings.

The Three Ruling Gods

There are three lords: in heaven, and on the earth and in the waters, and they are known as the Three Ruling Gods. They are all brothers, and are descended from the father of the Monk of the Yangtze-kiang. When the latter was sailing on the river he was cast into the water by a robber. But he did not drown, for a Triton came his way who took him along with him to the dragon-castle. And when the Dragon-King saw him he realized at once that there was something extraordinary about the Monk, and he married him to his daughter.

From their early youth his three sons showed a preference for the hidden wisdom. And together they went to an island in the sea. There they seated themselves and began to meditate. They heard nothing, they saw nothing, they spoke not a word and they did not move. The birds came and nested in their hair; the spiders came and wove webs across their faces; worms and insects came and crawled in and out of their noses and ears. But they paid no attention to any of them.

After they had meditated thus for a number of years, they obtained the hidden wisdom and became gods. And the Lord made them the Three Ruling Gods. The heavens make things, the earth completes things, and the waters create things. The

Three Ruling Gods sent out the current of their primal power to aid in ordering all to this end. Therefore they are also known as the primal gods, and temples are erected to them all over the earth.

If you go into a temple you will find the Three Ruling Gods all seated on one pedestal. They wear women's hats upon their heads, and hold scepters in their hands, like kings. But he who sits on the last place, to the right, has glaring eyes and wears a look of rage. If you ask why this is you are told: "These three were brothers and the Lord made them the Ruling Gods. So they talked about the order in which they were to sit. And the youngest said: 'To-morrow morning, before sunrise, we will meet here. Whoever gets here first shall have the seat of honor in the middle; the second one to arrive shall have the second place, and the third the third.' The two older brothers were satisfied. The next morning, very early, the youngest came first, seated himself in the middle place, and became the god of the waters. The middle brother came next, sat down on the left, and became the god of the heavens. Last of all came the oldest brother. When he saw that his brothers were already sitting in their places, he was disgusted and yet he could not say a word. His face grew red with rage, his eyeballs stood forth from their sockets like bullets, and his veins swelled like bladders. And he seated himself on the right and became god of the earth." The artisans who make the images of the gods noticed this, so they always represent him thus.

A Legend of Confucius

When Confucius came to the earth, the Kilin, that strange beast which is the prince of all four-footed animals, and only appears when there is a great man on earth, sought the child and spat out a jade whereon was written: "Son of the Watercrystal you are destined to become an uncrowned king!" And Confucius grew up, studied diligently, learned wisdom and came to be a saint. He did much good on earth, and ever since his death has been reverenced as the greatest of teachers and masters. He had foreknowledge of many things. And even after he had died he gave evidence of this.

Once, when the wicked Emperor Tsin Schi Huang had conquered all the other kingdoms, and was traveling through the entire empire, he came to the homeland of Confucius. And he found his grave. And, finding his grave, he wished to have it opened and see what was in it. All his officials advised him not to do so, but he would not listen to them. So a passage was dug into the grave, and in its main chamber they found a coffin, whose wood appeared to be quite fresh. When struck it sounded like metal. To the left of the coffin was a door, which led into an inner chamber. In this chamber stood a bed, and a table with books and clothing, all as though meant for the use of a living person. Tsin Schi Huang seated himself on the bed and looked down. And there on the floor stood two shoes of red silk, whose tips were adorned with a woven pattern of clouds. A bamboo staff leaned against the wall. The Emperor, in jest, put on the shoes, took the staff and left the grave. But as he did so a tablet suddenly appeared before his eyes on which stood the following lines:

O'er kingdoms six Tsin Schi Huang his army led,
To ope my grave and find my humble bed;
He steals my shoes and takes my staff away
To reach Schakiu—and his last earthly day!

Tsin Schi Huang was much alarmed, and had the grave closed again. But when he reached Schakiu he fell ill of a hasty fever of which he died.

The God of War

The God of War, Guan Di, was really named Guan Yu. At the time when the rebellion of the Yellow Turbans was raging throughout the empire, he, together with two others whom he met by the wayside, and who were inspired with the same love of country which possessed him, made a pact of friendship. One of the two was Liu Be, afterward emperor, the other was named Dschang Fe. The three met in a peach-orchard and swore to be brothers one to the other, although they were of different families. They sacrificed a white steed and vowed to be true to each other to the death.

Guan Yu was faithful, honest, upright and brave beyond all measure. He loved to read Confucius's "Annals of Lu," which tell of the rise and fall of empires. He aided his friend Liu Be to subdue the Yellow Turbans and to conquer the land of the four rivers. The horse he rode was known as the Red Hare, and could run a thousand miles in a day. Guan Yu had a knife shaped like a half-moon which was called the Green Dragon. His eyebrows were beautiful like those of the silk-butterflies, and his eyes were long-slitted like the eyes of the Phoenix. His face was scarlet-red in color, and his beard so long that it hung down over his stomach. Once, when he appeared before the emperor, the latter called him Duke Fairbeard, and presented him with a silken pocket in which to place his beard. He wore a garment of green brocade. Whenever he went into battle he showed invincible bravery. Whether he were opposed by a thousand armies or by ten thousand horsemen—he attacked them as though they were merely air.

Once the evil Tsau Tsau had incited the enemies of his master, the Emperor, to take the city by treachery. When Guan Yu heard of it he hastened up with an army to relieve the town. But he fell into an ambush, and, together with his son, was brought a captive to the capital of the enemy's land. The prince of that country would have been glad to have had him go over to his side; but Guan Yu swore that he would not yield to death himself. Thereupon father and son were slain. When he was dead, his horse Red Hare ceased to eat and died. A faithful captain of his, by name of Dschou Dsang, who was black-visaged and wore a great knife, had just invested a fortress when the news of the sad end of the duke reached him. And he, as well as other faithful followers would not survive their master, and perished.

At the time a monk, who was an old compatriot and acquaintance of Duke Guan was living in the Hills of the Jade Fountains. He used to walk at night in the moonlight.

Suddenly he heard a loud voice cry down out of the air: "I want my head back again!"

The monk looked up and saw Duke Guan, sword in hand, seated on his horse, just as he appeared while living. And at his right and left hand, shadowy figures in the clouds, stood his son Guan Ping and his captain, Dschou Dsang.

The monk folded his hands and said: "While you lived you were upright and faithful, and in death you have become a wise god; and yet you do not understand fate! If you insist on having your head back again, to whom shall the many thousands of your enemies who lost their lives through you appeal, in order to have life restored to them?"

When he heard this the Duke Guan bowed and disappeared. Since that time he has been without interruption spiritually active. Whenever a new dynasty is founded, his holy form may be seen. For this reason temples and sacrifices have been instituted for him, and he has been made one of the gods of the empire. Like Confucius, he received the great sacrifice of oxen, sheep and pigs. His rank increases with the passing of centuries. First he was worshipped as Prince Guan, later as King Guan, and then as the great god who conquers the demons. The last dynasty, finally, worships him as the great, divine Helper of the Heavens. He is also called the God of War, and is a strong deliverer in all need, when men are plagued by devils and foxes. Together with Confucius, the Master of Peace, he is often worshiped as the Master of War.

Tales of Saints and Magicians

The Halos of the Saints

The true gods all have halos around their heads. When the lesser gods and demons see these halos, they hide and dare not move. The Master of the Heavens on the Dragon-Tiger Mountain meets the gods at all times. One day the God of War came down to the mountain while the mandarin of the neighboring district was visiting the Master of the Heavens. The latter advised the mandarin to withdraw and hide himself in an inner chamber. Then he went out to receive the God of War. But the mandarin peeped through a slit in the door, and he saw the red face and green garment of the God of War as he stood there, terrible and awe-inspiring. Suddenly a red halo flashed up above his head, whose beams penetrated into the inner chamber so that the mandarin grew blind in one eye. After a time the God of War went away again, and the Master of the Heavens accompanied him. Suddenly Guan Di said, with alarm: "Confucius is coming! The halo he wears illumines the whole world. I cannot endure its radiance even a thousand miles away, so I must hurry and get out of the way!" And with that he stepped into a cloud and disappeared. The Master of the Heavens then told the mandarin what had happened, and added: "Fortunately you did not see the God of War face to face! Whoever does not possess the greatest virtue and the greatest wisdom, would be melted by the red glow of his halo." So saying he gave him a pill of the elixir of life to eat, and his blind eye gradually regained its sight.

It is also said that scholars wear a red halo around their heads which devils, foxes and ghosts fear when they see it.

There was once a scholar who had a fox for a friend. The fox came to see him at night, and went walking with him in the villages. They could enter the houses, and see all that was going on, without people being any the wiser. But when at a distance the fox saw a red halo hanging above a house he would not enter it. The scholar asked him why not.

"Those are all celebrated scholars," answered the fox. "The greater the halo, the more extensive is their knowledge. I dread them and do not dare enter their houses."

Then the man said: "But I am a scholar, too! Have I no halo which makes you fear me, instead of going walking with me?"

"There is only a black mist about your head," answered the fox. "I have never yet seen it surrounded by a halo."

The scholar was mortified and began to scold him; but the fox disappeared with a horse-laugh.

Laotsze

LAOTSZE IS REALLY OLDER THAN HEAVEN AND EARTH PUT TOGETHER. HE IS THE YELLOW Lord or Ancient, who created this world together with the other four. At various times he has appeared on earth, under various names. His most celebrated incarnation, however, is that of Laotsze, "The Old Child," which name he was given because he made his appearance on earth with white hair.

He acquired all sorts of magic powers by means of which he extended his life-span. Once he hired a servant to do his bidding. He agreed to give him a hundred pieces of copper daily; yet he did not pay him, and finally he owed him seven million, two hundred thousand pieces of copper. Then he mounted a black steer and rode to the West. He wanted to take his servant along. But when they reached the Han-Gu pass, the servant refused to go further, and insisted on being paid. Yet Laotsze gave him nothing.

When they came to the house of the guardian of the pass, red clouds appeared in the sky. The guardian understood this sign and knew that a holy man was drawing near. So he went out to meet him and took him into his house. He questioned him with regard to hidden knowledge, but Laotsze only stuck out his tongue at him and would not say a word. Nevertheless, the guardian of the pass treated him with the greatest respect in his home. Laotsze's servant told the servant of the guardian that his master owed him a great deal of money, and begged the latter to put in a good word for him. When the guardian's servant heard how large a sum it was, he was tempted to win so wealthy a man for a son-in-law, and he married him to his daughter. Finally the guardian heard of the matter and came to Laotsze together with the servant. Then Laotsze said to his servant: "You rascally servant. You really should have been dead long ago. I hired you, and since I was poor and could give you no money, I gave you a life-giving talisman to eat. That is how you still happen to be alive. I said to you: 'If you will follow me into the West, the land of Blessed Repose, I will pay you your wages in yellow gold. But you did not wish to do this.'" And with that he patted his servant's neck. Thereupon the latter opened his mouth, and spat out the life-giving talisman. The magic signs written on it with cinnabar, quite fresh and well-preserved, might still be seen. But the servant suddenly collapsed and turned into a heap of dry bones. Then the guardian of the pass cast himself to earth and pleaded for him. He promised to pay the servant for Laotsze and begged the latter to restore him to life. So Laotsze placed the talisman among the bones and at once the servant came to life again. The guardian of the pass paid him his wages and dismissed him. Then he adored Laotsze as his master, and the latter taught him the art of eternal life, and left him his teachings, in five thousand words, which the guardian wrote down. The book which thus came into being is the Tao Teh King, "The Book of the Way and Life." Laotsze then disappeared from the eyes of men. The guardian of the pass however, followed his teachings, and was given a place among the immortals.

The Ancient Man

Once upon a time there was a man named Huang An. He must have been well over eighty and yet he looked like a youth. He lived on cinnabar and wore no clothing. Even in winter he went about without garments. He sat on a tortoise three feet long. Once he was asked: "About how old might this tortoise be?" He answered: "When Fu Hi first invented fish-nets and eel-pots he caught this tortoise and gave it to me. And since then I have worn its shield quite flat sitting on it. The creature dreads the radiance of the sun and moon, so it only sticks its head out of its shell once in two thousand years. Since I have had the beast, it has already stuck its head out five times." With these words he took his tortoise on his back and went off. And the legend arose that this man was ten thousand years old.

The Eight Immortals

I

There is a legend which declares that Eight Immortals dwell in the heavens. The first is named Dschung Li Kuan. He lived in the time of the Han dynasty, and discovered the wonderful magic of golden cinnabar, the philosopher's stone. He could melt quicksilver and burn lead and turn them into yellow gold and white silver. And he could fly through the air in his human form. He is the chief of the Eight Immortals.

The second is named Dschang Go. In primal times he gained hidden knowledge. It is said that he was really a white bat, who turned into a man. In the first days of the Tang dynasty an ancient with a white beard and a bamboo drum on his back, was seen riding backward on a black ass in the town of Tschang An. He beat the drum and sang, and called himself old Dschang Go. Another legend says that he always had a white mule with him which could cover a thousand miles in a single day. When he had reached his destination he would fold up the animal and put it in his trunk. When he needed it again, he would sprinkle water on it with his mouth, and the beast would regain its first shape.

The third is named Lu Yuan or Lu Dung Bin (The Mountain Guest). His real name was Li, and he belonged to the ruling Tang dynasty. But when the Empress Wu seized the throne and destroyed the Li family to almost the last man, he fled with his wife into the heart of the mountains. They changed their names to Lu, and, since they lived in hiding in the caverns in the rocks, he called himself the Mountain Guest or the Guest of the Rocks. He lived on air and ate no bread. Yet he was fond of flowers. And in the course of time he acquired the hidden wisdom.

In Lo Yang, the capital city, the peonies bloomed with special luxuriance. And there dwelt a flower fairy, who changed herself into a lovely maiden with whom Guest of the Rocks, when he came to Lo Yang, was wont to converse. Suddenly along came the Yellow Dragon, who had taken the form of a handsome youth. He mocked the flower fairy. Guest of the Rocks grew furious and cast his flying sword at him, cutting off his head. From that time onward he fell back again into the world of mundane pleasure and death. He sank down into the dust of the diurnal, and was no longer able to wing his way to the upper regions. Later he met Dschung Li Kuan, who delivered him, and then he was taken up in the ranks of the Immortals.

Willowelf was his disciple. This was an old willow-tree which had drawn into itself the most ethereal powers of the sunrays and the moonbeams, and had thus been able to assume the shape of a human being. His face is blue and he has red hair. Guest of the Rocks received him as a disciple. Emperors and kings of future times honor Guest of the Rocks as the ancestor and master of the pure sun. The people call him Grandfather Lu. He is very wise and powerful. And therefore the people still stream into Grandfather Lu's temples to obtain oracles and pray for good luck. If you want to know whether you will be successful or not in an undertaking, go to the temple, light incense and bow your head to earth. On the altar is a bamboo goblet, in which are some dozens of little lottery sticks. You must shake them while kneeling, until one of the sticks flies out. On the lottery-stick is inscribed a number. This number must then be looked up in the Book of Oracles, where it is accompanied by a four-line stanza. It is said that fortune and misfortune, strange to think, occur to one just as foretold by the oracle.

The fourth Immortal is Tsau Guo Gui (Tsau the Uncle of the State). He was the younger brother of the Empress Tsau, who for a time ruled the land. For this reason he was called the Uncle of the State. From his earliest youth he had been a lover of the hidden wisdom. Riches and honors were no more to him than dust. It was Dschung Li Kuan who aided him to become immortal.

The fifth is called Lan Tsai Ho. Nothing is known of his true name, his time nor his family. He was often seen in the market-place, clad in a torn blue robe and wearing only a single shoe, beating a block of wood and singing the nothingness of life.

The sixth Immortal is known as Li Tia Guai (Li with the iron crutch). He lost his parents in early youth and was brought up in his older brother's home. His sister-in-law treated him badly and never gave him enough to eat. Because of this he fled into the hills, and there learned the hidden wisdom.

Once he returned in order to see his brother, and said to his sister-in-law: "Give me something to eat!" She answered: "There is no kindling wood on hand!" He replied: "You need only to prepare the rice. I can use my leg for kindling wood, only you must not say that the fire might injure me, and if you do not no harm will be done."

His sister-in-law wished to see his art, so she poured the rice into the pot. Li stretched one of his legs out under it and lit it. The flames leaped high and the leg burned like coal.

When the rice was nearly boiled his sister-in-law said: "Won't your leg be injured?"

And Li replied angrily: "Did I not warn you not to say anything! Then no harm would have been done. Now one of my legs is lamed." With these words he took an iron poker and fashioned it into a crutch for himself. Then he hung a bottle-gourd on his back, and went into the hills to gather medicinal herbs. And that is why he is known as Li with the Iron Crutch.

It is also told of him that he often was in the habit of ascending into the heavens in the spirit to visit his master Laotsze. Before he left he would order a disciple to watch his body and soul within it, so that the latter did not escape. Should seven days have gone by without his spirit returning, then he would allow his soul to leave the empty tenement. Unfortunately, after six days had passed, the disciple was called to the death-bed of his mother, and when the master's spirit returned on the evening of the seventh day, the life had gone out of its body. Since there was no place for his spirit in his own body, in his despair he seized upon the first handy body from which the vital essence had not yet dispersed. It was the body of a neighbor, a lame cripple, who had just died, so that from that time on the master appeared in his form.

The seventh Immortal is called Hang Siang Dsi. He was the nephew of the famous Confucian scholar Han Yu, of the Tang dynasty. From his earliest youth he cultivated the arts of the deathless gods, left his home and became a Taoist. Grandfather Lu awakened him and raised him to the heavenly world. Once he saved his uncle's life. The latter had been driven from court, because he had objected when the emperor sent for a bone of Buddha with great pomp. When he reached the Blue Pass in his flight, a deep snowfall had made the road impassable. His horse had floundered in a snow-drift, and he himself was well-nigh frozen. Then Hang Siang Dsi suddenly appeared, helped him and his horse out of the drift, and brought them safely to the nearest inn along the Blue Pass. Han Yu sang a verse, in which the lines occurred:

"Tsin Ling Hill 'mid clouds doth lie,
And home is far, beyond my sight!
Round the Blue Pass snow towers high,
And who will lead the horse aright?"

Suddenly it occurred to him that several years before, Hang Siang Dsi had come to his house to congratulate him on his birthday. Before he had left, he had written these words on a slip of paper, and his uncle had read them, without grasping their meaning. And now he was unconsciously singing the very lines of that song that his nephew had written. So he said to Hang Siang Dsi, with a sigh: "You must be one of the Immortals, since you were able thus to foretell the future!"

And thrice Hang Siang Dsi sought to deliver his wife from the bonds of earth. For when he left his home to seek the hidden wisdom, she sat all day long yearning for his presence. Hang Siang Dsi wished to release her into immortality, but he feared she was not capable of translation. So he appeared to her in various forms, in order to try her, once as a beggar, another time as a wandering monk. But his wife did not grasp her opportunities. At last he took the shape of a lame Taoist, who sat on a mat, beat a block of wood and read sutras before the house.

His wife said: "My husband is not at home. I can give you nothing."

The Taoist answered: "I do not want your gold and silver, I want you. Sit down beside me on the mat, and we will fly up into the air and you shall find your husband again!"

Hereupon the woman grew angry and struck at him with a cudgel.

Then Hang Siang Dsi changed himself into his true form, stepped on a shining cloud and was carried aloft. His wife looked after him and wept loudly; but he had disappeared and was not seen again.

The eighth Immortal is a girl and was called Ho Sian Gu. She was a peasant's daughter, and though her step-mother treated her harshly she remained respectful and industrious. She loved to give alms, though her step-mother tried to prevent her. Yet she was never angry, even when her step-mother beat her. She had sworn not to marry, and at last her step-mother did not know what to do with her. One day, while she was cooking rice, Grandfather Du came and delivered her. She was still holding the rice-spoon in her hand as she ascended into the air. In the heavens she was appointed to sweep up the fallen flowers at the Southern Gate of Heaven.

II

Once upon a time there was a poor man, who at last had no roof to shelter him and not a bite to eat. So, weary and worn, he lay down beside a little temple of the field-god that stood by the roadside and fell asleep. And he dreamed that the old, white-bearded field-god came out of his little shrine and said to him: "I know of a means to help you! To-morrow the Eight Immortals will pass along this road. Cast yourself down before them and plead to them!"

When the man awoke he seated himself beneath the great tree beside the field-god's little temple, and waited all day long for his dream to come true. At last, when the sun had nearly sunk, eight figures came down the road, which the beggar clearly recognized as those of the Eight Immortals. Seven of them were hurrying as fast as they could, but one among them, who had a lame leg, limped along after the rest. Before him—it was Li Tia Guai—the man cast himself to earth. But the lame Immortal did not want to bother with him, and told him to go away. Yet the poor man would not give over pleading with him, begging that he might go with them and be one of the Immortals, too. That would be impossible, said the cripple. Yet, as the poor man did not cease his prayers and would not leave him, he at last said: "Very well, then, take hold of my coat!" This the man did and off they went in flying haste over paths and fields, on and on, and even further on. Suddenly they stood together high up on the tower of Pong-lai-schan, the ghost mountain by the Eastern Sea. And, lo, there stood the rest of the Immortals as well! But they were very discontented with the companion whom Li Tia Guai had brought along. Yet since the poor man pleaded so earnestly, they too allowed themselves to be moved, and said to him: "Very well! We will now leap down into the sea. If you follow us you may also become an Immortal!" And one after another the seven leaped down into the sea. But when it came to the man's turn he was frightened, and would not dare the leap. Then the cripple said to him: "If you are afraid, then you cannot become an Immortal!"

"But what shall I do now?" wailed the man, "I am far from my home and have no money!" The cripple broke off a fragment of the battlement of the tower, and thrust it into the man's hand; then he also leaped from the tower and disappeared into the sea like his seven companions.

When the man examined the stone in his hand more closely, he saw that it was the purest silver. It provided him with traveling money during the many weeks it took him to reach his home. But by that time the silver was completely used up, and he found himself just as poor as he had been before.

The Two Scholars

Once upon a time there were two scholars. One was named Liu Tschen and the other Yuan Dschau. Both were young and handsome. One spring day they went together into the hills of Tian Tai to gather curative herbs. There they came to a little valley where peach-trees blossomed luxuriantly on either side. In the middle of the valley was a cave, where two maidens stood under the blossoming trees, one of them clad in red garments, the other in green. And they were beautiful beyond all telling. They beckoned to the scholars with their hands.

"And have you come?" they asked. "We have been waiting for you overlong!"

Then they led them into the cave and served them with tea and wine.

"I have been destined for the lord Liu," said the maiden in the red gown; "and my sister is for the lord Yuan!"

And so they were married. Every day the two scholars gazed at the flowers or played chess so that they forgot the mundane world completely. They only noticed that at times the peach-blossoms on the trees before the cave opened, and at others that they fell from the boughs. And, at times, unexpectedly, they felt cold or warm, and had to change the clothing they were wearing. And they marveled within themselves that it should be so.

Then, one day, they were suddenly overcome by homesickness. Both maidens were already aware of it.

"When our lords have once been seized with homesickness, then we may hold them no longer," said they.

On the following day they prepared a farewell banquet, gave the scholars magic wine to take along with them and said:

"We will see one another again. Now go your way!"

And the scholars bade them farewell with tears.

When they reached home the gates and doors had long since vanished, and the people of the village were all strangers to them. They crowded about the scholars and asked who they might be.

"We are Liu Tschen and Yuan Dschau. Only a few days ago we went into the hills to pick herbs!"

With that a servant came hastening up and looked at them. At last he fell at Liu Tschen's feet with great joy and cried: "Yes, you are really my master! Since you went away, and we had no news of any kind regarding you some seventy years or more have passed."

Thereupon he drew the scholar Liu through a high gateway, ornamented with bosses and a ring in a lion's mouth, as is the custom in the dwellings of those of high estate.

And when he entered the hall, an old lady with white hair and bent back, leaning on a cane, came forward and asked: "What man is this?"

"Our master has returned again," replied the servant. And then, turning to Liu he added: "That is the mistress. She is nearly a hundred years old, but fortunately is still strong and in good health."

Tears of joy and sadness filled the old lady's eyes.

"Since you went away among the immortals, I had thought that we should never see each other again in this life," said she. "What great good fortune that you should have returned after all!"

And before she had ended the whole family, men and women, came streaming up and welcomed him in a great throng outside the hall.

And his wife pointed out this one and that and said: "That is so and so, and this is so and so!"

At the time the scholar had disappeared there had been only a tiny boy in his home, but a few years old. And he was now an old man of eighty. He had served the empire in a high office, and had already retired to enjoy his old age in the ancestral gardens. There were three grand-children, all celebrated ministers; there were more than ten great-grand-children, of whom five had already passed their examinations for the doctorate; there were some twenty great-great-grand-children, of whom the oldest had just returned home after having passed his induction examinations for the magistracy with honor. And the little ones, who were carried in their parents' arms, were not to be counted. The grand-children, who were away, busy with their duties, all asked for leave and returned home when they heard that their ancestor had returned. And the girl grand-children, who had married into other families, also came. This filled

Liu with joy, and he had a family banquet prepared in the hall, and all his descendants, with their wives and husbands sat about him in a circle. He himself and his wife, a white-haired, wrinkled old lady, sat in their midst at the upper end. The scholar himself still looked like a youth of twenty years, so that all the young people in the circle looked around and laughed.

Then the scholar said: "I have a means of driving away old age!"

And he drew out his magic wine and gave his wife some of it to drink. And when she had taken three glasses, her white hair gradually turned black again, her wrinkles disappeared, and she sat beside her husband, a handsome young woman. Then his son and the older grand-children came up and all asked for a drink of the wine. And whichever of them drank only so much as a drop of it was turned from an old man into a youth. The tale was bruited abroad and came to the emperor's ears. The emperor wanted to call Liu to his court, but he declined with many thanks. Yet he sent the emperor some of his magic wine as a gift. This pleased the emperor greatly, and he gave Liu a tablet of honor, with the inscription:

The Common Home of Five Generations

Besides this he sent him three signs which he had written with his own imperial brush signifying:

Joy in longevity

As to the other of the two scholars, Yuan Dschau, he was not so fortunate. When he came home he found that his wife and child had long since died, and his grand-children and great-grand-children were mostly useless people. So he did not remain long, but returned to the hills. Yet Liu Tschen remained for some years with his family, then taking his wife with him, went again to the Tai Hills and was seen no more.

The Miserly Farmer

Once upon a time there was a farmer who had carted pears to market. Since they were very sweet and fragrant, he hoped to get a good price for them. A bonze with a torn cap and tattered robe stepped up to his cart and asked for one. The farmer repulsed him, but the bonze did not go. Then the farmer grew angry and began to call him names. The bonze said: "You have pears by the hundred in your cart. I only ask for one. Surely that does you no great injury. Why suddenly grow so angry about it?"

The bystanders told the farmer that he ought to give the bonze one of the smaller pears and let him go. But the farmer would not and did not. An artisan saw the whole affair from his shop, and since the noise annoyed him, he took some money, bought a pear and gave it to the bonze.

The bonze thanked him and said: "One like myself, who has given up the world, must not be miserly. I have beautiful pears myself, and I invite you all to eat them with me." Then some one asked: "If you have pears then why do you not eat your own?" He answered: "I first must have a seed to plant."

And with that he began to eat the pear with gusto. When he had finished, he held the pit in his hand, took his pick-ax from his shoulder; and dug a hole a couple of inches deep. Into this he thrust the pit, and covered it with earth. Then he asked the folk in the market place for water, with which to water it. A pair of curiosity seekers brought him hot water from the hostelry in the street, and with it the bonze watered the pit. Thousands of eyes were turned on the spot. And the pit could already be seen to sprout. The sprout grew and in a moment it had turned into a tree. Branches and leaves burgeoned out from it. It began to blossom and soon the fruit had ripened: large, fragrant pears, which hung in thick clusters from the boughs. The bonze climbed into the tree and handed down the pears to the bystanders. In a moment all the pears had been eaten up. Then the bonze took his pick-ax and cut down the tree. Crash, crash! so it went for a while, and the tree was felled. Then he took the tree on his shoulder and walked away at an easy gait.

When the bonze had begun to make his magic, the farmer, too, had mingled with the crowd. With neck outstretched and staring eyes he had stood there and had entirely forgotten the business he hoped to do with his pears. When the bonze had gone off he turned around to look after his cart. His pears had all disappeared. Then he realized that the pears the bonze had divided had been his own. He looked more closely, and the axle of his cart had disappeared. It was plainly evident that it had been chopped off quite recently. The farmer fell into a rage and hastened after the bonze as fast as ever he could. And when he turned the corner, there lay the missing piece from the axle by the city wall. And then he realized that the pear-tree which the bonze had chopped down must have been his axle. The bonze, however, was nowhere to be found. And the whole crowd in the market burst out into loud laughter.

Sky O'Dawn

Once upon a time there was a man who took a child to a woman in a certain village, and told her to take care of him. Then he disappeared. And because the dawn was just breaking in the sky when the woman took the child into her home, she called him Sky O'Dawn. When the child was three years old, he would often look up to the heavens and talk with the stars. One day he ran away and many months passed before he came home again. The woman gave him a whipping. But he ran away again, and did not return for a year. His foster-mother was frightened, and asked: "Where have you been all year long?" The boy answered: "I only made a quick trip to the Purple Sea. There the water stained my clothes red. So I went to the spring at which the sun turns in, and washed them. I went away in the morning and I came back at noon. Why do you speak about my having been gone a year?"

Then the woman asked: "And where did you pass on your way?"

The boy answered: "When I had washed my clothes, I rested for a while in the City of the Dead and fell asleep. And the King-Father of the East gave me red chestnuts and rosy dawn-juice to eat, and my hunger was stilled. Then I went to the dark skies and drank the yellow dew, and my thirst was quenched. And I met a black tiger and wanted to ride home on his back. But I whipped him too hard, and he bit me in the leg. And so I came back to tell you about it."

Once more the boy ran away from home, thousands of miles, until he came to the swamp where dwelt the Primal Mist. There he met an old man with yellow eyebrows and asked him how old he might be. The old man said: "I have given up the habit of eating, and live on air. The pupils of my eyes have gradually acquired a green glow, which enables me to see all hidden things. Whenever a thousand years have passed I turn around my bones and wash the marrow. And every two thousand years I scrape my skin to get rid of the hair. I have already washed my bones thrice and scraped my skin five times."

Afterward Sky O'Dawn served the Emperor Wu of the Han dynasty. The Emperor, who was fond of the magic arts, was much attached to him. One day he said to him: "I wish that the empress might not grow old. Can you prevent it?"

Sky O'Dawn answered: "I know of only one means to keep from growing old."

The Emperor asked what herbs one had to eat. Sky O'Dawn replied: "In the North-East grow the mushrooms of life. There is a three-legged crow in the sun who always wants to get down and eat them. But the Sun-God holds his eyes shut and does not let him get away. If human beings eat them they become immortal, when animals eat them they grow stupefied."

"And how do you know this?" asked the Emperor.

"When I was a boy I once fell into a deep well, from which I could not get out for many decades. And down there was an immortal who led me to this herb. But one has to pass through a red river whose water is so light that not even a feather can swim on it. Everything that touches its surface sinks to the depths. But the man pulled off one of his shoes and gave it to me. And I crossed the water on the shoe, picked the herb and ate it. Those who dwell in that place weave mats of pearls and precious stones. They led me to a spot before which hung a curtain of delicate, colored skin. And they gave me a pillow carved of black jade, on which were graven sun and moon, clouds and thunder. They covered me with a dainty coverlet spun of the hair of a hundred gnats. A cover of that kind is very cool and refreshing in summer. I felt of it with my hands, and it seemed to be formed of water; but when I looked at it more closely, it was pure light."

Once the Emperor called together all his magicians in order to talk with them about the fields of the blessed spirits. Sky O'Dawn was there, too, and said: "Once I was wandering about the North Pole and I came to the Fire-Mirror Mountain. There neither sun nor moon shines. But there is a dragon who holds a fiery mirror in his jaws in order to light up the darkness. On the mountain is a park, and in the park is a lake. By the lake grows the glimmer-stalk grass, which shines like a lamp of gold. If you pluck it and use it for a candle, you can see all things visible, and the shapes of the spirits as well. It even illuminates the interior of a human being."

Once Sky O'Dawn went to the East, into the country of the fortunate clouds. And he brought back with him from that land a steed of the gods, nine feet high. The Emperor asked him how he had come to find it.

So he told him: "The Queen-Mother of the West had him harnessed to her wagon when she went to visit the King-Father of the East. The steed was staked out in the field of the mushrooms of life. But he trampled down several hundred of them. This made the King-Father angry, and he drove the steed away to the heavenly river. There I found him and rode him home. I rode three times around the sun, because I had fallen asleep on the steed's back. And then, before I knew it, I was here. This steed can catch up with the sun's shadow. When I found him he was quite thin and as sad as an aged donkey. So I mowed the grass of the country of the fortunate clouds, which grows once every two-thousand years on the Mountain of the Nine Springs and fed it to the horse; and that made him lively again."

The Emperor asked what sort of a place the country of the fortunate clouds might be. Sky O'Dawn answered: "There is a great swamp there. The people prophesy fortune and misfortune by the air and the clouds. If good fortune is to befall a house, clouds of five colors form in the rooms, which alight on the grass and trees and turn into a colored dew. This dew tastes as sweet as cider."

The Emperor asked whether he could obtain any of this dew. Sky O'Dawn replied: "My steed could take me to the place where it falls four times in the course of a single day!"

And sure enough he came back by evening, and brought along dew of every color in a crystal flask. The Emperor drank it and his hair grew black again. He gave it to his highest officials to drink, and the old grew young again and the sick became well.

Once, when a comet appeared in the heavens, Sky O'Dawn gave the Emperor the astrologer's wand. The Emperor pointed it at the comet and the comet was quenched.

Sky O'Dawn was an excellent whistler. And whenever he whistled in full tones, long drawn out, the motes in the sunbeams danced to his music.

Once he said to a friend: "There is not a soul on earth who knows who I am with the exception of the astrologer!"

When Sky O'Dawn had died, the Emperor called the astrologer to him and asked: "Did you know Sky O'Dawn?"

He replied: "No!"

The Emperor said: "What do you know?"

The astrologer answered: "I know how to gaze on the stars."

"Are all the stars in their places?" asked the Emperor.

"Yes, but for eighteen years I have not seen the Star of the Great Year. Now it is visible once more."

Then the Emperor looked up toward the skies and sighed: "For eighteen years Sky O'Dawn kept me company, and I did not know that he was the Star of the Great Year!"

King Mu of Dschou

In the days of King Mu of Dschou a magician came out of the uttermost West, who could walk through water and fire, and pass through metal and stone. He could make mountains and rivers change place, shift about cities and castles, rise into emptiness without falling, strike against solid matter without finding it an obstruction; and he knew a thousand transformations in all their inexhaustible variety. And he could not only change the shape of things but he could change men's thoughts. The King honored him like a god, and served him as he would a master. He resigned his own apartments that the magician might be lodged in them, had beasts of sacrifice brought to offer him, and selected sweet singers to give him pleasure. But the rooms in the King's palace were too humble—the magician could not dwell in them; and the King's singers were not musical enough to be allowed to be near him. So King Mu had a new palace built for him. The work of bricklayers and carpenters, of painters and stainers left nothing to be desired with regard to skill. The King's treasury was empty when the tower had reached its full height. It was a thousand fathoms high, and rose above the top of the mountain before the capital. The King selected maidens, the loveliest and most dainty, gave them fragrant essences, had their eyebrows curved in lines of beauty, and adorned their hair and ears with jewels. He garbed them in fine cloth, and with white silks fluttering about them, and had their faces painted white and their eyebrows stained black. He had them put on armlets of precious stones and mix sweet-smelling herbs. They filled the palace and sang the songs of the ancient kings in order to please the magician. Every month the most costly garments were brought him, and every morning the most delicate food. The magician allowed them to do so, and since he had no choice, made the best of it.

Not long afterward the magician invited the King to go traveling with him. The King grasped the magician's sleeve, and thus they flew up through the air to the middle of the skies. When they stopped they found they had reached the palace of the magician. It was built of gold and silver, and adorned with pearls and precious stones. It towered high over the clouds and rain; and none could say whereon it rested. To the eye it had the appearance of heaped-up clouds. All that it offered the senses was different from the things of the world of men. It seemed to the King as though he were bodily present in the midst of the purple depths of the city of the air, of the divine harmony of the spheres, where the Great God dwells. The King looked down, and his castles and pleasure-houses appeared to him like hills of earth and heaps of straw. And there the King remained for some decades and thought no more of his kingdom.

Then the magician again invited the King to go traveling with him once more. And in the place to which they came there was to be seen neither sun nor moon above, nor rivers or sea below. The King's dazzled eyes could not see the radiant shapes which showed themselves; the King's dulled ears could not hear the sounds which played about them. It seemed as though his body were dissolving in confusion; his thoughts began to stray, and consciousness threatened to leave him. So he begged the magician to return. The magician put his spell upon him, and it seemed to the King as though he were falling into empty space.

When he regained consciousness, he was sitting at the same place where he had been sitting when the magician had asked him to travel with him for the first time. The servants waiting on him were the same, and when he looked down, his goblet was not yet empty, and his food had not yet grown cold.

The King asked what had happened. And the servants answered, "The King sat for a space in silence." Whereupon the King was quite bereft of reason, and it was three months before he regained his right mind. Then he questioned the magician. The magician said: "I was traveling with you in the spirit, O King! What need was there for the body to go along? And the place in which we stayed at that time was no less real than your own castle and your own gardens. But you are used only to permanent conditions, therefore visions which dissolve so suddenly appear strange to you."

The King was content with the explanation. He gave no further thought to the business of government and took no more interest in his servants, but resolved to travel afar. So he had the eight famous steeds harnessed, and accompanied by a few faithful retainers, drove a thousand miles away. There he came to the country of the great hunters. The great hunters brought the King the blood of the white brant to drink, and washed his feet in the milk of mares and cows. When the King and his followers had quenched their thirst, they drove on and camped for the night on the slope of the Kunlun Mountain, south of the Red River. The next day they climbed to the peak of Kunlun Mountain and gazed at the castle of the Lord of the Yellow Earth. Then they traveled on to the Queen-Mother of the West. Before they got there they had to pass the Weak River. This is a river whose waters will bear neither floats nor ships. All that attempts to float over it sinks into its depths. When the King reached the shore, fish and turtles, crabs and salamanders came swimming up and formed a bridge, so that he could drive across with the wagon.

It is said of the Queen-Mother of the West that she goes about with hair unkempt, with a bird's beak and tiger's teeth, and that she is skilled in playing the flute. Yet this is not her true figure, but that of a spirit who serves her, and rules over the Western sky. The Queen-Mother entertained King Mu in her castle by the Springs of Jade. And she gave him rock-marrow to drink and fed him with the fruit of the jade-trees. Then she sang him a song and taught him a magic formula by means of which one could obtain long life. The Queen-Mother of the West gathers the immortals around her, and gives them to eat of the peaches of long life; and then they come to her with wagons with purple canopies, drawn by flying dragons. Ordinary mortals sink in the Weak River when they try to cross. But she was kindly disposed to King Mu.

When he took leave of her, he also went on to the spot where the sun turns in after running three thousand miles a day. Then he returned again to his kingdom.

When King Mu was a hundred years old, the Queen-Mother of the West drew near his palace and led him away with her into the clouds.

And from that day on he was seen no more.

The King of Huai Nan

THE KING OF HUAI NAN WAS A LEARNED MAN OF THE HAN DYNASTY. SINCE HE WAS OF the blood royal the emperor had given him a kingdom in fee. He cultivated the society of scholars, could interpret signs and foretell the future. Together with his scholars he had compiled the book which bears his name.

One day eight aged men came to see him. They all had white beards and white hair. The gate-keeper announced them to the King. The King wished to try them, so he sent back the gate-keeper to put difficulties in the way of their entrance. The latter said to them: "Our King is striving to learn the art of immortal life. You gentlemen are old and feeble. How can you be of aid to him? It is unnecessary for you to pay him a visit."

The eight old men smiled and said: "Oh, and are we too old to suit you? Well, then we will make ourselves young!" And before they had finished speaking they had turned themselves into boys of fourteen and fifteen, with hair-knots as black as silk and faces like peach-blossoms. The gate-keeper was frightened, and at once informed the King of what had happened. When the King heard it, he did not even take time to slip into his shoes, but hurried out barefoot to receive them. He led them into his palace, had rugs of brocade spread for them, and beds of ivory set up, fragrant herbs burned and tables of gold and precious stones set in front of them. Then he bowed before them as pupils do before a teacher, and told them how glad he was that they had come.

The eight boys changed into old men again and said: "Do you wish to go to school to us, O King? Each one of us is master of a particular art. One of us can call up wind and rain, cause clouds and mists to gather, rivers to flow and mountains to heave themselves up, if he wills it so. The second can cause high mountains to split asunder and check great streams in their course. He can tame tigers and panthers and soothe serpents and dragons. Spirits and gods do his bidding. The third can send out doubles, transform himself into other shapes, make himself invisible, cause whole armies to disappear, and turn day into night. The fourth can walk through the air and clouds, can stroll on the surface of the waves, pass through walls and rocks and cover a thousand miles in a single breath. The fifth can enter fire without burning, and water without drowning. The winter frost cannot chill him, nor the summer heat burn him. The sixth can create and transform living creatures if he feel inclined. He can form birds and beasts, grasses and trees. He can transplace houses and castles. The seventh can bake lime so that it turns to gold, and cook lead so that it turns to silver; he can mingle water and stone so that the bubbles effervesce and turn into pearls. The eighth can ride on dragons and cranes to the eight poles of the world, converse with the immortals, and stand in the presence of the Great Pure One."

The King kept them beside him from morning to night, entertained them and had them show him what they could do. And, true enough, they could do everything just as they had said. And now the King began to distill the elixir of life with their aid. He had finished, but not yet imbibed it when a misfortune overtook his family. His son had been playing with a courtier and the latter had heedlessly wounded him. Fearing that the prince might punish him, he joined other discontented persons and excited a revolt. And the emperor, when he heard of it, sent one of his captains to judge between the King and the rebels.

The eight aged men spoke: "It is now time to go. This misfortune has been sent you from heaven, O King! Had it not befallen you, you would not have been able to resolve to leave the splendors and glories of this world!"

They led him on to a mountain. There they offered sacrifices to heaven, and buried gold in the earth. Then they ascended into the skies in bright daylight. The footprints of the eight aged men and of the king were imprinted in the rock of the mountain, and may be seen there to this very day. Before they had left the castle, however, they had set what was left of the elixir of life out in the courtyard. Hens and hounds picked and licked it up, and all flew up into the skies. In Huai Nan to this very day the crowing of cocks and the barking of hounds may be heard up in the skies, and it is said that these are the creatures who followed the King at the time.

One of the King's servants, however, followed him to an island in the sea, whence he sent him back. He told that the King himself had not yet ascended to the skies, but had only become immortal and was wandering about the world. When the emperor heard of the matter he regretted greatly that he had sent soldiers into the King's land and thus driven him out. He called in magicians to aid him, in hope of meeting the eight old men himself. Yet, for all that he spent great sums, he was not successful. The magicians only cheated him.

Old Dschang

Once upon a time there was a man who went by the name of Old Dschang. He lived in the country, near Yangdschou, as a gardener. His neighbor, named Sir We, held an official position in Yangdschou. Sir We had decided that it was time for his daughter to marry, so he sent for a match-maker and commissioned her to find a suitable husband. Old Dschang heard this, and was pleased. He prepared food and drink, entertained the match-maker, and told her to recommend him as a husband. But the old match-maker went off scolding.

The next day he invited her to dinner again and gave her money. Then the old match-maker said: "You do not know what you wish! Why should a gentleman's beautiful daughter condescend to marry a poor old gardener like yourself? Even though you had money to burn, your white hair would not match her black locks. Such a marriage is out of the question!"

But Old Dschang did not cease to entreat her: "Make an attempt, just one attempt, to mention me! If they will not listen to you, then I must resign myself to my fate!"

The old match-maker had taken his money, so she could not well refuse, and though she feared being scolded, she mentioned him to Sir We. He grew angry and wanted to throw her out of the house.

"I knew you would not thank me," said she, "but the old man urged it so that I could not refuse to mention his intention."

"Tell the old man that if this very day he brings me two white jade-stones, and four hundred ounces of yellow gold, then I will give him my daughter's hand in marriage."

But he only wished to mock the old man's folly, for he knew that the latter could not give him anything of the kind. The match-maker went to Old Dschang and delivered the message. And he made no objection; but at once brought the exact quantity of gold and jewels to Sir We's house. The latter was very much frightened and when his wife heard of it, she began to weep and wail loudly. But the girl encouraged her mother: "My father has given his word now and cannot break it. I will know how to bear my fate."

So Sir We's daughter was married to Old Dschang. But even after the wedding the latter did not give up his work as a gardener. He spaded the field and sold vegetables as usual, and his wife had to fetch water and build the kitchen fire herself. But she did her work without false shame and, though her relatives reproached her, she continued to do so.

Once an aristocratic relative visited Sir We and said: "If you had really been poor, were there not enough young gentlemen in the neighborhood for your daughter? Why did you have to marry her to such a wrinkled old gardener? Now that you have thrown her away, so to speak, it would be better if both of them left this part of the country."

Then Sir We prepared a banquet and invited his daughter and Old Dschang to visit him. When they had had sufficient to eat and drink he allowed them to get an inkling of what was in his mind.

Said Old Dschang: "I have only remained here because I thought you would long for your daughter. But since you are tired of us, I will be glad to go. I have a little country house back in the hills, and we will set out for it early to-morrow morning."

The following morning, at break of dawn, Old Dschang came with his wife to say farewell. Sir We said: "Should we long to see you at some later time, my son can make inquiries." Old Dschang placed his wife on a donkey and gave her a straw hat to wear. He himself took his staff and walked after.

A few years passed without any news from either of them. Then Sir We and his wife felt quite a longing to see their daughter and sent their son to make inquiries. When the latter got back in the hills he met a plow-boy who was plowing with two yellow steers. He asked him: "Where is Old Dschang's country house?" The plow-boy left the plow in the harrow, bowed and answered: "You have been a long time coming, sir! The village is not far from here: I will show you the way."

They crossed a hill. At the foot of the hill flowed a brook, and when they had crossed the brook they had to climb another hill. Gradually the landscape changed. From the top of the hill could be seen a valley, level in the middle, surrounded by abrupt crags and shaded by green trees, among which houses and towers peeped forth. This was the country house of Old Dschang. Before the village flowed a deep brook full of clear, blue water. They passed over a stone bridge and reached the gate. Here flowers and trees grew in luxurious profusion, and peacocks and cranes flew about. From the distance could be heard the sound of flutes and of stringed instruments. Crystal-clear tones rose to the clouds. A messenger in a purple robe received the guest at the gate and led him into a hall of surpassing splendor. Strange fragrances filled the air, and there was a ringing of little bells of pearl. Two maid-servants came forth to greet him, followed by two rows of beautiful girls in a long processional. After them a man in a flowing turban, clad in scarlet silk, with red slippers, came floating along. The guest saluted him. He was serious and dignified, and at the same time seemed youthfully fresh. At first We's son did not recognize him, but when he looked more closely, why it was Old Dschang! The latter said with a smile: "I am pleased that the long road to travel has not prevented your coming. Your sister is just combing her hair. She will welcome you in a moment." Then he had him sit down and drink tea.

After a short time a maid-servant came and led him to the inner rooms, to his sister. The beams of her room were of sandalwood, the doors of tortoise-shell and the windows inlaid with blue jade; her curtains were formed of strings of pearls and the steps leading into the room of green nephrite. His sister was magnificently gowned, and far more beautiful than before. She asked him carelessly how he was getting along, and what her parents were doing; but was not very cordial. After a splendid meal she had an apartment prepared for him.

"My sister wishes to make an excursion to the Mountain of the Fairies," said Old Dschang to him. "We will be back about sunset, and you can rest until we return."

Then many-colored clouds rose in the courtyard, and dulcet music sounded on the air. Old Dschang mounted a dragon, while his wife and sister rode on phoenixes and their attendants on cranes. So they rose into the air and disappeared in an easterly direction. They did not return until after sunset.

Old Dschang and his wife then said to him: "This is an abode of the blessed. You cannot remain here overlong. To-morrow we will escort you back."

On the following day, when taking leave, Old Dschang gave him eighty ounces of gold and an old straw hat. "Should you need money," said he, "you can go to Yangdschou and inquire in the northern suburb for old Wang's drug-shop. There you can collect ten million pieces of copper. This hat is the order for them." Then he ordered his plow-boy to take him home again.

Quite a few of the folks at home, to whom he described his adventures, thought that Old Dschang must be a holy man, while others regarded the whole thing a magic vision.

After five or six years Sir We's money came to an end. So his son took the straw hat to Yangdschou and there asked for old Wang. The latter just happened to be standing in his drug-shop, mixing herbs. When the son explained his errand he said: "The money is ready. But is your hat genuine?" And he took the hat and examined it. A young girl came from an inner room and said: "I wove the hat for Old Dschang myself. There must be a red thread in it." And sure enough, there was. Then old Wang gave young We the ten million pieces of copper, and the latter now believed that Old Dschang was really a saint. So he once more went over the hills to look for him. He asked the forest-keepers, but they could tell him naught. Sadly he retraced his steps and decided to inquire of old Wang, but he had also disappeared.

When several years had passed he once more came to Yangdschou, and was walking in the meadow before the city gate. There he met Old Dschang's plow-boy. The latter cried out: "How are you? How are you?" and drew out ten pounds of gold, which he gave to him, saying: "My mistress told me to give you this. My master is this very moment drinking tea with old Wang in the inn." Young We followed the plow-boy, intending to greet his brother-in-law. But when he reached the inn there was no one in sight. And when he turned around the plow-boy had disappeared as well. And since that time no one ever heard from Old Dschang again.

The Kindly Magician

ONCE UPON A TIME THERE WAS A MAN NAMED DU DSI TSCHUN. IN HIS YOUTH HE WAS a spendthrift and paid no heed to his property. He was given to drink and idling. When he had run through all his money, his relatives cast him out. One winter day he was walking barefoot about the city, with an empty stomach and torn clothes. Evening came on and still he had not found any food. Without end or aim he wandered about the market place. He was hungry, and the cold seemed well nigh unendurable. So he turned his eyes upward and began to lament aloud.

Suddenly an ancient man stood before him, leaning on a staff, who said: "What do you lack since you complain so?"

"I am dying of hunger," replied Du Dsi Tschun, "and not a soul will take pity on me!"

The ancient man said: "How much money would you need in order to live in all comfort?"

"If I had fifty thousand pieces of copper it would answer my purpose," replied Du Dsi Tschun.

The ancient said: "That would not answer."

"Well, then, a million!"

"That is still too little!"

"Well, then, three million!"

The ancient man said: "That is well spoken!" He fetched a thousand pieces of copper out of his sleeve and said: "That is for this evening. Expect me to-morrow by noon, at the Persian Bazaar!"

At the time set Du Dsi Tschun went there, and, sure enough, there was the ancient, who gave him three million pieces of copper. Then he disappeared, without giving his name.

When Du Dsi Tschun held the money in his hand, his love for prodigality once more awoke. He rode pampered steeds, clothed himself in the finest furs, went back to his wine, and led such an extravagant life that the money gradually came to an end. Instead of wearing brocade he had to wear cotton, and instead of riding horseback he went to the dogs. Finally he was again running about barefoot and in rags as before, and did not know how to satisfy his hunger. Once more he stood in the market-place and sighed. But the ancient was already there, took him by the hand and said: "Are you back already to where you were? That is strange! However, I will aid you once more!"

But Du Dsi Tschun was ashamed and did not want to accept his help. Yet the ancient insisted, and led him along to the Persian Bazaar. This time he gave him ten million pieces of copper, and Du Dsi Tschun thanked him with shame in his heart.

With money in hand, he tried to give time to adding to it, and saving in order to gain great wealth. But, as is always the case, it is hard to overcome ingrown faults. Gradually he began to fling his money away again, and gave free rein to all his desires. And once more his purse grew empty. In a couple of years he was as poor as ever he had been.

Then he met the ancient the third time, but was so ashamed of himself that he hid his face when he passed him.

The ancient seized his arm and said: "Where are you going? I will help you once more. I will give you thirty million. But if then you do not improve you are past all aid!"

Full of gratitude, Du Dsi Tschun bowed before him and said: "In the days of my poverty my wealthy relatives did not seek me out. You alone have thrice aided me. The money you give me to-day shall not be squandered, that I swear; but I will devote it to good works in order to repay your great kindness. And when I have done this I will follow you, if needs be through fire and through water."

The ancient replied: "That is right! When you have ordered these things ask for me in the temple of Laotsze beneath the two mulberry trees!"

Du Dsi Tschun took the money and went to Yangdschou. There he bought a hundred acres of the best land, and built a lofty house with many hundreds of rooms on the highway. And there he allowed widows and orphans to live. Then he bought a burial-place for his ancestors, and supported his needy relations. Countless people were indebted to him for their livelihood.

When all was finished, he went to inquire after the ancient in the temple of Laotsze. The ancient was sitting in the shade of the mulberry trees blowing the flute. He took Du Dsi Tschun along with him to the cloudy peaks of the holy mountains of the West. When they had gone some forty miles into the mountains, he saw a dwelling, fair and clean. It was surrounded by many-colored clouds, and peacocks and cranes were flying about it. Within the house was an herb-oven nine feet high. The fire burned with a purple flame, and its glow leaped along the walls. Nine fairies stood at the oven, and a green dragon and a white tiger crouched beside it. Evening came. The ancient was no longer clad like an ordinary man; but wore a yellow cap and wide, flowing garments. He took three pellets of the White Stone, put them into a flagon of wine, and gave them to Du Dsi Tschun to drink. He spread out a tiger-skin against the western wall of the inner chamber, and bade Du Dsi Tschun sit down on it, with his face turned toward the East. Then he said to him: "Now beware of speaking a single word—no matter what happens to you, whether you encounter powerful gods or terrible demons, wild beasts or ogres, or all the tortures of the nether world, or even if you see your own relatives suffer—for all these things are only deceitful images! They cannot harm you. Think only of what I have said, and let your soul be at rest!" And when he had said this the ancient disappeared.

Then Du Dsi Tschun saw only a large stone jug full of clear water standing before him. Fairies, dragon and tiger had all vanished. Suddenly he heard a tremendous crash, which made heaven and earth tremble. A man towering more than ten feet in height appeared. He called himself the great captain, and he and his horse were covered with golden armor. He was surrounded by more than a hundred soldiers, who drew their bows and swung their swords, and halted in the courtyard.

The giant called out harshly: "Who are you? Get out of my way!"

Du Dsi Tschun did not move. And he returned no answer to his questions.

Then the giant flew into a passion and cried with a thundering voice: "Chop off his head!"

But Du Dsi Tschun remained unmoved, so the giant went off raging.

Then a furious tiger and a poisonous serpent came up roaring and hissing. They made as though to bite him and leaped over him. But Du Dsi Tschun remained unperturbed in spirit, and after a time they dissolved and vanished.

Suddenly a great rain began to fall in streams. It thundered and lightninged incessantly, so that his ears rang and his eyes were blinded. It seemed as though the house would fall. The water rose to a flood in a few moments' time, and streamed up to the place where he was sitting. But Du Dsi Tschun remained motionless and paid no attention to it. And after a time the water receded.

Then came a great demon with the head of an ox. He set up a kettle in the middle of the courtyard, in which bubbled boiling oil. He caught Du Dsi Tschun by the neck with an iron fork and said: "If you will tell me who you are I will let you go!"

Du Dsi Tschun shut his eyes and kept silent. Then the demon picked him up with the fork and flung him into the kettle. He withstood the pain, and the boiling oil did not harm him. Finally the demon dragged him out again, and drew him down the steps of the house before a man with red hair and a blue face, who looked like the prince of the nether world. The latter cried: "Drag in his wife!"

After a time Du Dsi Tschun's wife was brought on in chains. Her hair was torn and she wept bitterly.

The demon pointed to Du Dsi Tschun and said: "If you will speak your name we will let her go!"

But he answered not a word.

Then the prince of evil had the woman tormented in all sorts of ways. And she pleaded with Du Dsi Tschun: "I have been your wife now for ten years. Will you not speak one little word to save me? I can endure no more!" And the tears ran in streams from her eyes. She screamed and scolded. Yet he spoke not a word.

Thereupon the prince of evil shouted: "Chop her into bits!" And there, before his eyes, it seemed as though she were really being chopped to pieces. But Du Dsi Tschun did not move.

"The scoundrel's measure is full!" cried the prince of evil. "He shall dwell no longer among the living! Off with his head!" And so they killed him, and it seemed to him that his soul fled his body. The ox-headed demon dragged him down into the nether regions, where he tasted all the tortures in turn. But Du Dsi Tschun remembered the words of the ancient. And the tortures, too, seemed bearable. So he did not scream and said not a word.

Now he was once more dragged before the prince of evil. The latter said: "As punishment for his obstinacy this man shall come to earth again in the shape of a woman!"

The demon dragged him to the wheel of life and he returned to earth in the shape of a girl. He was often ill, had to take medicine continually, and was pricked and burned with hot needles. Yet he never uttered a sound. Gradually he grew into a beautiful maiden. But since he never spoke, he was known as the dumb maid. A scholar finally took him for his bride, and they lived in peace and good fellowship. And a son came to them who, in the course of two years was already beyond measure wise and intelligent. One day the father was carrying the son on his arm. He spoke jestingly to his wife and said: "When I look at you it seems to me that you are not really dumb. Won't you say one little word to me? How delightful it would be if you were to become my speaking rose!"

The woman remained silent. No matter how he might coax and try to make her smile, she would return no answer.

Then his features changed: "If you will not speak to me, it is a sign that you scorn me; and in that case your son is nothing to me, either!" And with that he seized the boy and flung him against the wall.

But since Du Dsi Tschun loved this little boy so dearly, he forgot the ancient's warning, and cried out: "Oh, oh!"

And before the cry had died away Du Dsi Tschun awoke as though from a dream and found himself seated in his former place. The ancient was there as well. It must have been about the fifth hour of the night. Purple flames rose wildly from the oven, and flared up to the sky. The whole house caught fire and burned like a torch.

"You have deceived me!" cried the ancient. Then he seized him by the hair and thrust him into the jug of water. And in a minute the fire went out. The ancient spoke: "You overcame joy and rage, grief and fear, hate and desire, it is true; but love you had not driven from your soul. Had you not cried out when the child was flung against the wall, then my elixir would have taken shape and you would have attained immortality. But in the last moment you failed me. Now it is too late. Now I can begin brewing my elixir of life once more from the beginning and you will remain a mere mortal man!"

Du Dsi Tschun saw that the oven had burst, and that instead of the philosopher's stone it held only a lump of iron. The ancient man cast aside his garments and chopped it up with a magic knife. Du Dsi Tschun took leave of him and returned to Yangdschou, where he lived in great affluence. In his old age he regretted that he had not completed his task. He once more went to the mountain to look for the ancient. But the ancient had vanished without leaving a trace.

The Flower-Elves

Once upon a time there was a scholar who lived retired from the world in order to gain hidden wisdom. He lived alone and in a secret place. And all about the little house in which he dwelt he had planted every kind of flower, and bamboos and other trees. There it lay, quite concealed in its thick grove of flowers. With him he had only a boy servant, who dwelt in a separate hut, and who carried out his orders. He was not allowed to appear before his master unless summoned. The scholar loved his flowers as he did himself. Never did he set his foot beyond the boundaries of his garden.

It chanced that once there came a lovely spring evening. Flowers and trees stood in full bloom, a fresh breeze was blowing, the moon shone clearly. And the scholar sat over his goblet and was grateful for the gift of life.

Suddenly he saw a maiden in dark garments come tripping up in the moonlight. She made a deep courtesy, greeted him and said: "I am your neighbor. We are a company of young maids who are on our way to visit the eighteen aunts. We should like to rest in this court for awhile, and therefore ask your permission to do so."

The scholar saw that this was something quite out of the common, and gladly gave his consent. The maiden thanked him and went away.

In a short time she brought back a whole crowd of maids carrying flowers and willow branches. All greeted the scholar. They were charming, with delicate features, and slender, graceful figures. When they moved their sleeves, a delightful fragrance was exhaled. There is no fragrance known to the human world which could be compared with it.

The scholar invited them to sit down for a time in his room. Then he asked them: "Whom have I really the honor of entertaining? Have you come from the castle of the Lady in the Moon, or the Jade Spring of the Queen-Mother of the West?"

"How could we claim such high descent?" said a maiden in a green gown, with a smile. "My name is Salix." Then she presented another, clad in white, and said: "This is Mistress Prunophora"; then one in rose, "and this is Persica"; and finally one in a dark-red gown, "and this is Punica. We are all sisters and we want to visit the eighteen zephyr-aunts to-day. The moon shines so beautifully this evening and it is so charming here in the garden. We are most grateful to you for taking pity on us."

"Yes, yes," said the scholar.

Then the sober-clad servant suddenly announced: "The zephyr-aunts have already arrived!"

At once the girls rose and went to the door to meet them.

"We were just about to visit you, aunts," they said, smiling. "This gentleman here had just invited us to sit for a moment. What a pleasant coincidence that you aunts have come here, too. This is such a lovely night that we must drink a goblet of nectar in honor of you aunts!"

Thereon they ordered the servant to bring what was needed.

"May one sit down here?" asked the aunts.

"The master of the house is most kind," replied the maids, "and the spot is quiet and hidden."

And then they presented the aunts to the scholar. He spoke a few kindly words to the eighteen aunts. They had a somewhat irresponsible and airy manner. Their words fairly gushed out, and in their neighborhood one felt a frosty chill.

Meanwhile the servant had already brought in table and chairs. The eighteen aunts sat at the upper end of the board, the maids followed, and the scholar sat down with them at the lowest place. Soon the entire table was covered with the most delicious foods and most magnificent fruits, and the goblets were filled with a fragrant nectar. They were delights such as the world of men does not know! The moon shone brightly and the flowers exhaled intoxicating odors. After they had partaken of food and drink the maids rose, danced and sung. Sweetly the sound of their singing echoed through the falling gloam, and their dance was like that of butterflies fluttering about the flowers. The scholar was so overpowered with delight that he no longer knew whether he were in heaven or on earth.

When the dance had ended, the girls sat down again at the table, and drank the health of the aunts in flowing nectar. The scholar, too, was remembered with a toast, to which he replied with well-turned phrases.

But the eighteen aunts were somewhat irresponsible in their ways. One of them, raising her goblet, by accident poured some nectar on Punica's dress. Punica, who was young and fiery, and very neat, stood up angrily when she saw the spot on her red dress.

"You are really very careless," said she, in her anger. "My other sisters may be afraid of you, but I am not!"

Then the aunts grew angry as well and said: "How dare this young chit insult us in such a manner!"

And with that they gathered up their garments and rose.

All the maids then crowded about them and said: "Punica is so young and inexperienced! You must not bear her any ill-will! To-morrow she shall go to you switch in hand, and receive her punishment!"

But the eighteen aunts would not listen to them and went off. Thereupon the maids also said farewell, scattered among the flower-beds and disappeared. The scholar sat for a long time lost in dreamy yearning.

On the following evening the maids all came back again.

"We all live in your garden," they told him. "Every year we are tormented by naughty winds, and therefore we have always asked the eighteen aunts to protect us. But yesterday Punica insulted them, and now we fear they will help us no more. But we know that you have always been well disposed toward us, for which we are heartily grateful. And now we have a great favor to ask, that every New Year's day you make a small scarlet flag, paint the sun, moon and five planets on it, and set it up in the eastern part of the garden. Then we sisters will be left in peace and will be protected from all evil. But since New Year's day has passed for this year, we beg that you will set up the flag on the twenty-first of this month. For the East Wind is coming and the flag will protect us against him!"

The scholar readily promised to do as they wished, and the maids all said with a single voice: "We thank you for your great kindness and will repay it!" Then they departed and a sweet fragrance filled the entire garden.

The scholar, however, made a red flag as described, and when early in the morning of the day in question the East Wind really did begin to blow, he quickly set it up in the garden.

Suddenly a wild storm broke out, one that caused the forests to bend, and broke the trees. The flowers in the garden alone did not move.

Then the scholar noticed that Salix was the willow; Prunophora the plum; Persica the peach, and the saucy Punica the Pomegranate, whose powerful blossoms the wind cannot tear. The eighteen zephyr-aunts, however, were the spirits of the winds.

In the evening the flower-elves all came and brought the scholar radiant flowers as a gift of thanks.

"You have saved us," they said, "and we have nothing else we can give you. If you eat these flowers you will live long and avoid old age. And if you, in turn, will protect us every year, then we sisters, too, will live long."

The scholar did as they told him and ate the flowers. And his figure changed and he grew young again like a youth of twenty. And in the course of time he attained the hidden wisdom and was placed among the Immortals.

The Spirit of the Wu-Lian Mountain

To the west of the gulf of Kiautschou is the Wu-Lian Mountain, where there are many spirits. Once upon a time a scholar who lived there was sitting up late at night, reading. And, as he stepped out before the house, a storm rose up suddenly, and a monster stretched out his claws and seized him by the hair. And he lifted him up in the air and carried him away. They passed by the tower which looks out to sea, a Buddhist temple in the hills. And in the distance, in the clouds, the scholar saw the figure of a god in golden armor. The figure looked exactly like the image of Weto which was in the tower. In its right hand it held an iron mace, while its left pointed toward the monster, and it looked at it with anger. Then the monster let the scholar fall, right on top of the tower, and disappeared. No doubt the saint in the tower had come to the scholar's aid, because his whole family worshiped Buddha dutifully.

When the sun rose the priest came and saw the scholar on his tower. He piled up hay and straw on the ground; so that he could jump down without hurting himself. Then he took the scholar home, yet there where the monster had seized his hair, the hair remained stiff and unyielding. It did not improve until half a year had gone by.

The King of the Ants

Once upon a time there was a scholar, who wandered away from his home and went to Emmet village. There stood a house which was said to be haunted. Yet it was beautifully situated and surrounded by a lovely garden. So the scholar hired it. One evening he was sitting over his books, when several hundred knights suddenly came galloping into the room. They were quite tiny, and their horses were about the size of flies. They had hunting falcons and dogs about as large as gnats and fleas.

They came to his bed in the corner of the room, and there they held a great hunt, with bows and arrows: one could see it all quite plainly. They caught a tremendous quantity of birds and game, and all this game was no larger than little grains of rice.

When the hunt was over, in came a long procession with banners and standards. They wore swords at their side and bore spears in their hands, and came to a halt in the north-west corner of the room. They were followed by several hundred serving-men. These brought with them curtains and covers, tents and tent-poles, pots and kettles, cups and plates, tables and chairs. And after them some hundreds of other servants carried in all sorts of fine dishes, the best that land and water had to offer. And several hundred more ran to and fro without stopping, in order to guard the roads and carry messages.

The scholar gradually accustomed himself to the sight. Although the men were so very small he could distinguish everything quite clearly.

Before long, a bright colored banner appeared. Behind it rode a personage wearing a scarlet hat and garments of purple. He was surrounded by an escort of several thousands. Before him went runners with whips and rods to clear the way.

Then a man wearing an iron helmet and with a golden ax in his hand cried out in a loud voice: "His Highness is graciously pleased to look at the fish in the Purple Lake!" Whereupon the one who wore the scarlet hat got down from his horse, and, followed by a retinue of several hundred men, approached the saucer which the scholar used for his writing-ink. Tents were put up on the edge of the saucer and a banquet was prepared. A great number of guests sat down to the table. Musicians and dancers stood ready. There was a bright confusion of mingled garments of purple and scarlet, crimson and green. Pipes and flutes, fiddles and cymbals sounded, and the dancers moved in the dance. The music was very faint, and yet its melodies could be clearly distinguished. All that was said, too, the table-talk and orders, questions and calls, could be quite distinctly heard.

After three courses, he who wore the scarlet hat said: "Quick! Make ready the nets and lines for fishing!"

And at once nets were thrown out into the saucer which held the water in which the scholar dipped his brush. And they caught hundreds of thousands of fishes. The one with the scarlet hat contented himself with casting a line in the shallow waters of the saucer, and caught a baker's dozen of red carp.

Then he ordered the head cook to cook the fish, and the most varied dishes were prepared with them. The odor of roasting fat and spices filled the whole room.

And then the wearer of the scarlet hat in his arrogance, decided to amuse himself at the scholar's expense. So he pointed to him and said: "I know nothing at all about the writings and customs of the saints and wise men, and still I am a king who is highly honored! Yonder scholar spends his whole life toiling over his books and yet he remains poor and gets nowhere. If he could make up his mind to serve me faithfully as one of my officials, I might allow him to partake of our meal."

This angered the scholar, and he took his book and struck at them. And they all scattered, wriggling and crawling out of the door. He followed them and dug up the earth in the place where they had disappeared. And there he found an ants' nest as large as a barrel, in which countless green ants were wriggling around. So he built a large fire and smoked them out.

The Little Hunting Dog

ONCE UPON A TIME, IN THE CITY OF SHANSI, THERE LIVED A SCHOLAR WHO FOUND the company of others too noisy for him. So he made his home in a Buddhist temple. Yet he suffered because there were always so many gnats and fleas in his room that he could not sleep at night.

Once he was resting on his bed after dinner, when suddenly two little knights with plumes in their helmets rode into the room. They might have been two inches high, and rode horses about the size of grasshoppers. On their gauntleted hands they held hunting falcons as large as flies. They rode about the room with great rapidity. The scholar had no more than set eyes on them when a third entered, clad like the others, but carrying a bow and arrows and leading a little hunting dog the size of an ant with him. After him came a great throng of footmen and horsemen, several hundred in all. And they had hunting falcons and hunting dogs by the hundred, too. Then the fleas and gnats began to rise in the air; but were all slain by the falcons. And the hunting dogs climbed on the bed, and sniffed along the walls trailing the fleas, and ate them up. They followed the trace of whatever hid in the cracks, and nosed it out, so that in a short space of time they had killed nearly all the vermin.

The scholar pretended to be asleep and watched them. And the falcons settled down on him, and the dogs crawled along his body. Shortly after came a man clad in yellow, wearing a king's crown, who climbed on an empty couch and seated himself there. And at once all the horsemen rode up, descended from their horses and brought him all the birds and game. They then gathered beside him in a great throng, and conversed with him in a strange tongue.

Not long after the king got into a small chariot and his bodyguards saddled their horses with the greatest rapidity. Then they galloped out with great cries of homage, till it looked as though some one were scattering beans and a heavy cloud of dust rose behind them.

They had nearly all of them disappeared, while the scholar's eyes were still fixed on them full of terror and astonishment, and he could not imagine whence they had come. He slipped on his shoes and looked; but they had vanished without a trace. Then he returned and looked all about his room; but there was nothing to be seen. Only, on a brick against the wall, they had forgotten a little hunting dog. The scholar quickly caught it and found it quite tame. He put it in his paint-box and examined it closely. It had a very smooth, fine coat, and wore a little collar around its neck. He tried to feed it a few bread-crumbs, but the little dog only sniffed at them and let them lie. Then it leaped into the bed and hunted up some nits and gnats in the folds of the linen, which it devoured. Then it returned and lay down. When the night had passed the scholar feared it might have run away; but there it lay, curled up as before. Whenever the scholar went to bed, the dog climbed into it and bit to death any vermin it could find. Not a fly or gnat dared alight while it was around. The scholar loved it like a jewel of price.

But once he took a nap in the daytime, and the little dog crawled into bed beside him. The scholar woke and turned around, supporting himself on his side. As he did so he felt something, and feared it might be his little dog. He quickly rose and looked, but it was already dead—pressed flat, as though cut out of paper!

But at any rate none of the vermin had survived it.

The Dragon After His Winter Sleep

ONCE THERE WAS A SCHOLAR WHO WAS READING IN THE UPPER STORY OF HIS HOUSE. It was a rainy, cloudy day and the weather was gloomy. Suddenly he saw a little thing which shone like a fire-fly. It crawled upon the table, and wherever it went it left traces of burns, curved like the tracks of a rainworm. Gradually it wound itself about the scholar's book and the book, too, grew black. Then it occurred to him that it might be a dragon. So he carried it out of doors on the book. There he stood for quite some time; but it sat uncurled, without moving in the least.

Then the scholar said: "It shall not be said of me that I was lacking in respect." With these words he carried back the book and once more laid it on the table. Then he put on his robes of ceremony, made a deep bow and escorted the dragon out on it again.

No sooner had he left the door, than he noticed that the dragon raised his head and stretched himself. Then he flew up from the book with a hissing sound, like a radiant streak. Once more he turned around toward the scholar, and his head had already grown to the size of a barrel, while his body must have been a full fathom in length. He gave one more snaky twist, and then there was a terrible crash of thunder and the dragon went sailing through the air.

The scholar then returned and looked to see which way the little creature had come. And he could follow his tracks hither and thither, to his chest of books.

The Spirits of the Yellow River

THE SPIRITS OF THE YELLOW RIVER ARE CALLED DAI WANG—GREAT KING. FOR many hundreds of years past the river inspectors had continued to report that all sorts of monsters show themselves in the waves of the stream, at times in the shape of dragons, at others in that of cattle and horses, and whenever such a creature makes an appearance a great flood follows. Hence temples are built along the river banks. The higher spirits of the river are honored as kings, the lower ones as captains, and hardly a day goes by without their being honored with sacrifices or theatrical performances. Whenever, after a dam has been broken, the leak is closed again, the emperor sends officials with sacrifices and ten great bars of Tibetan incense. This incense is burned in a great sacrificial censer in the temple court, and the river inspectors and their subordinates all go to the temple to thank the gods for their aid. These river gods, it is said, are good and faithful servants of former rulers, who died in consequence of their toil in keeping the dams unbroken. After they died their spirits became river-kings; in their physical bodies, however, they appear as lizards, snakes and frogs.

The mightiest of all the river-kings is the Golden Dragon-King. He frequently appears in the shape of a small golden snake with a square head, low forehead and four red dots over his eyes. He can make himself large or small at will, and cause the waters to rise and fall. He appears and vanishes unexpectedly, and lives in the mouths of the Yellow River and the Imperial Canal. But in addition to the Golden Dragon-King there are dozens of river-kings and captains, each of whom has his own place. The sailors of the Yellow River all have exact lists in which the lives and deeds of the river-spirits are described in detail.

The river-spirits love to see theatrical performances. Opposite every temple is a stage. In the hall stands the little spirit-tablet of the river-king, and on the altar in front of it a small bowl of golden lacquer filled with clean sand. When a little snake appears in it, the river-king has arrived. Then the priests strike the gong and beat the drum and read from the holy books. The official is at once informed and he sends for a company of actors. Before they begin to perform the actors go up to the temple, kneel, and beg the king to let them know which play they are to give. And the river-god picks one out and points to it with his head; or else he writes signs in the sand with his tail. The actors then at once begin to perform the desired play.

The river-god cares naught for the fortunes or misfortunes of human beings. He appears suddenly and disappears in the same way, as best suits him.

Between the outer and the inner dam of the Yellow River are a number of settlements. Now it often happens that the yellow water moves to the very edge of the inner walls. Rising perpendicularly, like a wall, it gradually advances. When people see it coming they hastily burn incense, bow in prayer before the waters, and promise the river-god a theatrical performance. Then the water retires and the word goes round: "The river-god has asked for a play again!"

In a village in that section there once dwelt a wealthy man. He built a stone wall, twenty feet high, around the village, to keep away the water. He did not believe in the spirits of the river, but trusted in his strong wall and was quite unconcerned.

One evening the yellow water suddenly rose and towered in a straight line before the village. The rich man had them shoot cannon at it. Then the water grew stormy, and surrounded the wall to such a height that it reached the openings in the battlements. The water foamed and hissed, and seemed about to pour over the wall. Then every one in the village was very much frightened. They dragged up the rich man and he had to kneel and beg for pardon. They promised the river-god a theatrical performance, but in vain; but when they promised to build him a temple in the middle of the village and give regular performances, the water sank more and more and gradually returned to its bed. And the village fields suffered no damage, for the earth, fertilized by the yellow slime, yielded a double crop.

Once a scholar was crossing the fields with a friend in order to visit a relative. On their way they passed a temple of the river-god where a new play was just being performed. The friend asked the scholar to go in with him and look on. When they entered the temple court they saw two great snakes upon the front pillars, who had wound themselves about the columns, and were thrusting out their heads as though watching the performance. In the hall of the temple stood the altar with the bowl of sand. In it lay a small snake with a golden body, a green head and red dots above his eyes. His neck was thrust up and his glittering little eyes never left the stage. The friend bowed and the scholar followed his example.

Softly he said to his friend: "What are the three river-gods called?"

"The one in the temple," was the reply, "is the Golden Dragon-King. The two on the columns are two captains. They do not dare to sit in the temple together with the king."

This surprised the scholar, and in his heart he thought: "Such a tiny snake! How can it possess a god's power? It would have to show me its might before I would worship it."

He had not yet expressed these secret thoughts before the little snake suddenly stretched forth his head from the bowl, above the altar. Before the altar burned two enormous candles. They weighed more than ten pounds and were as thick as small trees. Their flame burned like the flare of a torch. The snake now thrust his head into the middle of the candle-flame. The flame must have been at least an inch broad, and was burning red. Suddenly its radiance turned blue, and was split into two tongues. The candle was so enormous and its fire so hot that even copper and iron would have melted in it; but it did not harm the snake.

Then the snake crawled into the censer. The censer was made of iron, and was so large one could not clasp it with both arms. Its cover showed a dragon design in open-work. The snake crawled in and out of the holes in this cover, and wound his way through all of them, so that he looked like an embroidery in threads of gold. Finally all the openings of the cover, large and small, were filled by the snake. In order to do so, he must have made himself several dozen feet long. Then he stretched out his head at the top of the censer and once more watched the play.

Thereupon the scholar was frightened, he bowed twice, and prayed: "Great King, you have taken this trouble on my account! I honor you from my heart!"

No sooner had he spoken these words than, in a moment, the little snake was back in his bowl, and just as small as he had been before.

In Dsiningdschou they were celebrating the river-god's birthday in his temple. They were giving him a theatrical performance for a birthday present. The spectators crowded around as thick as a wall, when who should pass but a simple peasant from the country, who said in a loud voice: "Why, that is nothing but a tiny worm! It is a great piece of folly to honor it like a king!"

Before ever he had finished speaking the snake flew out of the temple. He grew and grew, and wound himself three times around the stage. He became as thick around as a small pail, and his head seemed like that of a dragon. His eyes sparkled like golden lamps, and he spat out red flame with his tongue. When he coiled and uncoiled the whole stage trembled and it seemed as though it would break down. The actors stopped their music and fell down on the stage in prayer. The whole multitude was seized with terror and bowed to the ground. Then some of the old men came along, cast the peasant on the ground, and gave him a good thrashing. So he had to cast himself on his knees before the snake and worship him. Then all heard a noise as though a great many firecrackers were being shot off. This lasted for some time, and then the snake disappeared.

East of Shantung lies the city of Dongschou. There rises an observation-tower with a great temple. At its feet lies the water-city, with a sea-gate at the North, through which the flood-tide rises up to the city. A camp of the boundary guard is established at this gate.

Once upon a time there was an officer who had been transferred to this camp as captain. He had formerly belonged to the land forces, and had not yet been long at his new post. He gave some friends of his a banquet, and before the pavilion in which they feasted lay a great stone shaped somewhat like a table. Suddenly a little snake was seen crawling on this stone. It was spotted with green, and had red dots on its square head. The soldiers were about to kill the little creature, when the captain went out to look into the matter. When he had looked he laughed and said: "You must not harm him! He is the river-king of Dsiningdschou. When I was stationed in Dsiningdschou he sometimes visited me, and then I always gave sacrifices and performances in his honor. Now he has come here expressly in order to wish his old friend luck, and to see him once more."

There was a band in camp; the bandsmen could dance and play like a real theatrical troupe. The captain quickly had them begin a performance, had another banquet with wine and delicate foods prepared, and invited the river-god to sit down to the table.

Gradually evening came and yet the river-god made no move to go.

So the captain stepped up to him with a bow and said: "Here we are far removed from the Yellow River, and these people have never yet heard your name spoken. Your visit has been a great honor for me. But the women and fools who have crowded together chattering outside, are afraid of hearing about you. Now you have visited your old friend, and I am sure you wish to get back home again."

With these words he had a litter brought up; cymbals were beaten and fire-works set off, and finally a salute of nine guns was fired to escort him on his way. Then the little snake crawled into the litter, and the captain followed after. In this order they reached the port, and just when it was about time to say farewell, the snake was already swimming in the water. He had grown much larger, nodded to the captain with his head, and disappeared.

Then there were doubts and questionings: "But the river-god lives a thousand miles away from here, how does he get to this place?"

Said the captain: "He is so powerful that he can get to any place, and besides, from where he dwells a waterway leads to the sea. To come down that way and swim to sea is something he can do in a moment's time!"

The Dragon-Princess

In the Sea of Dungting there is a hill, and in that hill there is a hole, and this hole is so deep that it has no bottom.

Once a fisherman was passing there who slipped and fell into the hole. He came to a country full of winding ways which led over hill and dale for several miles. Finally he reached a dragon-castle lying in a great plain. There grew a green slime which reached to his knees. He went to the gate of the castle. It was guarded by a dragon who spouted water which dispersed in a fine mist. Within the gate lay a small hornless dragon who raised his head, showed his claws, and would not let him in.

The fisherman spent several days in the cave, satisfying his hunger with the green slime, which he found edible and which tasted like rice-mush. At last he found a way out again. He told the district mandarin what had happened to him, and the latter reported the matter to the emperor. The emperor sent for a wise man and questioned him concerning it.

The wise man said: "There are four paths in this cave. One path leads to the southwest shore of the Sea of Dungting, the second path leads to a valley in the land of the four rivers, the third path ends in a cave on the mountain of Lo-Fu and the fourth in an island of the Eastern Sea. In this cave dwells the seventh daughter of the Dragon-King of the Eastern Sea, who guards his pearls and his treasure. It happened once in the ancient days, that a fisherboy dived into the water and brought up a pearl from beneath the chin of a black dragon. The dragon was asleep, which was the reason the fisherboy brought the pearl to the surface without being harmed. The treasure which the daughter of the Dragon-King has in charge is made up of thousands and millions of such jewels. Several thousands of small dragons watch over them in her service. Dragons have the peculiarity of fighting shy of wax. But they are fond of beautiful jade-stones, and of kung-tsing, the hollowgreen wood, and like to eat swallows. If one were to send a messenger with a letter, it would be possible to obtain precious pearls."

The emperor was greatly pleased, and announced a large reward for the man who was competent to go to the dragon-castle as his messenger.

The first man to come forward was named So Pi-Lo. But the wise man said: "A great-great-great-great-grandfather of yours once slew more than a hundred of the dragons of the Eastern Sea, and was finally himself slain by the dragons. The dragons are the enemies of your family and you cannot go."

Then came a man from Canton, Lo-Dsi-Tschun, with his two brothers, who said that his ancestors had been related to the Dragon-King. Hence they were well liked by the dragons and well known to them. They begged to be entrusted with the message.

The wise man asked: "And have you still in your possession the stone which compels the dragons to do your will?"

"Yes," said they, "we have brought it along with us."

The wise man had them show him the stone; then he spoke: "This stone is only obeyed by the dragons who make clouds and send down the rain. It will not do for the dragons who guard the pearls of the sea-king." Then he questioned them further: "Have you the dragon-brain vapor?"

When they admitted that they had not, the wise man said: "How then will you compel the dragons to yield their treasure?"

And the emperor said: "What shall we do?"

The wise man replied: "On the Western Ocean sail foreign merchants who deal in dragon-brain vapor. Some one must go to them and seek it from them. I also know a holy man who is an adept in the art of taming dragons, and who has prepared ten pounds of the dragon-stone. Some one should be sent for that as well."

The emperor sent out his messengers. They met one of the holy man's disciples and obtained two fragments of dragon-stone from him.

Said the wise man: "That is what we want!"

Several more months went by, and at last a pill of dragon-brain vapor had also been secured. The emperor felt much pleased and had his jewelers carve two little boxes of the finest jade. These were polished with the ashes of the Wutung-tree. And he had an essence prepared of the very best hollowgreen wood, pasted with sea-fish lime, and hardened in the fire. Of this two vases were made. Then the bodies and the clothing of the messengers were rubbed with tree-wax, and they were given five hundred roasted swallows to take along with them.

They went into the cave. When they reached the dragon-castle, the little dragon who guarded the gate smelled the tree-wax, so he crouched down and did them no harm. They gave him a hundred roasted swallows as a bribe to announce them to the daughter of the Dragon-King. They were admitted to her presence and offered her the jade caskets, the vases and the four hundred roasted swallows as gifts. The dragon's daughter received them graciously, and they unfolded the emperor's letter.

In the castle there was a dragon who was over a thousand years old. He could turn himself into a human being, and could interpret the language of human beings. Through him the dragon's daughter learned that the emperor was sending her the gifts, and she returned them with a gift of three great pearls, seven smaller pearls and a whole bushel of ordinary pearls. The messengers took leave, rode off with their pearls on a dragon's back, and in a moment they had reached the banks of the Yangtze-kiang. They made their way to Nanking, the imperial capital, and there handed over their treasure of gems.

The emperor was much pleased and showed them to the wise man. He said: "Of the three great pearls one is a divine wishing-pearl of the third class, and two are black dragon-pearls of medium quality. Of the seven smaller pearls two are serpent-pearls, and five are mussel-pearls. The remaining pearls are in part sea-crane pearls, in part snail and oyster-pearls. They do not approach the great pearls in value, and yet few will be found to equal them on earth."

The emperor also showed them to all his servants. They, however, thought the wise man's words all talk, and did not believe what he said.

Then the wise man said: "The radiance of wishing-pearls of the first class is visible for forty miles, that of the second class for twenty miles, and that of the third for ten miles. As far as their radiance carries, neither wind nor rain, thunder nor lightning, water, fire nor weapons may reach. The pearls of the black dragon are nine-colored and glow by night. Within the circle of their light the poison of serpents and worms is powerless. The serpent-pearls are seven-colored, the mussel-pearls five-colored. Both shine by night. Those most free from spots are the best. They grow within the mussel, and increase and decrease in size as the moon waxes and wanes."

Some one asked how the serpent and sea-crane pearls could be told apart, and the wise man answered: "The animals themselves recognize them."

Then the emperor selected a serpent-pearl and a sea-crane pearl, put them together with a whole bushel of ordinary pearls, and poured the lot out in the courtyard. Then a large yellow serpent and a black crane were fetched and placed among the pearls. At once the crane took up a sea-crane pearl in his bill and began to dance and sing and flutter around. But the serpent snatched at the serpent-pearl, and wound himself about it in many coils. And when the people saw this they acknowledged the truth of the wise man's words. As regards the radiance of the larger and smaller pearls it turned out, too, just as the wise man had said.

In the dragon-castle the messengers had enjoyed dainty fare, which tasted like flowers, herbs, ointment and sugar. They had brought a remnant of it with them to the capital; yet exposed to the air it had become as hard as stone. The emperor commanded that these fragments be preserved in the treasury. Then he bestowed high rank and titles on the three brothers, and made each one of them a present of a thousand rolls of fine silk stuff. He also had investigated why it was that the fisherman, when he chanced upon the cave, had not been destroyed by the dragons. And it turned out that his fishing clothes had been soaked in oil and tree-wax. The dragons had dreaded the odor.

Help in Need

Some twenty miles east of Gingdschou lies the Lake of the Maidens. It is several miles square and surrounded on all sides by thick green thickets and tall forests. Its waters are clear and dark-blue. Often all kinds of wondrous creatures show themselves in the lake. The people of the vicinity have erected a temple there for the Dragon Princess. And in times of drought all make pilgrimage there to offer up prayers.

West of Gingdschou, two hundred miles away, is another lake, whose god is named Tschauna, and who performs many miracles. During the time of the Tang dynasty there lived in Gingdschou a mandarin by name of Dschou Bau. While he was in office it chanced that in the fifth month clouds suddenly arose in the sky, piling themselves up like mountains, among which wriggled dragons and serpents; they rolled up and down between the two seas. Tempest and rain, thunder and lightning arose so that houses fell to pieces, trees were torn up by the roots, and much damage was done the crops. Dschou Bau took the blame upon himself, and prayed to the heavens that his people might be pardoned.

On the fifth day of the sixth month he sat in his hall of audience and gave judgment; and suddenly he felt quite weary and sleepy. He took off his hat and laid down on the cushions. No sooner had he closed his eyes than he saw a warrior in helmet and armor, with a halberd in his hand, standing on the steps leading to the hall, who announced: "A lady is waiting outside who wishes to enter!" Dschou Bau asked him: "Who are you?" The answer was: "I am your door-keeper. In the invisible world I already have been performing this duty for many years." Meanwhile two figures clad in green came up the steps, knelt before him and said: "Our mistress has come to visit you!" Dschou Bau rose. He beheld lovely clouds, from which fell a fine rain, and strange fragrances enchanted him. Suddenly he saw a lady clad in a simple gown, but of surpassing beauty, float down from on high, with a retinue of many female servants. These were all neat and clean in appearance, and waited upon the lady as though she were a princess. When the latter entered the hall she raised her arms in greeting. Dschou Bau came forward to meet her and invited her to be seated. From all sides bright-colored clouds came floating in, and the courtyard was filled with a purple ether. Dschou Bau had wine and food brought and entertained them all in the most splendid way. But the goddess sat staring straight before her with wrinkled brows, and seemed to feel very sad. Then she rose and said with a blush: "I have been living in this neighborhood for many years. A wrong which has been done me, permits me to pass the bounds of what is fitting, and encourages me to ask a favor of you. Yet I do not know whether you wish to save me!"

"May I hear what it is all about," answered Dschou Bau. "If I can help you, I will be glad to place myself at your disposal."

The goddess said: "For hundreds of years my family has been living in the depth of the Eastern Sea. But we were unfortunate in that our treasures excited the jealousy of men. The ancestor of Pi-Lo nearly destroyed our entire clan by fire. My ancestors had to fly and hide themselves. And not long ago, our enemy Pi-Lo himself wanted to deliver an imperial letter in the cave of the Sea of Dungting. Under the pretext of begging for pearls and treasures, he wished to enter the dragon-castle and destroy our family. Fortunately a wise man saw through his treacherous purpose, and Lo-Dsi-Tschun and his brothers were sent in his stead. Yet my people did not feel safe from future attacks. For this reason they withdrew to the distant West. My father has done much good to mankind and hence is highly honored there. I am his ninth daughter. When I was sixteen I was wedded to the youngest son of the Rock-Dragon. But my good husband had a fiery temper, which often caused him to offend against the laws of courtesy, and in less than a year's time the punishment of heaven was his portion. I was left alone and returned to the home of my parents. My father wished me to marry again; but I had promised to remain true to the memory of my husband, and made a vow not to comply with my father's wish. My parents grew angry, and I was obliged to retire to this place in view of their anger. That was three years ago. Who could imagine that the contemptible dragon Tschauna, who was seeking a wife for his youngest brother, would try to force the wedding-gift upon me? I refused to accept it; but Tschauna knew how to gain his point with my father, and was determined to carry out his intention. My father, regardless of my wishes, promised me to him. And then the dragon Tschauna appeared with his youngest brother and wanted to carry me off by sheer force of arms. I encountered him with fifty faithful followers, and we fought on the meadow before the city. We were defeated, and I am more than ever afraid that Tschauna will attempt to drag me off. So I have plucked up courage to beg you to lend me your mercenaries so that I may beat off my foes and remain as I am. If you will help me I will be grateful to you till the end of my days."

Dschou Bau answered: "You come from a noble family. Have you no kinsfolk who will hasten to help you in your need, that you are compelled to turn to a mortal man?"

"It is true that my kinsfolk are far-famed and numerous. If I were to send out letters and they came to my aid, they would rub out that scaly scoundrel Tschauna as one might rub garlic. But my deceased husband offended the high heavens and he has not yet been pardoned. And my parents' will, too, is opposed to mine, so that I dare not call upon my kinsfolk for help. You will understand my need." Then Dschou Bau promised to help her, and the princess thanked him and departed.

When he awoke, he sighed long thinking over his strange experience. And the following day he sent off fifteen hundred soldiers to stand guard by the Lake of the Maidens.

On the seventh day of the sixth month Dschou Bau rose early. Darkness still lay before the windows, yet it seemed to him as though he could glimpse a man before the curtain. He asked who it might be. The man said: "I am the princess's adviser. Yesterday you were kind enough to send soldiers to aid us in our distress. But they were all living men, and such cannot fight against invisible spirits. You will have to send us soldiers of yours who have died, if you wish to aid us."

Dschou Bau reflected for a time, and then it occurred to him that of course such must be the case. So he had his field-secretary examine the roster to see how many of his soldiers had fallen in battle. And the latter counted up to some two thousand foot-soldiers and five-hundred horsemen. Dschou Bau appointed his deceased officer Mong Yuan as their leader, and wrote his commands on a paper which he burned, in order thus to place them at the princess's disposal. The living soldiers he recalled. When they were being reviewed in the courtyard after their return, a soldier suddenly fell unconscious. It was not until early the following morning that he came to his senses again. He was questioned and replied: "I saw a man clad in red who approached me and said: 'Our princess is grateful for the aid your master has so kindly given her. Yet she still has a request to make and has asked me to call you.' I followed him to the temple. The princess bade me come forward and said to me: 'I thank your master from my heart for sending me the ghost soldiers, but Mong Yuan, their leader is incapable. Yesterday the robbers came with three thousand men, and Mong Yuan was beaten by them. When you return and again see your master, say that I earnestly beg him to send me a good general. Perhaps that will save me in my need.' Then she had me led back again and I regained consciousness."

When Dschou Bau had heard these words, which seemed to fit strangely well with what he had dreamed, he thought he would try to see if this were really the case. Therefore he chose his victorious general Dschong Tschong-Fu to take the place of Mong Yuan. That evening he burned incense, offered wine and handed over to the princess this captain's soul.

On the twenty-sixth of the month news came from the general's camp that he had suddenly died at midnight on the thirteenth. Dschou Bau was frightened, and sent a man to bring him a report. The latter informed him that the general's heart had hardly ceased to beat, and that, in spite of the hot summer weather, his body was free from any trace of decay. So the order was given not to bury him.

Then one night an icy, spectral wind arose, which whirled up sand and stones, broke trees and tore down houses. The standing corn in the fields was blown down. The storm lasted all day. Finally, the crash of a terrific thunderbolt was heard, and then the skies cleared and the clouds scattered. That very hour the dead general began to breathe painfully on his couch, and when his attendants came to him, he had returned to life again.

They questioned him and he told them: "First I saw a man in a purple gown riding a black horse, who came up with a great retinue. He dismounted before the door. In his hand he held a decree of appointment which he gave me, saying: 'Our princess begs you most respectfully to become her general. I hope that you will not refuse.' Then he brought forth gifts and heaped them up before the steps. Jade-stones, brocades, and silken garments, saddles, horses, helmets and suits of mail—he heaped them all up in the courtyard. I wished to decline, but this he would not allow, and urged me to enter his chariot with him. We drove a hundred miles and met a train of three-hundred armored horsemen who had ridden out to escort me. They led me to a great city, and before the city a tent had been erected in which played a band of musicians. A high official welcomed me. When I entered the city the onlookers were crowded together like walls. Servants ran to and fro bearing orders. We passed through more than a dozen gates before we reached the princess. There I was requested to dismount and change my clothes in order to enter the presence of the princess, for she wished to receive me as her guest. But I thought this too great an honor and greeted her below, on the steps. She, however, invited me to seat myself near her in the hall. She sat upright in all her incomparable beauty, surrounded by female attendants adorned with the richest jewels. These plucked lute-strings and played flutes. A throng of servitors stood about in golden girdles with purple tassels, ready to carry out her commands. Countless crowds were assembled before the palace. Five or six visitors sat in a circle about the princess, and a general led me to my place. The princess said to me: 'I have begged you to come here in order to entrust the command of my army to you. If you will break the power of my foe I will reward you richly.' I promised to obey her. Then wine was brought in, and the banquet was served to the sound of music. While we were at table a messenger entered: 'The robber Tschauna has invaded our land with ten thousand footmen and horsemen, and is approaching our city by various roads. His way is marked by columns of fire and smoke!' The guests all grew pale with terror when they heard the news. And the princess said: 'This is the foe because of whom I have sought your aid. Save me in my hour of need!' Then she gave me two chargers, a suit of golden armor, and the insignia of a commander-in-chief, and bowed to me. I thanked her and went, called together the captains, had the army mustered and rode out before the city. At several decisive points I placed troops in ambush. The enemy was already approaching in great force, careless and unconcerned, intoxicated by his former victories. I sent out my most untrustworthy soldiers in advance, who allowed themselves to be beaten in order to lure him on. Light-armed men then went out against him, and retreated in skirmish order. And thus he fell into my ambush. Drums and kettledrums sounded together, the ring closed around them on all sides and the robber army suffered a grievous defeat. The dead lay about like hemp-stalks, but little Tschauna succeeded in breaking through the circle. I sent out the light horsemen after him, and they seized him before the tent of the enemy's commanding general. Hastily I sent word to the princess, and she reviewed the prisoners before the palace. All the people, high and low, streamed together, to acclaim her. Little Tschauna was about to be executed in the market place when a messenger came spurring up with a command from the princess's father to pardon him. The princess did not dare to disobey. So he was dismissed to his home after he had sworn to give up all thought of realizing his traitorous plans. I was loaded with benefits as a reward for my victory. I was invested with an estate with three thousand peasants, and was given a palace, horses and wagons, all sorts of jewels, men-servants and women-servants, gardens and forests, banners and suits of mail. And my subordinate officers, too, were duly rewarded. On the following day a banquet was held, and the princess herself filled a goblet, sent it to me by one of her attendants, and said: 'Widowed early in life, I opposed the wishes of my stern father and fled to this spot. Here the infamous Tschauna harassed me and well-nigh put me to shame. Had not your master's great kindness and your own courage come to my assistance, hard would have been my lot!' Then she began to thank me and her tears of emotion flowed like a stream. I bowed and begged her to grant me leave of absence, so that I might look after my family. I was given a month's leave and the following day she dismissed me with a splendid retinue. Before the city a pavilion had been erected in which I drank the stirrup-cup. Then I rode away and when I arrived before our own gate a thunder-peal crashed and I awoke."

Thereupon the general wrote an account of what had happened to Dschou Bau, in which he conveyed the princess's thanks. Then he paid no further heed to worldly matters, but set his house in order and turned it over to his wife and son. When a month had passed, he died without any sign of illness.

That same day one of his officers was out walking. Suddenly he saw a heavy cloud of dust rising along the highway, while flags and banners darkened the sun. A thousand knights were escorting a man who sat his horse proudly and like a hero. And when the officer looked at his face, it was the general Dschong Tschong-Fu. Hastily he stepped to the edge of the road, in order to allow the cavalcade to pass, and watched it ride by. The horsemen took the way to the Lake of the Maidens, where they disappeared.

The Disowned Princess

At the time that the Tang dynasty was reigning there lived a man named Liu I, who had failed to pass his examinations for the doctorate. So he traveled home again. He had gone six or seven miles when a bird flew up in a field, and his horse shied and ran ten miles before he could stop him. There he saw a woman who was herding sheep on a hillside. He looked at her and she was lovely to look upon, yet her face bore traces of hidden grief. Astonished, he asked her what was the matter.

The woman began to sob and said: "Fortune has forsaken me, and I am in need and ashamed. Since you are kind enough to ask I will tell you all. I am the youngest daughter of the Dragon-King of the Sea of Dungting, and was married to the second son of the Dragon-King of Ging Dschou. Yet my husband ill-treated and disowned me. I complained to my step-parents, but they loved their son blindly and did nothing. And when I grew insistent they both became angry, and I was sent out here to herd sheep." When she had done, the woman burst into tears and lost all control of herself. Then she continued: "The Sea of Dungting is far from here; yet I know that you will have to pass it on your homeward journey. I should like to give you a letter to my father, but I do not know whether you would take it."

Liu I answered: "Your words have moved my heart. Would that I had wings and could fly away with you. I will be glad to deliver the letter to your father. Yet the Sea of Dungting is long and broad, and how am I to find him?"

"On the southern shore of the Sea stands an orange-tree," answered the woman, "which people call the tree of sacrifice. When you get there you must loosen your girdle and strike the tree with it three times in succession. Then some one will appear whom you must follow. When you see my father, tell him in what need you found me, and that I long greatly for his help."

Then she fetched out a letter from her breast and gave it to Liu I. She bowed to him, looked toward the east and sighed, and, unexpectedly, the sudden tears rolled from the eyes of Liu I as well. He took the letter and thrust it in his bag.

Then he asked her: "I cannot understand why you have to herd sheep. Do the gods slaughter cattle like men?"

"These are not ordinary sheep," answered the woman; "these are rain-sheep."

"But what are rain-sheep?"

"They are the thunder-rams," replied the woman.

And when he looked more closely he noticed that these sheep walked around in proud, savage fashion, quite different from ordinary sheep.

Liu I added: "But if I deliver the letter for you, and you succeed in getting back to the Sea of Dungting in safety, then you must not use me like a stranger."

The woman answered: "How could I use you as a stranger? You shall be my dearest friend."

And with these words they parted.

In course of a month Liu I reached the Sea of Dungting, asked for the orange-tree and, sure enough, found it. He loosened his girdle, and struck the tree with it three times. At once a warrior emerged from the waves of the sea, and asked: "Whence come you, honored guest?"

Liu I said: "I have come on an important mission and want to see the King."

The warrior made a gesture in the direction of the water, and the waves turned into a solid street along which he led Liu I. The dragon-castle rose before them with its thousand gates, and magic flowers and rare grasses bloomed in luxurious profusion. The warrior bade him wait at the side of a great hall.

Liu I asked: "What is this place called?"

"It is the Hall of the Spirits," was the reply.

Liu I looked about him: all the jewels known to earth were there in abundance. The columns were of white quartz, inlaid with green jade; the seats were made of coral, the curtains of mountain crystal as clear as water, the windows of burnished glass, adorned with rich lattice-work. The beams of the ceiling, ornamented with amber, rose in wide arches. An exotic fragrance filled the hall, whose outlines were lost in darkness.

Liu I had waited for the king a long time. To all his questions the warrior replied: "Our master is pleased at this moment to talk with the priest of the sun up on the coral-tower about the sacred book of the fire. He will, no doubt, soon be through."

Liu I went on to ask: "Why is he interested in the sacred book of the fire?"

The reply was: "Our master is a dragon. The dragons are powerful through the power of water. They can cover hill and dale with a single wave. The priest is a human being. Human beings are powerful through fire. They can burn the greatest palaces by means of a torch. Fire and water fight each other, being different in their nature. For that reason our master is now talking with the priest, in order to find a way in which fire and water may complete each other."

Before they had quite finished there appeared a man in a purple robe, bearing a scepter of jade in his hand.

The warrior said: "This is my master!"

Liu I bowed before him.

The king asked: "Are you not a living human being? What has brought you here?"

Liu I gave his name and explained: "I have been to the capital and there failed to pass my examination. When I was passing by the Ging Dschou River, I saw your daughter, whom you love, herding sheep in the wilderness. The winds tousled her hair, and the rain drenched her. I could not bear to see her trouble and spoke to her. She complained that her husband had cast her out and wept bitterly. Then she gave me a letter for you. And that is why I have come to visit you, O King!"

With these words he fetched out his letter and handed it to the king. When the latter had read it, he hid his face in his sleeve and said with a sigh: "It is my own fault. I picked out a worthless husband for her. Instead of securing her happiness I have brought her to shame in a distant land. You are a stranger and yet you have been willing to help her in her distress, for which I am very grateful to you." Then he once more began to sob, and all those about him shed tears. Thereupon the monarch gave the letter to a servant who took it into the interior of the palace; and soon the sound of loud lamentations rose from the inner rooms.

The king was alarmed and turned to an official: "Go and tell them within not to weep so loudly! I am afraid that Tsian Tang may hear them."

"Who is Tsian Tang?" asked Liu I.

"He is my beloved brother," answered the king. "Formerly he was the ruler of the Tsian-Tang River, but now he has been deposed."

Liu I asked: "Why should the matter be kept from him?"

"He is so wild and uncontrollable," was the reply, "that I fear he would cause great damage. The deluge which covered the earth for nine long years in the time of the Emperor Yau was the work of his anger. Because he fell out with one of the kings of heaven, he caused a great deluge that rose and covered the tops of five high mountains. Then the king of heaven grew angry with him, and gave him to me to guard. I had to chain him to a column in my palace."

Before he had finished speaking a tremendous turmoil arose, which split the skies and made the earth tremble, so that the whole palace began to rock, and smoke and clouds rose hissing and puffing. A red dragon, a thousand feet long, with flashing eyes, blood-red tongue, scarlet scales and a fiery beard came surging up. He was dragging along through the air the column to which he had been bound, together with its chain. Thunders and lightnings roared and darted around his body; sleet and snow, rain and hail-stones whirled about him in confusion. There was a crash of thunder, and he flew up to the skies and disappeared.

Liu I fell to earth in terror. The king helped him up with his own hand and said: "Do not be afraid! That is my brother, who is hastening to Ging Dschou in his rage. We will soon have good news!"

Then he had food and drink brought in for his guest. When the goblet had thrice made the rounds, a gentle breeze began to murmur and a fine rain fell. A youth clad in a purple gown and wearing a lofty hat entered. A sword hung at his side. His appearance was manly and heroic. Behind him walked a girl radiantly beautiful, wearing a robe of misty fragrance. And when Liu I looked at her, lo, it was the dragon-princess whom he had met on his way! A throng of maidens in rosy garments received her, laughing and giggling, and led her into the interior of the palace. The king, however, presented Liu I to the youth and said: "This is Tsian Tang, my brother!"

Tsian Tang thanked him for having brought the message. Then he turned to his brother and said: "I have fought against the accursed dragons and have utterly defeated them!"

"How many did you slay?"

"Six hundred thousand."

"Were any fields damaged?"

"The fields were damaged for eight hundred miles around."

"And where is the heartless husband?"

"I ate him alive!"

Then the king was alarmed and said: "What the fickle boy did was not to be endured, it is true. But still you were a little too rough with him; in future you must not do anything of the sort again." And Tsian Tang promised not to.

That evening Liu I was feasted at the castle. Music and dancing lent charm to the banquet. A thousand warriors with banners and spears in their hands stood at attention. Trombones and trumpets resounded, and drums and kettledrums thundered and rattled as the warriors danced a war-dance. The music expressed how Tsian Tang had broken through the ranks of the enemy, and the hair of the guest who listened to it rose on his head in terror. Then, again, there was heard the music of strings, flutes and little golden bells. A thousand maidens in crimson and green silk danced around. The return of the princess was also told in tones. The music sounded like a song of sadness and plaining, and all who heard it were moved to tears. The King of the Sea of Dungting was filled with joy. He raised his goblet and drank to the health of his guest, and all sorrow departed from them. Both rulers thanked Liu I in verses, and Liu I answered them in a rimed toast. The crowd of courtiers in the palace-hall applauded. Then the King of the Sea of Dungting drew forth a blue cloud-casket in which was the horn of a rhinoceros, which divides the water. Tsian Tang brought out a platter of red amber on which lay a carbuncle. These they presented to their guest, and the other inmates of the palace also heaped up embroideries, brocades and pearls by his side. Surrounded by shimmer and light Liu I sat there, smiling, and bowed his thanks to all sides. When the banquet was ended he slept in the Palace of Frozen Radiance.

On the following day another banquet was held. Tsian Tang, who was not quite himself, sat carelessly on his seat and said: "The Princess of the Dungting Sea is handsome and delicately fashioned. She has had the misfortune to be disowned by her husband, and to-day her marriage is annulled. I should like to find another husband for her. If you were agreeable it would be to your advantage. But if you were not willing to marry her, you may go your way, and should we ever meet again we will not know each other."

Liu I was angered by the careless way in which Tsian Tang spoke to him. The blood rose to his head and he replied: "I served as a messenger, because I felt sorry for the princess, but not in order to gain an advantage for myself. To kill a husband and carry off a wife is something an honest man does not do. And since I am only an ordinary man, I prefer to die rather than do as you say."

Tsian Tang rose, apologized and said: "My words were over-hasty. I hope you will not take them ill!" And the King of the Dungting Sea also spoke kindly to him, and censured Tsian Tang because of his rude speech. So there was no more said about marriage.

On the following day Liu I took his leave, and the Queen of the Dungting Sea gave a farewell banquet in his honor.

With tears the queen said to Liu I: "My daughter owes you a great debt of gratitude, and we have not had an opportunity to make it up to you. Now you are going away and we see you go with heavy hearts!"

Then she ordered the princess to thank Liu I.

The princess stood there, blushing, bowed to him and said: "We will probably never see each other again!" Then tears choked her voice.

It is true that Liu I had resisted the stormy urging of her uncle, but when he saw the princess standing before him in all the charm of her loveliness, he felt sad at heart; yet he controlled himself and went his way. The treasures which he took with him were incalculable. The king and his brother themselves escorted him as far as the river.

When, on his return home, he sold no more than a hundredth part of what he had received, his fortune already ran into the millions, and he was wealthier than all his neighbors. He decided to take a wife, and heard of a widow who lived in the North with her daughter. Her father had become a Taoist in his later years and had vanished in the clouds without ever returning. The mother lived in poverty with the daughter; yet since the girl was beautiful beyond measure she was seeking a distinguished husband for her.

Liu I was content to take her, and the day of the wedding was set. And when he saw his bride unveiled on the evening of her wedding day, she looked just like the dragon-princess. He asked her about it, but she merely smiled and said nothing.

After a time heaven sent them a son. Then she told her husband: "To-day I will confess to you that I am truly the Princess of Dungting Sea. When you had rejected my uncle's proposal and gone away, I fell ill of longing, and was near death. My parents wanted to send for you, but they feared you might take exception to my family. And so it was that I married you disguised as a human maiden. I had not ventured to tell you until now, but since heaven has sent us a son, I hope that you will love his mother as well."

Then Liu I awoke as though from a deep sleep, and from that time on both were very fond of each other.

One day his wife said: "If you wish to stay with me eternally, then we cannot continue to dwell in the world of men. We dragons live ten thousand years, and you shall share our longevity. Come back with me to the Sea of Dungting!"

Ten years passed and no one knew where Liu I, who had disappeared, might be. Then, by accident, a relative went sailing across the Sea of Dungting. Suddenly a blue mountain rose up out of the water.

The seamen cried in alarm: "There is no mountain on this spot! It must be a water-demon!"

While they were still pointing to it and talking, the mountain drew near the ship, and a gaily-colored boat slid from its summit into the water. A man sat in the middle, and fairies stood at either side of him. The man was Liu I. He beckoned to his cousin, and the latter drew up his garments and stepped into the boat with him.

But when he had entered the boat it turned into a mountain. On the mountain stood a splendid castle, and in the castle stood Liu I, surrounded with radiance, and with the music of stringed instruments floating about him.

They greeted each other, and Liu I said to his cousin: "We have been parted no more than a moment, and your hair is already gray!"

His cousin answered: "You are a god and blessed: I have only a mortal body. Thus fate has decreed."

Then Liu I gave him fifty pills and said: "Each pill will extend your life for the space of a year. When you have lived the tale of these years, come to me and dwell no longer in the earthly world of dust, where there is nothing but toil and trouble."

Then he took him back across the sea and disappeared.

His cousin, however, retired from the world, and fifty years later, and when he had taken all the pills, he disappeared and was never seen again.

Fox-Fire

ONCE UPON A TIME THERE WAS A STRONG YOUNG FARMER WHO CAME HOME LATE ONE evening from market. His way led him past the gardens of a wealthy gentleman, in which stood a number of tall buildings. Suddenly he saw something shining floating in the air inside the gardens, something which glowed like a ball of crystal. He was astonished, and climbed the wall around the gardens, but there was not a human being in sight; all he saw was, at a distance, something which appeared to be a dog, looking up at the moon. And whenever it blew its breath out a ball of fire came out of its mouth, and rose to the moon. And whenever it drew its breath in the ball sank down again, and it caught it in its jaws. And so it went on without a stop. Then the farmer realized that it was a fox, who was preparing the elixir of life. He hid in the grass and waited until the ball of fire came down again, at about the height of his own head. Then he stepped hastily from his hiding-place, took it away and at once swallowed it. And he could feel it glow as it passed down his throat into his stomach. When the fox saw what had happened he grew angry. He looked furiously at the farmer, but feared his strength. For this reason he did not dare attack him, but went angrily on his way.

From that time on the farmer-boy could make himself invisible, was able to see ghosts and devils, and had intercourse with the spirit-world. In cases of sickness, when people lay unconscious, he could call back their souls, and if some one had committed a sin he could plead for them. He earned much money owing to these gifts.

When he reached his fiftieth year, he withdrew from all things and would no longer exercise his arts. One summer evening he was sitting in his courtyard, enjoying the cool air. While there he drank a number of goblets of wine, and by midnight had fallen fast asleep. Suddenly he awoke, feeling ill. It seemed as though some one were patting him on the back, and before he knew it, the ball of fire had leaped out from his throat. At once a hand reached for it and a voice said: "For thirty long years you kept my treasure from me, and from a poor farmer-lad you have grown to be a wealthy man. Now you have enough, and I would like to have my fire-ball back again!"

Then the man knew what had happened, but the fox was gone.

The Talking Silver Foxes

THE SILVER FOXES RESEMBLE OTHER FOXES, BUT ARE YELLOW, FIRE-RED OR WHITE in color. They know how to influence human beings, too. There is a kind of silver fox which can learn to speak like a man in a year's time. These foxes are called "Talking Foxes."

South-west of the bay of Kaiutschou there is a mountain by the edge of the sea, shaped like a tower, and hence known as Tower Mountain. On the mountain there is an old temple with the image of a goddess, who is known as the Old Mother of Tower Mountain. When children fall ill in the surrounding villages, the magicians often give orders that paper figures of them be burned at her altar, or little lime images of them be placed around it. And for this reason the altar and its surroundings are covered with hundreds of fig ures of children made in lime. Paper flowers, shoes and clothing are also brought to the Old Mother, and lie in a confusion of colors. The pilgrimage festivals take place on the third day of the third month, and the ninth day of the ninth month, and then there are theatrical performances, and the holy writings are read. And there is also an annual fair. The girls and women of the neighborhood burn incense and pray to the goddess. Parents who have no children go there and pick out one of the little children made of lime, and tie a red thread around its neck, or even secretly break off a small bit of its body, dissolve it in water and drink it. Then they pray quietly that a child may be sent them.

Behind the temple is a great cave where, in former times, some talking foxes used to live. They would even come out and seat themselves on the point of a steep rock by the wayside. When a wanderer came by they would begin to talk to him in this fashion: "Wait a bit, neighbor; first smoke a pipe!" The traveler would look around in astonishment, to see where the voice came from, and would become very much frightened. If he did not happen to be exceptionally brave, he would begin to perspire with terror, and run away. Then the fox would laugh: "Hi hi!"

Once a farmer was plowing on the side of the mountain. When he looked up he saw a man with a straw hat, wearing a mantle of woven grass and carrying a pick across his shoulder coming along the way.

"Neighbor Wang," said he, "first smoke a pipeful and take a little rest! Then I will help you plow."

Then he called out "Hu!" the way farmers do when they talk to their cattle.

The farmer looked at him more closely and saw then that he was a talking fox. He waited for a favorable opportunity, and when it came gave him a lusty blow with his ox-whip. He struck home, for the fox screamed, leaped into the air and ran away. His straw hat, his mantle of woven grass and the rest he left lying on the ground. Then the farmer saw that the straw hat was just woven out of potato-leaves; he had cut it in two with his whip. The mantle was made of oak-leaves, tied together with little blades of grass. And the pick was only the stem of a kau-ling plant, to which a bit of brick had been fastened.

Not long after, a woman in a neighboring village became possessed. A picture of the head priest of the Taoists was hung up in her room, but the evil spirit did not depart. Since there were none who could exorcise devils in the neighborhood, and the trouble she gave was unendurable, the woman's relatives decided to send to the temple of the God of War and beg for aid.

But when the fox heard of it he said: "I am not afraid of your Taoist high-priest nor of your God of War; the only person I fear is your neighbor Wang in the Eastern village, who once struck me cruelly with his whip."

This suited the people to a T. They sent to the Eastern village, and found out who Wang was. And Wang took his ox-whip and entered the house of the possessed woman.

Then he said in a deep voice: "Where are you? Where are you? I have been on your trail for a long time. And now, at last, I have caught you!"

With that he snapped his whip.

The fox hissed and spat and flew out of the window.

They had been telling stories about the talking fox of Tower Mountain for more than a hundred years when one fine day, a skillful archer came to that part of the country who saw a creature like a fox, with a fiery-red pelt, whose back was striped with gray. It was lying under a tree. The archer aimed and shot off its hind foot.

At once it said in a human voice: "I brought myself into this danger because of my love for sleep; but none may escape their fate! If you capture me you will get at the most no more than five thousand pieces of copper for my pelt. Why not let me go instead? I will reward you richly, so that all your poverty will come to an end."

But the archer would not listen to him. He killed him, skinned him and sold his pelt; and, sure enough, he received five thousand pieces of copper for it.

From that time on the fox-spirit ceased to show itself.

The Constable

In a city in the neighborhood of Kaiutschou there once lived a constable by the name of Dung. One day when he returned from a hunt after thieves the twilight had already begun to fall. So before he waded through the stream that flowed through the city he sat down on the bank, lit a pipe and took off his shoes. When he looked up, he suddenly saw a man in a red hat dressed as a constable crouching beside him.

Astonished, he inquired: "Who are you? Your clothes indicate that you are a member of our profession, but I have never yet seen you among the men of our local force. Tell me, pray, whence you come?"

The other answered: "I am weary, having come a long journey, and would like to enjoy a pipeful of tobacco in your company. I am sure you will not object to that."

Dung handed him a pipe and tobacco.

But the other constable said: "I do not need them. Just you keep on smoking. It is enough for me to enjoy the odor."

So they chatted awhile together, and together waded through the stream. And gradually they became quite confidential and the stranger said: "I will be quite frank with you. I am the head constable of the Nether World, and am subject to the Lord of the Great Mountain. You yourself are a constable of reputation here in the upper world. And, because of my skill, I have standing in the world below. Since we are so well suited to each other, I should like to enter into a bond of brotherhood with you."

Dung was agreeable and asked: "But what really brings you here?"

Said the other: "In your district there lives a certain Wang, who was formerly superintendent of the granaries, and at that time caused the death of an officer. This man has now accused him in the Nether World. The King of the Nether World cannot come to a decision in the case, and therefore has asked the Lord of the Great Mountain to settle it. The Lord of the Great Mountain has ordered that Wang's property and life be shortened. First his property is to be sequestered here in the upper world, and then his soul is to be dragged to the nether one. I have been sent out by the Judge of the Dead to fetch him. Yet the established custom is, when some one is sent for, that the constable has first to report to the god of the city. The god of the city then issues a summons, and sends one of his own spirit constables to seize the soul and deliver it over to me. Only then may I take it away with me."

Dung asked him further particulars; but the other merely said: "Later on you will see it all for yourself."

When they reached the city Dung invited his colleague to stay at his home, and entertained him with wine and food. But the other only talked and touched neither the goblet nor the chop-sticks.

Said Dung: "In my haste I could not find any better meal for you. I am afraid it is not good enough."

But his guest replied: "Oh no, I am already surfeited and satisfied! We spirits feed only on odors; in which respect we differ from men."

It was late at night before he set out to visit the temple of the city god.

No sooner did morning dawn than he reappeared to take farewell and said: "Now all is in order: I am off! In two years' time you will go to Taianfu, the city near the Great Mountain, and there we will meet again."

Dung began to feel ill at ease. A few days later, in fact, came the news that Wang had died. The district mandarin journeyed to the dead man's natal village in order to express his sympathy. Among his followers was Dung. The inn-keeper there was a tenant of Wang's.

Dung asked him: "Did anything out of the ordinary happen when Sir Wang died?"

"It was all very strange," answered the inn-keeper, "and my mother who had been very busy in his house, came home and fell into a violent fever. She was unconscious for a day and a night, and could hardly breathe. She came to on the very day when the news of Sir Wang's death was made public, and said: 'I have been to the Nether World and I met him there. He had chains about his neck and several devils were dragging him along. I asked him what he had done, but he said: "I have no time to tell you now. When you return ask my wife and she will tell you all!"' And yesterday my mother went there and asked her. And Wang's wife told her with tears: 'My master was an official, but for a long time he did not make any head-way. He was superintendent of the granaries in Nanking, and in the same city was a high officer, with whom my master became very intimate. He always came to visit at our house and he and my master would talk and drink together. One day my master said to him: "We administrative mandarins have a large salary and a good income besides. You are an officer, and have even reached the second step in rank, yet your salary is so small that you cannot possibly make it do. Have you any other income aside from it?" The officer replied: "We are such good friends that I know I can speak openly to you. We officers are compelled to find some additional sources of revenue in order that our pockets may not be altogether empty. When we pay our men we make a small percentage of gains on the exchange; and we also carry more soldiers on our rosters than there actually are present. If we had to live on our salaries we would die of hunger!"

"'When my husband heard him say this he could not rid himself of the idea that by disclosing these criminal proceedings the State would be indebted to him, and that it would surely aid his plans for advancement. On the other hand, he reflected that it would not be right to abuse his friend's confidence. With these ideas in his mind he retired to his inner rooms. In the courtyard stood a round pavilion. Lost in heavy thought, he crossed his hands behind his back, and for a long time walked round and round the pavilion. Finally he said with a sigh: "Charity begins at home; I will sacrifice my friend!" Then he drew up his report, in which the officer was indicted. An imperial order was issued, the matter was investigated, and the officer was condemned to death. My husband, however, was at once increased in rank, and from that time on advanced rapidly. And with the exception of myself no one ever knew anything of the matter.' When my mother told them of her encounter with Wang in the Nether World, the whole family burst into loud weeping. Four tents full of Buddhist and Taoist priests were sent for, who fasted and read masses for thirty-five days in order that Wang might be delivered. Whole mountains of paper money, silk and straw figures were burned, and the ceremonies have not as yet come to an end."

When Dung heard this he was very much frightened.

Two years later he received an order to journey to Taianfu in order to arrest some robbers there. He thought to himself: "My friend, the spirit, must be very powerful indeed, to have known about this trip so far in advance. I must inquire for him. Perhaps I will see him again."

When he reached Taianfu he sought out an inn.

The inn-keeper received him with the words: "Are you Master Dung, and have you come from the bay of Kaiutschou?"

"I am the man," answered Dung, alarmed, "how do you happen to know me?"

The inn-keeper replied: "The constable of the temple of the Great Mountain appeared to me last night and said: 'To-morrow a man by the name of Dung who is a good friend of mine is coming from the bay of Kaiutschou!' And then he described your appearance and your clothes to me exactly, and told me to make careful note of them, and when you came to treat you with the greatest consideration, and to take no pay from you, since he would repay me lavishly. So when I saw you coming everything was exactly as my dreams had foretold, and I knew you at once. I have already prepared a quiet room for you, and beg that you will condescend to make yourself at ease."

Joyfully Dung followed him, and the inn-keeper waited on him with the greatest consideration, and saw that he had great plenty to eat and to drink.

At midnight the spirit arrived. Without having opened the door, he stood by Dung's bedside, gave him his hand, and asked how things had gone with him since he had last seen him.

Dung answered all his questions and thanked him into the bargain for appearing to the inn-keeper in a dream.

He continued to live for some days at the inn. During the day he went walking on the Great Mountain and at night his friend came to visit him and talked with him, and at the same time asked him what had happened to Sir Wang.

"His sentence has already been spoken," answered the other. "This man pretended to be conscientious, and traitorously brought about the death of his friend. Of all sins there is no greater sin than this. As a punishment he will be sent forth again into the world as an animal." Then he added: "When you reach home you must take constant care of your health. Fate has allowed you seventy-eight years of mortal life. When your time is up I will come to fetch you myself. Then I will see that you obtain a place as constable in the Nether World, where we can always be together."

When he had said this, he disappeared.

The Dangerous Reward

ONCE UPON A TIME A MAN NAMED HU-WU-BAU, WHO LIVED NEAR THE GREAT MOUNTAIN, went walking there one day. And there, under a tree, he met a messenger in a red robe who called out to him: "The Lord of the Great Mountain would like to see you!" The man was much frightened, but dared offer no objection. The messenger bade him shut his eyes, and when he was allowed to open them again after a short time, he found himself standing before a lofty palace. He entered it to see the god. The latter had a meal prepared for him and said: "I only sent for you to-day because I had heard you intended traveling to the West. And in that case I should like to give you a letter to take to my daughter."

"But where is your daughter?" asked the man.

"She is married to the river-god," was the reply. "All you need to do is to take along the letter lying there. When you reach the middle of the Yellow River, beat against the side of the ship and call out: 'Greencoat!' Then some one will appear and take the letter from you."

And with these words he handed Hu-Wu-Bau the letter, and he was taken back again to the upper world.

When he came to the Yellow River on his journey, he did what the Lord of the Great Mountain had told him, and cried: "Greencoat!" And sure enough, a girl in green garments rose from the water, took him by the hand and told him to close his eyes. Then she led him into the palace of the river-god and he delivered the letter. The river-god entertained him splendidly, and thanked him as best he knew how. At parting he said: "I am grateful that you have made this long journey to see me. I have nothing to give you, however, save this pair of green silk shoes. While you are wearing them you can keep on walking as long as you like and never grow weary. And they will give you the second sight, so that you will be able to see the spirits and gods."

The man thanked him for the gift and returned to his ship. He continued on his journey to the West, and after a year had passed, came back again. When he reached the Great Mountain, he thought it would be fit and proper to report to the god. So he once more knocked against the tree and gave his name. In a moment the red-clad messenger appeared and led him to the Lord of the Mountain. So he reported that he had delivered the letter to the river-god, and how all things were there, and the Lord of the Mountain thanked him. During the meal which the god had prepared for him, he withdrew for a few moments to a quiet spot. Suddenly he saw his deceased father, bound and loaded with chains, who together with several hundred other criminals, was doing menial labor.

Moved to tears, he asked: "O my father, why are you here?"

His father replied: "During my life on earth I happened to tread on bread, hence I was condemned to hard labor at this spot. I have passed two years in this manner, yet their bitterness has been unspeakable. Since you are acquainted with the Lord of the Mountain, you might plead for me, and beg him to excuse me from this task and make me the field-god in our village."

His son promised to do so, and went back and pleaded with the Lord of the Mountain as he had agreed. The latter seemed inclined to listen to his prayer, yet said warningly: "The quick and the dead tread different paths. It is not well for the dead and the living to abide near one another permanently."

The man returned home. Yet, in about a year's time nearly all his children had died. In the terror of his heart he turned to the Lord of the Great Mountain. He beat on the tree; the red-coat came and led him into the palace. There he told of his misfortune and begged the god to protect him. The Lord of the Mountain smiled: "Did I not tell you in the start that the quick and the dead tread different paths, and that it is not well if they abide near each other permanently? Now you see what has happened!" Yet he sent his messenger to fetch the man's father. The father came and the god spake to him as follows: "I forgave you your offense and sent you back to your home as A field-god. It was your duty to bring happiness to your family. Instead, nearly all of your grand-children have died off. Why is this?"

And the father said: "I had been away from home so long that I was overjoyed to return. Besides I had meat and drink in overflowing measure. So I thought of my little grand-children and called them to me."

Then the Lord of the Great Mountain appointed another field-god for that village, and also gave the father another place. And from that time no further misfortune happened to the family of Hu-Wu-Bau.

Retribution

Once upon a time there was a boy named Ma, whose father taught him himself, at home. The window of the upper story looked out on the rear upon a terrace belonging to old Wang, who had a garden of chrysanthemums there. One day Ma rose early, and stood leaning against the window, watching the day dawn. And out came old Wang from his terrace and watered his chrysanthemums. When he had just finished and was going in again, along came a water-carrier, bearing two pails on his shoulders, who seemed to want to help him. But the old man grew annoyed and motioned him off. Yet the water-carrier insisted on mounting the terrace. So they pulled each other about on the terrace-edge. It had been raining, the terrace was slippery, its border high and narrow, and when the old man thrust back the water-carrier with his hand, the latter lost his balance, slipped and tumbled down the slope. Then the old man hastened down to pick him up; but the two pails had fallen on his chest and he lay there with feet outstretched. The old man was extremely frightened. Without uttering a sound, he took hold of the water-carrier's feet, and dragged him through the back door to the bank of the stream which flowed by the garden. Then he fetched the pails and set them down beside the corpse. After that he went home, locked the door and went to bed again.

Little Ma, in spite of his youth, thought it would be better to say nothing about an affair of this kind, in which a human life was involved. He shut the window and withdrew. The sun rose higher, and soon he heard a clamor without: "A dead man is lying on the river-bank!" The constable gave notice, and in the afternoon the judge came up to the beating of gongs, and the inspector of the dead knelt down and uncovered the corpse; yet the body showed no wound. So it was said: "He slipped and fell to his death!" The judge questioned the neighbors, but the neighbors all insisted that they knew nothing of the matter. Thereupon the judge had the body placed in a coffin, sealed it with his seal, and ordered that the relatives of the deceased be found. And then he went his way.

Nine years passed by, and young Ma had reached the age of twenty-one and become a baccalaureate. His father had died, and the family was poor. So it came about that in the same room in which he had formerly studied his lessons, he now gathered a few pupils about him, to instruct them.

The time for examinations drew near. Ma had risen early, in order to work. He opened the window and there, in the distant alley, he saw a man with two pails gradually drawing nearer. When he looked more closely, it was the water-carrier. Greatly frightened, he thought that he had returned to repay old Wang. Yet he passed the old man's door without entering it. Then he went a few steps further to the house of the Lis; and there went in. The Lis were wealthy people, and since they were near neighbors the Mas and they were on a visiting footing. The matter seemed very questionable to Ma, and he got up and followed the water-carrier.

At the door of Li's house he met an old servant who was just coming out and who said: "Heaven is about to send a child to our mistress! I must go buy incense to burn to the gods in order to show our gratitude!"

Ma asked: "Did not a man with two pails of water on his shoulder just go in?"

The servant said there had not, but before he had finished speaking a maid came from the house and said: "You need not go to buy incense, for I have found some. And, through the favor of heaven, the child has already come to us." Then Ma began to realize that the water-carrier had returned to be born again into the life of earth, and not to exact retribution. He wondered, though, for what merit of his the former water-carrier happened to be re-born into so wealthy a family. So he kept the matter in mind, and from time to time inquired as to the child's well-being.

Seven more years went by, and the boy gradually grew up. He did not show much taste for learning, but he loved to keep birds. Old Wang was still strong and healthy. And though he was by this time more than eighty years old, his love for his chrysanthemums had only increased with age.

One day Ma once more rose early, and stood leaning against his window. And he saw old Wang come out upon his terrace and begin to water his chrysanthemums. Little Li sat in the upper story of his house flying his pigeons. Suddenly some of the pigeons flew down on the railing of the flower-garden. The boy was afraid they might fly off and called them, but the pigeons did not move. The boy did not know what to do: he picked up stones and threw them at the birds. By mistake one of them struck old Wang. The old man started, slipped, and fell down over the terrace. Time passed and he did not rise. He lay there with his feet outstretched. The boy was very much frightened. Without uttering a sound he softly closed his window and went away. The sun gradually rose higher, and the old man's sons and grandsons all came out to look for him. They found him and said: "He slipped and fell to his death!" And they buried him as was the custom.

The Ghost Who Was Foiled

THERE ARE GHOSTS OF MANY KINDS, BUT THE GHOSTS OF THOSE WHO HAVE HUNG themselves are the worst. Such ghosts are always coaxing other living people to hang themselves from the beams of the roof. If they succeed in persuading some one to hang himself, then the road to the Nether World is open to them, and they can once more enter into the wheel of transformation. The following story of such a ghost is told by persons worthy of belief.

Once upon a time there lived a man in Tsing Tschoufu who had passed his military examination, and had been ordered to Tsinanfu to report for duty. It was at the season of rains. So it happened that evening came on before he could reach the town-inn where he had expected to pass the night. Just as the sun was setting he reached a small village and asked for a night's lodging. But there were only poor families in the village who had no room for him in their huts. So they directed him to an old temple which stood outside the village, and said he could spend the night there.

The images of the gods in the temple were all decayed, so that one could not distinguish one from the other. Thick spider-webs covered the entrance, and the dust lay inches high everywhere. So the soldier went out into the open, where he found an old flight of steps. He spread out his knapsack on a stone step, tied his horse to an old tree, took his flask from his pocket and drank—for it had been a hot day. There had been a heavy rain, but it had just cleared again. The new moon was on the decline. The soldier closed his eyes and tried to sleep.

Suddenly he heard a rustling sound in the temple, and a cool wind passed over his face and made him shudder. And he saw a woman come out of the temple, dressed in an old dirty red gown, and with a face as white as a chalk wall. She stole past quietly as though she were afraid of being seen. The soldier knew no fear. So he pretended to be asleep and did not move, but watched her with half-shut eyes. And he saw her draw a rope from her sleeve and disappear. Then he knew that she was the ghost of one who had hung herself. He got up softly and followed her, and, sure enough, she went into the village.

When she came to a certain house she slipped into the court through a crack in the door. The soldier leaped over the wall after her. It was a house with three rooms. In the rear room a lamp was burning dimly. The soldier looked through the window into the room, and there was a young woman of about twenty sitting on the bed, sighing deeply, and her kerchief was wet through with tears. Beside her lay a little child, asleep. The woman looked up toward the beam of the ceiling. One moment she would weep and the next she would stroke the child. When the soldier looked more closely, there was the ghost sitting up on the beam. She had passed the rope around her neck and was hanging herself in dumb show. And whenever she beckoned with her hand the woman looked up toward her. This went on for some time.

Finally the woman said: "You say it would be best for me to die. Very well, then, I will die; but I cannot part from my child!"

And once more she burst into tears. But the ghost merely laughed and coaxed her again.

So the woman said determinedly: "It is enough. I will die!"

With these words she opened her chest of clothes, put on new garments, and painted her face before the mirror. Then she drew up a bench and climbed up on it. She undid her girdle and knotted it to the beam. She had already stretched forth her neck and was about to leap from the bench, when the child suddenly awoke and began to cry. The woman climbed down again and soothed and quieted her child, and while she was petting it she wept, so that the tears fell from her eyes like a string of pearls. The ghost frowned and hissed, for it feared to lose its prey. In a short time the child had fallen asleep again, and the woman once more began to look aloft. Then she rose, again climbed on the bench, and was about to lay the noose about her neck when the soldier began to call out loudly and drum on the window-pane. Then he broke it and climbed into the room. The woman fell to the ground and the ghost disappeared. The soldier recalled the woman to consciousness, and then he saw something hanging down from the beam, like a cord without an end. Knowing that it belonged to the ghost of the hanged woman he took and kept it.

Then he said to the woman: "Take good care of your child! You have but one life to lose in this world!"

And with that he went out.

Then it occurred to him that his horse and his baggage were still in the temple. And he went there to get them. When he came out of the village there was the ghost, waiting for him in the road.

The ghost bowed and said: "I have been looking for a substitute for many years, and to-day, when it seemed as though I should really get one, you came along and spoiled my chances. So there is nothing more for me to do. Yet there is something which I left behind me in my hurry. You surely must have found it, and I will ask you to return it to me. If I only have this one thing, my not having found a substitute will not worry me."

Then the soldier showed her the rope and said with a laugh: "Is this the thing you mean? Why, if I were to give it back to you then some one is sure to hang themselves. And that I could not allow."

With these words he wound the rope around his arm, drove her off and said: "Now be off with you!"

But then the ghost grew angry. Her face turned greenish-black, her hair fell in wild disorder down her neck, her eyes grew bloodshot, and her tongue hung far out of her mouth. She stretched forth both hands and tried to seize the soldier, but he struck out at her with his clenched fist. By mistake he hit himself in the nose and it began to bleed. Then he sprinkled a few drops of blood in her direction and, since the ghosts cannot endure human blood, she ceased her attack, moved off a few paces and began to abuse him. This she did for some time, until the cock in the village began to crow. Then the ghost disappeared.

In the meantime the farmer-folk of the village had come to thank the soldier. It seems that after he had left the woman her husband had come home, and asked his wife what had happened. And then for the first time he had learned what had occurred. So they all set out together along the road in order to look for the soldier outside the village. When they found him he was still beating the air with his fists and talking wildly. So they called out to him and he told them what had taken place. The rope could still be seen on his bare arm; yet it had grown fast to it, and surrounded it in the shape of a red ring of flesh.

The day was just dawning, so the soldier swung himself into his saddle and rode away.

The Punishment of Greed

ONCE UPON A TIME THERE LIVED A MAN SOUTH OF THE YANGTZE-KIANG. HE HAD taken a position as a teacher in Sutschoufu, on the border of Shantung. But when he got there he found that the schoolhouse had not yet been completed. Yet a two-story building in the neighborhood had been rented, in which the teacher was to live and hold school in the meantime. This house stood outside the village, not far from the river bank. A broad plain, overgrown with tangled brush, stretched out from it on every side. The teacher was pleased with the view.

Well, one evening he was standing in the door of his house watching the sun go down. The smoke that rose from the village chimneys gradually merged with the twilight shadows. All the noises of the day had died away. Suddenly, off in the distance, along the river bank, he beheld a fiery gleam. He hurried away at once in order to see what it might be. And there, on the bank, he found a wooden coffin, from which came the radiance he had noticed. Thought the teacher to himself: "The jewels with which they adorn the dead on their journey shine by night. Perhaps there are gems in the coffin!" And greed awoke in his heart, and he forgot that a coffin is a resting-place of the dead and should be respected. He took up a large stone, broke the cover of the coffin, and bent over to look more closely. And there in the coffin lay a youth. His face was as white as paper, he wore a mourning turban on his head, his body was wrapped in hempen garments, and he wore straw sandals on his feet. The teacher was greatly frightened and turned to go away. But the corpse had already raised itself to a sitting posture. Then the teacher's fear got the better of him, and he began to run. And the corpse climbed out of its coffin and ran after him. Fortunately the house was not far away. The teacher ran as fast as he could, flew up the steps and locked the door after him. Gradually he caught his breath again. Outside there was not a sound to be heard. So he thought that perhaps the corpse had not followed him all the way. He opened the window and peered down. The corpse was leaning against the wall of the house. Suddenly it saw that the window had been opened, and with one leap it bounded up and in through it. Overcome by terror, the teacher fell down the stairs of the house, and rolled unconscious to the bottom of the flight. And when he did so the corpse fell down on the floor of the room above.

At the time the school children had all long since gone home. And the owner of the house lived in another dwelling, so that no one knew anything about what had happened. On the following morning the children came to school as usual. They found the door locked, and when they called no one answered. Then they broke down the door and found their teacher lying unconscious on the ground. They sprinkled him with ginger, but it took a long time before he woke from his coma. When they asked he told them all that had occurred. Then they all went upstairs and took away the corpse. It was taken outside the village limits and burned, and the bones which remained were once more laid in the coffin. But the teacher said, with a sigh: "Because of a moment's greed, I nearly lost my life!" He resigned his position, returned home and never, through all the days of his life, did he speak of gain again.

The Night on the Battlefield

Once upon a time there was a merchant, who was wandering toward Shantung with his wares, along the road from the South. At about the second watch of the night, a heavy storm blew up from the North. And he chanced to see an inn at one side of the road, whose lights were just being lit. He went in to get something to drink and order lodgings for the night, but the folk at the inn raised objections. Yet an old man among them took pity on his unhappy situation and said: "We have just prepared a meal for warriors who have come a long distance, and we have no wine left to serve you. But there is a little side room here which is still free, and there you may stay overnight." With these words he led him into it. But the merchant could not sleep because of his hunger and thirst. Outside he could hear the noise of men and horses. And since all these proceedings did not seem quite natural to him, he got up and looked through a crack in the door. And he saw that the whole inn was filled with soldiers, who were sitting on the ground, eating and drinking, and talking about campaigns of which he had never heard. After a time they began calling to each other: "The general is coming!" And far off in the distance could be heard the cries of his bodyguard. All the soldiers hurried out to receive him. Then the merchant saw a procession with many paper lanterns, and riding in their midst a man of martial appearance with a long beard. He dismounted, entered the inn, and took his place at the head of the board. The soldiers mounted guard at the door, awaiting his commands, and the inn-keeper served food and drink, to which the general did full justice.

When he had finished his officers entered, and he said to them: "You have now been underway for some time. Go back to your men. I shall rest a little myself. It will be time enough to beat the assembly when the order to advance is given."

The officers received his commands and withdrew. Then the general called out: "Send Asti in!" and a young officer entered from the left side of the house. The people of the inn locked the gates and withdrew for the night, while Asti conducted the long-haired general to a door at the left, through a crack of which shone the light of a lamp.

The merchant stole from his room and looked through the crack in the door. Within the room was a bed of bamboo, without covers or pillows. The lamp stood on the ground. The long-bearded general took hold of his head. It came off and he placed it on the bed. Then Asti took hold of his arms. These also came off and were carefully placed beside the head. Then the old general threw himself down on the bed crosswise, and Asti took hold of his body, which came apart below the thighs, and the two legs fell to the ground. Then the lamp went out. Overcome by terror the merchant hurried back to his room as fast as he could, holding his sleeves before his eyes, and laid down on his bed, where he tossed about sleepless all night.

At last he heard a cock crow in the distance. He was shivering. He took his sleeves from his face and saw that dawn was stealing along the sky. And when he looked about him, there he was lying in the middle of a thick clump of brush. Round about him was a wilderness, not a house, not even a grave was to be seen anywhere. In spite of being chilled, he ran about three miles till he came to the nearest inn. The inn-keeper opened the door and asked him with astonishment where he came from at that early hour. So the merchant told him his experiences and inquired as to the sort of place at which he had spent the night. The inn-keeper shook his head: "The whole neighborhood is covered with old battlefields," was his reply, "and all sorts of supernatural things take place on them after dark."

The Kingdom of the Ogres

In the land of Annam there once dwelt a man named Su, who sailed the seas as a merchant. Once his ship was suddenly driven on a distant shore by a great storm. It was a land of hills broken by ravines and green with luxuriant foliage, yet he could see something along the hills which looked like human dwellings. So he took some food with him and went ashore. No sooner had he entered the hills than he could see at either hand the entrances to caves, one close beside the other, like a row of beehives. So he stopped and looked into one of the openings. And in it sat two ogres, with teeth like spears and eyes like fiery lamps. They were just devouring a deer. The merchant was terrified by this sight and turned to flee; but the ogres had already noticed him and they caught him and dragged him into their cave. Then they talked to each other with animal sounds, and were about to tear his clothes from his body and devour him. But the merchant hurriedly took a bag of bread and dried meat out and offered it to them. They divided it, ate it up and it seemed to taste good to them. Then they once more went through the bag; but he gestured with his hand to show them that he had no more.

Then he said: "Let me go! Aboard my ship I have frying-pans and cooking-pots, vinegar and spices. With these I could prepare your food."

The ogres did not understand what he was saying, however, and were still ferocious. So he tried to make them understand in dumb show, and finally they seemed to get an idea of his meaning. So they went to the ship with him, and he brought his cooking gear to the cave, collected brush-wood, made a fire and cooked the remains of the deer. When it was done to a turn he gave them some of it to eat, and the two creatures devoured it with the greatest satisfaction. Then they left the cave and closed the opening with a great rock. In a short space of time they returned with another deer they had caught. The merchant skinned it, fetched fresh water, washed the meat and cooked several kettles full of it. Suddenly in came a whole herd of ogres, who devoured all he had cooked, and became quite animated over their eating. They all kept pointing to the kettle, which seemed too small to them. When three or four days had passed, one of the ogres dragged in an enormous cooking-pot on his back, which was thenceforth used exclusively.

Now the ogres crowded about the merchant, bringing him wolves and deer and antelopes, which he had to cook for them, and when the meat was done they would call him to eat it with them.

Thus a few weeks passed and they gradually came to have such confidence in him that they let him run about freely. And the merchant listened to the sounds which they uttered, and learned to understand them. In fact, before very long he was able to speak the language of the ogres himself. This pleased the latter greatly, and they brought him a young ogre girl and made her his wife. She gave him valuables and fruit to win his confidence, and in course of time they grew much attached to each other.

One day the ogres all rose very early, and each one of them hung a string of radiant pearls about his neck. They ordered the merchant to be sure and cook a great quantity of meat. The merchant asked his wife what it all meant.

"This will be a day of high festival," answered she, "we have invited the great king to a banquet."

But to the other ogres she said: "The merchant has no string of pearls!"

Then each of the ogres gave him five pearls and his wife added ten, so that he had fifty pearls in all. These his wife threaded and hung the pearl necklace about his neck, and there was not one of the pearls which was not worth at least several hundred ounces of silver.

Then the merchant cooked the meat, and having done so left the cave with the whole herd in order to receive the great king. They came to a broad cave, in the middle of which stood a huge block of stone, as smooth and even as a table. Round it were stone seats. The place of honor was covered with a leopard-skin, and the rest of the seats with deerskins. Several dozen ogres were sitting around the cave in rank and file.

Suddenly a tremendous storm blew up, whirling around the dust in columns, and a monster appeared who had the figure of an ogre. The ogres all crowded out of the cave in a high state of excitement to receive him. The great king ran into the cave, sat down with his legs outstretched, and glanced about him with eyes as round as an eagle's. The whole herd followed him into the cave, and stood at either hand of him, looking up to him and folding their arms across their breasts in the form of a cross in order to do him honor.

The great king nodded, looked around and asked: "Are all the folk of the Wo-Me hills present?"

The entire herd declared that they were.

Then he saw the merchant and asked: "From whence does he hail?"

His wife answered for him, and all spoke with praise of his art as a cook. A couple of ogres brought in the cooked meat and spread it out on the table. Then the great king ate of it till he could eat no more, praised it with his mouth full, and said that in the future they were always to furnish him with food of this kind.

Then he looked at the merchant and asked: "Why is your necklace so short?"

With these words he took ten pearls from his own necklace, pearls as large and round as bullets of a blunderbuss. The merchant's wife quickly took them on his behalf and hung them around his neck; and the merchant crossed his arms like the ogres and spoke his thanks. Then the great king went off again, flying away like lightning on the storm.

In the course of time heaven sent the merchant children, two boys and a girl. They all had a human form and did not resemble their mother. Gradually the children learned to speak and their father taught them the language of men. They grew up, and were soon so strong that they could run across the hills as though on level ground.

One day the merchant's wife had gone out with one of the boys and the girl and had been absent for half-a-day. The north wind was blowing briskly, and in the merchant's heart there awoke a longing for his old home. He took his son by the hand and went down to the sea-shore. There his old ship was still lying, so he climbed into it with his boy, and in a day and a night was back in Annam again.

When he reached home he loosened two of his pearls from his chain, and sold them for a great quantity of gold, so that he could keep house in handsome style. He gave his son the name of Panther, and when the boy was fourteen years of age he could lift thirty hundred weight with ease. Yet he was rough by nature and fond of fighting.

The general of Annam, astonished at his bravery, appointed him a colonel, and in putting down a revolt his services were so meritorious that he was already a general of the second rank when but eighteen.

At about this time another merchant was also driven ashore by a storm on the island of Wo-Me. When he reached land he saw a youth who asked him with astonishment: "Are you not from the Middle Kingdom?"

The merchant told him how he had come to be driven ashore on the island, and the youth led him to a little cave in a secret valley. Then he brought deer-flesh for him to eat, and talked with him. He told him that his father had also come from Annam, and it turned out that his father was an old acquaintance of the man to whom he was talking.

"We will have to wait until the wind blows from the North," said the youth, "then I will come and escort you. And I will give you a message of greeting to take to my father and brother."

"Why do you not go along yourself and hunt up your father?" asked the merchant.

"My mother does not come from the Middle Kingdom," replied the youth. "She is different in speech and appearance, so it cannot well be."

One day the wind blew strongly from the North, and the youth came and escorted the merchant to his ship, and ordered him, at parting, not to forget a single one of his words.

When the merchant returned to Annam, he went to the palace of Panther, the general, and told him all that had happened. When Panther listened to him telling about his brother, he sobbed with bitter grief. Then he secured leave of absence and sailed out to sea with two soldiers. Suddenly a typhoon arose, which lashed the waves until they spurted sky-high. The ship turned turtle, and Panther fell into the sea. He was seized by a creature and flung up on a strand where there seemed to be dwellings. The creature who had seized him looked like an ogre, so Panther addressed him in the ogre tongue. The ogre, surprised, asked him who he was, and Panther told him his whole story.

The ogre was pleased and said: "Wo-Me is my old home, but it lies about eight thousand miles away from here. This is the kingdom of the poison dragons."

Then the ogre fetched a ship and had Panther seat himself in it, while he himself pushed the ship before him through the water so that it clove the waves like an arrow. It took a whole night, but in the morning a shoreline appeared to the North, and there on the strand stood a youth on look-out. Panther recognized his brother. He stepped ashore and they clasped hands and wept. Then Panther turned around to thank the ogre, but the latter had already disappeared.

Panther now asked after his mother and sister and was told that both were well and happy, so he wanted to go to them with his brother. But the latter told him to wait, and went off alone. Not long after he came back with their mother and sister. And when they saw Panther, both wept with emotion. Panther now begged them to return with him to Annam.

But his mother replied: "I fear that if I went, people would mock me because of my figure."

"I am a high officer," replied Panther, "and people would not dare to insult you."

So they all went down to the ship together with him. A favorable wind filled their sails and they sped home swiftly as an arrow flies. On the third day they reached land. But the people whom they encountered were all seized with terror and ran away. Then Panther took off his mantle and divided it among the three so that they could dress themselves.

When they reached home and the mother saw her husband again, she at once began to scold him violently because he had said not a word to her when he went away. The members of his family, who all came to greet the wife of the master of the house, did so with fear and trembling. But Panther advised his mother to learn the language of the Middle Kingdom, dress in silks, and accustom herself to human food. This she agreed to do; yet she and her daughter had men's clothing made for them. The brother and sister gradually grew more fair of complexion, and looked like the people of the Middle Kingdom. Panther's brother was named Leopard, and his sister Ogrechild. Both possessed great bodily strength.

But Panther was not pleased to think that his brother was so uneducated, so he had him study. Leopard was highly gifted; he understood a book at first reading; yet he felt no inclination to become a man of learning. To shoot and to ride was what he best loved to do. So he rose to high rank as a professional soldier, and finally married the daughter of a distinguished official.

It was long before Ogrechild found a husband, because all suitors were afraid of their mother-in-law to be. But Ogrechild finally married one of her brother's subordinates. She could draw the strongest bow, and strike the tiniest bird at a distance of a hundred paces. Her arrow never fell to earth without having scored a hit. When her husband went out to battle she always accompanied him, and that he finally became a general was largely due to her. Leopard was already a field marshal at the age of thirty, and his mother accompanied him on his campaigns. When a dangerous enemy drew near, she buckled on armor, and took a knife in her hand to meet him in place of her son. And among the enemies who encountered her there was not a single one who did not flee from her in terror. Because of her courage the emperor bestowed upon her the title of "The Superwoman."

The Maiden Who Was Stolen Away

In the western portion of the old capital city of Lo Yang there was a ruined cloister, in which stood an enormous pagoda, several hundred stories high. Three or four people could still find room to stand on its very top.

Not far from it there lived a beautiful maiden, and one very hot summer's day she was sitting in the courtyard of her home, trying to keep cool. And as she sat there a sudden cyclone came up and carried her off. When she opened her eyes, there she was on top of the pagoda, and beside her stood a young man in the dress of a student.

He was very polite and affable, and said to her: "It seems as though heaven had meant to bring us together, and if you promise to marry me, we will be very happy." But to this the maiden would not agree. So the student said that until she changed her mind she would have to remain on the pagoda-top. Then he produced bread and wine for her to satisfy her hunger and thirst, and disappeared.

Thereafter he appeared each day and asked her whether she had changed her mind, and each day she told him she had not. When he went away he always carefully closed the openings in the pagoda-top with stones, and he had also removed some of the steps of the stairs, so that she could not climb down. And when he came to the pagoda-top he always brought her food and drink, and he also presented her with rouge and powder, dresses and mandarin-coats and all sorts of jewelry. He told her he had bought them in the market place. And he also hung up a great carbuncle-stone so that the pagoda-top was bright by night as well as by day. The maiden had all that heart could wish, and yet she was not happy.

But one day when he went away he forgot to lock the window. The maiden spied on him without his knowing it, and saw that from a youth he turned himself into an ogre, with hair as red as madder and a face as black as coal. His eyeballs bulged out of their sockets, and his mouth looked like a dish full of blood. Crooked white fangs thrust themselves from his lips, and two wings grew from his shoulders. Spreading them, he flew down to earth and at once turned into a man again.

The maiden was seized with terror and burst into tears. Looking down from her pagoda she saw a wanderer passing below. She called out, but the pagoda was so high that her voice did not carry down to him. She beckoned with her hand, but the wanderer did not look up. Then she could think of nothing else to do but to throw down the old clothes she had formerly worn. They fluttered through the air to the ground.

The wanderer picked up the clothes. Then he looked up at the pagoda, and quite up at the very top he saw a tiny figure which looked like that of a girl; yet he could not make out her features. For a long time he wondered who it might be, but in vain. Then he saw a light.

"My neighbor's daughter," said he to himself, "was carried away by a magic storm. Is it possible that she may be up there?"

So he took the clothes with him and showed them to the maiden's parents, and when they saw them they burst into tears.

But the maiden had a brother, who was stronger and braver than any one for miles around. When the tale had been told him he took a heavy ax and went to the pagoda. There he hid himself in the tall grass and waited for what would happen. When the sun was just going down, along came a youth, tramping the hill. Suddenly he turned into an ogre, spread his wings and was about to fly. But the brother flung his ax at him and struck him on the arm. He began to roar loudly, and then fled to the western hills. But when the brother saw that it was impossible to climb the pagoda, he went back and enlisted the aid of several neighbors. With them he returned the following morning and they climbed up into the pagoda. Most of the steps of the stairway were in good condition for the ogre had only destroyed those at the top. But they were able to get up with a ladder, and then the brother fetched down his sister and brought her safely home again.

And that was the end of the enchantment.

The Flying Ogre

There once lived in Sianfu an old Buddhist monk, who loved to wander in lonely places. In the course of his wanderings he once came to the Kuku-Nor, and there he saw a tree which was a thousand feet high and many cords in breadth. It was hollow inside and one could see the sky shining down into it from above.

When he had gone on a few miles, he saw in the distance a girl in a red coat, barefoot, and with unbound hair, who was running as fast as the wind. In a moment she stood before him.

"Take pity on me and save my life!" said she to him.

When the monk asked her what was the trouble, she replied: "A man is pursuing me. If you will tell him you have not seen me, I will be grateful to you all my life long!"

With that she ran up to the hollow tree and crawled into it.

When the monk had gone a little further, he met one who rode an armored steed. He wore a garment of gold, a bow was slung across his shoulders, and a sword hung at his side. His horse ran with the speed of lightning, and covered a couple of miles with every step. Whether it ran in the air or on the ground, its speed was the same.

"Have you seen the girl in the red coat?" asked the stranger. And when the monk replied that he had seen nothing, the other continued: "Bonze, you should not lie! This girl is not a human being, but a flying ogre. Of flying ogres there are thousands of varieties, who bring ruin to people everywhere. I have already slain a countless number of them, and have pretty well done away with them. But this one is the worst of all. Last night the Lord of the Heavens gave me a triple command, and that is the reason I have hurried down from the skies. There are eight thousand of us under way in all directions to catch this monster. If you do not tell the truth, monk, then you are sinning against heaven itself!"

Upon that the monk did not dare deceive him, but pointed to the hollow tree. The messenger of the skies dismounted, stepped into the tree and looked about him. Then he once more mounted his horse, which carried him up the hollow trunk and out at the end of the tree. The monk looked up and could see a small, red flame come out of the tree-top. It was followed by the messenger of the skies. Both rose up to the clouds and disappeared. After a time there fell a rain of blood. The ogre had probably been hit by an arrow or captured.

Afterward the monk told the tale to the scholar who wrote it down.

Black Arts

The wild people who dwell in the South-West are masters of many black arts. They often lure men of the Middle Kingdom to their country by promising them their daughters in marriage, but their promises are not to be trusted. Once there was the son of a poor family, who agreed to labor for three years for one of the wild men in order to become his son-in-law. At the end of that time the wedding was celebrated, and the couple were given a little house for a home. But no sooner had they entered it than the wife warned her husband to be on his guard, since her parents did not like him, and would seek to do him harm. In accordance with the custom she entered the house first with a lighted lantern, but when the bridegroom followed her she had disappeared. And thus it went, day by day. During the daytime she was there, but when evening came she disappeared. And one day, not long after they had been married, his wife said to him: "To-morrow morning my mother celebrates her birthday, and you must go to congratulate her. They will offer you tea and food. The tea you may drink, but be sure not to touch any of the food. Keep this in mind!"

So the following day the wife and husband went to her mother's home and offered their congratulations. Her parents seemed highly pleased, and served them with tea and sweets. The son-in-law drank, but ate nothing, though his wife's parents, with kind words and friendly gestures, kept urging him to help himself. At last the son-in-law did not know what to do, and thought that surely they could mean him no ill. And seeing the fresh caught eels and crabs on the plate before him, he ate a little of them. His wife gave him a reproachful glance, and he offered some excuse for taking his leave.

But his mother-in-law said: "This is my birthday. You simply must taste my birthday noodles!"

With that she placed a great dish before him, filled with noodles that looked like threads of silver, mingled with fat meat, and spiced with fragrant mushrooms. During all the time he had been living in the country the son-in-law had never yet seen such an appetizing dish. Its pleasant odor rose temptingly to his nostrils, and he could not resist raising his chop-sticks. His wife glanced over at him, but he pretended that he did not see her.

She coughed significantly, but he acted as though he did not hear. Finally she trod on his foot under the table; and then he regained control of himself.

He had not as yet eaten half of the food and said: "My hunger is satisfied."

Then he took leave, and went off with his wife.

"This is a serious matter," said the latter. "You would not listen to my words, and now you will surely have to die!"

But still he did not believe her, until he suddenly felt terrible pains, which soon grew unbearable, so that he fell to the ground unconscious. His wife at once hung him up by the feet from the beam of the roof, and put a panful of glowing charcoal under his body, and a great jar of water, into which she had poured sesame oil, in front of the fire, directly below his mouth. And when the fire had heated him thoroughly, he suddenly opened his mouth—and can you imagine what came out of it? A squirming, crawling mass of poisonous worms, centipedes, toads and tadpoles, who all fell into the jar of water. Then his wife untied him, carried him to bed, and gave him wine mingled with realgar to drink. Then he recovered.

"What you ate in the belief that they were eels and crabs," said his wife, "were nothing but toads and tadpoles, and the birthday noodles were poisonous worms and centipedes. But you must continue to be careful. My parents know that you have not died, and they will think up other evil plans."

A few days later his father-in-law said to him: "There is a large tree growing on the precipice which juts over the cave. In it is the nest of the phoenix. You are still young and able to climb, so go there quickly and fetch me the eggs!"

His son-in-law went home and told his wife.

"Take long bamboo poles," said she, "and tie them together, and fasten a curved sword at the top. And take these nine loaves of bread and these hens' eggs, there are seven times seven of them. Carry them along with you in a basket. When you come to the spot you will see a large nest up in the branches. Do not climb the tree, but chop it down with the curved sword. Then throw away your poles, and run for dear life. Should a monster appear and follow you, throw him the loaves of bread, three loaves at a time, and finally throw down the eggs on the ground and make for home as quickly as you can. In this way you may escape the danger which threatens you."

The man noted all she said exactly and went. And sure enough he saw the bird's nest—it was as large as a round pavilion. Then he tied his curved sword to the poles, chopped at the tree with all his strength, laid down his poles on the ground and never looked around but ran for dear life. Suddenly he heard the roaring of a thunder-storm rising above him. When he looked up he saw a great dragon, many fathoms long and some ten feet across. His eyes gleamed like two lamps and he was spitting fire and flame from his maw. He had stretched out two feelers and was feeling along the ground. Then the man swiftly flung the loaves into the air. The dragon caught them, and it took a little time before he had devoured them. But no sooner had the man gained a few steps than the dragon once more came flying after him. Then he flung him more loaves and when the loaves came to an end, he turned over his basket so that the eggs rolled over the ground. The dragon had not yet satisfied his hunger and opened his greedy jaws wide. When he suddenly caught sight of the eggs, he descended from the air, and since the eggs were scattered round about, it took some time before he had sucked them all. In the meantime the man succeeded in escaping to his home.

When he entered the door and saw his wife, he said to her, amid sobs: "It was all I could do to escape, and I am lucky not to be in the dragon's stomach! If this sort of thing keeps up much longer I am bound to die!"

With these words he kneeled and begged his wife pitifully to save his life.

"Where is your home?" asked his wife.

"My home is about a hundred miles away from here, in the Middle Kingdom, and my old mother is still living. The only thing that worries me is that we are so poor."

His wife said: "I will flee with you, and we will find your mother. And waste no regrets on your poverty."

With that she gathered up all the house held in the way of pearls and precious stones, put them in a bag and had her husband tie it around his waist. Then she also gave him an umbrella, and in the middle of the night they climbed the wall with the aid of a ladder, and stole away.

His wife had also said to him: "Take the umbrella on your back and run as fast as ever you can! Do not open it, and do not look around! I will follow you in secret."

So he turned North and ran with all his might and main. He had been running for a day and a night, had covered nearly a hundred miles, and passed the boundaries of the wild people's country, when his legs gave out and he grew hungry. Before him lay a mountain village. He stopped at the village gate to rest, drew some food from his pocket and began to eat. And he looked around without being able to see his wife.

Said he to himself: "Perhaps she has deceived me after all, and is not coming with me!"

After he had finished eating, he took a drink from a spring, and painfully dragged himself further. When the heat of the day was greatest a violent mountain rain suddenly began to fall. In his haste he forgot what his wife had told him and opened his umbrella. And out fell his wife upon the ground.

She reproached him: "Once more you have not listened to my advice. Now the damage has been done!"

Quickly she told him to go to the village, and there to buy a white cock, seven black tea-cups, and half a length of red nettlecloth.

"Do not be sparing of the silver pieces in your pocket!" she cried after him as he went off.

He went to the village, attended to everything, and came back. The woman tore the cloth apart, made a coat of it and put it on. No sooner had they walked a few miles before they could see a red cloud rising up in the South, like a flying bird.

"That is my mother," said the woman.

In a moment the cloud was overhead. Then the woman took the black tea-cups and threw them at it. Seven she threw and seven fell to earth again. And then they could hear the mother in the cloud weeping and scolding, and thereupon the cloud disappeared.

They went on for about four hours. Then they heard a sound like the noise of silk being torn, and could see a cloud as black as ink, which was rushing up against the wind.

"Alas, that is my father!" said the woman. "This is a matter of life and death, for he will not let us be! Because of my love for you I will now have to disobey the holiest of laws!"

With these words she quickly seized the white cock, separated its head from its body, and flung the head into the air. At once the black cloud dissolved, and her father's body, the head severed from the trunk, fell down by the edge of the road. Then the woman wept bitterly, and when she had wept her fill they buried the corpse. Thereupon they went together to her husband's home, where they found his old mother still living. They then undid the bag of pearls and jewels, bought a piece of good ground, built a fine house, and became wealthy and respected members of the community.

Historic Legends

The Sorcerer of the White Lotus Lodge

Once upon a time there was a sorcerer who belonged to the White Lotus Lodge. He knew how to deceive the multitude with his black arts, and many who wished to learn the secret of his enchantments became his pupils.

One day the sorcerer wished to go out. He placed a bowl which he covered with another bowl in the hall of his house, and ordered his pupils to watch it. But he warned them against uncovering the bowl to see what might be in it.

No sooner had he gone than the pupils uncovered the bowl and saw that it was filled with clear water. And floating on the water was a little ship made of straw, with real masts and sails. They were surprised and pushed it with their fingers till it upset. Then they quickly righted it again and once more covered the bowl. By that time the sorcerer was already standing among them. He was angry and scolded them, saying: "Why did you disobey my command?"

His pupils rose and denied that they had done so.

But the sorcerer answered: "Did not my ship turn turtle at sea, and yet you try to deceive me?"

On another evening he lit a giant candle in his room, and ordered his pupils to watch it lest it be blown out by the wind. It must have been at the second watch of the night and the sorcerer had not yet come back. The pupils grew tired and sleepy, so they went to bed and gradually fell asleep. When they woke up again the candle had gone out. So they rose quickly and re-lit it. But the sorcerer was already in the room, and again he scolded them.

"Truly we did not sleep! How could the light have gone out?"

Angrily the sorcerer replied: "You let me walk fifteen miles in the dark, and still you can talk such nonsense!"

Then his pupils were very much frightened.

In the course of time one of his pupils insulted the sorcerer. The latter made note of the insult, but said nothing. Soon after he told the pupil to feed the swine, and no sooner had he entered the sty than his master turned him into a pig. The sorcerer then at once called in a butcher, sold the pig to the man, and he went the way of all pigs who go to the butcher.

One day this pupil's father turned up to ask after his son, for he had not come back to his home for a long time. The sorcerer told him that his son had left him long ago. The father returned home and inquired everywhere for his son without success. But one of his son's fellow-pupils, who knew of the matter, informed the father. So the father complained to the district mandarin. The latter, however, feared that the sorcerer might make himself invisible. He did not dare to have him arrested, but informed his superior and begged for a thousand well-armed soldiers. These surrounded the sorcerer's home and seized him, together with his wife and child. All three were put into wooden cages to be transported to the capital.

The road wound through the mountains, and in the midst of the hills up came a giant as large as a tree, with eyes like saucers, a mouth like a plate, and teeth a foot long. The soldiers stood there trembling and did not dare to move.

Said the sorcerer: "That is a mountain spirit. My wife will be able to drive him off."

They did as he suggested, unchained the woman, and she took a spear and went to meet the giant. The latter was angered, and he swallowed her, tooth and nail. This frightened the rest all the more.

The sorcerer said: "Well, if he has done away with my wife, then it is my son's turn!"

So they let the son out of his cage. But the giant swallowed him in the same way. The rest all looked on without knowing what to do.

The sorcerer then wept with rage and said: "First he destroys my wife, and then my son. If only he might be punished for it! But I am the only one who can punish him!"

And, sure enough, they took him out of his cage, too, gave him a sword, and sent him out against the giant. The sorcerer and the giant fought with each other for a time, and at last the giant seized the sorcerer, thrust him into his maw, stretched his neck and swallowed him. Then he went his way contentedly.

And now when it was too late, the soldiers realized that the sorcerer had tricked them.

The Three Evils

Once upon a time, in the old days, there lived a young man by the name of Dschou Tschu. He was of more than ordinary strength, and no one could withstand him. He was also wild and undisciplined, and wherever he was, quarrels and brawls arose. Yet the village elders never ventured to punish him seriously. He wore a high hat on his head, adorned with two pheasants' wings. His garments were woven of embroidered silk, and at his side hung the Dragonspring sword. He was given to play and to drinking, and his hand was inclined to take that which belonged to others. Whoever offended him had reason to dread the consequences, and he always mixed into disputes in which others were engaged. Thus he kept it up for years, and was a pest throughout the neighborhood.

Then a new mandarin came to that district. When he had arrived, he first went quietly about the country and listened to the people's complaints. And they told him that there were three great evils in that district.

Then he clothed himself in coarse garments, and wept before Dschou Tschu's door. Dschou Tschu was just coming from the tavern, where he had been drinking. He was slapping his sword and singing in a loud voice.

When he reached his house he asked: "Who is weeping here so pitifully?"

And the mandarin replied: "I am weeping because of the people's distress."

Then Dschou Tschu saw him and broke out into loud laughter.

"You are mistaken, my friend," said he. "Revolt is seething round about us like boiling water in a kettle. But here, in our little corner of the land, all is quiet and peaceful. The harvest has been abundant, corn is plentiful, and all go happily about their work. When you talk to me about distress I have to think of the man who groans without being sick. And who are you, tell me that, who instead of grieving for yourself, are grieving for others? And what are you doing before my door?"

"I am the new mandarin," replied the other. "Since I left my litter I have been looking about in the neighborhood. I find the people are honest and simple in their way of life, and every one has sufficient to wear and to eat. This is all just as you state. Yet, strange to say, when the elders come together, they always sigh and complain. And if they are asked why, they answer: 'There are three great evils in our district!' I have come to ask you to do away with two of them, as to the third, perhaps I had better remain silent. And this is the reason I weep before your door."

"Well, what are these evils?" answered Dschou Tschu. "Speak freely, and tell me openly all that you know!"

"The first evil," said the mandarin, "is the evil dragon at the long bridge, who causes the water to rise so that man and beast are drowned in the river. The second evil is the tiger with the white forehead, who dwells in the hills. And the third evil, Dschou Tschu—is yourself!"

Then the blush of shame mounted to the man's cheek, and he bowed and said: "You have come here from afar to be the mandarin of this district, and yet you feel such sympathy for the people? I was born in this place and yet I have only made our elders grieve. What sort of a creature must I be? I beg that you will return home again. I will see to it that matters improve!"

Then he ran without stopping to the hills, and hunted the tiger out of his cave. The latter leaped into the air so that the whole forest was shaken as though by a storm. Then he came rushing up, roaring, and stretching out his claws savagely to seize his enemy. Dschou Tschu stepped back a pace, and the tiger lit on the ground directly in front of him. Then he thrust the tiger's neck to the ground with his left hand, and beat him without stopping with his right, until he lay dead on the earth. Dschou Tschu loaded the tiger on his back and went home.

Then he went to the long bridge. He undressed, took his sword in his hand, and thus dived into the water. No sooner had he disappeared, than there was a boiling and hissing, and the waves began to foam and billow. It sounded like the mad beating of thousands of hoofs. After a time a stream of blood shot up from the depths, and the water of the river turned red. Then Dschou Tschu, holding the dragon in his hand, rose out of the waves.

He went to the mandarin and reported, with a bow: "I have cut off the dragon's head, and have also done away with the tiger. Thus I have happily accomplished your command. And now I shall wander away so that you may be rid of the third evil as well. Lord, watch over my country, and tell the elders that they need sorrow no more!"

When he had said this he enlisted as a soldier. In combat against the robbers he gained a great reputation and once, when the latter were pressing him hard, and he saw that he could not save himself, he bowed to the East and said: "The day has come at last when I can atone for my sin with my life!" Then he offered his neck to the sword and died.

How Three Heroes Came by Their Deaths Because of Two Peaches

At the beginning of his reign Duke Ging of Tsi loved to draw heroes about him. Among those whom he attached to him were three of quite extraordinary bravery. The first was named Gung Sun Dsia, the second Tian Kai Giang, the third Gu I Dsi. All three were highly honored by the prince, but the honor paid them made them presumptuous, they kept the court in a turmoil, and overstepped the bounds of respect which lie between a prince and his servants.

At the time Yan Dsi was chancellor of Tsi. The duke consulted him as to what would be best to do. And the chancellor advised him to give a great court banquet and invite all his courtiers. On the table, the choicest dish of all, stood a platter holding four magnificent peaches.

Then, in accordance with his chancellor's advice, the Duke rose and said: "Here are some magnificent peaches, but I cannot give one to each of you. Only those most worthy may eat of them. I myself reign over the land, and am the first among the princes of the empire. I have been successful in holding my possessions and power, and that is my merit. Hence one of the peaches falls to me. Yan Dsi sits here as my chancellor. He regulates communications with foreign lands and keeps the peace among the people. He has made my kingdom powerful among the kingdoms of the earth. That is his merit, and hence the second peach falls to him. Now there are but two peaches left; yet I cannot tell which ones among you are the worthiest. You may rise yourselves and tell us of your merits. But whoever has performed no great deeds, let him hold his tongue!"

Then Gung Sun Dsia beat upon his sword, rose up and said: "I am the prince's captain general. In the South I besieged the kingdom of Lu, in the West I conquered the kingdom of Dsin, in the North I captured the army of Yan. All the princes of the East come to the Duke's court and acknowledge the overlordship of Tsi. That is my merit. I do not know whether it deserves a peach."

The Duke replied: "Great is your merit! A peach is your just due!"

Then Tian Kai Giang rose, beat on the table, and cried: "I have fought a hundred battles in the army of the prince. I have slain the enemy's general-in-chief, and captured the enemy's flag. I have extended the borders of the Duke's land till the size of his realm has been increased by a thousand miles. How is it with my merit?"

The Duke said: "Great is your merit! A peach is your just due!"

Then Gu I Dsi arose; his eyes started from their sockets, and he shouted with a loud voice: "Once, when the Duke was crossing the Yellow River, wind and waters rose. A river-dragon snapped up one of the steeds of the chariot and tore it away. The ferry-boat rocked like a sieve and was about to capsize. Then I took my sword and leaped into the stream. I fought with the dragon in the midst of the foaming waves. And by reason of my strength I managed to kill him, though my eyes stood out of my head with my exertions. Then I came to the surface with the dragon's head in one hand, and holding the rein of the rescued horse in the other, and I had saved my prince from drowning. Whenever our country was at war with neighboring states, I refused no service. I commanded the van, I fought in single combat. Never did I turn my back on the foe. Once the prince's chariot stuck fast in the swamp, and the enemy hurried up on all sides. I pulled the chariot out, and drove off the hostile mercenaries. Since I have been in the prince's service I have saved his life more than once. I grant that my merit is not to be compared with that of the prince and that of the chancellor, yet it is greater than that of my two companions. Both have received peaches, while I must do without. This means that real merit is not rewarded, and that the Duke looks on me with disfavor. And in such case how may I ever show myself at court again!"

With these words he drew his sword and killed himself.

Then Gung Sun Dsia rose, bowed twice, and said with a sigh: "Both my merit and that of Tian Kai Giang does not compare with Gu I Dsi's and yet the peaches were given us. We have been rewarded beyond our deserts, and such reward is shameful. Hence it is better to die than to live dishonored!"

He took his sword and swung it, and his own head rolled on the sand.

Tian Kai Giang looked up and uttered a groan of disgust. He blew the breath from his mouth in front of him like a rainbow, and his hair rose on end with rage. Then he took sword in hand and said: "We three have always served our prince bravely. We were like the same flesh and blood. The others are dead, and it is my duty not to survive them!"

And he thrust his sword into his throat and died.

The Duke sighed incessantly, and commanded that they be given a splendid burial. A brave hero values his honor more than his life. The chancellor knew this, and that was why he purposely arranged to incite the three heroes to kill themselves by means of the two peaches.

How the River-God's Wedding Was Broken Off

At the time of the seven empires there lived a man by the name of Si-Men Bau, who was a governor on the Yellow River. In this district the river-god was held in high honor. The sorcerers and witches who dwelt there said: "Every year the river-god looks for a bride, who must be selected from among the people. If she be not found then wind and rain will not come at the proper seasons, and there will be scanty crops and floods!" And then, when a girl came of age in some wealthy family, the sorcerers would say that she should be selected. Whereupon her parents, who wished to protect their daughter, would bribe them with large sums of money to look for some one else, till the sorcerers would give in, and order the rich folk to share the expense of buying some poor girl to be cast into the river. The remainder of the money they would keep for themselves as their profit on the transaction. But whoever would not pay, their daughter was chosen to be the bride of the river-god, and was forced to accept the wedding gifts which the sorcerers brought her. The people of the district chafed grievously under this custom.

Now when Si-Men entered into office, he heard of this evil custom. He had the sorcerers come before him and said: "See to it that you let me know when the day of the river-god's wedding comes, for I myself wish to be present to honor the god! This will please him, and in return he will shower blessings on my people." With that he dismissed them. And the sorcerers were full of praise for his piety.

So when the day arrived they gave him notice. Si-Men dressed himself in his robes of ceremony, entered his chariot and drove to the river in festival procession. The elders of the people, as well as the sorcerers and the witches were all there. And from far and near men, women and children had flocked together in order to see the show. The sorcerers placed the river-bride on a couch, adorned her with her bridal jewels, and kettledrums, snaredrums and merry airs vied with each other in joyful sound.

They were about to thrust the couch into the stream, and the girl's parents said farewell to her amid tears. But Si-Men bade them wait and said: "Do not be in such a hurry! I have appeared in person to escort the bride, hence everything must be done solemnly and in order. First some one must go to the river-god's castle, and let him know that he may come himself and fetch his bride."

And with these words he looked at a witch and said: "You may go!" The witch hesitated, but he ordered his servants to seize her and thrust her into the stream. After which about an hour went by.

"That woman did not understand her business," continued Si-Men, "or else she would have been back long ago!" And with that he looked at one of the sorcerers and added: "Do you go and do better!" The sorcerer paled with fear, but Si-Men had him seized and cast into the river. Again half-an-hour went by.

Then Si-Men pretended to be uneasy. "Both of them have made a botch of their errand," said he, "and are causing the bride to wait in vain!" Once more he looked at a sorcerer and said: "Do you go and hunt them up!" But the sorcerer flung himself on the ground and begged for mercy. And all the rest of the sorcerers and witches knelt to him in a row, and pleaded for grace. And they took an oath that they would never again seek a bride for the river-god.

Then Si-Men held his hand, and sent the girl back to her home, and the evil custom was at an end forever.

Dschang Liang

Dschang Liang was a native of one of those states which had been destroyed by the Emperor Tsin Schi Huang. And Dschang Liang determined to do a deed for his dead king's sake, and to that end gathered followers with whom to slay Tsin Schi Huang.

Once Tsin Schi Huang was making a progress through the country. When he came to the plain of Bo Lang, Dschang Liang armed his people with iron maces in order to kill him. But Tsin Schi Huang always had two traveling coaches which were exactly alike in appearance. In one of them he sat himself, while in the other was seated another person. Dschang Liang and his followers met the decoy wagon, and Dschang Liang was forced to flee from the Emperor's rage. He came to a ruined bridge. An icy wind was blowing, and the snowflakes were whirling through the air. There he met an old, old man wearing a black turban and a yellow gown. The old man let one of his shoes fall into the water, looked at Dschang Liang and said: "Fetch it out, little one!"

Dschang Liang controlled himself, fetched out the shoe and brought it to the old man. The latter stretched out his foot to allow Dschang Liang to put it on, which he did in a respectful manner. This pleased the old man and he said: "Little one, something may be made of you! Come here to-morrow morning early, and I will have something for you."

The following morning at break of dawn, Dschang Liang appeared. But the old man was already there and reproached him: "You are too late. To-day I will tell you nothing. To-morrow you must come earlier."

So it went on for three days, and Dschang Liang's patience was not exhausted. Then the old man was satisfied, brought forth the Book of Hidden Complements, and gave it to him. "You must read it," said he, "and then you will be able to rule a great emperor. When your task is completed, seek me at the foot of the Gu Tschong Mountain. There you will find a yellow stone, and I will be by that yellow stone."

Dschang Liang took the book and aided the ancestor of the Han dynasty to conquer the empire. The emperor made him a count. From that time forward Dschang Liang ate no human food and concentrated in spirit. He kept company with the four whitebeards of the Shang Mountain, and with them shared the sunset roses in the clouds. Once he met two boys who were singing and dancing:

"Green the garments you should wear,
If to heaven's gate you'd fare;
There the Golden Mother greet,
Bow before the Wood Lord's feet!"

When Dschang Liang heard this, he bowed before the youths, and said to his friends: "Those are angel children of the King Father of the East. The Golden Mother is the Queen of the West. The Lord of Wood is the King Father of the East. They are the two primal powers, the parents of all that is male and female, the root and fountain of heaven and earth, to whom all that has life is indebted for its creation and nourishment. The Lord of Wood is the master of all the male saints, the Golden Mother is the mistress of all the female saints. Whoever would gain immortality, must first greet the Golden Mother and then bow before the King Father. Then he may rise up to the three Pure Ones and stand in the presence of the Highest. The song of the angel children shows the manner in which the hidden knowledge may be acquired."

At about that time the emperor was induced to have some of his faithful servants slain. Then Dschang Liang left his service and went to the Gu Tschong Mountain. There he found the old man by the yellow stone, gained the hidden knowledge, returned home, and feigning illness loosed his soul from his body and disappeared.

Later, when the rebellion of the "Red Eyebrows" broke out, his tomb was opened. But all that was found within it was a yellow stone. Dschang Liang was wandering with Laotsze in the invisible world.

Once his grandson Dschang Dau Ling went to Kunlun Mountain, in order to visit the Queen Mother of the West. There he met Dschang Liang. Dschang Dau Ling gained power over demons and spirits, and became the first Taoist pope. And the secret of his power has been handed down in his family from generation to generation.

Old Dragonbeard

At the time of the last emperor of the Sui dynasty, the power was in the hands of the emperor's uncle, Yang Su. He was proud and extravagant. In his halls stood choruses of singers and bands of dancing girls, and serving-maids stood ready to obey his least sign. When the great lords of the empire came to visit him he remained comfortably seated on his couch while he received them.

In those days there lived a bold hero named Li Dsing. He came to see Yang Su in humble clothes in order to bring him a plan for the quieting of the empire.

He made a low bow to which Yang Su did not reply, and then he said: "The empire is about to be troubled by dissension and heroes are everywhere taking up arms. You are the highest servant of the imperial house. It should be your duty to gather the bravest around the throne. And you should not rebuff people by your haughtiness!"

When Yang Su heard him speak in this fashion he collected himself, rose from his place, and spoke to him in a friendly manner.

Li Dsing handed him a memorial, and Yang Su entered into talk with him concerning all sorts of things. A serving-maid of extraordinary beauty stood beside them. She held a red flabrum in her hand, and kept her eyes fixed on Li Dsing. The latter at length took his leave and returned to his inn.

Later in the day some one knocked at his door. He looked out, and there, before the door, stood a person turbaned and gowned in purple, and carrying a bag slung from a stick across his shoulder.

Li Dsing asked who it was and received the answer: "I am the fan-bearer of Yang Su!"

With that she entered the room, threw back her mantle and took off her turban. Li Dsing saw that she was a maiden of eighteen or nineteen.

She bowed to him, and when he had replied to her greeting she began: "I have dwelt in the house of Yang Su for a long time and have seen many famous people, but none who could equal you. I will serve you wherever you go!"

Li Dsing answered: "The minister is powerful. I am afraid that we will plunge ourselves into misfortune."

"He is a living corpse, in whom the breath of life grows scant," said the fan-bearer, "and we need not fear him."

He asked her name, and she said it was Dschang, and that she was the oldest among her brothers and sisters.

And when he looked at her, and considered her courageous behavior and her sensible words, he realized that she was a girl of heroic cast, and they agreed to marry and make their escape from the city in secret. The fan-bearer put on men's clothes, and they mounted horses and rode away. They had determined to go to Taiyuanfu.

On the following day they stopped at an inn. They had their room put in order and made a fire on the hearth to cook their meal. The fan-bearer was combing her hair. It was so long that it swept the ground, and so shining that you could see your face in it. Li Dsing had just left the room to groom the horses. Suddenly a man who had a long curling mustache like a dragon made his appearance. He came along riding on a lame mule, threw down his leather bag on the ground in front of the hearth, took a pillow, made himself comfortable on a couch, and watched the fan-bearer as she combed her hair. Li Dsing saw him and grew angry; but the fan-bearer had at once seen through the stranger. She motioned Li Dsing to control himself, quickly finished combing her hair and tied it in a knot.

Then she greeted the guest and asked his name.

He told her that he was named Dschang.

"Why, my name is also Dschang," said she, "so we must be relatives!"

Thereupon she bowed to him as her elder brother.

"How many are there of you brothers?" she then inquired.

"I am the third," he answered, "and you?"

"I am the oldest sister."

"How fortunate that I should have found a sister to-day," said the stranger, highly pleased.

Then the fan-bearer called to Li Dsing through the door and said: "Come in! I wish to present my third brother to you!"

Then Li Dsing came in and greeted him.

They sat down beside each other and the stranger asked: "What have you to eat?"

"A leg of mutton," was the answer.

"I am quite hungry," said the stranger.

So Li Dsing went to the market and brought bread and wine. The stranger drew out his dagger, cut the meat, and they all ate in company. When they had finished he fed the rest of the meat to his mule.

Then he said: "Sir Li, you seem to be a moneyless knight. How did you happen to meet my sister?"

Li Dsing told him how it had occurred.

"And where do you wish to go now?"

"To Taiyuanfu," was the answer.

Said the stranger: "You do not seem to be an ordinary fellow. Have you heard anything regarding a hero who is supposed to be in this neighborhood?"

Li Dsing answered: "Yes, indeed, I know of one, whom heaven seems destined to rule."

"And who might he be?" inquired the other.

"He is the son of Duke Li Yuan of Tang, and he is no more than twenty years of age."

"Could you present him to me some time?" asked the stranger.

And when Li Dsing has assured him he could, he continued: "The astrologers say that a special sign has been noticed in the air above Taiyuanfu. Perhaps it is caused by the very man. To-morrow you may await me at the Fenyang Bridge!"

With these words he mounted his mule and rode away, and he rode so swiftly that he seemed to be flying.

The fan-bearer said to him: "He is not a pleasant customer to deal with. I noticed that at first he had no good intentions. That is why I united him to us by bonds of relationship."

Then they set out together for Taiyuanfu, and at the appointed place, sure enough, they met Dragonbeard. Li Dsing had an old friend, a companion of the Prince of Tang.

He presented the stranger to this friend, named Liu Wendsing, saying: "This stranger is able to foretell the future from the lines of the face, and would like to see the prince."

Thereupon Liu Wendsing took him in to the prince. The prince was clothed in a simple indoor robe, but there was something impressive about him, which made him remarked among all others. When the stranger saw him, he fell into a profound silence, and his face turned gray. After he had drunk a few flagons of wine he took his leave.

"That man is a true ruler," he told Li Dsing. "I am almost certain of the fact, but to be sure my friend must also see him."

Then he arranged to meet Li Dsing on a certain day at a certain inn.

"When you see this mule before the door, together with a very lean jackass, then you may be certain I am there with my friend."

On the day set Li Dsing went there and, sure enough he saw the mule and the jackass before the door. He gathered up his robe and descended to the upper story of the inn. There sat old Dragonbeard and a Taoist priest over their wine. When the former saw Li Dsing he was much pleased, bade him sit down and offered him wine. After they had pledged each other, all three returned to Liu Wendsing. He was engaged in a game of chess with the prince. The prince rose with respect and asked them to be seated.

As soon as the Taoist priest saw his radiant and heroic countenance he was disconcerted, and greeted him with a low bow, saying: "The game is up!"

When they took their leave Dragonbeard said to Li Dsing: "Go on to Sianfu, and when the time has come, ask for me at such and such a place."

And with that he went away snorting.

Li Dsing and the fan-bearer packed up their belongings, left Taiyuanfu and traveled on toward the West. At that time Yang Su died, and great disturbance arose throughout the empire.

In the course of a few days Li Dsing and his wife reached the meeting-place appointed by Dragonbeard. They knocked at a little wooden door, and out came a servant, who led them through long passages. When they emerged magnificent buildings arose before them, in front of which stood a crowd of slave girls. Then they entered a hall in which the most valuable dowry that could be imagined had been piled up: mirrors, clothes, jewelry, all more beautiful than earth is wont to show. Handsome slave girls led them to the bath, and when they had changed their garments their friend was announced. He stepped in clad in silks and fox-pelts, and looking almost like a dragon or a tiger. He greeted his guests with pleasure and also called in his wife, who was of exceptional loveliness. A festive banquet was served, and all four sat down to it. The table was covered with the most expensive viands, so rare that they did not even know their names. Flagons and dishes and all the utensils were made of gold and jade, and ornamented with pearls and precious stones. Two companies of girl musicians alternately blew flutes and chalameaus. They sang and danced, and it seemed to the visitors that they had been transported to the palace of the Lady of the Moon. The rainbow garments fluttered, and the dancing girls were beautiful beyond all the beauty of earth.

After they had banqueted, Dragonbeard commanded his servitors to bring in couches upon which embroidered silken covers had been spread. And after they had seen everything worth seeing, he presented them with a book and a key.

Then he said: "In this book are listed the valuables and the riches which I possess. I make you a wedding-present of them. Nothing great may be undertaken without wealth, and it is my duty to endow my sister properly. My original intention had been to take the Middle Kingdom in hand and do something with it. But since a ruler has already arisen to reign over it, what is there to keep me in this country? For Prince Tang of Taiyuanfu is a real hero, and will have restored order within a few years' time. You must both of you aid him, and you will be certain to rise to high honors. You, my sister, are not alone beautiful, but you have also the right way of looking at things. None other than yourself would have been able to recognize the true worth of Li Dsing, and none other than Li Dsing would have had the good fortune to encounter you. You will share the honors which will be your husband's portion, and your name will be recorded in history. The treasures which I bestow upon you, you are to use to help the true ruler. Bear this in mind! And in ten years' time a glow will rise far away to the South-east, and it shall be a sign that I have reached my goal. Then you may pour a libation of wine in the direction of the South-east, to wish me good fortune!"

Then, one after another, he had his servitors and slave-girls greet Li Dsing and the fan-bearer, and said to them: "This is your master and your mistress!"

When he had spoken these words, he took his wife's hand, they mounted three steeds which were held ready, and rode away.

Li Dsing and his wife now established themselves in the house, and found themselves possessed of countless wealth. They followed Prince Tang, who restored order to the empire, and aided him with their money. Thus the great work was accomplished, and after peace had been restored throughout the empire, Li Dsing was made Duke of We, and the fan-bearer became a duchess.

Some ten years later the duke was informed that in the empire beyond the sea a thousand ships had landed an army of a hundred thousand armored soldiers. These had conquered the country, killed its prince, and set up their leader as its king. And order now reigned in that empire.

Then the duke knew that Dragonbeard had accomplished his aim. He told his wife, and they robed themselves in robes of ceremony and offered wine in order to wish him good fortune. And they saw a radiant crimson ray flash up on the South-eastern horizon. No doubt Dragonbeard had sent it in answer. And both of them were very happy.

How Molo Stole the Lovely Rose-Red

At the time when the Tang dynasty reigned over the Middle Kingdom, there were master swordsmen of various kinds. Those who came first were the saints of the sword. They were able to take different shapes at will, and their swords were like strokes of lightning. Before their opponents knew they had been struck their heads had already fallen. Yet these master swordsmen were men of lofty mind, and did not lightly mingle in the quarrels of the world. The second kind of master swordsmen were the sword heroes. It was their custom to slay the unjust, and to come to the aid of the oppressed. They wore a hidden dagger at their side and carried a leather bag at their belt. By magic means they were able to turn human heads into flowing water. They could fly over roofs and walk up and down walls, and they came and went and left no trace. The swordsmen of the lowest sort were the mere bought slayers. They hired themselves out to those who wished to do away with their enemies. And death was an everyday matter to them.

Old Dragonbeard must have been a master swordsman standing midway between those of the first and of the second order. Molo, however, of whom this story tells, was a sword hero.

At that time there lived a young man named Tsui, whose father was a high official and the friend of the prince. And the father once sent his son to visit his princely friend, who was ill. The son was young, handsome and gifted. He went to carry out his father's instructions. When he entered the prince's palace, there stood three beautiful slave girls, who piled rosy peaches into a golden bowl, poured sugar over them and presented them to him. After he had eaten he took his leave, and his princely host ordered one of the slave girls, Rose-Red by name, to escort him to the gate. As they went along the young man kept looking back at her. And she smiled at him and made signs with her fingers. First she would stretch out three fingers, then she would turn her hand around three times, and finally she would point to a little mirror which she wore on her breast. When they parted she whispered to him: "Do not forget me!"

When the young man reached home his thoughts were all in confusion. And he sat down absent-mindedly like a wooden rooster. Now it happened that he had an old servant named Molo, who was an extraordinary being.

"What is the trouble, master," said he. "Why are you so sad? Do you not want to tell your old slave about it?"

So the boy told him what had occurred, and also mentioned the signs the girl had made to him in secret.

Said Molo: "When she stretched out three fingers, it meant that she is quartered in the third court of the palace. When she turned round her hand three times, it meant the sum of three times five fingers, which is fifteen. When she pointed at the little mirror, she meant to say that on the fifteenth, when the moon is round as a mirror, at midnight, you are to go for her."

Then the young man was roused from his confused thoughts, and was so happy he could hardly control himself.

But soon he grew sad again and said: "The prince's palace is shut off as though by an ocean. How would it be possible to win into it?"

"Nothing easier," said Molo. "On the fifteenth we will take two pieces of dark silk and wrap ourselves up in them, and thus I will carry you there. Yet there is a wild dog on guard at the slave girl's court, who is strong as a tiger and watchful as a god. No one can pass by him, so he must be killed."

When the appointed day had come, the servant said: "There is no one else in the world who can kill this dog but myself!"

Full of joy the youth gave him meat and wine, and the old man took a chain-hammer and disappeared with it.

And after no more time had elapsed than it takes to eat a meal he was back again and said: "The dog is dead, and there is nothing further to hinder us!"

At midnight they wrapped themselves in dark silk, and the old man carried the youth over the tenfold walls which surrounded the palace. They reached the third gateway and the gate stood ajar. Then they saw the glow of a little lamp, and heard Rose-Red sigh deeply. The entire court was silent and deserted. The youth raised the curtain and stepped into the room. Long and searchingly Rose-Red looked at him, then seized his hand.

"I knew that you were intelligent, and would understand my sign language. But what magic power have you at your disposal, that you were able to get here?"

The youth told her in detail how Molo had helped him.

"And where is Molo?" she asked.

"Outside, before the curtain," was his answer.

Then she called him in and gave him wine to drink from a jade goblet and said: "I am of good family and have come here from far away. Force alone has made me a slave in this palace. I long to leave it. For though I have jasper chop-sticks with which to eat, and drink my wine from golden flagons, though silk and satin rustle around me and jewels of every kind are at my disposal, all these are but so many chains and fetters to hold me here. Dear Molo, you are endowed with magic powers. I beg you to save me in my distress! If you do, I will be glad to serve your master as a slave, and will never forget the favor you do me."

The youth looked at Molo. Molo was quite willing. First he asked permission to carry away Rose-Red's gear and jewels in sacks and bags. Three times he went away and returned until he had finished. Then he took his master and Rose-Red upon his back, and flew away with them over the steep walls. None of the watchmen of the prince's palace noticed anything out of the way. At home the youth hid Rose-Red in a distant room.

When the prince discovered that one of his slave-girls was missing, and that one of his wild dogs had been killed, he said: "That must have been some powerful sword hero!" And he gave strict orders that the matter should not be mentioned, and that investigations should be made in secret.

Two years passed, and the youth no longer thought of any danger. Hence, when the flowers began to bloom in the spring, Rose-Red went driving in a small wagon outside the city, near the river. And there one of the prince's servants saw her, and informed his master. The latter sent for the youth, who, since he could not conceal the matter, told him the whole story exactly as it had happened.

Said the prince: "The whole blame rests on Rose-Red. I do not reproach you. Yet since she is now your wife I will let the whole matter rest. But Molo will have to suffer for it!"

So he ordered a hundred armored soldiers, with bows and swords, to surround the house of the youth, and under all circumstances to take Molo captive. But Molo drew his dagger and flew up the high wall. Thence he looked about him like a hawk. The arrows flew as thick as rain, but not one hit him. And in a moment he had disappeared, no one knew where.

Yet ten years later one of his former master's servants ran across him in the South, where he was selling medicine. And he looked exactly as he had looked ten years before.

The Golden Canister

In the days of the Tang dynasty there lived a certain count in the camp at Ludschou. He had a slave who could play the lute admirably, and was also so well versed in reading and writing that the count employed her to indite his confidential letters.

Once there was a great feast held in the camp. Said the slave-girl: "The large kettledrum sounds so sad to-day; some misfortune must surely have happened to the kettledrummer!"

The count sent for the kettledrummer and questioned him.

"My wife has died," he replied, "yet I did not venture to ask for leave of absence. That is why, in spite of me, my kettledrum sounded so sad."

The count allowed him to go home.

At that time there was much strife and jealousy among the counts along the Yellow River. The emperor wished to put an end to their dissensions by allying them to each other by marriages. Thus the daughter of the Count of Ludschou had married the son of the old Count of Webo. But this did not much improve matters. The old Count of Webo had lung trouble, and when the hot season came it always grew worse, and he would say: "Yes, if I only had Ludschou! It is cooler and I might feel better there!"

So he gathered three thousand warriors around him, gave them good pay, questioned the oracle with regard to a lucky day, and set out to take Ludschou by force.

The Count of Ludschou heard of it. He worried day and night, but could see no way out of his difficulties. One night, when the water-clock had already been set up, and the gate of the camp had been locked, he walked about the courtyard, leaning on his staff. Only his slave-girl followed him.

"Lord," said she, "it is now more than a month since sleep and appetite have abandoned you! You live sad and lonely, wrapped up in your grief. Unless I am greatly deceived it is on account of Webo."

"It is a matter of life and death," answered the count, "of which you women understand nothing."

"I am no more than a slave-girl," said she, "and yet I have been able to guess the cause of your grief."

The count realized that there was meaning in her words and replied: "You are in truth an extraordinary girl. It is a fact that I am quietly reflecting on some way of escape."

The slave-girl said: "That is easily done! You need not give it a thought, master! I will go to Webo and see how things are. This is the first watch of the night. If I go now, I can be back by the fifth watch."

"Should you not succeed," said the count, "you merely bring misfortune upon me the more quickly."

"A failure is out of the question," answered the slave-girl.

Then she went to her room and prepared for her journey. She combed her raven hair, tied it in a knot on the top of her head, and fastened it with a golden pin. Then she put on a short garment embroidered with purple, and shoes woven of dark silk. In her breast she hid a dagger with dragon-lines graved on it, and upon her forehead she wrote the name of the Great God. Then she bowed before the count and disappeared.

The count poured wine for himself and waited for her, and when the morning horn was blown, the slave-girl floated down before him as light as a leaf.

"Did all go well?" asked the count.

"I have done no discredit to my mission," replied the girl.

"Did you kill any one?"

"No, I did not have to go to such lengths. Yet I took the golden canister at the head of Webo's couch along as a pledge."

The count asked what her experience had been, and she began to tell her story:

"I set out when the drums were beating their first tattoo and reached Webo three hours before midnight. When I stepped through the gate, I could see the sentries asleep in their guard-rooms. They snored so that it sounded like thunder. The camp sentinels were pacing their beats, and I went in through the left entrance into the room in which the Count of Webo slept. There lay your relative on his back behind the curtain, plunged in sweet slumber. A costly sword showed from beneath his pillow; and beside it stood an open canister of gold. In the canister were various slips. On one of them was set down his age and the day of his birth, on another the name of the Great Bear God. Grains of incense and pearls were scattered over it. The candles in the room burned dimly, and the incense in the censers was paling to ash. The slave-girls lay huddled up, round about, asleep. I could have drawn out their hair-pins and raised their robes and they would not have awakened. Your relative's life was in my hand, but I could not bring myself to kill him. So I took the golden canister and returned. The water-clock marked the third hour when I had finished my journey. Now you must have a swift horse saddled quickly, and must send a man to Webo to take back the golden canister. Then the Lord of Webo will come to his senses, and will give up his plans of conquest."

The Count of Ludschou at once ordered an officer to ride to Webo as swiftly as possible. He rode all day long and half the night and finally arrived. In Webo every one was excited because of the loss of the golden canister. They were searching the whole camp rigorously. The messenger knocked at the gate with his riding-whip, and insisted on seeing the Lord of Webo. Since he came at so unusual an hour the Lord of Webo guessed that he was bringing important information, and left his room to receive the messenger. The latter handed him a letter which said: "Last night a stranger from Webo came to us. He informed us that with his own hands he had taken a golden canister from beside your bed. I have not ventured to keep it and hence am sending it back to you by messenger." When the Lord of Webo saw the golden canister he was much frightened. He took the messenger into his own room, treated him to a splendid meal, and rewarded him generously.

On the following day he sent the messenger back again, and gave him thirty thousand bales of silk and a team of four horses along as a present for his master. He also wrote a letter to the Count of Ludschou:

"My life was in your hand. I thank you for having spared me, regret my evil intentions and will improve. From this time forward peace and friendship shall ever unite us, and I will let no thought to the contrary enter my mind. The citizen soldiery I have gathered I will use only as a protection against robbers. I have already disarmed the men and sent them back to their work in the fields."

And thenceforward the heartiest friendship existed between the two relatives North and South of the Yellow River.

One day the slave-girl came and wished to take leave of her master.

"In my former existence," said the slave-girl, "I was a man. I was a physician and helped the sick. Once upon a time I gave a little child a poison to drink by mistake instead of a healing draught, and the child died. This led the Lord of Death to punish me, and I came to earth again in the shape of a slave-girl. Yet I remembered my former life, tried to do well in my new surroundings, and even found a rare teacher who taught me the swordsman's art. Already I have served you for nineteen years. I went to Webo for you in order to repay your kindness. And I have succeeded in shaping matters so that you are living at peace with your relatives again, and thus have saved the lives of thousands of people. For a weak woman this is a real service, sufficient to absolve me of my original fault. Now I shall retire from the world and dwell among the silent hills, in order to labor for sanctity with a clean heart. Perhaps I may thus succeed in returning to my former condition of life. So I beg of you to let me depart!"

The count saw that it would not be right to detain her any longer. So he prepared a great banquet, invited a number of guests to the farewell meal, and many a famous knight sat down to the board. And all honored her with toasts and poems.

The count could no longer hide his emotion, and the slave-girl also bowed before him and wept. Then she secretly left the banquet-hall, and no human being ever discovered whither she had gone.

Yang Gui Fe

The favorite wife of the emperor Ming Huang of the Tang dynasty was the celebrated Yang Gui Fe. She so enchanted him by her beauty that he did whatever she wished him to do. But she brought her cousin to the court, a gambler and a drinker, and because of him the people began to murmur against the emperor. Finally a revolt broke out, and the emperor was obliged to flee. He fled with his entire court to the land of the four rivers.

But when they reached a certain pass his own soldiers mutinied. They shouted that Yang Gui Fe's cousin was to blame for all, and that he must die or they would go no further. The emperor did not know what to do. At last the cousin was delivered up to the soldiers and was slain. But still they were not satisfied.

"As long as Yang Gui Fe is alive she will do all in her power to punish us for the death of her cousin, so she must die as well!"

Sobbing, she fled to the emperor. He wept bitterly and endeavored to protect her; but the soldiers grew more and more violent. Finally she was hung from a pear-tree by a eunuch.

The emperor longed so greatly for Yang Gui Fe that he ceased to eat, and could no longer sleep. Then one of his eunuchs told him of a man named Yang Shi Wu, who was able to call up the spirits of the departed. The emperor sent for him and Yang Shi Wu appeared.

That very evening he recited his magic incantations, and his soul left its body to go in search of Yang Gui Fe. First he went to the Nether World, where the shades of the departed dwell. Yet no matter how much he looked and asked he could find no trace of her. Then he ascended to the highest heaven, where sun, moon and stars make their rounds, and looked for her in empty space. Yet she was not to be found there, either. So he came back and told the emperor of his experience. The emperor was dissatisfied and said: "Yang Gui Fe's beauty was divine. How can it be possible that she had no soul!"

The magician answered: "Between hill and valley and amid the silent ravines dwell the blessed. I will go back once more and search for her there."

So he wandered about on the five holy hills, by the four great rivers and through the islands of the sea. He went everywhere, and finally came to fairyland.

The fairy said: "Yang Gui Fe has become a blessed spirit and dwells in the great south palace!"

So the magician went there and knocked on the door. A maiden came out and asked what he wanted, and he told her that the emperor had sent him to look for her mistress. She let him in. The way led through broad gardens filled with flowers of jade and trees of coral, giving forth the sweetest of odors. Finally they reached a high tower, and the maiden raised the curtain hanging before a door. The magician kneeled and looked up. And there he saw Yang Gui Fe sitting on a throne, adorned with an emerald headdress and furs of yellow swans' down. Her face glowed with rosy color, yet her forehead was wrinkled with care.

She said: "Well do I know the emperor longs for me! But for me there is no path leading back to the world of men! Before my birth I was a blessed sky-fairy, and the emperor was a blessed spirit as well. Even then we loved each other dearly. Then, when the emperor was sent down to earth by the Lord of the Heavens, I, too, descended to earth and found him there among men. In twelve years' time we will meet again. Once, on the evening of the seventh day, when we stood looking up at the Weaving Maiden and the Herd Boy, we swore eternal love. The emperor had a ring, which he broke in two. One half he gave to me, the other he kept himself. Take this half of mine, bring it to the emperor, and tell him not to forget the words we said to each other in secret that evening. And tell him not to grieve too greatly because of me!"

With that she gave him the ring, with difficulty suppressing her sobs. The magician brought back the ring with him. At sight of it the emperor's grief broke out anew.

He said: "What we said to each other that evening no one else has ever learned! And now you bring me back her ring! By that sign I know that your words are true and that my beloved has really become a blessed spirit."

Then he kept the ring and rewarded the magician lavishly.

The Monk of the Yangtze-kiang

Buddhism took its rise in southern India, on the island of Ceylon. It was there that the son of a Brahminic king lived, who had left his home in his youth, and had renounced all wishes and all sensation. With the greatest renunciation of self he did penance so that all living creatures might be saved. In the course of time he gained the hidden knowledge and was called Buddha.

In the days of the Emperor Ming Di, of the dynasty of the Eastern Hans, a golden glow was seen in the West, a glow which flashed and shone without interruption.

One night the emperor dreamed that he saw a golden saint, twenty feet in height, barefoot, his head shaven, and clothed in Indian garb enter his room, who said to him: "I am the saint from the West! My gospel must be spread in the East!"

When the ruler awoke he wondered about this dream, and sent out messengers to the lands of the West in order to find out what it meant.

Thus it was that the gospel of Buddha came to China, and continued to gain in influence up to the time of the Tang dynasty. At that time, from emperors and kings down to the peasants in the villages, the wise and the ignorant alike were filled with reverence for Buddha. But under the last two dynasties his gospel came to be more and more neglected. In these days the Buddhist monks run to the houses of the rich, read their sutras and pray for pay. And one hears nothing of the great saints of the days gone by.

At the time of the Emperor Tai Dsung, of the Tang dynasty, it once happened that a great drought reigned in the land, so that the emperor and all his officials erected altars everywhere in order to plead for rain.

Then the Dragon-King of the Eastern Sea talked with the Dragon of the Milky Way and said: "To-day they are praying for rain on earth below. The Lord of the Heavens has granted the prayer of the King of Tang. To-morrow you must let three inches of rain fall!"

"No, I must let only two inches of rain fall," said the old dragon.

So the two dragons made a wager, and the one who lost promised as a punishment to turn into a mud salamander.

The following day the Highest Lord suddenly issued an order saying that the Dragon of the Milky Way was to instruct the wind and cloud spirits to send down three inches of rain upon the earth. To contradict this command was out of the question.

But the old dragon thought to himself: "It seems that the Dragon-King had a better idea of what was going to happen than I had, yet it is altogether too humiliating to have to turn into a mud salamander!" So he let only two inches of rain fall, and reported back to the heavenly court that the command had been carried out.

Yet the Emperor Tai Dsung then offered a prayer of thanks to heaven. In it he said: "The precious fluid was bestowed upon us to the extent of two inches of depth. We beg submissively that more may be sent down, so that the parched crops may recover!"

When the Lord of the Heavens read this prayer he was very angry and said: "The criminal Dragon of the Milky Way has dared diminish the rain which I had ordered. He cannot be suffered to continue his guilty life. So We Dschong, who is a general among men on earth, shall behead him, as an example for all living beings."

In the evening the Emperor Tai Dsung had a dream. He saw a giant enter his room, who pleaded with hardly restrained tears: "Save me, O Emperor! Because of my own accord I diminished the rainfall, the Lord of the Heavens, in his anger, has commanded that We Dschong behead me to-morrow at noon. If you will only prevent We Dschong from falling asleep at that time, and pray that I may be saved, misfortune once more may pass me by!"

The emperor promised, and the other bowed and left him.

The following day the emperor sent for We Dschong. They drank tea together and played chess.

Toward noon We Dschong suddenly grew tired and sleepy; but he did not dare take his leave. The emperor, however, since one of his pawns had been taken, fixed his gaze for a moment on the chess-board and pondered, and before he knew it We Dschong was already snoring with a noise like a distant thunder. The emperor was much frightened, and hastily called out to him; but he did not awake. Then he had two eunuchs shake him, but a long time passed before he could be aroused.

"How did you come to fall asleep so suddenly?" asked the emperor.

"I dreamed," replied We Dschong, "that the Highest God had commanded me to behead the old dragon. I have just hewn off his head, and my arm still aches from the exertion."

And before he had even finished speaking a dragon's head, as large as a bushel-measure, suddenly fell down out of the air. The emperor was terribly frightened and rose.

"I have sinned against the old dragon," said he. Then he retired to the inner chambers of his palace and was confused in mind. He remained lying on his couch, closed his eyes, said not a word, and breathed but faintly.

Suddenly he saw two persons in purple robes who had a summons in their hands. They spoke to him as follows: "The old Dragon of the Milky Way has complained against the emperor in the Nether World. We beg that you will have the chariot harnessed!"

Instinctively the emperor followed them, and in the courtyard there stood his chariot before the castle, ready and waiting. The emperor entered it, and off they went flying through the air. In a moment they had reached the city of the dead. When he entered he saw the Lord of the High Mountain sitting in the midst of the city, with the ten princes of the Nether World in rows at his right and left. They all rose, bowed to him and bade him be seated.

Then the Lord of the High Mountain said: "The old Dragon of the Milky Way has really committed a deed which deserved punishment. Yet Your Majesty has promised to beg the Highest God to spare him, which prayer would probably have saved the old dragon's life. And that this matter was neglected over the chess-board might well be accounted a mistake. Now the old dragon complains to me without ceasing. When I think of how he has striven to gain sainthood for more than a thousand years, and must now fall back into the cycle of transformations, I am really depressed. It is for this reason I have called together the princes of the ten pits of the Nether World, to find a way out of the difficulty, and have invited Your Majesty to come here to discuss the matter. In heaven, on earth and in the Nether World only the gospel of Buddha has no limits. Hence, when you return to earth great sacrifices should be made to the three and thirty lords of the heavens. Three thousand six hundred holy priests of Buddha must read the sutras in order to deliver the old dragon so that he may rise again to the skies, and keep his original form. But the writings and readings of men will not be enough to ensure this. It will be necessary to go to the Western Heavens and thence bring words of truth."

This the emperor agreed to, and the Lord of the Great Mountain and the ten princes of the Nether World rose and said as they bowed to him: "We beg that you will now return!"

Suddenly Tai Dsung opened his eyes again, and there he was lying on his imperial couch. Then he made public the fact that he was at fault, and had the holiest among the priests of Buddha sent for to fetch the sutras from the Western Heavens. And it was Huan Dschuang, the Monk of the Yangtze-kiang, who in obedience to this order, appeared at court.

The name of this Huan Dschuang had originally been Tschen. His father had passed the highest examinations during the reign of the preceding emperor, and had been intrusted with the office of district mandarin on the Yangtze-kiang. He set out with his wife for this new district, but when their ship reached the Yellow River it fell in with a band of robbers. Their captain slew the whole retinue, threw father Tschen into the river, took his wife and the document appointing him mandarin, went to the district capital under an assumed name and took charge of it. All the serving-men whom he took along were members of his robber-band. Tschen's wife, however, together with her little boy, he imprisoned in a tower room. And all the servants who attended her were in the confidence of the robbers.

Now below the tower was a little pond, and in this pond rose a spring which flowed beneath the walls to the Yellow River. So one day Tschen's wife took a little basket of bamboo, pasted up the cracks and laid her little boy in the basket. Then she cut her finger, wrote down the day and hour of the boy's birth on a strip of silk paper with the blood, and added that the boy must come and rescue her when he had reached the age of twelve. She placed the strip of silk paper beside the boy in the basket, and at night, when no one was about, she put the basket in the pond. The current carried it away to the Yangtze-kiang, and once there it drifted on as far as the monastery on the Golden Hill, which is an island lying in the middle of the river. There a priest who had come to draw water found it. He fished it out and took it to the monastery.

When the abbot saw what had been written in blood, he ordered his priests and novices to say nothing about it to any one. And he brought up the boy in the monastery.

When the latter had reached the age of five, he was taught to read the holy books. The boy was more intelligent than any of his fellow-students, soon grasped the meaning of the sacred writings, and entered more and more deeply into their secrets. So he was allowed to take the vows, and when his head had been shaven was named: "The Monk of the Yangtze-kiang."

By the time he was twelve he was as large and strong as a grown man. The abbot, who knew of the duty he still had to perform, had him called to a quiet room. There he drew forth the letter written in blood and gave it to him.

When the monk had read it he flung himself down on the ground and wept bitterly. Thereupon he thanked the abbot for all that the latter had done for him. He set out for the city in which his mother dwelt, ran around the yamen of the mandarin, beat upon the wooden fish and cried: "Deliverance from all suffering! Deliverance from all suffering!"

After the robber who had slain his father had slipped into the post he held by false pretences, he had taken care to strengthen his position by making powerful friends. He even allowed Tschen's wife, who had now been a prisoner for some ten years, a little more liberty.

On that day official business had kept him abroad. The woman was sitting at home, and when she heard the wooden fish beaten so insistently before the door and heard the words of deliverance, the voice of her heart cried out in her. She sent out the serving-maid to call in the priest. He came in by the back door, and when she saw that he resembled his father in every feature, she could no longer restrain herself, but burst into tears. Then the monk of the Yangtze-kiang realized that this was his mother and he took the bloody writing out and gave it to her.

She stroked it and said amid sobs: "My father is a high official, who has retired from affairs and dwells in the capital. But I have been unable to write to him, because this robber guarded me so closely. So I kept alive as well as I could, waiting for you to come. Now hurry to the capital for the sake of your father's memory, and if his honor is made clear then I can die in peace. But you must hasten so that no one finds out about it."

The monk then went off quickly. First he went back to his cloister to bid farewell to his abbot; and then he set out for Sianfu, the capital.

Yet by that time his grandfather had already died. But one of his uncles, who was known at court, was still living. He took soldiers and soon made an end of the robbers. But the monk's mother had died in the meantime.

From that time on, the Monk of the Yangtze-kiang lived in a pagoda in Sianfu, and was known as Huan Dschuang. When the emperor issued the order calling the priests of Buddha to court, he was some twenty years of age. He came into the emperor's presence, and the latter honored him as a great teacher. Then he set out for India.

He was absent for seventeen years. When he returned he brought three collections of books with him, and each collection comprised five-hundred and forty rolls of manuscript. With these he once more entered the presence of the emperor. The emperor was overjoyed, and with his own hand wrote a preface of the holy teachings, in which he recorded all that had happened. Then the great sacrifice was held to deliver the old Dragon of the Milky Way.

LITERARY FAIRY TALES

The Heartless Husband

IN OLDEN TIMES HANCHOW WAS THE CAPITAL OF SOUTHERN CHINA, AND FOR THAT reason a great number of beggars had gathered there. These beggars were in the habit of electing a leader, who was officially entrusted with the supervision of all begging in the town. It was his duty to see that the beggars did not molest the townsfolk, and he received a tenth of their income from all his beggar subjects. When it snowed or rained, and the beggars could not go out to beg, he had to see to it that they had something to eat, and he also had to conduct their weddings and funerals. And the beggars obeyed him in all things.

Well, it happened that there was a beggar king of this sort in Hanchow by the name of Gin, in whose family the office had been handed down from father to son for seven generations. What they had taken in by way of beggars' pence they had lent out on interest, and so the family had gradually become well-to-do, and finally even rich.

The old beggar-king had lost his wife at the age of fifty. But he had an only child, a girl who was called "Little Golden Daughter." She had a face of rare beauty and was the jewel of his love. She had been versed in the lore of books from her youth up, and could write, improvise poems and compose essays. She was also experienced in needlework, a skilled dancer and singer, and could play the flute and zither. The old beggar-king above all else wanted her to have a scholar for a husband. Yet because he was a beggar-king the distinguished families avoided him, and with those who were of less standing than himself he did not wish to have anything to do. So it came about that Little Golden Daughter had reached the age of eighteen without being betrothed.

Now at that time there dwelt in Hanchow, near the Bridge of Peace, a scholar by the name of Mosu. He was twenty years of age, and universally popular because of his beauty and talent. His parents were both dead, and he was so poor that he could hardly manage to keep alive. His house and lot had long since been mortgaged or sold, and he lived in an abandoned temple, and many a day passed at whose end he went hungry to bed.

A neighbor took pity on him and said to him one day: "The beggar-king has a child named Little Golden Daughter, who is beautiful beyond all telling. And the beggar-king is rich and has money, but no son to inherit it. If you wish to marry into his family his whole fortune would in the end come to you. Is that not better than dying of hunger as a poor scholar?"

At that time Mosu was in dire extremity. Hence, when he heard these words he was greatly pleased. He begged the neighbor to act as a go-between in the matter.

So the latter visited the old beggar-king and talked with him, and the beggar-king talked over the matter with Little Golden Daughter, and since Mosu came from a good family and was, in addition, talented and learned, and had no objection to marrying into their family, they were both much pleased with the prospect. So they agreed to the proposal, and the two were married.

So Mosu became a member of the beggar-king's family. He was happy in his wife's beauty, always had enough to eat and good clothes to wear. So he thought himself lucky beyond his deserts, and lived with his wife in peace and happiness.

The beggar-king and his daughter, to whom their low estate was a thorn in the flesh, admonished Mosu to be sure to study hard. They hoped that he would make a name for himself and thus reflect glory on their family as well. They bought books for him, old and new, at the highest prices, and they always supplied him liberally with money so that he could move in aristocratic circles. They also paid his examination expenses. So his learning increased day by day, and the fame of it spread through the entire district. He passed one examination after another in rapid succession, and at the age of twenty-three was appointed mandarin of the district of Wu We. He returned from his audience with the emperor in ceremonial robes, high on horseback.

Mosu had been born in Hanchow, so the whole town soon knew that he had passed his examination successfully, and the townsfolk crowded together on both sides of the street to look at him as he rode to his father-in-law's house. Old and young, women and children gathered to enjoy the show, and some idle loafer called out in a loud voice:

"The old beggar's son-in-law has become a mandarin!"

Mosu blushed with shame when he heard these words. Speechless and out of sorts he seated himself in his room. But the old beggar-king in the joy of his heart did not notice his ill humor. He had a great festival banquet prepared, to which he invited all his neighbors and good friends. But most of the invited guests were beggars and poor folk, and he insisted that Mosu eat with them. With much difficulty Mosu was induced to leave his room. Yet when he saw the guests gathered around the table, as ragged and dirty as a horde of hungry devils, he retired again with disdain. Little Golden Daughter, who realized how he felt, tried to cheer him up again in a hundred and one ways, but all in vain.

A few days later Mosu, with his wife and servants, set out for the new district he was to govern. One goes from Hanchow to Wu We by water. So they entered a ship and sailed out to the Yangtze-kiang. At the end of the first day they reached a city where they anchored. The night was clear and the moon-rays glittered on the water, and Mosu sat in the front part of the ship enjoying the moonlight. Suddenly he chanced to think of the old beggar-king. It was true that his wife was wise and good, but should heaven happen to bless them with children, these children would always be the beggar's nephews and nieces, and there was no way of preventing such a disgrace. And thus thinking a plan occurred to him. He called Little Golden Daughter out of the cabin to come and enjoy the moonlight, and she came out to him happily. Men servants and maid servants and all the sailors had long since gone to sleep. He looked about him on all sides, but there was no one to be seen. Little Golden Daughter was standing at the front of the ship, thinking no evil, when a hand suddenly thrust her into the water. Then Mosu pretended to be frightened, and began to call out: "My wife made a misstep and has fallen into the water!"

And when they heard his words, the servants hurried up and wanted to fish her out.

But Mosu said: "She has already been carried away by the current, so you need not trouble yourselves!" Then he gave orders to set sail again as soon as possible.

Now who would have thought that owing to a fortunate chance, Sir Hu, the mandarin in charge of the transportation system of the province, was also about to take charge of his department, and had anchored in the same place. He was sitting with his wife at the open window of the ship's cabin, enjoying the moonlight and the cool breeze.

Suddenly he heard some one crying on the shore, and it sounded to him like a girl's voice. He quickly sent people to assist her, and they brought her aboard. It was Little Golden Daughter.

When she had fallen into the water, she had felt something beneath her feet which held her up so that she did not sink. And she had been carried along by the current to the river-bank, where she crept out of the water. And then she realized that her husband, now that he had become distinguished, had forgotten how poor he had been, and for all she had not been drowned, she felt very lonely and abandoned, and before she knew it her tears began to flow. So when Sir Hu asked her what was the matter, she told him the whole story. Sir Hu comforted her.

"You must not shed another tear," said he. "If you care to become my adopted daughter, we will take care of you."

Little Golden Daughter bowed her thanks. But Hu's wife ordered her maids to bring other clothes to take the place of the wet ones, and to prepare a bed for her. The servants were strictly bidden to call her "Miss," and to say nothing of what had occurred.

So the journey continued and in a few days' time Sir Hu entered upon his official duties. Wu We, where Mosu was district mandarin, was subject to his rule, and the latter made his appearance in order to visit his official superior. When Sir Hu saw Mosu he thought to himself: "What a pity that so highly gifted a man should act in so heartless a manner!"

When a few months had passed, Sir Hu said to his subordinates: "I have a daughter who is very pretty and good, and would like to find a son-in-law to marry into my family. Do you know of any one who might answer?"

His subordinates all knew that Mosu was young and had lost his wife. So they unanimously suggested him.

Sir Hu replied: "I have also thought of that gentleman, but he is young and has risen very rapidly. I am afraid he has loftier ambitions, and would not care to marry into my family and become my son-in-law."

"He was originally poor," answered his people, "and he is your subordinate. Should you care to show him a kindness of this sort, he will be sure to accept it joyfully, and will not object to marrying into your family."

"Well, if you all believe it can be done," said Sir Hu, "then pay him a visit and find out what he thinks about it. But you must not say that I have sent you."

Mosu, who was just then reflecting how he might win Sir Hu's favor, took up the suggestion with pleasure, and urgently begged them to act as his go-between in the matter, promising them a rich reward when the connection was established.

So they went back again and reported to Sir Hu.

He said: "I am much pleased that the gentleman in question does not disdain this marriage. But my wife and I are extremely fond of this daughter of ours, and we can hardly resign ourselves to giving her up. Sir Mosu is young and aristocratic, and our little daughter has been spoiled. If he were to ill-treat her, or at some future time were to regret having married into our family, my wife and I would be inconsolable. For this reason everything must be clearly understood in advance. Only if he positively agrees to do these things would I be able to receive him into my family."

Mosu was informed of all these conditions, and declared himself ready to accept them. Then he brought gold and pearls and colored silks to Sir Hu's daughter as wedding gifts, and a lucky day was chosen for the wedding. Sir Hu charged his wife to talk to Little Golden Daughter.

"Your adopted father," said she, "feels sorry for you, because you are lonely, and therefore has picked out a young scholar for you to marry."

But Little Golden Daughter replied: "It is true that I am of humble birth, yet I know what is fitting. It chances that I agreed to cast my lot with Mosu for better or for worse. And though he has shown me but little kindness, I will marry no other man so long as he lives. I cannot bring myself to form another union and break my troth."

And thus speaking the tears poured from her eyes. When Sir Hu's wife saw that nothing would alter her resolve, she told her how matters really stood.

"Your adopted father," said she, "is indignant at Mosu's heartlessness. And although he will see to it that you meet again, he has said nothing to Mosu which would lead him to believe that you are not our own daughter. Therefore Mosu was delighted to marry you. But when the wedding is celebrated this evening, you must do thus and so, in order that he may taste your just anger."

When she had heard all this, Little Golden Daughter dried her tears, and thanked her adopted parents. Then she adorned herself for the wedding.

The same day, late at evening, Mosu came to the house wearing golden flowers on his hat, and a red scarf across his breast, riding on a gaily trapped horse, and followed by a great retinue. All his friends and acquaintances came with him in order to be present at the festival celebration.

In Sir Hu's house everything had been adorned with colored cloths and lanterns. Mosu dismounted from his horse at the entrance of the hall. Here Sir Hu had spread a festival banquet to which Mosu and his friends were led. And when the goblet had made the rounds three times, serving-maids came and invited Mosu to follow them to the inner rooms. The bride, veiled in a red veil, was led in by two maid-servants. Following the injunctions of the master of the ceremony, they worshiped heaven and earth together, and then the parents-in-law. Thereupon they went into another apartment. Here brightly colored candles were burning, and a wedding dinner had been prepared. Mosu felt as happy as though he had been raised to the seventh heaven.

But when he wanted to leave the room, seven or eight maids with bamboo canes in their hands appeared at each side of the door, and began to beat him without mercy. They knocked his bridal hat from his head, and then the blows rained down upon his back and shoulders. When Mosu cried for help he heard a delicate voice say: "You need not kill that heartless bridegroom of mine completely! Ask him to come in and greet me!"

Then the maids stopped beating him, and gathered about the bride, who removed her bridal veil.

Mosu bowed with lowered head and said: "But what have I done?"

Yet when he raised his eyes he saw that none other than his wife, Little Golden Daughter, was standing before him.

He started with fright and cried: "A ghost, a ghost!" But all the servants broke out into loud laughter.

At last Sir Hu and his wife came in, and the former said: "My dear son-in-law, you may rest assured that my adopted daughter, who came to me while I was on my way to this place, is no ghost."

Then Mosu hastily fell on his knees and answered: "I have sinned and beg for mercy!" And he kowtowed without end.

"With that I have nothing to do," remarked Sir Hu, "if our little daughter only gets along well with you, then all will be in order."

But Little Golden Daughter said: "You heartless scoundrel! In the beginning you were poor and needy. We took you into our family, and let you study so that you might become somebody, and make a name for yourself. But no sooner had you become a mandarin and a man of standing, than your love turned into enmity, and you forgot your duty as a husband and pushed me into the river. Fortunately, I found my dear adopted parents thereby. They fished me out, and made me their own child, otherwise I would have found a grave in the bellies of the fishes. How can I honorably live again with such a man as you?"

With these words she began to lament loudly, and she called him one hard-hearted scoundrel after another.

Mosu lay before her, speechless with shame, and begged her to forgive him.

Now when Sir Hu noticed that Little Golden Daughter had sufficiently relieved herself by her scolding, he helped Mosu up and said to him: "My dear son-in-law, if you repent of your misdeed, Little Golden Daughter will gradually cease to be angry. Of course you are an old married couple; yet as you have renewed your vows this evening in my house, kindly do me a favor and listen to what I have to say: You, Mosu, are weighed with a heavy burden of guilt, and for that reason you must not resent your wife's being somewhat indignant, but must have patience with her. I will call in my wife to make peace between you."

With these words Sir Hu went out and sent in his wife who finally, after a great deal of difficulty, succeeded in reconciling the two, so that they agreed once more to take up life as husband and wife.

And they esteemed and loved each other twice as much as they had before. Their life was all happiness and joy. And later, when Sir Hu and his wife died, they mourned for them as if in truth they had been their own parents.

Giauna the Beautiful

Once upon a time there was a descendant of Confucius. His father had a friend, and this friend held an official position in the South and offered the young man a place as secretary. But when the latter reached the town where he was to have been active, he found that his father's friend had already died. Then he was much embarrassed, seeing that he did not have the means to return home again. So he was glad to take refuge in the Monastery of Puto, where he copied holy books for the abbot.

About a hundred paces west of the monastery stood a deserted house. One day there had been a great snowfall, and as young Kung accidentally passed by the door of the house, he noticed a well dressed and prepossessing youth standing there who bowed to him and begged him to approach. Now young Kung was a scholar, and could appreciate good manners. Finding that the youth and himself had much in common, he took a liking to him, and followed him into the house. It was immaculately clean; silk curtains hung before the doors, and on the walls were pictures of good old masters. On a table lay a book entitled: "Tales of the Coral Ring." Coral Ring was the name of a cavern.

Once upon a time there lived a monk at Puto who was exceedingly learned. An aged man had led him into the cave in question, where he had seen a number of volumes on the book stands. The aged man had said: "These are the histories of the various dynasties." In a second room were to be found the histories of all the peoples on earth. A third was guarded by two dogs. The aged man explained: "In this room are kept the secret reports of the immortals, telling the arts by means of which they gained eternal life. The two dogs are two dragons." The monk turned the pages of the books, and found that they were all works of ancient times, such as he had never seen before. He would gladly have remained in the cave, but the old man said: "That would not do!" and a boy led him out again. The name of that cave, however, was the Coral Ring, and it was described in the volume which lay on the table.

The youth questioned Kung regarding his name and family, and the latter told him his whole history. The youth pitied him greatly and advised him to open a school.

Kung answered with a sigh: "I am quite unknown in the neighborhood, and have no one to recommend me!"

Said the youth: "If you do not consider me altogether too unworthy and stupid, I should like to be your pupil myself."

Young Kung was overjoyed. "I should not dare to attempt to teach you," he replied, "but together we might dedicate ourselves to the study of science." He then asked why the house had been standing empty for so long.

The youth answered: "The owner of the house has gone to the country. We come from Shensi, and have taken the house for a short time. We only moved in a few days ago."

They chatted and joked together gaily, and the young man invited Kung to remain overnight, ordering a small boy to light a pan of charcoal.

Then he stepped rapidly into the rear room and soon returned saying: "My father has come."

As Kung rose an aged man with a long, white beard and eyebrows stepped into the room and said, greeting him: "You have already declared your willingness to instruct my son, and I am grateful for your kindness. But you must be strict with him and not treat him as a friend."

Then he had garments of silk, a fur cap, and shoes and socks of fur brought in, and begged Kung to change his clothes. Wine and food were then served. The cushions and covers of the tables and chairs were made of stuffs unknown to Kung, and their shimmering radiance blinded the eye. The aged man retired after a few beakers of wine, and then the youth showed Kung his essays. They were all written in the style of the old masters and not in the new-fangled eight-section form.

When he was asked about this, the youth said with a smile: "I am quite indifferent to winning success at the state examinations!" Then he turned to the small boy and said: "See whether the old gentleman has already fallen asleep. If he has, you may quietly bring in little Hiang-Nu."

The boy went off, and the youth took a lute from an embroidered case. At once a serving-maid entered, dressed in red, and surpassingly beautiful. The youth bade her sing "The Lament of the Beloved," and her melting tones moved the heart. The third watch of the night had passed before they retired to sleep.

On the following morning all rose early and study began. The youth was exceptionally gifted. Whatever he had seen but once was graven in his memory. Hence he made surprising progress in the course of a few months. The old custom was followed of writing an essay every five days, and celebrating its completion with a little banquet. And at each banquet Hiang-Nu was sent for.

One evening Kung could not remove his glance from Hiang-Nu. The youth guessed his thoughts and said to him: "You are as yet unmarried. Early and late I keep thinking as to how I can provide you with a charming life companion. Hiang-Nu is the serving-maid of my father, so I cannot give her to you."

Said Kung: "I am grateful to you for your friendly thought. But if the girl you have in mind is not just as beautiful as Hiang-Nu, then I would rather do without."

The youth laughed: "You are indeed inexperienced if you think that Hiang-Nu is beautiful. Your wish is easily fulfilled."

Thus half a year went by and the monotonous rainy season had just began. Then a swelling the size of a peach developed in young Kung's breast, which increased over night until it was as large as a tea-cup. He lay on his couch groaning with pain, and unable to eat or to sleep. The youth was busy day and night nursing him, and even the old gentleman asked how he was getting along.

Then the youth said: "My little sister Giauna alone is able to cure this illness. Please send to grandmother, and have her brought here!"

The old gentleman was willing, and he sent off his boy.

The next day the boy came back with the news that Giauna would come, together with her aunt and her cousin A-Sung.

Not long after the youth led his sister into the room. She was not more than thirteen or fourteen years of age, enchantingly beautiful, and slender as a willow-tree. When the sick man saw her he forgot all his pain and his spirits rose.

The youth said to his sister Giauna: "This is my best friend, whom I love as a brother! I beg of you, little sister, to cure him of his illness!"

The maiden blushed with confusion; then she stepped up to the sick-bed. While she was feeling his pulse, it seemed to him as though she brought the fragrance of orchards with her.

Said the maiden with a smile: "No wonder that this illness has befallen him. His heart beats far too stormily. His illness is serious but not incurable. Now the blood which has flowed has already gathered, so we will have to cut to cure."

With that she took her golden armlet from her arm and laid it on the aching place. She pressed it down very gently, and the swelling rose a full inch above the armlet so that it enclosed the entire swelling. Then she loosed a pen-knife with a blade as thin as paper from her silken girdle. With one hand she held the armlet, and with the other she took the knife and lightly passed it around the bottom of the ring. Black blood gushed forth and ran over mattress and bed. But young Kung was so enchanted by the presence of the beautiful Giauna that not only did he feel no pain, but his one fear was that the whole affair might end too soon, and that she would disappear from his sight. In a moment the diseased flesh had been cut away, and Giauna had fresh water brought and cleansed the wound. Then she took a small red pellet from her mouth, and laid it on the wound, and when she turned around in a circle, it seemed to Kung as though she drew out all the inflammation in steam and flames. Once more she turned in a circle, and he felt his wound itch and quiver, and when she turned for the third time, he was completely cured.

The maiden took the pellet into her mouth again and said: "Now all is well!" Then she hastened into the inner room. Young Kung leaped up in order to thank her.

True, he was now cured of his illness, but his thoughts continued to dwell on Giauna's pretty face. He neglected his books and sat lost in day-dreams.

His friend had noticed it and said to him: "I have at last succeeded, this very day, in finding an attractive life companion for you."

Kung asked who she might be.

"The daughter of my aunt, A-Sung. She is seventeen years of age, and anything but homely."

"I am sure she is not as beautiful as Giauna," thought Kung. Then he hummed the lines of a song to himself:

"Who once has seen the sea close by,
All rivers shallow streams declares;
Who o'er Wu's hill the clouds watched fly,
Says nothing with that view compares."

The youth smiled. "My little sister Giauna is still very young," said he. "Besides, she is my father's only daughter, and he would not like to see her marry some one from afar. But my cousin A-Sung is not homely either. If you do not believe me, wait until they go walking in the garden, and then you may take a look at them without their knowing it."

Kung posted himself at the open window on the look-out, and sure enough, he saw Giauna come along leading another girl by the hand, a girl so beautiful that there was none other like her. Giauna and she seemed to be sisters, only to be told apart by a slight difference in age.

Then young Kung was exceedingly happy and begged his friend to act for him in arranging the marriage, which the latter promised to do. The next day he came to Kung, and told him amid congratulations that everything was arranged. A special court was put in order for the young pair, and the wedding was celebrated. Young Kung felt as though he had married a fairy, and the two became very fond of each other.

One day Kung's friend came to him in a state of great excitement and said: "The owner of this house is coming back, and my father now wishes to return to Shensi. The time for us to part draws near, and I am very sad!"

Kung wished to accompany them, but his friend advised him to return to his own home.

Kung mentioned the difficulties in the way, but the youth replied: "That need not worry you, because I will accompany you."

After a time the father came, together with A-Sung, and made Kung a present of a hundred ounces of gold. Then the youth took Kung and his wife by the hand, and told them to close their eyes. As soon as they did so off they went through the air like a storm-wind. All Kung could notice was that the gale roared about his ears.

When some time had passed the youth cried: "Now we have arrived!" Kung opened his eyes and saw his old home, and then he knew that his friend was not of human kind.

Gaily they knocked at the door of his home. His mother opened it and when she saw that he had brought along so charming a wife she was greatly pleased. Then Kung turned around to his friend, but the latter had already disappeared.

A-Sung served her mother-in-law with great devotion, and her beauty and virtue was celebrated far and near. Soon after young Kung gained the doctorate, and was appointed inspector of prisons in Shensi. He took his wife along with him, but his mother remained at home, since Shensi was too far for her to travel. And heaven gave A-Sung and Kung a little son.

But Kung became involved in a dispute with a traveling censor. The latter complained about Kung and he was dismissed from his po st.

So it happened that one day he was idling about before the city, when he saw a handsome youth riding a black mule. When he looked more closely he saw that it was his old friend. They fell into each others' arms, laughing and weeping, and the youth led him to a village. In the midst of a thick grove of trees which threw a deep shade, stood a house whose upper stories rose to the skies. One could see at a glance that people of distinction lived there. Kung now inquired after sister Giauna, and was told that she had married. He remained over night and then went off to fetch his wife.

In the meantime Giauna arrived. She took A-Sung's little son in her arms and said: "Cousin, this is a little stranger in our family!"

Kung greeted her, and again thanked her for the kindness she had shown him in curing his illness.

She answered with a smile: "Since then you have become a distinguished man, and the wound has long since healed. Have you still not forgotten your pain?"

Then Giauna's husband arrived, and every one became acquainted. And after that they parted.

One day the youth came sadly to Kung and said: "We are threatened by a great misfortune to-day. I do not know whether you would be willing to save us!"

Kung did not know what it might be; but he gladly promised his aid. Then the youth called up the entire family and they bowed down in the outer court.

He began: "I will tell you the truth just as it is. We are foxes. This day we are threatened by the danger of thunder. If you care to save us, then there is a hope that we may manage to stay alive; if not, then take your child and go, so that you are not involved in our danger."

But Kung vowed that he would share life and death with them.

Then the youth begged him to stand in the door with a sword in his hand, and said: "Now when the thunder begins to roll you must stand there and never stir."

Suddenly dark clouds rose in the sky, and the heavens grew gloomy as if night were closing down. Kung looked about him, but the buildings had all disappeared, and behind him he could only see a high barrow, in which was a large cave whose interior was lost in darkness. In the midst of his fright he was surprised by a thunderbolt. A heavy rain poured down in streams, and a storm wind arose which rooted up the tallest trees. Everything glimmered before his eyes and his ears were deafened. But he held his sword in his hand, and stood as firm as a rock. Suddenly in the midst of black smoke and flashes of lightning, he saw a monster with a pointed beak and long claws, which was carrying off a human body. When he looked more closely he recognized by the dress that it was Giauna. He leaped up at the monster and struck at him with his sword, and at once Giauna fell to the ground. A tremendous crash of thunder shook the earth, and Kung fell down dead.

Then the tempest cleared away, and the blue sky appeared once more.

Giauna had regained consciousness, and when she saw Kung lying dead beside her she said amid sobs: "He died for my sake! Why should I continue to live?"

A-Sung also came out, and together they carried him into the cave. Giauna told A-Sung to hold his head while her brother opened his mouth. She herself took hold of his chin, and brought out her little red pellet. She pressed it against his lips with her own, and breathed into his lungs. Then the breath came back to his throat with a rattling noise, and in a short time he was himself once more.

So there was the whole family reunited again, and none of its members had come to harm. They gradually recovered from their fright, and were quite happy: when suddenly a small boy brought the news that Giauna's husband and his whole family had been killed by the thunder. Giauna broke down, weeping, and the others tried to comfort her.

Finally Kung said: "It is not well to dwell too long amid the graves of the dead. Will you not come home with me?"

Thereupon they packed up their belongings and went with him. He assigned a deserted garden, which he carefully walled off, to his friend and his family as a dwelling-place. Only when Kung and A-Sung came to visit them was the bolt drawn. Then Giauna and her brother played chess, drank tea and chatted with them like members of the same family.

But Kung's little son had a somewhat pointed face, which resembled a fox's, and when he went along the street, the people would turn around and say: "There goes the fox-child!"

The Frog Princess

THERE WHERE THE YANGTZE-KIANG HAS COME ABOUT HALF-WAY ON ITS COURSE TO THE sea, the Frog King is worshiped with great devotion. He has a temple there and frogs by the thousand are to be found in the neighborhood, some of them of enormous size. Those who incur the wrath of the god are apt to have strange visitations in their homes. Frogs hop about on tables and beds, and in extreme cases they even creep up the smooth walls of the room without falling. There are various kinds of omens, but all indicate that some misfortune threatens the house in question. Then the people living in it become terrified, slaughter a cow and offer it as a sacrifice. Thus the god is mollified and nothing further happens.

In that part of the country there once lived a youth named Sia Kung-Schong. He was handsome and intelligent. When he was some six or seven years of age, a serving-maid dressed in green entered his home. She said that she was a messenger from the Frog King, and declared that the Frog King wished to have his daughter marry young Sia. Old Sia was an honest man, not very bright, and since this did not suit him, he declined the offer on the plea that his son was still too young to marry. In spite of this, however, he did not dare look about for another mate for him.

Then a few years passed and the boy gradually grew up. A marriage between him and a certain Mistress Giang was decided upon.

But the Frog King sent word to Mistress Giang: "Young Sia is my son-in-law. How dare you undertake to lay claim to what does not belong to you!" Then Father Giang was frightened, and took back his promise.

This made Old Sia very sad. He prepared a sacrifice and went to his temple to pray. He explained that he felt unworthy of becoming the relation of a god. When he had finished praying a multitude of enormous maggots made their appearance in the sacrificial meat and wine, and crawled around. He poured them out, begged forgiveness, and returned home filled with evil forebodings. He did not know what more he could do, and had to let things take their course.

One day young Sia went out into the street. A messenger stepped up to him and told him, on the part of the Frog King that the latter urgently requested Sia to come to him. There was no help for it; he had to follow the messenger. He led him through a red gateway into some magnificent, high-ceilinged rooms. In the great hall sat an ancient man who might have been some eighty years of age. Sia cast himself down on the ground before him in homage. The old man bade him rise, and assigned him a place at the table. Soon a number of girls and women came crowding in to look at him. Then the old man turned to them and said: "Go to the room of the bride and tell her that the bridegroom has arrived!"

Quickly a couple of maids ran away, and shortly after an old woman came from the inner apartments, leading a maiden by the hand, who might have been sixteen years of age, and was incomparably beautiful. The old man pointed to her and said: "This is my tenth little daughter. It seemed to me that you would make a good pair. But your father has scorned us because of our difference in race. Yet one's marriage is a matter that is of life-long importance. Our parents can determine it only in part. In the end it rests mainly with one's self."

Sia looked steadily at the girl, and a fondness for her grew in his heart. He sat there in silence. The old man continued: "I knew very well that the young gentleman would agree. Go on ahead of us, and we will bring you your bride!"

Sia said he would, and hurried to inform his father. His father did not know what to do in his excitement. He suggested an excuse and wanted to send Sia back to decline his bride with thanks. But this Sia was not willing to do. While they were arguing the matter, the bride's carriage was already at the door. It was surrounded by a crowd of greencoats, and the lady entered the house, and bowed politely to her parents-in-law. When the latter saw her they were both pleased, and the wedding was announced for that very evening.

The new couple lived in peace and good understanding. And after they had been married their divine parents-in-law often came to their house. When they appeared dressed in red, it meant that some good fortune was to befall them; when they came dressed in white, it signified that they were sure to make some gain. Thus, in the course of time, the family became wealthy.

But since they had become related to the gods the rooms, courtyards and all other places were always crowded with frogs. And no one ventured to harm them. Sia Kung-Schong alone was young and showed no consideration. When he was in good spirits he did not bother them, but when he got out of sorts he knew no mercy, and purposely stepped on them and killed them.

In general his young wife was modest and obedient; yet she easily lost her temper. She could not approve her husband's conduct. But Sia would not do her the favor to give up his brutal habit. So she scolded him because of it and he grew angry.

"Do you imagine," he told her, "that because your parents can visit human beings with misfortune, that a real man would be afraid of a frog?"

His wife carefully avoided uttering the word "frog," hence his speech angered her and she said: "Since I have dwelt in your house your fields have yielded larger crops, and you have obtained the highest selling prices. And that is something after all. But now, when young and old, you are comfortably established, you wish to act like the fledgling owl, who picks out his own mother's eyes as soon as he is able to fly!"

Sia then grew still more angry and answered: "These gifts have been unwelcome to me for a long time, for I consider them unclean. I could never consent to leave such property to sons and grandsons. It would be better if we parted at once!"

So he bade his wife leave the house, and before his parents knew anything about it, she was gone. His parents scolded him and told him to go at once and bring her back. But he was filled with rage, and would not give in to them.

That same night he and his mother fell sick. They felt weak and could not eat. The father, much worried, went to the temple to beg for pardon. And he prayed so earnestly that his wife and son recovered in three days' time. And the Frog Princess also returned, and they lived together happily and contented as before.

But the young woman sat in the house all day long, occupied solely with her ornaments and her rouge, and did not concern herself with sewing and stitching. So Sia Kung-Schong's mother still had to look out for her son's clothes.

One day his mother was angry and said: "My son has a wife, and yet I have to do all the work! In other homes the daughter-in-law serves her mother-in-law. But in our house the mother-in-law must serve the daughter-in-law."

This the princess accidentally heard. In she came, much excited, and began: "Have I ever omitted, as is right and proper, to visit you morning and evening? My only fault is that I will not burden myself with all this toil for the sake of saving a trifling sum of money!" The mother answered not a word, but wept bitterly and in silence because of the insult offered her.

Her son came along and noticed that his mother had been weeping. He insisted on knowing the reason, and found out what had happened. Angrily he reproached his wife. She raised objections and did not wish to admit that she had been in the wrong. Finally Sia said: "It is better to have no wife at all than one who gives her mother-in-law no pleasure. What can the old frog do to me after all, if I anger him, save call misfortunes upon me and take my life!" So he once more drove his wife out of the house.

The princess left her home and went away. The following day fire broke out in the house, and spread to several other buildings. Tables, beds, everything was burned.

Sia, in a rage because of the fire, went to the temple to complain: "To bring up a daughter in such a way that she does not please her parents-in-law shows that there is no discipline in a house. And now you even encourage her in her faults. It is said the gods are most just. Are there gods who teach men to fear their wives? Incidentally, the whole quarrel rests on me alone. My parents had nothing to do with it. If I was to be punished by the ax and cord, well and good. You could have carried out the punishment yourself. But this you did not do. So now I will burn your own house in order to satisfy my own sense of justice!"

With these words he began piling up brush-wood before the temple, struck sparks and wanted to set it ablaze. The neighbors came streaming up, and pleaded with him. So he swallowed his rage and went home.

When his parents heard of it, they grew pale with a great fear. But at night the god appeared to the people of a neighboring village, and ordered them to rebuild the house of his son-in-law. When day began to dawn they dragged up building-wood and the workmen all came in throngs to build for Sia. No matter what he said he could not prevent them. All day long hundreds of workmen were busy. And in the course of a few days all the rooms had been rebuilt, and all the utensils, curtains and furniture were there as before. And when the work had been completed the princess also returned. She climbed the stairs to the great room, and acknowledged her fault with many tender and loving words. Then she turned to Sia Kung-Schong, and smiled at him sideways. Instead of resentment joy now filled the whole house. And after that time the princess was especially peaceable. Two whole years passed without an angry word being said.

But the princess had a great dislike for snakes. Once, by way of a joke, young Sia put a small snake into a parcel, which he gave her and told her to open. She turned pale and reproached him. Then Sia-Kung-Schong also took his jest seriously, and angry words passed.

At last the princess said: "This time I will not wait for you to turn me out. Now we are finally done with one another!" And with that she walked out of the door.

Father Sia grew very much alarmed, beat his son himself with his staff, and begged the god to be kind and forgive. Fortunately there were no evil consequences. All was quiet and not a sound was heard.

Thus more than a year passed. Sia-Kung-Schong longed for the princess and took himself seriously to task. He would creep in secret to the temple of the god, and lament because he had lost the princess. But no voice answered him. And soon afterward he even heard that the god had betrothed his daughter to another man. Then he grew hopeless at heart, and thought of finding another wife for himself. Yet no matter how he searched he could find none who equaled the princess. This only increased his longing for her, and he went to the home of the Yuans, to a member of which family it was said she had been promised. There they had already painted the walls, and swept the courtyard, and all was in readiness to receive the bridal carriage. Sia was overcome with remorse and discontent. He no longer ate, and fell ill. His parents were quite stunned by the anxiety they felt on his account, and were incapable of helpful thought.

Suddenly while he was lying there only half-conscious, he felt some one stroke him, and heard a voice say: "And how goes it with our real husband, who insisted on turning out his wife?"

He opened his eyes and it was the princess.

Full of joy he leaped up and said: "How is it you have come back to me?" The princess answered: "To tell the truth, according to your own habit of treating people badly, I should have followed my father's advice and taken another husband. And, as a matter of fact, the wedding gifts of the Yuan family have been lying in my home for a long time. But I thought and thought and could not bring myself to do so. The wedding was to have been this evening and my father thought it shameful to have the wedding gifts carried back. So I took the things myself and placed them before the Yuan's door. When I went out my father ran out beside me: 'You insane girl,' he said, 'so you will not listen to what I say! If you are ill-treated by Sia in the future I wash my hands of it. Even if they kill you you shall not come home to me again!'"

Moved by her faithfulness the tears rolled from Sia's eyes. The servants, full of joy, hurried to the parents to acquaint them with the good news. And when they heard it they did not wait for the young people to come to them, but hastened themselves to their son's rooms, took the princess by the hand and wept. Young Sia, too, had become more settled by this time, and was no longer so mischievous. So he and his wife grew to love each other more sincerely day by day.

Once the princess said to him: "Formerly, when you always treated me so badly, I feared that we would not keep company into our old age. So I never asked heaven to send us a child. But now that all has changed, and I will beg the gods for a son."

And, sure enough, before long Sia's parents-in-law appeared in the house clad in red garments, and shortly after heaven sent the happy pair two sons instead of one.

From that time on their intercourse with the Frog-King was never interrupted. When some one among the people had angered the god, he first tried to induce young Sia to speak for him, and sent his wife and daughter to the Frog Princess to implore her aid. And if the princess laughed, then all would be well.

The Sia family has many descendants, whom the people call "the little frog men." Those who are near them do not venture to call them by this name, but those standing further off do so.

Rose of Evening

On the fifth day of the fifth month the festival of the Dragon Junk is held along the Yangtze-kiang. A dragon is hollowed out of wood, painted with an armor of scales, and adorned with gold and bright colors. A carved red railing surrounds this ship, and its sails and flags are made of silks and brocade. The after part of the vessel is called the dragon's tail. It rises ten feet above the water, and a board which floats in the water is tied to it by means of a cloth. Upon this board sit boys who turn somersaults, stand on their heads, and perform all sorts of tricks. Yet, being so close to the water their danger is very great. It is the custom, therefore, when a boy is hired for this purpose, to give his parents money before he is trained. Then, if he falls into the water and is drowned, no one has him on their conscience. Farther South the custom differs in so much that instead of boys, beautiful girls are chosen for this purpose.

In Dschen-Giang there once lived a widow named Dsiang, who had a son called Aduan. When he was no more than seven years of age he was extraordinarily skillful, and no other boy could equal him. And his reputation increasing as he grew, he earned more and more money. So it happened that he was still called upon at the Dragon Junk Festival when he was already sixteen.

But one day he fell into the water below the Gold Island and was drowned. He was the only son of his mother, and she sorrowed over him, and that was the end of it.

Yet Aduan did not know that he had been drowned. He met two men who took him along with them, and he saw a new world in the midst of the waters of the Yellow River. When he looked around, the waves of the river towered steeply about him like walls, and a palace was visible, in which sat a man wearing armor and a helmet. His two companions said to him: "That is the Prince of the Dragon's Cave!" and bade him kneel.

The Prince of the Dragon's Cave seemed to be of a mild and kindly disposition and said: "We can make use of such a skillful lad. He may take part in the dance of the willow branches!"

So he was brought to a spot surrounded by extensive buildings. He entered, and was greeted by a crowd of boys who were all about fourteen years of age.

An old woman came in and they all called out: "This is Mother Hia!" And she sat down and had Aduan show his tricks. Then she taught him the dance of the flying thunders of Tsian-Tang River, and the music that calms the winds on the sea of Dung-Ting. When the cymbals and kettle-drums reechoed through all the courts, they deafened the ear. Then, again, all the courts would fall silent. Mother Hia thought that Aduan would not be able to grasp everything the very first time; so she taught him with great patience. But Aduan had understood everything from the first, and that pleased old Mother Hia. "This boy," said she, "equals our own Rose of Evening!"

The following day the Prince of the Dragon's Cave held a review of his dancers. When all the dancers had assembled, the dance of the Ogres was danced first. Those who performed it all wore devil-masks and garments of scales. They beat upon enormous cymbals, and their kettle-drums were so large that four men could just about span them. Their sound was like the sound of a mighty thunder, and the noise was so great that nothing else could be heard. When the dance began, tremendous waves spouted up to the very skies, and then fell down again like star-glimmer which scatters in the air.

The Prince of the Dragon Cave hastily bade the dance cease, and had the dancers of the nightingale round step forth. These were all lovely young girls of sixteen. They made a delicate music with flutes, so that the breeze blew and the roaring of the waves was stilled in a moment. The water gradually became as quiet as a crystal world, transparent to its lowest depths. When the nightingale dancers had finished, they withdrew and posted themselves in the western courtyard.

Then came the turn of the swallow dancers. These were all little girls. One among them, who was about fifteen years of age, danced the dance of the giving of flowers with flying sleeves and waving locks. And as their garments fluttered, many-colored flowers dropped from their folds, and were caught up by the wind and whirled about the whole courtyard. When the dance had ended, this dancer also went off with the rest of the girls to the western courtyard. Aduan looked at her from out the corner of his eye, and fell deeply in love with her. He asked his comrades who she might be and they told him she was named "Rose of Evening."

But the willow-spray dancers were now called out. The Prince of the Dragon Cave was especially desirous of testing Aduan. So Aduan danced alone, and he danced with joy or defiance according to the music. When he looked up and when he looked down his glances held the beat of the measure. The Dragon Prince, enchanted with his skill, presented him with a garment of five colors, and gave him a carbuncle set in golden threads of fish-beard for a hair-jewel. Aduan bowed his thanks for the gift, and then also hastened to the western courtyard. There all the dancers stood in rank and file. Aduan could only look at Rose of Evening from a distance, but still Rose of Evening returned his glances.

After a time Aduan gradually slipped to the end of his file and Rose of Evening also drew near to him, so that they stood only a few feet away from each other. But the strict rules allowed no confusion in the ranks, so they could only gaze and let their souls go out to each other.

Now the butterfly dance followed the others. This was danced by the boys and girls together, and the pairs were equal in size, age and the color of their garments. When all the dances had ended, the dancers marched out with the goose-step. The willow-spray dancers followed the swallow dancers, and Aduan hastened in advance of his company, while Rose of Evening lingered along after hers. She turned her head, and when she spied Aduan she purposely let a coral pin fall from her hair. Aduan hastily hid it in his sleeve.

When he had returned, he was sick with longing, and could neither eat nor sleep. Mother Hia brought him all sorts of dainties, looked after him three or four times a day, and stroked his forehead with loving care. But his illness did not yield in the least. Mother Hia was unhappy, and yet helpless.

"The birthday of the King of the Wu River is at hand," said she. "What is to be done?"

In the twilight there came a boy, who sat down on the edge of Aduan's bed and chatted with him. He belonged to the butterfly dancers, said he, and asked casually: "Are you sick because of Rose of Evening?" Aduan, frightened, asked him how he came to guess it. The other boy said, with a smile: "Well, because Rose of Evening is in the same case as yourself."

Disconcerted, Aduan sat up and begged the boy to advise him. "Are you able to walk?" asked the latter. "If I exert myself," said Aduan, "I think I could manage it."

So the boy led him to the South. There he opened a gate and they turned the corner, to the West. Once more the doors of the gate flew open, and now Aduan saw a lotus field about twenty acres in size. The lotus flowers were all growing on level earth, and their leaves were as large as mats and their flowers like umbrellas. The fallen blossoms covered the ground beneath the stalks to the depth of a foot or more. The boy led Aduan in and said, "Now first of all sit down for a little while!" Then he went away.

After a time a beautiful girl thrust aside the lotus flowers and came into the open. It was Rose of Evening. They looked at each other with happy timidity, and each told how each had longed for the other. And they also told each other of their former life. Then they weighted the lotus-leaves with stones so that they made a cozy retreat, in which they could be together, and promised to meet each other there every evening. And then they parted.

Aduan came back and his illness left him. From that time on he met Rose of Evening every day in the lotus field.

After a few days had passed they had to accompany the Prince of the Dragon Cave to the birthday festival of the King of the Wu River. The festival came to an end, and all the dancers returned home. Only, the King had kept back Rose of Evening and one of the nightingale dancers to teach the girls in his castle.

Months passed and no news came from Rose of Evening, so that Aduan went about full of longing and despair. Now Mother Hia went every day to the castle of the god of the Wu River. So Aduan told her that Rose of Evening was his cousin, and entreated her to take him along with her so that he could at least see her a single time. So she took him along, and let him stay at the lodge-house of the river-god for a few days. But the indwellers of the castle were so strictly watched that he could not see Rose of Evening even a single time. Sadly Aduan went back again.

Another month passed and Aduan, filled with gloomy thoughts, wished that death might be his portion.

One day Mother Hia came to him full of pity, and began to sympathize with him. "What a shame," said she, "that Rose of Evening has cast herself into the river!"

Aduan was extremely frightened, and his tears flowed resistlessly. He tore his beautiful garments, took his gold and his pearls, and went out with the sole idea of following his beloved in death. Yet the waters of the river stood up before him like walls, and no matter how often he ran against them, head down, they always flung him back.

He did not dare return, since he feared he might be questioned about his festival garments, and severely punished because he had ruined them. So he stood there and knew not what to do, while the perspiration ran down to his ankles. Suddenly, at the foot of the water-wall he saw a tall tree. Like a monkey he climbed up to its very top, and then, with all his might, he shot into the waves.

And then, without being wet, he found himself suddenly swimming on the surface of the river. Unexpectedly the world of men rose up once more before his dazzled eyes. He swam to the shore, and as he walked along the river-bank, his thoughts went back to his old mother. He took a ship and traveled home.

When he reached the village, it seemed to him as though all the houses in it belonged to another world. The following morning he entered his mother's house, and as he did so, heard a girl's voice beneath the window saying: "Your son has come back again!" The voice sounded like the voice of Rose of Evening, and when she came to greet him at his mother's side, sure enough, it was Rose of Evening herself.

And in that hour the joy of these two who were so fond of each other overcame all their sorrow. But in the mother's mind sorrow and doubt, terror and joy mingled in constant succession in a thousand different ways.

When Rose of Evening had been in the palace of the river-king, and had come to realize that she would never see Aduan again, she determined to die, and flung herself into the waters of the stream. But she was carried to the surface, and the waves carried and cradled her till a ship came by and took her aboard. They asked whence she came. Now Rose of Evening had originally been a celebrated singing girl of Wu, who had fallen into the river and whose body had never been found. So she thought to herself that, after all, she could not return to her old life again. So she answered: "Madame Dsiang, in Dschen-Giang is my mother-in-law." Then the travelers took passage for her in a ship which brought her to the place she had mentioned. The widow Dsiang first said she must be mistaken, but the girl insisted that there was no mistake, and told Aduan's mother her whole story. Yet, though the latter was charmed by her surpassing loveliness, she feared that Rose of Evening was too young to live a widow's life. But the girl was respectful and industrious, and when she saw that poverty ruled in her new home, she took her pearls and sold them for a high price. Aduan's old mother was greatly pleased to see how seriously the girl took her duties.

Now that Aduan had returned again Rose of Evening could not control her joy. And even Aduan's old mother cherished the hope that, after all, perhaps her son had not died. She secretly dug up her son's grave, yet all his bones were still lying in it. So she questioned Aduan. And then, for the first time, the latter realized that he was a departed spirit. Then he feared that Rose of Evening might regard him with disgust because he was no longer a human being. So he ordered his mother on no account to speak of it, and this his mother promised. Then she spread the report in the village that the body which had been found in the river had not been that of her son at all. Yet she could not rid herself of the fear that, since Aduan was a departed spirit, heaven might refuse to send him a child.

In spite of her fear, however, she was able to hold a grandson in her arms in course of time. When she looked at him, he was no different from other children, and then her cup of joy was filled to overflowing.

Rose of Evening gradually became aware of the fact that Aduan was not really a human being. "Why did you not tell me at once?" said she. "Departed spirits who wear the garments of the dragon castle, surround themselves with a soul-casing so heavy in texture that they can no longer be distinguished from the living. And if one can obtain the lime made of dragon-horn which is in the castle, then the bones may be glued together in such wise that flesh and blood will grow over them again. What a pity that we could not obtain the lime while we were there!"

Aduan sold his pearl, for which a merchant from foreign parts gave him an enormous sum. Thus his family grew very wealthy. Once, on his mother's birthday, he danced with his wife and sang, in order to please her. The news reached the castle of the Dragon Prince and he thought to carry off Rose of Evening by force. But Aduan, alarmed, went to the Prince, and declared that both he and his wife were departed spirits. They examined him and since he cast no shadow, his word was taken, and he was not robbed of Rose of Evening.

The Ape Sun Wu Kung

Far, far away to the East, in the midst of the Great Sea there is an island called the Mountain of Flowers and Fruits. And on this mountain there is a high rock. Now this rock, from the very beginning of the world, had absorbed all the hidden seed power of heaven and earth and sun and moon, which endowed it with supernatural creative gifts. One day the rock burst, and out came an egg of stone. And out of this stone egg a stone ape was hatched by magic power. When he broke the shell he bowed to all sides. Then he gradually learned to walk and to leap, and two streams of golden radiance broke from his eyes which shot up to the highest of the castles of heaven, so that the Lord of the Heavens was frightened. So he sent out the two gods, Thousandmile-Eye and Fine-Ear, to find out what had happened. The two gods came back and reported: “The rays shine from the eyes of the stone ape who was hatched out of the egg which came from the magic rock. There is no reason for uneasiness.”

Little by little the ape grew up, ran and leaped about, drank from the springs in the valleys, ate the flowers and fruits, and time went by in unconstrained play.

One day, during the summer, when he was seeking coolness, together with the other apes on the island, they went to the valley to bathe. There they saw a waterfall which plunged down a high cliff. Said the apes to each other: “Whoever can force his way through the waterfall, without suffering injury, shall be our king.” The stone ape at once leaped into the air with joy and cried: “I will pass through!” Then he closed his eyes, bent down low and leaped through the roar and foam of the waters. When he opened his eyes once more he saw an iron bridge, which was shut off from the outer world by the waterfall as though by a curtain.

At its entrance stood a tablet of stone on which were graven the words: “This is the heavenly cave behind the water-curtain on the Blessed Island of Flowers and Fruits.” Filled with joy, the stone ape leaped out again through the waterfall and told the other apes what he had found. They received the news with great content, and begged the stone ape to take them there. So the tribe of apes leaped through the water on the iron bridge, and then crowded into the cave castle where they found a hearth with a profusion of pots, cups and platters. But all were made of stone. Then the apes paid homage to the stone ape as their king, and he was given the name of Handsome King of the Apes. He appointed long-tailed, ring-tailed and other monkeys to be his officials and counselors, servants and retainers, and they led a blissful life on the Mountain, sleeping by night in their cave castle, keeping away from birds and beasts, and their king enjoyed untroubled happiness. In this way some three hundred years went by.

One day, when the King of the Apes sat with his subjects at a merry meal, he suddenly began to weep. Frightened, the apes asked him why he so suddenly grew sad amid all his bliss. Said the King: “It is true that we are not subject to the law and rule of man, that birds and beasts do not dare attack us, yet little by little we grow old and weak, and some day the hour will strike when Death, the Ancient, will drag us off! Then we are gone in a moment, and can no longer dwell upon earth!” When the apes heard these words, they hid their faces and sobbed. But an old ape, whose arms were connected in such a way that he could add the length of one to that of the other, stepped forth from the ranks. In a loud tone of voice he said: “That you have hit upon this thought, O King, shows the desire to search for truth has awakened you! Among all living creatures, there are but three kinds who are exempt from Death’s power: the

Buddhas, the blessed spirits and the gods. Whoever attains one of these three grades escapes the rod of re-birth, and lives as long as the Heavens themselves."

The King of the Apes said: "Where do these three kinds of beings live?" And the old ape replied: "They live in caves and on holy mountains in the great world of mortals." The King was pleased when he heard this, and told his apes that he was going to seek out gods and sainted spirits in order to learn the road to immortality from them. The apes dragged up peaches and other fruits and sweet wine to celebrate the parting banquet, and all made merry together.

On the following morning the Handsome King of the Apes rose very early, built him a raft of old pine trees and took a bamboo staff for a pole. Then he climbed on the raft, quite alone, and poled his way through the Great Sea. Wind and waves were favorable and he reached Asia. There he went ashore. On the strand he met a fisherman. He at once stepped up to him, knocked him down, tore off his clothes and put them on himself. Then he wandered around and visited all famous spots, went into the market-places, the densely populated cities, learned how to conduct himself properly, and how to speak and act like a well-bred human being. Yet his heart was set on learning the teaching of the Buddhas, the blessed spirits and the holy gods. But the people of the country in which he was were only concerned with honors and wealth. Not one of them seemed to care for life. Thus he went about until nine years had passed by unnoticed. Then he came to the strand of the Western Sea and it occurred to him: "No doubt there are gods and saints on the other side of the sea!" So he built another raft, floated it over the Western Sea and reached the land of the West. There he let his raft drift, and went ashore. After he had searched for many days, he suddenly saw a high mountain with deep, quiet valleys. As the Ape King went toward it, he heard a man singing in the woods, and the song sounded like one the blessed spirits might sing. So he hastily entered the wood to see who might be singing. There he met a wood-chopper at work. The Ape King bowed to him and said: "Venerable, divine master, I fall down and worship at your feet!" Said the wood-chopper: "I am only a workman; why do you call me divine master?" "Then, if you are no blessed god, how comes it you sing that divine song?" The wood-chopper laughed and said: "You are at home in music. The song I was singing was really taught me by a saint." "If you are acquainted with a saint," said the Ape King, "he surely cannot live far from here. I beg of you to show me the way to his dwelling." The wood-chopper replied: "It is not far from here. This mountain is known as the Mountain of the Heart. In it is a cave where dwells a saint who is called 'The Discerner.' The number of his disciples who have attained blessedness is countless. He still has some thirty to forty disciples gathered about him.

You need only follow this path which leads to the South, and you cannot miss his dwelling." The Ape King thanked the wood-chopper and, sure enough, he came to the cave which the latter had described to him. The gate was locked and he did not venture to knock. So he leaped up into a pine tree, picked pine-cones and devoured the seed. Before long one of the saint's disciples came and opened the door and said: "What sort of a beast is it that is making such a noise?" The Ape King leaped down from his tree, bowed, and said: "I have come in search of truth. I did not venture to knock." Then the disciple had to laugh and said: "Our master was seated lost in meditation, when he told me to lead in the seeker after truth who stood without the gate, and here you really are. Well, you may come along with me!" The Ape King smoothed his clothes, put his hat on straight, and stepped in. A long passage led past magnificent buildings and quiet hidden huts to the place where the master was sitting upright on a seat of white marble. At his right and left stood his disciples, ready to serve him. The Ape King flung himself down on the ground and greeted the master humbly. In answer to his questions he told him how he had found his way to him. And when he was asked his name, he said: "I have no name. I am the ape who came out of the stone." So the master said: "Then I will give you a name. I name you Sun Wu Kung." The Ape King thanked him, full of joy, and thereafter he was called Sun Wu Kung. The master ordered his oldest disciple to instruct Sun Wu Kung in sweeping and cleaning, in going in and out, in good manners, how to labor in the field and how to water the gardens. In the course of time he learned to write, to burn incense and read the sutras. And in this way some six or seven years went by.

One day the master ascended the seat from which he taught, and began to speak regarding the great truth. Sun Wu Kung understood the hidden meaning of his words, and commenced to jerk about and dance in his joy. The master reproved him: "Sun Wu Kung, you have still not laid aside your wild nature! What do you mean by carrying on in such an unfitting manner?" Sun Wu Kung bowed and answered: "I was listening attentively to you when the meaning of your words was disclosed to my heart, and without thinking I began to dance for joy. I was not giving way to my wild nature." Said the master: "If your spirit has really awakened, then I will announce the great truth to you. But there are three hundred and sixty ways by means of which one may reach this truth. Which way shall I teach you?" Said Sun Wu Kung: "Whichever you will, O Master!" Then the Master asked: "Shall I teach you the way of magic?" Said Sun Wu Kung: "What does magic teach one?" The Master replied: "It teaches one to raise up spirits, to question oracles, and to foretell fortune and misfortune." "Can one secure eternal life by means of it?" inquired Sun Wu Kung. "No," was the answer.

"Then I will not learn it." "Shall I teach you the sciences?" "What are the sciences?" "They are the nine schools of the three faiths. You learn how to read the holy books, pronounce incantations, commune with the gods, and call the saints to you." "Can one gain eternal life by means of them?" "No." "Then I will not learn them." "The way of repose is a very good way." "What is the way of repose?" "It teaches how to live without nourishment, how to remain quiescent in silent purity, and sit lost in meditation." "Can one gain eternal life in this way?" "No." "Then I will not learn it." "The way of deeds is also a good way." "What does that teach?" "It teaches one to equalize the vital powers, to practice bodily exercise, to prepare the elixir of life and to hold one's breath." "Will it give one eternal life?" "Not so." "Then I will not learn it! I will not learn it!" Thereupon the Master pretended to be angry, leaped down from his stand, took his cane and scolded: "What an ape! This he will not learn, and that he will not learn! What are you waiting to learn, then?" With that he gave him three blows across the head, retired to his inner chamber, and closed the great door after him.

The disciples were greatly excited, and overwhelmed Sun Wu Kung with reproaches. Yet the latter paid no attention to them, but smiled quietly to himself, for he had understood the riddle which the Master had given him to solve. And in his heart he thought: "His striking me over the head three times meant that I was to be ready at the third watch of the night. His withdrawing to his inner chamber and closing the great door after him, meant that I was to go in to him by the back door, and that he would make clear the great truth to me in secret." Accordingly he waited until evening, and made a pretense of lying down to sleep with the other disciples. But when the third watch of the night had come he rose softly and crept to the back door. Sure enough it stood ajar. He slipped in and stepped before the Master's bed. The Master was sleeping with his face turned toward the wall, and the ape did not venture to wake him, but knelt down in front of the bed. After a time the Master turned around and hummed a stanza to himself:

"A hard, hard grind,
Truth's lesson to expound.
One talks oneself deaf, dumb and blind,
Unless the right man's found."

Then Sun Wu Kung replied: "I am waiting here reverentially!"

The Master flung on his clothes, sat up in bed and said harshly: "Accursed ape! Why are you not asleep? What are you doing here?"

Sun Wu Kung answered: "Yet you pointed out to me yesterday that I was to come to you at the third watch of the night, by the back door, in order to be instructed in the truth. Therefore I have ventured to come. If you will teach me in the fulness of your grace, I will be eternally grateful to you."

Thought the Master to himself: "There is real intelligence in this ape's head, to have made him understand me so well." Then he replied: "Sun Wu Kung, it shall be granted you! I will speak freely with you. Come quite close to me, and then I will show you the way to eternal life."

With that he murmured into his ear a divine, magical incantation to further the concentration of his vital powers, and explained the hidden knowledge word for word. Sun Wu Kung listened to him eagerly, and in a short time had learned it by heart. Then he thanked his teacher, went out again and lay down to sleep. From that time forward he practiced the right mode of breathing, kept guard over his soul and spirit, and tamed the natural instincts of his heart. And while he did so three more years passed by. Then the task was completed.

One day the Master said to him: "Three great dangers still threaten you. Every one who wishes to accomplish something out of the ordinary is exposed to them, for he is pursued by the envy of demons and spirits. And only those who can overcome these three great dangers live as long as the heavens."

Then Sun Wu Kung was frightened and asked: "Is there any means of protection against these dangers?"

Then the Master again murmured a secret incantation into his ear, by means of which he gained the power to transform himself seventy-two times.

And when no more than a few days had passed Sun Wu Kung had learned the art.

One day the Master was walking before the cave in the company of his disciples. He called Sun Wu Kung up to him and asked: "What progress have you made with your art? Can you fly already?"

"Yes, indeed," said the ape.

"Then let me see you do so."

The ape leaped into the air to a distance of five or six feet from the ground. Clouds formed beneath his feet, and he was able to walk on them for several hundred yards. Then he was forced to drop down to earth again.

The Master said with a smile: "I call that crawling around on the clouds, not floating on them, as do the gods and saints who fly over the whole world in a single day. I will teach you the magic incantation for turning somersaults on the clouds. If you turn one of those somersaults you advance eighteen thousand miles at a clip."

Sun Wu Kung thanked him, full of joy, and from that time on he was able to move without limitation of space in any direction.

One day Sun Wu Kung was sitting together with the other disciples under the pine-tree by the gate, discussing the secrets of their teachings. Finally they asked him to show them some of his transforming arts. Sun Wu Kung could not keep his secret to himself, and agreed to do so.

With a smile he said: "Just set me a task! What do you wish me to change myself into?"

They said: "Turn yourself into a pine-tree."

So Sun Wu Kung murmured a magic incantation, turned around—and there stood a pine-tree before their very eyes. At this they all broke out into a horse-laugh. The Master heard the noise and came out of the gate, dragging his cane behind him.

"Why are you making such a noise?" he called out to them harshly.

Said they: "Sun Wu Kung has turned himself into a pine-tree, and this made us laugh."

"Sun Wu Kung, come here!" said the Master. "Now just tell me what tricks you are up to? Why do you have to turn yourself into a pine-tree? All the work you have done means nothing more to you than a chance to make magic for your companions to wonder at. That shows that your heart is not yet under control."

Humbly Sun Wu Kung begged his forgiveness.

But the Master said: "I bear you no ill will, but you must go away."

With tears in his eyes Sun Wu Kung asked him: "But where shall I go?"

"You must go back again whence you came," said the Master. And when Sun Wu Kung sadly bade him farewell, he threatened him: "Your savage nature is sure to bring down evil upon you some time. You must tell no one that you are my pupil. If you so much as breathe a word about it, I will fetch your soul and lock it up in the nethermost hell, so that you cannot escape for a thousand eternities."

Sun Wu Kung replied: "I will not say a word! I will not say a word!"

Then he once more thanked him for all the kindness shown him, turned a somersault and climbed up to the clouds.

Within the hour he had passed the seas, and saw the Mountain of Flowers and Fruits lying before him. Then he felt happy and at home again, let his cloud sink down to earth and cried: "Here I am back again, children!" And at once, from the valley, from behind the rocks, out of the grass and from amid the trees came his apes. They came running up by thousands, surrounded and greeted him, and inquired as to his adventures. Sun Wu Kung said: "I have now found the way to eternal life, and need fear Death the Ancient no longer." Then all the apes were overjoyed, and competed with each other in bringing flowers and fruits, peaches and wine, to welcome him. And again they honored Sun Wu Kung as the Handsome Ape King.

Sun Wu Kung now gathered the apes about him and questioned them as to how they had fared during his absence.

Said they: "It is well that you have come back again, great king! Not long ago a devil came here who wanted to take possession of our cave by force. We fought with him, but he dragged away many of your children and will probably soon return."

Sun Wu Kung grew very angry and said: "What sort of a devil is this who dares be so impudent?"

The apes answered: "He is the Devil-King of Chaos. He lives in the North, who knows how many miles away. We only saw him come and go amid clouds and mist."

Sun Wu Kung said: "Wait, and I will see to him!" With that he turned a somersault and disappeared without a trace.

In the furthest North rises a high mountain, upon whose slope is a cave above which is the inscription: "The Cave of the Kidneys." Before the door little devils were dancing. Sun Wu Kung called harshly to them: "Tell your Devil-King quickly that he had better give me my children back again!" The little devils were frightened, and delivered the message in the cave. Then the Devil-King reached for his sword and came out. But he was so large and broad that he could not even see Sun Wu Kung. He was clad from head to foot in black armor, and his face was as black as the bottom of a kettle. Sun Wu Kung shouted at him: "Accursed devil, where are your eyes, that you cannot see the venerable Sun?" Then the devil looked to the ground and saw a stone ape standing before him, bare-headed, dressed in red, with a yellow girdle and black boots. So the Devil-King laughed and said: "You are not even four feet high, less than thirty years of age, and weaponless, and yet you venture to make such a commotion." Said Sun Wu Kung: "I am not too small for you; and I can make myself large at will. You scorn me because I am without a weapon, but my two fists can thresh to the very skies." With that he stooped, clenched his fists and began to give the devil a beating. The devil was large and clumsy, but Sun Wu Kung leaped about nimbly. He struck him between the ribs and between the wind and his blows fell ever more fast and furious. In his despair the devil raised his great knife and aimed a blow at Sun Wu Kung's head. But the latter avoided the blow, and fell back on his magic powers of transformation. He pulled out a hair, put it in his mouth, chewed it, spat it out into the air and said: "Transform yourself!" And at once it turned into many hundreds of little apes who began to attack the devil. Sun Wu Kung, be it said, had eighty-four thousand hairs on his body, every single one of which he could transform. The little apes with their sharp eyes, leaped around with the greatest rapidity. They surrounded the Devil-King on all sides, tore at his clothes, and pulled at his legs, until he finally measured his length on the ground. Then Sun Wu Kung stepped up, tore his knife from his hand, and put an end to him. After that he entered the cave and released his captive children, the apes. The transformed hairs he drew to him again, and making a fire, he burned the evil cave to the ground. Then he gathered up those he had released, and flew back with them like a storm-wind to his cavern on the Mountain of Flowers and Fruits, joyfully greeted by all the apes.

After Sun Wu Kung had obtained possession of the Devil-King's great knife, he exercised his apes every day. They had wooden swords and lances of bamboo, and played their martial music on reed pipes. He had them build a camp so that they would be prepared for all dangers. Suddenly the thought came to Sun Wu Kung: "If we go on this way, perhaps we may incite some human or animal king to fight with us, and then we would not be able to withstand him with our wooden swords and bamboo lances!" And to his apes he said: "What should be done?" Four baboons stepped forward and said: "In the capital city of the Aulai empire there are warriors without number. And there coppersmiths and steelsmiths are also to be found. How would it be if we were to buy steel and iron and have those smiths weld weapons for us?"

A somersault and Sun Wu Kung was standing before the city moat. Said he to himself: "To first buy the weapons would take a great deal of time. I would rather make magic and take some." So he blew on the ground. Then a tremendous storm-wind arose which drove sand and stones before it, and caused all the soldiers in the city to run away in terror. Then Sun Wu Kung went to the armory, pulled out one of his hairs, turned it into thousands of little apes, cleared out the whole supply of weapons, and flew back home on a cloud.

Then he gathered his people about him and counted them. In all they numbered seventy-seven thousand. They held the whole Mountain in terror, and all the magic beasts and spirit princes who dwelt on it. And these came forth from seventy-two caves and honored Sun Wu Kung as their head.

One day the Ape King said: "Now you all have weapons; but this knife which I took from the Devil-King is too light, and no longer suits me. What should be done?"

Then the four baboons stepped forward and said: "In view of your spirit powers, O king, you will find no weapon fit for your use on all the earth! Is it possible for you to walk through the water?"

The Ape King answered: "All the elements are subject to me and there is no place where I cannot go."

Then the baboons said: "The water at our cave here flows into the Great Sea, to the castle of the Dragon-King of the Eastern Sea. If your magic power makes it possible, you could go to the Dragon-King and let him give you a weapon."

This suited the Ape King. He leaped on the iron bridge and murmured an incantation. Then he flung himself into the waves, which parted before him and ran on till he came to the palace of water-crystal. There he met a Triton who asked who he was. He mentioned his name and said: "I am the Dragon-King's nearest neighbor, and have come to visit him." The Triton took the message to the castle, and the Dragon-King of the Eastern Sea came out hastily to receive him. He bade him be seated and served him with tea.

Sun Wu Kung said: "I have learned the hidden knowledge and gained the powers of immortality. I have drilled my apes in the art of warfare in order to protect our mountain; but I have no weapon I can use, and have therefore come to you to borrow one."

The Dragon-King now had General Flounder bring him a great spear. But Sun Wu Kung was not satisfied with it. Then he ordered Field-Marshal Eel to fetch in a nine-tined fork, which weighed three thousand six hundred pounds. But Sun Wu Kung balanced it in his hand and said: "Too light! Too light! Too light!"

Then the Dragon-King was frightened, and had the heaviest weapon in his armory brought in. It weighed seven thousand two hundred pounds. But this was still too light for Sun Wu Kung. The Dragon-King assured him that he had nothing heavier, but Sun Wu Kung would not give in and said: "Just look around!"

Finally the Dragon-Queen and her daughter came out, and said to the Dragon-King: "This saint is an unpleasant customer with whom to deal. The great iron bar is still lying here in our sea; and not so long ago it shone with a red glow, which is probably a sign it is time for it to be taken away."

Said the Dragon-King: "But that is the rod which the Great Yu used when he ordered the waters, and determined the depth of the seas and rivers. It cannot be taken away."

The Dragon-Queen replied: "Just let him see it! What he then does with it is no concern of ours."

So the Dragon-King led Sun Wu Kung to the measuring rod. The golden radiance that came from it could be seen some distance off. It was an enormous iron bar, with golden clamps on either side.

Sun Wu Kung raised it with the exertion of all his strength, and then said: "It is too heavy, and ought to be somewhat shorter and thinner!"

No sooner had he said this than the iron rod grew less. He tried it again, and then he noticed that it grew larger or smaller at command. It could be made to shrink to the size of a pin. Sun Wu Kung was overjoyed and beat about in the sea with the rod, which he had let grow large again, till the waves spurted mountain-high and the dragon-castle rocked on its foundations. The Dragon-King trembled with fright, and all his tortoises, fishes and crabs drew in their heads.

Sun Wu Kung laughed, and said: "Many thanks for the handsome present!" Then he continued: "Now I have a weapon, it is true, but as yet I have no armor. Rather than hunt up two or three other households, I think you will be willing to provide me with a suit of mail."

The Dragon-King told him that he had no armor to give him.

Then the ape said: "I will not leave until you have obtained one for me." And once more he began to swing his rod.

"Do not harm me!" said the terrified Dragon-King, "I will ask my brothers."

And he had them beat the iron drum and strike the golden gong, and in a moment's time all the Dragon-King's brothers came from all the other seas. The Dragon-King talked to them in private and said: "This is a terrible fellow, and we must not rouse his anger! First he took the rod with the golden clamps from me, and now he also insists on having a suit of armor. The best thing to do would be to satisfy him at once, and complain of him to the Lord of the Heavens later."

So the brothers brought a magic suit of golden mail, magic boots and a magic helmet.

Then Sun Wu Kung thanked them and returned to his cave. Radiantly he greeted his children, who had come to meet him, and showed them the rod with the golden clamps. They all crowded up and wished to pick it up from the ground, if only a single time; but it was just as though a dragon-fly had attempted to overthrow a stone column, or an ant were trying to carry a great mountain. It would not move a hair's breadth. Then the apes opened their mouths and stuck out their tongues, and said: "Father, how is it possible for you to carry that heavy thing?" So he told them the secret of the rod and showed them its effects. Then he set his empire in order, and appointed the four baboons field-marshals; and the seven beast-spirits, the ox-spirit, the dragon-spirit, the bird-spirit, the lion-spirit and the rest also joined him.

One day he took a nap after dinner. Before he did so he had let the bar shrink, and had stuck it in his ear. While he was sleeping he saw two men come along in his dream, who had a card on which was written "Sun Wu Kung." They would not allow him to resist, but fettered him and led his spirit away. And when they reached a great city the Ape King gradually came to himself. Over the city gate he saw a tablet of iron on which was engraved in large letters: "The Nether World."

Then all was suddenly clear to him and he said: "Why, this must be the dwelling-place of Death! But I have long since escaped from his power, and how dare he have me dragged here!" The more he reflected the wilder he grew. He drew out the golden rod from his ear, swung it and let it grow large. Then he crushed the two constables to mush, burst his fetters, and rolled his bar before him into the city. The ten Princes of the Dead were frightened, bowed before him and asked: "Who are you?"

Sun Wu Kung answered: "If you do not know me then why did you send for me and have me dragged to this place? I am the heaven-born saint Sun Wu Kung of the Mountain of Flowers and Fruits. And now, who are you? Tell me your names quickly or I will strike you!"

The ten Princes of the Dead humbly gave him their names.

Sun Wu Kung said: "I, the Venerable Sun, have gained the power of eternal life! You have nothing to say to me! Quick, let me have the Book of Life!"

They did not dare defy him, and had the scribe bring in the Book. Sun Wu Kung opened it. Under the head of "Apes," No. 1350, he read: "Sun Wu Kung, the heaven-born stone ape. His years shall be three hundred and twenty-four. Then he shall die without illness."

Sun Wu Kung took the brush from the table and struck out the whole ape family from the Book of Life, threw the Book down and said: "Now we are even! From this day on I will suffer no impertinences from you!"

With that he cleared a way for himself out of the Nether World by means of his rod, and the ten Princes of the Dead did not venture to stay him, but only complained of him afterward to the Lord of the Heavens.

When Sun Wu Kung had left the city he slipped and fell to the ground. This caused him to wake, and he noticed he had been dreaming. He called his four baboons to him and said: "Splendid, splendid! I was dragged to Death's castle and I caused considerable uproar there. I had them give me the Book of Life, and I struck out the mortal hour of all the apes!" And after that time the apes on the Mountain no longer died, because their names had been stricken out in the Nether World.

But the Lord of the Heavens sat in his castle, and had all his servants assembled about him. And a saint stepped forward and presented the complaint of the Dragon-King of the Eastern Sea. And another stepped forward and presented the complaint of the ten Princes of the Dead. The Lord of the Heavens glanced through the two memorials. Both told of the wild, unmannerly conduct of Sun Wu Kung. So the Lord of the Heavens ordered a god to descend to earth and take him prisoner. The Evening Star came forward, however, and said: "This ape was born of the purest powers of heaven and earth and sun and moon. He has gained the hidden knowledge and has become an immortal. Recall, O Lord, your great love for all that which has life, and forgive him his sin! Issue an order that he be called up to the heavens, and be given a charge here, so that he may come to his senses. Then, if he again oversteps your commands, let him be punished without mercy." The Lord of the Heavens was agreeable, had the order issued, and told the Evening Star to take it to Sun Wu Kung. The Evening Star mounted a colored cloud and descended on the Mountain of Flowers and Fruits.

He greeted Sun Wu Kung and said to him: "The Lord had heard of your actions and meant to punish you. I am the Evening Star of the Western Skies, and I spoke for you. Therefore he has commissioned me to take you to the skies, so that you may be given a charge there."

Sun Wu Kung was overjoyed and answered: "I had just been thinking I ought to pay Heaven a visit some time, and sure enough, Old Star, here you have come to fetch me!"

Then he had his four baboons come and said to them impressively: "See that you take good care of our Mountain! I am going up to the heavens to look around there a little!"

Then he mounted a cloud together with the Evening Star and floated up. But he kept turning his somersaults, and advanced so quickly that the Evening Star on his cloud was left behind. Before he knew it he had reached the Southern Gate of Heaven and was about to step carelessly through. The gate-keeper did not wish to let him enter, but he did not let this stop him. In the midst of their dispute the Evening Star came up and explained matters, and then he was allowed to enter the heavenly gate. When he came to the castle of the Lord of the Heavens, he stood upright before it, without bowing his head.

The Lord of the Heavens asked: "Then this hairy face with the pointed lips is Sun Wu Kung?"

He replied: "Yes, I am the Venerable Sun!"

All the servants of the Lord of the Heavens were shocked and said: "This wild ape does not even bow, and goes so far as to call himself the Venerable Sun. His crime deserves a thousand deaths!"

But the Lord said: "He has come up from the earth below, and is not as yet used to our rules. We will forgive him."

Then he gave orders that a charge be found for him. The marshal of the heavenly court reported: "There is no charge vacant anywhere, but an official is needed in the heavenly stables." Thereupon the Lord made him stablemaster of the heavenly steeds. Then the servants of the Lord of the Heavens told him he should give thanks for the grace bestowed on him. Sun Wu Kung called out aloud: "Thanks to command!" took possession of his certificate of appointment, and went to the stables in order to enter upon his new office.

Sun Wu Kung attended to his duties with great zeal. The heavenly steeds grew sleek and fat, and the stables were filled with young foals. Before he knew it half a month had gone by. Then his heavenly friends prepared a banquet for him.

While they were at table Sun Wu Kung asked accidentally: "Stablemaster? What sort of a title is that?"

"Why, that is an official title," was the reply.

"What rank has this office?"

"It has no rank at all," was the answer.

"Ah," said the ape, "is it so high that it outranks all other dignities?"

"No, it is not high, it is not high at all," answered his friends. "It is not even set down in the official roster, but is quite a subordinate position. All you have to do is to attend to the steeds. If you see to it that they grow fat, you get a good mark; but if they grow thin or ill, or fall down, your punishment will be right at hand."

Then the Ape King grew angry: "What, they treat me, the Venerable Sun, in such a shameful way!" and he started up. "On my Mountain I was a king, I was a father! What need was there for him to lure me into his heaven to feed horses? I'll do it no longer! I'll do it no longer!"

Hola, and he had already overturned the table, drawn the rod with the golden clamps from his ear, let it grow large and beat a way out for himself to the Southern gate of Heaven. And no one dared stop him.

Already he was back in his island Mountain and his people surrounded him and said: "You have been gone for more than ten years, great king! How is it you do not return to us until now?"

The Ape King said: "I did not spend more than about ten days in Heaven. This Lord of the Heavens does not know how to treat his people. He made me his stablemaster, and I had to feed his horses. I am so ashamed that I am ready to die. But I did not put up with it, and now I am here once more!"

His apes eagerly prepared a banquet to comfort him. While they sat at table two horned devil-kings came and brought him a yellow imperial robe as a present. Filled with joy he slipped into it, and appointed the two devil-kings leaders of the vanguard. They thanked him and began to flatter him: "With your power and wisdom, great king, why should you have to serve the Lord of the Heavens? To call you the Great Saint who is Heaven's Equal would be quite in order."

The ape was pleased with this speech and said: "Good, good!" Then he ordered his four baboons to have a flag made quickly, on which was to be inscribed: "The Great Saint Who Is Heaven's Equal." And from that time on he had himself called by that title.

When the Lord of the Heavens learned of the flight of the ape, he ordered Li Dsing, the pagoda-bearing god, and his third son, Notscha, to take the Ape King prisoner. They sallied forth at the head of a heavenly warrior host, laid out a camp before his cave, and sent a brave warrior to challenge him to single combat. But he was easily beaten by Sun Wu Kung and obliged to flee, and Sun Wu Kung even shouted after him, laughing: "What a bag of wind! And he calls himself a heavenly warrior! I'll not slay you. Run along quickly and send me a better man!"

When Notscha saw this he himself hurried up to do battle.

Said Sun Wu Kung to him: "To whom do you belong, little one? You must not play around here, for something might happen to you!"

But Notscha cried out in a loud voice: "Accursed ape! I am Prince Notscha, and have been ordered to take you prisoner!" And with that he swung his sword in the direction of Sun Wu Kung.

"Very well," said the latter, "I will stand here and never move."

Then Notscha grew very angry, and turned into a three-headed god with six arms, in which he held six different weapons. Thus he rushed on to the attack.

Sun Wu Kung laughed. "The little fellow knows the trick of it! But easy, wait a bit! I will change shape, too!"

And he also turned himself into a figure with three heads and with six arms, and swung three gold-clamp rods. And thus they began to fight. Their blows rained down with such rapidity that it seemed as though thousands of weapons were flying through the air. After thirty rounds the combat had not yet been decided. Then Sun Wu Kung hit upon an idea. He secretly pulled out one of his hairs, turned it into his own shape, and let it continue the fight with Notscha. He himself, however, slipped behind Notscha, and gave him such a blow on the left arm with his rod that his knees gave way beneath him with pain, and he had to withdraw in defeat.

So Notscha told his father Li Dsing: "This devil-ape is altogether too powerful! I cannot get the better of him!" There was nothing left to do but to return to the

Heavens and admit their overthrow. The Lord of the Heavens bowed his head, and tried to think of some other hero whom he might send out.

Then the Evening Star once more came forward and said: "This ape is so strong and so courageous, that probably not one of us here is a match for him. He revolted because the office of stablemaster appeared too lowly for him. The best thing would be to temper justice with mercy, let him have his way, and appoint him Great Saint Who Is Heaven's Equal. It will only be necessary to give him the empty title, without combining a charge with it, and then the matter would be settled." The Lord of the Heavens was satisfied with this suggestion, and once more sent the Evening Star to summon the new saint. When Sun Wu Kung heard that he had arrived, he said: "The old Evening Star is a good fellow!" and he had his army draw up in line to give him a festive reception. He himself donned his robes of ceremony and politely went out to meet him.

Then the Evening Star told him what had taken place in the Heavens, and that he had his appointment as Great Saint Who Is Heaven's Equal with him.

Thereupon the Great Saint laughed and said: "You also spoke in my behalf before, Old Star! And now you have again taken my part. Many thanks! Many thanks!"

Then when they appeared together in the presence of the Lord of the Heavens the latter said: "The rank of Great Saint Who Is Heaven's Equal is very high. But now you must not cut any further capers."

The Great Saint expressed his thanks, and the Lord of the Heavens ordered two skilled architects to build a castle for him East of the peach-garden of the Queen-Mother of the West. And he was led into it with all possible honors.

Now the Saint was in his element. He had all that heart could wish for, and was untroubled by any work. He took his ease, walked about in the Heavens as he chose, and paid visits to the gods. The Three Pure Ones and the Four Rulers he treated with some little respect; but the planetary gods and the lords of the twenty-eight houses of the moon, and of the twelve zodiac signs, and the other stars he addressed familiarly with a "Hey, you!" Thus he idled day by day, without occupation among the clouds of the Heavens. On one occasion one of the wise said to the Lord of the Heavens: "The holy Sun is idle while day follows day. It is to be feared that some mischievous thoughts may occur to him, and it might be better to give him some charge."

So the Lord of the Heavens summoned the Great Saint and said to him: "The life-giving peaches in the garden of the Queen-Mother will soon be ripe. I give you the charge of watching over them. Do your duty conscientiously!"

This pleased the Saint and he expressed his thanks. Then he went to the garden, where the caretakers and gardeners received him on their knees.

He asked them: "How many trees in all are there in the garden?"

"Three thousand six hundred," replied the gardener. "There are twelve-hundred trees in the foremost row. They have red blossoms and bear small fruit, which ripens every three thousand years. Whoever eats it grows bright and healthy. The twelve hundred trees in the middle row have double blossoms and bear sweet fruit, which ripens every six thousand years. Whoever eats of it is able to float in the rose-dawn without aging. The twelve hundred trees in the last row bear red-striped fruit with small pits. They ripen every nine thousand years. Whoever eats their fruit lives eternally, as long as the Heavens themselves, and remains untouched for thousands of eons."

The Saint heard all this with pleasure. He checked up the lists and from that time on appeared every day or so to see to things. The greater part of the peaches in the last row were already ripe. When he came to the garden, he would on each occasion send away the caretakers and gardeners under some pretext, leap up into the trees, and gorge himself to his heart's content with the peaches.

At that time the Queen-Mother of the West was preparing the great peach banquet to which she was accustomed to invite all the gods of the Heavens. She sent out the fairies in their garments of seven colors with baskets, that they might pick the peaches. The caretaker said to them: "The garden has now been entrusted to the guardianship of the Great Saint Who is Heaven's Equal, so you will first have to announce yourselves to him." With that he led the seven fairies into the garden. There they looked everywhere for the Great Saint, but could not find him. So the fairies said: "We have our orders and must not be late. We will begin picking the peaches in the meantime!" So they picked several baskets full from the foremost row. In the second row the peaches were already scarcer. And in the last row there hung only a single half-ripe peach. They bent down the bough and picked it, and then allowed it to fly up again.

Now it happened that the Great Saint, who had turned himself into a peach-worm, had just been taking his noon-day nap on this bough. When he was so rudely awakened, he appeared in his true form, seized his rod and was about to strike the fairies.

But the fairies said: "We have been sent here by the Queen-Mother. Do not be angry, Great Saint!"

Said the Great Saint: "And who are all those whom the Queen-Mother has invited?"

They answered: "All the gods and saints in the Heavens, on the earth and under the earth."

"Has she also invited me?" said the Saint.

"Not that we know of," said the fairies.

Then the Saint grew angry, murmured a magic incantation and said: "Stay! Stay! Stay!"

With that the seven fairies were banned to the spot. The Saint then took a cloud and sailed away on it to the palace of the Queen-Mother.

On the way he met the Bare-Foot God and asked him: "Where are you going?"

"To the peach banquet," was the answer.

Then the Saint lied to him, saying: "I have been commanded by the Lord of the Heavens to tell all the gods and saints that they are first to come to the Hall of Purity, in order to practice the rites, and then go together to the Queen-Mother."

Then the Great Saint changed himself into the semblance of the Bare-Foot God and sailed to the palace of the Queen-Mother. There he let his cloud sink down and entered quite unconcerned. The meal was ready, yet none of the gods had as yet appeared. Suddenly the Great Saint caught the aroma of wine, and saw well-nigh a hundred barrels of the precious nectar standing in a room to one side. His mouth watered. He tore a few hairs out and turned them into sleep-worms. These worms crept into the nostrils of the cup-bearers so that they all fell asleep. Thereupon he enjoyed the delicious viands to the full, opened the barrels and drank until he was nearly stupefied. Then he said to himself: "This whole affair is beginning to make me feel creepy. I had better go home first of all and sleep a bit." And he stumbled out of the garden with uncertain steps. Sure enough, he missed his way, and came to the dwelling of Laotzse. There he regained consciousness. He arranged his clothing and went in. There was no one to be seen in the place, for at the moment Laotzse was at the God of Light's abode, talking to him, and with him were all his servants, listening. Since he found no one at home the Great Saint went as far as the inner chamber, where Laotzse was in the habit of brewing the elixir of life. Beside the stove stood five gourd containers full of the pills of life which had already been rolled. Said the Great Saint: "I had long since intended to prepare a couple of these pills. So it suits me very well to find them here." He poured out the contents of the gourds, and ate up all the pills of life. Since he had now had enough to eat and drink he thought to himself: "Bad, bad! The mischief I have done cannot well be repaired. If they catch me my life will be in danger. I think I had better go down to earth again and remain a king!" With that he made himself invisible, went out at the Western Gate of Heaven, and returned to the Mountain of Flowers and Fruits, where he told his people who received him the story of his adventures.

When he spoke of the wine-nectar of the peach garden, his apes said: "Can't you go back once more and steal a few bottles of the wine, so that we too may taste of it and gain eternal life?"

The Ape King was willing, turned a somersault, crept into the garden unobserved, and picked up four more barrels. Two of them he took under his arms and two he held in his hands. Then he disappeared with them without leaving a trace and brought them to his cave, where he enjoyed them together with his apes.

In the meantime the seven fairies, whom the Great Saint had banned to the spot, had regained their freedom after a night and a day. They picked up their baskets and told the Queen-Mother what had happened to them. And the cup-bearers, too, came hurrying up and reported the destruction which some one unknown had caused among the eatables and drinkables. The Queen-Mother went to the Lord of the Heavens to complain. Shortly afterward Laotzse also came to him to tell about the theft of the pills of life. And the Bare-Foot God came along and reported that he had been deceived by the Great Saint Who Is Heaven's Equal; and from the Great Saint's palace the servants came running and said that the Saint had disappeared and was nowhere to be found. Then the Lord of the Heavens was frightened, and said: "This whole mess is undoubtedly the work of that devilish ape!"

Now the whole host of Heaven, together with all the star-gods, the time-gods and the mountain-gods was called out in order to catch the ape. Li Dsing once more was its commander-in-chief. He invested the entire Mountain, and spread out the sky-net and the earth-net, so that no one could escape. Then he sent his bravest heroes into battle. Courageously the ape withstood all attacks from early morn till sundown. But by that time his most faithful followers had been captured. That was too much for him. He pulled out a hair and turned it into thousands of Ape-Kings, who all hewed about them with golden-clamped iron rods. The heavenly host was vanquished, and the ape withdrew to his cave to rest.

Now it happened that Guan Yin had also gone to the peach banquet in the garden, and had found out what Sun Wu Kung had done. When she went to visit the Lord of the Heavens, Li Dsing was just coming in, to report the great defeat which he had suffered on the Mountain of Flowers and Fruits. Then Guan Yin said to the Lord of the Heavens: "I can recommend a hero to you who will surely get the better of the ape. It is your grandson Yang Oerlang. He has conquered all the beast and bird spirits, and overthrown the elves in the grass and the brush. He knows what has to be done to get the better of such devils."

So Yang Oerlang was brought in, and Li Dsing led him to his camp. Li Dsing asked Yang Oerlang how he would go about getting the better of the ape.

Yang Oerlang laughed and said: "I think I will have to go him one better when it comes to changing shapes. It would be best for you to take away the sky-net so that our combat is not disturbed." Then he requested Li Dsing to post himself in the upper air with the magic spirit mirror in his hand, so that when the ape made himself invisible, he might be found again by means of the mirror. When all this had been arranged, Yang Oerlang went out in front of the cave with his spirits to give battle.

The ape leaped out, and when he saw the powerful hero with the three-tined sword standing before him he asked: "And who may you be?"

The other said: "I am Yang Oerlang, the grandson of the Lord of the Heavens!"

Then the ape laughed and said: "Oh yes, I remember! His daughter ran away with a certain Sir Yang, to whom heaven gave a son. You must be that son!"

Yang Oerlang grew furious, and advanced upon him with his spear. Then a hot battle began. For three hundred rounds they fought without decisive results. Then Yang Oerlang turned himself into a giant with a black face and red hair.

"Not bad," said the ape, "but I can do that too!"

So they continued to fight in that form. But the ape's baboons were much frightened. The beast and planet spirits of Yang Oerlang pressed the apes hard. They slew most of them and the others hid away. When the ape saw this his heart grew uneasy. He drew the magic giant-likeness in again, took his rod and fled. But Yang Oerlang followed hard on his heels. In his urgent need the ape thrust the rod, which he had turned into a needle, into his ear, turned into a sparrow, and flew up into the crest of a tree. Yang Oerlang who was following in his tracks, suddenly lost sight of him. But his keen eyes soon recognized that he had turned himself into a sparrow. So he flung away spear and crossbow, turned himself into a sparrow-hawk, and darted down on the sparrow. But the latter soared high into the air as a cormorant. Yang Oerlang shook his plumage, turned into a great sea-crane, and shot up into the clouds to seize the cormorant. The latter dropped, flew into a valley and dove beneath the waters of a brook in the guise of a fish. When Yang Oerlang reached the edge of the valley, and had lost his trail he said to himself: "This ape has surely turned himself into a fish or a crab! I will change my form as well in order to catch him." So he turned into a fish-hawk and floated above the surface of the water. When the ape in the water caught sight of the fish-hawk, he saw that he was Yang Oerlang. He swiftly swung around and fled, Yang Oerlang in pursuit. When the latter was no further away than the length of a beak, the ape turned, crept ashore as a water-snake and hid in the grass. Yang Oerlang, when he saw the water-snake creep from the water, turned into an eagle and spread his claws to seize the snake. But the water-snake sprang up and turned into the lowest of all birds, a speckled buzzard, and perched on the steep edge of a cliff. When Yang Oerlang saw that the ape had turned himself into so contemptible a creature as a buzzard, he would no longer play the game of changing form with him. He reappeared in his original form, took up his crossbow and shot at the bird. The buzzard slipped and fell down the side of the cliff. At its foot the ape turned himself into the chapel of a field-god. He opened his mouth for a gate, his teeth became the two wings of the door, his tongue the image of the god, and his eyes the windows. His tail was the only thing he did not know what to do with. So he let it stand up stiffly behind him in the shape of a flagpole. When Yang Oerlang reached the foot of the hill he saw the chapel, whose flagpole stood in the rear. Then he laughed and said: "That ape is really a devil of an ape! He wants to lure me into the chapel in order to bite me. But I will not go in. First I will break his windows for him, and then I will stamp down the wings of his door!" When the ape heard this he was much frightened. He made a bound like a tiger, and disappeared without a trace in the air. With a single somersault he reached Yang Oerlang's own temple. There he assumed Yang Oerlang's own form and stepped in. The spirits who were on guard were unable to recognize him. They received him on their knees. So the ape then seated himself on the god's throne, and had the prayers which had come in submitted to him.

When Yang Oerlang no longer saw the ape, he rose in the air to Li Dsing and said: "I was vying with the ape in changing shape. Suddenly I could no longer find him. Take a look in the mirror!" Li Dsing took a look in the magic spirit mirror and then he laughed and said: "The ape has turned himself into your likeness, is sitting in your temple quite at home there, and making mischief." When Yang Oerlang heard this he took his three-tined spear, and hastened to his temple. The door-spirits were frightened and said: "But father came in only this very minute! How is it that another one comes now?" Yang Oerlang, without paying attention to them, entered the temple and aimed his spear at Sun Wu Kung. The latter resumed his own shape, laughed and said: "Young sir, you must not be angry! The god of this place is now Sun Wu Kung." Without uttering a word Yang Oerlang assailed him. Sun Wu Kung took up his rod and returned the blows. Thus they crowded out of the temple together, fighting, and wrapped in mists and clouds once more gained the Mountain of Flowers and Fruits.

In the meantime Guan Yin was sitting with Laotzse, the Lord of the Heavens and the Queen-Mother in the great hall of Heaven, waiting for news. When none came she said: "I will go with Laotzse to the Southern Gate of Heaven and see how matters stand." And when they saw that the struggle had still not come to an end she said to Laotzse: "How would it be if we helped Yang Oerlang a little? I will shut up Sun Wu Kung in my vase."

But Laotzse said: "Your vase is made of porcelain. Sun Wu Kung could smash it with his iron rod. But I have a circlet of diamonds which can enclose all living creatures. That we can use!" So he flung his circlet through the air from the heavenly gate, and struck Sun Wu Kung on the head with it. Since he had his hands full fighting, the latter could not guard himself against it, and the blow on the forehead caused him to slip. Yet he rose again and tried to escape. But the heavenly hound of Yang Oerlang bit his leg until he fell to the ground. Then Yang Oerlang and his followers came up and tied him with thongs, and thrust a hook through his collar-bone so that he could no longer transform himself. And Laotzse took possession of his diamond circlet again, and returned with Guan Yin to the hall of Heaven. Sun Wu Kung was now brought in in triumph, and was condemned to be beheaded. He was then taken to the place of execution and bound to a post. But all efforts to kill him by means of ax and sword, thunder and lightning were vain. Nothing so much as hurt a hair on his head.

Said Laotzse: "It is not surprising. This ape has eaten the peaches, has drunk the nectar and also swallowed the pills of life. Nothing can harm him. The best thing would be for me to take him along and thrust him into my stove in order to melt the elixir of life out of him again. Then he will fall into dust and ashes."

So Sun Wu Kung's fetters were loosed, and Laotzse took him with him, thrust him into his oven, and ordered the boy to keep up a hot fire.

But along the edge of the oven were graven the signs of the eight elemental forces. And when the ape was thrust into the oven he took refuge beneath the sign of the wind, so that the fire could not injure him; and the smoke only made his eyes smart. He remained in the oven seven times seven days. Then Laotzse had it opened to take a look. As soon as Sun Wu Kung saw the light shine in, he could no longer bear to be shut up, but leaped out and upset the magic oven. The guards and attendants he threw to the ground and Laotzse himself, who tried to seize him, received such a push that he stuck his legs up in the air like an onion turned upside down. Then Sun Wu Kung took his rod out of his ear, and without looking where he struck, hewed everything to bits, so that the star-gods closed their doors and the guardians of the Heavens ran away. He came to the castle of the Lord of the Heavens, and the guardian of the gate with his steel whip was only just in time to hold him back. Then the thirty-six thunder gods were set at him, and surrounded him, though they could not seize him.

The Lord of the Heavens said: "Buddha will know what is to be done. Send for him quickly!"

So Buddha came up out of the West with Ananada and Kashiapa, his disciples. When he saw the turmoil he said: "First of all, let weapons be laid aside and lead out the Saint. I wish to speak with him!" The gods withdrew. Sun Wu Kung snorted and said: "Who are you, who dare to speak to me?" Buddha smiled and replied: "I have come out of the blessed West, Shakiamuni Amitofu. I have heard of the revolt you have raised, and am come to tame you!"

Said Sun Wu Kung: "I am the stone ape who has gained the hidden knowledge. I am master of seventy-two transformations, and will live as long as Heaven itself. What has the Lord of the Heavens accomplished that entitles him to remain eternally on his throne? Let him make way for me, and I will be satisfied!"

Buddha replied with a smile: "You are a beast which has gained magic powers. How can you expect to rule here as Lord of the Heavens? Be it known to you that the Lord of the Heavens has toiled for eons in perfecting his virtues. How many years would you have to pass before you could attain the dignity he has gained? And then I must ask you whether there is anything else you can do, aside from playing your tricks of transformation?"

Said Sun Wu Kung: "I can turn cloud somersaults. Each one carries me eighteen thousand miles ahead. Surely that is enough to entitle me to be the Lord of the Heavens?"

Buddha answered with a smile: "Let us make a wager. If you can so much as leave my hand with one of your somersaults, then I will beg the Lord of the Heavens to make way for you. But if you are not able to leave my hand, then you must yield yourself to my fetters."

Sun Wu Kung suppressed his laughter, for he thought: "This Buddha is a crazy fellow! His hand is not a foot long; how could I help but leap out of it?" So he opened his mouth wide and said: "Agreed!"

Buddha then stretched out his right hand. It resembled a small lotus-leaf. Sun Wu Kung leaped up into it with one bound. Then he said: "Go!" And with that he turned one somersault after another, so that he flew along like a whirlwind. And while he was flying along he saw five tall, reddish columns towering to the skies. Then he thought: "That is the end of the world! Now I will turn back and become Lord of the Heavens. But first I will write down my name to prove that I was there." He pulled out a hair, turned it into a brush, and wrote with great letters on the middle column: "The Great Saint Who Is Heaven's Equal." Then he turned his somersaults again until he had reached the place whence he had come. He leaped down from the Buddha's hand laughing and cried: "Now hurry, and see to it that the Lord of the Heavens clears his heavenly castle for me! I have been at the end of the world and have left a sign there!"

Buddha scolded: "Infamous ape! How dare you claim that you have left my hand? Take a look and see whether or not 'The Great Saint Who Is Heaven's Equal' is written on my middle finger!"

Sun Wu Kung was terribly frightened, for at the first glance he saw that this was the truth. Yet outwardly he pretended that he was not convinced, said he would take another look, and tried to make use of the opportunity to escape. But Buddha covered him with his hand, shoved him out of the gate of Heaven, and formed a mountain of water, fire, wood, earth and metal, which he softly set down on him to hold him fast. A magic incantation pasted on the mountain prevented his escape.

Here he was obliged to lie for hundreds of years, until he finally reformed and was released, in order to help the Monk of the Yangtze-kiang fetch the holy writings from out of the West. He honored the Monk as his master, and thenceforward was known as the Wanderer. Guan Yin, who had released him, gave the Monk a golden circlet. Sun Wu Kung was induced to put it on, and it at once grew into his flesh so that he could not remove it. And Guan Yin gave the Monk a magic formula by means of which the ring could be tightened, should the ape grow disobedient. But from that time on he was always polite and well-mannered.

Chinese Fables

How the Moon Became Beautiful

The Moon is very beautiful with his round, bright face which shines with soft and gentle light on all the world of man. But once there was a time when he was not so beautiful as he is now. Six thousand years ago the face of the Moon became changed in a single night. Before that time his face had been so dark and gloomy that no one liked to look at him, and for this reason he was always very sad.

One day he complained to the flowers and to the stars—for they were the only things that would ever look in his face.

He said, "I do not like to be the Moon. I wish I were a star or a flower. If I were a star, even the smallest one, some great general would care for me; but alas! I am only the Moon and no one likes me. If I could only be a flower and grow in a garden where the beautiful earth women come, they would place me in their hair and praise my fragrance and beauty. Or, if I could even grow in the wilderness where no one could see, the birds would surely come and sing sweet songs for me. But I am only the Moon and no one honors me."

The stars answered and said, "We can not help you. We were born here and we can not leave our places. We never had any one to help us. We do our duty, we work all the day and twinkle in the dark night to make the skies more beautiful.—But that is all we can do," they added, as they smiled coldly at the sorrowful Moon.

Then the flowers smiled sweetly and said, "We do not know how we can help you. We live always in one place—in a garden near the most beautiful maiden in all the world. As she is kind to every one in trouble we will tell her about you. We love her very much and she loves us. Her name is Tseh-N'io."

Still the Moon was sad. So one evening he went to see the beautiful maiden Tseh-N'io. And when he saw her he loved her at once. He said, "Your face is very beautiful. I wish that you would come to me, and that my face would be as your face. Your motions are gentle and full of grace. Come with me and we will be as one—and perfect. I know that even the worst people in all the world would have only to look at you and they would love you. Tell me, how did you come to be o beautiful?"

"I have always lived with those who were gentle and happy, and I believe that is the cause of beauty and goodness," answered Tseh-N'io.

And so the Moon went every night to see the maiden. He knocked on her window, and she came. And when he saw how gentle and beautiful she was, his love grew stronger, and he wished more and more to be with her always.

One day Tseh-N'io said to her mother, "I should like to go to the Moon and live always with him. Will you allow me to go?"

Her mother thought so little of the question that she made no reply, and Tseh-N'io told her friends that she was going to be the Moon's bride.

In a few days she was gone. Her mother searched everywhere but could not find her. And one of Tseh-N'io's friends said,—"She has gone with the Moon, for he asked her many times."

A year and a year passed by and Tseh-N'io, the gentle and beautiful earth maiden, did not return. Then the people said, "She has gone forever. She is with the Moon."

The face of the Moon is very beautiful now. It is happy and bright and gives a soft, gentle light to all the world. And there are those who say that the Moon is now like Tseh-N'io, who was once the most beautiful of all earth maidens.

The Animals' Peace Party

THE ANCIENT BOOKS SAY THAT THE PIG IS A VERY UNCLEAN ANIMAL AND OF NO GREAT use to the world or man, and one of them contains this story:

Once upon a time the horses and cattle gave a party. Although the pigs were very greedy, the horses said, "Let us invite them, and it may be we can settle our quarrels in this way and become better friends. We will call this a Peace Party.

"Generations and generations of pigs have broken through our fence, taken our food, drunk our water, and rooted up our clean green grass; but it is also true that the cattle children have hurt many young pigs.

"All this trouble and fighting is not right, and we know the Master wishes we should live at peace with one another. Do you not think it a good plan to give a Peace Party and settle this trouble?"

The cattle said, "Who will be the leader of our party and do the inviting? We should have a leader, both gentle and kind, to go to the pigs' home and invite them."

The next day a small and very gentle cow was sent to invite the pigs. As she went across to the pigs' yard, all the young ones jumped up and grunted, "What are you coming here for? Do you want to fight?"

"No, I do not want to fight," said the cow. "I was sent here to invite you to our party. I should like to know if you will come, so that I may tell our leader."

The young pigs and the old ones talked together and the old ones said, "The New Year feast will soon be here. Maybe they will have some good things for us to eat at the party. I think we should go."

Then the old pigs found the best talker in all the family, and sent word by him that they would attend the party.

The day came, and the pigs all went to the party. There were about three hundred all together.

When they arrived they saw that the leader of the cows was the most beautiful of all the herd and very kind and gentle to her guests.

After a while the leader spoke to them in a gentle voice and said to the oldest pig, "We think it would be a good and pleasant thing if there were no more quarrels in this pasture.

"Will you tell your people not to break down the fences and spoil the place and eat our food? We will then agree that the oxen and horses shall not hurt your children and all the old troubles shall be forgotten from this day."

Then one young pig stood up to talk. "All this big pasture belongs to the Master, and not to you," he said. "We can not go to other places for food.

"The Master sends a servant to feed us, and sometimes he sends us to your yard to eat the corn and potatoes.

"The servants clean our pen every day. When summer comes, they fill the ponds with fresh water for us to bathe in.

"Now, friends, can you not see that this place and this food all belongs to the Master? We eat the food and go wherever we like. We take your food only after you have finished. It would spoil on the ground if we did not do this.

"Answer this question—Do our people ever hurt your people? No; even though every year some of our children are killed by bad oxen and cows.

"What is your food? It is nothing; but our lives are worth much to us.

"Our Master never sends our people to work as he does the horses and oxen. He sends us food and allows us to play a year and a year the same, because he likes us best.

"You see the horses and oxen are always at work. Some pull wagons, others plow land for rice; and they must work—sick or well.

"Our people never work. Every day at happy time we play; and do you see how fat we are?

"You never see our bones. Look at the old horses and the old oxen. Twenty years' work and no rest!

"I tell you the Master does not honor the horses and oxen as he does the pigs.

"Friends, that is all I have to say. Have you any questions to ask? Is what I have said not the truth?"

The old cow said, "Moo, Moo," and shook her head sadly. The tired old horses groaned, "Huh, Huh," and never spoke a word.

The leader said, "My friends, it is best not to worry about things we can not know. We do not seem to understand our Master.

"It will soon be time for the New Year feast day; so, good night. And may the pig people live in the world as long and happily as the horses and the oxen, although our Peace Party did not succeed."

On their way home the little pigs made a big noise, and every one said, "We, we! We win, we win!"

Then the old horses and oxen talked among them- selves. "We are stronger, wiser, and more useful than the pigs," they said. "Why docs the Master treat us so?"

The Widow and Her Son

A widow had two sons, Yao-Pao, a lad yet in school, and Yao-Moi who tilled the soil. Yao-Moi, the elder, was a good man; he had worked hard for thirty years, but he had not gained riches. He sent Yao-Pao to school and served his mother well.

One year there were great rains. The grain all died in the ground and the people of that country had nothing to eat. Yao-Moi had debts which he could not pay, and when his harvest failed he became poorer than ever before.

Then there came a great famine and twenty thousand people died in that land. Yao-Moi killed his oxen to keep his mother and brother from starving. Last of all he killed the horses and mules, for it was yet six months before the time of harvest. Each time when he would kill for meat, the neighbors would come and beg food, and because he was sorry for them, he could not refuse.

One widow came many times until she was ashamed to beg longer from the little that he had. Finally she brought a girl child to him and said, "We are again starving. I will give you this girl for some meat. She is strong and can serve your mother." But Yao-Moi said, "No, I will give you the meat. I can not take your girl from you."

So he gave her meat once more, and she took the meat home to her son. But when it was gone and they were weak and fierce again with the death hunger, the widow said, "We shall all die, unless one dies to save the others. My son can not longer walk.

I will kill the girl child and save his life. He can then eat." Her son said, "No, do not kill the girl, trade her to Yao-Moi for meat." And the mother said, "Yao-Moi will soon starve, too, and then he will kill her. It is better that I do it"; and she took the big sharp knife to make it sharper.

She laid the girl child down on a bench and prepared to kill; but Yao-Moi passed by the house just then, and hearing the moans and screams he stopped to ask the reason. And the widow said, "We are starving. We will have a funeral to-day. We will now kill and eat each other that the last one may live until the time of the harvest." But Yao-Moi said, "Oh, no, do not kill the girl, I will take her home with me, and you can have meat in exchange for her"; and he took her to his home and gave the widow many pounds of meat for herself and her dying son.

Four months passed by. Yao-Moi had nothing in his own house to eat, and they were all starving—Yao-Moi, his mother, his little brother, and the girl.

When the death hunger came, and the mother saw that her sons must die, she said, "I will kill the girl." But Yao-Moi said, "No, I think we shall not die. Let us sleep to-night and see. I think something surely will come. Better kill me than the girl child."

So they went to bed that night. It was winter and the house was cold and dark. There was no wood, no light, no food; and they were starving.

Now, as the house grew more cold and dark, there came to them the quiet of a great despair and they all slept.

And Yao-Moi had a dream, and he saw an old man in flowing white garments, with a belt of gold around his waist. His hair was long and white, and his face was gentle and kind. And he called, "Yao-Moi! Yao-Moi! Yao-Moi! Hearken unto my words. Do you know how many people are dead in this land?"

Yao-Moi answered, "No, but I do know they are many, for only three among a hundred of all that were are now left."

And the old man said, "In every house but yours some have died, but those of your household are all alive: you have also saved the girl child. I know you are a good man. You have plowed the soil for thirty years, and have never complained about the heaven or the earth. The thunder and waters come, the winds blow and the earth quakes, and still you are patient and kind. You are good to your mother. You support your brother, send him to school, and are as a father to him. You have a kind heart for your neighbors' troubles. You live a good life and, because of this, you shall not starve. To-morrow morning you must arise early and go to the East Mountain by the wilderness. There you will find many meats and nuts and seeds. Bring them home to your family. I am a spirit sent from the Greatest One to earth."

After saying these things the man went out and Yao-Moi arose with great joy and told his family. Then he went to the East Mountain by the wilderness, where he found corn and peanuts and the meat of two hundred foxes already prepared to eat.

And he was very glad, and brought home much food and saved many lives.

The Evergreen Tree and the Wilderness Marigold

When the springtime comes in China, the marigold (long-life flower) grows everywhere—on the mountains, in the fields, and by the river side.

The marigold is very proud of its great family which is so numerous that the earth seems hardly large enough for it.

Once there was a marigold family that lived beneath an evergreen tree. They grew together all summer long, side by side, arms interwoven with arms, and leaves mingling with leaves.

Every year the tree grew larger, until at last no more sunshine or rain could come through its thick leaves and branches.

One day the marigold said to the evergreen tree, "Whom does this mountain belong to? You are only one, while our family grow in thousands everywhere. We have beautiful flowers from the summer time until the autumn comes. These flowers bear seeds that live through the winter, and in the spring another generation appears. In the summer time people come many miles to this mountain to see us.

"These people take our flowers home. Some of us they put in baskets and call basket flowers. Some they put in the maidens' hair and they call us maiden flowers. School boys like us on their tables and the pupils say we are their flowers. Old people gather us for their birthdays and we are called long-life flowers, and when maidens are married, our flowers are placed in a dish and they worship the Flower God, and call us the pure flower.

"So you see how pretty the names are that have been given us and how many people need us for their happiness.

"We must bring more and more flowers into the world, for there are not enough even yet.

"But we that live under your shade are not happy. You take away the sun so that he never shines on us, and when the rain comes, not a drop can reach our throats. The breeze comes, but never into our house—no fresh air, no sunshine, no rain, until we fear that we shall die.

"For eighty years our family has lived here. Our children sometimes say, 'We hope that next year we may have sunshine,' or 'We hope that we may soon have rain to drink.' Still no sunshine and no rain can reach us.

"You have destroyed many of our people. When will you allow us to have sun, rain, and air? Do you not know that you are killing us?"

Then the evergreen tree said, "My dear friend, I can not prevent this. Your people are more easily moved than I am. We are three brothers who have lived here hundreds of years and we are here forever. If our great bodies were moved we should die. It is you who should go away from here. Your seeds are light and it would be easy for them to go.

"When summer comes the children need us here. When the sun is hot the boys and girls sit under our shade, and even though we may kill some of your family, yet must we serve mankind. Do you not know that the children hang swings, and that women hang their babies' beds in our arms? The children also play ride-the-horse, and climb up in our arms, and have many games in our shade.

"Although we serve them and make them happy, yet they are not always kind to us, for sometimes they cut our bark. Students write words in my body with a sharp knife, but I can not prevent it. I have cried many years about this one thing and I would like to go away from here—but how can I move?

"I do not wish to hurt you, dear friend, any more than I wish to be hurt by others; but I am a mountain evergreen and must stand here forever. I hope you will be able to go, for we do not want to quarrel."

The marigold bowed her head and made no reply. And a deep silence came over the evergreen tree as he grew and grew, a year and a hundred years, and many, many more.

The Snail and the Bees

One day the king of the bees with his followers passed by the snail's door with a great noise. The mother snail said, "I have sixteen babies asleep on a leaf, and they must sleep fifteen days before they can walk. You will surely wake them. You are the noisiest creatures that pass my door. How can my children sleep? Yesterday your family and a crowd of your silly followers were here and made a great noise, and now to-day you come again. If I lose one baby because of all this, I will go to your house and destroy it. Then you will have no place to live. Do you know that this tree belongs to me? My master planted it twenty years ago, that I and my children might feed on its fruit. Every year your people come here when my tree has flowers upon it and take the honey away from them; and you not only rob me, but while you are doing it, you make loud and foolish noises. If you do not go away, I will call my master and my people."

The king bee answered, "You have no master in the world. You came from the dirt. Your ancestors all died in the wilderness and nobody even cared, because you are of no use to the world. Our name is Fon (Bee). People like us and they grow fat from our honey, which is better than medicine. My people live in all parts of the world. All mankind likes us and feeds us flowers. Do you think you are better than man?

"One day a bad boy tried to spoil our house, but his mother said, 'You spoil many things, but you shall not trouble the bees. They work hard every day and make honey for us. If you kill one bee-mother, her children will all leave us and in winter we shall have no honey for our bread.' And the boy obeyed. He might catch birds and goldfish, destroy flowers, do anything he wished, but he could not trouble us, because we are so useful. But you, slow creeper, are not good for anything."

Then the snail was angry and went to her house and said to her family, "The bees are our enemies. In fifteen days, five of you must go to their house and destroy it."

So they went. But when they reached the bee's house, they found no one there; and they said, "We are glad, for we can eat their honey." And they ate honey until sunset. Then the bee king and all his people in great numbers came with joyous singing, drumming, and dancing to their home.

When the bee king saw the five snails in his house he said, "Friends, this is not your home nor your food. Why do you come here and eat all our honey? But it is late, and you are welcome to stay overnight with us, if you do not hurt our children."

The big snail only laughed and answered, "This is very good honey. I have moved my family here. We will stay not only one night or two nights, but forever, and we will eat your honey for our food as long as it lasts."

The bee king said, "I will allow you to stay only one night here. You can not live in my house. You do no good thing to help. I am afraid even to let you stay one night. My honey may be all taken and the babies killed while we sleep to-night."

And he said to the wise old bees, "Do not sleep. We can not trust them."

The next morning the wise bees came and told the king, "Thirty-five babies died last night. The snails crept all about our house and poisoned them. And they left much mouth-dirt in the honey so that we fear it will kill even man to eat it. We must drive them away, O king."

"One day more and if they do not go, we will do some other thing," said the bee king.

Then he went to talk to the snails again and said, "Friends, you are looking fat; I know you are satisfied here and like my honey, but why do you kill my people and why do you spoil our honey? I think I know why. I believe you are an enemy, for I remember now that I met a snail mother some time ago, who scolded me and my people. I believe you are her children.

"Be that as it may, I now tell you that if you snails do not leave my house before to-morrow at midday, you die here."

"Do what you will," said the snail, "we will stay. We are a free people. We go where we will, we eat what we like, and just now we like honey. We shall eat all the honey you have, if we wish it. At any rate, we will stay now, for we would like to see what you can do that is so great."

Then the bee king looked grave and called all his soldiers together, and told them to prepare for battle. The first order was, "Make ready your wax until midday!" The second order was, "Sharpen your swords and be ready!"

The great army of thousands with sharpened stings was commanded to make the noise of battle and sting to the death if need be.

The snails were frightened at the battle cries and drew into their shells. Then the king ordered the soldiers to bring wax quickly. And while thousands of bees kept the snails frightened by the great noise of battle, other soldiers filled the snails' mouths with the wax; and in two hours they were sealed so that they could not move nor breathe.

The bee king then said to the snails, "At first I thought you were friends, and I offered you shelter for the night and all the honey you could eat. But you thought the Creator made the earth for you alone and nothing for any one else. With such natures as yours, if you were as large and powerful as the birds or the beasts, there would be no room for any other creature in all the world. Truly you spoke, when you said you would stay, for now you die."

Then the king moved all his people away to a new house and left the snails to die.

One day when the master came to get honey and saw the empty house and the five dead snails, he said, "This bee house, with all the honey, is poisoned. It must be cleansed."

And the dead snails and the spoiled honey were sunk into the earth together, but the bees lived on and were happy and useful.

The Proud Chicken

A WIDOW NAMED HONG-MO LIVED IN A LITTLE HOUSE NEAR THE MARKET PLACE. EVERY year she raised many hundreds of chickens, which she sold to support herself and her two children.

Each day the chickens went to the fields near by and hunted bugs, rice, and green things to cat.

The largest one was called the king of the chickens, because, of all the hundreds in the flock, he was the strongest. And for this reason he was the leader of them all.

He led the flock to new places for food. He could crow the loudest, and as he was the strongest, none dared oppose him in any way.

One day he said to the flock, "Let us go to the other side of the mountain near the wilderness to-day, and hunt rice, wheat, corn, and wild silkworms. There is not enough food here."

But the other chickens said, "We are afraid to go so far. There are foxes and eagles in the wilderness, and they will catch us."

The king of the chickens said, "It is better that all the old hens and cowards stay at home."

The king's secretary said, "I do not know fear. I will go with you." Then they started away together.

When they had gone a little distance, the secretary found a beetle, and just as he was going to swallow it, the king flew at him in great anger, saying, "Beetles are for kings, not for common chickens. Why did you not give it to me?" So they fought together, and while they were fighting, the beetle ran away and hid under the grass where he could not be found.

And the secretary said, "I will not fight for you, neither will I go to the wilderness with you." And he went home again.

At sunset the king came home. The other chickens had saved the best roosting place for him; but he was angry because none of them had been willing to go to the wilderness with him, and he fought first with one and then with another.

He was a mighty warrior, and therefore none of them could stand up against him. And he pulled the feathers out of many of the flock.

At last the chickens said, "We will not serve this king any longer. We will leave this place. If Hong-Mo will not give us another home, we will stay in the vegetable garden. We will do that two or three nights, and see if she will not give us another place to live."

So the next day, when Hong-Mo waited at sunset for the chickens to come home, the king was the only one who came.

And she asked the king, "Where are all my chickens?"

But he was proud and angry, and said, "They are of no use in the world. I would not care if they always stayed away."

Hong-Mo answered, "You are not the only chicken in the world. I want the others to come back. If you drive them all away, you will surely see trouble."

But the king laughed and jumped up on the fence and crowed—"Nga-Un-Gan-Yu-Na" (coo-ka-doodle-doo-oo) in a loud voice. "I don't care for you! I don't care for you!"

Hong-Mo went out and called the chickens, and she hunted long through the twilight until the dark night came, but she could not find them. The next morning early she went to the vegetable garden, and there she found her chickens. They were glad to see her, and bowed their heads and flew to her.

Hong-Mo said, "What are you doing? Why do you children stay out here, when I have given you a good house to live in?"

The secretary told her all about the trouble with the king.

Hong-Mo said, "Now you must be friendly to each other. Come with me, and I will bring you and your king together. We must have peace here."

When the chickens came to where the king was, he walked about, and scraped his wings on the ground, and sharpened his spurs. His people had come to make peace, and they bowed their heads and looked happy when they saw their king. But he still walked about alone and would not bow.

He said, "I am a king—always a king. Do you know that? You bow your heads and think that pleases me. But what do I care? I should not care if there was never another chicken in the world but myself. I am king."

And he hopped up on a tree and sang some war songs. But suddenly an eagle who heard him, flew down and caught him in his talons and carried him away. And the chickens never saw their proud, quarrelsome king again.

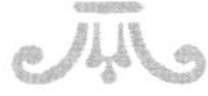

The Lemon Tree and the Pumelo

ONCE A LEMON TREE AND A PUMELO TREE LIVED AND GREW TOGETHER IN AN old orchard.

When the springtime came, they opened wide their beautiful blossoms and were very happy.

And all the children came to visit them, and their hearts were glad with the joy of springtime.

When the warm winds blew, they bowed their heads and waved their blossom-covered arms until they looked like gay little flower girls dancing in the sunshine.

Then the birds came together, and sang sweet songs to the fragrant, happy trees, and their joy lasted from spring until summer.

But once in the summer time the Lemon Tree talked all night long, telling the Pumelo Tree of a great sorrow that had come to her. And she said, "I wish I were a Pumelo Tree, for I have learned that the children of men do not like my children so well as they like yours.

"The first born of my family are thrown away or destroyed. The second generation are taken from me and put in the sunshine for twenty days before they are liked. They are never seen in the market places as your children are, for it is said we are too bitter and sour.

"My children are not well thought of. Ah me! I wish I were not a Lemon Tree.

"Why did the Creator make your children so sweet that they have a good name in all the world, while mine are sour and bitter?

"My flowers are the same as your flowers. My trees are liked the same as yours, but my fruit is almost despised.

"When the Moon feast day of the eighth month and fifteenth day comes, then your children have a happy time for they are honored in every family. When the New Year feast day comes, your children are placed on the first table and every one says, 'Oh, how beautiful!'

"Women and girls like to kiss your children's sweet faces. Oh, Mrs. Pumelo, I should like to be as great a blessing to the world as you are."

And the Pumelo said, "My dear friend, do not say these sad words to me. I feel sure that some day you will be loved as much as I am.

"Did you know that the master spoke of your beauty to-day?"

"What did he say?" asked the Lemon Tree.

"He said, 'How beautiful the Lemon Tree is! I think I shall try to graft the branches of the Lemon Tree on to the Pumelo Tree.'

"Wait until another springtime comes and you will see how much your children will be honored. How happy we shall be together when you come to grow with me and I with you."

So the next year the master and his son brought a sharp knife and cut the Lemon Tree's branches, and fastened them to the Pumelo Tree.

The first fruit came and the children danced for joy.

"How queer to see lemons growing on the Pumelo Tree!" they said.

And the lemons were no longer bitter and sour, but wore so pleasant to taste and so fair to look upon that many were saved for the coming feast day.

The Lemon Tree saw that her children were honored, and she was very happy.

Her heart was grateful to the Pumelo Tree who had raised her children to honored places.

And from that time the Lemon Tree and the Pumelo both had the same body and the same mind, the same happiness and the same friends, through many generations forever.

Woo Sing and the Mirror

ONE DAY WOO SING'S FATHER BROUGHT HOME A MIRROR FROM THE GREAT CITY.

Woo Sing had never seen a mirror before. It was hung in the room while he was out at play, so when he came in he did not understand what it was, but thought he saw another boy.

This made him very happy, for he thought the boy had come to play with him.

He spoke to the stranger in a very friendly way, but received no reply.

He laughed and waved his hand at the boy in the glass, who did the same thing, in exactly the same way.

Then Woo Sing thought, "I will go closer. It may be that he does not hear me." But when he began to walk, the other boy imitated him.

Woo Sing stopped to think about these strange actions, and he said to himself, "This boy mocks me, he does everything that I do"; and the more he thought about it, the angrier he became, and soon he noticed that the boy became angry too.

So Woo Sing grew very much enraged and struck the boy in the glass, but he only hurt his hand and he went crying to his father.

The father said, "The boy you saw was your own image. This should teach you an important lesson, my son. You ought never to show your anger before other people. You struck the boy in the glass and hurt only yourself.

"Now remember, that in real life when you strike without cause you will hurt yourself most of all."

Two Mothers and a Child

WOO-LIU-MAI'S (SWEET SMELLING FLOWER) HUSBAND DIED WHEN HER BOY BABY was just two days old. She was young—only fifteen—and had loved her husband much; and now she felt very lonely and sad. In her heart she wondered why the gods had taken him away from her and the little baby, who needed him so much; but she was a good woman and patient, and never complained to the heavens or to her friends.

One day she felt that she must talk to somebody about it all. So she went to her mother-in-law and said, "Mother, to-morrow is the New Year Day and we must make merry and buy firecrackers and incense for the temple. We have thirty gods in our house and we worship often, but they do not help us any. They would not keep my husband alive and let us be happy together."

Woo-Liu-Mai's mother-in-law answered, "My child, we can see many people worse off than we are. Look at the poor—and there are many of them. They have no houses to live in. They go around to many market places, begging rice and sweet potatoes. They walk all the time and lose their health trying to get enough food to keep alive. Sometimes they walk from early morning to the dark night and get only one little meal.

"And, daughter, do you not know how many people are frozen and die by the wayside in the cold winter? The New Year brings them two or three days of happiness, then all the rest of the year they are hungry and sad.

"You married my son very young and you are not yet old. You have a good house to live in, plenty of clothes to wear, and a little son, I think you have great blessings from the gods. To-morrow is the New Year Day, and we will buy some pretty red paper to cut in a thousand pieces and hang on our walls, doors, beds, and vases.

"We will make a happy New Year and worship the gods. We will open our door wide and our friends who are happy will come to us and make the New Year call. We will cook the two sweet potatoes, one for you and one-half for me, and the other half for the child. Now see what a happy New Year we shall have."

But on the morning of the New Year early, Woo-Liu-Mai awoke and found her child dead in the bed by her side, and she ran sobbing her great despair, to her mother-in-law.

"We will not hang up the red paper on the door or any place, mother, for our happiness is all dead now. We will have a funeral in three days."

Woo-Liu-Mai's mother then took a piece of blue cloth and nailed it to the door, so that people would know that some one was dead there and would not come near the house for fear of bad luck. And she laid the child on a cloth and covered him with another cloth until the third day, when he would be buried.

When people passed by and saw the blue cloth on the door, they thought the mother-in-law, who was old, must be dead.

The second day Woo-Liu-Mai went to her own mother's home, which was some distance from there, and said, "Mother, my child is dead. Just as the New Year Day came, in the morning early, before the sunrise—so he died."

Woo-Liu-Mai's sisters, cousins, and neighbors came to comfort her, because they were sorry. She was now both a widow and childless. In China it is bad to be a widow, but to be both widowed and childless makes of a woman almost an outcast.

One favorite cousin, Woo-Lau-Chan, a very good woman who loved Woo-Liu-Mai like a sister, had a baby just the age of the one who had died, and when she heard the news, she thought much in her heart of her cousin's great sorrow. "How can my cousin find comfort in life any more?" she said in her mind. "She lost her husband when so young and now she has lost her only child. The first happiness lost—the second happiness lost. A widowed woman has nothing more to expect in life. Oh, I want to do something for her. Clothes, money, bracelets, jewelry, can not comfort her without her child."

Woo-Lau-Chan then dressed herself and took up her sleeping child and ran to the house where the dead baby lay. She was brave and went into the dark empty room, and no one saw her. She never thought or cared about the bad luck it might bring, nor of herself in any way. She thought only of the great sorrow of the dead child's mother.

The still body lay on the floor; she took off its clothes and put them on her own baby, and she waited until he had had milk and slept again; then she laid him on the floor and took the body of the dead child and went out into the great forest, where she left it.

She then went back to her cousin with a happy smiling face and said, "Woo-Liu-Mai, I wish you would come with me to your home."

"No," said Woo-Liu-Mai sadly, "I will go to-morrow and bury my child. I will stay here until then."

"But you can not wait until to-morrow. Come with me now. The gods told me in a dream last night that your child would live again. Kwoh-King may now be crying for milk. Come, go now."

But Woo-Liu-Mai said, "No, it can not be. You tell me what is not true. I go to-morrow to bury my dead."

Just then word came from the mother-in-law, "Your child is alive. Come home."

Woo-Liu-Mai went home and saw the child sitting on the grandmother's lap. And the grandmother said, "Three days your child lay on the floor as if dead. His face is changed, his body is changed. Strange, he seems not like the same baby, but he is alive, alive."

Then they thanked the gods with great joy, and the boy grew and was wise beyond the number of his years.

Woo-Liu-Mai's heart was now filled with great peace, and she no longer complained even in secret against the gods.

Woo-Lau-Chan, the real mother, kept her secret well and no one knew, but in her heart she said,

"The time will come, when I must tell my son all. When the years have grown old, Kwoh-King, his children and his children's children will bow in reverence to the ancestors who brought them into life, and it is right that he should know the truth and have his own birthright."

But in his youth she said, "Not now, for the judgment of youth is unstable and he might forsake Woo-Liu-Mai, and leave her again sorrowful."

When Kwoh-King was seven years old, he began school, and he learned fast. But in time the money was nearly gone and Woo-Liu-Mai was too poor to send him longer to the nearest school.

One of her cousins who was a teacher sent word that he would teach the child, so he was sent to the school where he need not pay. When Kwoh-King was sixteen years old, he finished his studies with great honor. He was still wiser than his years and went to work for the government, soon being given a high state position.

Then his mother, Woo-Lau-Chan, who was also a widow, wrote the whole truth to Kwoh-King and to the government—his father's name, his mother's name, his home, his house—all with great care.

And the two mothers, the mother who raised him and the mother who bore him, were called by the government; and when the Emperor heard this story, they were given a beautiful house, and Kwoh-King lived near and took loving care of them both as long as they lived.

The Boy Who Would Not Tell a Lie

SI-MA-QUONG LIVED IN THE PROVINCE OF SZE-CHUEN. WHEN HE WAS YOUNG (ABOUT six years old) he played with a dog and a cat, but they hunted all night long for food in the wilderness, and his mother feared he might get the devil-sickness from them. So one day his father paid much silver for Wa-Na-Juch, a bird with a beautiful song, for his son to play with.

Wa-Na-Juch hopped on Si-Ma-Quong's lap and shoulder and ate from his hand. He was a very handsome bird, and he sang all day long.

One day he flew out to the lake to bathe, and Si-Ma-Quong was very happy watching him. Then he ran and told his mother, "Mü-Tsing, I saw the bird bathe in the lake. I think the water is too cold for him. Give him a good hot bath, as you give me."

His mother said, "In winter you have a warm bath, but not too hot."

When she bathed Si-Ma-Quong, she showed him why the water must not be too hot for the bird, and he seemed to understand. But the next day when his mother went out, Si-Ma-Quong said to his bird, "Wa-Na-Juch, do you want a bath?" And the bird said, "Chi-Chi," which the boy thought meant "Yes, Yes."

He put some clean hot water in a dish, and called the bird, but it would not even go near the water.

This made Si-Ma-Quong angry. "You tell me a lie, and that is very bad," he said to the bird. "You said, 'Yes, Yes,' when I asked if you wanted a bath. Now, I will bathe you as Mü-Tsing bathes me."

He then put the bird in the hot water, but it chirped loudly and tried to get away. "Do not cry and be a bad bird," said Si-Ma-Quong. "I cry sometimes, too, when Mü-Tsing bathes me," but in two or three minutes, the bird lay still and he put it on the table to dry.

When his mother came, he said, "Mü-Tsing, my bird is cold. He is on the table. I think he wants some clothes. Give him my fur jacket and make him warm, so he will stand up and sing."

His mother did not know about the bath, so she said, "Oh no, the bird needs no jacket. He wears a feather jacket."

She then went into the room and saw the bird lying on the table, and she said, "He is dead. Who did this, Si-Ma-Quong? He is wet. Did he go to the pond? I think you killed him. If you did, your father will surely beat you, arid he will never bring you another bird."

And Si-Ma-Quong cried and said, "Yes, I did it. I put him in hot water. I bathed him just as you bathe me. At first he would not go in, but I made him. Then he cried, 'Chi-Chi-Chee.' Will you tell my father? I think he will forgive me, if I tell him the truth. He did the last time I did wrong."

When time came for the evening meal, his mother called him, but he would not eat. He said, "I am sorry about Wa-Na-Juch, and I can not eat food. Wait until my father comes, so that I may tell him all I have done."

Once Si-Ma-Quong and two other boys were trying to peel fruit that grew in a neighbor's garden, but the peach skins were tight and the boys were not skilled. Their task seemed not likely to be finished, when a man passing by said, "I will tell you how to peel the peaches. Get boiling water, drop the peaches in and take them out in a very little time, and then you can pull off their skins easily."

The man whose peaches they were peeling came soon, and saw that the task was finished. He looked at the fruit and said, "I never saw fruit peeled with so little waste. How did you do it?"

They showed him the hot water and he said, "You are very wise to know first this way of peeling fruit. I will give a piece of silver to each of the boys who made the discovery."

He asked the other two, "Did you?" and "Did you?" and they both said, "Yes." He then gave them the silver, but Si-Ma-Quong said, "No, I do not want the silver. We did not ourselves know how to remove the peach skins. A strange man showed us."

Now these two things happened when Si-Ma-Quong was very young; and he lived seventy-two years and served his emperor and his nation wisely. He did many great things, because he was true in the little things. So history says that this man, who never spoke falsely as a child, youth, or man, was one of the greatest men in the Chinese nation.

A Great Repentance and a Great Forgiveness

LIANG-SHENG-YU WAS ONE OF THE GREAT GENERALS OF CHINA. HE HAD SERVED HIS kingdom wisely for many years, when there was a war of four nations. Liang-Sheng-Yü conquered the other nations, and put them under the authority of his king.

He was also called Seung-Foo, or the great Helper of the King. He was given this honorable title because he had served two generations of kings—father and son.

One day Liang-Sheng-Yü reproved the general, Liang-Po, in the presence of the king. Liang-Po was angry because of this and said to himself, "Although Liang-Sheng-Yü is a great general, he should not say these things to me in the king's presence. He has found fault before the king. I will now find fault with him and accuse him before the king. The king forgave me, only because he knew I had done many good things for the kingdom."

He went to his home, but he could not sleep, for his heart burned with anger. In the morning his face was yet cast down with sorrow, for he could not forget his great disgrace before the king. His wife questioned him, "What troubled you last night?" But he only answered, "Do not ask."

A servant brought his morning meal, but it was to him as if it had no taste. And the wine-servant gave him wine, but it tasted as water. Another servant brought him water to bathe, and he said, "It is too cold." But the water was such as it always had been.

Three days passed by and the heart of Tiang-Po changed not. Then he went to the house of a friend. On the way, while still at some distance, he saw Liang-Sheng-Yü coming and he tried to meet him and talk with him. But Liang-Sheng-Yü walked by on the other side and would not see.

Liang-Po said to himself, "This is a strange and terrible thing. I was never his enemy; why is he so long angry? Why will he not face me? With him I served the king many years, I can not see why he should turn away from me. He is wrong, wrong."

He went home and wrote a letter to Liang-Sheng-Yü saying, "I saw you on the Wun-Chung Street to-day and I desired to meet you and tell you many things. I believe you wished not to see me, for you walked on the other side, with your face turned from me. So my heart has another sorrow. I would see you to- morrow, soon after the morning meal, and I invite you to come to my house and eat the noon meal with me."

But when the servant had brought Liang-Sheng-Yü the letter and he had read it, he threw it into the fire and said not a word. The servant saw and went home and told Liang-Po.

Fifty days after this, word came that the Chaa-Kwa Kingdom was about to make war against the Juo Kingdom.

The king, therefore, sent word to the general, Liang-Po, and to the great helper, Liang-Sheng-Yü, saying, "I want you to come at once to me, your king."

When he received the word, Liang-Po said, "I think there will be a great war with the Chaa-Kwa Kingdom." So he waited before going to the king, and gave orders that four thousand soldiers should make ready for battle.

They made ready, and for two days Liang-Po delayed his going. But Liang-Sheng-Yü was already with the king. And in his heart he had fear, for he thought, "Liang-Po will not come. I have made him feel shame before the king. I have done wrong. But if he comes not, our nation is surely lost. We can not go into battle without him."

The king asked him, "Why has not the general, Liang-Po, come into my presence? We can not have war without the general. Without him we can not even send an answer to the Chaa-Kwa Kingdom."

Liang-Sheng-Yü answered and said, "Before I sleep this night, I will see the general." Then he went to his home and told his servants, "I have not time for food. I must see General Liang-Po." And he bade them cut a bundle of thorn sticks, which he took and carried to Liang-Po's house.

It was the time of Nyi-Kang (Everything Quiet) when Liang-Sheng-Yü came to General Liang-Po's house. He knocked on the door three or four times before the servants opened it and asked, "Who is here?" He answered, "I am Liang-Sheng-Yü. Tell your master I must see him to-night, or I die."

Liang-Po dressed himself and came to the door. There he saw an old man with head so bowed as to conceal his face. He wore old clothes, and he carried a sword on his back and a bundle of thorn sticks in his hands. And he knelt on the floor.

General Liang-Po said, "Who is this?" Then Liang-Sheng-Yü, the great and proud helper of two generations of kings, said, "I wish to see General Liang-Po."

His face was still close to the floor and his voice trembled as he spoke. "General Liang-Po," he said, "I was against you before the king and I have learned that the fault was mine. I found you right, and I am guilty, not you. I have done you great wrong. General Liang-Po, my sword is on my back and a bundle of thorn sticks is in my hand. Take the sticks and beat me. Take the sword and cut off my head. We can not make war to-morrow, if we are not at peace to-night."

Then Liang-Po, the great general, helped Liang-Sheng-Yü upon his feet and said, "No, we have always been friends. We will be friends forever, and together we will serve our king. I wish you to forgive me. I wish the king, too, to forgive me, for I have also made mistakes. We will all forgive and be forgiven—then we will surely be friends."

The two great men bowed down together and worshiped the Creator, and they both swore that from that time they would have the same mind.

The Man Who Loved Money Better than Life

In ancient times there was an old woodcutter who went to the mountain almost every day to cut wood.

It was said that this old man was a miser who hoarded his silver until it changed to gold, and that he cared more for gold than anything else in all the world.

One day a wilderness tiger sprang at him and though he ran he could not escape, and the tiger carried him off in its mouth.

The woodcutter's son saw his father's danger, and ran to save him if possible. He carried a long knife, and as he could run faster than the tiger, who had a man to carry, he soon overtook them.

His father was not much hurt, for the tiger held him by his clothes. When the old woodcutter saw his son about to stab the tiger he called out in great alarm:

"Do not spoil the tiger's skin! Do not spoil the tiger's skin! If you can kill him without cutting holes in his skin we can get many pieces of silver for it. Kill him, but do not cut his body."

While the son was listening to his father's instructions the tiger suddenly dashed off into the forest, carrying the old man where the son could not reach him, and he was soon killed.

And the wise man who told this story said, "Ah, this old man's courage was foolishness. His love for money was stronger than his love for life itself."

The Hen and the Chinese Mountain Turtle

Four hundred and fifty years ago in Sze-Cheung Province, Western China, there lived an old farmer named Ah-Po.

The young farmers all said Ah-Po knew everything. If they wanted to know when it would rain, they asked Ah-Po, and when he said, "It will not rain to-morrow," or "You will need your bamboo-hat this time to-morrow," it was as he said. He knew all about the things of nature and how to make the earth yield best her fruits and seeds, and some said he was a prophet.

One day Ah-Po caught a fine mountain turtle. It was so large that it took both of Ah-Po's sons to carry it home. They tied its legs together and hung it on a strong stick, and each son put an end of the stick on his shoulder.

Ah-Po said, "We will not kill the turtle. He is too old to eat, and I think we will keep him and watch the rings grow around his legs each year." So they gave him a corner in the barnyard and fed him rice and water.

Ah-Po had many chickens, and for three months the turtle and chickens lived in peace with each other. But one day all the young chickens came together and laughed at the turtle. Then they said to him, "Why do you live here so long? Why do you not go back to your own place? This small barnyard corner is not so good as your cave in the wilderness. You have only a little sand and grass to live on here. The servant feeds you, but she never gives you any wilderness fruits. You are very large, and you take up too much room. We need all the room there is here. You foolish old thing, do you think our fathers and mothers want you? No. There is not one of our people who likes you. Besides, you are not clean. You make too much dirt. The servant girl gave you this water to drink, and your water bowl is even now upside down. You scatter rice on our floor. Too many flies come here to see you, and we do not like flies."

The turtle waited until they had all finished scolding. Then he said, "Do you think I came here myself? Who put me here, do you know? Do you suppose I like to be in jail? You need not be jealous. I never ate any rice that belonged to you or your family. I am not living in your house. What are you complaining about? If our master should take your whole family and sell it, he would only get one piece of silver. Who and what are you to talk so much? Wait and see; some day I may have the honored place."

Some of the chickens went home and told their mother, "We had an argument with the turtle to-day and he had the last word. To-morrow we want you to go with us and show him that a chicken can argue, as well as a turtle."

The next day all the chickens of the barnyard went to see the turtle. And the old hen said, "My children came here to play yesterday, and you scolded them and drove them away. You said all my family were not worth one piece of silver. You think you are worth many pieces of gold, I suppose. No one likes you. Your own master would not cat you. And the market people would never buy a thing so old and tough as you are. But I suppose you will have to stay here in our yard a thousand years or so, until you die. Then they will carry you to the wilderness and throw you into the Nobody-Knows Lake."

Then the turtle answered and said, "I am a mountain turtle. I come from a wise family, and it is not easy for even man to catch me. Educated men, doctors, know that I am useful for sickness, but if all the people knew the many ways they could use me, I think there would soon be no more turtles in the world. Many Chinese know that my skin is good for skin disease, and my forefeet are good for the devil-sickness in children, as they drive the devil away; and then my shells are good for sore throat, and my stomach is good for stomach-ache, and my bones are good for tooth- ache. Do you remember that not long ago our master brought three turtle eggs to feed your children? I heard him say, 'Those little chickens caught cold in that damp place, and so I must give them some turtle eggs.' I saw your children eat those three eggs, and in two or three days they were well.

"So you see the turtle is a useful creature in the world, even to chickens. Why do you not leave me in peace? As I must stay here against my will, it is not right that your children should trouble me. Sometimes they take all my rice and I go hungry, for our master will not allow me to go outside of this fence to hunt food for myself. I never come to your house and bother you, but your children will not even let me live in peace in the little corner our master gave me. If I had a few of my own people here with me, as you have, I think you would not trouble me. But I have only myself, while you are many.

"Yesterday your children scolded me and disturbed my peace. To-day you come again; and to-morrow and many to-morrows will see generations and still more unhatched generations of chickens coming here to scold me, I fear; for the length of life of a cackling hen is as a day to me—a mountain turtle. I know the heaven is large, I know the earth is large and made for all creatures alike. But you think the heavens and the earth were both made for you and your chickens only. If you could drive me away to-day, you would try to-morrow to drive the dog away, and in time you would think the master himself ought not to have enough of your earth and air to live in. This barnyard is large enough for birds, chickens, ducks, geese, and pigs. It makes our master happy to have us all here."

The chickens went away ashamed. Talking to each other about it, they said, "The turtle is right. It is foolish to want everything. We barnyard creatures must live at peace with each other until we die. The barnyard is not ours; we use it only a little while."

The Boy of Perfect Disposition

About two thousand four hundred and twenty years ago, Tsen-Tsze was a child and lived in San-Szi Province. For twenty-one years he studied many things with the great teacher, Confucius. And the first great moral law of Confucius he obeyed, not only in his acts, but in his heart, even when beaten for a thing he did not understand. And it is not on record that any other man has ever done this.

In earliest childhood, he always loved and reverenced his father and mother. In the morning when he arose he went to see his parents before he would have the morning meal.

One day Tsen-Tsze's mother went away to visit his grandparents. When she left, she said, "Dear son, I will return in one day. You and your father will be happy for a day without me." And he knelt and bowed his head to worship his mother at parting.

The evening came and she did not return, and Tsen-Tsze could not eat food or sleep that night from anxiety for his mother. And when the maid servant called him for the morning meal, he said, "No; I can not eat food until I see my mother's face." But his father said, "You must eat and go to school."

"I can not eat food or study books until my mo ther comes," said Tsen-Tsze, and word was sent his teacher who said, "You are not quite wise, Tsen-Tsze. If your mother should die, would you then no longer study? I hope to see you soon at school."

At midday his mother came. Then he had food, and went to school and studied his lessons.

When he came home from school, he always went to see where his parents were before going to play. At meal time he would not take food until his father and mother began eating. When he met an old person on the street, he uncovered his head and stood aside respectfully to let him pass before he went on.

These and all other customs of courtesy were observed and honored by Tsen-Tsze. At school he studied his lessons faithfully, and never left tasks unfinished. Every day he asked his teacher, "Have I done any wrong to-day?"—so great was his desire to know the right and to do all that he knew.

One day Tsen-Tsze's father beat him with a long Kia-Tsa (stick). When he got up from the floor he came and took his father's hand and asked, "Father, did I do wrong? Tell me what it was." But his father's face was red with anger, and he would not explain.

Tsen-Tsze went out to the schoolroom and took his music box and came again before his father's face, and sat down on the floor and played and sang to him. He sang,

"Every father loves his son,
Of this all men are sure.
Each child will need the stick sometimes,
To keep his nature pure."

And he said, "I read in history about many famous men who were great because they were gentle. I hope I shall be like them. History says their fathers gave them the stick when young." But the anger had not all left his father's face, and he brought him a cup of tea and said, "Father, are you thirsty?"

Then he took his father's hand and went to the garden where the birds were singing. He put a flower on his father's breast and asked, "Father, do you like that? I do."

All this caused Tsen-Tsze's father to think, and in his heart he said, "This boy is not like other children of his age." And so long as he had life, he never beat his son again.

Tsen-Tsze became a great scholar and finished all his studies when he was only twenty-five years old. And he was a wise and good man.

His own generation and all the generations of man that have come after him have studied about him, and have wished to be as he was.

What the Yen Tzi Taught the Hunter

One day a hunter was looking for a fox in the wilderness, when suddenly he saw thousands of birds coming toward the river, and he lay quite still and waited for them all to come.

The Yen Tzi, or Kind Birds, were talking together, and the hunter listened. One asked, "Is all our company here?"

And the Leader Bird said, "No, little One-Month-Old and Two-Month and Mrs. This-Year are not here yet."

And the Leader Bird said to the Lookout Birds, "You must go after them and help them to the river before five days. Our boats are dried and ready to sail. It is growing cold and we must all go south together."

So the Lookout Birds flew all around the country to hunt the lost birds. They found one with a broken wing, and a little one with not enough wing feathers to fly far, and one with a wound in his leg made by a hunter, and others that were tired or very hungry. They found every missing bird, and this great family of friends were soon all together again.

But while the Lookout Birds were seeking the lost ones from their own family, they heard another bird cry, "Save me! save me, too!" And they stopped and said, "Who is calling? Some one must be in trouble." They flew to a lemon tree and saw a Tailor Bird with her leg all covered with blood. The Kind Birds said, "Friend, how came you in such trouble? What is your name and where do you live?"

The Tailor Bird said, "I live in the South Province, eight hundred miles away. I came here to see my friends and relatives. Three of my children are with me, and we were on our way home to the south. We had gone sixty miles, when I asked my children to stop and rest in this lemon tree, and now I do not even know where they are. I fear the hunter got them. I am hurt, too, and I do not think I shall ever see my home again. I shall lose my life here, I fear."

The Yen Tzi heard all the Tailor Bird said. They talked together and were sorry for her who had no one to care for her, for they knew her children had been killed by the hunter. "If we do not save her life, she will surely die," they said.

So they asked, "Would you like to go with us? We know you eat different food. We live on rice and fruit and a few bugs. We do not know that you can live as we do. And we must ride on our boats, many, many hours."

The Tailor Bird answered, "Yes, I will go gladly, and will eat what you have and cause you no trouble."

The Kind Birds helped the Tailor Bird to their company and put her in one of their boats, and two or three birds fed her and cared for her until she was well. The hunter who told this story said, "I have learned many things by watching and studying the habits of the Kind Birds. I will never kill birds again."

A Lesson from Confucius

Confucius once heard two of his pupils quarreling. One was of a gentle nature and was called by all the students a peaceful man. The other had a good brain and a kind heart, but was given to great anger. If he wished to do a thing, he did it, and no man could prevent; if any one tried to hinder him, he would show sudden and terrible rage.

One day, after one of these fits of temper, the blood came from his mouth, and, in great fear, he went to Confucius. "What shall I do with my body?" he asked, "I fear I shall not live long. It may be better that I no longer study and work. I am your pupil and you love me as a father. Tell me what to do for my body."

Confucius answered, "Tsze-Lu, you have a wrong idea about your body. It is not the study, not the work in school, but your great anger that causes the trouble.

"I will help you to see this. You remember when you and Nou-Wui quarreled. He was at peace and happy again in a little time, but you were very long in overcoming your anger. You can not expect to live long if you do that way. Every time one of the pupils says a thing you do not like, you are greatly enraged. There are a thousand in this school. If each offends you only once, you will have a fit of temper a thousand times this year. And you will surely die, if you do not use more self-control. I want to ask you some questions:—

"How many teeth have you?"

"I have thirty-two, teacher."

"How many tongues?"

"Just one."

"How many teeth have you lost?"

"I lost one when I was nine years old, and four when I was about twenty-six years old."

"And your tongue—is it still perfect?"

"Oh, yes."

"You know Mun-Gun, who is quite old?"

"Yes, I know him well."

"How many teeth do you think he had at your age?"

"I do not know."

"How many has he now?"

"Two, I think. But his tongue is perfect, though he is very old."

"You see the teeth are lost because they are strong, and determined to have everything they desire. They are hard and hurt the tongue many times, but the tongue never hurts the teeth. Yet, it endures until the end, while the teeth are the first of man to decay. The tongue is peaceful and gentle with the teeth. It never grows angry and fights them, even when they are in the wrong. It always helps them do their work, in preparing man's food for him, although the teeth never help the tongue, and they always resist everything.

"And so it is with man. The strongest to resist, is the first to decay; and you, Tsze-Lu, will be even so if you learn not the great lesson of self-control."

The Wind, the Clouds, and the Snow

I

Once there was a great quarrel between the winds, the clouds, and the snow.

And suddenly, without any warning, there came the angry roar of the thunder and the sharp cracking of the forked lightning as it separated the heavens.

Then the north winds, the south winds, the east winds, and the west winds came together a thousand and a thousand strong.

And the sun was no longer seen, for the earth was covered with a deep blackness as of the night. The clouds were coming to the cast, but the wind drove them all back to the west side of the heavens and finally much hail and snow were thrown down to the earth.

The clouds said to the snow, "Why do you go to earth? You are not wanted there. In the warm south land you are never welcomed. Your people would be killed at once if they went there. Even here you are allowed to stay only for a short time."

"We do not come to this earth for our own pleasure," answered the snow. "It was pleasanter where we were. We came to earth to help its people."

At this the clouds frowned until their faces became black and they said, "We can not believe that."

"It is true," answered the snow. "In the summer time you will see how the people cry for pressed snow. They pay three pennies for one little cup of water that we have made cold.

"You say we are not liked in the south land, but we tell you that the south-land people send many oxen, horses, and men to the north to find the snow.

"They pack us in the storehouses so that we may last until the hot weather, and when the summer fever comes all people need us."

"You have been studying this one great need of man a long time, we think," and the clouds bowed in scornful mock sympathy.

"We do many good things for man," continued the snow. "Thunder and lightning do him much harm and he fears them greatly; but the Creator sends us to comfort him. The lightning disappears from the earth for a time when the season of our appearance comes."

"You should wear a crown," suggested the clouds sneeringly.

"A king who wore one—the old King Dai-Sung—once said of us, 'Oh, snow, snow, how beautiful you are. It is good for flowers, good for grass, and good for trees that you are here.'

"And he said to the rose bushes, shrubs, and trees who were asleep, 'If you wish beauty in the spring time, you must have our friend the snow in the winter.'

"He laid his hand gently on his horses' necks and said, 'True helpers that are both feet and legs to me, it will soon be time for the green grass to appear. You will have plenty this year, for we had a thick cover of snow this winter.

"'It will soon be hot weather, but I do not fear the heat, for I have plenty of hard snow, pressed and packed for the summer time.'

"So you see the snow is useful to man. We could have stayed where we were in the sky and kept clean, and we need not have worked hard flying all the way down to the ground.

"We never hear that the clouds do any good thing," said the snow.

"The time may come when you will have finished talking," said the clouds. "Then we can tell you some things."

"We saw the big Ti-San Mountain to-day," continued the snow, "and many of the cloud children were playing around its summit, but what good did they do? None.

"A hunter was looking for wild beasts and your children were naughty and covered his eyes so that he could not see. Do you remember how he scolded your children and said, 'I do not like these cloudy, foggy days'?

"Once the General San Chi led his soldiers to fight against his nation's enemy, and one night he went out to learn how many of the enemy could be seen.

"The moon and stars tried to help him, but you came and covered them and it grew so dark that he lost his way. Then the enemy took his horse and gun and he nearly lost his life.

"He hid in a cave and said, 'Those clouds have caused my death, I fear.' He lay in the dark cave until the morning came and he could see to find his way.

"We do not see why the Creator made clouds to hang around in the sky from north to south, and east to west," said the snow, angrily.

II

JUST THEN THE CLOUDS' LAWYER, THE WIND, CAME TO DEFEND THEM. "WHOM ARE you scolding?" he asked.

"You think the Creator should have made the snow king of a world, I suppose, and that there is no place or use for the clouds.

"You talk so much that we can not find opportunity to tell what we are good for. You are not the only helper of man and of growing things in the hot summer time.

"Do you remember when the great General Dhi-Sing led five thousand soldiers to battle? They traveled over mountains and through wild places until they were worn and weary.

"They found water to drink by the Gold Mine Mountain and stopped there to rest; but there were no trees or growing things on that mountain and they could find no shade.

"The sun sent down great heat and they suffered so that they could not rest. Then they held their faces up to heaven and in anguish they cried, 'Oh, sun, why shine so hot to-day?'

Then they looked to the east and saw our brother, the cloud, beginning to appear.

"'Why do you not come to us, and cover the face of the sun that we may have shade and rest?' they pleaded of the cloud; and so our brother came and stood between the earth and the sun.

"'Oh, this is rest, rest,' said the soldiers in great relief. 'How we wish that the cloud might always shield us from the burning fire of the sun.'

"And not only the soldiers, but all the farmers and woodcutters ask us to help them in the time when the sun comes close."

"Can you do only this one thing?" asked the snow, coldly.

"Who carries the rain and the snow through the sky?" asked the wind.

"I tell you there would be no rain nor snow but for the help of the wind and the clouds.

"You know well that the rain is made from the ocean water.

"One day the water said to the cloud, 'Friend, I should like to journey around and around the sky, but I have no wings, and can not fly. My body is so heavy that I can not move it, and I never expect to take this trip unless you, my friend, help me.'

"And so we lifted the water and helped it step by step until we floated it through the air. Our first cloud faces were very light, but after we had traveled five or six miles through the sky our faces changed to gray, and when we had gone one thousand miles our faces became black and the farmers said, 'We shall soon have rain.'

"Do you know why the faces of clouds grow black?" asked the wind.

"Anger makes things black," said the snow, "but why should we know, for of ourselves we never change color."

"It was because great strength was being put forth to travel through the sky," argued the wind, "for soon the drops of water said, 'We are tired and want to go back to earth again.'

"Then we said to the water, 'The earth people need you and all growing things need you. It is good that you go.'

"And on the place where that water fell there had been no rain for three years.

"The king had bowed his head a thousand times before our father and mother and had cried, 'Oh, rain cloud, why are you so long in coming?'

"We heard the earth king's cry, and that night the mother of clouds said to us, 'My children, you must go down to earth and help its people or they will perish.' So we called all our brothers and sisters to go at the same time, and we went to earth and saved a million and a million lives.

"The greatest wrong you have done is to forget who helped you when you were needy," continued the wind.

"Do you remember that you once lived in the ocean, river, or lake? At that time I do believe that you were not well liked. In the sea you were in the lowest class and worked hard every day and night.

"When the wind came and blew you into waves you would always call out in a big rough voice, 'Muh; Muh; Spsh; Sph -s -s.'

"You were restless and unhappy, and tried and tried to escape from that place, and the cloud mother pitied you.

"She said, 'I am very sorry. We will bring them up here with us,' and she asked the sun's help to do it.

"For a day and a day, a night and a night, you were carried up, up to the first section. But you were not satisfied then, and you were taken to very high seats.

"You wanted the best places and would do no work unless the winds pushed and the clouds carried you. So we took you up high where we lived and had a happy time.

"Now you have forgotten all this. Who helped you up? Who made you pure?" But the snow did not answer.

Finally the snow said, "Yes, our family is from the rivers and seas. We had forgotten. If we had only thought, we should have been more grateful."

The sun was judge, and he said, "We decide this case in favor of the wind and the clouds."

The Fish and the Flowers

Once there was a Chinese merchant who sold flowers and fish. In the winter time the flowers and fish each had a separate house to live in, but one very cold winter the merchant said to his servants, "I think we must put the lily bulbs in the house with the fish. It is warmer there."

And a thousand and a thousand narcissus bulbs which were growing for the great feast of the New Year were moved into the house with the fish.

This made the fish angry and that night they scolded the narcissus.

"Friends," said the fishes, "this is not your place and we will not have you here.

"We do not like your odor. You will spoil our people. When men pass by our door they will see only you.

"They will never see our family. You can not help or do any good here; so you must go.

"Every day a hundred and a hundred merchants and students come to visit us. If you stand by our door they will surely think the fish are all gone and there is nothing but flowers left.

"We do not want our place to smell so strongly of flowers. We do not like it. It is very bad and makes us sick."

The narcissus answered, "Strange, but we were thinking of that same thing.

"Some people say that fishes have a bad odor, but I never heard it said of our flowers. I think I will say no more about it. Let others decide."

Then another flower spoke and said to the one who had been talking, "Hush, sister, this is not our house. We will go to-morrow. Let the fishes say what they will about us, and do not quarrel with them. All people know we are not bad and that our fragrance is sweet."

When the morning sunshine came, the doors were opened, and a thousand and a thousand flowers had blossomed in the night, and the people said, "Oh, how sweet! Even a fish house can be made pleasant. We wish it could be like this all the time."

And one visitor said, "How sweet this place is! Do fishes or flowers live here?" And when he saw, he said, "It is too bad to put delicate flowers in evil smelling places."

Then three students came to buy flowers. The servants brought three pots from the fish house, and the students said, "We do not want pots from the fish house. Give us others. These have a disagreeable smell, like the fishes."

The fishes heard all and were even more angry at the flowers. But the flowers heard and were happy, and they said, "How foolish to quarrel and try to put evil on others."

The Hen, the Cat, and the Birds

Once a farmer's boy caught three young wood larks. He took them home and gave them his best and largest cage to live in. Soon they were happy and sang almost all day long.

Every one liked the birds very much, excepting the cat and the hen.

One day the sun shone very hot and the birds tried to get out of the cage. They wanted to fly in the trees and bushes.

The farmer's boy knew what they wanted and hung their cage in the tree.

He said to himself, "I think my birds will like this. They can get acquainted with other birds. I know birds should go with birds. That is their happiness."

Then the wood larks sang loud and long, for they were glad to be in the trees.

An old hen was sitting on some eggs near by, and her little ones were just beginning to come out of the shells. The singing of the birds made her angry and she said to them, "Will you stop that noise for a time so that I may hear my little ones call? I can not hear a word my children say. That is not a pretty song, anyway. When other birds sing, their songs are sweet; but your noise hurts my ears. Why do you sing all the time? No one likes to hear you.

"That foolish boy did not know much about birds, or he would not have caught you. There are plenty of other birds in the mountain. The thrush and the kind-birds are good, with fine voices and clean and beautiful feathers.

"Why could not that foolish boy catch them? They are the birds I like. They are kind to chickens and like to live with us, but you wood larks are our enemies, and our children fear to come near you."

The birds made no reply to the hen's scolding. They sang and were happy and did not seem to notice her.

This only made the hen more angry, and when the cat passed by her door, she said, "Good morning, Mrs. Cat. Do you know we have much trouble since our enemies, the wood larks, came here to live? They are always trying to get out of the cage. I think they want to hurt my children—or yours," she added slyly.

"Do you hear their harsh ugly voices all the day? I can not sleep, I can not find any comfort here since those birds have come."

"Our master's son brought them," said the cat, "and we can not help ourselves. What would you do about it?"

"I told you," said the hen, "that I do not like those birds. They should be killed or driven away."

"I do not like them very well either," replied the cat. "Cats and birds do not go well together. Cats like birds to eat you know, but then men like chickens. If you do not want them here, we can do this. At mid-day, when the master's son lets the birds out for a bath, they sit a while in the sun to dry their feathers. When you see them come out, call 'Cluck, cluck,' and I will come and catch them or drive them away."

When the time came for the birds to take their bath, the cat was asleep. The hen called loudly. The cat heard her and crept quietly to the place where the birds were bathing.

But one of the birds saw the cat and said to her, "Mrs. Cat, what are you trying to do? We know what the hen said to you about us last night. I heard her advise you to kill us or drive us away. Is this not true?

"The old hen does not wish us to live here; but then the rats and mice do not like you to live here either. I warn you not to put your paws on us. If you kill us, the master's boy will kill you, and he will kill and cook the hen. Do you know how much he loves us?

"Every morning before the sun shines, he is up; and do you know where he goes? He goes to the river to catch the baby swims (little fish) for us. He goes to the mountain and catches grasshoppers for us, and from the fields he brings us seeds and rice.

"He works hard for us. Sometimes he brings other toys here just to hear our songs. He spent much money for our cage and our gem-stone water dishes.

"Every day the master asks his son, 'How are your birds, my son?'

"One day our brother would not eat food and the boy said to his father, 'What ails my bird, father? All the foods are here, but he will not eat.'

"The father answered, 'I will call a doctor.'

"And the doctor came and said, 'The bird has fever. Give him some Da-Wong-Sai and Tseng-Chu-Mi and he will be well soon.' The boy paid the doctor for this; so you see how well he loves us.

"When we do not like to stay in the house he hangs us out in the trees so that we can talk with other birds.

"Now, Mrs. Cat, do you see how well we are cared for? Go back and tell the old hen not to talk about us. Do not notice what she says against us, for if you kill us, as the hen wishes you to do, you will surely have no life left in the world.

"You see how cunning the hen is. She will not do the thing herself, but wants you to do it. That proves that she is your enemy as well as ours.

"Oh, Mrs. Cat, do not be foolish. You have three little ones to care for. If you lose your life by taking ours, who will care for your children? Will the hen do it? I think not."

When the cat heard such wisdom from a little bird she said, "Well! Well! Well! I think you are right," and went away.

The Boy Who Wanted the Impossible

TSING-CHING (PURE GOLD) WAS FOUR YEARS OLD WHEN HIS PARENTS SENT HIM TO A "baby school" for the first time and told him that the teacher could tell him everything he would like to know.

When he saw a queer bird flying around he asked his teacher, "What kind of thing is that in the air?" His teacher told him, "A bird," and that to be a bird meant to fly around and sing in every place and make music for the people.

The boy said, "Can I not do it?" His teacher said, "Yes, you can sing music for the people, but you can not fly unless you get wings."

Tsing-Ching replied, "Yes, I can do that, too. My grandmother told me about a spirit with wings."

His teacher said, "If your grandmother told you that, you can try and see. You may be a man with wings sometime."

Just then the servant girl that his mother had sent came to fetch him home from school.

When they reached the park by his home, Tsing-Ching said, "Lau-Mai, I want that long ladder and a long stick." The nurse-girl did not know what he would do with them, but she finally had to give him both to keep him from crying. She was afraid his mother would hear him cry and that she would come out and scold her for not taking better care of the child.

As he took the long ladder he said, "Now I am going to be a bird." His nurse said, "You can not be a bird, Tsing-Ching. Birds fly. You can not fly. Why are you trying to climb up the ladder? That is not the way to be a bird."

Lau-Mai helped him up two or three steps, when his mother called her to come in and she left him there for a little time.

He climbed up, up, nine steps by himself—and fell down. But he was not hurt, nor did he cry; he had no fear—he thought of but one thing—he was going to be a bird.

Suddenly his mother came and saw him again trying to climb up the ladder and asked, "What are you doing, Tsing-Ching?"

He answered, "I want to be a bird; wait, I will try again. I know that birds fly in the air, not on the ground. I can not fly on earth. If I get up high in the air, then I know I can fly."

His mother thought he wanted to climb up and get a bird; she looked all around and said, "There is no bird up there now."

"But, Ah-Ma, I want to be a bird."

The servant Lau-Mai came just then and explained to his mother. His mother said he was a foolish boy, and gave him food and sent him to school again.

In two hours the teacher sent all the boys out to play. They ran to the pond where the gold-fish were, for they liked to watch them swim in the water.

After exercise, they all went into the schoolroom and Tsing-Ching told his teacher, "I saw many goldfish swimming in the pond. Did you know that, teacher? A man fed them rice and they all came out for him. They seemed so happy, they shook their tails and waved their fins and swam up and down and all around in the cool water. Oh, I should like to be a fish."

His teacher said, "Learn lessons now." But Tsing-Ching could not study; he could only think, think about the fish. Soon he asked that he might go out to drink. Then he went to the pond and took off his clothes, but the gardener saw him and asked, "What are you doing, boy? This is school-time."

"I want to be a fish," said Tsing-Ching.

The gardener thought he wanted to catch the fish and said, "The fish are for your eyes and not for your hands. Do not disturb them."

Tsing-Ching sat down and waited until the gardener went away. Then he stepped into the water and talked to the fish.

"I am going to be one of you now," he said. "Come to me and show me how to swim with you." But they all hurried away.

For half an hour he splashed in the shallow water, trying to swim, until the teacher thought, "Where is Tsing-Ching?" and sent a boy to see. He found him in the pond and asked him to come into the schoolroom, saying the teacher would punish him if he did not.

"No," said Tsing-Ching, "I shall be a fish; I told the teacher I was going to be a fish." And so the boy went back and told the teacher, who hardly knew what to think.

Finally he went out with a stick and asked, "Tsing-Ching, what are you doing here? Do you know this is school-time? Do you know that you were allowed only to go out for a drink and not to stay here and play? You have done wrong."

"Why, teacher, I told you that I wanted to be a fish," said Tsing-Ching. "I do not want books or exercises. I am going to be a fish and I will not go to school. Mother said you teach everything; now teach me to be a fish."

His teacher said, "How foolish you are, Tsing-Ching; you are a boy, a man. You can learn many things better than to be a fish. Come with me now."

That night when Tsing-Ching was walking with his mother and nurse out by the water, he saw the summer moon shining in the lake.

"How strange, Ah-Ma, the moon is under the lake! See, it raises the lake and shakes it all the time. I want it. What kind of a white ball is it?"

Then his mother told him that the moon was in the sky, not in the lake, and she explained and showed him. And when he saw the moon in the sky, he said, "I know that it is not the moon in the lake, for it shakes. It is not quiet like that one in the sky. It is a silver ball, I know."

He asked so many questions that his mother grew tired of answering and let him ask unnoticed. Then he wandered away a little distance and threw stones in the water. And the waters waved and the white ball danced so prettily that he wanted it very much. He waded into the lake, deeper, deeper, until he fell down. He screamed and swallowed the water, and it took a long time to make him alive again, after his mother took him out of the lake.

When the neighbors heard about it, they said, "Foolish boy; not satisfied to do the things he can—he is always wanting things he can not have."

Many people in this world are like Tsing-Ching.

The Boy Who Became Hsao-Tsze

THIS IS THE TRUE STORY OF A BOY WHO OBEYED PERFECTLY ALL HIS LIFE THE LAW of Confucius concerning honor to parents.

Few have been able to do this. Among a people of many millions who have kept record over four thousand years, only twenty-four men have been found worthy of the great honor of being called Hsao-Tsze.

Twelve hundred years ago, in Chê-Kiong Province, there lived a poor widow and her son, Wong Ziang. The father had died when Wong-Ziang was a baby, and the time came when they had only their little home left and not even one piece of silver to buy food with.

So the mother went to many places daily and asked food for herself and child. For seven long years, every day in the cold rain or in the sunshine, this poor widow begged food and kept herself and child from starving.

She was a good woman and never complained even to the heavens, and in her heart she said many times, "No mother should be sorrowful when she has a good son. My boy is true without being taught. Many mothers have sons, but they are not as this one."

When Wong-Ziang was fourteen years old, he said to his' mother, "Ah-Ma, I will seek work and we will have food. You must rest now."

In the morning early he went to the market place and asked work of many people. At midday, when the laborers left the market place, they said, "You are too young to work here."

As he was hungry, he went to a merchant's house and asked for food; and because he was a gentle boy and pleaded so earnestly, the merchant told his cook to give him food. Wong-Ziang would not eat the food, but took it home to his mother.

Ninety times Wong-Ziang left home at sunrise. He sought work all day, and every night he took food home to his mother and comforted her with, "I soon will find work. Ah Ma. One man says he will want me soon; or, a man told me of yet another place to seek work," and in many other ways he comforted his mother.

When he gave her the food he brought, she would say, "You eat, too." But he would always answer, "I have had mine; you eat first." And when she had finished eating, he would eat of what was left.

One time Wong-Ziang's mother fell sick. He said, "I will go for the doctor." But his mother said, "I have no silver. Wait and you will soon have work. I think I shall be well then."

But Wong-Ziang ran to the city of Nim-Chu and asked the doctor to come to his mother. He said to him as they went to his mother's house:

"My mother did not get up at sunrise. She is weak and sick and can not eat food. She does not want a doctor, as we have no silver, but I believe you will wait and, when I get work, I will pay you." The doctor said, "I always help the poor when I can, and will not charge you this time."

When they reached the widow's home, the doctor made the examination of the tongue, the eyes, and the pulse. He then said, "She is very weak. I will leave medicine, but it is better that she eat good food that she likes. Twice in five days, she should have a carp fish boiled in rice wine. But it is winter and the river is frozen. I know not how you will get that fish," and then he went away.

Wong-Ziang gave his mother the medicine, and she asked, "What did the doctor say about me?"

"He said you needed a carp fish cooked in rice wine so that you may be strong," answered Wong-Ziang. "It is very easy for me to find one. I am going now to the river."

But the mother said, "Not now, my son. Wait until spring. The river is covered with ice."

"I will see," said Wong-Ziang; and he put on his fishing clothes.

His mother said, "I fear you will die, if you go into the water."

"I will see first if there are any fish," said he.

When Wong-Ziang reached the river, he saw it was covered with ice. He made a great hole in the ice and went in, and after swimming and diving for some time, he caught a fish for his mother.

But his breath almost left him in the cold water, and when he came out, he could not stand on the ice.

He fell down, and his clothes froze to the ice with the net and the fish he had caught.

"He is gone a long time," thought his mother. She called a servant girl who was passing, and said, "Ah Moi, will you go down to the River Ching-Ki, and see if my boy is there?"

Ah Moi went and saw the boy and the fish in the net lying frozen on the ice together.

She called, "Wong-Ziang," but when no answer came back to her, she thought, "He is dead," and ran in fear. But she met a farmer who was riding a cow and she told him, "Wong-Ziang is dead on the ice." The farmer left his cow and went with her to see.

The farmer took off his own coat and wrapped it around the boy. He carried him in his arms and said to the servant. "I think he is not dead. Take the fish and net at once to Wong-Ziang's mother."

In an hour Wong-Ziang came to life again. He arose and cooked the fish for his mother. And in fifteen days she was well.

Soon after this, Wong-Ziang was given work in the next village as cook for a rich professor who had many pupils.

One day he went to the wilderness to cut wood. His mother knew that her boy worked hard, and so she went with him to help and they worked until sunset.

Suddenly a small tiger came out of the forest toward the mother, and from fear she became as one dead. Wong-Ziang screamed and made a great noise. He threw his clothes at the beast and it ran away. Then he carried his mother home, and the neighbors who had watched him all his life said, "Wong-Ziang will become a Hsao-Tsze if he is always like this."

Wong-Ziang had seen twenty-one years when his mother died, and he had never left her for one day in all his life. He was liked by his teachers, schoolmates, and neighbors, for they said, "We can learn a great lesson from Wong-Ziang who has loved and honored his mother perfectly."

While his mother was living, Wong-Ziang worked for her and spent little time or money in study; but after she died, he studied hard. When his work in the professor's kitchen was done each day, he always sat outside the schoolroom door where he heard the teacher giving lessons to his pupils.

For seven years he studied in this way before the teacher, Liao-Tsai, knew; but one day he found out what Wong-Ziang had been doing. In time he came to love him as his own son and he asked him, "Would you like to be my Chi-tsze (son by adoption)?"

And Wong-Ziang said, "I would, but I am poor and unlearned, and you are rich and honored. It could not be."

But his teacher said, "I want you in my school. I have had many pupils, but none that have worked and learned as you have. I have known many sons, but none of them served and honored his parents so faithfully. Think about this two or three days and then give me your answer."

After three days Wong-Ziang decided: and he came to Liao-Tsai, his teacher, and, kneeling down before him, he bowed his head low. And after this time he was as the professor's own son.

In sixteen years, Wong-Ziang graduated from the great University with highest honors. He had studied all the books of the Chinese schools and was now a Han-Ling (Ph.D.).

He served his nation and emperor wisely and had a high state position for more than twenty years. The people called him Zien-Zan before the emperor. But when he came home to his native province where people had known his deeds all his life, they bowed their heads low in affection, and called him, "Hsao-Tsze."

The Hunter, the Snipe, and the Bivalve

YUNG-MOI WAS ONE OF THE VERY WISE MEN OF CHINA. HE HAD LIVED IN THE mountains and studied the books of Confucius for twenty years, and afterward he taught others.

He taught school for ten years, and because of his wisdom had many pupils—over two thousand in all. He was now sixty years old and greatly respected by many people.

One day he thought he would give a party for his scholars. So he sent them all word and asked that each one repeat a story at the party.

After he had invited his guests, he thought, "I, too, must have a story ready for to-morrow night. What shall it be?" And he walked down to the river, thinking.

There he saw two creatures in the edge of the river fighting. One was the great bivalve; the other was a snipe that had been hunting for fish in the river.

They fought long and hard, until a hunter with a gun and net passed by and saw them. He made no noise and came close, close, but they were so busy trying to kill each other that they could not see him. So he caught them both and took them home in his net.

Yung-Moi, the wise teacher, thought deeply and said to himself, "There is meaning in all this," and he walked slowly back to his schoolroom.

He sat down at his desk and thought, and he stirred the ink in his ink-dish, not knowing what he did.

Then he wrote this story and said: "In my mind this is a strange thing. The snipe is a fine creature in the air. He has two wings and has great power to do for himself.

"Small fishes swim in the water and the snipe can take any one he wants, but he can not five in the home of the bivalve, or try to take life away from him without perishing himself.

"If he had power to go under the water and live, there would be no small fishes in the river, and if he were big, like the eagle or bear, there would soon be no fishes in the world. I am glad the Creator made him a small creature and not too powerful.

"The bivalve—he has great power to live under the water. Small swimming things can not escape if they pass by his door, but if he could move about like other fishes with his great power and his appetite for many fish, I think the mother of all fishes could not make enough for his greedy mouth, for now he opens his doors all day long and takes in the creatures that swim by.

"I had fish from the river last night for my evening meal, but I think they never passed the bivalve's house or he would have had them for his supper.

"When the bivalve and snipe fought together, each one thought, 'I have great power; I want what you have, and I will kill you and get it for myself.'

"The snipe saw the bivalve's door open and he thought, 'What nice white meat; I will have it,' and he picked at it. The bivalve shut his doors tight and held the snipe so that he could not get away.

"And they fought; each one trying to kill the other, until the hunter came and caught them both. Then the hunter took the snipe and the bivalve home and said to his wife, 'We will have a good supper to-night.' And his wife looked and was very glad to have two such savory things at one time. The hunter said, 'Cook the bivalve well done, and we will put some Tung-Ku and Cho-Chen-Cho with it. Save the shells and put them away carefully to dry, and I will sell them to the man who makes furniture, for inlaying his tables.

" 'The pearls that were in this bivalve will bring me much silver from the jeweler. I will ask my mother to come here for supper. The bivalve is enough for us all, and my mother will be glad. She has never before eaten of a bivalve.

" 'The snipe, I will not kill. I will keep him to show to my son and nephew. Give him rice to eat and some water to drink, and keep him in the cage. To-morrow I will give him some fish and in a few days I will take him to the school teacher. Then, when I train him to sing, I will take him to the market place and sell him for much silver.' "

At the party on the evening of the next day, all the pupils told stories. At last the teacher repeated the story of the fight between the swimming and flying creatures.

"Now, I will ask you a question," he said to the pupils. "If the snipe flies in the air, can man catch him? And if the bivalve stays under the cave in the river, can man injure him?"

And the pupils all said, "No, teacher."

"Well, it was sad that the snipe and the bivalve were caught yesterday. Can you tell me why?"

"We do not know," said the scholars.

And the teacher said, "They are happy and powerful creatures when they do no harm to each other. The snipe flies in the air, the bivalve swims in his home, the sea, and each has happiness according to his kind.

"Now you see these two creatures fought together, the snipe and the bivalve, and they did not succeed by fighting. The hunter is the only one that succeeded.

"It is so with the three nations now at war. They are like the hunter, the snipe, and the bivalve. They ought to live in peace. They are lost when they fight among themselves."

Then Yung-Moi drew a picture of the warring countries for his pupils.

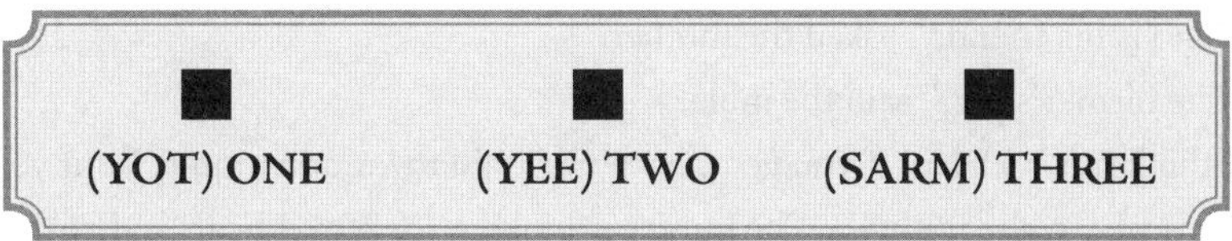

"One and Three represent two nations at war with each other. One asks Two's permission to pass an army through his country that he may fight Three. While the army of One is away from home, the people get in a fight among themselves and civil war follows. Number Two takes advantage of the situation and in the absence of Number One's army (who is trying to overpower Three), conquers Number One easily. Number Two then owns the nations One and Two, and with this added strength goes to the land of Number Three and conquers him, so that all three countries now belong to Number Two."

The Mule and the Lion

One night the lion was very hungry, but as the creatures of the wilderness knew and feared him even from afar, he could not find food. So he went to visit the young mule that lived near the farmer's house, and when he saw her he smiled blandly and asked, "What do you eat, fair Lii, to make you so sleek and fat? What makes your hair so smooth and beautiful? I think your master gives you tender fresh grass and fat young pig to eat."

The mule answered, "No, I am fat because I am gentle. My hair is beautiful because I do not fight with other creatures. But why do you come here, Sii? Are you hungry? I believe you are seeking for food."

The lion said, "Oh, no, I am not hungry. I only walk around to get the cool, fresh air. And then the night is very beautiful. The moon hangs up in the clear sky with the stars and makes a soft light, and so I came to visit you. Would you not like to take a walk with me? I will take you to visit my friend, the pig. I never go to his house alone; I always take a friend with me."

The mule asked, "Shall we go to any other place?"

"Yes," answered the lion, "I think we will go to visit another friend of mine who lives not far away."

Then the mule asked his mother, "Will you allow me to go with Sii to see his friend?"

"Who is his friend?" asked the mother.

"The farmer's pig," said the mule.

"I think it is no harm if you go only there," said the mother mule. "But you must not go anywhere else with Sii. The hunter is looking for him, I hear, and you must be careful. Do not trust him fully, for I fear he will tempt you to go to some other place or into some wrong thing. If I allow you to go, you must come home before midnight. The moon will not be gone then and you can see to find your way."

So the lion and the mule went to visit the pig who lived in a house in the farmer's yard. But as soon as the pig saw the lion, he called out in a loud voice to his mother.

The lion said, "He is afraid of me. I will hide and you may go in first."

When the pig saw that the mule was alone, he thought the lion had gone. He opened his door wide and was very friendly to the mule, saying, "Come in."

But the lion jumped from his hiding place and caught the pig as he came to the door. The pig called to his mother in great fear. And the mule begged the lion, saying, "Let the poor little creature go free."

But the lion said, "No, indeed, I have many pigs at my house. It is better for him to go with me."

Then the lion carried the pig, while the mule followed. Soon they came to where a fine looking dog lay on some hay behind a net. The lion did not seem to see the net, for he dropped the pig and tried to catch the dog who cried loudly for mercy.

But the lion said to the foolish mule, "See how rude the dog is to us. We came to visit him and he makes a loud noise and tries to call the hunter so that he will drive us away. I have never been so insulted. Come here, Lii-Tsze, at once and help me!"

The mule went to the lion and the net fell and caught them both. At sunrise the hunter came and found the mule and the lion in his net. The mule begged earnestly and said, "Hunter, you know me and you know my mother. We are your friends and we do no wrong. Set me free, oh hunter, set me free!"

The hunter said, "No, I will not set you free. You may be good, but you are in bad company and must take what it brings. I will take you and the lion both to the market place and sell you for silver. That is my right. I am a hunter. If you get in my net, that is your business. If I catch you, that is my business."

The Fa-Nien-Ts'ing and the Mön-Tien-Sing

CONFUCIUS HAD LABORED TEACHING THE PEOPLE RIGHTEOUSNESS FOR MANY FORGOTTEN moons. One day he said to himself:

"I have taught many years and I will now rest a while." He thought for a few days and said, "Where shall I go to find rest?" Then he spoke to Tsze-Lu, Yen-Yuen, and Tsze-Kong, his faithful pupils, saying, "I have been thinking that I would now rest for three moons and visit the Tai-San Mountain, but I do not wish to go alone. I should like you to go with me. Where on the mountain is the best place, do you think?"

"On the southwest side where the sun shines warm and the wind does not blow cold," answered Tsze-Kong. And Tsze-Lu, Tsze-Kong, and Yen-Yuen went to their own rooms and planned the journey.

After ten days Confucius and his pupils went to the Tai-San Mountain to rest for the three moons; but even there his pupils studied, for they took their books with them.

As Confucius walked on the Tai-San Mountain he said, "How great and beautiful are the things made by the Creator; even the trees, bushes, and flowers are beyond man's understanding." Then he went to the temple and saw the images of honored men, and when he looked at the face of Dai-Yee, the Just, he said, "You are very great. We remember and honor you, and other generations yet to come will remember and honor you."

When he had walked another half-mile, he grew tired and sat down under the Fa-Nien-Ts'ing tree, and soon he slept.

Suddenly he heard a noise. He awoke thinking his pupils had come, but seeing no man he lay down again to sleep. Once more he heard the same noise, and looking upward he saw the Mön-Tien-Sing and the Fa-Nien-Ts'ing trees looking into each other's faces; but they were not happy. The Mön-Tien-Sing's face was distorted with anger, and in great wrath she said to the Fa-Nien-Ts'ing, "If I were the Creator, I would not allow you to live. A year and a year passes by and you do not grow. You eat much food and you have more earth than I, and still you do not grow. I never heard that you did any good thing since you were born, and it is said you have lived here five hundred years. Your branches are crooked and your bark is rough.

"You are not even good to look upon. Do you think the children of men care for you? No, for you have neither flowers nor fruit. If people sit under your shade when the wind blows hard, I should think your sharp, ugly leaves would fall on them and stick them.

"It is a strange thing that the woodcutter does not chop you down—useless thing. If I were the Creator, I would not allow the sun to shine on you, nor would I give you rain to drink. I would cause the wind to blow hard until you fell down dead.

"You see I have the sweetest of flowers and the people all like me. One day two women passed by here and one of them said, 'Mön-Tien-Sing, how I wish that I might take you with me. You are so beautiful, but I fear you do not like me. Three times I have gathered your flowers for my hair, but I was careless and passed by a bush and it did but touch them when their lovely petals all fell to the earth. I wish that I might take you to my garden, and that you would grow there and open your beautiful flowers every third moon forever.'

"My name is Mön-Tien-Sing which means Flowers-every-three-moons. If you do not know another meaning it has, I will tell you.

"When you look in the sky on a summer night do you know how many stars are there? Even man can not count a clear sky filled with shining stars. I am Mön-Tien-Sing. Mön means full; Tien means heaven; and Sing means stars:—'sky filled with stars'—that is my name. I grow very fast. Every three moons I bear a thousand and a thousand flowers. I do not need servants to care for me, for I grow everywhere. Even the chickens and birds like me. They come to me and eat my seeds and grow fat.

"If I were the Creator, the Mön-Tien-Sing would grow everywhere in all the world, and fill the earth with its sweetness, but oh, I wish I could go away from you. I do not like even to see you, and here I must stand always by your side. Your branches are too strong; for when the wind blows, they come close and hurt me and spoil my beautiful flowers. I will pray the Creator to bring a woodcutter and cut you down to-day—useless, evil thing."

The Fa-Nien-Ts'ing did not answer, though he bowed his head in shame. He knew well that he was ugly and that his leaves were sharp and his bark rough, but he said to himself, "I know in my heart that some day, some one will like me, too. For the Creator made me and he surely made me for good. I will keep patient and wait."

In about three moons the cold days came and all things were frozen. The rivers stood still, the flowers were no longer seen, the trees and shrubs threw all their leaves to the ground. But the Fa-Nien-Ts'ing held his head up and smiled bravely, and he kept his leaves and they grew green and green. Then he said to himself, "The cool wind is good for me. The frost does me no harm. I feel better. This is my happy time, for the people like to have green in their houses now. To-day they came to the mountain and they found no other thing that was yet green but my leaves.

"A young man was about to be married. He could find no flowers. So he took some of my leaves and branches to put in his house. The birds come to me for shelter from the cold wind and snow. They say the Fa-Nien-Ts'ing is a good home for them.

"The winter is cold, cold every day, but I grow greener and greener. The woodcutter comes and stands by my side and says that I keep the cold wind away from him. I know the Creator made me for good."

Then Confucius awoke. He looked up, and he looked down, and he looked all about him. There was no living thing near except the Fa-Nien-Ts'ing and the Mön-Tien-Sing, and he said:

"It was a dream, but surely I heard the Mön-Tien-Sing trying to quarrel with the Fa-Nien-Ts'ing. I know that the things of the world have deep meaning, and this is my lesson: I would not be as the Mön-Tien-Sing, but I wish to be like the Fa-Nien-Ts'ing."

He arose and laid his hand gently on the Fa-Nien- Ts'ing and said, "The time is long that you stand here, patient one. The cold heart of winter does not change your nature more than it does that of birds, beasts, men, or even your enemy, the Mön-Tien-Sing.

"The cold weather makes you better, for you grow green as the springtime, and there is no other tree, bush, or flower which can do this. When the frost of winter comes, where are the flowers, where are the leaves, where are all the growing things of beauty? Where is the grass, where is the green of the field? They are gone. The first cold wintry wind of adversity takes them one by one, but you alone can withstand sorrow and grow even more beautiful.

"Your life is a lesson to me. I am serving the king and serving the people, but there are few who like me now. Three kings have tried to kill me, though my doctrine is to serve the world and help every one.

"But kings will not listen to my teaching, and my brothers try to drive me away, as the Mön-Tien-Sing wished to drive away the Fa-Nien-Ts'ing. For four days I went without food, and many were the enemies around and against me at that time when the king banished me. But I know that it is my duty to live and teach in the world, although it is winter for me and the cold winds of adversity blow and the hearts of my people seem hard and cold like rocks of ice. I hope I will be as the Fa-Nien-Ts'ing, and stand firmly on the mountain of righteousness forever, that I, Confucius, may do good to a wintry world.

"I would not be as the Mön-Tien-Sing. It is covered in the morning with the flowers of beauty which it drops before the evening. It is beautiful, for an hour, but is frail beyond all of its kind. It bears no fruit and its flowers last but a day, while the Fa-Nien-Ts'ing is strong of heart and mind, though a world is against him."

The Body that Deserted the Stomach

MAN'S BODY IS A PERFECT AND WONDERFUL THING. HIS HANDS ARE STRONG TO DO; his feet are strong to walk; his nose judges whether things are good to eat; his ears hear clearly; his eyes help him to see all the things of the world and to study books; his brain can think great thoughts. And so we call the body of man a *perfect* thing.

But one day the different parts of man's body quarreled among themselves about the work. Many complaints were brought against the stomach. The hands and feet said, "We work all day and yet we are nothing. Do you know whom we work for?"

The eyes said, "We find many chickens, fish, eggs, and much rice and tea for the stomach. He takes all and does no work for it. He does not even think. And though he never does anything for us, we are always working for him."

Then they all agreed to refuse to work longer for the stomach. They said, "To-morrow we will tell the heart and have him judge who is to be blamed."

So the next day the tongue told the brain about it, and the brain said, "I will see the judge to-night."

When the heart heard the story he said, "Yes, you are right. If all of you lie down and refuse to help the stomach; if you do not give him any rice or meat for food, or any tea for drink, he will learn then that he can not live without you."

In a little time the stomach wanted food and said to the hands, "Give me a piece of fish, some rice, and a cup of tea." The hands were quiet and said nothing.

Then the stomach said to the feet, "Will you go out and have Men- Yen bring me a bowl of chop-suey-meen? I am hungry."

The feet answered, "No, sir, we will not work for you any more." And they lay down.

The stomach cried for food, but all said, "We do not care; we will not work for him."

After a while the eyes found they could not see well; and in the theater hall next door the drums drummed hard, but the ears could not hear. The heart-judge said, "How is it now with the stomach?" The brain answered, "We are not working for him, nor helping him any more, and I believe he is going to die. I fear that I, too, will die and that all the others will die. I do not believe we have done right in deserting the stomach. Do you not think it best to tell the feet to go out and bring the stomach some chop-suey-meen? If he had that, he might help us again. We shall all surely die unless we have his aid."

But the unwise judge said, "Let him get his own food; let him do his work for himself."

"He can not do that," said the brain. "He lives in a place with great walls around him, so he can not get out. The hands and the feet have always brought his food to him."

The judge said, "Has he spoken about it to-day?"

And the brain answered, "No."

So they agreed to leave the stomach to himself one day longer.

But that night they were all found dead together, for they could not live without each other.

The Proud Fox and the Crab

One day a fox said to a crab, "Crawling thing, did you ever run in all your life?"

"Yes," said the crab, "I run very often from the mud to the grass and back to the river."

"Oh, shame," said the fox, "that is no distance to run. How many feet and legs have you? I have only four. Why, if I had as many feet as you have, I would run at least six times as fast as you do. Did you know that you are really a very slow, stupid creature? Though I have only four feet I run ten times as far as you do. I never heard of any one with so many feet as you have, running so slowly."

The crab said, "Would you like to run a race with a stupid creature like me? I will try to run as fast as you. I know I am small, so suppose we go to the scales and see how much heavier you are. As you are ten times larger than I, of course you will have to run ten times faster.

"Another reason why you can run so fast is because you have such a fine tail and hold it so high. If you would allow me to put it down, I do not think you could run any faster than I."

"Oh, very well," said the fox, contemptuously, "do as you like, and still the race will be so easy for me that I will not even need to try. Your many legs and your stupid head do not go very well together. Now, if I had my sense and all of your legs, no creature in the forest could outrun me. As it is, there are none that can outwit me. I am known as the sharp-witted. Even man says, 'Qui-kwat-wui-lai' (sly as a fox). So do what you will, stupid one."

"If you will let me tie your beautiful tail down so it will stay," said the crab, "I am sure I can win the race."

"Oh, no, you can not," said the fox. "But I will prove to even your stupid, slow brain that it will make no difference. Now, how do you wish that I should hold my tail?"

Said the crab, "If you will allow me to hang something on your tail to hold it down, I am sure you can not run faster than I."

"Do as you like," said the fox.

"Allow me to come nearer," said the crab, "and when I have it fastened to your tail, I will say 'Ready!' Then you are to start."

So the crab crawled behind and caught the fox's tail with his pincers and said, "Ready!" The fox ran and ran until he was tired. And when he stopped, there was the crab beside him.

"Where are you now?" said the crab. "I thought you were to run ten times faster than I. You are not even ahead of me with all your boasting."

The fox, panting for breath, hung his head in shame and went away where he might never see the crab again.

A Little Chinese Rose

One day Mai-Qwai (Little Rose) ran home angry to her mother saying, "Mü-Tsing, I do not want my name to be Rose any longer. I was in Dun-Qure's garden just now, and she asked me, 'Which flower do you like best of all in our garden?' and I said I liked my name-flower best.

"Then they all laughed and said, 'We do not. Do you not see the thorns on the roses? When we pass near we tear our dresses. When we touch them the blood flows from our hands. No, we do not like the roses. The baby cow does not like them either. They stick her nose when she tries to eat, and even mother can not pick them without scissors. Once when she had a large bunch of roses, little sister tried to get one and it stuck her hands and face so that she cried many hours. Other flowers do not make trouble like that, and we do not see why any one likes the rose best. We think it very foolish to like a trouble flower and be named for it.'

"I do not like my name-flower any more, Mü-Tsing, and I do not want to bear its name."

"Do not cry, dear child," said her mother, "and I will tell you some things about the rose. Do you like rose sugar?"

"Yes, very much," Rose answered, her face growing bright.

"And rose oil?"

"Oh, yes, Mü-Tsing."

"I thought you did not like the rose. So you ought not to like the good things it makes."

"But, Mü-Tsing, tell me why did the rose god make the rose grow with so many thorns? Other flowers are not like that."

"Listen, dear child. If the rose tree were like other trees and still had its beautiful flowers, I think we should never have any for ourselves. They would be too easily gathered. The rose god was very wise and put thorns all around his beautiful flower. When he made it, he gave it an odor so sweet that all the gods stopped working on the day it was finished. The thorns mean, Honor the rose which grows forever. The cows can not touch it, and the pigs never go near it, and careless children or wasteful people can not destroy it. Do you see, dear, why the rose must have thorns?"

The next morning Rose found in her room a beautiful new rose pillow made of the sweet-smelling petals. When she laid her head on this fragrant pillow she said, "Mü-Tsing, I do not wish to change my name."

The Eagle and the Rice Birds

Once a mother eagle had a nest with three eggs in it and she was very happy while waiting for her three children to come from the eggs. But one day, two schoolboys, named Jeung-Po and Hui-Yin, who knew of her nest, talked together and one of them said, "Did you know that the eagle likes the rice birds?" And the other boy replied, "No, she does not, for I have seen her drive them away."

But the one named Jeung-Po said, "Not only can I make an eagle like a rice bird, but I can make them change natures and live with each other."

"You can not do that," answered Hui-Yin.

"Will you give me a piece of silver if I can make the eagle like the rice birds and take them as friends?"

And Hui-Yin said, "Yes, I will give you a piece of silver if you do that, but I know you can not." And so they clapped hands.

So Jeung-Po went his way hunting, hunting many birds, until finally he found a rice bird's nest with five eggs in it. He took three of the eggs and put them in the mother eagle's nest and then he took the three eggs from the eagle's nest to the nest of the rice bird.

In twenty-five days the eagle's nest had three baby birds in it and Jeung-Po was glad. One day he heard the mother eagle saying to her three babies:

"I do not know why your feathers are not as mine, and your voices are so different and you are such very little things. I will go and ask my oldest son to come here to-morrow, and see if he can tell me why you are so."

On the next day the eagle's son came to visit his mother, and he said, "Ah-Ma, I am glad to see my three little brothers, but their faces are not like yours or mine."

"I know that what you say is true," said the eagle mother. "I wished you to come, so that we might talk of this strange thing. You are my child, and they are mine, but they are not like you and me."

"I will see what they eat," said the eagle son. Then he gave them a piece of meat, but they could not eat it.

"They want rice all the time," the eagle mother told him. "They will not eat meat." The mystery was so great that the eagles could not understand.

Soon the strange nestlings were flying with the eagle mother. One day she took them to a pleasant place to play, and on their way home they passed a rice bird who called to them. The mother eagle said, "Do not go with him. Come with me." But the little ones would not listen. And when the rice bird said, "Chi-Chi," and flew down to a rice field, the three little ones left the eagle mother and went with the rice bird.

The eagle mother called many times, but her strange children would not come to her. Then she said to the rice bird, "Why did my children follow your call and not mine? How did you teach them in one breath what I have not been able to teach them in all their lives?"

And the rice-bird father said, "They are not your children. They belong to the rice-bird mother. She is coming now; see for yourself."

Soon sixteen rice birds flew near and the eagle mother saw that they were all like her children. The rice bird said, "You see, it is as I told you."

"But they must be my children," said the eagle mother. "I can not understand this, for I never had children like them before. My other children were like me and they never behaved in this way. But I will take them home again and feed them, and when they grow older they may become like me and the others of my family."

"It will never be so," said the rice bird. "I am sure of that. You need not hope that these children will ever be eagles. You see they do not eat meat, they eat rice. They know the rice bird's call without being taught. They do not speak the same dialect that you speak, nor sing the same songs. They are surely rice birds and you can not keep them longer in your home."

The eagle mother tried again and again to call her children and they only said, "Chic, chic," which meant that they would not come. She waited long, but they refused to go with her. Then she chided the rice birds and said, "You are a bad company, and you have tempted my children to join you. Why do you not tell them to come home with me, their mother? If you do not cease your evil actions, I shall eat you or drive you away."

The eagle mother flew away alone to the mountain, and she sat on a great rock and waited long for her children to come home.

The night came, but her little ones did not return. In her heart the eagle mother knew they were lost to her. All the dark night she cried aloud in her grief. In the morning she hunted long, but she could not find them. She said to herself:

"This is a strange and dreadful thing that has come to me. I remember that I once heard a quarrel-bird say that some of her children had left her in this same way, and she believed some bad boy had changed her eggs. For she had six yellow children in her nest, and when they could fly they went away with the yellow song birds. She found her own children one day in a camphor tree. I wish that I might find my own children."

Just then she met the quarrel-bird mother, and she asked her, "How did you find your own children?"

And the quarrel-bird mother said, "I was passing by the camphor tree when I saw the little ones alone, and I asked, 'What are you doing here?' And they said, 'Eating nuts!'

"'Do you like nuts?' I asked.

"'Oh yes, very well.'

"'Where did you come from?' I said.

"'We came from the yellow-bird family.'

"' But you do not look like the yellow birds.'

"'No, and we did not talk nor eat as they did.'

"'Where is your home now?'

"'We have no home.'

"'Why do you not live with the yellow-bird mother?'

"'We were not happy there. The others do not eat nor drink, nor sing as we do. We are not fond of them, nor they of us.'

"'You are like me and mine,' I told them. And we looked at each other and saw the same feathers and the same color. Then they asked me where my home was and I told them under a rock of the Wu-Toa Mountain. So they went with me, and my house and my food were pleasant to them. In some way—though we could not tell how—we knew in our hearts that we belonged to each other. And we were happy, happy."

The eagle mother thought long about the story of the quarrel-bird, and the next morning she left her nest early and went to the wilderness to seek her lost children. On the way, she met a cousin eagle who asked her, "Why are you crying and crying?"

The eagle mother answered and said, "I have lost three children. Have you seen any—lost in the wilderness? I could not sleep all last night, for a great trouble has come to me."

The eagle cousin said, "I saw three eagle children pass here. They went to the Fah-Nim tree and ate of its fruit. They were playing there, and seemed to be happy."

The eagle mother went to the Fah-Nim tree and saw three little eagles; and she said, "Children, how did you come here?"

The little eagles answered her, "We are not your children. Why do you call us? We have had no mother since we were born. The rice bird left us when we were small. She said we were not her children. Then an eagle came along and gave us food until we could fly."

The eagle mother said, "You look like my older children, and I believe you are mine. Would you like to go with me and see our home?"

Then the little eagles talked together and said, "She is very kind to us. Of course we do not know her, but we might go and see her home."

So they went, and in that eagle mother's house, they soon knew her for their mother and she knew her own children.

And Jeung-Po lost the money, for it was proved that he could not change nature. Each bird went back to its own kind. The eagle is always an eagle, and the rice bird is always a rice bird.

The Children and the Dog

Woo-Hsing lived near the market place and all the children thought him a very wonderful man. He trained fine dogs to do almost everything but talk. If one wanted a dog educated, Woo-Hsing was the man to take him to. Whether for hunting, for performing tricks in public places or from door to door—anything, all things, Woo-Hsing could teach his dogs. This is why the children thought him a wonderful man.

It came time for Woo-Hsing's little boy to learn how to teach dogs. So one day he brought his son a very young one from the market place. Then he told him how the dog should be taught. It would take three years to teach him all: to play soldier with a gun, to dance, to bow his head, to kneel, to play churn the rice, to swim in water with a boy on his back, or to take a basket and go from door to door and beg rice and money for his master. Even then his training was not complete until he could hunt the fox, the gibbon, the mouse-deer, and other animals.

Woo-Hsing's little boy had been named Yiong-Yueng, which in Chinese means "Forever." The reason for the name was this: Woo-Hsing had been given many sons, but they had all died young, so when the last one came he named him Forever, for he said, "He will then live a long time and I shall not be childless."

Yiong-Yueng called his dog Hsi-Long, which means "for fun." He was a very wise dog and learned so many tricks in a short time, that he was known and admired by all the boys in the country around.

One day a crowd of children coming home from school met Hsi-Long in the road. They all shouted, "Here is Yiong-Yueng's dog. Now we will have some fun and make him do all his tricks for us."

So one boy said, "Here, Hsi-Long! Come here," but the dog would not even notice him. Then another boy pulled his tail because he would not obey; and Hsi-Long bit the boy's finger and growled, and the boy ran home crying.

Another boy said, "Now see me. I will make him take me on his back for a swim in the water as he takes Yiong-Yueng"; and he caught Hsi-Long roughly and tried to pull him in the water. But the dog pulled his clothes and growled so fiercely that the boys scattered and ran home.

One of the boys, Ah-Gum, told his mother what had happened, and how angry they all were at the dog, who needed a beating, as they thought. "When Yiong-Yueng has visitors, Hsi-Long kneels and bows and does all his tricks for him; why would he not do them for us, Ah-Ma? How can we make him do the tricks for us?"

"Well, my son," said his mother, "you wanted the dog to do many things for you. Have you ever done anything for the dog? You are a stranger to him. Did you ever give him anything to eat or drink?

"Try this," continued the mother. "To-morrow, take a bowl of rice, put a little meat and gravy with it, and give it to the dog. Speak kindly to him and pet him. Do this two or three times and he will surely like and trust you. Then he will do for you all he knows how to do.

"You will find people in the world are just the same, my son. Do not expect people to do things for you when you do nothing for them, for that is not right. You must give, if you expect to receive, and it is better to give first."

The Two Mountains

THE KWUNG-LUN MOUNTAIN IS VERY HIGH—TEN THOUSAND FEET OR MORE. MOST of the time his head is covered with the clouds and, since he was born, no man has ever found the way to climb where he might look in the face of the great Kwung-Lun. And the eagles and the San-Chi birds live always with him.

One day Kwung-Lun spoke to the Tai-San Mountain who lived near, and said, "I am the highest mountain in the world. I am the steepest and most honorable of all the mountains here. The farmers come to me; from the morning until the evening sun they come and cut the great rocks from my base. And from the earliest light, until the darkness gathers about my head, the birds sing for me. I have the San-Chi birds. They wear the most beautiful feather in the world. It shines in the sun and has a different glory for the moon. Man gives more gold for this than for any other feather that is on the earth. The San-Chi is mine. I feed him and he lives always with me.

"Yesterday, a teacher and his scholars came here and I heard him tell them this story about Confucius:—

"'One day, Confucius was talking to the young King Loa-Bai, and he asked the king, "Have you ever been to the Kwung-Lun Mountain?" And the king answered, "No." Then Confucius showed him a beautiful fan made of feathers from the San-Chi birds. "Did you ever see feathers like these?" he asked.

"'"I am a king and I have seen many things," said the young king, "but never have I beheld colors of such wondrous beauty. I will give you one thousand pieces of silver if you will bring me a fan like this one."

"'And Confucius answered, "If I can persuade you to do one thing that I desire greatly I will give you the fan, for I should not like to sell it. I could not well take silver in exchange for it, as it was given to my honored ancestor, my great-great-grandfather. But as I have said, if you will take my advice concerning a certain matter, you shall have the fan."

"'"I will be advised by you," said the young king. "What do you wish me to do?"

"'"You are a king of great strength," said Confucius. "You have more soldiers than any other king. But if you were a lion, you would not kill all the other animals in the wilderness to show your great strength. Or, if you were the greatest fish in the waters, you would not swallow all the weaker fish."

"'The young king answered, "No, I would not! If I were a lion, I would let all the weaker creatures dance before me in happiness and safety."

"'"You are a strong, great king," said Confucius. "Other kingdoms are weaker than your own. Their kings do not wish to fight, unless they must. If you will take my advice and will not force them to war for six years, you shall have many gifts from these kingdoms. You shall have this wonderful fan made of the feathers from one hundred and twenty San-Chi birds, and gold and ivory, with beautiful carving; and you shall have gems of many colors and battle-horses and bears' feet. If you will be advised by me, the other nations will give you these things."

"'"How soon shall I have these things?" the young king asked.

"'"In one year," Confucius replied, "you shall have them. I must have time to go again to the rulers of these kingdoms."

"'So the king agreed to do as Confucius desired; and Confucius said, "I now give you my fan, and if in one year it is as I say, the fan is yours. But if you begin warring with any other nation in that time, you must return the gift to me."

"'Then Confucius went to see the rulers of the weaker kingdoms, and four gave promises of peace and sent gifts to the young king. But one of the kings would not give tribute, neither would he say when he would begin war.

"'When a year had almost passed, the young king reported to Confucius, "Four kings only have sent me gifts. Does the other nation wish war, or will its king send me a gift as the others have done?"

"'"Will you not take my fan as a gift from me, and let the small weak nation go?" said Confucius.

"'Then the king became very angry. He tore his long robe and said, "I will swallow up the nation that is my enemy. We will have war now."

"'"The year of your promise is not yet gone," said Confucius. "If you do that, you must return the priceless fan." And the young king gave Confucius his fan and went away.

"'The king gave his general the order to make ready for war. But in a few hours he repented of what he had done, for he prized the fan of Confucius above all gold or jewels, and he ordered his general to cease preparing for battle. And he further ordered that a Jeh-Shung—good talker—be sent with this message to Confucius.

"'"I, the king, am sick at heart. I wish you to come to mc and bring with you the fan which I prize above all gems. I will not battle with the weaker kingdom."

"'"I have important work and can not come to-day," answered Confucius, "but in one more day I will see the king."

"'Then the king was very happy again, for his heart was set on possessing the fan.

"'When the next day came, the king sent the most honorable chair (carried by eight men), and went himself to meet Confucius, who held in his hand the priceless fan, for well he knew the heart of the young king.

"'And when he drew near, the king could not see Confucius. He saw only the sparkling colors of the fan he so desired. And Confucius said, "I thought you were going to destroy the weaker nation. Why do you wish me to come here?"

"'Then the king bowed to Confucius and said, "I am in the wrong. I have thought deeply about this, and I will take your advice and keep peace. Now, will you give me the fan?"

"'"No, you are not to have the fan on the agreement which you broke, for when you sent me away you prepared to make war on the weaker nation," said Confucius,

"'And the young King fell with his face to the ground and his attendants came to care for him.

"'"If you will make a new agreement," said Confucius, "and promise that you will never be the first to go to war, I will give you this fan that you so desire."

"'The young king made the agreement. And the fan was given him by Confucius. And the king said to himself, "This fan is more than many kingdoms to me. In all the world of man, there is nothing else so beautiful. My heart has desired above all things this wonderful fan of the San-Chi feathers and the rare carving."'"

When the Kwung-Lun Mountain had told this story to the Tai-San Mountain, he said, "Although I have the San-Chi birds, the most beautiful of all creation, yet it is to me a strange thing that a thousand and a thousand people bow their heads and worship you, while I stand here and am hardly noticed.

"You give no great thing to the people. You have no beauty. You are not tall and grand. Your head is not higher than the clouds. You can not see the dark and secret caves of the thunder, and the hidden places of the beginning of the storm. You never gave feathers, more beautiful even than flowers, to a king. Why do the people worship you instead of me? The hunter comes to me and the farmer takes my stones, but they forget me, the giver. Now, tell me truly, why do people love and worship you instead of me?"

And the Tai-San Mountain answered, "I will tell you why. You are very haughty. You are stiff and stony and proud, from your base to your summit. Your nature is not kind. The children can not play in your lap. In the summer time when the people come for the fruit and grain harvest, you give them nothing; and they can not come to you to choose the San-Da. It hurts their feet to walk among your rocks and stones. No one can visit you. You do not welcome them. How can they worship you?

"I am lower and of a gentler nature. The birds come to me to make their nests, and people always gather about me in the summer time. My heart is open and every one knows me well and loves me."

A Chinese Prodigal Son

I

KONG-HWA'S FATHER AND MOTHER WERE FARMERS. THEY HAD A PLEASANT HOME and would have been very happy together, but after Kong-Hwa was four years old, he was a bad, disobedient boy.

He would not listen to his mother's teachings. She was a good woman and tried by different ways to make him do right. In school he was considered a very bright boy and learned fast, but he would not obey his teacher.

Kong-Hwa was only seven years old when he came home one day with his books. He had run away from school.

As he came into the room where his mother was working, he cried out, "Mü-Ts'ing, why do you do that?"

She was cutting into little bits a fine large piece of cloth that she had woven to make the family clothes of. "Why do you spoil the cloth, mother?"

"Yes, my son, it is true I spoil the cloth. It is now good for nothing. It will not make clothes for your father, clothes for yourself, nor clothes for me. It is wasted, and will not be of use even for dust cloths. It is not good for anything. Do you know why I did that, my boy?"

"No, Mü-Ts'ing, why did you do it?"

"For this reason, my son: I am anxious that you shall be good and study your lessons in school every day, and I hope and hope that after a while you will be a good and wise man and do something for your father, your mother, and your nation. And I also hoped to make your clothes out of this cloth.

"But your teacher says you run away, go to the see- saw, play in the water, climb trees, throw stones at the little birds all day and will not study.

"You are using your time as I have used the nice new cloth—cutting it up in useless little pieces. I once thought you were a wise child, but you are not. You are very foolish."

Kong-Hwa cried and felt sad, while his mother talked, and then he said, "I will go back to school to-morrow. Now can you mend the cloth or make another piece, Mü-Ts'ing?"

"I will wait and see if you really mean to be a good boy," said his mother.

The next morning he arose early, took his books, and went directly to school; but in a few days he was as bad as before.

The school children and the neighbors complained about the boy who did so much mischief. His mother had only the one little son, and as they came to her with complaints, she felt that she could almost die with grief.

She lay awake all night thinking, "What can I do to teach my boy the good? Who can give a boy lessons if not his own mother? Oh, I must think of some way."

Next morning Kong-Hwa was up at the usual time and went into the kitchen for food. But the kitchen was dark; there was no fire, no food.

He said to himself, "It is queer; so late and no breakfast." He went to his mother's room and called, "Mü-Ts'ing"; but there was no answer. He then went close to her bed and touched her, but she did not move.

He then ran to his aunt and told her to go and see—that his mother was surely dead.

She answered, "It may be that the gods have taken her away because you have been such a bad boy. Now will you be a better boy?" And he promised. Then she ran to her sister's home to see if she was dead.

Kong-Hwa stayed outside trembling with fear, while his aunt went in. She soon saw that her sister was not dead and told of the promise of Kong-Hwa.

"Did my boy think I was dead?" asked his mother. "Well, keep him at your house for two or three days and send him to school. Let him think, and think, and he may be a better boy."

Kong-Hwa's aunt told him that if he learned his lessons and obeyed his teacher, it might be the gods would allow his mother to stay with him after all.

While his aunt prepared breakfast for him, he asked many questions. "What did you do with my mother? Will there be a funeral?"

"Never mind," said the aunt, "go to school and do not be so bad any more, and we shall see what hap- pens. It may be your mother will live again."

II

For two days Kong-Hwa was good—no schoolmate complained, no neighbor complained. He studied his lessons and obeyed his teacher. Then he went again to his mother's house. He saw that she was alive, and in a few days he was again as bad as ever.

"I can not teach him, he must learn things for himself," said his mother; "I do not know what else I can do."

And it was so until he was twelve years old. His mother tried to help him to do right, but it seemed of no use.

Shortly after he was twelve years old, he came home from school one day and said, "Mü-Ts'ing, I want to go to Siang-Sze. I will leave school. No one likes me; no one plays with me. I do not like school and I will not go anymore. I shall be a merchant and make money."

His mother thought he was too young to know what he wanted, and so paid little attention to him. But he insisted, and finally she said, "Go to your father."

His father was surprised and asked, "You wish to make money? How can you make money without money? Siang-Sze is a long way off and it will cost you much to go there. Then you will need more to be a merchant."

Kong-Hwa said, "Give me enough to reach Siang-Sze and I will go." He insisted until his father beat him and said, "Now go back to school. I will hear no more of this."

Kong-Hwa was keen and determined. He borrowed money, quietly, a little here and a little there, and then he ran away to Siang-Sze.

For many days his mother tried to find him. She did not think he would go far by himself. Finally she learned that he had gone to Siang-Sze and gave up searching for him.

Nine years had gone by when a man from Siang-Sze told of seeing Kong-Hwa there. His parents wrote to him, but no answer came. Thirteen years passed by and they thought, "We shall never see his face again."

One day Kong-Hwa, who still lived in Siang-Sze, said to a friend, "I must go home now, if I can get money enough. I have learned some life lessons and now I am going."

His friend said, "We have good times in Siang-Sze. Why do you leave?"

"It is not the place where I ought to be," answered Kong-Hwa. "I have tried many things here and in all the thirteen years have not had success. No one will have me for a bookkeeper. I tried to be a merchandise agent, and in two months I was discharged. I then worked in a bank for forty days, when they paid my salary and told me to go. To-morrow I need money to pay my rent, three months due; but I have no money. I order clothes, and they say, 'No money, no clothes.' I ask friends to lend me some, and they do not even answer me.

"I see now I have been very foolish. I have been here thirteen years and I try to have a good time. I drink, I smoke, I dance, I go to theaters and halls every night—every night. I spend all of my money when I have work. Now I have no work; all my friends have left me; they will not trust me for a piece of silver. I have been very bad. I was a bad boy at home. My mother was good and gave me many lessons which I would not learn.

"Because my mother was so good, I have no excuse for my miserable condition now. I must go home and show her I am sorry at last. I know now that in all the world there is no friend like a mother.

"I will write to her to-morrow and say in my letter, 'Mü-Ts'ing, I am going to leave the opium, theater, and dance—all bad things.' I will ask her to send me money to come home, and I will then take my father's place on the farm.

"I will take the oxen and plow the rice fields, plant the com, and tell my father to rest. I will help my mother so she need not cook nor do any other work. There is no one like father and mother, and no place but my home for me now."

Kong-Hwa wrote the letter and sent it by a friend, telling him to say "good words" for him; for he felt that he deserved nothing after causing his parents so much sorrow.

"Thirteen long years and at last a letter from our dear son," cried Kong-Hwa's mother.

His parents were filled with joy and asked the bearer of the good news all about him. How long would it take for the letter and money that they would send to reach him? Would he come at once?

His mother wrote: "My son, Kong-Hwa, come to our home. We feel that you will do what you say in your letter. The house, the land, and all we have is yours and we will rejoice to have you come and care for them. The time will seem long until you are here."

Kong-Hwa went to his parents as soon as the letter and money came to him. And he was a good man from that time and served his parents and made their old age glad. He did everything as he had said he would. He took the oxen and plowed the rice fields. He planted the corn, and he helped his mother in the house, and all were happy.

The Lion and the Mosquitoes

One day Ah-Fou's father said to him, "Come here, my boy, and I will tell you a story. Do you remember the great lion we saw one day, which Ah-Kay caught? You know a strong rope held him, and he roared and tried to free himself until he died. Then when Ah-Kay took him from the net, he looked at the rope and the bamboo carefully, and found five of the great ropes broken.

"How strong is the lion? Twenty children like you could not break one strand of that great rope. But the lion broke five complete ropes. He is the strongest of all animals. He catches many creatures for his food, but once he lost a battle with one of the least of the wilderness creatures. Do you know what it was?"

"A bird could fight and then fly away. Was it a bird?"

"No, my son."

"A man is stronger than a lion."

"No, do you not remember the woodcutter who could put down five strong men? One night a wilderness lion caught and killed him."

"Then what was the smallest of all creatures of the wilderness that battled with a lion?"

The father said, "I will tell you the story: Once in the summer time the lion was very thirsty. But the sun had taken all the water near the lion's home and he went to many places seeking for it. In time he found an old well, but the water was not fresh. As the lion was very thirsty he said, 'I must drink, even though the water is stale.'

"But when he reached down into the old well, he found that it was the home of all the mosquitoes of the wilderness.

"The mosquitoes said to the lion, 'Go away, we do not want you. This is our home and we are happy. We do not wish the lion, the fox, or the bear to come here. You are not our friend. Why do you come?'

"The lion roared and said, 'Weak and foolish things! I am the lion. It is you that should go away, for I have come to drink. This is my wilderness, and I am king. Do you know, weak things, that when I come out from my place and send forth my voice, all the creatures of the wilderness shake like leaves and bow their heads to me? What are you that you should have a place you call your home and tell me that I may or I may not?'

"Then the mosquitoes answered, 'You are only one. You speak as if you were many. Our people had this old well for a home before your roar was heard in the wilderness. And many generations of us have been born here. This home is ours, and we are they that say who shall come or go. And yet you come and tell us to go out of our own door. If you do not leave us, we will call our people, and you shall know trouble.'

"But the lion held his head high with pride and anger and said, 'What are you, oh small of the small? I will kill every one of your useless people. When I drink, I will open my mouth only a little wider, and you shall be swallowed like the water. And to-morrow, I shall forget that I drank to-day.'

" 'Boastful one,' said the mosquitoes, 'we do not believe that you have the power to destroy all our people. If you wish battle, we shall see. We know your name is great and that all animals bow their heads before you; but our people can kill you.'

"The lion jumped high in his rage and said, 'No other creature in the wilderness has dared to say these things to me—the king. Have I come to the vile well of the silly mosquitoes for wisdom?' And he held his head high, and gave the mighty roar of battle, and made ready to kill all the mosquitoes.

"Then the mosquitoes, big and little, flew around him. Many went into his ears, and the smallest ones went into his nose, and the big old ones went into his mouth to sting. A thousand and a thousand hung in the air, just over his head and made a great noise, and the lion soon knew that he could not conquer.

"He roared and jumped, and two of his front feet went down into the well. The well was narrow and deep and he could not get out, for his two hind feet were in the air and his head hung downward. And as he died, he said to himself:

"'My pride and anger have brought me this fate. Had I used gentle words, the mosquitoes might have given me water for my thirst. I was wise and strong in the wilderness, and even the greatest of the animals feared my power. But I fought with the mosquitoes and I die—not because I have not strength to overcome, but because of the foolishness of anger.'"

The Thief and the Elephant

Six hundred years ago the people of Southern China trained elephants and taught them to do many useful things. They worked for farmers and woodcutters, and helped make the roads twice a year; for an elephant could do many times more work than any other animal. So wise were the elephants that the people grew superstitious about them, believing they could see even into the heart of man.

A judge named Ko-Kia-Yong had an elephant that was trained to do this wonderful thing, so it was said. Three cases which were brought before him, were decided by a wise old elephant which he owned. And this is the way one of the decisions was made:

A man came before the judge and said that some robbers had been in his house during the night and had taken his gold and jewels—all that he had; and he asked the judge to find and punish the thieves.

In three months, five robbers had been found. When they were brought to the judge, they bowed before him and each one said, "I have never stolen anything."

The man and woman who had been robbed were called. And the woman said, "That man with the long gray hair is the one who robbed us."

The judge asked, "Are you sure it is he, and how do you know?"

She answered, "Yes, I remember. He took the bracelet from my arm and I looked into his face."

"Did the other four rob you also?" asked the judge.

The woman answered, "I do not know."

But the judge said, "The man who you say is a robber, seems not like one to me. His face is kind and gentle. I can not decide according to your testimony. I know of but one way to find out, and we shall soon know the truth in this matter. My elephant shall be brought in to examine the men. He can read the mind and heart of man; and those who are not guilty need have no fear, for he will surely know the one who has done this deed."

Four of the men looked glad.

They were stripped and stood naked—all but the cloth—before the judge and the law of the nation, and the elephant was brought in.

Then the judge said to the elephant, "Examine these men and tell us which is the robber." The elephant touched with his trunk each of the five accused men, from his head to his feet.

And the white-haired man and the three others stood still and laughed at the elephant with happy faces; for they knew in their hearts they were not guilty and they thought the elephant knew. But the fifth man shivered with fear and his face changed to many colors. While the elephant was examining him, the judge said, "Do your duty," and rapped loudly. The elephant took the guilty man and threw him down on the floor, dead.

Then the judge said to the four guiltless men, "You may go." And to the woman he said, "Be careful whom you accuse." Then he said to the elephant, "Food and water are waiting for you. I hope you may live a long time, and help me to judge wisely."

After this many wise men who were not superstitious went to the judge and said:

"We know that your elephant can not read the heart and mind of man. What kind of food do you give him and what do you teach him? Man himself lives only from sixty to one hundred years and he knows little. How could an elephant read the heart of man, a thing which man, himself, can not do? Did the spirit of a dead man grow wise and enter that elephant? We pray that you explain."

And Ko-Kio-Yong, the wise judge, laughed and said, "My elephant eats and drinks as other elephants do. I think he surely does not know a robber from an honest man, but this is a belief among our people. The honest man believes it and has no fear, because he has done no wrong. The thief believes it, and is filled with terror. Trial before the elephant is only confession through fear."

The General, the Bird, and the Ant

The people of the north nation were causing the king, Ting Ming Wong, much trouble, and one day he ordered his general, Gui Süt Yun, to declare war on them.

The brave general prepared to march north at once. He led an army of twenty-five thousand cavalry, followed by one thousand infantry.

By the time they reached Mau Tin Lang the soldiers were very tired, for they had then marched ten days. Orders were given that they rest for three days before proceeding.

The weather was very warm, and on the second day there was no more water, not even to drink. The soldiers dug wells in many places, hoping to find water; but each time they were disappointed.

A report was then made to the general, Gui Süt Yun, which said, "The men and horses are near death for the lack of water."

Then the general ordered many men to go in different directions within a radius of ten miles to search for water.

The following morning two hundred men were dead, and still no water could be found.

Then the general, Gui Süt Yun, said, "We must all die here if we do not find water. If it is within one hundred miles, I will find it." He then mounted his favorite war horse, and rode until both he and the horse were ready to die with the terrible thirst. He tried to feed his horse with green leaves; but he was weak and suffering, and the general lay down for rest and sleep.

He cried in bitterness of spirit. Then he looked up to heaven and said:

"Has our king done a great wrong or have our soldiers done evil? Why should we perish here in a strange land? In the hour that I rest and sleep here, may a spirit show me the path that leads out of this great trouble.

"It may be that if the north kingdom is right, we shall die here and not even go to battle. But if we are right, this thing should not be. When we first came here, there was plenty of water. Why did the earth drink up this water and leave us to die? As I sleep, may a spirit show me the meaning of all this."

Then he slept. And he saw one of the great wilderness ants; and a bird flew down to eat the ant. But the ant spoke and said, "I know that you birds try to eat our family all the time. But it is not right that one creature should eat another. You have power to overcome any ant and cat it if you wish, but man has charge of this world. When the hunter comes you cannot escape his arrow or his net.

"It is not right that one creature should be against another creature. Go your way, and I will go my way, so that I may find food for my children.

"I have one hundred and fifty eggs in my nest now and I hope every one will soon hatch. Then my children will depend on me to help them. They will all die if you eat me, their parent. The earth has much grain, wheat, and rice. These are enough for your food."

Then the bird answered, "Tell me what makes you so wise. I am a bird. I am much handsomer than you and I have a beautiful song. The children of men all like me. It is true, as you say, the hunter does catch my people sometimes. But there are many men who raise birds in their own houses and teach them to sing. Then they take us to the music hall or theater where they get money for our songs.

"One member of the bird family carries letters for man; and our feathers are used to make feather balls for the children to play with. So you see, birds are very useful. But as for the ant I can not see how he is useful to man or beast."

"Oh, you are mistaken," said the ant earnestly. "Do you see this general here? He needs me to help him now. Do you know why he is lying here? He and his war horse are near death for the lack of water. Soon more than a thousand soldiers will be dead. Then the north nation will take this general's nation, and his people will no longer have a country. But I will save them.

"Long ago our people saved a nation. Once there was a war between the east and the west nations, and the general, Hai Hau, nearly perished for water, even as this general here is doing. But my people always build their homes near water, and he followed their road and they showed him the way to water and saved many lives."

Then the bird opened his mouth and laughed scornfully, "Chic, Chic, I do not believe that story. You are speaking falsely. I know of one very evil thing your people have done, which I will tell you about.

"Men built a great tower on the North Mountain once, and soon it fell to earth again. After a time they discovered the cause of this trouble. It was not the wind, nor the storm, nor the rain, nor even the earthquake that shook the tower down. It was found that ants had eaten the wood and this caused it to break and fall.

"Birds do not make trouble in the world. Ants do. But I will give you fair warning, that if you do not do this good thing you boast of, I will eat you at once."

The ant answered, "You shall yet see that I am able to save this general, his soldiers, and his horses."

The ant then went straight to the general's ear and said to him, "Do you remember General Hai Hau who was lost in this wilderness? If you will go to the forest, you will see a black street full of my people. They will lead you to their nests near the great cave spring in the wilderness, which was named Hai Hau for the general who discovered it. It is only a half mile from here."

Then the general, Gui Süt Yun, awoke and said, "Strange, but I surely heard an ant and a bird talking together while I slept. Where is my map? I did not know of the cave of Hai Hau."

He found the great cave spring, and he and his horse drank. Then he hurried back to the soldiers, and their lives were saved.

The Three Girls Who Went to a Boys' School

There were thirty-five scholars in the school at Qui-Chu, and three were girls. The boys played by themselves and the three girls played together.

One day the teacher said to his mother, "I think I shall have the girls dress in boys' clothes next year, if they come to school."

"Why will you do this?" asked his mother.

"Because the boys do not like girls in the school. They will not play, read, or write with them. They tease them and laugh at them. I fear the girls must leave the school next year, and they are only nine years old. But we shall see."

When the next year came, the mother was willing to do as her son said. She took some cloth and made boys' clothes for the three girls, which she put on them to see how they would look dressed as boys.

When the girls were dressed, they looked at each other and laughed. "What will you do with the ear-holes, grandmother?" they asked. "Surely the boys will know we are girls."

The mother called her son and asked him, "What shall we do with the ear-holes? They look like boys now, save for that one thing. I fear the girls can not go to school."

"I will see," replied her son. He thought much for two days. Then he went to find an old doctor in the next village, far enough away so that no one would know. He asked the doctor, "Can you close the ear-holes so that girls' ears will be as boys'?"

"Oh, yes," answered the doctor, "I can if you will pay me." Then the doctor came and put something in the ear-holes and colored it so that it looked like skin, and the grandmother was satisfied to send the girls to school.

But the teacher forgot and called them girls' names. The others laughed at the three boys with funny names, but they did not seem to remember them.

Five or six months went by, and the boys had not yet learned that the three scholars with the pretty names were the girls of last year. Then one boy came to the teacher and asked, "Why do those boys have girls' names? I wish to know."

The teacher thought a moment and said, "Lily—Beauty—Moon. That boy was called Lily, I think, because he was so red when he was a little baby. The mother thought he ought to be called 'Red,' but that is not a pretty name for a baby, and so they called him Lily.

"And do you not think that Beauty's name suits him? He is the handsomest boy in the school. I think his mother called him Beauty because he was such a pretty baby. He is as pretty as a girl. I think it is right that he should be called Beauty. Moon's name is suitable for him, too. You know he is gentle and fair. Did you ever see a more gentle boy in school? I think he was always very gentle and fair, and so his mother gave him that name. All his friends like him as they do the moon."

The boy ran away and told the other pupils what his teacher had said about the three boys with the pretty names.

New Year came, and each boy had to write his name on a piece of paper and hand it to the teacher, so that he could give them their school names. Eight gave their names as Beauty, and seventeen as Moon, while all the others wanted to be called Lily. They expected the teacher would allow them to have those as their school names.

In the summer time the scholars had a vacation and the teacher went away for a time.

One day they were all on the playground playing "Theater." They took nine of the prettiest boys and put red and white on their faces and dressed them like ladies and bound their feet to make them small. Six boys put on false beards. Then they piled up chairs and tables high to make a mountain, and the boys with bound feet were to cross over to the other side. The boys who had to climb over the mountain from the opposite side were careless, and when all met at the top, they tumbled and fell down in a heap. One boy broke his arm, one broke his finger, and one hurt his eye. The other boys did not stay to help or see what they could do for those who were hurt. All but the three girls, who were dressed like boys, ran away in fear, and left the wounded children lying on the ground.

One girl ran for the doctor. The other two stayed and gave the hurt ones water to drink, fanned their faces, kept the flies away, and cared for them like little mothers.

In a few minutes the doctor came. He asked, "What were you doing, boys?" The boys were so hurt and scared that they could not talk, but the girls told how it had all happened.

The doctor bound up the broken arm and finger, and dressed the bruised eye. He was a good doctor and said, "These boys must lie still several days. They can not get up without my orders; now who is willing to take care of them?"

"We will help," said the three girls.

The teacher came back and school began again. When he called for the names of the pupils, they gave those which they liked best—Lily, Beauty, and Moon—as before, but the teacher said, "No, these names are all wrong.

"There is only one Lily, one Beauty, and one Moon in this school now. You boys can not use the names I gave you. You had beautiful names, but your acts were not beautiful.

"You ran away when your schoolmates were hurt. You had no pity for them. Had it not been for Lily, Beauty, and Moon, they would have died. These names mean something. Beauty makes the world a pleasant place for us to live in. The Moon shines and gives us soft light. The Lily gives us beauty and sweet-smelling odors.

"Your acts were not like the names. After this, when boys want such names they must do something to be worthy of them."

The Rattan Vine and the Rose Tree

In the San-Wui district, in the garden of a rich merchant, lived the Lon-da-Tang (rattan vine) and the Mui-Kwi (rose tree).

One day the rose tree said to the rattan vine, "Lon-da-Tang, please tell me how you grow so fast. What do you eat that you are able to go any where you wish? Nothing seems to hurt you. Nothing seems to stop you, not even the stone fences or the clay roofs. You have no fear, and there seems to be no danger for you. You care not for the heat of the sun when he is close in the summer time. The rain comes down with a rushing noise from dark places in the heavens, and you are not afraid. The wind blows hard and bends our heads to the earth, but you seem not even to heed it."

Then the Lon-da-Tang with a proud and happy summer face answered the rose tree, "Mui-Kwi-Si (Mrs. Rose Tree), you should be made to leave this garden. I would not allow you to grow here if I were master.

"I have known you five or six years. The master put you in the earth and gave you much dirt to feed upon. He gives you water every morning. In the winter time he gives you a cover and a bed of straw. He trims your branches and serves you in many ways. And yet you do not grow.

"You are nine years old now, and only five or six feet tall, while I am only four years old and my branches measure many thousands of feet. You bear a few flowers in the summer, and that is all you can do. You have no fruit and not many leaves. You stand still in the garden and do nothing useful. You ought to be ashamed. Do you see my branches? Although I have been here but four years, I now reach over this house and am climbing the fence on the other side. Next year, I shall go and cover up another house.

"The master likes me in summer, because I keep the hot sun from the roof and make his house cool. The children like me, too. Sometimes they climb in my arms and swing. And the fence likes me, because I cover it so thickly that I protect it from the children and the pigs. The birds build their nests high in my arms and they like me also. The bugs like me, because I give them a home and they feed upon my leaves. So the master knows that I am good for many things.

"The birds would not go to you, because you are so small; they can not build a nest upon you. The master's wife does not care much for you, because you have so many thorns that she finds it hard to gather your flowers. You are pretty, but who cares about that? The fence is high and no one sees you. And so you stand there and do nothing."

Then the rose tree replied, "Lon-da-Tang, with all your boasting, you can not even stand alone. I can at least do that. I know I am not large, and the birds do not build their nests with me. I can not grow so fast as you, but my children are known to the whole great world of mankind, and are called the sweetest of all flowers.

"And besides, I am independent. I do not lean upon other things. If your house or your fence falls down, where then will be your vain boastful head?

"I care not what you say of me, whether you think a rose is good or bad, strong or weak. I do not wish to lean on the fence or roof as you do. Some day, when the house and fence grow old, they will fall down, and what will you do then?"

Soon after this, there came a great storm. In San-Wiu many houses were partly destroyed and the fences fell to the ground. The roof of the merchant's house was blown off. The proud rattan vine, Lon-da-Tang, was broken in many places, and his head lay low on the earth.

But the rose tree stood firm. And she laughed and said to the rattan, "I told you that it was dangerous to lean upon other things and never to learn to stand by yourself. I would not trust any house or fence to do my standing for me. I would rather be independent. I grow all the leaves, stems, and flowers I want, and so I stand here forever. The north wind comes and I bow my head to the south. Then the south wind comes and opens my beautiful flowers. I am the rose tree, and in my own strength I stand."

The Melon and the Professor

WU-KIAO WAS A PROFESSOR IN A LARGE CHINESE UNIVERSITY, AND A VERY PROUD and learned man. Hundreds of students were under his teaching, and many thousands honored him. When he went out of his house, five people followed, singing and playing the drum all the way down the street, and eight men carried his chair,. At home he had six servants about him. During each meal, thirty dishes were served at his table.

The professor was a great man. Through his wisdom and out of his deep knowledge, he explained all questions to the people.

One day Wu-Kiao sat in the shade of a tree in his garden. He turned his head and saw a watermelon lying on the ground, nearly covered with its green leaves. Then, seeing the fig tree with many figs on it, he said, "I think the Creator should have made the melon grow on this tree."

He touched the tree and said, "How strong you are; you could bear larger fruit like the watermelon." And he said to the vine, "You, so thin and small, should bear small fruit like the fig. Things are not well ordered. Mistakes are made in creation." Just then a fig dropped from the tree on his nose, and he was a little bruised.

Then he said, "I was wrong. If the fig tree bore fruit as large as the watermelon and dropped it on my nose, I think I should be killed. It would be a dangerous tree to all people. I must study more carefully. I know many things and many people; and if I study and think more deeply, it may be I shall come to know that the Creator's works are perfect."

Some Chinese Ghosts

The Soul of the Great Bell

She hath spoken, and her words still resound in his ears.
HAO-KHIEOU-TCHOUAN: C. IX.

THE WATER-CLOCK MARKS THE HOUR IN THE *TA-CHUNG SZ'*—IN THE TOWER OF THE Great Bell: now the mallet is lifted to smite the lips of the metal monster—the vast lips inscribed with Buddhist texts from the sacred *Fa-hwa-King*, from the chapters of the holy *Ling-yen-King*! Hear the great bell responding!—how mighty her voice, though tongueless!—*KO-NGAI!* All the little dragons on the high-tilted eaves of the green roofs shiver to the tips of their gilded tails under that deep wave of sound; all the porcelain gargoyles tremble on their carven perches; all the hundred little bells of the pagodas quiver with desire to speak. *KO-NGAI!*—all the green-and-gold tiles of the temple are vibrating; the wooden goldfish above them are writhing against the sky; the uplifted finger of Fo shakes high over the heads of the worshippers through the blue fog of incense! *KO-NGAI!*—What a thunder tone was that! All the lacquered goblins on the palace cornices wriggle their fire-colored tongues! And after each huge shock, how wondrous the multiple echo and the great golden moan and, at last, the sudden sibilant sobbing in the ears when the immense tone faints away in broken whispers of silver—as though a woman should whisper, "*Hiai!*" Even so the great bell hath sounded every day for well-nigh five hundred years—*Ko-Ngai*: first with stupendous clang, then with immeasurable moan of gold, then with silver murmuring of "*Hiai!*" And there is not a child in all the many-colored ways of the old Chinese city who does not know the story of the great bell—who cannot tell you why the great bell says *Ko-Ngai* and *Hiai*!

Now, this is the story of the great bell in the Ta-chung sz', as the same is related in the *Pe-Hiao-Tou-Choue*, written by the learned Yu-Pao-Tchen, of the City of Kwang-tchau-fu.

Nearly five hundred years ago the Celestially August, the Son of Heaven, Yong-Lo, of the "Illustrious," or Ming, dynasty, commanded the worthy official Kouan-Yu that he should have a bell made of such size that the sound thereof might be heard for one hundred *li*. And he further ordained that the voice of the bell should be strengthened with brass, and deepened with gold, and sweetened with silver; and that the face and the great lips of it should be graven with blessed sayings from the sacred books, and that it should be suspended in the center of the imperial capital, to sound through all the many-colored ways of the City of Pe-king.

Therefore the worthy mandarin Kouan-Yu assembled the master-molders and the renowned bell-smiths of the empire, and all men of great repute and cunning in foundry work; and they measured the materials for the alloy, and treated them skillfully, and prepared the molds, the fires, the instruments, and the monstrous melting-pot for fusing the metal. And they labored exceedingly, like giants—neglecting only rest and sleep and the comforts of life; toiling both night and day in obedience to Kouan-Yu, and striving in all things to do the behest of the Son of Heaven.

But when the metal had been cast, and the earthen mold separated from the glowing casting, it was discovered that, despite their great labor and ceaseless care, the result was void of worth; for the metals had rebelled one against the other—the gold had scorned alliance with the brass, the silver would not mingle with the molten iron. Therefore the molds had to be once more prepared, and the fires rekindled, and the metal remelted, and all the work tediously and toilsomely repeated. The Son of Heaven heard, and was angry, but spake nothing.

A second time the bell was cast, and the result was even worse. Still the metals obstinately refused to blend one with the other; and there was no uniformity in the bell, and the sides of it were cracked and fissured, and the lips of it were slagged and split asunder; so that all the labor had to be repeated even a third time, to the great dismay of Kouan-Yu. And when the Son of Heaven heard these things, he was angrier than before; and sent his messenger to Kouan-Yu with a letter, written upon lemon-colored silk, and sealed with the seal of the Dragon, containing these words:—

> From the Mighty Yong-Lo, the Sublime Tait-Sung, the Celestial and August—whose reign is called "Ming"—to Kouan-Yu the Fuh-yin: Twice thou hast betrayed the trust we have deigned graciously to place in thee; if thou fail a third time in fulfilling our command, thy head shall be severed from thy neck. Tremble, and obey!

Now, Kouan-Yu had a daughter of dazzling loveliness, whose name—Ko-Ngai—was ever in the mouths of poets, and whose heart was even more beautiful than her face. Ko-Ngai loved her father with such love that she had refused a hundred worthy suitors rather than make his home desolate by her absence; and when she had seen the awful yellow missive, sealed with the Dragon-Seal, she fainted away with fear for her father's sake. And when her senses and her strength returned to her, she could not rest or sleep for thinking of her parent's danger, until she had secretly sold some of her jewels, and with the money so obtained had hastened to an astrologer, and paid him a great price to advise her by what means her father might be saved from the peril impending over him. So the astrologer made observations of the heavens, and marked the aspect of the Silver Stream (which we call the Milky Way), and examined the signs of the Zodiac—the *Hwang-tao,* or Yellow Road,—and consulted the table of the Five *Hin*, or Principles of the Universe, and the mystical books of the alchemists. And after a long silence, he made answer to her, saying: "Gold and brass will never meet in wedlock, silver and iron never will embrace, until the flesh of a maiden be melted in the crucible; until the blood of a virgin be mixed with the metals in their fusion." So Ko-Ngai returned home sorrowful at heart; but she kept secret all that she had heard, and told no one what she had done.

At last came the awful day when the third and last effort to cast the great bell was to be made; and Ko-Ngai, together with her waiting-woman, accompanied her father to the foundry, and they took their places upon a platform overlooking the toiling of the molders and the lava of liquefied metal. All the workmen wrought their tasks in silence; there was no sound heard but the muttering of the fires. And the muttering deepened into a roar like the roar of typhoons approaching, and the blood-red lake of metal slowly brightened like the vermilion of a sunrise, and the vermilion was transmuted into a radiant glow of gold, and the gold whitened blindingly, like the silver face of a full moon. Then the workers ceased to feed the raving flame, and all fixed their eyes upon the eyes of Kouan-Yu; and Kouan-Yu prepared to give the signal to cast.

But ere ever he lifted his finger, a cry caused him to turn his head; and all heard the voice of Ko-Ngai sounding sharply sweet as a bird's song above the great thunder of the fires—"*For thy sake, O my Father!*" And even as she cried, she leaped into the white flood of metal; and the lava of the furnace roared to receive her, and spattered monstrous flakes of flame to the roof, and burst over the verge of the earthen crater, and cast up a whirling fountain of many-colored fires, and subsided quakingly, with lightnings and with thunders and with mutterings.

Then the father of Ko-Ngai, wild with his grief, would have leaped in after her, but that strong men held him back and kept firm grasp upon him until he had fainted away and they could bear him like one dead to his home. And the serving-woman of Ko-Ngai, dizzy and speechless for pain, stood before the furnace, still holding in her hands a shoe, a tiny, dainty shoe, with embroidery of pearls and flowers—the shoe of her beautiful mistress that was. For she had sought to grasp Ko-Ngai by the foot as she leaped, but had only been able to clutch the shoe, and the pretty shoe came off in her hand; and she continued to stare at it like one gone mad.

But in spite of all these things, the command of the Celestial and August had to be obeyed, and the work of the molders to be finished, hopeless as the result might be. Yet the glow of the metal seemed purer and whiter than before; and there was no sign of the beautiful body that had been entombed therein. So the ponderous casting was made; and lo! when the metal had become cool, it was found that the bell was beautiful to look upon, and perfect in form, and wonderful in color above all other bells. Nor was there any trace found of the body of Ko-Ngai; for it had been totally absorbed by the precious alloy, and blended with the well-blended brass and gold, with the intermingling of the silver and the iron. And when they sounded the bell, its tones were found to be deeper and mellower and mightier than the tones of any other bell,—reaching even beyond the distance of one hundred *li*, like a pealing of summer thunder; and yet also like some vast voice uttering a name, a woman's name,—the name of Ko-Ngai!

And still, between each mighty stroke there is a long low moaning heard; and ever the moaning ends with a sound of sobbing and of complaining, as though a weeping woman should murmur, "*Hiai!*" And still, when the people hear that great golden moan they keep silence; but when the sharp, sweet shuddering comes in the air, and the sobbing of "*Hiai!*" then, indeed, all the Chinese mothers in all the many-colored ways of Pe-king whisper to their little ones: *"Listen! that is Ko-Ngai crying for her shoe! That is Ko-Ngai calling for her shoe!"*

The Story of Ming-Y

The ancient words of Kouei—Master of Musicians in the Courts of the
Emperor Yao:
When ye make to resound the stone melodious, the Ming-Khieou—
When ye touch the lyre that is called Kin, or the guitar that is called Ssé—
Accompanying their sound with song—
Then do grandfather and the father return;
Then do the ghosts of the ancestors come to hear.

Do you ask me who she was—the beautiful Siё-Thao? For a thousand years and more the trees have been whispering above her bed of stone. And the syllables of her name come to the listener with the lisping of the leaves; with the quivering of many-fingered boughs; with the fluttering of lights and shadows; with the breath, sweet as a woman's presence, of numberless savage flowers—*Sië-Thao*. But, saving the whispering of her name, what the trees say cannot be understood; and they alone remember the years of Sië-Thao. Something about her you might, nevertheless, learn from any of those *Kiang-kou-jin*—those famous Chinese story-tellers, who nightly narrate to listening crowds, in consideration of a few *tsien*, the legends of the past. Something concerning her you may also find in the book entitled "Kin-Kou-Ki-Koan," which signifies in our tongue: "The Marvelous Happenings of Ancient and of Recent Times." And perhaps of all things therein written, the most marvelous is this memory of Sië-Thao:—

Five hundred years ago, in the reign of the Emperor Houng-Wou, whose dynasty was Ming, there lived in the City of Genii, the city of Kwang-tchau-fu, a man celebrated for his learning and for his piety, named Tien-Pelou. This Tien-Pelou had one son, a beautiful boy, who for scholarship and for bodily grace and for polite accomplishments had no superior among the youths of his age. And his name was Ming-Y.

Now when the lad was in his eighteenth summer, it came to pass that Pelou, his father, was appointed Inspector of Public Instruction at the city of Tching-tou; and Ming-Y accompanied his parents thither. Near the city of Tching-tou lived a rich man of rank, a high commissioner of the government, whose name was Tchang, and who wanted to find a worthy teacher for his children. On hearing of the arrival of the new Inspector of Public Instruction, the noble Tchang visited him to obtain advice in this matter; and happening to meet and converse with Pelou's accomplished son, immediately engaged Ming-Y as a private tutor for his family.

Now as the house of this Lord Tchang was situated several miles from town, it was deemed best that Ming-Y should abide in the house of his employer. Accordingly the youth made ready all things necessary for his new sojourn; and his parents, bidding him farewell, counseled him wisely, and cited to him the words of Lao-tseu and of the ancient sages:

> "By a beautiful face the world is filled with love; but Heaven may never be deceived thereby. Shouldst thou behold a woman coming from the East, look thou to the West; shouldst thou perceive a maiden approaching from the West, turn thine eyes to the East."

If Ming-Y did not heed this counsel in after days, it was only because of his youth and the thoughtlessness of a naturally joyous heart.

And he departed to abide in the house of Lord Tchang, while the autumn passed, and the winter also.

When the time of the second moon of spring was drawing near, and that happy day which the Chinese call *Hoa-tchao*, or, "The Birthday of a Hundred Flowers," a longing came upon Ming-Y to see his parents; and he opened his heart to the good Tchang, who not only gave him the permission he desired, but also pressed into his hand a silver gift of two ounces, thinking that the lad might wish to bring some little memento to his father and mother. For it is the Chinese custom, on the feast of Hoa-tchao, to make presents to friends and relations.

That day all the air was drowsy with blossom perfume, and vibrant with the droning of bees. It seemed to Ming-Y that the path he followed had not been trodden by any other for many long years; the grass was tall upon it; vast trees on either side interlocked their mighty and moss-grown arms above him, beshadowing the way; but the leafy obscurities quivered with bird-song, and the deep vistas of the wood were glorified by vapors of gold, and odorous with flower-breathings as a temple with incense. The dreamy joy of the day entered into the heart of Ming-Y; and he sat him down among the young blossoms, under the branches swaying against the violet sky, to drink in the perfume and the light, and to enjoy the great sweet silence. Even while thus reposing, a sound caused him to turn his eyes toward a shady place where wild peach-trees were in bloom; and he beheld a young woman, beautiful as the pinkening blossoms themselves, trying to hide among them. Though he looked for a moment only, Ming-Y could not avoid discerning the loveliness of her face, the golden purity of her complexion, and the brightness of her long eyes, that sparkled under a pair of brows as daintily curved as the wings of the silkworm butterfly outspread. Ming-Y at once turned his gaze away, and, rising quickly, proceeded on his journey. But so much embarrassed did he feel at the idea of those charming eyes peeping at him through the leaves, that he suffered the money he had been carrying in his sleeve to fall, without being aware of it. A few moments later he heard the patter of light feet running behind him, and a woman's voice calling him by name. Turning his face in great surprise, he saw a comely servant-maid, who said to him, "Sir, my mistress bade me pick up and return you this silver which you dropped upon the road." Ming-Y thanked the girl gracefully, and requested her to convey his compliments to her mistress. Then he proceeded on his way through the perfumed silence, athwart the shadows that dreamed along the forgotten path, dreaming himself also, and feeling his heart beating with strange quickness at the thought of the beautiful being that he had seen.

It was just such another day when Ming-Y, returning by the same path, paused once more at the spot where the gracious figure had momentarily appeared before him. But this time he was surprised to perceive, through a long vista of immense trees, a dwelling that had previously escaped his notice—a country residence, not large, yet elegant to an unusual degree. The bright blue tiles of its curved and serrated double roof, rising above the foliage, seemed to blend their color with the luminous azure of the day; the green-and-gold designs of its carven porticos were exquisite artistic mockeries of leaves and flowers bathed in sunshine. And at the summit of terrace-steps before it, guarded by great porcelain tortoises, Ming-Y saw standing the mistress of the mansion—the idol of his passionate fancy—accompanied by the same waiting-maid who had borne to her his message of gratitude. While Ming-Y looked, he perceived that their eyes were upon him; they smiled and conversed together as if speaking about him; and, shy though he was, the youth found courage to salute the fair one from a distance. To his astonishment, the young servant beckoned him to approach; and opening a rustic gate half veiled by trailing plants bearing crimson flowers, Ming-Y advanced along the verdant alley leading to the terrace, with mingled feelings of surprise and timid joy. As he drew near, the beautiful lady withdrew from sight; but the maid waited at the broad steps to receive him, and said as he ascended:

"Sir, my mistress understands you wish to thank her for the trifling service she recently bade me do you, and requests that you will enter the house, as she knows you already by repute, and desires to have the pleasure of bidding you good-day."

Ming-Y entered bashfully, his feet making no sound upon a matting elastically soft as forest moss, and found himself in a reception-chamber vast, cool, and fragrant with scent of blossoms freshly gathered. A delicious quiet pervaded the mansion; shadows of flying birds passed over the bands of light that fell through the half-blinds of bamboo; great butterflies, with pinions of fiery color, found their way in, to hover a moment about the painted vases, and pass out again into the mysterious woods. And noiselessly as they, the young mistress of the mansion entered by another door, and kindly greeted the boy, who lifted his hands to his breast and bowed low in salutation. She was taller than he had deemed her, and supplely-slender as a beauteous lily; her black hair was interwoven with the creamy blossoms of the *chu-sha-kih*; her robes of pale silk took shifting tints when she moved, as vapors change hue with the changing of the light.

"If I be not mistaken," she said, when both had seated themselves after having exchanged the customary formalities of politeness, "my honored visitor is none other than Tien-chou, surnamed Ming-Y, educator of the children of my respected relative, the High Commissioner Tchang. As the family of Lord Tchang is my family also, I cannot but consider the teacher of his children as one of my own kin."

"Lady," replied Ming-Y, not a little astonished, "may I dare to inquire the name of your honored family, and to ask the relation which you hold to my noble patron?"

"The name of my poor family," responded the comely lady, "is *Ping*—an ancient family of the city of Tching-tou. I am the daughter of a certain Sië of Moun-hao; Sië is my name, likewise; and I was married to a young man of the Ping family, whose name was Khang. By this marriage I became related to your excellent patron; but my husband died soon after our wedding, and I have chosen this solitary place to reside in during the period of my widowhood."

There was a drowsy music in her voice, as of the melody of brooks, the murmurings of spring; and such a strange grace in the manner of her speech as Ming-Y had never heard before. Yet, on learning that she was a widow, the youth would not have presumed to remain long in her presence without a formal invitation; and after having sipped the cup of rich tea presented to him, he arose to depart. Sië would not suffer him to go so quickly.

"Nay, friend," she said; "stay yet a little while in my house, I pray you; for, should your honored patron ever learn that you had been here, and that I had not treated you as a respected guest, and regaled you even as I would him, I know that he would be greatly angered. Remain at least to supper."

So Ming-Y remained, rejoicing secretly in his heart, for Sië seemed to him the fairest and sweetest being he had ever known, and he felt that he loved her even more than his father and his mother. And while they talked the long shadows of the evening slowly blended into one violet darkness; the great citron-light of the sunset faded out; and those starry beings that are called the "Three Councillors," who preside over life and death and the destinies of men, opened their cold bright eyes in the northern sky. Within the mansion of Sië the painted lanterns were lighted; the table was laid for the evening repast; and Ming-Y took his place at it, feeling little inclination to eat, and thinking only of the charming face before him. Observing that he scarcely tasted the dainties laid upon his plate, Sië pressed her young guest to partake of wine; and they drank several cups together. It was a purple wine, so cool that the cup into which it was poured became covered with vapory dew; yet it seemed to warm the veins with strange fire. To Ming-Y, as he drank, all things became more luminous as by enchantment; the walls of the chamber appeared to recede, and the roof to heighten; the lamps glowed like stars in their chains, and the voice of Sië floated to the boy's ears like some far melody heard through the spaces of a drowsy night. His heart swelled;

his tongue loosened; and words flitted from his lips that he had fancied he could never dare to utter. Yet Sië sought not to restrain him; her lips gave no smile; but her long bright eyes seemed to laugh with pleasure at his words of praise, and to return his gaze of passionate admiration with affectionate interest.

"I have heard," she said, "of your rare talent, and of your many elegant accomplishments. I know how to sing a little, although I cannot claim to possess any musical learning; and now that I have the honor of finding myself in the society of a musical professor, I will venture to lay modesty aside, and beg you to sing a few songs with me. I should deem it no small gratification if you would condescend to examine my musical compositions."

"The honor and the gratification, dear lady," replied Ming-Y, "will be mine; and I feel helpless to express the gratitude which the offer of so rare a favor deserves."

The serving-maid, obedient to the summons of a little silver gong, brought in the music and retired. Ming-Y took the manuscripts, and began to examine them with eager delight. The paper upon which they were written had a pale yellow tint, and was light as a fabric of gossamer; but the characters were antiquely beautiful, as though they had been traced by the brush of Heï-song Ché-Tchoo himself,—that divine Genius of Ink, who is no bigger than a fly; and the signatures attached to the compositions were the signatures of Youen-tchin, Kao-pien, and Thou-mou—mighty poets and musicians of the dynasty of Thang! Ming-Y could not repress a scream of delight at the sight of treasures so inestimable and so unique; scarcely could he summon resolution enough to permit them to leave his hands even for a moment.

"O Lady!" he cried, "these are veritably priceless things, surpassing in worth the treasures of all kings. This indeed is the handwriting of those great masters who sang five hundred years before our birth. How marvelously it has been preserved! Is not this the wondrous ink of which it was written: '*Po-nien-jou-chi, i-tien-jou-ki*—After centuries I remain firm as stone, and the letters that I make like lacquer'? And how divine the charm of this composition!—the song of Kao-pien, prince of poets, and Governor of Sze-tchouen five hundred years ago!"

"Kao-pien! darling Kao-pien!" murmured Sië, with a singular light in her eyes. "Kao-pien is also my favorite. Dear Ming-Y, let us chant his verses together, to the melody of old—the music of those grand years when men were nobler and wiser than to-day."

And their voices rose through the perfumed night like the voices of the wonder-birds—of the Fung-hoang—blending together in liquid sweetness. Yet a moment, and Ming-Y, overcome by the witchery of his companion's voice, could only listen in speechless ecstasy, while the lights of the chamber swam dim before his sight, and tears of pleasure trickled down his cheeks.

So the ninth hour passed; and they continued to converse, and to drink the cool purple wine, and to sing the songs of the years of Thang, until far into the night. More than once Ming-Y thought of departing; but each time Sië would begin, in that silver-sweet voice of hers, so wondrous a story of the great poets of the past, and of the women whom they loved, that he became as one entranced; or she would sing for him a song so strange that all his senses seemed to die except that of hearing. And at last, as she paused to pledge him in a cup of wine, Ming-Y could not restrain himself from putting his arm about her round neck and drawing her dainty head closer to him, and kissing the lips that were so much ruddier and sweeter than the wine. Then their lips separated no more;—the night grew old, and they knew it not.

The birds awakened, the flowers opened their eyes to the rising sun, and Ming-Y found himself at last compelled to bid his lovely enchantress farewell. Sië, accompanying him to the terrace, kissed him fondly and said, "Dear boy, come hither as often as you are able—as often as your heart whispers you to come. I know that you are not of those without faith and truth, who betray secrets; yet, being so young, you might also be sometimes thoughtless; and I pray you never to forget that only the stars have been the witnesses of our love. Speak of it to no living person, dearest; and take with you this little souvenir of our happy night."

And she presented him with an exquisite and curious little thing—a paper-weight in likeness of a couchant lion, wrought from a jade-stone yellow as that created by a rainbow in honor of Kong-fu-tze. Tenderly the boy kissed the gift and the beautiful hand that gave it. "May the Spirits punish me," he vowed, "if ever I knowingly give you cause to reproach me, sweetheart!" And they separated with mutual vows.

That morning, on returning to the house of Lord Tchang, Ming-Y told the first falsehood which had ever passed his lips. He averred that his mother had requested him thenceforward to pass his nights at home, now that the weather had become so pleasant; for, though the way was somewhat long, he was strong and active, and needed both air and healthy exercise. Tchang believed all Ming-Y said, and offered no objection. Accordingly the lad found himself enabled to pass all his evenings at the house of the beautiful Sië. Each night they devoted to the same pleasures which had made their first acquaintance so charming: they sang and conversed by turns; they played at chess—the learned game invented by Wu-Wang, which is an imitation of war; they composed pieces of eighty rhymes upon the flowers, the trees, the clouds, the streams, the birds, the bees. But in all accomplishments Sië far excelled her young sweetheart. Whenever they played at chess, it was always Ming-Y's general, Ming-Y's *tsiang*, who was surrounded and vanquished; when they composed verses, Sië's poems were ever superior to his in harmony of word-coloring, in elegance of form, in classic loftiness of thought. And the themes they selected were always the most difficult,—those of the poets of the Thang dynasty; the songs they sang were also the songs of five hundred years before,—the songs of Youen-tchin, of Thou-mou, of Kao-pien above all, high poet and ruler of the province of Sze-tchouen.

So the summer waxed and waned upon their love, and the luminous autumn came, with its vapors of phantom gold, its shadows of magical purple.

Then it unexpectedly happened that the father of Ming-Y, meeting his son's employer at Tching-tou, was asked by him: "Why must your boy continue to travel every evening to the city, now that the winter is approaching? The way is long, and when he returns in the morning he looks fordone with weariness. Why not permit him to slumber in my house during the season of snow?"

And the father of Ming-Y, greatly astonished, responded: "Sir, my son has not visited the city, nor has he been to our house all this summer. I fear that he must have acquired wicked habits, and that he passes his nights in evil company—perhaps in gaming, or in drinking with the women of the flower-boats."

But the High Commissioner returned: "Nay! that is not to be thought of. I have never found any evil in the boy, and there are no taverns nor flower-boats nor any places of dissipation in our neighborhood. No doubt Ming-Y has found some amiable youth of his own age with whom to spend his evenings, and only told me an untruth for fear that I would not otherwise permit him to leave my residence. I beg that you will say nothing to him until I shall have sought to discover this mystery; and this very evening I shall send my servant to follow after him, and to watch whither he goes."

Pelou readily assented to this proposal, and promising to visit Tchang the following morning, returned to his home. In the evening, when Ming-Y left the house of Tchang, a servant followed him unobserved at a distance. But on reaching the most obscure portion of the road, the boy disappeared from sight as suddenly as though the earth had swallowed him. After having long sought after him in vain, the domestic returned in great bewilderment to the house, and related what had taken place. Tchang immediately sent a messenger to Pelou.

In the mean time Ming-Y, entering the chamber of his beloved, was surprised and deeply pained to find her in tears. "Sweetheart," she sobbed, wreathing her arms around his neck, "we are about to be separated forever, because of reasons which I cannot tell you. From the very first I knew this must come to pass; and nevertheless it seemed to me for the moment so cruelly sudden a loss, so unexpected a misfortune, that I could not prevent myself from weeping! After this night we shall never see each other again, beloved, and I know that you will not be able to forget me while you live; but I know also that you will become a great scholar, and that honors and riches will be showered upon you, and that some beautiful and loving woman will console you for my loss. And now let us speak no more of grief; but let us pass this last evening joyously, so that your recollection of me may not be a painful one, and that you may remember my laughter rather than my tears."

She brushed the bright drops away, and brought wine and music and the melodious *kin* of seven silken strings, and would not suffer Ming-Y to speak for one moment of the coming separation. And she sang him an ancient song about the calmness of summer lakes reflecting the blue of heaven only, and the calmness of the heart also, before the clouds of care and of grief and of weariness darken its little world. Soon they forgot their sorrow in the joy of song and wine; and those last hours seemed to Ming-Y more celestial than even the hours of their first bliss.

But when the yellow beauty of morning came their sadness returned, and they wept. Once more Sië accompanied her lover to the terrace-steps; and as she kissed him farewell, she pressed into his hand a parting gift—a little brush-case of agate, wonderfully chiseled, and worthy the table of a great poet. And they separated forever, shedding many tears.

Still Ming-Y could not believe it was an eternal parting. "No!" he thought, "I shall visit her tomorrow; for I cannot now live without her, and I feel assured that she cannot refuse to receive me." Such were the thoughts that filled his mind as he reached the house of Tchang, to find his father and his patron standing on the porch awaiting him.

Ere he could speak a word, Pelou demanded: "Son, in what place have you been passing your nights?"

Seeing that his falsehood had been discovered, Ming-Y dared not make any reply, and remained abashed and silent, with bowed head, in the presence of his father. Then Pelou, striking the boy violently with his staff, commanded him to divulge the secret; and at last, partly through fear of his parent, and partly through fear of the law which ordains that "*the son refusing to obey his father shall be punished with one hundred blows of the bamboo*," Ming-Y faltered out the history of his love.

Tchang changed color at the boy's tale. "Child," exclaimed the High Commissioner, "I have no relative of the name of Ping; I have never heard of the woman you describe; I have never heard even of the house which you speak of. But I know also that you cannot dare to lie to Pelou, your honored father; there is some strange delusion in all this affair."

Then Ming-Y produced the gifts that Sië had given him—the lion of yellow jade, the brush-case of carven agate, also some original compositions made by the beautiful lady herself. The astonishment of Tchang was now shared by Pelou. Both observed that the brush-case of agate and the lion of jade bore the appearance of objects that had lain buried in the earth for centuries, and were of a workmanship beyond the power of living man to imitate; while the compositions proved to be veritable master-pieces of poetry, written in the style of the poets of the dynasty of Thang.

"Friend Pelou," cried the High Commissioner, "let us immediately accompany the boy to the place where he obtained these miraculous things, and apply the testimony of our senses to this mystery. The boy is no doubt telling the truth; yet his story passes my understanding." And all three proceeded toward the place of the habitation of Sië.

But when they had arrived at the shadiest part of the road, where the perfumes were most sweet and the mosses were greenest, and the fruits of the wild peach flushed most pinkly, Ming-Y, gazing through the groves, uttered a cry of dismay. Where the azure-tiled roof had risen against the sky, there was now only the blue emptiness of air; where the green-and-gold façade had been, there was visible only the flickering of leaves under the aureate autumn light; and where the broad terrace had extended, could be discerned only a ruin—a tomb so ancient, so deeply gnawed by moss, that the name graven upon it was no longer decipherable. The home of Sië had disappeared!

All suddenly the High Commissioner smote his forehead with his hand, and turning to Pelou, recited the well-known verse of the ancient poet Tching-Kou:—

"Surely the peach-flowers blossom over the tomb of SIË-THAO."

"Friend Pelou," continued Tchang, "the beauty who bewitched your son was no other than she whose tomb stands there in ruin before us! Did she not say she was wedded to Ping-Khang? There is no family of that name, but Ping-Khang is indeed the name of a broad alley in the city near. There was a dark riddle in all that she said. She called herself Sië of Moun-Hiao: there is no person of that name; there is no street of that name; but the Chinese characters *Moun* and *hiao*, placed together, form the character *Kiao*. Listen! The alley Ping-Khang, situated in the street Kiao, was the place where dwelt the great courtesans of the dynasty of Thang! Did she not sing the songs of Kao-pien? And upon the brush-case and the paper-weight she gave your son, are there not characters which read, '*Pure object of art belonging to Kao, of the city of Pho-hai*'? That city no longer exists; but the memory of Kao-pien remains, for he was governor of the province of Sze-tchouen, and a mighty poet. And when he dwelt in the land of Chou, was not his favorite the beautiful wanton Sië—Sië-Thao, unmatched for grace among all the women of her day? It was he who made her a gift of those manuscripts of song; it was he who gave her those objects of rare art. Sië-Thao died not as other women die. Her limbs may have crumbled to dust; yet something of her still lives in this deep wood,—her Shadow still haunts this shadowy place."

Tchang ceased to speak. A vague fear fell upon the three. The thin mists of the morning made dim the distances of green, and deepened the ghostly beauty of the woods. A faint breeze passed by, leaving a trail of blossom-scent—a last odor of dying flowers,—thin as that which clings to the silk of a forgotten robe; and, as it passed, the trees seemed to whisper across the silence, "*Sië-Thao.*"

Fearing greatly for his son, Pelou sent the lad away at once to the city of Kwang-tchau-fu. And there, in after years, Ming-Y obtained high dignities and honors by reason of his talents and his learning; and he married the daughter of an illustrious house, by whom he became the father of sons and daughters famous for their virtues and their accomplishments. Never could he forget Sië-Thao; and yet it is said that he never spoke of her,—not even when his children begged him to tell them the story of two beautiful objects that always lay upon his writing-table: a lion of yellow jade, and a brush-case of carven agate.

The Legend of Tchi-Niu

A sound of gongs, a sound of song—the song of the builders building the dwellings of the dead:—

Khiû tchî yîng-yîng.
    Toû tchî hoûng-hoûng.
    Tchŭ tchî tông-tông.
    Siŏ liú pîng-pîng.

In the quaint commentary accompanying the text of that holy book of Lao-tseu called *Kan-ing-p'ien* may be found a little story so old that the name of the one who first told it has been forgotten for a thousand years, yet so beautiful that it lives still in the memory of four hundred millions of people, like a prayer that, once learned, is forever remembered. The Chinese writer makes no mention of any city nor of any province, although even in the relation of the most ancient traditions such an omission is rare; we are only told that the name of the hero of the legend was Tong-yong, and that he lived in the years of the great dynasty of Han, some twenty centuries ago.

Tong-Yong's mother had died while he was yet an infant; and when he became a youth of nineteen years his father also passed away, leaving him utterly alone in the world, and without resources of any sort; for, being a very poor man, Tong's father had put himself to great straits to educate the lad, and had not been able to lay by even one copper coin of his earnings. And Tong lamented greatly to find himself so destitute that he could not honor the memory of that good father by having the customary rites of burial performed, and a carven tomb erected upon a propitious site. The poor only are friends of the poor; and among all those whom Tong knew; there was no one able to assist him in defraying the expenses of the funeral. In one way only could the youth obtain money—by selling himself as a slave to some rich cultivator; and this he at last decided to do. In vain his friends did their utmost to dissuade him; and to no purpose did they attempt to delay the accomplishment of his sacrifice by beguiling promises of future aid. Tong only replied that he would sell his freedom a hundred times, if it were possible, rather than suffer his father's memory to remain unhonored even for a brief season. And furthermore, confiding in his youth and strength, he determined to put a high price upon his servitude—a price which would enable him to build a handsome tomb, but which it would be well-nigh impossible for him ever to repay.

* * *

Accordingly he repaired to the broad public place where slaves and debtors were exposed for sale, and seated himself upon a bench of stone, having affixed to his shoulders a placard inscribed with the terms of his servitude and the list of his qualifications as a laborer. Many who read the characters upon the placard smiled disdainfully at the price asked, and passed on without a word; others lingered only to question him out of simple curiosity; some commended him with hollow praise; some openly mocked his unselfishness, and laughed at his childish piety. Thus many hours wearily passed, and Tong had almost despaired of finding a master, when there rode up a high official of the province—a grave and handsome man, lord of a thousand slaves, and owner of vast estates. Reining in his Tartar horse, the official halted to read the placard and to consider the value of the slave. He did not smile, or advise, or ask any questions; but having observed the price asked, and the fine strong limbs of the youth, purchased him without further ado, merely ordering his attendant to pay the sum and to see that the necessary papers were made out.

Thus Tong found himself enabled to fulfill the wish of his heart, and to have a monument built which, although of small size, was destined to delight the eyes of all who beheld it, being designed by cunning artists and executed by skillful sculptors. And while it was yet designed only, the pious rites were performed, the silver coin was placed in the mouth of the dead, the white lanterns were hung at the door, the holy prayers were recited, and paper shapes of all things the departed might need in the land of the Genii were consumed in consecrated fire. And after the geomancers and the necromancers had chosen a burial-spot which no unlucky star could shine upon, a place of rest which no demon or dragon might ever disturb, the beautiful *chih* was built. Then was the phantom money strewn along the way; the funeral procession departed from the dwelling of the dead, and with prayers and lamentation the mortal remains of Tong's good father were borne to the tomb.

Then Tong entered as a slave into the service of his purchaser, who allotted him a little hut to dwell in; and thither Tong carried with him those wooden tablets, bearing the ancestral names, before which filial piety must daily burn the incense of prayer, and perform the tender duties of family worship.

Thrice had spring perfumed the breast of the land with flowers, and thrice had been celebrated that festival of the dead which is called *Siu-fan-ti*, and thrice had Tong swept and garnished his father's tomb and presented his fivefold offering of fruits and meats. The period of mourning had passed, yet he had not ceased to mourn for his parent. The years revolved with their moons, bringing him no hour of joy, no day of happy rest; yet he never lamented his servitude, or failed to perform the rites of ancestral worship—until at last the fever of the rice-fields laid strong hold upon him, and he could not arise from his couch; and his fellow-laborers thought him destined to die. There was no one to wait upon him, no one to care for his needs, inasmuch as slaves and servants were wholly busied with the duties of the household or the labor of the fields—all departing to toil at sunrise and returning weary only after the sundown.

Now, while the sick youth slumbered the fitful slumber of exhaustion one sultry noon, he dreamed that a strange and beautiful woman stood by him, and bent above him and touched his forehead with the long, fine fingers of her shapely hand. And at her cool touch a weird sweet shock passed through him, and all his veins tingled as if thrilled by new life. Opening his eyes in wonder, he saw verily bending over him the charming being of whom he had dreamed, and he knew that her lithe hand really caressed his throbbing forehead. But the flame of the fever was gone, a delicious coolness now penetrated every fiber of his body, and the thrill of which he had dreamed still tingled in his blood like a great joy. Even at the same moment the eyes of the gentle visitor met his own, and he saw they were singularly beautiful, and shone like splendid black jewels under brows curved like the wings of the swallow. Yet their calm gaze seemed to pass through him as light through crystal; and a vague awe came upon him, so that the question which had risen to his lips found no utterance. Then she, still caressing him, smiled and said: "I have come to restore thy strength and to be thy wife. Arise and worship with me."

Her clear voice had tones melodious as a bird's song; but in her gaze there was an imperious power which Tong felt he dare not resist. Rising from his couch, he was astounded to find his strength wholly restored; but the cool, slender hand which held his own led him away so swiftly that he had little time for amazement. He would have given years of existence for courage to speak of his misery, to declare his utter inability to maintain a wife; but something irresistible in the long dark eyes of his companion forbade him to speak; and as though his inmost thought had been discerned by that wondrous gaze, she said to him, in the same clear voice, "*I will provide.*" Then shame made him blush at the thought of his wretched aspect and tattered apparel; but he observed that she also was poorly attired, like a woman of the people—wearing no ornament of any sort, nor even shoes upon her feet. And before he had yet spoken to her, they came before the ancestral tablets; and there she knelt with him and prayed, and pledged him in a cup of wine—brought he knew not from whence—and together they worshipped Heaven and Earth. Thus she became his wife.

A mysterious marriage it seemed, for neither on that day nor at any future time could Tong venture to ask his wife the name of her family, or of the place whence she came, and he could not answer any of the curious questions which his fellow-laborers put to him concerning her; and she, moreover, never uttered a word about herself, except to say that her name was Tchi. But although Tong had such awe of her that while her eyes were upon him he was as one having no will of his own, he loved her unspeakably; and the thought of his serfdom ceased to weigh upon him from the hour of his marriage. As through magic the little dwelling had become transformed: its misery was masked with charming paper devices—with dainty decorations created out of nothing by that pretty jugglery of which woman only knows the secret.

Each morning at dawn the young husband found a well-prepared and ample repast awaiting him, and each evening also upon his return; but the wife all day sat at her loom, weaving silk after a fashion unlike anything which had ever been seen before in that province. For as she wove, the silk flowed from the loom like a slow current of glossy gold, bearing upon its undulations strange forms of violet and crimson and jewel-green: shapes of ghostly horsemen riding upon horses, and of phantom chariots dragon-drawn, and of standards of trailing cloud. In every dragon's beard glimmered the mystic pearl; in every rider's helmet sparkled the gem of rank. And each day Tchi would weave a great piece of such figured silk; and the fame of her weaving spread abroad. From far and near people thronged to see the marvelous work; and the silk-merchants of great cities heard of it, and they sent messengers to Tchi, asking her that she should weave for them and teach them her secret. Then she wove for them, as they desired, in return for the silver cubes which they brought her; but when they prayed her to teach them, she laughed and said, "Assuredly I could never teach you, for no one among you has fingers like mine." And indeed no man could discern her fingers when she wove, any more than he might behold the wings of a bee vibrating in swift flight.

The seasons passed, and Tong never knew want, so well did his beautiful wife fulfill her promise,— "*I will provide*"; and the cubes of bright silver brought by the silk-merchants were piled up higher and higher in the great carven chest which Tchi had bought for the storage of the household goods.

One morning, at last, when Tong, having finished his repast, was about to depart to the fields, Tchi unexpectedly bade him remain; and opening the great chest, she took out of it and gave him a document written in the official characters called *li-shu*. And Tong, looking at it, cried out and leaped in his joy, for it was the certificate of his manumission. Tchi had secretly purchased her husband's freedom with the price of her wondrous silks!

"Thou shalt labor no more for any master," she said, "but for thine own sake only. And I have also bought this dwelling, with all which is therein, and the tea-fields to the south, and the mulberry groves hard by—all of which are thine."

Then Tong, beside himself for gratefulness, would have prostrated himself in worship before her, but that she would not suffer it.

Thus he was made free; and prosperity came to him with his freedom; and whatsoever he gave to the sacred earth was returned to him centupled; and his servants loved him and blessed the beautiful Tchi, so silent and yet so kindly to all about her. But the silk-loom soon remained untouched, for Tchi gave birth to a son—a boy so beautiful that Tong wept with delight when he looked upon him. And thereafter the wife devoted herself wholly to the care of the child.

Now it soon became manifest that the boy was not less wonderful than his wonderful mother. In the third month of his age he could speak; in the seventh month he could repeat by heart the proverbs of the sages, and recite the holy prayers; before the eleventh month he could use the writing-brush with skill, and copy in shapely characters the precepts of Lao-tseu. And the priests of the temples came to behold him and to converse with him, and they marveled at the charm of the child and the wisdom of what he said; and they blessed Tong, saying: "Surely this son of thine is a gift from the Master of Heaven, a sign that the immortals love thee. May thine eyes behold a hundred happy summers!"

It was in the Period of the Eleventh Moon: the flowers had passed away, the perfume of the summer had flown, the winds were growing chill, and in Tong's home the evening fires were lighted. Long the husband and wife sat in the mellow glow—he speaking much of his hopes and joys, and of his son that was to be so grand a man, and of many paternal projects; while she, speaking little, listened to his words, and often turned her wonderful eyes upon him with an answering smile. Never had she seemed so beautiful before; and Tong, watching her face, marked not how the night waned, nor how the fire sank low, nor how the wind sang in the leafless trees without.

All suddenly Tchi arose without speaking, and took his hand in hers and led him, gently as on that strange wedding-morning, to the cradle where their boy slumbered, faintly smiling in his dreams. And in that moment there came upon Tong the same strange fear that he knew when Tchi's eyes had first met his own—the vague fear that love and trust had calmed, but never wholly cast out, like unto the fear of the gods. And all unknowingly, like one yielding to the pressure of mighty invisible hands, he bowed himself low before her, kneeling as to a divinity. Now, when he lifted his eyes again to her face, he closed them forthwith in awe; for she towered before him taller than any mortal woman, and there was a glow about her as of sunbeams, and the light of her limbs shone through her garments. But her sweet voice came to him with all the tenderness of other hours, saying:

"Lo! my beloved, the moment has come in which I must forsake thee; for I was never of mortal born, and the Invisible may incarnate themselves for a time only. Yet I leave with thee the pledge of our love—this fair son, who shall ever be to thee as faithful and as fond as thou thyself hast been. Know, my beloved, that I was sent to thee even by the Master of Heaven, in reward of thy filial piety, and that I must now return to the glory of His house: I am the Goddess Tchi-Niu."

Even as she ceased to speak, the great glow faded; and Tong, re-opening his eyes, knew that she had passed away forever—mysteriously as pass the winds of heaven, irrevocably as the light of a flame blown out. Yet all the doors were barred, all the windows unopened. Still the child slept, smiling in his sleep. Outside, the darkness was breaking; the sky was brightening swiftly; the night was past. With splendid majesty the East threw open high gates of gold for the coming of the sun; and, illuminated by the glory of his coming, the vapors of morning wrought themselves into marvelous shapes of shifting color,—into forms weirdly beautiful as the silken dreams woven in the loom of Tchi-Niu.

The Return of Yen-Tchin-King

Before me ran, as a herald runneth, the Leader of the Moon;
And the Spirit of the Wind followed after me,—quickening his flight.

LI-SAO

IN THE THIRTY-EIGHTH CHAPTER OF THE HOLY BOOK, *KAN-ING-P'IEN*, WHEREIN THE Recompense of Immortality is considered, may be found the legend of Yen-Tchin-King. A thousand years have passed since the passing of the good Tchin-King; for it was in the period of the greatness of Thang that he lived and died.

Now, in those days when Yen-Tchin-King was Supreme Judge of one of the Six August Tribunals, one Li-hi-lié, a soldier mighty for evil, lifted the black banner of revolt, and drew after him, as a tide of destruction, the millions of the northern provinces. And learning of these things, and knowing also that Hi-lié was the most ferocious of men, who respected nothing on earth save fearlessness, the Son of Heaven commanded Tchin-King that he should visit Hi-lié and strive to recall the rebel to duty, and read unto the people who followed after him in revolt the Emperor's letter of reproof and warning. For Tchin-King was famed throughout the provinces for his wisdom, his rectitude, and his fearlessness; and the Son of Heaven believed that if Hi-lié would listen to the words of any living man steadfast in loyalty and virtue, he would listen to the words of Tchin-King. So Tchin-King arrayed himself in his robes of office, and set his house in order; and, having embraced his wife and his children, mounted his horse and rode away alone to the roaring camp of the rebels, bearing the Emperor's letter in his bosom. "I shall return; fear not!" were his last words to the gray servant who watched him from the terrace as he rode.

And Tchin-King at last descended from his horse, and entered into the rebel camp, and, passing through that huge gathering of war, stood in the presence of Hi-lié. High sat the rebel among his chiefs, encircled by the wave-lightning of swords and the thunders of ten thousand gongs: above him undulated the silken folds of the Black Dragon, while a vast fire rose bickering before him. Also Tchin-King saw that the tongues of that fire were licking human bones, and that skulls of men lay blackening among the ashes. Yet he was not afraid to look upon the fire, nor into the eyes of Hi-lié; but drawing from his bosom the roll of perfumed yellow silk upon which the words of the Emperor were written, and kissing it, he made ready to read, while the multitude became silent. Then, in a strong, clear voice he began:—

> "The words of the Celestial and August, the Son of Heaven, the Divine Ko-Tsu-Tchin-Yao-ti, unto the rebel Li-Hi-lié and those that follow him."

And a roar went up like the roar of the sea—a roar of rage, and the hideous battle-moan, like the moan of a forest in storm—"*Hoo! hoo-oo-oo-oo!*"—and the sword-lightnings brake loose, and the thunder of the gongs moved the ground beneath the messenger's feet. But Hi-lié waved his gilded wand, and again there was silence. "Nay!" spake the rebel chief; "let the dog bark!" So Tchin-King spake on:—

> "Knowest thou not, O most rash and foolish of men, that thou leadest the people only into the mouth of the Dragon of Destruction? Knowest thou not, also, that the people of my kingdom are the first-born of the Master of Heaven? So it hath been written that he who doth needlessly subject the people to wounds and death shall not be suffered by Heaven to live! Thou who wouldst subvert those laws founded by the wise—those laws in obedience to which may happiness and prosperity alone be found—thou art committing the greatest of all crimes—the crime that is never forgiven!
>
> "O my people, think not that I your Emperor, I your Father, seek your destruction. I desire only your happiness, your prosperity, your greatness; let not your folly provoke the severity of your Celestial Parent. Follow not after madness and blind rage; hearken rather to the wise words of my messenger."

"*Hoo! hoo-oo-oo-oo-oo!*" roared the people, gathering fury. "*Hoo! hoo-oo-oo-oo!*"—till the mountains rolled back the cry like the rolling of a typhoon; and once more the pealing of the gongs paralyzed voice and hearing. Then Tchin-King, looking at Hi-lié, saw that he laughed, and that the words of the letter would not again be listened to. Therefore he read on to the end without looking about him, resolved to perform his mission in so far as lay in his power. And having read all, he would have given the letter to Hi-lié; but Hi-lié would not extend his hand to take it. Therefore Tchin-King replaced it in his bosom, and folding his arms, looked Hi-lié calmly in the face, and waited.

Again Hi-lié waved his gilded wand; and the roaring ceased, and the booming of the gongs, until nothing save the fluttering of the Dragon-banner could be heard. Then spake Hi-lié, with an evil smile:

"Tchin-King, O son of a dog! if thou dost not now take the oath of fealty, and bow thyself before me, and salute me with the salutation of Emperors—even with the *luh-kao*, the triple prostration—into that fire thou shalt be thrown."

But Tchin-King, turning his back upon the usurper, bowed himself a moment in worship to Heaven and Earth; and then rising suddenly, ere any man could lay hand upon him, he leaped into the towering flame, and stood there, with folded arms, like a God.

Then Hi-lié leaped to his feet in amazement, and shouted to his men; and they snatched Tchin-King from the fire, and wrung the flames from his robes with their naked hands, and extolled him, and praised him to his face. And even Hi-lié himself descended from his seat, and spoke fair words to him, saying: "O Tchin-King, I see thou art indeed a brave man and true, and worthy of all honor; be seated among us, I pray thee, and partake of whatever it is in our power to bestow!"

But Tchin-King, looking upon him unswervingly, replied in a voice clear as the voice of a great bell:

"Never, O Hi-lié, shall I accept aught from thy hand, save death, so long as thou shalt continue in the path of wrath and folly. And never shall it be said that Tchin-King sat him down among rebels and traitors, among murderers and robbers."

Then Hi-lié in sudden fury, smote him with his sword; and Tchin-King fell to the earth and died, striving even in his death to bow his head toward the South—toward the place of the Emperor's palace—toward the presence of his beloved Master.

Even at the same hour the Son of Heaven, alone in the inner chamber of his palace, became aware of a Shape prostrate before his feet; and when he spake, the Shape arose and stood before him, and he saw that it was Tchin-King. And the Emperor would have questioned him; yet ere he could question, the familiar voice spake, saying:

"Son of Heaven, the mission confided to me I have performed; and thy command hath been accomplished to the extent of thy humble servant's feeble power. But even now must I depart, that I may enter the service of another Master."

And looking, the Emperor perceived that the Golden Tigers upon the wall were visible through the form of Tchin-King; and a strange coldness, like a winter wind, passed through the chamber; and the figure faded out. Then the Emperor knew that the Master of whom his faithful servant had spoken was none other than the Master of Heaven.

Also at the same hour the gray servant of Tchin-King's house beheld him passing through the apartments, smiling as he was wont to smile when he saw that all things were as he desired.

"Is it well with thee, my lord?" questioned the aged man.

And a voice answered him: "It is well"; but the presence of Tchin-King had passed away before the answer came.

So the armies of the Son of Heaven strove with the rebels. But the land was soaked with blood and blackened with fire; and the corpses of whole populations were carried by the rivers to feed the fishes of the sea; and still the war prevailed through many a long red year. Then came to aid the Son of Heaven the hordes that dwell in the desolations of the West and North—horsemen born, a nation of wild archers, each mighty to bend a two-hundred-pound bow until the ears should meet. And as a whirlwind they came against rebellion, raining raven-feathered arrows in a storm of death; and they prevailed against Hi-lié and his people. Then those that survived destruction and defeat submitted, and promised allegiance; and once more was the law of righteousness restored. But Tchin-King had been dead for many summers.

And the Son of Heaven sent word to his victorious generals that they should bring back with them the bones of his faithful servant, to be laid with honor in a mausoleum erected by imperial decree. So the generals of the Celestial and August sought after the nameless grave and found it, and had the earth taken up, and made ready to remove the coffin.

But the coffin crumbled into dust before their eyes; for the worms had gnawed it, and the hungry earth had devoured its substance, leaving only a phantom shell that vanished at touch of the light. And lo! as it vanished, all beheld lying there the perfect form and features of the good Tchin-King. Corruption had not touched him, nor had the worms disturbed his rest, nor had the bloom of life departed from his face. And he seemed to dream only—comely to see as upon the morning of his bridal, and smiling as the holy images smile, with eyelids closed, in the twilight of the great pagodas.

Then spoke a priest, standing by the grave: "O my children, this is indeed a Sign from the Master of Heaven; in such wise do the Powers Celestial preserve them that are chosen to be numbered with the Immortals. Death may not prevail over them, neither may corruption come nigh them. Verily the blessed Tchin-King hath taken his place among the divinities of Heaven!"

Then they bore Tchin-King back to his native place, and laid him with highest honors in the mausoleum which the Emperor had commanded; and there he sleeps, incorruptible forever, arrayed in his robes of state. Upon his tomb are sculptured the emblems of his greatness and his wisdom and his virtue, and the signs of his office, and the Four Precious Things: and the monsters which are holy symbols mount giant guard in stone about it; and the weird Dogs of Fo keep watch before it, as before the temples of the gods.

The Tradition of the Tea-Plant

Sang a Chinese heart fourteen hundred years ago:—
There is Somebody of whom I am thinking.
Far away there is Somebody of whom I am thinking.
A hundred leagues of mountains lie between us:—
Yet the same Moon shines upon us, and the passing Wind breathes upon us both.

"Good is the continence of the eye;
Good is the continence of the ear;
Good is the continence of the nostrils;
Good is the continence of the tongue;
Good is the continence of the body;
Good is the continence of speech; Good is all . . . ."

Again the Vulture of Temptation soared to the highest heaven of his contemplation, bringing his soul down, down, reeling and fluttering, back to the World of Illusion. Again the memory made dizzy his thought, like the perfume of some venomous flower. Yet he had seen the bayadère for an instant only, when passing through Kasí upon his way to China—to the vast empire of souls that thirsted after the refreshment of Buddha's law, as sun-parched fields thirst for the life-giving rain. When she called him, and dropped her little gift into his mendicant's bowl, he had indeed lifted his fan before his face, yet not quickly enough; and the penalty of that fault had followed him a thousand leagues—pursued after him even into the strange land to which he had come to hear the words of the Universal Teacher. Accursed beauty! surely framed by the Tempter of tempters, by Mara himself, for the perdition of the just! Wisely had Bhagavat warned his disciples:

"O ye Çramanas, women are not to be looked upon! And if ye chance to meet women, ye must not suffer your eyes to dwell upon them; but, maintaining holy reserve, speak not to them at all. Then fail not to whisper unto your own hearts, 'Lo, we are Çramanas, whose duty it is to remain uncontaminated by the corruptions of this world, even as the Lotus, which suffereth no vileness to cling unto its leaves, though it blossom amid the refuse of the wayside ditch.'"

Then also came to his memory, but with a new and terrible meaning, the words of the Twentieth-and-Third of the Admonitions:—

> Of all attachments unto objects of desire, the strongest indeed is the attachment to form. Happily, this passion is unique; for were there any other like unto it, then to enter the Perfect Way were impossible.

How, indeed, thus haunted by the illusion of form, was he to fulfill the vow that he had made to pass a night and a day in perfect and unbroken meditation? Already the night was beginning! Assuredly, for sickness of the soul, for fever of the spirit, there was no physic save prayer. The sunset was swiftly fading out. He strove to pray:—

> *O the Jewel in the Lotus!*
>
> Even as the tortoise withdraweth its extremities into its shell, let me, O Blessed One, withdraw my senses wholly into meditation!
>
> *O the Jewel in the Lotus!*
>
> For even as rain penetrateth the broken roof of a dwelling long uninhabited, so may passion enter the soul uninhabited by meditation.
>
> *O the Jewel in the Lotus!*
>
> Even as still water that hath deposited all its slime, so let my soul, O Tathâgata, be made pure! Give me strong power to rise above the world, O Master, even as the wild bird rises from its marsh to follow the pathway of the Sun!
>
> *O the Jewel in the Lotus!*
>
> By day shineth the sun, by night shineth the moon; shineth also the warrior in harness of war; shineth likewise in meditations the Çramana. But the Buddha at all times, by night or by day, shineth ever the same, illuminating the world.
>
> *O the Jewel in the Lotus!*
>
> Let me cease, O thou Perfectly Awakened, to remain as an Ape in the World-Forest, forever ascending and descending in search of the fruits of folly. Swift as the twining of serpents, vast as the growth of lianas in a forest, are the all-encircling growths of the Plant of Desire.
>
> *O the Jewel in the Lotus!*

Vain his prayer, alas! vain also his invocation! The mystic meaning of the holy text—the sense of the Lotus, the sense of the Jewel—had evaporated from the words, and their monotonous utterance now served only to lend more dangerous definition to the memory that tempted and tortured him. *O the jewel in her ear!* What lotus-bud more dainty than the folded flower of flesh, with its dripping of diamond-fire! Again he saw it, and the curve of the cheek beyond, luscious to look upon as beautiful brown fruit. How true the Two Hundred and Eighty-Fourth verse of the Admonitions!

> So long as a man shall not have torn from his heart even the smallest rootlet of that liana of desire which draweth his thought toward women, even so long shall his soul remain fettered.

And there came to his mind also the Three Hundred and Forty-Fifth verse of the same blessed book, regarding fetters:

> In bonds of rope, wise teachers have said, there is no strength; nor in fetters of wood, nor yet in fetters of iron. Much stronger than any of these is the fetter of *concern for the jeweled earrings of women.*

"Omniscient Gotama!" he cried—"all-seeing Tathâgata! How multiform the Consolation of Thy Word! how marvelous Thy understanding of the human heart! Was this also one of Thy temptations?—one of the myriad illusions marshaled before Thee by Mara in that night when the earth rocked as a chariot, and the sacred trembling passed from sun to sun, from system to system, from universe to universe, from eternity to eternity?"

O the jewel in her ear! The vision would not go! Nay, each time it hovered before his thought it seemed to take a warmer life, a fonder look, a fairer form; to develop with his weakness; to gain force from his enervation. He saw the eyes, large, limpid, soft, and black as a deer's; the pearls in the dark hair, and the pearls in the pink mouth; the lips curling to a kiss, a flower-kiss; and a fragrance seemed to float to his senses, sweet, strange, soporific—a perfume of youth, an odor of woman. Rising to his feet, with strong resolve he pronounced again the sacred invocation; and he recited the holy words of the *Chapter of Impermanency*:

> Gazing upon the heavens and upon the earth ye must say, *These are not permanent*. Gazing upon the mountains and the rivers, ye must say, *These are not permanent*. Gazing upon the forms and upon the faces of exterior beings, and beholding their growth and their development, ye must say, *These are not permanent*.

And nevertheless! how sweet illusion! The illusion of the great sun; the illusion of the shadow-casting hills; the illusion of waters, formless and multiform; the illusion of—Nay, nay I what impious fancy! Accursed girl! yet, yet! why should he curse her? Had she ever done aught to merit the malediction of an ascetic? Never, never! Only her form, the memory of her, the beautiful phantom of her, the accursed phantom of her! What was she? An illusion creating illusions, a mockery, a dream, a shadow, a vanity, a vexation of spirit! The fault, the sin, was in himself, in his rebellious thought, in his untamed memory. Though mobile as water, intangible as vapor, Thought, nevertheless, may be tamed by the Will, may be harnessed to the chariot of Wisdom—must be!—that happiness be found. And he recited the blessed verses of the "Book of the Way of the Law":—

> *All forms are only temporary*. When this great truth is fully comprehended by any one, then is he delivered from all pain. This is the Way of Purification.
>
> *All forms are subject unto pain*. When this great truth is fully comprehended by any one, then is he delivered from all pain. This is the Way of Purification.
>
> *All forms are without substantial reality*. When this great truth is fully comprehended by any one, then is he delivered from all pain. This is the way of . . .

Her form, too, unsubstantial, unreal, an illusion only, though comeliest of illusions? She had given him alms! Was the merit of the giver illusive also—illusive like the grace of the supple fingers that gave? Assuredly there were mysteries in the Abhidharma impenetrable, incomprehensible! . . . It was a golden coin, stamped with the symbol of an elephant—not more of an illusion, indeed, than the gifts of Kings to the Buddha! Gold upon her bosom also, less fine than the gold of her skin. Naked between the silken sash and the narrow breast-corselet, her young waist curved glossy and pliant as a bow. Richer the silver in her voice than in the hollow *pagals* that made a moonlight about her ankles! But her smile!—the little teeth like flower-stamens in the perfumed blossom of her mouth!

O weakness! O shame! How had the strong Charioteer of Resolve thus lost his control over the wild team of fancy! Was this languor of the Will a signal of coming peril, the peril of slumber? So strangely vivid those fancies were, so brightly definite, as about to take visible form, to move with factitious life, to play some unholy drama upon the stage of dreams! "O Thou Fully Awakened!" he cried aloud, "help now thy humble disciple to obtain the blessed wakefulness of perfect contemplation! let him find force to fulfill his vow! suffer not Mara to prevail against him!" And he recited the eternal verses of the Chapter of Wakefulness:—

Completely and eternally awake are the disciples of Gotama! Unceasingly, by day and night, their thoughts are fixed upon the Law.

Completely and eternally awake are the disciples of Gotama! Unceasingly, by day and night, their thoughts are fixed upon the Community.

Completely and eternally awake are the disciples of Gotama! Unceasingly, by day and night, their thoughts are fixed upon the Body.

Completely and eternally awake are the disciples of Gotama! Unceasingly, by day and night, their minds know the sweetness of perfect peace.

Completely and eternally awake are the disciples of Gotama! Unceasingly, by day and night, their minds enjoy the deep peace of meditation.

There came a murmur to his ears; a murmuring of many voices, smothering the utterances of his own, like a tumult of waters. The stars went out before his sight; the heavens darkened their infinities: all things became viewless, became blackness; and the great murmur deepened, like the murmur of a rising tide; and the earth seemed to sink from beneath him. His feet no longer touched the ground; a sense of supernatural buoyancy pervaded every fiber of his body: he felt himself floating in obscurity; then sinking softly, slowly, like a feather dropped from the pinnacle of a temple. Was this death? Nay, for all suddenly, as transported by the Sixth Supernatural Power, he stood again in light—a perfumed, sleepy light, vapory, beautiful—that bathed the marvelous stree ts of some Indian city. Now the nature of the murmur became manifest to him; for he moved with a mighty throng, a people of pilgrims, a nation of worshippers. But these were not of his faith; they bore upon their foreheads the smeared symbols of obscene gods! Still, he could not escape from their midst; the mile-broad human torrent bore him irresistibly with it, as a leaf is swept by the waters of the Ganges. Rajahs were there with their trains, and princes riding upon elephants, and Brahmins robed in their vestments, and swarms of voluptuous dancing-girls, moving to chant of *kabit* and *damâri*. But whither, whither? Out of the city into the sun they passed, between avenues of banyan, down colonnades of palm. But whither, whither?

Blue-distant, a mountain of carven stone appeared before them—the Temple, lifting to heaven its wilderness of chiseled pinnacles, flinging to the sky the golden spray of its decoration. Higher it grew with approach, the blue tones changed to gray, the outlines sharpened in the light. Then each detail became visible: the elephants of the pedestals standing upon tortoises of rock; the great grim faces of the capitals; the serpents and monsters writhing among the friezes; the many-headed gods of basalt in their galleries of fretted niches, tier above tier; the pictured foulnesses, the painted lusts, the divinities of abomination. And, yawning in the sloping precipice of sculpture, beneath a frenzied swarming of gods and Gopia—a beetling pyramid of limbs and bodies interlocked—the Gate, cavernous and shadowy as the mouth of Siva, devoured the living multitude.

The eddy of the throng whirled him with it to the vastness of the interior. None seemed to note his yellow robe, none even to observe his presence. Giant aisles intercrossed their heights above him; myriads of mighty pillars, fantastically carven, filed away to invisibility behind the yellow illumination of torch-fires. Strange images, weirdly sensuous, loomed up through haze of incense. Colossal figures, that at a distance assumed the form of elephants or garuda-birds, changed aspect when approached, and revealed as the secret of their design an interplaiting of the bodies of women; while one divinity rode all the monstrous allegories—one divinity or demon, eternally the same in the repetition of the sculptor, universally visible as though self-multiplied. The huge pillars themselves were symbols, figures, carnalities; the orgiastic spirit of that worship lived and writhed in the contorted bronze of the lamps, the twisted gold of the cups, the chiseled marble of the tanks. . . .

How far had he proceeded? He knew not; the journey among those countless columns, past those armies of petrified gods, down lanes of flickering lights, seemed longer than the voyage of a caravan, longer than his pilgrimage to China! But suddenly, inexplicably, there came a silence as of cemeteries; the living ocean seemed to have ebbed away from about him, to have been engulfed within abysses of subterranean architecture! He found himself alone in some strange crypt before a basin, shell-shaped and shallow, bearing in its center a rounded column of less than human height, whose smooth and spherical summit was wreathed with flowers. Lamps similarly formed, and fed with oil of palm, hung above it. There was no other graven image, no visible divinity. Flowers of countless varieties lay heaped upon the pavement; they covered its surface like a carpet, thick, soft; they exhaled their ghosts beneath his feet. The perfume seemed to penetrate his brain—a perfume sensuous, intoxicating, unholy; an unconquerable languor mastered his will, and he sank to rest upon the floral offerings.

The sound of a tread, light as a whisper, approached through the heavy stillness, with a drowsy tinkling of *pagals*, a tintinnabulation of anklets. All suddenly he felt glide about his neck the tepid smoothness of a woman's arm. *She, she!* his Illusion, his Temptation; but how transformed, transfigured!—preternatural in her loveliness, incomprehensible in her charm! Delicate as a jasmine-petal the cheek that touched his own; deep as night, sweet as summer, the eyes that watched him.

"Heart's-thief," her flower-lips whispered—"heart's-thief, how have I sought for thee! How have I found thee! Sweets I bring thee, my beloved; lips and bosom; fruit and blossom. Hast thirst? Drink from the well of mine eyes! Wouldst sacrifice? I am thine altar! Wouldst pray? I am thy God!"

Their lips touched; her kiss seemed to change the cells of his blood to flame. For a moment Illusion triumphed; Mara prevailed! . . . With a shock of resolve the dreamer awoke in the night—under the stars of the Chinese sky.

Only a mockery of sleep! But the vow had been violated, the sacred purpose unfulfilled! Humiliated, penitent, but resolved, the ascetic drew from his girdle a keen knife, and with unfaltering hands severed his eyelids from his eyes, and flung them from him.

"O Thou Perfectly Awakened!" he prayed, "thy disciple hath not been overcome save through the feebleness of the body; and his vow hath been renewed. Here shall he linger, without food or drink, until the moment of its fulfillment."

And having assumed the hieratic posture—seated himself with his lower limbs folded beneath him, and the palms of his hands upward, the right upon the left, the left resting upon the sole of his upturned foot—he resumed his meditation.

Dawn blushed; day brightened. The sun shortened all the shadows of the land, and lengthened them again, and sank at last upon his funeral pyre of crimson-burning cloud. Night came and glittered and passed. But Mara had tempted in vain. This time the vow had been fulfilled, the holy purpose accomplished.

And again the sun arose to fill the world with laughter of light; flowers opened their hearts to him; birds sang their morning hymn of fire worship; the deep forest trembled with delight; and far upon the plain, the eaves of many-storied temples and the peaked caps of the city-towers caught aureate glory. Strong in the holiness of his accomplished vow, the Indian pilgrim arose in the morning glow. He started for amazement as he lifted his hands to his eyes. What! was everything a dream? Impossible! Yet now his eyes felt no pain; neither were they lidless; not even so much as one of their lashes was lacking. What marvel had been wrought? In vain he looked for the severed lids that he had flung upon the ground; they had mysteriously vanished. But lo! there where he had cast them two wondrous shrubs were growing, with dainty leaflets eyelid-shaped, and snowy buds just opening to the East.

Then, by virtue of the supernatural power acquired in that mighty meditation, it was given the holy missionary to know the secret of that newly created plant—the subtle virtue of its leaves. And he named it, in the language of the nation to whom he brought the Lotos of the Good Law, "TE"; and he spake to it, saying:—

"Blessed be thou, sweet plant, beneficent, life-giving, formed by the spirit of virtuous resolve! Lo! the fame of thee shall yet spread unto the ends of the earth; and the perfume of thy life be borne unto the uttermost parts by all the winds of heaven! Verily, for all time to come men who drink of thy sap shall find such refreshment that weariness may not overcome them nor languor seize upon them;—neither shall they know the confusion of drowsiness, nor any desire for slumber in the hour of duty or of prayer. Blessed be thou!"

And still, as a mist of incense, as a smoke of universal sacrifice, perpetually ascends to heaven from all the lands of earth the pleasant vapor of TE, created for the refreshment of mankind by the power of a holy vow, the virtue of a pious atonement.

The Tale of the Porcelain-God

> It is written in the *Fong-ho-chin-tch'ouen*, that whenever the artist Thsang-Kong was in doubt, he would look into the fire of the great oven in which his vases were baking, and question the Guardian-Spirit dwelling in the flame. And the Spirit of the Oven-fires so aided him with his counsels, that the porcelains made by Thsang-Kong were indeed finer and lovelier to look upon than all other porcelains. And they were baked in the years of Khang-hí—sacredly called Jin Houang-tí.

WHO FIRST OF MEN DISCOVERED THE SECRET OF THE *KAO-LING*, OF THE *PE-TUN-TSE*—the bones and the flesh, the skeleton and the skin, of the beauteous Vase? Who first discovered the virtue of the curd-white clay? Who first prepared the ice-pure bricks of *tun*: the gathered-hoariness of mountains that have died for age; blanched dust of the rocky bones and the stony flesh of sun-seeking Giants that have ceased to be? Unto whom was it first given to discover the divine art of porcelain?

Unto Pu, once a man, now a god, before whose snowy statues bow the myriad populations enrolled in the guilds of the potteries. But the place of his birth we know not; perhaps the tradition of it may have been effaced from remembrance by that awful war which in our own day consumed the lives of twenty millions of the Black-haired Race, and obliterated from the face of the world even the wonderful City of Porcelain itself—the City of King-te-chin, that of old shone like a jewel of fire in the blue mountain-girdle of Feou-liang.

Before his time indeed the Spirit of the Furnace had being; had issued from the Infinite Vitality; had become manifest as an emanation of the Supreme Tao. For Hoang-ti, nearly five thousand years ago, taught men to make good vessels of baked clay; and in his time all potters had learned to know the God of Oven-fires, and turned their wheels to the murmuring of prayer. But Hoang-ti had been gathered unto his fathers for thrice ten hundred years before that man was born destined by the Master of Heaven to become the Porcelain-God.

And his divine ghost, ever hovering above the smoking and the toiling of the potteries, still gives power to the thought of the shaper, grace to the genius of the designer, luminosity to the touch of the enamelist. For by his heaven-taught wisdom was the art of porcelain created; by his inspiration were accomplished all the miracles of Thao-yu, maker of the *Kia-yu-ki*, and all the marvels made by those who followed after him;—

All the azure porcelains called *You-kouo-thien-tsing*; brilliant as a mirror, thin as paper of rice, sonorous as the melodious stone *Khing*, and colored, in obedience to the mandate of the Emperor Chi-tsong, "blue as the sky is after rain, when viewed through the rifts of the clouds." These were, indeed, the first of all porcelains, likewise called *Tchai-yao*, which no man, howsoever wicked, could find courage to break, for they charmed the eye like jewels of price;—

And the *Jou-yao*, second in rank among all porcelains, sometimes mocking the aspect and the sonority of bronze, sometimes blue as summer waters, and deluding the sight with mucid appearance of thickly floating spawn of fish;—

And the *Kouan-yao*, which are the Porcelains of Magistrates, and third in rank of merit among all wondrous porcelains, colored with colors of the morning,—skyey blueness, with the rose of a great dawn blushing and bursting through it, and long-limbed marsh-birds flying against the glow;

Also the *Ko-yao*—fourth in rank among perfect porcelains—of fair, faint, changing colors, like the body of a living fish, or made in the likeness of opal substance, milk mixed with fire; the work of Sing-I, elder of the immortal brothers Tchang;

Also the *Ting-yao*—fifth in rank among all perfect porcelains—white as the mourning garments of a spouse bereaved, and beautiful with a trickling as of tears—the porcelains sung of by the poet Son-tong-po;

Also the porcelains called *Pi-se-yao*, whose colors are called "hidden," being alternately invisible and visible, like the tints of ice beneath the sun—the porcelains celebrated by the far-famed singer Sin-in;

Also the wondrous *Chu-yao*—the pallid porcelains that utter a mournful cry when smitten—the porcelains chanted of by the mighty chanter, Thou-chao-ling;

Also the porcelains called *Thsin-yao*, white or blue, surface-wrinkled as the face of water by the fluttering of many fins. . . . And ye can see the fish!

Also the vases called *Tsi-hong-khi*, red as sunset after a rain; and the *T'o-t'ai-khi*, fragile as the wings of the silkworm-moth, lighter than the shell of an egg;

Also the *Kia-tsing*—fair cups pearl-white when empty, yet, by some incomprehensible witchcraft of construction, seeming to swarm with purple fish the moment they are filled with water;

Also the porcelains called *Yao-pien*, whose tints are transmuted by the alchemy of fire; for they enter blood-crimson into the heat, and change there to lizard-green, and at last come forth azure as the cheek of the sky;

Also the *Ki-tcheou-yao*, which are all violet as a summer's night; and the *Hing-yao* that sparkle with the sparklings of mingled silver and snow;

Also the *Sieouen-yao*—some ruddy as iron in the furnace, some diaphanous and ruby-red, some granulated and yellow as the rind of an orange, some softly flushed as the skin of a peach;

Also the *Tsoui-khi-yao*, crackled and green as ancient ice is; and the *Tchou-fou-yao*, which are the Porcelains of Emperors, with dragons wriggling and snarling in gold; and those *yao* that are pink-ribbed and have their angles serrated as the claws of crabs are;

Also the *Ou-ni-yao*, black as the pupil of the eye, and as lustrous; and the *Hou-tien-yao*, darkly yellow as the faces of men of India; and the *Ou-kong-yao*, whose color is the dead-gold of autumn-leaves;

Also the *Long-kang-yao*, green as the seedling of a pea, but bearing also paintings of sun-silvered cloud, and of the Dragons of Heaven;

Also the *Tching-hoa-yao*—pictured with the amber bloom of grapes and the verdure of vine-leaves and the blossoming of poppies, or decorated in relief with figures of fighting crickets;

Also the *Khang-hi-nien-ts'ang-yao*, celestial azure sown with star-dust of gold; and the *Khien-long-nien-thang-yao*, splendid in sable and silver as a fervid night that is flashed with lightnings.

Not indeed the *Long-Ouang-yao*—painted with the lascivious *Pi-hi*, with the obscene *Nan-niu-ssé-sie*, with the shameful *Tchun-hoa*, or "Pictures of Spring"; abominations created by command of the wicked Emperor Moutsong, though the Spirit of the Furnace hid his face and fled away;

But all other vases of startling form and substance, magically articulated, and ornamented with figures in relief, in cameo, in transparency—the vases with orifices belled like the cups of flowers, or cleft like the bills of birds, or fanged like the jaws of serpents, or pink-lipped as the mouth of a girl; the vases flesh-colored and purple-veined and dimpled, with ears and with earrings; the vases in likeness of mushrooms, of lotus-flowers, of lizards, of horse-footed dragons woman-faced; the vases strangely translucid, that simulate the white glimmering of grains of prepared rice, that counterfeit the vapory lace-work of frost, that imitate the efflorescences of coral;—

Also the statues in porcelain of divinities: the Genius of the Hearth; the Long-pinn who are the Twelve Deities of Ink; the blessed Lao-tseu, born with silver hair; Kong-fu-tse, grasping the scroll of written wisdom; Kouan-in, sweetest Goddess of Mercy, standing snowy-footed upon the heart of her golden lily; Chi-nong, the god who taught men how to cook; Fo, with long eyes closed in meditation, and lips smiling the mysterious smile of Supreme Beatitude; Cheou-lao, god of Longevity, bestriding his aerial steed, the white-winged stork; Pou-t'ai, Lord of Contentment and of Wealth, obese and dreamy; and that fairest Goddess of Talent, from whose beneficent hands eternally streams the iridescent rain of pearls.

And though many a secret of that matchless art that Pu bequeathed unto men may indeed have been forgotten and lost forever, the story of the Porcelain-God is remembered; and I doubt not that any of the aged *Jeou-yen-liao-kong*, any one of the old blind men of the great potteries, who sit all day grinding colors in the sun, could tell you Pu was once a humble Chinese workman, who grew to be a great artist by dint of tireless study and patience and by the inspiration of Heaven. So famed he became that some deemed him an alchemist, who possessed the secret called *White-and-Yellow*, by which stones might be turned into gold; and others thought him a magician, having the ghastly power of murdering men with horror of nightmare, by hiding charmed effigies of them under the tiles of their own roofs; and others, again, averred that he was an astrologer who had discovered the mystery of those Five Hing which influence all things—those Powers that move even in the currents of the star-drift, in the milky *Tien-ho*, or River of the Sky. Thus, at least, the ignorant spoke of him; but even those who stood about the Son of Heaven, those whose hearts had been strengthened by the acquisition of wisdom, wildly praised the marvels of his handicraft, and asked each other if there might be any imaginable form of beauty which Pu could not evoke from that beauteous substance so docile to the touch of his cunning hand.

And one day it came to pass that Pu sent a priceless gift to the Celestial and August: a vase imitating the substance of ore-rock, all aflame with pyritic scintillation—a shape of glittering splendor with chameleons sprawling over it; chameleons of porcelain that shifted color as often as the beholder changed his position. And the Emperor, wondering exceedingly at the splendor of the work, questioned the princes and the mandarins concerning him that made it. And the princes and the mandarins answered that he was a workman named Pu, and that he was without equal among potters, knowing secrets that seemed to have been inspired either by gods or by demons. Whereupon the Son of Heaven sent his officers to Pu with a noble gift, and summoned him unto his presence.

So the humble artisan entered before the Emperor, and having performed the supreme prostration—thrice kneeling, and thrice nine times touching the ground with his forehead—awaited the command of the August.

And the Emperor spake to him, saying: "Son, thy gracious gift hath found high favor in our sight; and for the charm of that offering we have bestowed upon thee a reward of five thousand silver *liang*. But thrice that sum shall be awarded thee so soon as thou shalt have fulfilled our behest. Hearken, therefore, O matchless artificer! it is now our will that thou make for us a vase having the tint and the aspect of living flesh, but—mark well our desire!—*of flesh made to creep by the utterance of such words as poets utter—flesh moved by an Idea, flesh horripilated by a Thought!* Obey, and answer not! We have spoken."

Now Pu was the most cunning of all the *P'ei-se-kong*—the men who marry colors together; of all the *Hoa-yang-kong*, who draw the shapes of vase-decoration; of all the *Hoei-sse-kong*, who paint in enamel; of all the *T'ien-thsai-kong*, who brighten color; of all the *Chao-lou-kong*, who watch the furnace-fires and the porcelain-ovens. But he went away sorrowing from the Palace of the Son of Heaven, notwithstanding the gift of five thousand silver *liang* which had been given to him. For he thought to himself: "Surely the mystery of the comeliness of flesh, and the mystery of that by which it is moved, are the secrets of the Supreme Tao. How shall man lend the aspect of sentient life to dead clay? Who save the Infinite can give soul?"

Now Pu had discovered those witchcrafts of color, those surprises of grace, that make the art of the ceramist. He had found the secret of the *feng-hong*, the wizard flush of the Rose; of the *hoa-hong*, the delicious incarnadine; of the mountain-green called *chan-lou*; of the pale soft yellow termed *hiao-hoang-yeou*; and of the *hoang-kin*, which is the blazing beauty of gold. He had found those eel-tints, those serpent-greens, those pansy-violets, those furnace-crimsons, those carminates and lilacs, subtle as spirit-flame, which our enamelists of the Occident long sought without success to reproduce. But he trembled at the task assigned him, as he returned to the toil of his studio, saying: "How shall any miserable man render in clay the quivering of flesh to an Idea—the inexplicable horripilation of a Thought? Shall a man venture to mock the magic of that Eternal Molder by whose infinite power a million suns are shapen more readily than one small jar might be rounded upon my wheel?"

Yet the command of the Celestial and August might never be disobeyed; and the patient workman strove with all his power to fulfill the Son of Heaven's desire. But vainly for days, for weeks, for months, for season after season, did he strive; vainly also he prayed unto the gods to aid him; vainly he besought the Spirit of the Furnace, crying: "O thou Spirit of Fire, hear me, heed me, help me! how shall I—a miserable man, unable to breathe into clay a living soul—how shall I render in this inanimate substance the aspect of flesh made to creep by the utterance of a Word, sentient to the horripilation of a Thought?"

For the Spirit of the Furnace made strange answer to him with whispering of fire: *"Vast thy faith, weird thy prayer! Has Thought feet, that man may perceive the trace of its passing? Canst thou measure me the blast of the Wind?"*

Nevertheless, with purpose unmoved, nine-and-forty times did Pu seek to fulfill the Emperor's command; nine-and-forty times he strove to obey the behest of the Son of Heaven. Vainly, alas! did he consume his substance; vainly did he expend his strength; vainly did he exhaust his knowledge: success smiled not upon him; and Evil visited his home, and Poverty sat in his dwelling, and Misery shivered at his hearth.

Sometimes, when the hour of trial came, it was found that the colors had become strangely transmuted in the firing, or had faded into ashen pallor, or had darkened into the fuliginous hue of forest-mold. And Pu, beholding these misfortunes, made wail to the Spirit of the Furnace, praying: "O thou Spirit of Fire, how shall I render the likeness of lustrous flesh, the warm glow of living color, unless thou aid me?"

And the Spirit of the Furnace mysteriously answered him with murmuring of fire: *"Canst thou learn the art of that Infinite Enameler who hath made beautiful the Arch of Heaven—whose brush is Light; whose paints are the Colors of the Evening?"*

Sometimes, again, even when the tints had not changed, after the pricked and labored surface had seemed about to quicken in the heat, to assume the vibratility of living skin—even at the last hour all the labor of the workers proved to have been wasted; for the fickle substance rebelled against their efforts, producing only crinklings grotesque as those upon the rind of a withered fruit, or granulations like those upon the skin of a dead bird from which the feathers have been rudely plucked. And Pu wept, and cried out unto the Spirit of the Furnace: "O thou Spirit of Flame, how shall I be able to imitate the thrill of flesh touched by a Thought, unless thou wilt vouchsafe to lend me thine aid?"

And the Spirit of the Furnace mysteriously answered him with muttering of fire: *"Canst thou give ghost unto a stone? Canst thou thrill with a Thought the entrails of the granite hills?"*

Sometimes it was found that all the work indeed had not failed; for the color seemed good, and all faultless the matter of the vase appeared to be, having neither crack nor wrinkling nor crinkling; but the pliant softness of warm skin did not meet the eye; the flesh-tinted surface offered only the harsh aspect and hard glimmer of metal. All their exquisite toil to mock the pulpiness of sentient substance had left no trace; had been brought to nought by the breath of the furnace. And Pu, in his despair, shrieked to the Spirit of the Furnace: "O thou merciless divinity! O thou most pitiless god!—thou whom I have worshipped with ten thousand sacrifices!—for what fault hast thou abandoned me? for what error hast thou forsaken me? How may I, most wretched of men! ever render the aspect of flesh made to creep with the utterance of a Word, sentient to the titillation of a Thought, if thou wilt not aid me?"

And the Spirit of the Furnace made answer unto him with roaring of fire: *"Canst thou divide a Soul? Nay! . . . Thy life for the life of thy work!—thy soul for the soul of thy Vase!"*

And hearing these words Pu arose with a terrible resolve swelling at his heart, and made ready for the last and fiftieth time to fashion his work for the oven.

One hundred times did he sift the clay and the quartz, the *kao-ling* and the *tun;* one hundred times did he purify them in clearest water; one hundred times with tireless hands did he knead the creamy paste, mingling it at last with colors known only to himself. Then was the vase shapen and reshapen, and touched and retouched by the hands of Pu, until its blandness seemed to live, until it appeared to quiver and to palpitate, as with vitality from within, as with the quiver of rounded muscle undulating beneath the integument. For the hues of life were upon it and infiltrated throughout its innermost substance, imitating the carnation of blood-bright tissue, and the reticulated purple of the veins; and over all was laid the envelope of sun-colored *Pe-kia-ho*, the lucid and glossy enamel, half diaphanous, even like the substance that it counterfeited—the polished skin of a woman. Never since the making of the world had any work comparable to this been wrought by the skill of man.

Then Pu bade those who aided him that they should feed the furnace well with wood of *tcha*; but he told his resolve unto none. Yet after the oven began to glow, and he saw the work of his hands blossoming and blushing in the heat, he bowed himself before the Spirit of Flame, and murmured: "O thou Spirit and Master of Fire, I know the truth of thy words! I know that a Soul may never be divided! Therefore my life for the life of my work!—my soul for the soul of my Vase!"

And for nine days and for eight nights the furnaces were fed unceasingly with wood of *tcha*; for nine days and for eight nights men watched the wondrous vase crystallizing into being, rose-lighted by the breath of the flame. Now upon the coming of the ninth night, Pu bade all his weary comrades retire to, rest, for that the work was well-nigh done, and the success assured. "If you find me not here at sunrise," he said, "fear not to take forth the vase; for I know that the task will have been accomplished according to the command of the August." So they departed.

But in that same ninth night Pu entered the flame, and yielded up his ghost in the embrace of the Spirit of the Furnace, giving his life for the life of his work—his soul for the soul of his Vase.

And when the workmen came upon the tenth morning to take forth the porcelain marvel, even the bones of Pu had ceased to be; but lo! the Vase lived as they looked upon it: seeming to be flesh moved by the utterance of a Word, creeping to the titillation of a Thought. And whenever tapped by the finger it uttered a voice and a name—the voice of its maker, the name of its creator: PU.

And the son of Heaven, hearing of these things, and viewing the miracle of the vase, said unto those about him: "Verily, the Impossible hath been wrought by the strength of faith, by the force of obedience! Yet never was it our desire that so cruel a sacrifice should have been; we sought only to know whether the skill of the matchless artificer came from the Divinities or from the Demons,—from heaven or from hell. Now, indeed, we discern that Pu hath taken his place among the gods." And the Emperor mourned exceedingly for his faithful servant. But he ordained that godlike honors should be paid unto the spirit of the marvelous artist, and that his memory should be revered forevermore, and that fair statues of him should be set up in all the cities of the Celestial Empire, and above all the toiling of the potteries, that the multitude of workers might unceasingly call upon his name and invoke his benediction upon their labors.